Beginning
Access 97
VBA Programming

Robert Smith
David Sussman

Wrox Press Ltd.®

Beginning Access 97 VBA Programming

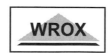

Published by Wrox Press Ltd. 30 Lincoln Road, Olton, Birmingham, B27 6PA , UK.
Printed in Canada
1 2 3 4 5 TRI 99 98 97

ISBN 1-861000-86-3

Trademark Acknowledgements

Credits

Authors
Robert Smith
David Sussman

Editors
Timothy Briggs
Victoria Hudgson

Managing Editor
John Franklin

Technical Reviewers
Ben Chapman
Darren Gill
Robert Hernady
Mike Joy
David Liske

Technical Reviewers
Douglas Sapola
Douglas Shand
David Skowronski
David Vogt
Bernard Wong

Cover/Design/Layout
Andrew Guillaume
Graham Butler

Copy Edit/Index
Simon Gilks

Proof Readers
Jeremy Beacock
Anthea Elston
Dominic Shakeshaft

Author Biographies

Robert Smith has been developing applications with Access since its first release in 1992. A graduate of Oxford University, Robert was recently the Strategy Director of Edinburgh-based IT consultancy, Amethyst Ltd. Now, however, he has got a proper job and spends most of his time working with Access and SQL Server, providing consultancy in client-server design and development issues, and—less successfully—trying to hit his 3-wood straighter.

David is a freelance developer and trainer in Edinburgh. He too has been using Access since its first release, and now specialises in training and developing client/server solutions around Access, Visual Basic and SQL Server. Most of his spare time is spent trying to persuade Rob—even less successfully—that they ought to be working instead of playing golf.

Author Acknowledgements

Rob would like to dedicate this book to all the developers at Amethyst for their hard work, resolute determination and warped sense of humour; to Dr. Farrell for giving his all to the cause and being a great pal besides; and, of course, to Valerie for being patient and beautiful throughout.

Dave would like, firstly, to thank the Wrox team, especially Dave, Tim and Victoria, who showed much patience when things got tight—Rob and I wrote the words, but we all made the book. Thanks also to mum, for feeding me for a week—next time I stay I won't be writing! But mostly to Jan—"you're forever in my heart, and your smile is only a phone call away".

Beginning
Access 97
VBA Programming

Chapter 11: Error Handling, Debugging and Testing 317

Chapter 12: Class Modules — 369

Chapter 13: Optimizing the Database — 397

Introduction

Who is This Book For?

You can achieve a lot in Access without any programming at all. However, if you're serious about database development and want to endow your application with a professional and intelligent interface, you need to know how to use code to control your tables and forms. That is what Beginning Access 97 VBA Programming will teach you.

The focus of the book is the programming language that underlies Access 97—Visual Basic for Applications (VBA). This is the language that Microsoft are making standard across the whole Office suite of applications. If you learn to program in VBA for Access, you'll find that you also have an easy ride when it comes to working with Excel, Project and, of course, Microsoft's popular programming language—Visual Basic itself.

There are two types of user, in particular, who will benefit from this book:

▶ You have some experience of Access, but have not yet begun to learn Visual Basic for Applications. You have spent a bit of time familiarizing yourself with the different Access objects—tables, forms, queries and reports, and have probably used macros to achieve some degree of automation. You have not programmed before, but are keen to tap into the power that VBA offers.

▶ You are familiar with Access and have programmed Access 2 using Access Basic. However, you want, or need, a quick primer on how to program in VBA. If this is the case, you may want to skim quickly through Chapters 1 to 3 and start your serious reading at Chapter 4. You'll find plenty of useful information and handy tips to keep your attention from straying in the rest of the book.

What's Covered in This Book

Beginning Access 97 VBA Programming covers everything that you need to gain the confidence to go away and experiment on your own. Programming is an art and cannot simply be taught—like anything worth doing in life, it's a question of practice-makes-perfect. This book will provide the necessary information to get you up and running and will show you enough interesting and practical examples to whet your appetite and ensure that your experiences with VBA don't end with the last page of this book.

We'll start off by looking at exactly why you need to learn VBA. Chapter 1 will familiarize you with the sample database included on the CD that comes with this book and then poses a few problems that really need solving to perfect the application. As you'll see, the only way to get what you want from the database is to use VBA.

We'll then move on to explain how Access is **event-driven**, and what this means in programming terms. We'll examine the events that Access responds to and look at the fundamentals of programming, introducing you to the coding environment and basic principles such as variables, control structures, data types and functions. We'll also look at how objects are arranged in Access—which will help you really get what you want from code.

Once we have a basis on which to build, we'll start to look at how we can use VBA in a more practical sense, looking at how to create recordsets and other objects at run-time, how to import data from, and export it to, other applications, and how to work with reports. We'll also look at some issues that you must bear in mind when programming any application—how to find and correct errors, and how to optimize your applications. In the later part of the book, we'll take a look at some more advanced topics such as working in a multi-user environment, using libraries and add-ins, and communicating with other ActiveX-enabled applications. We'll also be finding out about what's new in Access 97 such as class modules and user-defined objects, and the Internet features. Finally, we'll look at those finishing touches that will add polish to your application.

What You Need to Use This Book

Apart from a bit of time and a willingness to learn, you'll need access to a PC running Windows 95/Windows NT Workstation and Access 97. Also, for some of the chapters you really need a copy of Office 97 and access to the Internet to take full advantage of the examples.

The CD

The CD contains all the sample databases from the book, both in an installation **.exe** and in an uncompressed, read-only format. To install the examples from the CD, double click on the **Setup.exe** file and follow the instructions. In order to install all the samples on the CD, you'll need a hard drive with at least 20Mb of free space. It's important to use and develop the samples from the disc as they form a fundamental part of the teaching process of the book.

Apart from miscellaneous support materials for chapters of the book, the disc also contains some utilities to help you develop applications with Access 97. Have a look at the **\Tools\ReadMe.doc** for details.

The Whisky Shop

Included with the CD is a sample application, designed around a fictitious liquor store, the Whisky Shop. We'll look at this application through the various stages of its design and development. Notice that we have included a version of the database for each chapter of the book, **Whisky1.mdb** through **Whisky18.mdb**, and a final, completed version, **Whisky.mdb**. The versions for each chapter allow you to work through all the examples in that particular chapter. If you want to make life a little easier on yourself, you can skip to the next database along, which will contain all the completed examples from the previous chapter. We do recommend, however, that you use the relevant database as you go along, and try all the examples yourself.

Conventions

We use a number of different styles of text and layout in the book to help differentiate between the various styles of information. Here are examples of the styles we use along with explanations of what they mean:

Try It Out—How Do They Work?

1 These are examples that you should work through.

2 Each step has a number.

3 Follow the steps through with your copy of the databases.

How It Works

After each Try-It-Out, the code we've typed is explained in the context of the theory that we're looking at.

 Extra details, for your information, come in boxes like this.

Background information will look like this.

Not-to-be-missed information looks like this.

Bulleted information is shown like this:

- **Important Words** are in a bold type font
- Words that appear on the screen, such as menu options, are a similar font to the one used on screen, e.g. the File menu
- Keys that you press on the keyboard, like *Ctrl* and *Enter*, are in italics
- All file, function names and other code snippets are in this style: **Whisky.mdb**

Code shown for the first time, or other, relevant code, is in the following format,

```
Dim intVariable1 As Integer

intVariable1 = intVariable1 + 1
Debug.Print intVariable1
```

while less important code, or that seen before, looks like this:

```
intvariable1 = intvariable1 + 1
```

Tell Us What You Think

We have tried to make this book accurate, enjoyable and worthwhile. But what really matters is whether or not you find it useful, and we would appreciate your views and comments. You can return the the reply card in the back of the book, or contact us at:

feedback@wrox.com
http://www.wrox.com
or
http://www.wrox.co.uk

Designing Applications

Access 97 is a powerful database and application development tool. With it you can create not only databases, but also complete applications. Turning a collection of tables, forms, queries and reports into a tightly integrated whole requires an overall design plan. It also requires some 'glue' to bind those objects together. This chapter walks you through the steps involved in creating an application and, in the process, defines the need for an underlying language to manipulate your database objects. By the end of the chapter you'll wonder how you ever got this far without Visual Basic for Applications.

In this chapter we will:

▶ Define what an Access application really is

▶ Introduce you to the design and implementation of the database you'll be working with throughout the book

▶ Create some forms to allow users to interact with our application

▶ Identify the need to automate our user interface and use macros to do it

▶ Show how macros really can't do the job and why we need Visual Basic for Applications

What is an Access Application?

Becoming proficient in Access is not an end in itself—the end is to create useful and effective applications. Different people may have different ideas as to what the word 'application' really means, so let's clear up any misunderstandings:

An Access application is a collection of objects that cooperate to perform a common task.

An Access application consists of various objects—tables, forms, reports, queries and so on—that are all usually contained within a single **.mdb** file. It is also possible, and sometimes advisable, to split the 'front-end' (user interface elements) and 'back-end' (tables) of your application into separate **.mdb** files. Later on, in Chapter 8 we will look at some of the issues involved in splitting the database in two like this.

Designing an Application

The starting point for creating a successful Access application is to have a clear idea of what your users want the application to do. You need to know this before you can even start to think about how to design it. Then, once you have worked out the primary purpose of the application and have an idea about how it will fit together, you can move on to more specific questions:

▶ What data you will need to store

▶ How you should structure the data

▶ What queries and forms you will need

While this chapter doesn't pretend to be a primer on database design, it's instructive to take this as our starting point.

The analysis that goes into your application is, in some ways, the most important step—good analysis and design should make the actual building of the application a formality (in theory!). If you make mistakes during the analysis and design phases of your application and don't spot them, once you start to build your application you will build in the mistakes too. It's always faster (and therefore cheaper) to spend time looking for and correcting mistakes during the analysis and design phases, than it is during the build phase.

During the analysis phase, you must develop a full understanding of what the users expect from the system. If you're dealing with users who have little technical knowledge, it's up to you to explain what the system can offer them. Remember that *you* are in charge now. And, as with everything in life, you will be blamed far more often for failures than you will be praised for ingenuity!

The Construction Metaphor

Traditionally, applications have been designed and built using what some people call the 'construction' metaphor, i.e. in the same way that projects in the construction industry are carried out. If you were responsible for building a bridge, the steps you would take would be:

▶ Consult with the authorities to determine the location of the bridge

▶ Design the construction of the bridge

▶ Build the bridge

▶ Get paid and hand the bridge over to the authorities

This way of working is fine for building bridges. After all, even though it may take two years to build the bridge, it's unlikely that the requirements will change in that time. The design settled upon at the start of the project will be as valid after two years as it was at the start. Unfortunately, the same can't be said of the applications we have to build!

The problem with using the construction metaphor when designing applications is that your end-users' requirements will change while the application is being built. Legal requirements, new business imperatives, the changing market place—all of these are dynamic factors which mean that even though you may have come up with a valid design at the start of the build phase, the design may no longer be valid once this phase is over.

Settling on a Design

So how do you solve this problem? Well, the first thing is to talk to the people who will be using your application. One method is to develop **prototypes** of your application to explain how it will work. You can build the application in small stages (iterations) and at the end of each iteration, discuss and redefine the design with the end-users. In this way, by making small changes here and there as you go along, you can ensure that you end up with an application that suits the end-users' requirements. Access is very well suited to this style of development, as it enables the developer to make design changes quickly and easily. Note, however, that even when using this method, you must still spend time defining the end-users' requirements before you start.

A prototype is like a newborn baby. It has the capability to excite those who receive it with the possibilities that it promises. But it should also encapsulate all the elements required in the adult version. The arms and legs may not be coordinated, but they are still there!

When you're developing the design, don't think of any part of the system as superficial and not really worth your attention. The screen color might be a small formality to you, but to someone that may have to use the system on a day-to-day basis and stare at the screen for most of the day, the screen color is as important as the file structures are to you. Pale green lettering on a light blue background may appeal for an instant, but the novelty soon wears off! Remember, also, that overuse and misuse of color will make your application look amateurish.

How Does Visual Basic for Applications Influence the Design?

Once you have completed your design, you should have the answers to these two questions:

- What data items (or entities) and application objects do you need?
- How should those entities and objects fit together?

This book is not about how to design the data items and application objects that make up your application—you should know enough about tables, forms, reports and queries from your previous exploration of Access. This book is about how you use Visual Basic for Applications (VBA) to control the way those objects behave as part of the overall system. On one level, you can think of VBA as the 'glue' that holds the whole application together.

The best way to understand how VBA fits into your application is, of course, not through theory but through practice. In this chapter, we're going to run through the process of starting to create an application (the Malt Whisky Shop database that's on the example CD). At a certain point we'll hit a wall—where we need our application to display some intelligence. We'll then look at our options for solving the problem: VBA or macros, and explain why VBA is the best and, at times, the only choice.

You'll probably find that this chapter covers a lot of familiar territory. However, you should take the time to read through it, as it will also acquaint you with the Malt Whisky Shop application, so that when the crunch moment comes and we turn to VBA, we will have a familiar database to experiment with. So please bear with us.

The Malt Whisky Shop Application

The various stages of development of the Malt Whisky Shop application are available on the CD that accompanies the book. The first one that you need is **Whisky1.mdb**.

Creating the Malt Whisky Shop Application

The Malt Whisky Shop application is, as the name suggests, an application that has been designed to track orders for the Malt Whisky Shop, a fictitious liquor store. The first step in any project is to establish what services the system should provide and what constraints will influence the project. This step is known as **requirements analysis**. The analysis for the Malt Whisky Shop project reveals that the system should store information about the following things:

- Information about the items held in stock
- The orders taken for delivery of those whiskies
- The companies that ordered them
- The people who work for those companies

Also, at this stage, we can identify that entering and maintaining contact information is a key component of the system, and there must be a form for these tasks that's easy to use. In fact, this contact information form is going to be one of the forms that we will look at in quite a bit of detail in these early chapters.

Once we identify these **data entities** (Person, Whisky, Order and Company), we need to identify their characteristics or **attributes**. For example, the Person data entity has attributes such as Name and DOB (Date of Birth), while the Whisky entity has attributes such as WhiskyName and Price.

After the data entities and their attributes have been determined, we can then make the data entities into tables and give them fields corresponding to their attributes. Each table is also assigned an ID field that is used as a primary key. The design at this stage looks like this:

Company	Person	Whisky	Order
CompanyID	PersonID	WhiskyID	OrderID
Name	Company	Name	Company
Turnover	Salutation	Distillery	OrderNumber
Notes	FirstName	Region	OrderDate
InvoiceTemplate	MiddleName	Label	SentDate
Address	LastName	Age	PaidDate
Town	Suffix	Strength	Whisky
Postcode	DoB	DistillationDate	Quantity
Country		Peatiness	
		Notes	
		Price	

10

Removing Redundant Information

Once we have identified all the attributes of the entities and created the tables, we should tackle the normal problems of redundant and duplicate information. For example, for each company with more than one address, the information about that company's turnover and notes is repeated for each site. For this reason we further subdivide our design from the original four tables (one for each of our main entities)—initially creating a Location table.

Further analysis reveals that we need details about currencies in different countries, so that we can work out, via the currency rate, the price at which the whisky retails in the country's own currency. This leads to the Country table.

Also, because different bottlings of a particular whisky have different characteristics and are priced differently, we need a Bottling table. We end up with a modified design that looks like this:

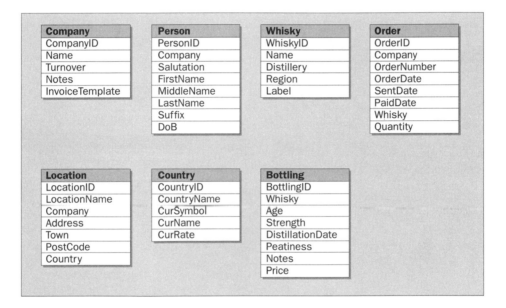

Relationships between the Entities and Attributes

The final design stage involves relating the tables to each other. The Company and Location tables need linking, as the user may wish to browse the address of each of the sites of a company in the Location table while checking the general notes about the company as a whole from the Company table. Therefore, a reference is created to join the CompanyID in the Location table with CompanyID in the Company table.

Similarly the Country table should be referred to from the Location table to indicate that a single country can contain many company locations.

We want to link the data in the Order table to the company who made the order. In fact, we need to link it to the location that made the order, rather than just the company. This is because different locations can place orders independently of each other. Therefore, the Order table is linked to the Location table rather than the Company table. The people whom we are concerned with are located at different sites as well, so a reference is created between the Location and Person tables on the LocationID fields.

Finally, the Order table also needs linking to the Bottling table. This in turn requires the creation of a separate table. Orders are made by one location for several different bottlings. If we keep our design as it is in the diagram above, each order can only be made for one bottling—there would have to be a new order for each different bottling required. It's easier if one order can include all the different bottlings to be supplied to the one location. Therefore, we need a new table to store the quantity of each of the bottlings needed, together with the OrderID and the BottlingID. There would be several different entries in this table with the same OrderID, so we needed a new identifier, which is unique for this table. The table is the OrderLine table.

The illustration below shows our final design with all the data entities and their attributes, and the relationships that now exist between the data entities.

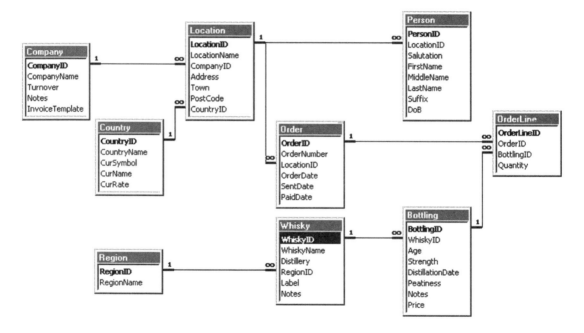

Typical Dilemmas Regarding the Storage of Information

Take a look at the Person table that holds information about our contacts at each company location. Our requirements analysis indicates that we need to store the names of these contacts in the database. It turns out that our store needs to export a list of contact names in the format "LastName, FirstName" to its head office on a six-monthly basis for marketing purposes. But we need the names in "FirstName LastName" format for our invoices. So in which format do we store the names? Should we have a single Name field or should we break it down into FirstName and LastName fields?

If we store the name in separate fields, it's easy enough to assemble them into either of the required formats. But if the name is stored in a single field, we'll have to parse it every time we want the last name part. Storing a name in separate fields also allows us to index the LastName field. An index is a data structure that allows us to look up values more quickly, just like the index in a book does. Given that it is likely that we will want to search for people by their last name, it would be sensible to index this field in the Person table, as this index will speed up such searches.

Having decided that the name should be split into its constituent parts, we ask what other parts may be required. The user may reply "Title, first name, last name, and perhaps a middle name. There isn't usually a suffix." Whenever you come across the words 'perhaps' or 'usually' in the analysis phase, you should beware! Just because you may not always know the middle name or suffix doesn't mean that you won't need fields for them. You can, of course, make it optional to enter middle names or suffixes, but you must have fields set up in the first place.

Of course, it isn't just the Person table that requires such careful design. All of the tables do. But this one example should give a good indication of the care needed when structuring the other tables and fields. Look at the structure of the Location table. Why do you think that the address information has been broken into four fields, instead of being held in a single field? The answer is that by breaking it into four fields we make it easier for our users to analyze their orders by town, country and zip code (postcode) individually. This would be difficult, if not impossible, if the address was stored in a single field.

Note, however, that only one field is used for the first part of the address (i.e. the lines that precede the town, country and zip code).

Address	Corpus Christi College
	Merton Street
Town	Oxford
Postcode	OX1 4JF
Country	England

Even though this first part of the address might contain more than one line we can store it in a single field, because Access allows us to store and display multi-line values. We store these in one field because they logically belong together and you shouldn't need to split them up at all. Sometimes you will see databases with tables that store this part of the address in multiple fields, because the database cannot easily handle carriage returns as part of the data in a field. That's not a problem with Access though.

The other advantage with storing the first part of the address in a single field is that it makes it a lot easier to amend the address. Just imagine if you had stored the above address with a separate field for every line of the address and then had to change it to:

The Bursar's Buildings
Corpus Christi College
Merton Street
Oxford
OX1 4JF
England

Entering and Viewing Data

So far, we've considered the need for careful analysis and table design. But that's only the start. Now we have to consider how the users of our system are going to enter information into the tables. Of course, they could type information straight into the tables in datasheet mode, but that would be inelegant and inefficient and would make it difficult to check data entry properly. We need to put an acceptable face on our application and shield the users from the complexity of the table structure. After all, just because we need to store name information in separate fields, that doesn't mean that the users need to enter the name in four text boxes. It would be useful if the users could enter Mr James Alexander III as a single entry and leave the application to break the name into its constituent elements behind the scenes.

Designing a Form

The simplest way to create a quick-and-easy form is to use one of the Form Wizards. Using a wizard to produce a form will give you all the fields you require from one or more tables. This is great, but sometimes you'll need to add extra functionality to the form, in which case you'll have to hand-turn it yourself. We're going to use a Form Wizard to create the form that was identified as key to the application—the form for maintaining contact information.

Try It Out—Creating a Form Using the AutoForm Wizard

1 Load up the database file **Whisky1.mdb**. In the Database window, select the Tables tab and then the Person table.

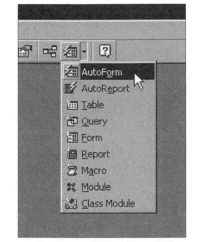

2 Click the down arrow next to the **New Object** button on the toolbar and select **AutoForm** from the drop-down menu.

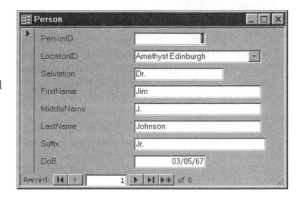

3 Access will now generate a form with all the fields from the **Person** table and display the first record.

This is OK, but it's not perfect. There are several things that you can improve:

▶ The form caption is **Person**, which isn't very instructive to the user.

▶ You will probably want to hide the **PersonID** field, as it's of little relevance to the user.

▶ The labels on the form are generated from the field names in **Person**. These should be changed to make them more meaningful.

▶ The navigation buttons at the bottom of the form are a bit small and fiddly—remember this is a key form and must be as easy to use as possible.

▶ Finally, as we mentioned previously, it would be good if we could allow the user to enter the contact's name in a single field and then parse it into its constituent parts behind the scenes, so that it could be stored in the five fields in our table. This would also have the added benefit of taking up less space on the screen.

So let's change the form so that it looks a little more professional.

Try It Out—Changing a Form's Appearance in Design View

1 Save the form you've just created by choosing <u>S</u>ave from the <u>F</u>ile menu or by hitting *Ctrl + S*. A dialog box will appear allowing you to type in a name for the form. Call it frmPerson:

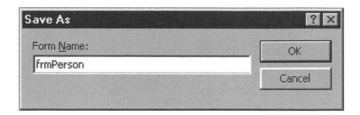

2 Now switch to Design view for the newly-saved form by selecting <u>D</u>esign View from the <u>V</u>iew menu or by clicking the Design View button.

3 We can now attempt to make the changes which we highlighted earlier. To change the form's caption, you bring up the form's property sheet by double-clicking the Form Selector (the small gray box in the upper left corner of the form where the rulers meet), or by clicking the Properties button on the toolbar.

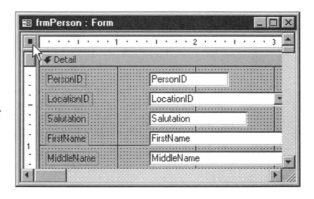

4 When the Properties window appears, make sure that the Format tab is selected and then change the text of the Caption property to Company Contacts.

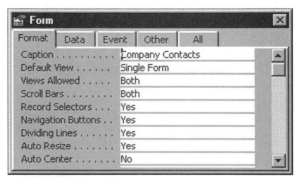

5 Next we must delete the PersonID text box and its label. To do this, you must select the text box on the form by clicking it once, then hit the *Delete* key. The PersonID text box and its label will be deleted:

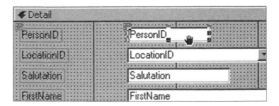

6 Next we'll change the caption on the LocationID label. To do this, you select the LocationID label (not the text box) on the form and, in the property sheet, change the caption from LocationID to Location. Change the captions on the other labels as well, until you're happy that they all read well. You may need to resize the labels as well if you are altering their captions.

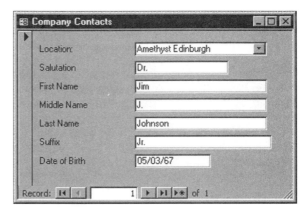

7 Finally, change the form back to Form View to see the changes you've made. You can do this by selecting Form View from the View menu or by clicking the button which has replaced the Design View button.

We've now made the first three of the changes we decided on after creating our initial form. But what about the other two? We still need to:

▶ Put more manageable navigation buttons on the screen

▶ Create a single text box that's capable of accepting a person's name and breaking it into its constituent elements

This is where things get a little more advanced!

Creating Navigation Buttons

To make the form easier to use, we can place some command buttons on the screen to replace the present navigation buttons. We can then use macros to move through the records behind the form. A macro is simply a stored collection of instructions that correspond to the actions that a user might carry out. So, in this case, our macro would contain the instructions to move to the next, previous, first or last records.

Of course, this book is about VBA, not macros. However, using them here will help show you their limitations....

Try It Out—Adding Simple Navigation Buttons to a Form

1 Switch back to Design view. We're going to use headers and footers, so go to the <u>V</u>iew menu and select the Form <u>H</u>eader/Footer option. A header section and footer section will then appear on the form. We don't have to add the buttons to the footer of the form. We could add them to the Detail section of the form instead. However, putting them on the footer keeps them in one place and we don't have to worry about them getting in the way if we decide to change around the other controls in the Detail section.

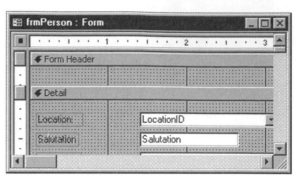

2 Next we must remove the navigation buttons that Access supplies by default. So, double click the Form Selector to bring up the form's property sheet and on the property sheet's Format tab, change the value of the Navigation Buttons property from Yes to No. You can do this by double-clicking the property value or by clicking on the arrow and selecting No from the drop-down list that appears.

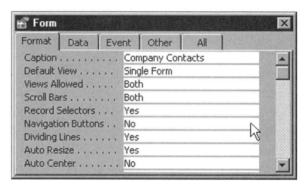

Now you can add the first of your own navigation buttons. We'll start by creating a Next Record button.

3 Make sure that the toolbox is visible by clicking the Toolbox button on the toolbar:

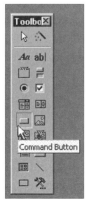

4 Then, make sure the Control Wizards button isn't depressed (that's the one with the magic wand on it) and select the Command Button tool from the toolbox. This will allow us to place a command button on the form.

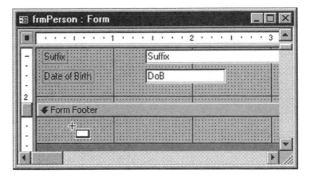

5 A good place for the navigation buttons to appear is in the form footer we created earlier, so click in the form footer to place the first command button.

6 Now go to the property sheet and change the Name property of the button (found under the Other tab) to cmdNext and its Caption property (found under the Format tab) to Next.

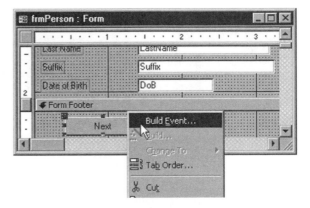

7 Now we must instruct the button to display the next record whenever it is clicked. To do this, you right-click on the button and select Build Event... from the pop-up menu which appears.

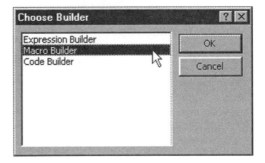

8 This will, in turn, bring up the Choose Builder dialog. For the moment, we want to use a macro, so select Macro Builder and hit the OK button.

9 We've said that we want a macro behind the button, so Access now helps us to build it. It displays the macro design window and asks us for the name that we want to give the macro. We will call it macNextButton so you should type in macNextButton and then press OK.

10 Now we get to specify the macro commands which will be carried out when we hit the command button. We want the button to make the form go to the next record. To get it to do this, you must select the down arrow in the Action column and select GoToRecord from the drop-down list that appears.

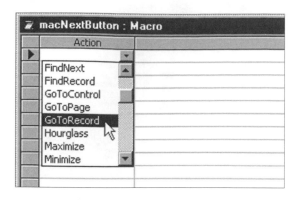

11 We then need to specify which record we want the command button to move us to. Click in the Record box in the lower pane of the screen, click the down arrow and select which record you want to go to from the drop-down list. We want to go to the next record, so make sure Next is selected. In fact, Next is the default selection in the drop-down list.

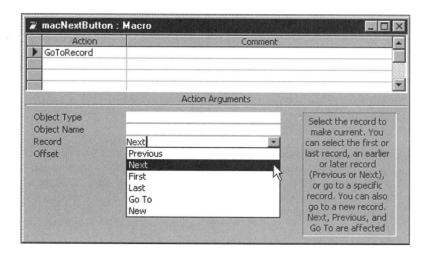

12 Now close the macro window and choose Yes when prompted to save the macro you have just created. Then change the frmPerson form to Form view and save the changes you made to it. When you open the form in form view, there should be a navigation button on it that allows you to move forward through the records in the form.

If you look at the button's properties, you will see that the name of the macro is listed in the **On Click** property on the **Event** tab. This is how Access knows to run the macro when the button is clicked. The macro name was inserted automatically into the event property because you right-clicked the button to select **Build Event....** If you had built the macro yourself, you could still make Access use it whenever you click the cmdNext button, but you would have to insert the macro's name manually into the `Event` property before it would work.

13 Finally, complete the form by adding navigation buttons to enable you to move to the previous, first, last and new records. You should be able to work out how to do this simply enough by referring to the steps described above.

The Finished Product

So there we have it! Your own hand-crafted navigation buttons! You can customize these further if you wish—you may want to change the caption on the Next button to add a 'greater than' sign (>). You may even want to add a tooltip by modifying the ControlTipText property of each button.

You can also provide a hotkey for each of the buttons. This allows the user to activate the button from the keyboard by pressing *Alt* and a particular letter. To set this up, you simply type an ampersand (&) in the button's Caption property, before the letter that you want to activate the button. So, for example, if you typed &New, the user could select the button by pressing *Alt-N*. The hot-key (in this case N) will appear underlined on the button.

Once you have added the other buttons, your form should look something similar to the one shown below.

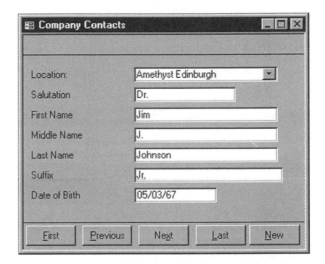

The form looks better but it's still not perfect. Try clicking the First button to move to the first record. Now try clicking the Previous button to move to the previous record. Obviously, there's no record previous to the first record, so an error occurs and an error message box appears.

Wouldn't it be better if the buttons were intelligent and only allowed you to click them if they represented a valid choice? In other words, if you were already at the first record, the Previous button should appear grayed out or **disabled**.

Sure, you may say, but how? There doesn't appear to be any way to determine where you are in the recordset when you're using macros. So how is it done? You have just come across one of the shortcomings of macros. Macros are good at automating simple tasks, but they're less useful when the task (or the logic behind the task) becomes more complex. The only way to make these buttons intelligent is to use VBA.

Macros or VBA?

Obviously, there are some simple tasks that can be performed happily by macros, but the example above should have highlighted one of their limitations. We could create navigation buttons using macros, but we could not disable or enable them according to where we were in the records behind the form. That may not be a problem for some people, but if you want a slick interface that will win over your end-users, you'll probably want to enable and disable buttons. And remember, our analysis showed that this form is a key component. Our users will be sitting in front of this screen a lot, so we want to get it right.

Why You Should Use VBA

The advantages that VBA has over macros can be summarized as follows:

VBA enables you to provide complex functionality.
You'll remember that when we tried to move back from the first record we encountered an error and Access displayed an error message. What if we wanted to display our own error message instead? This type of intelligence isn't possible with macros. We'll look at how to do this in Chapter 2.

You can trap (i.e. intercept) and handle errors using VBA.
Handling errors is impossible with macros but simple enough with VBA. Also, in some circumstances, you *have* to handle errors yourself. If you don't, your application could easily crash!

VBA is faster to execute than macros.
Code is executed faster than macros. Although you may not notice the difference in a one-line macro, the difference in speed becomes more noticeable the longer and more complex the macro you are creating. Since speed is normally a critical factor in impressing end-users, we have another notch in favor of VBA.

Using VBA makes your database easier to maintain.
Macros are completely separate from the objects which call them. Although we created the navigation button macro from within the form, the macro is actually stored as a separate object in the database window. Click the Macros tab and you'll see it's there. In contrast, you can save VBA code with the form itself. This means that if you want to move the form into another database, the code automatically goes with it. With macros, you would have to find out for yourself which macros you needed to take as well.

Using VBA allows you to interact with other applications.
With VBA you are able to make full use of OLE automation. This is a facility which allows you to access the functionality of applications like Excel and Word from within your Access application. It also allows you to control Access programmatically from applications like Excel and Word. More on this in Chapter 16.

Using VBA gives you more programmatic control.
Macros are good at performing set tasks where there's little need for flexibility. They can't pass variables from one macro to another in the form of parameters, are unable to ask for and receive input from the user, and they have extremely limited methods for controlling the sequence in which actions are performed.

VBA is easier to read.

Because you can only view one set of Action arguments at a time in the lower pane of the macro window, it is difficult to see the details of a macro. You have to select each action one after the other and look at its arguments in turn. In contrast, VBA with its colour-coded text and Full Module View is very easy to read.

VBA is common to all Microsoft applications (well, almost!)

And, finally, VBA is the language on which all Microsoft applications are now standardizing. VBA code written in Access 97 is easily portable to Excel and vice versa. In contrast, macros are highly specific to their native application.

When to Use Macros

By this stage, you may be wondering why you should ever bother to use macros if VBA has so much in its favor! Well, there are still a couple of things that you can't do in VBA that you need macros for. These are:

 Trapping certain keystrokes throughout the application

 Carrying out a series of actions whenever a database is opened (this is done via the Autoexec macro)

But, these apart, you'll find that with VBA you can do all you could with macros and lots more besides.

> **FYI** In previous versions of Access, you also had to use macros if you wanted to create custom menu bars or attach custom functionality to buttons on toolbars. However, in Access 97, both of these tasks are now achieved from the <u>C</u>ustomize... dialog box available from <u>T</u>oolbars on the <u>V</u>iew menu.

Before we move on to Chapter 2 and completely discard macros in favor of VBA, let's just take a look at the two things mentioned above where we still need macros.

Trapping Keystrokes Throughout an Application

Something you may want to do to make your application more user-friendly is to assign frequently-used actions to certain keystrokes. For example, you may want your application to print the current record when your users hit *Ctrl+P.*

We have already seen that on a specific form you can implement a hotkey by using an ampersand (&) in the caption for a control. That's what we did with the navigation button on the Company Contacts form.

However, if you want to implement a global keyboard shortcut—one that is available throughout your application—you can do so by creating a special macro. You need to save the macro with the name Autokeys, as this is the name of the macro in which Access 97 looks for keyboard shortcuts.

First create a new macro. To display the Macro Name column, click on the Macro Names button on the toolbar. This button toggles the column between visible and invisible. You can also do this by selecting Macro Names from the View menu.

Then you specify the keystroke which you wish to instigate the required action in the Macro Name column and the action itself in the Action column. For example, the following macro will cause the currently selected records to be printed whenever *Ctrl+P* is pressed.

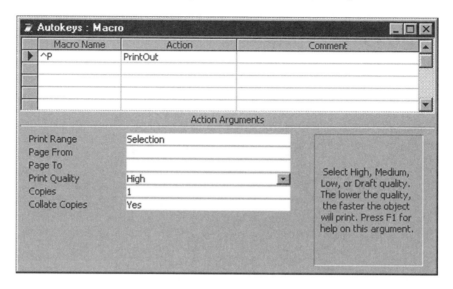

The lower pane of the macro window lists the arguments which you can pass to the PrintOut action to define exactly how it should operate. For example, we've specified Selection as the Print Range argument. This causes Access to only print out those records that were selected when the key combination *Ctrl+P* was pressed. If we had only wanted to print out the first two pages of the currently selected object, we could have chosen Pages as the Print Range argument and then typed 1 as the Page From argument and 2 as the Page To argument, like this:

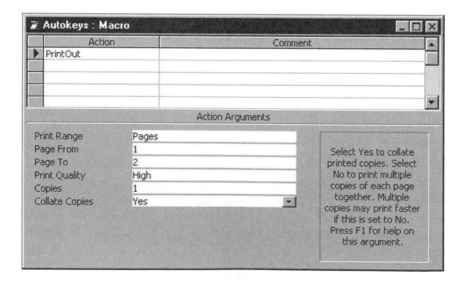

The caret sign (^) is used to indicate that the *Ctrl* key is held down at the same time as the *P* key. For more information on these key codes, search Access Help using the phrase "Autokeys Key Combinations"

Carrying Out Actions when a Database is Opened—the Autoexec Macro

When you open up an existing database, the first thing that Access does is to set any options which have been specified in the Tools/Startup... dialog. After this it checks to see if a macro called Autoexec is present. If it is, then Access executes it immediately. This handy feature allows you to carry out actions such as writing a record to a log file to indicate that your application is running.

> *Users of versions of Access 2.x and earlier should note that many of the conventional uses of the Autoexec macro have now been replaced by the Startup... option on the Tools menu. If you're converting an application from a version 2.x or earlier, you may want to remove the functionality from the Autoexec macro and use the Startup... dialog instead.*

If you want to perform an action whenever the database is opened, but want to get the benefits of using VBA, rather than macros, then you should write a procedure in VBA and call the procedure from the Autoexec macro. You can do this by using the RunCode action in your Autoexec macro:

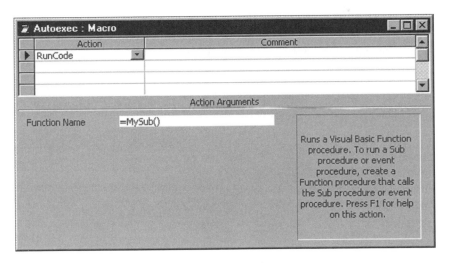

In this situation, when the database opens, the Autoexec macro is executed and this causes the **MySub()** procedure—written in VBA—to be executed.

Be aware, however, that a user can prevent the Tools/Startup... options or the Autoexec macro from running by holding down the *Shift* key when the database is being opened.

You can prevent a user from bypassing the Tools/Startup... options and the Autoexec macro by setting the database's AllowBypassKey property to False. However, the AllowBypassKey property isn't available normally and so can't be set in the usual way. We'll look at how to set this property from VBA later on.

Moving to VBA

Macros have their purposes then, such as trapping certain keystrokes throughout the application but, while undoubtedly useful for some things, they don't offer the power of VBA. We've just demonstrated in a few pages how and where you should apply macros. We'll now use the rest of the book describing how and where you can use VBA.

Summary

In this chapter, we've worked our way through the process of creating part of an Access application with one aim in mind—to deliberately hit a brick wall. That brick wall is the implementation of the intelligent navigation buttons. We just can't implement them properly using macros. Instead, we need VBA.

You'll remember that there was another requirement that we haven't provided yet. We wanted the user to be able to enter their full name and let the application parse it into first name, last name, etc.. Well, you could sit there for a week with macros trying to get that to work and you wouldn't get anywhere. Again, it's a problem that can only be solved with VBA. We'll see how this can be achieved in Chapter 4.

So, in brief, we have covered:

- How to go about designing an application
- An introduction to the application that forms the basis of this book—**Whisky.mdb**
- Creating the main form for the application and adding custom navigation buttons
- Why macros aren't sufficient for our needs
- When to use VBA and when to use macros

In the next chapter, we'll look at how you can polish up the Company Contacts form using VBA. If this chapter has been a success, you'll be hungry for the power to solve the problems we've come up against—so let's get on with it.

Exercises

1   Access 97 introduces the Customize dialog (available from Toolbars on the View menu) to allow you to create custom menus, toolbars and shortcut menus—something which was only possible with macros in previous versions of Access. Make sure that you know how to take advantage of this powerful new dialog. Try adding a menu bar to the Customer Contacts form that allows the user to navigate through the records in the same way as the buttons in the form footer without using macros.

2   The Autokeys macro is used to associate macro actions with keyboard shortcuts. Try using the Autokeys macro to display the property window whenever you hit *F4*. When does this shortcut not work? What happens if you try to associate this action with *Alt+F4* and why?

Responding to Events

This chapter will introduce some fundamental concepts of programming in Access 97. Access operates in an event-driven environment so one of the first things you need to understand is just what events are and how to write code to respond to them.

We will also examine the environment in which you program, looking in particular at how Access stores your code. We'll end the chapter by writing a small program that begins to solve one of the problems set in Chapter 1—making the navigation buttons on the Company Contacts form intelligent.

So, in brief, we will:

▶ Explain what event-driven programming means and how it relates to Access 97

▶ Examine the VBA code window

▶ Write a simple VBA event handler

▶ Create the first intelligent navigation button

Event-driven Programming

This chapter introduces a concept that is fundamental to understanding how Access works— namely that the Windows family of operating systems and Windows applications such as Access 97 are **event-driven**. In other words, nothing happens in an Access 97 application unless it's in response to an event that Access has detected.

This isn't really a difficult concept to master. A lot of the time we are event-driven ourselves! The phone rings, so we respond by picking up the receiver. We feel hungry, so we make ourselves a cheese sandwich. The sun goes down, so we turn the light on so that we can see. This is event-driven behavior. It's as simple as that.

Looking at these examples, we can break down event-driven behavior into three steps:

> **An external or internal event occurs**
>
> An example of an external event is the sun going down or the telephone ringing. It's an event that requires the action of some entity (the sun or the telephone) other than ourselves. In contrast, when we feel hungry we are detecting an internal event.

> **The event is detected by the system**
>
> The event has to be one that can be detected by the system. We can't respond to the telephone ringing if it's in a house down the street out of earshot.

> **The system responds to the event**
>
> Finally, the system responds to the event with some action of its own, such as turning on the light or making a sandwich. Once this action has been taken the system returns to a dormant state until the next event occurs and is detected.

Obviously, Windows applications don't get hungry (except for memory!) and, with a bit of luck, the lights won't go out, so what are the events to which Windows applications respond? How are they detected? And how exactly do the applications respond?

Windows Events

We'll now take a look at something with which you should be very familiar. It is, of course, the Windows desktop:

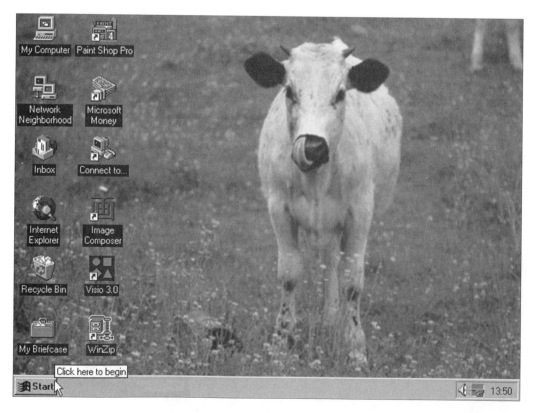

You see something like this whenever you start up Windows 95 or Windows NT. But then what do you do? Where do you go from here? As the tooltip in the lower-left corner of the screen suggests, one of the things you can do is to move the mouse over the Start button and click it. This is an event. In fact, this simple action represents a collection of several events. For example:

> **You move the mouse**

> This causes the **MouseMove** event, to which Windows responds by repainting the mouse pointer at different points on the screen, reflecting the movement of the mouse.

> **You click the mouse over the Start button**

> This causes a **Click** event to which Windows responds by displaying a pop-up menu, listing the options open to you.

These are simple actions which each set the same three steps in motion:

> An event occurs

> Windows detects the event

> Windows responds in some way

Let's take another example. When you start an application by double-clicking its shortcut, you cause a **DoubleClick** event to occur. Windows detects this event and responds by loading the application. Windows then goes back to waiting for the next event to occur.

> *Throughout this book, and in this chapter in particular, we will be talking a lot about the Windows family of operating systems. Although Windows 95 and Windows NT (both versions 3.5x and 4.0) do behave differently in some respects, for most of this chapter we will be able to treat the two operating systems as if they were the same. So, if we refer simply to Windows, you should understand that the point we are making refers equally to Windows NT and Windows 95. Where it is necessary to differentiate between the operating systems, we will call them by their specific titles. The 16-bit implementations of Windows (i.e. Windows 3.1 and Windows for Workgroups) will always be referred to by name.*

How Windows Handles Events

So far, all we have seen are some examples of events. Now let's look in a little more detail at how Windows handles events. Whenever Windows recognizes that an event has occurred, it generates one or more messages. Moving the mouse, pressing a key, clicking a mouse button—all these events cause Windows to create one or more associated messages. All of these messages are held in a system-wide message queue and each one is then passed to the message queue for the application to which it belongs.

As an example, if we have Microsoft Word open on our machine and we click the mouse button anywhere within the Microsoft Word window, Windows will detect that the **MouseDown** event has occurred, generate a **WM_MOUSEDOWN** message and then dispatch this message to Word's message queue. It's then up to Word to look at what is in its message queue and act accordingly. Word is able to inspect its message queue because it contains a piece of code called a **message loop**. This message loop has one purpose in life—to retrieve messages from the application's message queue and pass them to whichever of the windows within the Word application that needs to process the message.

FYI   The message generated when we clicked the mouse button was called WM_MOUSEDOWN. The WM prefix indicates the type of window that can interpret and process the message. A prefix of WM (Window Message) means that the message is intended for general windows, rather than any specific window type. Messages intended for specific window types have different prefixes such as TB for Toolbars and LB for List Box controls.

You should note that, with a couple of exceptions we don't need to worry about, these message queues operate on a first-in, first-out principle. Messages are processed in the order in which they were generated and placed in the application's message queue.

And, in essence, that's all you need to know! Windows programming in a couple of pages! OK, so there's more to it than that, but the overview above should help you to understand what is really happening beneath the hood when we talk about an application responding to an event.

> *Tools such as Spy which comes with the Windows Software Developer's Kit or WinSight included with Borland's Delphi enable you to eavesdrop on the messages which are being passed to individual windows. Alternatively, you can use one of the many OCXs (OLE custom controls) that allow you to do this, like Desaware's SpyWorks or WareWithAll's Message Blaster OCX. If you can, have a look at one of these in action. You'll be amazed at how many messages are generated, even when it looks like nothing is happening!*

So how does all of this impact Access 97? Well, Access 97 is a Windows application and so, like any Windows application, it receives and processes messages from Windows and thus responds to events. That much should be clear to you by this stage. However, where Access differs from a product like Notepad is that Access exposes some of these events to you as a developer and gives you the chance to add your own code to supplement its default behavior.

Event-driven vs. Traditional Programming Methods

At this stage, it's useful to contrast Access with a traditional MS-DOS-based application. This is because the two programming methods used differ widely and there's a good chance that, if you've programmed before, you might have used more traditional programming methods.

Traditional Programming Methods

In the MS-DOS environment, programmers had to devise their own methods for determining what to do when the user interacted with the program. For example, have a look at the following pseudo-code (English language that imitates computer code) which illustrates how a typical application might run:

```
Start
Loop While True
    Get Keystroke Into A
    If A="U" Then
        Get UserName Into B
        Display B at Col 20, Row 12
    If A = "X" Then
```

```
        Exit Loop
    End Loop
    End
```

The main thing to note about this program is that it has a fixed starting point and a fixed end. Once the program has started, a loop is initialized which continues until a keystroke is detected. If the user presses the *U* key, the program displays the user's name on the screen; if the *X* key is pressed, the program terminates.

Event-driven Methods

In Access, you would create the application like this:

▶ Create a form, **frmMain**

▶ Create a text box, **txtUserName**, on **frmMain**

▶ Create a command button, **cmdUserName**, on **frmMain**

▶ Change the caption of **cmdUserName** to "Your Name"

▶ Write code in the **Click** event handler, **cmdUserName_Click**, to change the caption of the text box, **txtUserName**, to display the user's name

▶ Create a second command button, **cmdExit**, on **frmMain**

▶ Change the caption of **cmdExit** to "Exit"

▶ Write code in the **Click** event handler, **cmdExit_Click**, to close the form **frmMain**

The first thing that stands out as being different when we look at this method of programming is that the developer creates objects (two command buttons, a text box and a form) and modifies their properties. Most of this creation is done graphically. This is not only quick, but also lets the developer see how the application looks on the screen and think about how it will work.

Secondly, in the MS-DOS-based code there was a strict order of processing. The programmer knew exactly in which order events would be processed. But in the Access example, the objects that we have created seem to be just lying around. Where is the starting point? How does the program check for user activity? Where is the end?

Well, the starting point occurs when the form, **frmMain**, is loaded. This causes all of the objects on the form (the two command buttons and the text box) to be displayed.

Windows itself then acts as the loop to check for user activity. If the Access application is active and Windows detects that a mouse button has been clicked over the application's windows, Windows passes a **MouseClick** message to Access. Access then determines whether the mouse was over either the **cmdUserName** or the **cmdExit** button and if it was, it runs the code that is contained in the event handler for that button.

If the mouse was over the **cmdUserName** button, the **Click** event handler for that button is invoked. This causes the text box object, **txtUserName**, to be modified so that it displays the name of the user.

If the mouse was over the **cmdExit** button, the **Click** event handler for that button is invoked. This unloads the form.

You can think of the two main differences between traditional MS-DOS-based applications and Access applications as:

- In Access, you create objects whose properties can be modified at design- or at run-time (i.e. when the application is running)
- In Access, you put code into event handlers which are automatically triggered when Windows determines that the relevant event has occurred

But that's enough theory for now. To see how this works in practice, let's look back at the navigation buttons that we created in the first chapter.

Handling Events with Macros

In Chapter 1 we designed a simple form that allowed the users of the Malt Whisky Store application to view, amend and add details of customers to the database. When we left it, we had put five navigation buttons on the bottom of the form. When clicked, these moved the user to the first, previous, next or last record, or added a new record. The form looked like this:

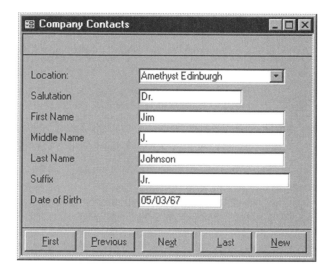

If you didn't implement all the Try It Outs detailed in Chapter 1, you can load up **Whisky2.mdb** from the accompanying CD which has the full code from that chapter.

To make the form useful, we implemented event handlers for the **Click** events of each of the five command buttons.

If that sounds like gobbledygook, let us paraphrase it. We wrote a macro for each button and linked that macro to the relevant button, so that it was executed when the button was clicked. The macros are event handlers. The event they handle is the **Click** event. So, yes, we implemented event handlers for the **Click** event of each of the five command buttons.

Let's look in a little more detail at what is happening behind these buttons. First, we'll look at the events to which the navigation buttons can respond.

Examining a Button's Event Properties

Open the form, **frmPerson**, that you created in Chapter 1. If you switch to Design view and click on the Event tab on the property sheet for the **cmdFirst** command button, you'll see the following:

There are twelve events to which the button **cmdFirst** can respond. And for one of those events, the **Click** event, there is a custom event handler. This is simply a macro, or piece of VBA code, that supplements Access' default response to an event.

You may be a little surprised (and concerned!) at the number of events to which your button can respond. The good news is that you only have to worry about the events that you specifically want to handle. If you don't specify your own custom event handler, Access will handle the event for you. This means that you don't need to write your own event handling code for every event.

For example, we haven't written a custom event handler for the **MouseDown** event of the **cmdFirst** button, yet when we press and hold down the mouse button over **cmdFirst**, the button is redrawn in a 'down' state to show that it has been depressed. That is because this is the default behavior for all buttons in Access. If we wanted Access to perform some additional action when the mouse was depressed over the button, we would need to implement a custom event handler with either a macro or VBA code.

We mentioned that the **Click** event has a custom event handler. When the **cmdFirst** button has the focus and Access receives a message from Windows indicating that the button has been clicked, Access first implements the button's default behavior and then runs the **macFirstButton** macro. You can look at the macro in detail by clicking the builder button (the one with the ellipsis or three dots on its face). This will open up the relevant macro sheet.

FYI

When we say that a button has the focus, we mean that the button is capable of receiving user input through the mouse or keyboard. If a text box has the focus, we can type text into it. If a button has the focus we can hit the spacebar or left mouse button to 'click' it and cause the **Click** event to occur. To prevent a control from receiving the focus, we can disable a control by setting its **Enabled** property to **False**.

Handling Events with VBA

The example that we looked at above uses a macro as a custom event handler. However, it's also possible to write a custom event handler in VBA. In fact, you will find that almost all event handlers in 'professional' applications are written in VBA. We looked at some of the reasons for this in Chapter 1. To recap, the most important are as follows:

> VBA allows you to program functionality that is too complex for a macro to handle

> VBA allows you to trap errors and handle them gracefully

> VBA executes faster than macros

> In a large application, using macros can 'clutter' your database with objects, making it hard to maintain

> VBA allows you to interact with other applications using Automation

In short, VBA gives you more control. Bearing this in mind, we'll rewrite our event handlers using VBA. However, before we can start writing code, we should take a quick look at the environment in which we'll be working.

The Access Programming Environment

Load **Whisky2.mdb** if you haven't done so already and press *F11* to view the database window if it is not already showing. Then highlight **frmPerson** on the Forms sheet and select Code from the View menu.

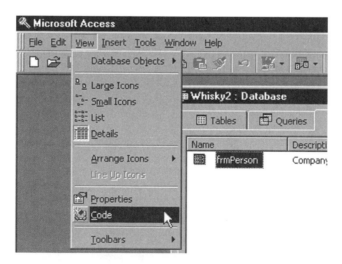

The form will open in Design view, and then the module window will appear.

This is where you can type in code.

You may not see the line Option Explicit in your module window. We'll look at what this means later in the chapter, so don't worry about it now.

Modules and Procedures

Modules are where Access stores your code and are used as a way of grouping related chunks of code (known as **procedures**) together. If it makes things easier, think of a filing cabinet at the office—you might use the top drawer for product detail files, the second for customer files and the third for invoices and sales details. The drawers of a filing cabinet allow you to store similar files together, but in a way that keeps them separate from each other. In the same way, a module allows you to store related chunks of code—for example, the Malt Whisky Store database has several modules, including one each for the code examples from each chapter of the book.

Form and Report Modules

Forms and reports can also have a built-in module that contains all the code for that form or report, including both event and general procedures. This module is kept completely within the form or report object—so if you copy a form which has a module, its module is copied as well. As you have seen, you can display the code for a form or report by selecting Code from the View menu.

> *Unlike previous versions of Access, new forms and reports do not automatically have a module associated with them. Instead, the module is only created if you decide to use VBA code in your form.*

Standard Modules

Standard modules, on the other hand, exist outside of forms or reports as objects in their own right, and are used for creating procedures that aren't associated with any one form or report in particular. For example, you may have a standard module that contains specific functions that your company uses. These may carry out complex calculations such as wind loading in a construction company, or they may format and check the text of a site-visit report in line with your company's safety policy. A prime example of a stand-alone module is one where you store all of those useful little chunks of code that you collect over time; for example, functions that convert **Null** values to zero (as in the Access sample **Northwind** database), or which format a string so that only the first character of each word is capitalized.

As these modules are separate from forms and reports, you create and view them on the Modules tab in the main database window, using the New and Design buttons. And, of course, you can easily copy the modules into other Access databases without having to worry about which form or report they are stored in.

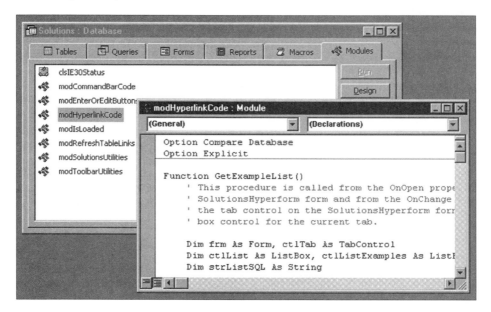

Class Modules

New to this version of Access are class modules. These appear with standard modules and you can view them on the Modules tab in the database window. You can use class modules to create and define custom objects. You can then create instances of those objects in code. We shall look at how you can use these class modules in more detail in Chapter 12.

FYI

In fact, class modules did exist in Access 95, but only behind forms and reports. A form or report module is actually a type of class module but cannot exist without its associated form or report object. In contrast, the new class modules in Access 97 can exist on their own.

Module Contents

Now you know where the modules are and how to access them, but what do they actually contain? Let's have a look at the module window in more detail:

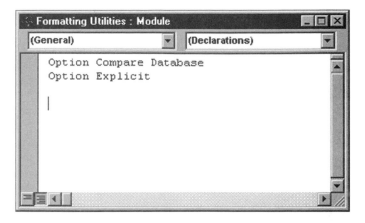

When you open a module window, you see two combo boxes at the top. These enable you to access the different procedures stored in the module. The combo box to the left allows you to select the object whose code you wish to view. With standard modules, the only option available will be **(General)** since standard modules don't contain objects, but for a form or report module, this combo box will contain a list of all the objects that the form or report contains in alphabetical order:

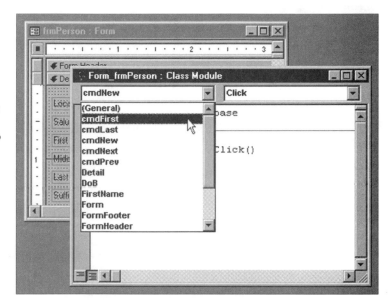

Once you have selected the required object in the left combo box, you can use the right combo box to select the events for that object:

So, for example, this screenshot shows where you would type the event handler for the form's **Load** event.

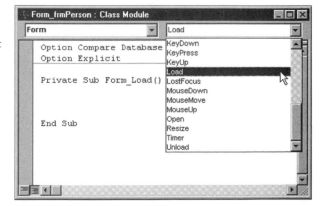

The (General) Object

The **(General)** object isn't really an object at all. Instead, it's where everything that relates to the module as a whole goes. So, in a form or report module, you could put procedures here that aren't event procedures, but are procedures that are general to the form. In standard modules, all procedures go in this section.

Options

You also set **Options** in the **(General)** section of a module. Every module has certain options that can be set using statements commencing with the **Option** keyword:

Option Base

This statement allows you to set the default lower limit for arrays. This is normally **0**. Arrays are explained later on in the book, so you don't need to worry about this at the moment.

Option Compare

This is one statement that you will frequently see. It determines how Access compares strings. Normally, this is set to **Database**, but it can be **Binary** or **Text** as well.

When **Option Compare Binary** is set, Access will use the internal binary representation of characters when comparing them in that module. This means that it will regard lower and upper case versions of the same letter as different. It also means that when Access sorts values it will place all upper-case letters before all lower-case letters, so whereas a word beginning with a upper-case **Z** is placed after one starting with an uppercase **Y**; a word beginning with a lower-case **a** is placed after both of these.

Option Compare Database, which is the default setting, causes Access to use the database's sort order when comparing strings in that module. The sort order of the database is determined by what the setting of the <u>N</u>ew Database Sort Order option on the General tab of the <u>T</u>ools/ <u>O</u>ptions... dialog was when the database was created.

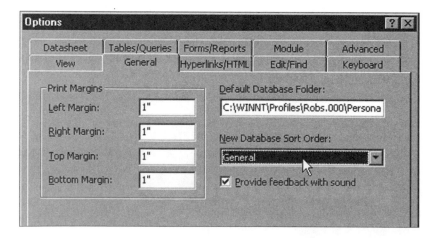

If the value in the New Database Sort Order drop-down box is General, then the database will be created with a sort order defined by the system locale. We can change the system locale by using the Regional Settings utility in the Control Panel. As well as defining the sort order, the system locale also affects other features such as the way that dates are formatted or how currency values are displayed.

Alternatively, if we want to use a sort order different from that specified by the system locale, we can select a different sort order in the New Database Sort Order drop-down box.

Changes we make to the the New Database Sort Order drop-down box are only reflected in new database that are created after we change the setting. Note, however, that when we tell Access to compact a database, it physically creates a new database into which it compacts the old. This means that the new database that is created will have the new sort order. In fact, this is the recommended way of changing the sort order of a database.

Option Compare Text is similar to **Option Compare Database** except that string comparisons are not case sensitive.

Option Explicit

This is the most useful of the options. If it's set, it means that all variables have to be declared before being used. You will see why this is a good idea in later chapters. You can turn on **Option Explicit** by selecting Options from the Tools menu and turning on Require Variable Declaration in the Module page.

Option Private

This makes the whole module private, so that none of the code within it can be accessed from another module. This saves you having to use the **Private** keyword on each procedure. Again, we'll explain these concepts in more detail in later chapters, so don't worry too much about them for now.

You will not normally need to modify any of these **Option** settings in day-to-day use. The only one to keep an eye on is **Option Explicit**. We'll look at the reasons for that in the next chapter.

Declarations

As well as setting options, the **(General)** section can also be used to declare external functions, variables and constants which apply to the whole module. We'll look at this subject in more detail in the next chapter.

VBA Event Handlers

Let's return now to our navigation buttons, and replace the macros that we built in the first chapter with VBA code. When you create an event handler in VBA, you are writing a **subprocedure** or **subroutine**. We'll create a VBA subprocedure that operates the Last button on the form and takes us to the last record in our database....

Try It Out—Writing VBA Event Handlers

1 Close down the module window if you have it open and, with the **frmPerson** form open in Design view, display the property sheet for the command button **cmdLast**.

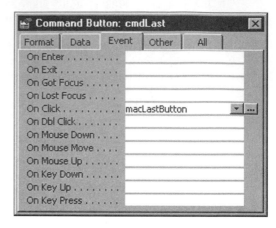

2 Select the On Click event property and delete the name of its event handler. Note that by doing this you aren't deleting the actual macro. You are just telling Access that the macro is no longer to be used as the event handler for the click event of the **cmdLast** button.

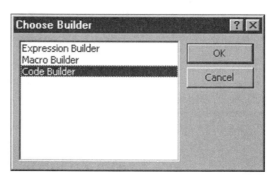

3 Click the builder button (with the ellipsis) to the right of the On Click event property. This will bring up a dialog asking how you want to build your event handler.

4 This time round we want to use VBA to write the event handler, so you should select the Code Builder option and hit the OK button. Access now displays the VBA module window.

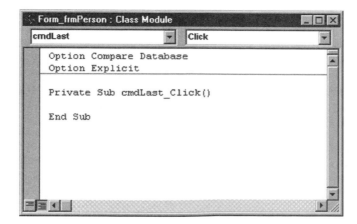

The lines that you can see here form the VBA event procedure for the click event of the **cmdLast** button. We can tell that by looking at the two combo boxes at the top of the window. In other words, the code here is what will be executed when the **cmdLast** button is clicked at run-time.

Notice also that the screenshot shows the **Declarations** section of the module as well. This is because the module window is set to Full Module View. You can switch between having the entire module displayed or having just a single procedure displayed by checking and unchecking the Full Module View checkbox on the Module tab of the Tools/Options... dialog. You can also do this by clicking the small buttons in the bottom left of the module window.

The procedure starts with the line:

```
Private Sub cmdLast_Click()
```

and ends with the line:

```
End Sub
```

Everything that goes between those two lines will be executed when the button is clicked. At the moment there is just a blank line, so nothing would happen if **cmdLast** were clicked. It's time to write some code!

5 Type the following line of code in the module window, making sure you don't forget the two commas.

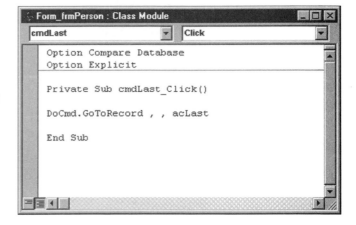

Don't be concerned if Access throws something that looks like tooltips at you while you are typing in this line. These features—Auto List Members and Auto Quick Info—are discussed a little later in this chapter, but you can ignore them for the moment.

6 Now close the module window. The words [Event Procedure] now appear against the On Click event property in the property sheet for **cmdLast**. This indicates that a VBA procedure now handles the click event rather than a macro.

7 Switch the form to Form view and click the Last button. If you've done everything correctly, you will be taken to the last record in the database. Congratulations! You have written your first VBA procedure!

How It Works

OK, so let's have a look in more detail at the code you typed in:

```
DoCmd.GoToRecord , , acLast
```

It's really quite simple. We'll look at each part in turn.

The **DoCmd** at the start of the line indicates that we want Access to carry out an **action**. In other words, we want Access to do something that we could have performed using either the keyboard or a macro. The action that we want to carry out is the **GoToRecord** action. This is what would happen if we selected G̲o To from the Edit menu when the form's open in Form view. You will remember this is also the name of the action we selected in the macro that was originally behind this button.

Once we've specified the action, we need to tell Access to which record we want to go. This is the purpose of the constant **acLast**—the record we want is the last record. (We'll be looking at constants in Chapter 3.)

The two commas before **acLast** indicate that there are additional arguments we could have supplied to make our code more specific. In this case, we could have specified the type of object we want to move within (in our case a form) and the name of the object, **frmPerson**. So, we could have written the code like this:

```
DoCmd.GoToRecord acForm, "frmPerson", acLast
```

If we omit these two arguments, Access will assume that we mean the current object. This is fine in our case, so we can leave the optional arguments out. However, we still have to insert a commas to indicate where arguments have been omitted. So that's how we end up with the line of code:

```
DoCmd.GoToRecord , , acLast
```

In Access 2 and earlier you would have used the **DoCmd** action. This was replaced in Access 95 with the **DoCmd** object. This means that instead of typing **DoCmd GoToRecord** you type **DoCmd.GoToRecord** (note the intervening period). In other words, in Access 95 and Access 97 you are invoking the **GoToRecord** method of the **DoCmd** object.

What are Actions and Methods?

At this stage you might be getting a little confused over just what the difference is between actions and methods. After all, there is a **GoToRecord** action and a **GoToRecord** method and they both do the same thing. What's the difference?

Actions are the building blocks of **macros**. Many of them correspond to tasks carried out by the user through the Access user interface by selecting items from a menu. Others allow you to perform different tasks that a user can't, such as displaying a message box or making the computer beep. The main thing to remember, however is that actions occur in macros.

Methods, however, occur in **VBA**. A method is used to make an object behave in a certain way and we'll look at the idea of methods and objects in more detail in Chapter 5. Because you cannot use actions outside of macros, you use methods to achieve the same ends in VBA. There are two objects whose methods you use to perform almost all of the macro actions in VBA. These are the **Application** object and the **DoCmd** object.

So, if we want to write a VBA statement that performs the same action as the **Quit** action in a macro, we would use the **Quit** method of the **Application** object.

```
Application.Quit
```

In fact, the **Application** object is the default object, so we can omit it and simply type this as our line of code.

```
Quit
```

Almost all of the macro actions, however, are mapped to methods of the **DoCmd** object. So if we want to write a line of VBA that does the same as the **Beep** macro action, we would write this:

```
DoCmd.Beep
```

There are only eight macro actions that don't have a corresponding method in VBA code. The VBA equivalents are listed below. Don't worry if they don't make much sense to you at the moment. Hopefully, they will make more sense as you read more of the book! Just bear in mind that the eight actions below don't have corresponding methods in VBA.

Action	Equivalent in VBA
AddMenu	Use **MenuBar** or **ShortcutMenuBar** properties
MsgBox	Use the **MsgBox** function
RunApp	Use the **Shell** function to run another application
RunCode	Run the function directly in VBA
SendKeys	Use the **SendKeys** statement
SetValue	Set the value directly in VBA
StopAllMacros	Not applicable
StopMacro	Not applicable

FYI

To find out the VBA equivalent of a macro action, simply look up the action in Access online help. If there is an equivalent VBA method, it will be described on the help page for the action.

Why is the Code in Different Colors?

One of the nice things about writing VBA in Access 97 is colored code. This is not just a pretty device. The different colors are used to distinguish the different components of code and can make your code easier to read. You can set these colors yourself on the Module tab of the Options... dialog on the Tools menu.

The colors really can make it easier for you to read and understand the code. For example, you can alter the color of the line of code that is due to be executed next. This makes it easier to see what is happening when you step through your code at run-time. Or you can choose to have all your comments in gray so that they don't appear too intrusive.

 Stepping through the code by running it line by line is useful for debugging the code. This is covered later in the book, in Chapter 11, "Debugging and Error Handling".

You can also use different colors to distinguish between the different types of word you use in your code. **Keywords**—reserved words, such as **DoCmd**, which always have a special meaning to Access—can be in one color, and **identifiers**—such as the names of forms you have created or messages you want to display—can be in another color. This can make it easier to understand what your code (or someone else's code!) is doing.

What were all those Popup Thingies?

Good question! Writing VBA in Access 97 is suddenly an altogether more animated affair than it was in previous versions of Access. Before you have finished typing even half a word you may find Access trying to butt in and finish the job for you. It all looks a bit disconcerting at first but, once you get used to the way it works, it can both make your code easier to write and less prone to errors. The proper terms for these popups are Auto List Members and Auto Quick Info. We'll look at them now in more detail.

> *The Auto List Members and Auto Quick Info features can be turned on and off via the* Module *tab of the Options... dialog on the Tools menu. Make sure that these options are checked if you want to observe the behavior described below.*

The Auto List Members feature of Access 97 suggests a list of all the valid words that can come next. (More specifically, it lists the relevant methods, properties, events, members or constants. We'll be looking at what these words mean in the next few chapters). You can see this at work if you type the phrase **DoCmd.** in the Module Window. As soon as you have done so, Access suggests a list of possible methods that could come next.

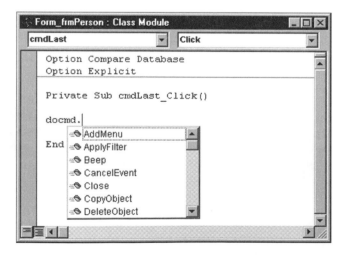

All of the words in the popup list box are valid methods that can follow the **DoCmd** object. We saw earlier how the **DoCmd** object allows us to carry out the same actions you can perform in macros. Well, once we have decided that we want to use the **DoCmd** object, the popup lists all of those actions for you.

You can select an item from the list by double-clicking it or by hitting either the *Tab* key or the space bar. Or, if you want, you can carry on typing your code. If you do carry on typing your code, Access will highlight the word that matches what you are typing most closely.

The other popup you may have seen is displayed by the Auto Quick Info feature. This one helps you to remember the syntax of difficult-to-remember commands. You'll see it whenever you type the name of a recognised function or subprocedure into the Module Window. So, in our example above, once you had typed **DoCmd.GotoRecord**, Access displayed the Auto Quick Info popup to help you with the rest of the command.

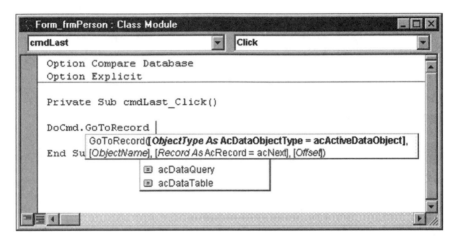

The popup window acts as an aide-memoire, to remind you what arguments you need to type in after **DoCmd.GoToRecord**. The next argument you need to type in is always highlighted in bold, and any optional arguments are displayed inside square brackets.

In the example above, the next argument we should type in is the **ObjectType** argument. There is even an Auto List Members popup behind the Auto Quick Info popup to list the possible values you can type in for the **ObjectType** argument! Since the **ObjectType** argument is shown in square brackets, we can ignore it as it is an optional argument. However, we still need to type a comma to acknowledge the fact that we have omitted the optional argument.

Typing the comma causes Access to highlight the next argument in the Auto Quick Info popup.

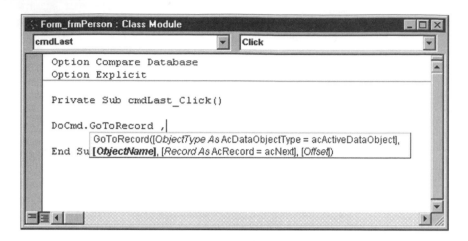

Again the argument is optional, so we can ignore it and simply type a comma in its place. The highlight then moves to the third argument.

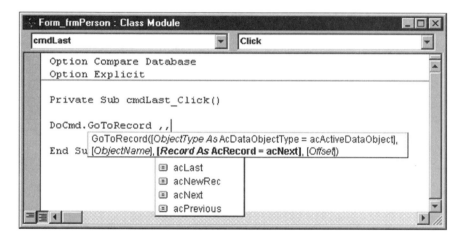

Even though the Record argument is optional, we want to use it, as this is the one that tells Access which record we want to move to. And what's cool is that Access displays an Auto List Members popup which lists the possible values we can supply for this argument. We can click acLast and Access inserts that argument in our line of code. The last argument, Offset, is also optional, so we can ignore it and just hit the *Enter* key to complete our line of code.

Auto List Members and Auto Quick Info aren't just gimmicks. They really help you to get your VBA code right first time without needing to spend time looking in Online Help or other manuals. I just love 'em!

What if I still Get It Wrong?

So we're none of us perfect! Even with Auto List Members and Auto Quick Info looking over our shoulder and telling us what to write we still make mistakes. Another way in which Access makes the job of writing code a bit easier is that it will inform you if you have made a mistake in a line of code. For example, you might have mistyped the line of code as:

```
Do Cmd GoToRecord , , acLast
```

Then, when you tried to move off the line, Access would have highlighted the line of code (and the word **Cmd**) and displayed this dialog box:

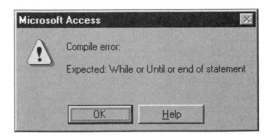

This indicates that the word **Do** must always be followed by the words **While** or **Until**, or else it must appear on its own. Of course, we don't want the word **Do**—we want to use **DoCmd**, which is something altogether different. This type of error is called a **syntax error**.

However, if the error is less obvious, Access may only be able to recognize the fact that it's an error when you try to run the code (i.e. when you click the button). This is called a **run-time error** and will result in a rather unfriendly dialog box being presented to the user when they click the button. For example, if you had missed out a comma and typed:

```
DoCmd.GoToRecord , acLast
```

Access wouldn't have generated a syntax error when you moved off the line but, when the **cmdLast** button was clicked at run-time, it would have interpreted **acLast** as the second argument (rather than the third) and would have displayed the following dialog box:

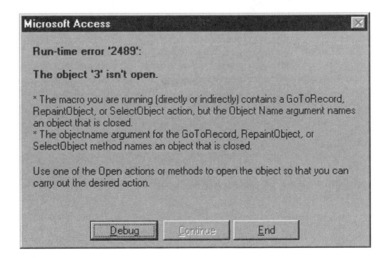

Here, **acLast** has the value 3 within VBA, a value that the missing optional parameter should not have. Later in the book we shall be looking at how to prevent these run-time errors and how to handle them more gracefully.

49

The third type of error that you can create when writing code occurs when the code that you type in is syntactically correct, but does not produce the desired effect. In this situation, the program appears to function normally, but in fact doesn't perform as you intended. For example, you may have accidentally typed:

```
DoCmd.GoToRecord , , acFirst
```

This is a **logic error** - you had intended to type **acLast** not **acFirst**. It might take some time for you or the users of your application to notice that the **cmdLast** button was moving the current record pointer to the first rather than the last record. You may also hear this type of error referred to as a **semantic error**.

Compiling Code

You've seen how Access checks for the more obvious errors as you type. However, there is another method that can be used to prevent errors. This is the process known as **compiling**, and is used to trap the less obvious errors that might crop up in your code. When your code is compiled, routine checks are performed—such as checking that variables have been declared (if **Option Explicit** has been set) and that procedures you call are named in your application. Compiling involves assembling the code in preparation for execution, but doesn't actually execute the code. To compile your code, you use the Compile Loaded Modules button on the toolbar.

Compiling can't catch all errors, but it will pick up general consistency problems in your code. If compiling doesn't produce any errors, then control is returned to you.

Where Now?

So far, we have looked at how to execute a procedure when the user clicks a button. Well, you may say, that's great but so what? It's not exactly an earth-shattering example of the power of VBA. After all, the VBA procedure does exactly what the macro did! True, but the purpose of this example was to show you how easy it is to write VBA. One simple line of code is all it takes. There will be plenty of time later on to look at some of the more complex things you can do with VBA. For the moment, we are just trying to familiarize ourselves with how to write VBA procedures.

In fact, Access 97 can now convert your macros to VBA for you. We'll use this feature to convert the event handlers behind the other four buttons to VBA.

You will only be able to carry out this next exercise if you selected Advanced Wizards to be installed as part of the Access setup. The advanced wizards are not included with the typical setup, but are available either by choosing custom setup when you first install Access or by selecting the Add/Remove Components option if you re-run setup after Access has been installed.

Try It Out—Converting Macros to VBA

1 Open the **frmPerson** form in Design view and then click the code button to view the code module. This should contain the event handler for the **Click** event of the **cmdLast** button.

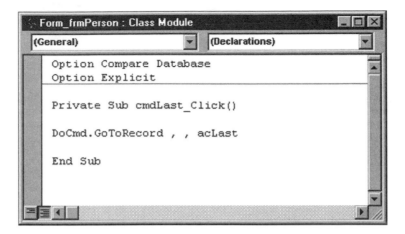

2 Check that the event handlers for the **Click** event of the other four buttons use the macros created in the earlier chapter, by clicking each button in turn and inspecting the On Click property on the Event tab of the property window. This should contain the name of the macro that handles the **Click** event.

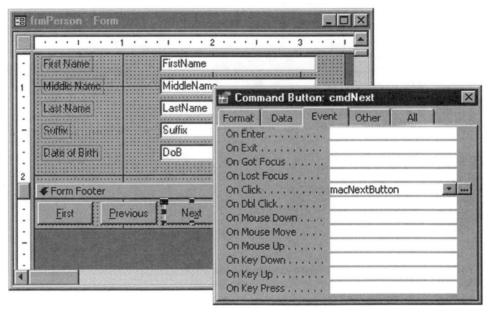

3 Now click Macro from the Tools menu and from the submenu which appears select Convert Form's Macros to Visual Basic.

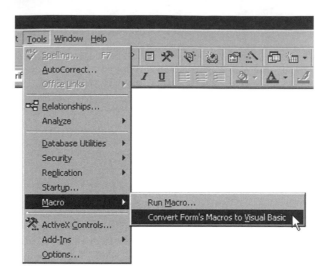

4 A dialog box will appear asking whether you want to add error handling and whether you want to include macro comments in the generated code. Make sure that both of these boxes are checked and then hit the Convert button.

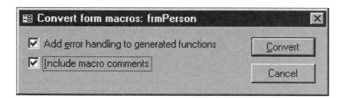

5 Access will then convert the macro-based event handlers behind the four remaining buttons into VBA and display a message box when it has succeeded in doing so. Click the code button to view the code module for the form and you will be able to view the newly generated event handlers. The code for the **Click** event of the **cmdFirst** button is shown below.

```
'-------------------------------------------------------------
' cmdFirst_Click
'
'-------------------------------------------------------------
Private Sub cmdFirst_Click()
On Error GoTo cmdFirst_Click_Err

    DoCmd.GoToRecord , "", acFirst


cmdFirst_Click_Exit:
    Exit Sub

cmdFirst_Click_Err:
    MsgBox Error$
```

```
        Resume cmdFirst_Click_Exit

    End Sub
```

How It Works

If you look at the code that Access creates when it converts the event-handling macro into VBA, you will see a familiar statement using the **DoCmd** object that we encountered earlier:

```
DoCmd.GoToRecord , "", acFirst
```

So what is the rest of the code which Access has inserted? Well, the first four lines are comments. These are remarks inserted, normally by the programmer, to explain the purpose of the code that follows them.

```
'------------------------------------------------------------
' cmdFirst_Click
'
'------------------------------------------------------------
```

Comments are denoted by an apostrophe, which prevents Access from trying to run these lines as if they were executable code. By default, Access displays comments in green, but you can change this via the Module tab of the Options... dialog on the Tools menu. If our macro had contained any comments, the Access Macro to VBA converter would have placed these before the appropriate line of code in the VBA procedure.

With the exception of the comments and the statement that uses the **DoCmd** object, the rest of the code generated by the converter is for error handling purposes. You may remember that one of the reasons for implementing VBA instead of macros was that 'VBA allows you to trap errors and handle them gracefully'. We'll be looking at error handling in more detail later on in the book.

Access Events

So where are we now? We have looked at what events are, and how fundamental they are to the operation of Windows and Access. We have also looked at how we can use macros and VBA to write event handlers. But so far we have only mentioned one or two events. We'll take a quick look at some of the more common events that can be handled within Access 97, what triggers them and how they can be useful to us. You can find a comprehensive list of all of the events that Access 97 handles in Appendix A. It should give you an idea of just how much you can achieve in Access through the careful use of event handlers.

Event Property	Belongs to...	Occurs...	Can be used for...
On Change	Controls on a form	after the contents of a control change. (e.g. by typing a character)	triggering the update of related controls on the form.
On Click	Forms, Controls and sections on a form	when the user clicks the mouse button over a form or control; when the user takes some action which has the same effect as clicking (e.g. pressing the spacebar to check a checkbox).	just about anything—this is one of the most used of all events, and is about the only event used with command buttons.
On Close	Forms, Reports	after a form or report has been closed and removed from the screen.	triggering the opening of the next form.
On Current	Forms	when the form is opened or requeried; after thefocus moves to a different record, but before the new record is displayed.	implementing intelligent navigation buttons (see example below).
On Dbl Click	Forms; Controls and sections on a form	when the user depresses and releases the left mouse button twice over the same object.	selecting an item in a list and carrying out the actions of the OK button in one go.
On Delete	Forms	when the user attempts to delete a record.	preventing the user from deleting records.
On Error	Forms; Reports	when a run-time database engine error occurs (but not a VBA error). We look at this in more detail in Chapter 11.	intercepting errors and displaying your own custom error messages.
On Mouse Move	Forms; Controls and sections on a form	when the mouse pointer moves over objects.	displaying X and Y coordinates of the mouse pointer.
On Mouse Up	Forms; Controls and sections on a form	when the user releases a mouse button.	detecting whether the user has a mouse button depressed when clicking an object.

FYI

The final column of the table is only intended to give an indication of the type of action that you can perform in the event handler. It isn't meant to be an exhaustive or comprehensive list of the uses of each event handler.

Also, the table above only lists the more commonly-used events. For a fuller listing, refer to Appendix A.

You will notice that the table lists event properties rather than events. An event property is a property that appears in the property sheet and allows you to handle a specific event. Therefore, in the example above, the event handler for the click event of the **cmdFirst** button, **cmdFirst_Click**, is exposed via the On Click event property in the property sheet.

Completing the Company Contacts Form

So how does all this help us? If you remember, our original mission in this chapter was to produce intelligent navigation buttons. That is to say, we need to create navigation buttons that disable themselves when they are unavailable. How can we do this? Well, first of all we'll show you the answer, and then we'll explain how it works.

Try It Out—Creating An 'Intelligent' Navigation Button

1 Open the **frmPerson** form in Design view.

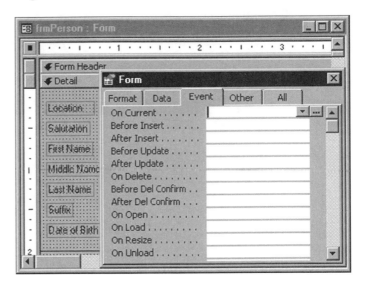

2 View the form's properties by double-clicking on the form selector at the top left, where the rulers meet.

3 Open the form's **Current** event procedure by clicking on the builder button to the right of the On Current property and selecting Code Builder.

4 Add the following code to the form's **Current** event procedure:

```
Private Sub Form_Current()
    'If the PersonID control in the form is empty then we are on the
    'new (blank) record. In this case, disable the Next button.
    'To do this we have to shift the focus first. If there is
    'a value, the button must be enabled.

    If IsNull(Me.PersonID) Then
        cmdPrev.SetFocus
        cmdNext.Enabled = False
```

```
Else
    cmdNext.Enabled = True
End If
End Sub
```

5 Close the form and save it when prompted. When you open the form again, what do you know! You've got an 'intelligent' Next button! When you get to the end of the records, the button becomes disabled. However, clicking the Previous button enables the Next button again.

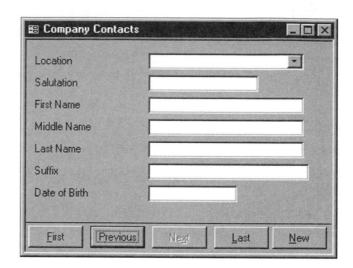

How Does It Work? The 'Intelligent' Navigation Button

Well, it looks simple enough, but bear in mind that we are only dealing with one button here—and in fact it's the easiest one to handle! The first thing is to note that we have used the On Current event property. We need to enable or disable the button as soon as the form is opened, and then whenever the user moves from one record to another. Looking through the list of events, there is only one that fits the bill, and that is the On Current event.

After determining which event handler to use, we must decide exactly what rules to follow for enabling and disabling the button. The records for this form come from the **Person** table, which contains a **PersonID** field. This is the primary key for the table, so it will always contain a value in every record. If the current record has no value in this field (i.e. if it's **Null**), then we must be on a new record—the last record in the recordset.

> *Remember that Access automatically provides a new blank record at the end of every updateable table or recordset. We must allow the user to move to this record so that they can enter details of a new contact.*

If we are on a new record, the Next button should be disabled. If not, it should be enabled. We get the value of the current record's **PersonID** field using **Me.PersonID**. The **Me** keyword simply indicates to Access that we want to use the current object's recordset (the current object is our **frmPerson** form). If this value is **Null**, we know we are on a new record.

However, it's not quite that easy—we can't just disable the Next button directly because it has the focus—it's just been clicked. If we disable an item that has the focus, we'll get a run-time error. So first we must move the focus somewhere else, and where better than to the Previous button. This is likely to be the one you want to use next anyway. To set the focus to a control, we just call its **SetFocus** method.

```
If IsNull(Me.PersonID) Then
    cmdPrev.SetFocus
    cmdNext.Enabled = False
```

You'll notice that to enable or disable a control, we just set its **Enabled** property to **True** or **False**.

As it stands, the button will be disabled when we hit a new record (or if the recordset is empty when the form opens), but it will also remain grayed out when we scroll to an existing record. We must re-enable it each time the current record is *not* a new one...

```
Else
    cmdNext.Enabled = True
End If
```

This code uses the **If...Then...Else** construct which may be new to you. This is pretty intuitive, but in case you aren't familiar with branching statements, they are explained in more detail in Chapter 4.

Summary

This chapter has given you your first taste of VBA code. It should also have given you some idea of how an application is built. As a developer, you build your forms and reports and then write code that causes the objects you have created to respond to events in a particular way. In an event-driven environment like Access, you can let the users decide the order in which your code modules are executed.

We have spent some time looking at the different events that can occur in Access and how these can be put to use. You have seen, for example, how the On Current event can be used to solve one of the tasks we set ourselves in Chapter 1—enabling and disabling navigation buttons depending on our position in the recordset. We shall complete this feature for all the buttons in Chapter 6, once you have a few more programming concepts under your belt.

To summarize then, you should now feel comfortable with:

- What events are
- How to make an Access object respond to an event
- The Access coding window
- What modules are and how Access uses them to store code
- How to use the On Current event to make a navigation button intelligent

In the next couple of chapters, we will be looking at the nuts and bolts of VBA so that you will be able to write your own event handlers more easily.

Exercises

1 One of the most important things to remember when working with events in VBA is the order in which events occur. For example, when you save a record on a form, several events occur, one after another. By looking at the list of events on the property sheet, try to work out the order in which they happen.

For the answer, look at the topic 'Find out when events occur' in the Access online help.

2 Take some time to read through the list of events and their uses. You will find that some events are more useful than others—in other words, you will find yourself writing custom event handlers for some events more often than others. Look at the list and try to think about which events you would most commonly handle with custom event handlers.

Creating Code

In the next two chapters, we are going to lay the foundations that will enable us to write some quite sophisticated programs later on in the book. We will be looking at how procedures are built up and how you can use variables to make your procedures generic—so you don't have to write a new piece of code every time your data changes.

In particular, we will be looking at:

▶ What procedures are and how you use them

▶ The differences between subroutines and functions

▶ What variables are and how they are used

▶ The different data types

▶ How to name your objects consistently

Procedures

You saw some examples of procedures (subroutines and functions) in Chapter 2, but exactly what they are and how they can be used has yet to be explained. As we'll see in just a moment, there is only one difference between a subroutine and a function, so we will use the generic term **procedure** to refer to them both.

A procedure is a (hopefully) small section of code, usually self-contained, which performs either a single task or a set of related tasks. So what's the reasons for breaking code down into small chunks? Well, one reason is that a small piece of code, such as a separate procedure, can be re-used in another application. That saves not only time, but also money, as less development and testing have to take place. It also allows maintenance of applications to be controlled more easily. Imagine a very large block of code that needed several changes—only one person could really do one change at once. If this was split into several procedures, then they could all be worked on together. You can also substitute one procedure for another if they both achieve the same purpose. The downside of this is that it may take more time initially. You will have to design your application to be structured from the very beginning, and this may slow down the initial development, but the paybacks are considerable. So, your first project may be slower, but at the end you will have a number of reusable components that can be slotted quickly into other projects.

Subroutines and Functions

So what's the difference between functions and subroutines? A subroutine is simply a small block of code that has a name. This piece of code can be used by calling its name, and is just like asking someone to do something for you. A function is similar, but unlike a subroutine it can tell you something when it's finished. So if you ask someone to do something for you, and they go away and do it, but don't tell you anything afterwards, then that's a subroutine. If they come back after they have done it and tell you something about it, then that's a function.

To make this a bit clearer, let's have a look at the 'making tea' example that all programming books use. Imagine that you want to create a procedure for making tea in the office. You could write it as follows:

```
Sub MakeTea()
    Go to kitchen.
    Boil kettle.
    Put milk in cup.
    Put tea bag in cup.
    When kettle is boiled, pour water into cup.
    When brewed for long enough, take out tea bag.
End Sub
```

Then, whenever someone wanted a cup of tea, you could simply call your **MakeTea()** procedure and it would perform all the necessary tasks for you.

This looks good, but things are never as simple as they first appear! What we've forgotten is that some people take sugar in their tea. Therefore, we need to tell the procedure whether or not to add sugar to the tea.

We can pass information to a procedure using **arguments**. These are simply variables (variables are discussed in more detail in the next section) that have been set elsewhere in the code and can pass the required information. This is just like someone writing down his or her tea order and passing it to you on your way to the kitchen. So, in this case, we need to pass an argument that lets the procedure know whether or not to add sugar.

```
Sub MakeTea (SugarIsRequired)
    Go to kitchen.
    Boil kettle.
    Put milk in cup.
    Put tea bag in cup.
    When kettle is boiled, pour water into cup.
    When brewed for long enough, take out tea bag.
    If SugarIsRequired then add sugar.
End Sub
```

You would call this procedure by specifying the name, **MakeTea()**, and whether or not sugar is required.

So that's that problem solved. What happens now, though, when someone asks for a cup of tea with sugar, but the sugar has run out? Well, you'll get your tea without sugar and you won't be told there's no sugar because the procedure does not include a way to get this information back to you. In other words, this is a **subroutine**.

We mentioned earlier that a **function** differs from a subroutine in that it can return a value to the place from which it was called. If we turn the **MakeTea** subroutine into a function, we can make it tell us whether all parts succeeded, so at least we'll know if we get a cup of tea with no sugar. Again, we need to tell the function whether or not we take sugar and we need to tell it the type of the value we want returned. In this case, we want a simple true or false value, so the type is Boolean (more on this later).

```
Function MakeTea(SugarIsRequired) As Boolean
    Go to kitchen.
    Boil kettle.
    Put milk in cup.
    Put tea bag in cup.
    When kettle is boiled, pour water into cup.
    When brewed for long enough, take out tea bag.
    If SugarIsRequired then add sugar.

    If all parts completed then
        MakeTea = True
    Else
        MakeTea = False
    End If

End Function
```

Don't worry if you can't follow every word in this example above—this is called pseudo-code and is not a real programming language. It's a way of writing in English (or your chosen language) the tasks that the procedure will do. All will become clear very soon. The important thing to understand here is that a procedure is a way of bundling several lines of code into a single unit. Then, every time you want to perform that particular task, you can just type one line of code containing the name of the procedure. This saves a lot of time and effort—not just because it is easier on the old fingers, but also because you'll avoid a lot of errors. This is what reuse is all about. You are investing time to create a piece of code that can be used more than once, and that's the payback. Because it's already written, you don't need to write it again.

Procedures are basically all there is to programming. Programming is simply a way of performing a number of small, simple tasks in order to carry out a slightly larger, more complex one. The tea making example was just programming—a set of instructions to carry out a task. And you thought it was going to be hard!

Procedure Declaration

To declare a procedure, there are several things you must know:

- What it is going to be called
- What arguments (if any) it will take
- Whether or not a result is needed, and what data type it will return

These things will depend on the program design, and once they are known, you can begin to construct your procedure. For example, a subroutine to print mailing labels might look like this:

```
Sub PrintMailingLabels (strLabelType As String)
    .
    .
    .
End Sub
```

Here, you have given the subroutine a sensible name, **PrintMailingLabels**, and it needs to know one piece of information—the type of labels to print. The words between the parentheses make up the argument: **strLabelType** is the name of the argument and **String** is the type of data it will hold. This subroutine would be called in the following fashion:

```
Call PrintMailingLabels ("Avery7163")
```

A function is slightly different:

```
Function PaymentStatus (datInvoiced As Date, datPaid As Date) As String
    If datPaid > (datInvoiced + 30) Then
        PaymentStatus = "Overdue"
    Else
        PaymentStatus = "OK"
    End If
End Function
```

Here, the function is called **PaymentStatus**. It takes two arguments, separated by commas, both of which are dates. Unlike a subroutine, a function has a return value. If you imagine the function as a question, then the return value is the answer to that question. So there's a good definition for you. A subroutine is 'Go and do this' and a function is 'What is the answer if you go and do this?'. In this example, the type of data being returned is a string value. To return the value from within the function, you simply set the function name to the value that you want returned. As you can see above, either **Overdue** or **OK** is returned, depending on whether the payment has been settled within the right number of days.

You can see from the **PaymentStatus** example that we have to supply values for both of the arguments when we call the function; if we don't, an error occurs. So, to call the procedure, we would use:

```
Result = PaymentStatus (datDateInvoiced, datDatePaid)
```

Result would be either **OK** or **Overdue**, depending on the actual dates. However, if we swap the two arguments around, we will get the wrong answer—the function will assume that the first argument is the date of the invoice. So the order of the arguments is vital. But there is a technique which we can use to supply the arguments in a different order....

Named Arguments

With named arguments, you can supply the arguments in any position simply by specifying the argument name in front of the argument and using a colon followed by an equals sign (**:=**) to separate the two:

```
Result = PaymentStatus (datPaid:= datDatePaid, datInvoiced:=
datDateInvoiced)
```

With a function that only takes two arguments, the benefits of this may seem minimal but, as the number of arguments increases, it can make the function easier to read. It is also a useful way to avoid errors—especially if the arguments take the same type of data. It's quite easy to forget which way round the two date arguments go, even in our simple function.

This technique is particularly useful when the function you are calling does not require you to provide values for *all* the arguments. You should, however, pick a style and use it consistently throughout your application. Don't chop and change your style according to the function as this can add confusion to maintenance.

Optional Arguments

A piece of code won't normally compile unless all calls to the procedure supply the correct number of arguments. However, you can change this behavior by specifying one or more arguments in the function itself as **optional**. Then you are not obliged to include values for these arguments when you call the procedure. For example, have a look at the following function:

```
Function PaymentStatus (datInvoiced As Date, _
                        Optional datPaid As Date) As String
```

The underscore character (_) is used in VBA as a line continuation character. It tells Access that the following line is not a new statement but should be read as part of the current line. We will be using it throughout this book due to the space limitations of the page. However, you should type these split lines without a carriage return (and without the underscore).

Note that you cannot use the line continuation character to split a text string. Anything that is written between quote marks must be on the same line.

You can call the function as:

```
Result = PaymentStatus (datDateInvoiced)
```

or:

```
Result = PaymentStatus (datInvoiced:=datDateInvoiced)
```

These are both quite legal, even though no value has been supplied for the **datPaid** argument.

Again, these methods really only come into their own when you have a lot of arguments. For example, the mythical function,

```
Function MeaningOfLife (arg1, arg2, arg3, arg4, arg5)
    If (arg2 + arg3 * arg4 - arg5) < 42 Then
        MeaningOfLife = arg1
    Else
        MeaningOfLife = 42
    End If
End Function
```

requires five arguments, so would need to be called as:

```
Result = MeaningOfLife (value1, value2, value3, value4, value5)
```

Depending on the values in the arguments, the function returns another value. However, if we didn't supply any arguments, it would still be able to return a sensible value—42. So we could make some or all of the arguments optional:

```
Function MeaningOfLife (arg1, arg2, arg3, Optional arg4, Optional arg5)
```

Now we can call the function and supply less than five arguments. The following are all acceptable:

```
Result = MeaningOfLife (value1, value2, value3)
Result = MeaningOfLife (value1, value2, value3, value4)
Result = MeaningOfLife (value1, value2, value3, , value5)
Result = MeaningOfLife (arg1:= value1, arg2:= value2, arg3:= value3)
Result = MeaningOfLife (arg1:= value1, arg2:= value2, arg3:= value3, _
arg5:= value5)
```

There are a few things to note here:

- If we use the normal calling convention (without named arguments), we need to indicate the position of each argument by including a comma to show that an optional argument is being omitted. This is the third example.

- If we use named arguments, we can save a lot of typing by supplying the required arguments and then just including any others for which we want to supply values. This saves a long line of commas in the call. Again this comes into its own with functions that have a great number of optional arguments. This is shown in the last example.

- Any arguments which are optional should be at the end of the list of arguments in the function declaration. This allows the function to be called with only the first (non-optional) arguments. If the last argument is not optional and earlier ones are, when you call the function you either have to supply an argument or include a comma for all the others, or use named arguments.

Handling Optional Arguments within a Procedure

So what happens if you call a procedure and omit values for the optional arguments? There is a special Access function **IsMissing** (the section below describes Access functions), which is used in conjunction with optional arguments, allowing you to determine whether optional arguments have been supplied or not. We can use it as follows:

```
Function PaymentStatus (datInvoiced As Date, Optional datPaid As Date) _
As String

    If IsMissing(datPaid) And Date() > (datInvoiced + 30) Or _
      datPaid > (datInvoiced + 30) Then
        PaymentStatus = "Overdue"
    Else
```

```
            PaymentStatus = "OK"
        End If

    End Function
```

You can read this bit of code as follows "If **datPaid** is missing and the current date is more than 30 days after the invoice date, *or* if the payment date is more than 30 days after the invoice date, then return "**Overdue**". Otherwise return "**OK**" ".

 Don't worry about the structure of this code just yet. Logical operators, like **And** and **Or,** and the precedence of such operators, are discussed in the next chapter.

The **IsMissing** function is used here to check whether an argument has been omitted. Notice how much more useful this makes the function. If we call it using,

```
    Result = PaymentStatus (datThisInvoice)
```

then the function notices that the date of payment is missing and assumes we mean today. This is most likely to be what you want and saves you having to supply today's date as part of the call to the function.

The **IsMissing** function is a really useful feature as it allows you to create generic procedures. Without it, you could often find that you end up creating two very similar procedures, just because one needs two arguments and the other needs three. With **IsMissing**, you can create just one procedure, with an optional argument.

Built-in Functions

IsMissing is an example of a built-in function—a procedure that is part of Access and, therefore, already available to you. These are effectively reusable functions—remember how we talked about those earlier. There are built-in functions for all kinds of tasks, including manipulating text and numbers, communicating with other applications, accessing databases, etc.. You will most likely have met some of the built-in functions before, especially if you have played around with Access' Expression Builder tool. The **Date()** function that we used in the procedure above is an example of a common built-in function. You can find a comprehensive list of built-in functions in Appendix B.

If Access doesn't supply the function you need, you can create your own with VBA and use them just as you would a built-in function. Such user-defined functions mean that you can build up a library of procedures that you use often and import it into other Access databases—thus saving yourself a great deal of development time when creating new applications. We will be creating a library database of a few common functions later in the book to show you how this can be done.

 Some of the Access wizards are written in VBA, which should give you an idea of the power of the language and what it is possible to achieve.

Variables

We have talked about and used variables in previous examples, so you have probably already got a feel for them. A variable is what VBA uses to store data in a subroutine or function. You can think of it as a container specifically designed to hold one thing. You can assign values to a variable and then perform calculations on those values by using the variable. By using variables rather than the value directly, you make your procedures re-usable. For example, in our `PaymentStatus` function, we automatically assumed that payment was due in 30 days. However, if you wished to make this date flexible, you could use a variable. We can adapt our example to use the variable `intLengthDue` in place of 30. `intLengthDue` can be set to any value you like, the advantage being that, in order to change the value of this number, you only have to do so once, rather than changing every occurrence of the number in the code. In our example, we've changed it to 40:

```
...
intLengthDue = 40
If datPaid > (datInvoiced + intLengthDue) Then
    PaymentStatus = "Overdue"
Else
    PaymentStatus = "OK"
End If
...
```

Variables are thus used to store data. You may be wondering why you need a storage method since Access uses tables to store data, but the answer is quite simple. Subroutines are usually only active for a short period of time, having been written to perform a small task. If Access needs to store some information temporarily, it is not really sensible to store it in a table—they are meant for more permanent data.

The real world is full of examples of temporary storage. Cans, bottles and cartons are all short lived items and, when the product is used, the container is discarded. This is similar in Access— you can create a container (a variable), use it to hold something (some data) and then discard it when it is no longer required.

Variable Types

Variable types (or **data types** as they are often known) are what you use to tell Access what kind of data is going to be stored in a variable. This way, Access knows how to store the variable and how to manipulate it when actions are performed upon it. You can compare this to cans and cartons in real life. Imagine being blindfolded and having to make a simple breakfast of cereal in the morning. You have two items in the fridge—a can of cola and a carton of milk. You can tell the difference just by the shape, and can thus avoid putting cola on your cornflakes. Access works in the same way. By knowing what the container is, it can tell the type of contents it will hold.

Declaring Variables

You tell Access what type of data is going to be stored in a variable by declaring it using the `Dim` statement with the `As Type` clause. This has to be done before you can assign a value to a variable

```
Dim intThisOne As Integer
```

This defines the variable **intThisOne** as being an **Integer** type.

 FYI It is common practice to include an indication of the type of value a variable stores at the start of its name—we've used **int** to mean **Integer**. We'll look at these naming conventions in more detail at the end of the chapter.

Once you've declared a variable as being of a certain type, you can assign it an appropriate value:

```
Function PaymentStatus (datInvoiced As Date,Optional datPaid As Date) _
                 As String
    Dim intLengthDue As Integer
    intLengthDue = 40
    If datPaid > (datInvoiced + intLengthDue) Then
        PaymentStatus = "Overdue"
    Else
        PaymentStatus = "OK"
    End If
End Function
```

The Variable Types

The following table shows the standard variable types and how they are used:

Variable	Range	Usage	Notes
String	Character data	`Dim strThis As String` `Dim sThis$`	
Integer	Whole numbers from -32,768 to 32,767	`Dim intThis As Integer` `Dim iThis%`	To determine which type to use, integer or long, you should answer the question "What is the highest value that I could possibly need?".
Long	Whole numbers from -2,147,483,648 to 2147,483,647	`Dim lngThis As Long` `Dim lThis&`	
Single	Positive or negative floating point number with 7 decimal places in the range $1.401298*10^{-45}$ to $3.402823*10^{38}$, or zero.	`Dim sngThis As Single` `Dim sngThis!`	Again, when choosing between single, double and currency, you must always make allowances for the data increasing in the future.

Table Continued on Following Page

Variable	Range	Usage	Notes
Double	Positive or negative floating point number with 15 decimal places in the range $4.94065645842147*10^{-324}$ to $1.79769313486231 * 10^{308}$, or zero.	`Dim dblThis As Double` `Dim dwThis#`	
Currency	Number with 4 decimal places in the range -922,337,203,685,477.5808 to 922,337,203,685,477.5807	`Dim curThis As Currency` `Dim cThis@`	Often the most accurate, as it doesn't suffer from rounding errors.
Boolean	For values which can only hold True or False	`Dim booThis As Boolean` `Dim bThis As Boolean`	
Date	Stores dates in the range 1 Jan 100 to 31 Dec 9999 and times in the range 00:00:00 to 23:59:59	`Dim datThis As Date`	
Byte	Single values from 0 to 255	`Dim bytThis As Byte` `Dim wThis As Byte`	Used to store binary data that can be passed to and from DLLs and OLE automation objects. You will probably never need to implement this data type.
Object	Any type of object, not just Access objects	`Dim objMyDB As Object` `Set objDatabase = OpenDatabase ("C:\My Documents \ABF.MDB")`	Unlike other variables, you assign object variables using the **Set** keyword.
Variant	Stores different types of data		See next section
Hyperlink	Stores text that identifies a hyperlink address	`Dim hypHomePage As Hyperlink`	This is discussed in more detail in the Internet chapter

You can see that we've included a column marked 'Usage'. This shows two ways of declaring the variables. The second way uses the shorthand syntax of a special character after the name. This is referred to as the **type declaration character** and can save a lot of typing, though it may make your code more difficult to understand.

FYI

It is important to make sure that variables are declared as the correct type, otherwise unpredictable results can occur when manipulating them.

Variants

We will look at the variant type in a little more detail as it is more complicated than the rest. It can store different kinds of data and is the default data type in Access 97. This means that if the **As *Type*** clause is omitted from a **Dim** statement, you will get a variant.

You can declare a variable as a variant and use it to store any of the types in the above table. Therefore, you can store numbers, text or whatever you like in a variant and Access will treat them as if they were that data type. The only types you cannot declare as variants are fixed length strings or types defined by the user. For example:

```
Dim varAnyVarType As Variant

varAnyVarType = 31
```

Here, **varAnyVarType** would be assumed to be an integer. You can manipulate the variant as though it was the assumed data type, so in this example you could add it to another integer:

```
Dim varAnyVarType As Variant

varAnyVarType = 31
varAnyVarType = varAnyVarType + 20
```

So far that's no advantage over a single data type, but if you ran the following code:

```
Dim varAnyVarType As Variant

varAnyVarType = 31.241
varAnyVarType = varAnyVarType & " is the square root of 976"
```

you would find that VBA automatically converts between types where necessary. Here, you've assigned **varAnyVarType** to a numeric variable and then appended a string to the end. The **&** symbol is what you use to add one string to another. This leaves us with a string containing 31.241 is the square root of 976. Compare this with another example:

```
Dim varAnyVarType As Variant

varAnyVarType = "23.45"
varAnyVarType = varAnyVarType + 10
```

This example first assigns a string (note the quote marks—these denote a string) to the variable and then performs a numeric addition on it. Access converts **varAnyVarType** from a string into a numeric variable containing **33.45**.

This seems fairly straightforward, but consider another example:

```
Dim varAnyVarType As Variant

varAnyVarType = 23.45
varAnyVarType = varAnyVarType + "10"
```

71

What do you think **varAnyVarType** holds now? Once again, it holds **33.45** because Access recognizes that the string **"10"** contains a number and converts it automatically.

> *With Access 2.0, you would have got a different answer in the above example. The string would not have been converted, so **varAnyVarType** would have held the string 23.4510.*

The examples above illustrate two important points:

▶ Access will convert variants into the appropriate type when they are used in expressions

▶ If you are joining strings together, use the **&** operator and not the **+** operator, otherwise you may get surprising results

If you use the **+** operator on variants, remember the following:

▶ If both of the values contain numbers, addition is performed.

▶ If both of the values contain strings, string concatenation (the process of adding one string onto another) is performed.

▶ If one of the values is a number and the other is a string, VBA attempts to convert the string into a number. If successful, the two values are added together. If unsuccessful, an error occurs.

Determining the Type of a Variant

As variants can hold different data types, you need to be able to find out what type a variant is currently holding. Access provides a function called **VarType** for this purpose. **VarType** returns a value that indicates which data type a **Variant** uses to store its contents. This data type is assumed and can change each time you place a value in the **Variant**, depending on what the value actually is. Remember that it's not the contents that directly control the **VarType**, but the way Access is storing them internally. The table below shows the values returned by this function and their meanings.

Value returned	What the variant contains	Value returned	What the variant contains
0	Empty (uninitialized)	8	String
1	Null (no valid data)	9	Object
2	Integer	10	Error value
3	Long integer	11	Boolean value
4	Single-precision floating-point number	12	Variant (used only with arrays of variants)
5	Double-precision floating-point number	13	A data access object
		14	Decimal value
6	Currency value	17	Byte value
7	Date value	8192	Array

The terms "empty" and "null" are discussed in some detail later in the chapter.

Let's have a look at how this function works.

Try It Out—Examining a Variant

1 Open up **Whisky3.mdb** and select the Modules tab from the main database window. Select New to create a new module.

2 Create a new procedure by selecting Procedure ... from the Insert menu or by clicking the Insert Procedure button on the toolbar. The diagram below shows the toolbar method.

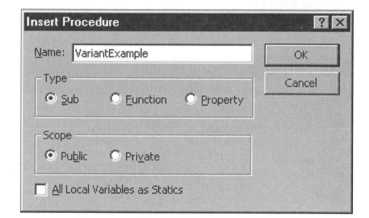

3 Select Sub as the Type and enter **VariantExample** for the subroutine name.

4 Now press *Return.* The module window will be displayed.

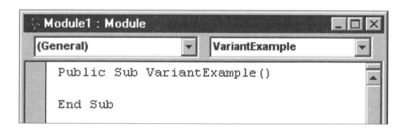

5 You can now test the examples we looked at just now and see how the **VarType** function works. Type in the following between the two lines:

```
Dim varAnyVarType As Variant

varAnyVarType = 31.241
varAnyVarType = varAnyVarType & " is the root of 976"
Debug.Print VarType (varAnyVarType)

varAnyVarType = 23.45
varAnyVarType = varAnyVarType + "10"
Debug.Print VarType (varAnyVarType)

varAnyVarType = 12 + 34
Debug.Print VarType (varAnyVarType)

varAnyVarType = 123456
Debug.Print VarType (varAnyVarType)

varAnyVarType = 123.456
Debug.Print VarType (varAnyVarType)
```

6 Now open the debug window by clicking the Debug Window button on the toolbar:

FYI The debug window allows you to call procedures directly without having to build a form. This is extremely useful when testing for and correcting errors (a process known as debugging) and will be covered in more detail in Chapter 11. For the moment, though, you are only going to use it to call your test procedures.

7 Now run the subroutine by typing **Call VariantExample** into the bottom pane of the window and, if you typed everything correctly, you will be presented with five numbers.

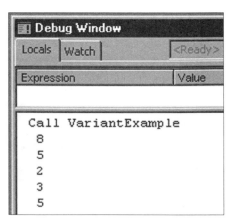

How It Works

The program we created ran five different types of 'calculation' using variants and returned a number after each. Remember that the numbers here represent the *type* of variant returned after each 'calculation' had been completed—not the *value* in **varAnyVarType**. The numbers differ depending on what the variant holds. Note that the **varAnyVarType** variable sets itself to a long type when the number assigned is too big for an integer, and that for any floating-point number, a variant becomes a double.

The Empty Value

When numeric variable types are declared, they have an initial value of 0, and strings are initially zero length strings (i.e. ""). When a variant data type is first declared, it is empty. The empty value is special in that it is not 0, a zero length string or the null value (described in the next section). A variant variable has the empty value before it is assigned a value. If a variant that has the empty value is used in an expression, either 0 or the empty string will be assumed, depending on the expression. For example:

```
Dim varAnyVarType As Variant

varAnyVarType = varAnyVarType + 1.23
```

This leaves **varAnyVarType** with the value **1.23**, since it was treated as 0 initially.
If you assign a value (or even 0, a zero length string, or the null value) to a variant, the empty value is replaced. So, simply assigning 0 or a zero length string to a variant does not make it empty again. To set a variant back to the empty value, you have to assign another empty variant to it. You can use the **IsEmpty** function to test for the empty value:

```
If IsEmpty(varAnyVarType) Then ...
```

The Null Value

The null value is another value special to a variant. In fact, a variant is the only data type that can hold this value—if you assign null to any other variable type, an error will occur. You can test for the null value with the **IsNull** function:

```
If IsNull(AnyVarType) Then ...
```

Unlike the empty value, if any part of an expression is null, then the whole expression becomes null. In general, null propagates through expressions. For example:

```
Sub VariantExample1 ()

Dim varAnyVarType As Variant

varAnyVarType = Null
varAnyVarType = varAnyVarType + 1.23

Debug.Print varAnyVarType

End Sub
```

This does not result in **1.23** like the empty example; it results in **Null**.

The next example demonstrates how the string concatenation operator & does not propagate nulls through an expression. It is the only one that doesn't.

Try It Out—How Null Propagates Through an Expression

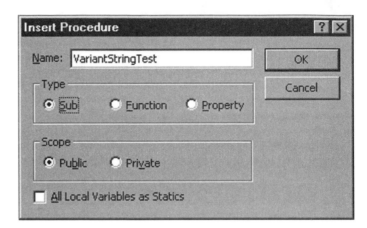

1 Click the Insert Procedure button on the toolbar, select Sub in the dialog displayed and call the new procedure **VariantStringTest**.

2 Type in the following lines of code:

```
Dim varFirstName As Variant
Dim varLastName  As Variant
Dim varFullName  As Variant

varFirstName = Null
varLastName = "Jones"

varFullName = varFirstName & varLastName

Debug.Print varFullName
```

3 Now run it in the debug window and watch what happens.

```
Call VariantStringTest
Jones
```

4 Now go back to the module window and try changing the **&** sign you typed in to a **+** and run the procedure again.

```
Call VariantStringTest
Null
```

How It Works

When you use **&**, and one of the expressions is a null value, it is treated as a zero length string. If both expressions had been null, then an empty string would have been returned. Using the **+** sign in the example, however, returned a null value. This is what happens if one (or both) of the expressions is null, because, when you add to them, nulls propagate as though they were numbers.

When to Use Variants

There are some good reasons for using variants, but there are also some very good reasons not to. Use variants because:

- They make coding very easy, since you don't have to worry about data types.
- They are the only data type to which null can be assigned. Database applications often use the null value to show data that is missing or unknown, so you often have to use a variant if you are unsure of the data.
- For the same reason, if you want to assign the values from a field in a table to a variable and there is *any* chance of the field being null, you should use the variant data type.

But remember that:

- They slow up your application because Access must determine the type of data stored in the variable whenever it is accessed.
- They can encourage bad programming. Assigning the proper data type to a variable allows Access to automatically prevent certain errors from occurring. As seen above, the variant data type circumvents this feature.

Before we move on to look at some other aspects of variables, we are going to look at an example that uses the date type. This is one of the more common data types, so it's as well to know how easy it is to use!

The Date Type

One of the most common requirements when handling dates in a business is to check that certain actions are happening within an allotted time—for example, checking that payments are received within 30 days, or that deliveries are sent out within 3 days. Let's have a look at how this can be done. We'll see how one of the functions we described earlier can be implemented in a different way, and how to specify dates in code....

Try It Out—Handling Dates

1 Click the Insert Procedure button on the toolbar and then select Function in the dialog displayed and call it **PaymentOverdue**.

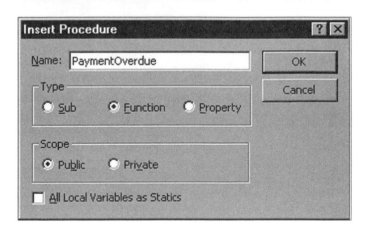

2 Type in the following code. Notice that **Public Function PaymentOverdue()** has been added for you, so you only need to type the arguments for this line.

```
Public Function PaymentOverdue (datDateInvoiced As Date, _
                                datDatePaid As Date) As String
    If DateDiff("d", datDateInvoiced, datDatePaid) > 30 Then
        PaymentOverdue = "Overdue"
    Else
        PaymentOverdue = "OK"
    End If
End Function
```

The function **DateDiff** takes three arguments. The first is the type of date unit you are referring to—in this case **"d"** for days (you could also use **"ww"** for weeks, **"m"** for months, etc. Check out the help file for full details). The second two arguments are the dates between which you want to find the difference.

3 Now go to the debug window and try the following two statements. Press *Return* after typing each one:

?PaymentOverdue(#01/01/95#,#05/10/95#)

?PaymentOverdue(#01/01/95#,#01/10/95#)

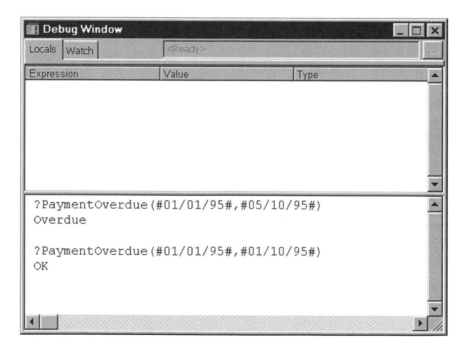

FYI Note the use of the question mark. If you put this before any VBA expression, it prints out the answer to it below. The question mark is used to put the 'question' to Access. Here we passed two dates to the function and it calculated the function and returned an answer.

How It Works

You shouldn't have too much of a problem understanding the code here—we've described the background to it earlier in the chapter. However, there are a couple of things to note. We've also introduced a new built-in Access function here—**DateDiff** and used it to calculate whether the two dates are 30 days apart.

When typing dates directly into code, you need to surround the date with two hash signs to inform Access that it is a date. If you don't do this, Access will read the slashes as division signs, work out the expression and then convert the result into a date or time.

If you assign numeric values to date variables, values to the left of the decimal point represent date information (the number of days) and those after it represent time information. Midnight, for example, is 0, and noon 0.5. Noon on the 6th January 1996 is actually stored by Access as the value **35070.5**. You should not need to use this, but it's useful to know, just in case you assign a **Double** to a Date.

Using Arithmetic with Dates

Using **DateDiff** for days is probably a bad example, but we used it here because it is a function many beginners use without realizing there is a much faster way. When working with dates, you can use normal arithmetic and get a great speed improvement. In our earlier examples, instead of the **DateDiff** function we used:

```
If (datDatePaid - datDateInvoiced) > 30 Then
```

Access knows that the two variables are dates and treats them as days—remember it stores them as values such as **35070.5**, where the fractional part is just the way of storing the time of day. Thus, you are just subtracting one day number from another. This sort of speed improvement can have great effect when used within loops or queries, since it is approximately fifty times faster than the **DateDiff** function. For values other than days (e.g. months and weeks), you will still have to use the **DateDiff** function.

The DatePart Function

Another good function is **DatePart** which will tell us which period of the year a certain date falls in. This is often useful when summing values, since you can extract totals on months and quarters. In the next example, you are going to create a query to show how easy it can be to analyze figures, just by using a few functions.

Try It Out—Using DatePart

1 Select the Queries tab from the database window and press the <u>N</u>ew button. (You needn't save changes to the module you created earlier.)

2 Select Design View from the dialog that appears and click OK.

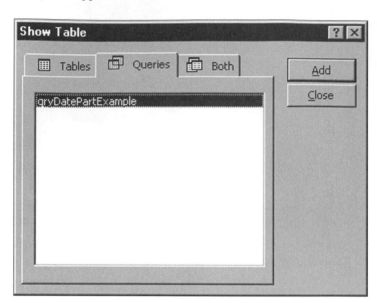

3 Select the Queries tab on the Show Table dialog and pick **qryDatePartExample**. Click the Add button and then Close.

4 Add all of the fields to the query grid in turn and then change it into a totals query by pressing the Totals button on the toolbar.

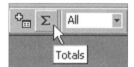

5 Now change the Total for the quantity field to Sum.

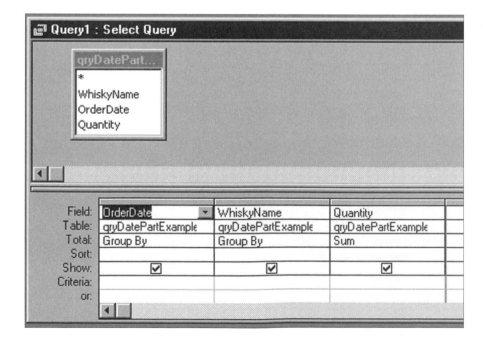

6 Place the cursor at the beginning of the **OrderDate** field and amend it so that it contains the following:

```
Month: DatePart ("m", [OrderDate])
```

7 Now run the query. You will see that the month column shows 1 to 12—the month of the year in which the order was placed.

WhiskyName	Month	SumOfQuantit
Aberlour	1	32
Aberlour	2	37
Aberlour	3	31
Aberlour	4	42
Aberlour	5	34
Aberlour	6	42
Aberlour	7	44
Aberlour	8	38
Aberlour	9	38
Aberlour	10	38
Aberlour	11	39
Aberlour	12	79
Ardbeg	1	27

Query1 : Select Query — Record: 1 of 552

You could also add another column to split this by year, allowing you to spot trends between months per year, or even the quarters of the year, for financial reporting:

```
Year: DatePart ("yyyy", [OrderDate])
Quarter: DatePart ("q", [OrderDate])
```

As you can see, dates are extremely easy to use. It's well worth familiarizing yourself with these functions.

Variable Declaration

Now that you have seen what data types you can use, let's look at the declaration in more detail, examining what names you can give variables and where variables can be declared and used. A variable name must conform to these four rules:

- It must begin with a letter
- It can only contain letters, numbers and the underscore character
- It must be 40 characters or less
- It cannot be a reserved word

Variable names are not case-sensitive. If you mistype the case of a variable in the body of a procedure, it will automatically change to the case it was in where it is declared—in the **Dim** statement. This can be quite handy when you have a long variable name which is made up from mixed case letters. You can type it all in one case throughout the code and then, when you have finished, you can just change it to the case you want in the declaration. Like magic, you will see it change in all other places as well.

VBA allows you to use variables without declaring them first. This may seem trivial, but look at the following section of code and consider the consequences:

```
Sub AreaOfCircle (dblRadius as Double)

    Dim dblArea As Double

    Area = 3.1415 * dblRadius * dblRadyus

    Debug.Print "The Area is " & dblArea

End Sub
```

You can see that **dblRadius** has been misspelled in one instance. As a result, the procedure will always print **0** as the area. This is because **dblRadyus** has no value and, therefore, defaults to **0**. Since typing errors are frequent, this is a very common mistake and the dangers are obvious. To avoid this problem, you should use the **Option Explicit** statement which you can type on the line after **Option Compare Database** in the **(General) (Declarations)** section of a module. This tells Access that you wish to be notified of any variables which have not been declared—a real necessity if your typing is as hopeless as mine.

> *Access 97 has a place where you can set this option. If you select* Options *from the* Tools *menu and select the* Module *tab, you will see a check-box labeled* Require Variable Declaration. *This makes sure that the* **Option Explicit** *is automatically added to your modules.*

There is no specified place where the declarations must go, but by convention they are all put together at the top of the procedure. This makes for a neat and tidy program, making life easier for you as you'll always know where to find them. This is also where you should declare constants, and should be stated as part of your coding standards. These are discussed in more detail at the end of the chapter.

Constants

Constants are like variables apart from the fact that, once you've assigned a value to them, you can't change them. That's why they are called constants—they never change. They are one of the most useful facilities you can use to improve the readability and maintainability of your code. You can liken a constant to an alias, giving us an easier way to store and remember certain details such as strings and numbers. In fact, Access supports three types of constants:

- Symbolic constants created with the **Const** statement
- Intrinsic constants, which are part of Access itself
- System-defined constants: **True**, **False** and **Null**

Symbolic Constants

Symbolic constants are added to your code using the **Const** statement. They allow you to create a meaningful name in place of a number:

```
Const csPi = 3.14159
```

The constant **csPi** can now be used throughout your code instead of the number. So what is the use of this? Well, the fact that they do not change is precisely why they are so useful. You can assign all of your constant values meaningful names and define them in one place. Your code will then become much clearer. So when you look at your code, 299792458 might not be that meaningful but defined as **csSpeedOfLight**, it makes much more sense. Also, you know that you're not going to need to change its value in a hurry.

Constants can be used anywhere in your code where you would use a variable. They can also be used in other constant definitions:

```
Const csMinute = 60
Const csHour = csMinute * 60
Const csDay = 24 * csHour
```

You also now apply types to constants, just as you can to other data types:

```
Const csPi As Double = 3.14159
```

This means that Access can recognize the data type it is dealing with and, therefore, can handle the constant in a more intelligent way—for example, it can permit arithmetic with the constant.

Intrinsic Constants

Intrinsic constants are exactly the same as symbolic ones, only they are automatically declared by Access. For example, the values returned by the function **VarType** are intrinsic constants. Let's have another look at the table shown earlier, only this time with an added column:

Value returned	What the variant contains	Constant
0	Empty (uninitialized)	vbEmpty
1	Null (no valid data)	vbNull
2	Integer	vbInteger
3	Long integer	vbLong
4	Single-precision floating-point number	vbSingle
5	Double-precision floating-point number	vbDouble
6	Currency value	vbCurrency
7	Date value	vbDate
8	String	vbString
9	Object	vbObject
10	Error value	vbError
11	Boolean value	vbBoolean

Table Continued on Following Page

83

Value returned	What the variant contains	Constant
12	Variant (used only with arrays of variants)	vbVariant
13	A data access object	vbDataObject
14	Decimal value	vbDecimal
17	Byte value	vbByte
8192	Array	vbArray

In Access 2.0, the variant constants were V_EMPTY, V_NULL etc., and these will still work, so don't worry if you have some old code. In fact, all of the intrinsic constants have changed to this new form, although the old form is still valid. Microsoft makes no claims, however, about future compatibility.

You can use these constants to test the result from the **VarType** function. For example, compare

```
If VarType(AnyVarType) = 2 Then ...
```

with:

```
If VarType(AnyVarType) = vbInteger Then ...
```

You can immediately see which is clearer.

There are also system-defined constants. The two most widely used are **True** and **False**. Many of Access' built-in functions return **True** or **False** as their result.

Variable Scope and Lifetime

Whether or not you can use a variable within a particular procedure depends on where the variable was declared, i.e. on the **scope** of a variable. Scope is the term given to the visibility of a variable, in other words, where it can be seen from. A variable that is created within a procedure can only be seen, and therefore can only be changed, from within that procedure. Its scope is **local** to the procedure. However, a variable can also be declared outside a procedure in the **(General) (Declarations)** section. In this case, it can be seen by all procedures in that module (and sometimes other modules as well). Thus, its scope is **public**.

The lifetime of a variable is defined by how long the variable can be seen for, in other words, how long it will contain the value assigned to it. Normally, local variables 'live' for as long as their procedure has the control—so when the procedure exits the variable ceases to exist. The next time the procedure is called, the local variables are recreated.

If you want local variables to exist even when the procedure exits, you can use the **Static** keyword. Making a variable static ensures that its contents are not lost. You can also declare a procedure as static, which makes all of the local variables within the procedure static.

A public variable exists as long as the database is open and retains its contents throughout the life of the program.

With Access 97, you can apply scope to the procedures themselves by using the `Public` and `Private` keywords. A `Private` procedure can only be called from within the module in which it is declared, whereas a `Public` procedure can be seen from everywhere.

A procedure has to be public for it to be called from the Debug Window. A private procedure is only visible to other procedures in the same module. So if you are creating private procedures and you need to test them from the Debug Window, you will have change them to public to test them. Don't forget to change them back though.

Let's look at these concepts in more detail.

Local Variables

You have already seen local variables in the **VariantExample** procedure and others that you created earlier. These procedures have variables called **varAnyVarType**. This shows that you can have variables of the same name in different procedures without them interfering with each other. Remember that the variables are local to the procedure, no matter where the procedure can be seen from. So local variables in a public procedure have the same scope are local variables in a private procedure—it is just the procedure that can be seen from outside, not the variables.

Let's have a look at some simple examples which illustrate this.

Try It Out—Local Variables

1 Create a new subroutine and call it **Procedure1**. Make sure it's a public procedure. Enter the following lines:

```
Dim intVariable1 As Integer
Dim intVariable2 As Integer

intVariable1 = 1
intVariable2 = 2

Debug.Print intVariable1
Debug.Print intVariable2
```

2 Now create another subroutine, **Procedure2**, with these lines:

```
Dim intVariable1 As Integer

intVariable1 = 100

Debug.Print intVariable1
```

3 Now you need a third subroutine, `TestLocal`, to call the first two:

```
Call Procedure1
Call Procedure2
```

4 Now open the debug window and run the `TestLocal` subroutine:

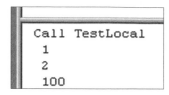

```
Call TestLocal
 1
 2
 100
```

If this is what you expected, then award yourself a gold star. The variables in **Procedure1** are only seen in that procedure. Likewise with the variable in **Procedure2**. With local variables, you can have the same variable name in different procedures without them affecting each other.

5 Now try accessing `intVariable2` from within **Procedure2** by adding the following line before the **End Sub**:

```
Debug.Print intVariable2
```

Before running the example again, think about what you expect to happen. . . OK, that's long enough. Now try typing **Call TestLocal** in the debug window again. Were you surprised? Whether yes or no, the answer is very obvious. **Procedure1** declared **intVariable2** as local. Therefore, no other procedure can see the variable. Don't forget to remove this last line, otherwise it will cause warning messages later.

Try It Out—Local Scope

Now let's look at another example to explain local scope.

1 Stop the module running by selecting the End button on the toolbar. Then create another Public subroutine, **TestLocal1**, and add the following lines:

```
Dim intVariable1 As Integer

intVariable1 = intVariable1 + 1
Debug.Print intVariable1
```

Here, you are adding 1 to the variable even though it has not been used before. This is allowed since an integer is set to 0 when first declared. This should give you a clue as to what happens when you run the program.

2 Now type **Call TestLocal1** in the debug window. Don't worry about the data that is already there - it won't affect what you are doing. Now type **Call TestLocal1** again. You should see:

```
Call TestLocal1
 1
Call TestLocal1
 1
```

You can see that **intVariable1** is reset each time the procedure is called.

 FYI Local variables only exist while a procedure has the control. When the procedure exits, local variables 'die'. When the procedure is called again, local variables are reset.

Static Variables

To allow a variable to retain its value over multiple calls, you must declare it as **Static**. This means that the variable is only initialized once—the first time the procedure is called. To declare a variable in this manner, you replace the **Dim** with **Static**:

```
Static intVariable1 As Integer
```

Try It Out—Static Variables

1 Stop the module running by selecting the End button on the toolbar. Then create another subroutine called **StaticScope**. Add the same code as before, but this time change the variable declaration line from **Dim** to **Static**:

```
Static intVariable1 As Integer

intVariable1 = intVariable1 + 1
Debug.Print intVariable1
```

2 Run the subroutine several times from the debug window.

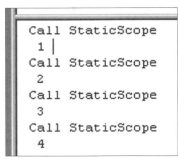

```
Call StaticScope
 1 |
Call StaticScope
 2
Call StaticScope
 3
Call StaticScope
 4
```

So, just by changing one word, you have dramatically altered the way the program works. You'll find this a useful feature; for example, you can use static variables to create a function that keeps a running total each time a new value is passed in, or one that keeps track of the number of times it has been called. This could be used, for instance, as a user name and password system for securing a system. You could limit the user to three tries before shutting the system down.

If you want all variables in a procedure to be static, just put **Static** before the procedure declaration:

```
Static Sub AllVariablesAreStatic()
```

All variables will now be **Static** irrespective of whether they are declared with **Static** or **Dim**.

Public Variables

If you need other procedures to see your variables, you must declare them as **public**. Public variables are very useful but they can also be easily abused, so you must take care when using them.

There are two types of public variable:

▶ Module variables, also known as form variables

▶ Public variables (yes, you have read that correctly!)

A module or form public variable is defined in the normal way with a **Dim** statement. However, it is not defined in a procedure, but in the **(General)** **(Declarations)** section of a form or module. It can then be seen by all procedures in that module or form. The following example demonstrates module variables.

Try It Out—Module Variables

We'll create two subroutines called **TestProc1** and **TestProc2** within the same module.

1 Move to the **(Declarations)** section of the module window and enter the following line under the **Option** statements:

```
Dim intModuleVariable As Integer
```

2 Now create a subroutine, **TestProc1**, as follows:

```
Sub TestProc1
   intModuleVariable = intModuleVariable + 1
End Sub
```

3 Now create another subroutine, **TestProc2**, as follows:

```
Sub TestProc2
Debug.Print intModuleVariable
End Sub
```

4 Try calling the two procedures to see what happens:

```
Call TestProc1
Call TestProc2
 1
Call TestProc1
Call TestProc2
 2
Call TestProc1
Call TestProc1
Call TestProc2
 4
```

Here you can see that, although neither procedure declared **intModuleVariable**, they can both access it. However, procedures in other modules or forms will not be able to access it.

 FYI   A module or form level variable has the scope of the module or form. If, for example, you declare a variable in the **(Declarations)** section of a form, all procedures in that form will have access to it. When the form is unloaded, the variable and its contents will die and will be reset when the form is next loaded.

5   Now add a third procedure, **TestProc3**, as follows:

```
Sub TestProc3
   Dim intModuleVariable As Integer
   intModuleVariable = 100
   Debug.Print intModuleVariable
End Sub
```

This declares **intModuleVariable** as a local when you already have it as a module level variable.

6   Run through the procedure again to see what happens:

```
Call TestProc1
Call TestProc2
 1
Call TestProc1
Call TestProc2
 2
Call TestProc1
Call TestProc1
Call TestProc2
 4
Call TestProc3
 100
Call TestProc2
 4
```

The call to **TestProc3** does not change its own (separate) variable **intModuleVariable**, but also does not affect the public **intModuleVariable** variable. Only its own copy is in scope within the procedure.

So, not only can you have procedures with local variables of the same name, but you can have local variables with the same names as public ones. In this case, the procedure with the local variable will always use its own variable, rather than the public one. You can probably see that it is not a very good idea to create local and public variables with the same name, as it can lead to confusion when looking at the code later. It is much better practice to use different names for your variables.

Public Public Variables

A public public variable is one which can be accessed from all modules and forms. They can only be created in modules, not within the **(Declarations)** section of a form. To declare a public variable, replace the **Dim** statement with **Public**:

```
Public intModuleVariable As Integer
```

This variable is now accessible to all modules and forms and has a lifetime until the database is closed.

You cannot declare **Public** variables within a procedure.

Public vs. Private

There are some general principles that you should bear in mind when deciding on the scope and lifetime of your variables:

▶ Unless you are writing a general routine, make procedures private. This is especially true if you are developing in teams or when writing add-ins, as then there is no danger of your procedure clashing with another of the same name. However you should never really have more than one procedure with the same name. The names of procedures should really be decided at the design time, especially to avoid this sort of confusion.

▶ Wherever possible, you should avoid manipulating variables that are declared outside a procedure. Instead, pass the value of the variable into the procedure using an argument. Inside the procedure, you can perform the calculations required and return the new value to the code that calls it. This not only protects you from errors that are difficult to find, but also makes your procedures far more generic and re-usable.

▶ Use public variables sparingly and with care. You will generally find that a small number of public variables are used in most programs. It is sometimes much easier to use a public variable than to have the same variable declared in several procedures and passed as a parameter. However, do not always take the easy route. Think about how a variable is going to be used and try to plan ahead.

Naming Conventions

Naming conventions are one of the most important concepts in programming and yet are rarely taught. It's easy to ignore the importance of a systematic approach to naming variables, etc.—but believe me, once you start programming in earnest, you'll realize that not only does a set of conventions make thinking up new names easier, but it is a godsend when it comes to understanding the code you have written. For example, if you follow a set of conventions, you will be able to tell at a glance a variable's type and where it was declared (that is, whether it is local or public). This will save you having to look for the variable declaration to find this out—a process which can be especially tedious if you have several modules and public variables.

Naming conventions are, of course, a matter of personal taste and you should use whichever set of standards you prefer. There are no hard and fast rules. All we can do is list our favorite set of conventions and let you make your own mind up...

Keep Names Meaningful

The first rule is to make variable names meaningful. They should describe what they hold. If you have a variable that holds someone's age, then call it **Age**. A birth date should be stored as **DateOfBirth**, or **date_of_birth**. We prefer the first method without the underscores, since we think it looks neater, but you can choose any style. The important point is to be consistent. If you have a system, then stick to it.

Prefix All Variables and Constants with their Type

If you use a prefix, you can easily see what type the variable is. For example, if **Age** was stored as an integer, then you should use **int** as the prefix, giving **intAge**. The prefix is lower case to separate it from the variable name. The most commonly used prefixes are listed below:

Variable Type	Prefixes
Integer	**int**
Long	**lng**
Single	**sng**
Double	**dbl**
Currency	**ccy**
String	**str**
Variant	**var**
Date	**dat**
Boolean	**boo**
Byte	**byt**
Object	**obj**
Hyperlink	**hyp**

It's also a good idea to add a double prefix for the variant type. Use **var** to denote that a variant is in use, but add another prefix to denote the type of data the variant will store. For example, if the age was to be stored in this way, you could use **intvarAge**.

Prefix All Variables with their Scope

Yet another prefix. Will it never stop? This is the last one and, in some ways, the most useful since it can be a great time saver. Use a prefix to denote the scope, i.e. whether it is a local, module or public variable. You can leave the prefix for local variables blank, since most will be local, but use **m** for module level, **g** for public variables and **s** for static variables. Thus if **Age** was a public variant holding an integer value, it would become **gintvarAge**.

OK, so in this case the prefixes are now almost as large as the variable name but, on the other hand, you can see everything about this variable from its name. What could be clearer?

Naming Conventions for Controls

In the same way that you use conventions for variables, you should also consider using them for controls on forms and reports, especially if you are going to refer to these controls in your code.

Control	Prefix
Chart (graph)	**cht**
Check box	**chk**
Combo box	**cbo**
Command button	**cmd**
Frame	**fra**
Label	**lbl**
Line	**lin**
List box	**lst**
Option button	**opt**
Option group	**grp**
Page break	**brk**
Rectangle	**rec**
Subform/report	**sub**
Text box	**txt**
Toggle button	**tgl**
Hyperlink	**hyp**

The principle is exactly the same as for variables and, again, will make your code easier to read:

```
Function GetName () As String

Dim strName As String

strName = txtFirstName & " " & txtLastName
GetName = strName

End Function
```

It immediately becomes obvious that the first and last names are stored on the form as text boxes.

Now that the use of ActiveX controls is becoming widespread, you may find you wish to use controls that do not fit into the above list. In this case just use a prefix which you find is suitable. For example, we will be looking at the Calendar control later on, and for this you could use **cal**.

Naming Conventions for Objects

The same principle should be applied to objects, both in code and in the database window. So when you save your tables, queries, forms, etc., follow the same principle:

Object	Prefix
Table	**tbl**
Query	**qry**
Form	**frm**
Report	**rep**
Macro	**mac**
Module	**mod**
Users	**usr**
Groups	**grp**
Containers	**con**
Documents	**doc**
Indexes	**idx**
Fields	**fld**
Property	**pty**
Pages	**pag**

You may not have come across many of these objects yet, but you will meet a few more as the book progresses.

All of this may seem rather cumbersome and a waste of effort, but as your programs become larger, you will find it essential to be able to identify different variables/controls/objects. If you start using conventions as you learn the language, it will soon become second nature and, after a while, you won't even have to think about it!

One of the greatest advantages of naming conventions is in maintenance. You will inevitable spend a proportion of time maintaining code, and not necessarily your own code. If a standard set of conventions has been used, it makes you job so much easier. You will automatically know where global variables are stored, what type variables are, and what their scope is, and the chance of introducing errors is automatically reduced. If you follow this procedure, then it benefits others who have to maintain your code. No one likes maintenance, we all want to write cool new apps, so the quicker and more efficient you can make the process the better.

As in every set of guidelines, there are always some exceptions to the rule. In this case, it's constants.

Constants

In the past, the general standard for constants has been to use upper case, with underscore separators. However, Microsoft has recently changed their standards. The variant constants used to be **V_INTEGER**, etc. (in all upper case), but have now changed to **vbInteger** (mixed case). Although this fits in with our proposed convention, it makes constants harder to spot and can, therefore, lead to confusion. What we propose is that you use a mixture of the old and new style, using **cs** as the prefix, and putting the name in upper case:

```
Const csCHRISTMAS_DAY As Date = #12/25/9700#
```

Using **cs** as the prefix also tends to separate constants from other variables.

 FYI   The really important thing to remember is consistency. Whichever style you choose, you should be consistent with its use. Don't think that just because you are writing a small program or a single procedure that naming conventions have no place. If you are going to use a style, then use it everywhere.

You notice that the Whisky application does not use a prefix for the tables, but it does for the queries. That's because we prefer this form, and as experienced developers we tend to remember (well most of the time, anyway) that these are tables.

The Access 97 Programming Environment

For those of you who have used previous versions of Access you may have noticed some snazzy new features that pop up in the module window as you type. These are Auto List Members and Auto Quick Info, and they follow what you are typing and help you along your way. These features can be disabled via the Modules tab of the Tools Options menu. Let's look at these features and see how they can speed up your coding, as well as helping you learn.

Try It Out—The Auto Features

1   Create a new module

2   Create a new function called **AutoTest**. You can use <u>P</u>rocedure... on the I<u>n</u>sert menu for this, or you could type it in yourself directly.

3   Declare a new variable, by typing

```
Dim intMonth As
```

Notice how the list pops up, showing what type of variables you can declare. Surprised at how many you can declare?

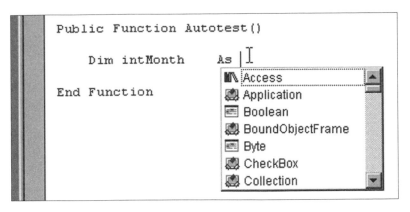

4 Start to type `Integer`, and see how the list follows you.

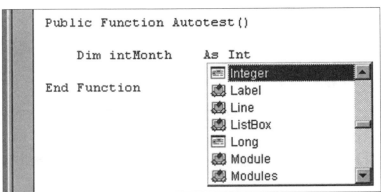

At this point, if the selection is the one you want you can hit the *Tab* or *Return* key, or the space bar, for it to fill in the rest for you. If it is not the selection you want then continue typing or move the highlight to the option you want. In this case you want an integer, so accept the suggested option.

5 Now type the following line, but don't type to fast. Make sure you stop after the first open parenthesis.

```
IntMonth = DatePart (
```

```
        IntMonth = DatePart (|
                            DatePart(Interval As String, Date, [FirstDayOfWeek As VbDayOfWeek = vbSunday],
        End Function          [FirstWeekOfYear As VbFirstWeekOfYear = vbFirstJan1])
```

Isn't that great? For those of you with memories like mine this is so useful, since you don't have to keep reaching for the manual or flicking to the help file. The argument list is there in front of you.

6 Continue typing, with the following and notice how the argument that you are on is highlighted in bold.

```
"q", #1-Jul-1997#,
```

Now you have come to an argument that only accepts certain values, so Access shows you those values.

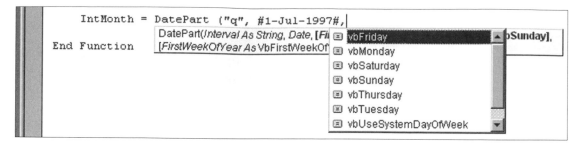

In this case you don't want any extra arguments, so delete the last comma and type a closing parenthesis to end the line.

This system also works for you own procedures, so let's see this in action too.

1 Create a new procedure as shown below

```
Function AddTogether(intOne As Integer, intTwo As Integer) As Integer

    AddTogether = intOne + intTwo

End Function
```

2 Now create another procedure that calls the first, but stop after the opening parenthesis again.

```
        Call AddTogether (|
                AddTogether(intOne As Integer, intTwo As Integer) As Integer
    End Sub
```

Although these examples have been simple, the auto-complete feature really becomes useful when you start dealing with OLE and working with objects, and you will see more of that later.

Summary

This chapter has covered some of the fundamental concepts of programming. We started off by looking at how you pass values to a procedure, and then the difference between a function and subroutine. We then looked at some examples of Access' built-in functions.

We have also introduced the concept of variables. You have seen the importance of declaring the right data type and why it matters where and how you declare the variable. Remember that, although it is tempting to make variables public, it is not always a good idea.

So then, to summarize, we have covered:

▶ Procedures and the differences between the two main types of procedure, functions and subroutines

▶ What variables are and how to declare them

▶ The different data types

▶ The different types of constant

▶ The scope of variables and constants within VBA

▶ Sensible naming conventions for variables, constants and menu items

▶ The new Access 97 Programming Environment

In the next chapter, we will embark on learning some keywords and some common programming techniques that will enable us to get on with some real programming in later chapters.

Exercises

1 Experiment with the **Format** function in queries to see how you can split dates into their different parts. See how it offers more flexibility than the **DataPart** function.

2 Using built-in functions create a procedure that generates random numbers. Then modify it to produce selected numbers for you favorite lottery—that way you can blame the computer when you don't win. And if you do win, try and remember your poor impoverished authors!

Controlling the Program

Most of the procedures that you have seen so far have been fairly simple—they start at the first line, finish at the last and execute the lines in between one after the other. However, depending upon the data in your forms and tables, you may find that you only want to execute certain lines of code, or, alternatively, execute a group of lines more than once. To do this, you have to introduce **control structures** into your code. These are what we'll look at in this chapter.

We'll cover:

- How to make decisions in a program
- How to perform repetitive tasks
- How to store variables in an array
- The difference between static and dynamic arrays
- How control structures are utilized within our sample application

Making Decisions

With VBA, you can test conditions and perform different operations depending on the results of the test. There are a series of statements that can be used to make these decisions, which we will look at here.

There are three main structures that are used in programming. Firstly, sequential, where we need to do things one after the other, or in a certain order. Next comes selection, where we often need to make a choice based upon some piece of information, so we either do one thing or another. Lastly comes looping, where we do the same thing over and over again. Let's see how these work.

If...Then...

We've already come across this statement when creating an intelligent navigation button. We'll now take a look at the structure of the statement and then run through a couple of examples. You use **If...Then** when you want to execute a piece of code only when a certain statement is true. It has two formats; the single line format is as follows:

```
If condition Then statement
```

and its multi-line format runs like this:

```
If condition Then
    statement
End If
```

Both of the above perform the same operation. The second example, however, allows more than one line as the **statement**. For example,

```
If strInName = "" Then Exit Function
```

is the same as:

```
If strInName = "" Then
    Exit Function
End If
```

Here, you test whether the argument **strInName** is an empty string (denoted by the two double quotes together), and if so, exit the function directly.

The expression can also contain other functions:

```
Sub Test()
Dim strSource As String
Dim strSearch As String
Dim strResult As String

strSource = "Beginning Access Programming"
strSearch = "Access"
```

```
If InStr(strSource, strSearch) Then
    strResult = strSearch
    strResult = strResult & " is in the source string"
End If
```

```
Debug.Print strResult
End Sub
```

This **If** statement uses one of Access' built-in functions. The **InStr** function checks to see if one string exists in another. **InStr** returns the position in the source string, **strSource**, where the search string, **strSearch**, was found. If it's not found, the function returns zero—which is equivalent to **False**.

If **InStr** returns a true value, i.e. if the word in **strSearch**, **"Access"**, is in **strSource**, then the code is executed. If not, nothing is done.

The **If** statement relies on the fact that, in VBA, expressions are either **True** or **False**. An expression is **False** if it evaluates to 0, and **True** otherwise. For example, both -1 and 1 are **True** expressions. So, if the above **If** statement finds the string in the prefix list, the value returned will be the start position in the string which, for an expression, evaluates to **True**. If it does not find it, 0 is returned and thus the expression is **False**.

If...Then...Else...

You can use the `If...Then...Else...` statement to decide which of two actions to perform. Imagine a lazy teacher in need of a system to write the reports on students, according to exam results:

```
If (intPercent > 50) Then
    strOutFinal = "Excellent"
Else
    strOutFinal = "Not so Excellent"
End If
```

This expression tests the value stored in `intPercent` against the value 50. If this is true, then `strOutFinal` is set to `"Excellent"`, otherwise, if it's false, it's set to `"Not so Excellent"`.

 Note that you can use any normal arithmetic operators within an `If` statement, such as +, -, *, /, <, > or = in conjunction with variables and values, to determine whether or not a condition is true.

ElseIf...

The `ElseIf` statement is used for joining a set of `If` conditions together. This is quite common when you need to check the results of several different conditions:

```
If (intPercent > 50) Then
    strOutFinal = "Excellent"
ElseIf (intPercent > 40) Then
    strOutFinal = "Fair to Middling"
Else
    strOutFinal = "Poor"
End If
```

If the first condition isn't true, the second is tried. If that isn't true, the `Else` statement is executed.

Logical Operators with the If statement

You can also make more complex queries with this statement by using logical operators. The three most common logical operators are **AND**, **OR** and **NOT**. You can use these to test a combination of expressions together to get a true or false answer. The answer is calculated via a set of truth tables which are applied for each operator:

AND	Expression 1	Expression 2	Result
	TRUE	TRUE	TRUE
	TRUE	FALSE	FALSE
	FALSE	TRUE	FALSE
	FALSE	FALSE	FALSE

OR	Expression 1	Expression 2	Result
	TRUE	TRUE	TRUE
	TRUE	FALSE	TRUE
	FALSE	TRUE	TRUE
	FALSE	FALSE	FALSE

NOT	Expression	Result
	TRUE	FALSE
	FALSE	TRUE

It's as easy, though, to use common sense to deduce what the answer should be. Think of it in terms of the English language; for example, if you are over 18 AND you have passed your driving test, it's true that you can drive. If you break the speed limit OR you rob a bank, it's true that you've broken the law. Let's apply it to our teaching example to make the criteria slightly more complex.

```
If (intMathPercent > 50 And intEnglishPercent > 50) Then
    strOutFinal = "Excellent"
ElseIf (intMathPercent > 50 Or intEnglishPercent > 50 ) Then
    strOutFinal = "Fair to Middling"
Else
    strOutFinal = "Poor"
End If
```

If you got over 50% in both of your main subjects, then you have excellent grades, but if you got 50% in only one of your main subjects, you have fair grades. You can also apply several operators together to get a result:

```
If (intMathPercent > 50 And intEnglishPercent > 50 And Not _
  intHistoryPercent < 40) Then
    strOutFinal = "Fairly Good"
End If
```

This time, the code determines that, if you got good grades in English and Math and you didn't fail in History, you have fairly good grades.

Select Case

There's no limit to the number of **ElseIf** statements that you can have:

```
If datOrderDate >= #7/1/97# Then
  .
  .
  .
ElseIf datOrderDate >= #6/1/97# And datOrderDate <= #6/30/97# Then
  .
  .
  .
ElseIf datOrderDate < #6/1/97# Then
  .
  .
  .
Else
  .
  .
  .
End If
```

FYI The # sign around the dates just tells Access that this is a date value, otherwise Access would take 6/1/97 as 6 divided by 1 divided by 97.

You can see that the code is starting to look messy. There's a much better way—using the **Select Case** statement:

```
Select Case datOrderDate
Case Is >= #7/1/97#
  .
  .
  .
Case #6/1/97# To #6/30/97#
  .
  .
  .
Case Else
  .
  .
  .
End Select
```

This is much clearer to read, even though it is slightly more lines of code. If **datOrderDate** is after the 1st July then the section of code under this **Case** statement would be executed. The second **Case** statement checks for **datOrderDate** being from June 1st to June 30th, and the **Case Else** will get run if **datOrderDate** is any other date. Adding a **Case Else** statement is not compulsory, but it's always a good idea to include one, just in case the variable you are testing has an unexpected value. Even if you don't think you need a **Case Else**, put one in anyway, and put an error message there. That way, if something does go wrong, you have already planned for it.

You can also test for more than one value with **Case**:

```
Select Case intMainCount
Case 1, 2, 3
    .
    .
    .
Case 4 To 6
    .
    .
    .
Case Else
    .
    .
    .
End Select
```

This shows two different ways of testing the condition. If **intMainCount** is **1**, **2** or **3**, the first section is executed. If it's between **4** and **6** inclusive, the second section is executed, and so on. You can achieve the same result using the **Is** keyword and an expression:

```
Select Case intMainCount
Case Is < 4
    .
    .
    .
Case Is < 7
    .
    .
    .
Case Else
    .
    .
    .
End Select
```

Here, if **intMainCount** is less than **4**, the first section is executed, and so on.

Note that, as soon as a true expression is found in a **Select Case** statement, no more expressions are checked. An expression must fail one test to get to the next. This means that if you have an expression that matches two **Case** statements, only the first will be executed.

Select Case isn't limited to numeric tests—you can also use strings:

```
    Select Case strSalutation
    Case "Mrs", "Miss", "Ms"
    .
    .
    .
    Case "Mr"
    .
    .
    .
    Case Else
    .
    .
    .
    End Select
```

You can also use the **To** form with strings:

```
    Case "Alfred" To "Bertrand"
```

This would be executed if the condition matched any string within the range specified. Don't be put off by the fact the string has a range. They can be tested alphabetically, so a value such as **"Basil"** would be accepted in such a condition, while **"Roy"** would be excluded.

As you can see, not only is the **Select Case** statement very flexible, but it can also greatly increase the clarity of your code.

IIf

There are certain places where you need to be able to return one of two values, but you can't use the **If** statement, 'so in these cases, you can use the **immediate if**, or **IIf**:

```
    strOutFinal = IIf (intPercent > 50, "Excellent", "Not So Excellent")
```

The **IIf** statement takes three arguments:

▶ The condition to test for
▶ The value to return if the condition was true
▶ The value to return if the condition was false

So, this is exactly the same as our first **If** statement:

```
    If (intPercent > 50) Then
        strOutFinal = "Excellent"
    Else
        strOutFinal = "Not so Excellent"
    End If
```

Some people prefer using the **IIf** since it looks slightly neater, as it's all on one line, but it can be a cause of confusion, especially for new programmers. There is also a major drawback of which you must be aware. When using the **IIf** statement, all three arguments are evaluated by VBA. "So what?" you may ask. Consider the following examples:

105

```
Function Divide (intNumber1 As Integer, intNumber2 As Integer) As Double

    If intNumber2 = 0 Then
        Divide = 0
    Else
        Divide = intNumber1 / intNumber2
    End If

End Function
```

```
Function Divide (intNumber1 As Integer, intNumber2 As Integer) As Double

    Divide = IIf (intNumber2 = 0, 0, intNumber1 / intNumber2)

End Function
```

The two functions look as though they should work the same, but this isn't the case. If **intNumber2** is 0, the second version will give a **Divide by Zero** error because **intNumber1 / intNumber2** is always evaluated. You must bear this in mind when you use **IIf**.

Because **IIf** evaluates all the arguments, it's slower to use than the normal **If** statement. Admittedly, you'll probably never notice this, but if you were to use **IIf** in a large loop, that small delay would gradually build up. You might not think that a small delay is a problem, but you can be sure that your users will think otherwise!

The real use for **IIf** is in queries and on forms and reports. You'll see examples of this later in the book.

Operator Precedence

When combining conditions and expressions, it's very important that you understand operator precedence. This defines the order in which parts of an expression are evaluated and is similar to the lessons that you learnt in mathematics when you were at school. The rules are recapped below and may, at first, seem complex, but do persevere. There are some examples later to make everything clear.

When operators from more than one category are combined in an expression, arithmetic operators are evaluated first, comparison operators next and logical operators last. Within these categories, the order of operator evaluation is shown below, from top downwards:

Arithmetic	Arithmetic Symbol
Exponentiation	^
Negation	–
Multiplication and Division	* /
Integer division	\
Modulo arithmetic	**Mod**
Addition and Subtraction	+ –
String concatenation	&

Some miscellaneous points are:

➤ All comparison operators, such as **=**, **<** and **Like**, have equal precedence. This means that they are evaluated from left to right as they appear in expressions.

➤ Arithmetic operators that appear two to a line are also evaluated from left to right.

➤ Operations within parentheses (brackets, like this) are always performed before those outside. However, normal precedence is maintained within the parentheses. This means that you can force the order in which evaluation takes place by using parentheses.

If that all sounds rather complex, don't worry. Here are some examples to help you.

You have four numbers, **A**, **B**, **C** and **D**, and you want to multiply the sum of **A** and **B** by the sum of **C** and **D**:

```
A = 1
B = 2
C = 3
D = 4

E = A + B * C + D
```

This doesn't produce **21**, but **11**, as multiplication has a higher precedence than addition. What happens is that **B** and **C** are multiplied, then **A** and **D** are added. To correct this, use:

```
E = (A + B) * (C + D)
```

This forces the additions to be performed first. However, in the example below, the parentheses have no effect although, to some, they make the intention clearer:

```
E = A * B + C * D
```

```
E = (A * B) + (C * D)
```

With expressions in **If** statements, you have to follow the same set of rules. You can liken **And** to ***** and **Or** to **+** in the previous examples, since **And** has a higher order of precedence. Imagine that **A**, **B**, **C**, and **D** are now expressions:

```
If A Or B And C Or D
```

Now **B And C** would be evaluated first. If this is not the intention, parentheses can be applied to clear up any confusion:

```
If (A Or B) And (C Or D)
```

Most of the time, you will find that your expressions are much simpler, but it's important to know what happens when things get more complicated.

FYI   If you are at all unsure of the order of precedence of an expression, use parentheses to force your meaning. If the order was correct anyway, then you won't have lost anything, plus you will have made your code clearer.

Repetition

We've now considered how to deal with conditions but, sometimes, you need to go through a portion of code several times to arrive at a certain condition. Performing repetitive tasks that would otherwise drive the user crazy is one of the best programming tricks on offer. You don't want to know if your computer has to check a database with 10,000 entries, adding an extra 1 to every international phone number each time the codes are changed, you only want to know when it's finished.

Loops

VBA provides the **For...Next** and **Do...Loop** statements to deal with these repetitive tasks. A loop is a piece of code that is executed repeatedly until a certain condition is met. We'll have a look at both these structures.

For...Next

The **For...Next** loop is useful when you know how many times you want to execute the statements within the loop:

```
For intLoop = 2 To intMainCount - 1 Step 2
    .
    .
    .
Next
```

This starts the **intLoop** at **2** and then executes the code between the **For** and **Next** statements. When the **Next** is reached, you go back to the **For** and add **2** to **intLoop**. This continues until **intLoop** equals **intMainCount - 1**.

The basic syntax is show below:

```
For counter = start To end [Step increment]
    ...
Next [counter]
```

where

counter	is the variable you assign to the loop
start	is the number with which you wish to start the loop
end	is the number with which to stop the loop
increment	is the number you add to *start* each time round the loop. (This is optional, and defaults to 1 if you omit the **Step** section.)

The argument *increment* can be either positive or negative, allowing loops to count both up and down. If you leave out the **Step** and *increment* part of a **For...Next** loop, Access will assume that you just want to increment the value by one each time. The *counter* after the **Next** statement is also optional and is usually left out. This isn't a bad thing but, if you have loops within loops, you may find that using the full form is clearer, since you can easily see to which loop a **Next** statement refers.

Do...Loop

The **For...Next** loop is ideal if you know how many times the loop is to be executed. There are occasions, however, when you want to perform loops until a certain condition is met. For those cases, you should use **Do...Loop**:

```
Do Until intSpeed > 100
    intSpeed = intSpeed + intAcceleration
    intTime = intTime + 1
Loop
```

This executes until the variable **intSpeed** is greater than 100. If the variable is already greater than 100, the loop isn't entered and the code isn't executed. There is a second form of this loop, however, which allows you to test the condition at the end of the loop instead of at the beginning:

```
Do
    intSpeed = intSpeed + intAcceleration
    intTime = intTime + 1
Loop Until intSpeed > 100
```

This is basically the same as the previous example, but the code in the loop is always executed at least once. Even if **intSpeed** is greater than 100 when the loop is first started, the code in the loop is still executed. This may cause errors if **intSpeed** is being used in other expressions.

You can also replace the **Until** with **While**, which allows loops to be performed *while* a condition is **True**, rather than *until* it is **False**.

Nested Control Structures

We have only looked at single control structures so far, but VBA does allow you to nest them. Here is a trivial function that executes a loop ten times and uses the **Mod** function (which divides two numbers and returns the remainder) to determine whether the loop counter **intLoop** is odd or even:

```
Sub OddEven()
Dim intLoop As Integer
Dim intMainCount As Integer
Dim strOutFinal As String

intMainCount = 10

For intLoop = 1 To intMainCount
    If (intLoop Mod 2 = 0) Then
        strOutFinal = "Even"
```

```
        Else
            strOutFinal = "Odd"
        End If
        Debug.Print intLoop, strOutFinal
    Next

    End Sub
```

Here, the **If** structure is nested inside the **For...Next** loop. The code for both structures is indented to make it clear where they start and end. There's no limit to the amount of nesting that can be performed, but if you nest too many loops you'll find that your code becomes almost impossible to read. If you need more than three or four levels of nesting, you should consider restructuring your code—perhaps by creating a new procedure.

Exiting a Control Structure

The loops that we have looked at so far have all started and stopped at set places. Suppose, though, that because of some action that took place in a loop, you need to exit it straight away, without reaching the condition that normally terminates it. In this case, you can use the **Exit** *structure* statement. For example:

```
For intLoop = 2 To intMainCount - 1
    If (intStopFlag) Then
        Exit For
    End If
    Debug.Print intLoop
Next
```

If the condition on the **If** line is true, (i.e. if there's a value other than zero in **intStopFlag**), the **Exit For** statement immediately exits from the loop, irrespective of the value of **intMainCount**.

You can also use the **Exit Sub** or **Exit Function** statement to immediately exit a procedure:

```
If strInName = "" Then Exit Function
```

This will directly exit the function if **strInName** is an empty string.

You'll now have a good idea of the power and versatility that a loop can offer. However, loops can also serve another very useful purpose which we will look at now. They can be used to populate **arrays**.

Arrays

Your first question is probably, "What is an array?" Earlier, we likened variables to cola cans—well, think of an array as a six-pack of your favorite cola. They are collections of variables, all with the same name and the same data type. Elements in an array are identified by their index—a number indicating their position in the array.

Arrays are used for collecting together a number of similar variables. Variables themselves are useful for holding specific information about a certain object, property or value. For example, if you want to store a number suggested by the user, you can create a variable to hold that value and then assign the value to the variable. These are the two lines of code that you would use to do that:

```
Dim intNum As Integer
intNum = InputBox("Please enter guess number 1", "Guess!")
```

The first line of code declares the variable as an integer. That is to say that the variable **intNum** will be able to hold any whole number between -32,768 and +32,767.

The second line of code assigns to the variable a number that has to be entered by the user. If you wanted the user to enter two numbers and you wanted to store the two values concurrently, you could create two variables as shown in the code below:

```
'Declare variables
Dim iNum As Integer
Dim iNum2 As Integer

'Assign values to variables
iNum = InputBox("Please enter guess number 1", "Guess!")
iNum2 = InputBox("Please enter guess number 2", "Guess!")
```

What if you want the user to be able to make five guesses...or twenty...or more? The answer is that your code could become very lengthy and repetitive. Given that the number of bugs in any program increases in proportion to the number of lines of code, you probably won't want to do this. What you need is a method for storing a collection of related variables together. That's just what an array provides.

The following are examples of items of data that you may want to collect in an array:

- The values of ten guesses made by the user
- Each individual letter making up a single string
- The enabled property of a number of different command buttons on a form
- The values of all the controls on a specific form

To show this at work, let's rewrite the code above to allow the user to make 10 initial guesses:

Try It Out—Declaring and Populating an Array

1 Open **Whisky4.mdb** if it's not open already, and select the Modules tab from the database window. Create a new module and type in the following function procedure:

```
Sub ArrayExample()

Dim i As Integer
Dim iNum(1 To 10) As Integer
```

```
For i = 1 To 10
    iNum(i) = InputBox("Please enter guess " & i, "Guess!")
Next I

For i = 1 To 10
    Debug.Print "Guess number " & i & " = " iNum(i)
Next i

End Sub
```

2 Run the **ArrayExample** procedure by typing **Call ArrayExample** in the debug window and hitting the *Enter* key. You'll be prompted to enter ten integers. Once you have entered the last of the ten integers, all ten will be displayed.

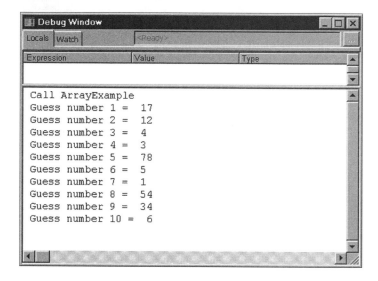

```
Debug Window
Locals  Watch           <Ready>

Expression        Value          Type


Call ArrayExample
Guess number 1 =   17
Guess number 2 =   12
Guess number 3 =   4
Guess number 4 =   3
Guess number 5 =   78
Guess number 6 =   5
Guess number 7 =   1
Guess number 8 =   54
Guess number 9 =   34
Guess number 10 =  6
```

How It Works

Declaring an array is easy. We simply place parentheses indicating the array's dimensions after its name. So, whereas

```
Dim intNum As Integer
```

declares an **Integer** type variable called **intNum,**

```
Dim intNum (1 To 10) As Integer
```

declares an array of ten **Integer** type variables called **intNum**. This tells Access that **intNum** is to hold ten separate values, each of which will be a whole number between -32,768 and 32,767.

Note that an array can hold any of the following data types:

Integer	**String**
Long	**Boolean**
Single	**Byte**
Double	**Date**
Variant	**Hyperlink**
Currency	

However, all elements of the array must be of the same data type. In other words, one array will not be able to store both strings and integers (although it could store **Variant** type variables with differing subtypes). We, of course, are just using integers. To return to our code:

```
For i = 1 To 10
    iNum(i) = InputBox("Please enter guess", "Guess!")
Next I
```

Now all that's needed is to populate the ten elements of the array with guesses from the user. Individual elements of the array are identified by their index (the number which appears in parentheses after the variable's name) so we create a simple **For...Next** loop and use the loop counter—in this case, the variable **i**—to refer to the elements of the array.

The ten elements of the **iNum** array are referred to as **iNum(1)**, **iNum(2)**, **iNum(3)**,...**iNum(10)**.

```
    iNum(i) = InputBox("Please enter guess " & i, "Guess!")
```

To make this rather tedious task easier on the user, we have also used the loop counter, **i**, to indicate to the user how many guesses they have had:

```
For i = 1 To 10
    Debug.Print "Guess number " & i & " = " iNum(i)
Next i
```

Having stored the results of all the guesses in an array, we then loop through the elements of the array to display the results in the debug window.

Note that, if we wanted to allow the user to make twenty guesses instead of ten, we need only alter three lines of code. In fact, we could reduce this to one line by replacing the value **10** in the code above with the constant **NO_OF_GUESSES**. The procedure would then look like this:

```
Sub ArrayExampleWithConstant()

Const NO_OF_GUESSES = 10
Dim i As Integer
Dim intNum(1 To NO_OF_GUESSES) As Integer

For i = 1 To NO_OF_GUESSES
    intNum(i) = InputBox("Please enter guess " & i, "Guess!")
Next i

For i = 1 To NO_OF_GUESSES
    Debug.Print "Guess number " & i & " = " intNum(i)
Next i

End Sub
```

To change the number of guesses that the user is allowed, we now need only to change the value of **NO_OF_GUESSES**.

Static Arrays

The examples above all made use of **static arrays**. That is to say, the number of elements in the array was fixed when the array was first declared. When you declare an array in this manner, the number of elements can't be changed.

 Don't confuse static arrays with static variables. A static variable is one which has been declared with the **Static** statement and preserves its values between calls. A static array is one whose dimensions are fixed when it is declared.

Static (i.e. fixed-dimension) arrays can be declared with any of the following statements **Dim**, **Static**, **Private** or **Public**.

For example, typing the following in the **Declarations** section of a form's code module would declare an array with a fixed number of elements which would be visible to all procedures in that form:

```
Option Compare Database
Option Explicit

Dim intNum(1 To 10) As Integer
```

whereas the following, if typed in the **Declarations** section of a standard code module, would declare an array with a fixed number of elements which was visible to all procedures throughout all code modules, forms and reports.

```
Option Compare Database
Option Explicit

Public intNum(1 To 10) As Integer
```

After you have created a static array, the elements of the array are initialized. The values with which they are initialized depend on the data type of the elements.

Data type	Initialization value
Any numeric	0
String (variable length)	Zero-length string (**""**)
String (fixed length)	A fixed length string of **Chr$(0)** characters
Variant	**Empty**

Upper and Lower Bounds

The bounds of an array are its lowest and highest indexes. The lower bound of an array need not be **1**. Had we wanted to, we could have typed:

```
Dim intNum(23 to 32) As Integer
```

114

This would also have given us an array which could hold a maximum of ten integers, but whose index would run from **23** to **32**. To populate this array, we could use the following **For...Next** loop:

```
For i = 23 To 32
    intNum(i) = ...
Next I
```

Alternatively, if we had wished, we could have omitted the lower bound and typed instead:

```
Dim intNum(10) As Integer
```

However, you should note that, if you do not explicitly specify a lower bound, Access will use **0** as the lower bound. In other words, the line of code above is evaluated as:

```
Dim intNum(0 to 10) As Integer
```

This means that the array **intNum()** will be able to hold eleven values.

If you want Access to use **1** instead of **0** as the default lower bound for arrays, you should include the following line of code in the **Declarations** section of the code module:

```
Option Base 1
```

Dynamic Arrays

You may not know at the outset how many elements are required in your array. In this case, you should declare a dynamic array. You do this by placing **empty** parentheses after the array name—you can still use the **Dim**, **Static**, **Private** or **Public** keywords. The **ReDim** statement is then used later in the procedure to dynamically set the lower and upper bounds of the array.

For example, we could modify our original procedure to allow the user to specify how many guesses they want:

```
Sub DynamicArrayExample()

Dim i As Integer
Dim intGuessCount As Integer
Dim intNum() As Integer

intGuessCount = InputBox("How many guesses do you want?")

ReDim intNum(1 To intGuessCount)

For i = 1 To intGuessCount
    intNum(i) = InputBox("Please enter guess " & i, _
                         "Guess!")
Next i

For i = 1 To intGuessCount
    Debug.Print "Guess number " & i & " = "; intNum(i)
```

```
    Next i

    End Sub
```

The **ReDim** statement can also be used to change the size of a dynamic array which already has a known number of elements set by a previous **ReDim** statement. For example, if you have an array of ten elements, declared with the following code:

```
Dim iNum() As Integer
...
...
ReDim iNum(1 To 10)
```

you can reduce the number of elements in the array later in the procedure to four, with the single line of code:

```
ReDim iNum(1 To 4)
```

Normally, when you change the size of an array, you lose *all* the values which were in that array—it is re-initialized. However, you can avoid this by using the **Preserve** keyword. The following line of code would have the same effect as the previous one, except that the values stored in **iNum(1)**, **iNum(2)**, **iNum(3)** and **iNum(4)** would remain unchanged.

```
ReDim Preserve iNum(1 To 4)
```

The same conventions regarding stating the lower and upper bounds of indexes to static arrays apply to dynamic arrays.

Using Control Structures

Right, now you're ready to put all of these structures together in one example! Don't worry though, this is not nearly as daunting as it sounds.

In this example, we will take the full name of the user and store each part in a separate variable of an array. To spice it up a bit, we're going to have to allow for the fact that some users may enter five parts of their name (title, first name, surname etc.) whereas others will just enter their surname. Also, we can't be sure how many spaces they will type between the different parts of the name. As you've guessed, we'll need to introduce you to some new functions to help. These are all part of Access—they are 'built-in' functions.

Some New Access Built-in Functions

The first three sets of functions are all involved with text and string handling and are used to manipulate the contents of strings. The last is a function to help you determine the number of items in an array. Here's a table summarizing what each of them does:

Function	Purpose	Example

Left$**, **Right$	The **Left$** function returns a specified number of characters from the left side of the string. The **Right$** function returns a specified number of characters from the right side of the string.	```strExample = "HalfTime"```
		```strResult1 = Left$(strExample,4)```
		```strResult2 = Right$(strExample,4)```
		strResult1 would equal **"Half"**
		strResult2 would equal **"Time"**

Len	This function returns a Long containing the number of characters a string contains.	```strExample = "Long"```
		```lngResult = Len(StrExample)```
		lngResult would equal 4

Ltrim$**, **Rtrim$, **Trim$**	The **LTrim$** function returns a string with all leading spaces removed. The **Rtrim$** function returns a string with all trailing spaces removed. The **Trim$** function returns a string with all the leading and trailing spaces removed.	```StrExample = " Doubtful"```
		```strResult = LTrim$(strExample)```
		strResult would contain **"Doubtful"**

UBound	This function returns a long containing the value of the largest available index for an array.	```Dim intExample (1 to 10) as Integer```
		```lngResult = UBound(intExample)```
		lngResult would equal 10

Without further ado, let's create the procedure....

Try It Out—Creating the Name Splitting Procedure

1 Open **Whisky4.mdb** if it's not open already, and select the Modules tab from the database window. Create a new module and add the following function procedure. If you want to save yourself typing it all in, you can find the procedure in Parse Name:

```
Sub FormEntryExample()

Dim strInName As String
Dim intSpacePos As Integer
Dim i As Integer

strInName = InputBox("Please enter your name", "Name splitter")
ReDim strTemp(0) As String

intSpacePos = InStr(strInName, " ")

Do Until intSpacePos = 0
    ReDim Preserve strTemp(UBound(strTemp) + 1)
    strTemp(UBound(strTemp)) = Trim$(Left$(strInName, intSpacePos - 1))
    strInName = LTrim$(Right$(strInName, Len(strInName) - intSpacePos))
    intSpacePos = InStr(strInName, " ")
Loop
```

```
For i = 1 To (UBound(strTemp))
    If strTemp(i) = "" Then
        Exit For
    End If
    Debug.Print strTemp(i)
Next i

Debug.Print strInName

End Sub
```

In this procedure you execute the first few statements *until* a condition is met, so the loop will only continue until **intSpacePos** equals **0**. In execution, this is similar to the **For Next** loop. When the **Do** loop starts, it make a first test of the condition. If it's false, the contents of the loop are executed. When the **Loop** statement is reached, control jumps back to the **Do** and the condition is tested again.

Note that **intSpacePos** is calculated again, just before the **Loop** statement. If this weren't the case, the loop would run forever.

2 Next open up the debug window and type in **Call FormEntryExample**.

3 Enter any example name in the dialog box that appears:

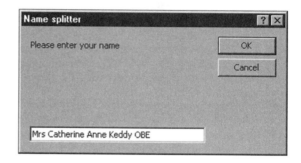

4 The program will then display the contents of each variable in the array that was created:

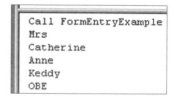

How It Works

After initial variable declarations, a dialog box is displayed asking the user for their name:

```
strInName = InputBox("Please enter your name", "Name splitter")
```

The two text parts that are required by the **InputBox** function are simply the prompt that the dialog box should display and the text for the input box's window title. The text that the user types is stored in the **strInName** variable when they click the OK button. When the user types in their name, they will separate the different parts with a space. Therefore, we can cycle through the name looking for spaces and placing each part in a different element of an array. Of course, the function won't work if they place just a full stop between parts of their name.

The diagram below illustrates what happens:

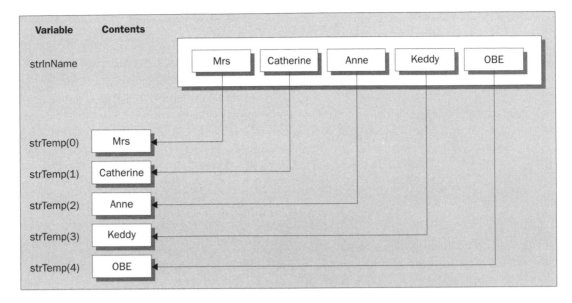

Have a look at the main chunk of the code and see if you can work out what it is doing:

```
intSpacePos = InStr(strInName, " ")
ReDim strTemp(0)

Do Until intSpacePos = 0
    ReDim Preserve strTemp(UBound(strTemp) + 1)
    strTemp(UBound(strTemp)) = Trim$(Left$(strInName, intSpacePos - 1))
    strInName = LTrim$(Right$(strInName, Len(strInName) - intSpacePos))
    intSpacePos = InStr(strInName, " ")
Loop
```

Again, we'll work through it line by line:

```
intSpacePos = InStr(strInName, " ")
```

The function **InStr** searches for one string within another and returns the position of that string (or 0 if the string was not found). Therefore, this line sets **intSpacePos** to point to the first space found in **strInName**.

```
ReDim strTemp(0)
```

We then allocate the first amount of storage for the array. At this stage, this is nothing but you will add elements to the array as you find them.

```
Do Until intSpacePos = 0
```

We can now start the loop. We'll execute the next lines until **intSpacePos** is 0 (that is, until there are no more spaces in the string).

```
ReDim Preserve strTemp(UBound(strTemp) + 1)
```

If the loop is executed, we know that we have found a space. Therefore, we can add an element to the array. The **UBound** function tells us how many elements we already have, and **Preserve** simply means that the existing contents of the array are kept in storage and not deleted when the array is resized. So all we're doing is adding another (empty) element to the collection at the end of the array.

```
strTemp(UBound(strTemp)) = Trim$(Left$(strInName, intSpacePos - 1))
```

The next line fills the new element with the word that you have found. As you have seen, **Trim$** gets rid of any extra space at the beginning and end of the string and **Left$** simply gets a number of characters from the left of a string. We want all those characters from **strInName** up to the space. Remember, the space was found earlier using InStr and its position was put into intSpacePos, so **(intSpacePos - 1)** is the character before the space.

```
strInName = LTrim$(Right$(strInName, Len(strInName) - intSpacePos))
```

Now you have extracted that word, you can remove it from the beginning of the original string, using the **Right$** function. Since we have used the characters to the left of the space, we now need **strInName** to contain just what's left—in other words, everything to the right of the space.

```
intSpacePos = InStr(strInName, " ")
```

Now that the string has been cut down, we can look for another space and continue the loop.

The following diagram illustrates how this works:

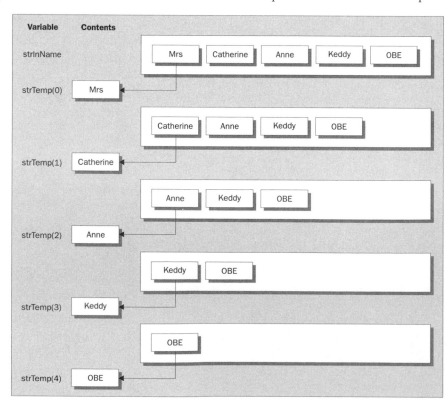

Using Control Structures in Whisky.mdb

Back in Chapter 1, we designed the **frmPeople** form in **Whisky.mdb** and noted that we wanted the user to be able to enter their name in one text box. Now maybe you'll see why we went through the previous example. We need to code our application so that it breaks a name up into its constituent parts and stores them in the relevant fields in our table.

You are now equipped to implement this feature. There is quite a bit of code involved, which we'll write and then look at in detail.

Try It Out—Parsing the User's Name

In Chapter 1, we created the **frmPerson** form. If you select Forms tab in the database window and open **frmMaintPerson**, you'll find that this is the same form. We need to start by adding a new field to the **frmMaintPerson** form.

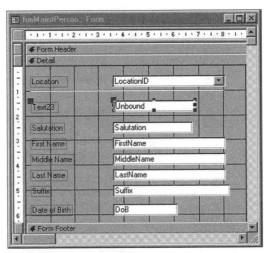

1 Open the **frmMaintPerson** in design mode and add a new unbound text box.

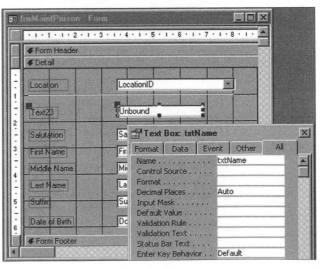

2 Change the text box's name to **txtName**. Then select the label next to it and change its caption to Name, and its name to **lblName**.

121

3 Select Tab Order... from the View menu and move the txtName row up, so it is just beneath LocationID. This ensures that when the user fills in the Location text box and presses *Tab*, the focus will move to the txtName text box.

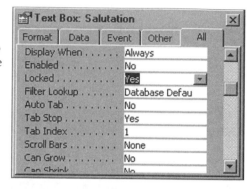

4 Now set the Enabled property of the text box to No and the Locked property to Yes for all of the following text boxes: Salutation, First Name, Middle Name, Last Name and Suffix. We are going to allow the user to enter their name in the new Name text box, so we must prevent access to these text boxes.

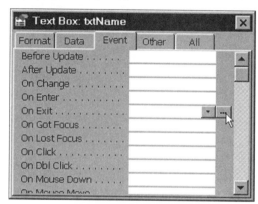

5 The function that actually breaks up (parses) the name into its constituent parts can be found in the Parse Name module. This is a more complicated version of the name parser that you created earlier. As the user enters the name in the **txtName** text box, it makes sense to call the function in the **On Exit** event handler for this text box. Select the **txtName** text box and go to the property sheet. Select the Event tab and click the builder button (the one with three dots) to the right of the On Exit event.

6 Select Code Builder and then enter the following code.

```
Private Sub txtName_Exit(Cancel As Integer)
    Dim intRetVal      As Integer
    Dim strSalutation  As String
    Dim strFirstName   As String
    Dim strMiddleName  As String
    Dim strLastName    As String
    Dim strSuffix      As String

    intRetVal = ParseName(strSalutation, strFirstName, _
        strMiddleName, strLastName, strSuffix, txtName)

    Salutation = strSalutation
    FirstName = strFirstName
    MiddleName = strMiddleName
    LastName = strLastName
    Suffix = strSuffix
    Me.Refresh
End Sub
```

This is a little 'wrapper' function to pass the values to and from the name parsing routine. We simply call the function, specifying the values of its six arguments. As a result, when the user moves off the Name text box, the individual parts of the names are automatically filled in. The current record is also refreshed so that changes are seen immediately. If you want to make the form even more user-friendly, you could hide the five redundant text boxes.

7 Before you can run the form, you need to update the **txtName** text box when the record changes, otherwise it will contain the name from the last record. You also need to make sure that the text box is cleared when you enter a new record. The code for this should be added to the section which checks for a new record and changes the state of the command button before exiting the event procedure. Select the form's property sheet and add the following code to the **On Current** event handler:

```
If IsNull(Me.PersonID) Then
    cmdPrev.SetFocus
    cmdNext.Enabled = False
    txtName = ""
Else
    cmdNext.Enabled = True
    txtName = BuildName(Salutation, FirstName, MiddleName, LastName, _
                        Suffix)
End If
```

8 Now you can finally run this function. Close the module window and the **frmMaintPerson** form (saving your changes) and go to the Forms tab of the database window. Open **frmMaintPerson** in form view and select the New button. First, you must select a location from the drop-down list in the LocationID combo box, after which you can enter a name in the Name text box, such as Dr Richard R Rowe Snr.

9 When you press *Tab* to move to the next control, all of the entries are automatically filled in for you. Since they are locked and disabled, you're left on the Date Of Birth text box. Once you've filled this in, the record is complete. Press the Previous button and then the Next button, just to confirm that it has successfully added to the database.

Of course, all of the hard work was done by the **ParseName** function in the module **Parse Name**. We'll take a look at that now.

How It Works—The Preparation

Open up the module called **Parse Name** and look at the **(General) (Declarations)** section:

```
Private Const csNAME_SAL    As Integer = &H1
Private Const csNAME_FIRST  As Integer = &H2
Private Const csNAME_MID    As Integer = &H4
Private Const csNAME_LAST   As Integer = &H8
Private Const csNAME_SUFFIX As Integer = &H10

Private Const csPREFIX_LIST As String = _
    ".MR.MRS.MISS.MS.M/S.MME.MMLLE.DR.SIR.PROF.LORD.MAJOR.COLONEL.LADY."
Private Const csSUFFIX_LIST As String = _
    ".I.II.III.IV.SR.SNR.JR.JNR.OBE."
```

The first five lines declare the constants that will be used to decide which parts of the name have been entered. They'll also be used as return values for the function which splits the name. The last two lines define the prefixes and suffixes. Because they are used in several places, we must declare them in the **(Declarations)** section to make them available to all the functions in the module.

You can have a look at the code that makes up the function by selecting **ParseName** in the Proc: combo box. The function has six arguments:

```
Function ParseName(strOutSal As String, strOutFirst As String, _
    strOutMiddle As String, strOutFinal As String, _
    strOutSuffix As String, ByVal strvarInName As Variant) As Integer
```

You will notice that the first five arguments all start **strOut**, which should indicate to you that they will be used to pass back the various parts of the person's name. By default, arguments are two-way: information can pass into and out of the function via them.

The last argument is the main one—this is what will hold the full name passed into the function. The argument is prefixed by a keyword that you have not yet encountered—**ByVal**. This means that the argument is one-way: data cannot be passed back via it.

FYI   ByVal is discussed in more detail in Chapter 10 where we look at aspects of advanced programming.

The six lines under the function definition declare the variables that we are working with:

```
Dim strTemp()       As String    ' Temporary work string
Dim intCount        As Integer   ' No. of elements in above string
Dim intSpacePos     As Integer   ' Position in string of space
Dim intLoop         As Integer   ' Loop index
Dim intParsename    As Integer   ' Return value
Dim intMainCount    As Integer   ' No. of elements - prefix & suffix
```

The parentheses after the first variable name indicate that this is an array. We don't specify how many items are needed because that will be decided later.

That covers the declarations. The next thing to look at is the code that actually makes the function do something.

Have a look at the code following the declarations. We'll take it line by line.

```
ParseName = 0
```

The first line sets the default return value for the function.

```
If IsBlank(strvarInName) Then Exit Function
```

We then check for a blank name. If the name you are searching does not have anything in it, there's nothing we can do and we need to exit the function directly.

```
StrvarInName = Trim$(strvarInName) & " "
```

The next line checks that the name entered doesn't have lots of leading or trailing spaces. There should be just one space on the end as this will be used in the search later on.

Next, we break the name up into its constituent parts, just like you saw in the earlier example. Once it's done, we have the various parts stored in the array **strTemp**.

That wraps up the preparation. We've already looked at how the function actually does the job of splitting the name up into its constituent parts in an earlier Try It Out, so let's skip further down the code to the line beginning with **intCount = UBound(strTemp)**.

How It Works—Analyzing the Array

We have the constituent parts of the name held in the elements of an array. The next task is to analyze which part is the salutation, which part is the first name etc.. If you think about it, you'll see that the first item doesn't have to be the salutation. If, for instance, the name didn't contain 'Mr', the first element of the array will contain their first name instead.

```
intCount = UBound(strTemp)
```

We start by setting a variable to tell us how many elements we have.

```
intMainCount = intCount
```

We then set another variable, **intMainCount**, to hold the count. We need two, as we'll be using them in different places.

```
If InStr(csPREFIX_LIST, "." & UCase$(strTemp(1)) & ".") Then
    intParsename = intParsename Or csNAME_SAL
    strOutSal = strTemp(1)
    intMainCount = intMainCount - 1
End If
```

This section of code checks to see if the first array element contains one of the permitted prefixes. Remember back to the constant declarations—the prefix constant has full stops around each prefix. You can now see why—**InStr** searches for one string within another, so if we put a full stop on either side of the string before we search, we can ensure that we find complete matches, rather than partial ones. If we are searching for **Mr**, we don't want **InStr** to find **Mrs**, which it could do if we didn't include the full stops or some other separator.

We need also to keep a note of which parts of the name we've found—remember there may be no salutation (such as "Mr") or suffix (such as "Snr"). We'll do this using **flags**. We've declared an integer variable **intParsename** which is initially zero. To appreciate how this works, you need to know a little about how numbers are stored in a computer. So we'll take a short detour....

Using an Integer Variable as a Set of Flags

Computers can only store values in two states (and these aren't California and Texas). Because they use voltages in RAM chips to store data, the only possible states are *on* and *off*. We can interpret these as YES and NO, or one and zero—on is 1, and off is 0. So, to store a number, we need to code it into a series of ones and zeros. The method used is called **binary coding**.

Binary is a base two number system as opposed to the decimal or base 10 system that we're all familiar with. When we see a number, such as 45, we automatically interpret it as 5 units and 4 tens. In decimal we have ten digits to work with (0 to 9) but binary only has one and zero so the bases go up by a factor of 2 rather than 10. This means we have units, twos, fours, eights, sixteens and so on as opposed to the units, tens, hundreds, thousands etc. of the decimal system.

Position	8	7	6	5	4	3	2	1
Decimal	10,000,000	1,000,000	100,000	10,000	1,000	100	10	1
Binary	128	64	32	16	8	4	2	1

So, to store 45 in binary we would have:

Position	8	7	6	5	4	3	2	1
Value	128	64	32	16	8	4	2	1
Stored	0	0	1	0	1	1	0	1

So much for the math lesson. We can also look at the individual positions simply as YES/NO flags. If position 1 means "Have we got a salutation entry?", we can store 1 in there to mean YES and 0 to mean NO. This is what we'll do in our code. You can see that we've already declared the variables which correspond to the position values:

```
Private Const csNAME_SAL    As Integer = &H1
Private Const csNAME_FIRST  As Integer = &H2
Private Const csNAME_MID    As Integer = &H4
Private Const csNAME_LAST   As Integer = &H8
Private Const csNAME_SUFFIX As Integer = &H10
```

The only extra complexity here is that we've used another different type of notation - hexadecimal. This is designed to make it easier to compare a number with its binary representation. Numbers below 10 are unchanged and, for the moment, just accept that &H10 means 16.

Looking at these in a binary table will make it clearer what we're doing:

Position	5	4	3	2	1
Value	16	8	4	2	1
Meaning	Suffix	Last Name	Middle Name	First Name	Salutation
csNAME_SAL	NO	NO	NO	NO	YES
csNAME_FIRST	NO	NO	NO	YES	NO
csNAME_MID	NO	NO	YES	NO	NO
csNAME_LAST	NO	YES	NO	NO	NO
csNAME_SUFFIX	YES	NO	NO	NO	NO

Back to the Code...

The **intParsename** variable is initially set to off (or 0) and to set the relevant flag, or bit, to on (or 1) we use the **OR** logical operator. You'll remember from earlier in the chapter that the **OR** operator gives a true result if either of its arguments are true.

So if we do find a salutation prefix, we set the flag:

```
intParsename = intParsename Or csNAME_SAL
```

This takes the current value of **intParsename** and **OR**s it with the value for a salutation. What we're effectively doing is updating the individual memory locations within the variable. Position 1 set to 1 means "We've got a salutation".

Position	8	7	6	5	4	3	2	1
Value Equivalent	128	64	32	16	8	4	2	1
Original **intParsename**	0	0	0	0	0	0	0	0
csNAME_SAL	0	0	0	0	0	0	0	1
Resulting **intParsename**	0	0	0	0	0	0	0	1

```
strOutSal = strTemp(1)
intMainCount = intMainCount - 1
```

Then we put the prefix in the salutation output string, and reduce the 'number of words' variable (**intMainCount**) by one, because we have already processed one string.

```
If InStr(csSUFFIX_LIST, "." & UCase$(strTemp(intCount))& ".") Then
    intParsename = intParsename Or csNAME_SUFFIX
    strOutSuffix = strTemp(intCount)
End If
```

We then repeat the same procedure for the suffix, this time using the last element in the array, the **csNAME_SUFFIX** value for the flag, and the suffix output string.

At this stage of the process **intParsename** would contain the value 00010001 if both a salutation and suffix are present:

Position	8	7	6	5	4	3	2	1
intParsename	0	0	0	0	0	0	0	1
csNAME_SUFFIX	0	0	0	1	0	0	0	0
OR Result	0	0	0	1	0	0	0	1

Now we come to the largest section of code where we extract the rest of the names and put them into their appropriate strings. At this stage, we will have one of three possible scenarios:

- There are three or more names, giving us a first name, a middle name and a last name
- There are two names, giving a first name and a last name
- There is only one name, giving a last name

The variable **intMainCount** holds the number of name parts remaining. To decide which parts of the name they represent and, therefore, place their values in the right output strings, we can use a **Select Case** statement.

```
Select Case intMainCount
Case 0
```

If **intMainCount** is equal to 0, it means there was only one word and this was either a salutation or a suffix—we have already handled it, so we can ignore the situation. This condition is also true if there were no words in the original name string.

```
Case 1
    If (intParsename And csNAME_SAL) Then
        strOutFinal = strTemp(2)
    Else
        strOutFinal = strTemp(1)
    End If
    intParsename = intParsename Or csNAME_LAST
```

If **intMainCount** is equal to 1, there's only one name. If the flag indicating a salutation is set, the first element of the array holds that salutation, so we use the second element. However, if the first element isn't filled, the last name must be there.

Here we've used the **AND** operator to check the value of our flag:

```
If (intParsename And csNAME_SAL) Then
```

Again, remembering back to earlier in the chapter, the **AND** operator will give a true result if both of its arguments are true. So, if we have previously set the salutation flag in **intParsename** and we **AND** it with the constant **csNAME_SAL**, we'll get a true result:

Position	8	7	6	5	4	3	2	1
Value Equivalent:	128	64	32	16	8	4	2	1
intParsename:	0	0	0	1	0	0	0	1
csNAME_SAL:	0	0	0	0	0	0	0	1
AND Result:	0	0	0	0	0	0	0	1

We therefore know the salutation is in the first element of the array, and use the second.

```
Case 2
    If (intParsename And csNAME_SAL) Then
        strOutFirst = strTemp(2)
```

128

```
    Else
        strOutFirst = strTemp(1)
    End If
    intParsename = intParsename Or csNAME_FIRST

    If (intParsename And csNAME_SUFFIX) Then
        strOutFinal = strTemp(intCount - 1)
    Else
        strOutFinal = strTemp(intCount)
    End If
    intParsename = intParsename Or csNAME_LAST
```

If **intMainCount** is equal to 2, there are two names. If the salutation flag is set, we assume that the first name is in the second element, otherwise we use the first. If the suffix flag is set, then the suffix is in the last element of the array (denoted by **intCount**), so the last name must be in the element before this. If the suffix flag isn't set, the last element must hold the last name. Notice how we set the flags in **intParsename** for each part of the name that we find, using the same **OR** method that we described earlier.

```
Case Else
    If (intParsename And csNAME_SAL) Then
        strOutFirst = strTemp(2)
    Else
        strOutFirst = strTemp(1)
    End If
    intParsename = intParsename Or csNAME_FIRST

    If (intParsename And csNAME_SUFFIX) Then
        strOutFinal = strTemp(intCount - 1)
    Else
        strOutFinal = strTemp(intCount)
    End If
    intParsename = intParsename Or csNAME_LAST
```

If **intMainCount** is not 0, 1 or 2 we can assume that all three names are present. In this case, we can take the first and last names in the same way that we did for **Case 2**.

```
For intLoop = 2 To intMainCount - 1
    If (intParsename And csNAME_SAL) Then
        strOutMiddle = Trim$(strOutMiddle) & " " & strTemp(intLoop + 1)
    Else
        strOutMiddle = Trim$(strOutMiddle) & " " & strTemp(intLoop)
    End If
    intParsename = intParsename Or csNAME_MID
Next
```

We then need to put any remaining names (there could be more than one) into the middle name string—we do this by looping over all the middle names, adding each element to the output string, **strOutMiddle**. If there is no prefix, then the loop starts at **intLoop = 2**, as the first of the middle names would be in the second element of the array. The last of the middle names would then be at **intMainCount - 1** (remember that **intMainCount** contains a count of the names only and does not include the prefix or suffix). If there is a prefix present, we simply add 1 to `intLoop` each time we loop, so that we can access the correct elements of the array.

```
End Select
```

We can then end the **Select** statement. The function is now completed.

```
ParseName = intParseName
```

All that remains to do is to return the flag, stating which elements are filled in. The function that calls it can then use **AND** to extract each flag and see whether we returned a value for that part of the name.

This has been a fairly complex function, so you should feel pretty pleased with yourself if you've managed to follow all the code. This example is a good demonstration of the power of VBA and how it can be used to greatly enhance an application.

Summary

This chapter has been a natural progression from the previous one. You have now seen how you can use program control to make your code more intelligent. We have taken your through three major programming techniques:

▶ Conditional structures (**If...Then** statements)
▶ Loops
▶ Arrays

Although there are some more advanced programming details in a later chapter, these are the major ones that you will use, so don't skip the intervening chapters, no matter how keen you are to start programming. Every chapter is another building block. In the next chapter, we'll look at the concept of objects within Access and how you can reference them and use them within VBA.

Exercises

1 Using a control structure, create a procedure to print a number out as a string, such as used on checks. For example, 120 should be printed as ONE TWO ZERO. Hint—Convert the number to a string first.

2 Convert the above function to use an array of strings for the words and replace one of the control structures. Now compare this version with the previous version and think about how this type of look-up can be used to improve the speed of functions within loops.

3 Create a user logon form that asks for a user name and a password and only lets the user carry on if the correct details have been entered. Think of two ways that you can use to make the user name case insensitive (so it ignores case)

Working with Objects

One of the most exciting new features of Access is the way in which certain object-oriented aspects of VBA are exposed to the programmer. In this chapter, we are going to look at the different objects within Access and how their structure provides the framework with which you can build better applications.

In particular we are going to look at:

- What objects are
- How they are used within Access 97
- The use of data access objects
- What collections are, and the different types in Access
- How to use properties and methods

Object-Oriented Programming

There is much talk these days about object-oriented programming, and much debate over what the term actually means. VBA has many object-oriented aspects to aid the programmer, some of which we will be considering in this chapter. There are several reasons why object-oriented aspects have been added to many languages, not just the Access programming language. The main problem is that current traditional languages (known as procedural languages) are failing to cope with contemporary trends such as:

- Reduced turnover time for many programming projects, but the same expectancy of high quality
- Applications of ever-increasing complexity and size
- An easier, more intuitive, graphical method for users to communicate their actions to the system
- The need to access data which is stored on many different platforms and systems in many different way
- The fact that programmers want to be able to efficiently re-use large portions of code in other applications

Of course, all of these problems also apply to Access and tackling them successfully will yield many benefits, but what puts many people off in the first place is the obscure and esoteric terminology in which object-oriented programming is often described. So let's start by defining our terms.

Objects

In the real world we use the word **object** to describe a whole number of things. A car, a computer, a house—they are all objects. An object can also be a collection of other objects: for example, a car is made up of a chassis, wheels, a transmission system and many other components which are objects in their own right.

The key thing about all these objects is that they know everything they need to know in order to do what they do. In other words, when the ignition key is turned, the battery, distributor and spark plugs know how to start the car; when the brake pedal is depressed, the braking mechanism knows how to slow the car down.

Likewise, in Access 97, a form is an object. It knows everything it needs to know in order to do what it does. When you hit the Cancel button, the form closes itself. When you hit the Minimize button, the form makes itself smaller.

Properties

All objects have **properties**. These are simply its characteristics. Just as a car has a size, weight and color, forms have their own properties. For example, they have a **Caption** property, a **Filter** property, a **DefaultView** property and so on... QueryDefs have properties such as an **SQL** property and an **Updatable** property. You can alter an object's properties either on the property sheet in design view, or with VBA code.

Methods

Methods are actions attached to objects. Our car might have a **LightsOn** method for turning on the headlights and a **LightsOff** method for extinguishing them. In Access, objects have methods for performing actions. For example, among the **Database** object's methods is the **OpenRecordset** method for creating a new recordset.

Classes

A **class** is a collection of objects which share the same properties and methods. Each object within a class is said to be an **instance** of that class. In the car analogy, a class might represent a model of car—for example, a Pontiac Firebird; individual Pontiac Firebirds would be instances of that class. There may also be **subclasses** within that class which **inherit** the properties and methods of the parent class, but also include their own properties and methods. For example, the Pontiac Firebird class may have subclasses of 2398cc, 2598cc, 2798cc and 2998cc for the four different engine sizes available.

The Advantages of Object-Orientation

The key advantage of object-orientation in development is that it promotes re-use. Because objects have their own self-contained properties and methods (this is called **encapsulation**), once you have built and tested an object, you or other developers can re-use the object in other code with minimal effort.

134

Using classes also opens up new vistas. Instead of creating objects from scratch, you can either **instantiate** (create a new instance of) an object from that class, or you can create a subclass which inherits the properties and methods of the parent class—again faster than creating an object from scratch.

Being able to re-use an object is of paramount importance when you're under pressure to create bug-free applications on time. Re-using objects reduces testing time dramatically, as objects need only be tested when they are first built. It also reduces the amount of errors because it takes less effort to instantiate an existing object than to build one from scratch.

Access 97 Objects

There are two sets of objects within Access. The first is the set of general Access objects:

Access Object	Description
Application	Microsoft Access itself
Control	A control on a form or report
DoCmd	Macro actions used in VBA
Debug	Debug window
Form	An open form, including sub-forms
Module	A code module
Report	An open report, including sub-reports
Screen	The screen display
Section	A form or report section, or a collection of sections
Pages	Pages of a tab control
References	References to other object libraries

The second set of objects is the set of data access objects, often referred to as **DAO**s. These are the objects concerned with data management:

Data Access Object	Description
Container	An object that contains information about other objects
Database	The open database
DBEngine	The database engine
Document	Information that the database engine manages about other objects
Error	Data access errors
Group	A group account in the database engine
Index	A table index
Parameter	A query parameter
Property	An object property
QueryDef	A saved query

Table Continued on Following Page

Data Access Object	Description
`Recordset`	A set of records defined by a table or query
`Relation`	A relationship between two tables or queries
`TableDef`	A saved table
`User`	A user account in the database engine
`Workspace`	An active database session

We will examine these data access objects in more detail in the rest of this chapter.

Collections

From the last table, you can see that a database is an object, and since a database is made up from other objects, you can conclude that objects can contain other objects. Forms, for example, contain controls, and tables contain fields. Objects that are contained in another object are grouped together in **collections**. Collections only contain objects of the same class. Hence, several forms in one object would be known as a **Forms** collection. Although you must be getting fed up of those cola cans by now (if you are, just imagine beer cans instead), your six pack would be a collection of cola cans. From this, you can deduce that a collection is really just an array. Most objects belong to collections and, to understand how these fit together, a hierarchical diagram is best. The one below shows the **data access object hierarchy** that contains the objects concerned with data management:

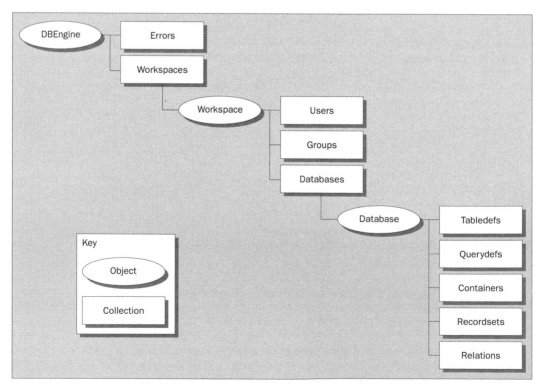

You may be surprised to find that the database is not at the top of this hierarchy. In fact, the top position is held by **DBEngine**. This is the database engine, the workhorse which processes all of your database requests and you will often find it referred to as the **Jet engine**. You may think this is an extremely bad joke (and you'd be right), but it actually stands for **Joint Engine Technology**. The Jet engine processes nearly everything you do in Access 97.

The DBEngine contains two collections: **Workspaces** and **Errors**. You can liken a workspace to an office at work. The building would be the DBEngine and each office would be a workspace. The **Errors** collection, unsurprisingly, contains a list of errors that have occurred in the DBEngine.

Almost all of your actions are processed by the Jet engine, and almost every action is performed on a data access object. It is therefore extremely important that you understand exactly what data access objects are and how they relate to each other. Once you understand this, you will find yourself much more at ease with Access and the way in which it handles its objects.

We'll start by looking at the data access objects and how they can be accessed. This will illustrate how objects can contain other objects and will show exactly how the above hierarchy works.

Try It Out—The Data Access Object Hierarchy

In this example, we'll be using the Debug window to show us the result of the code that we type in.

1 Load the sample database, **Whisky5.mdb**, and create a new module. Open the debug window, and type in the following:

```
?DBEngine.Workspaces(0).Name
```

Press *Enter* at the end of the line and you should see the following result:

#Default Workspace#

2 Now add **Database** into the line:

```
?DBEngine.Workspaces(0).Databases(0).Name
```

This time, you get the full name of the database.

3 How about adding another layer:

```
?DBEngine.Workspaces(0).Databases(0).TableDefs(0).Name
```

You should see Bottling, which is the first table.

4 Finally, try changing the index in the **TableDefs** collection from 0 to 4:

```
?DBEngine.Workspaces(0).Databases(0).TableDefs(4).Name
```

This gives a slightly unusual result:

MSysACEs

Let's have a look at what's happening here.

How It Works

The first thing to note is how you reference objects within a collection. Look again at the first line that you typed:

```
?DBEngine.Workspaces(0).Name
```

Notice that you use a full stop between the objects, and between the objects and their properties.

This line of code shows the name of the workspace that is currently in use. **DBEngine** is the top-level object and **Workspaces** is a collection of objects within it. Each object within this collection is a **Workspace**. Notice the difference in name is between singular and plural. Collections are plural, because they contain more than one object, whilst the object itself is singular. So **Workspaces** is plural, therefore it is the collection, and **Workspace** is singular, therefore it is the object.

Have a look at the adjacent diagram, which shows a small section of the object model in more detail:

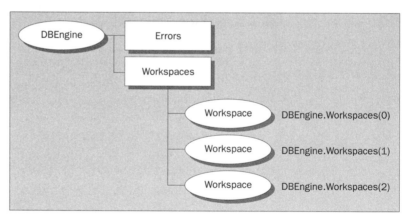

Here you can see how the collection is organized and that it is organized along the lines of an array. Each of these array elements is a single object—a **Workspace**. The **Name** at the end of the code line is not an object but a property of the workspace. It simply tells you what the object is called. In this case, it is #Default Workspace# because, by default, we only have one workspace set up. (You will probably never use more than the default workspace and you certainly won't need to use any more in this book.)

```
?DBEngine.Workspaces(0).Databases(0).Name
```

The second line adds another level to the hierarchy by adding the **Database** object. This gives the name of the database.

You will often see **DBEngine.Workspaces(0).Databases(0)** used to refer to the current database, but you can also use **CurrentDB()**. This is the preferred method because it creates a new instance of the current database and allows you to have more than one variable of type **Database**—avoiding conflicts if you are using Access on a network. The long syntax is used here to illustrate the object hierarchy.

```
?DBEngine.Workspaces(0).Databases(0).TableDefs(0).Name
```

The third section steps down another layer to the **TableDefs** collection. This is a list of all of the tables stored in the database. You may have been surprised that the name returned was MSysACEs, when you used the index of 4, instead of **Order**, which is the fifth table. This is because indexes into collections start at 0. This is one of the system tables used by Access and, since tables are stored in alphabetical order, this is in the middle of your tables. There are eight system tables, all of which start with **MSys**. A diagram explains the **TableDefs** collection clearly:

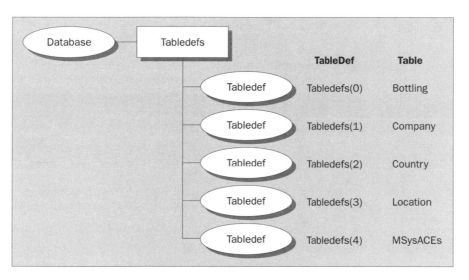

Using this method of gradually delving deeper into the hierarchy, you can see how easy it is to find out about all the objects that you have stored in the database.

Containers and Documents

The **Containers** and **Documents** collections are extremely important because they hold information about every saved object. So every table that you save appears in a collection under **Containers**. Simply put, a container is just a collection of objects, each of which is a saved object in the database. If you look at the main database window, each page is a container and the objects it shows are the documents. The term **document** is used as a generic description for an object stored in a container. You can liken this to pieces of paper in a folder. If you write the contents of each table on a sheet of paper and put them all together, you have a similar situation. The piece of paper is your **document**, and the folder is the **container**. Like other objects, this is stored as a hierarchy and is best shown with another diagram:

139

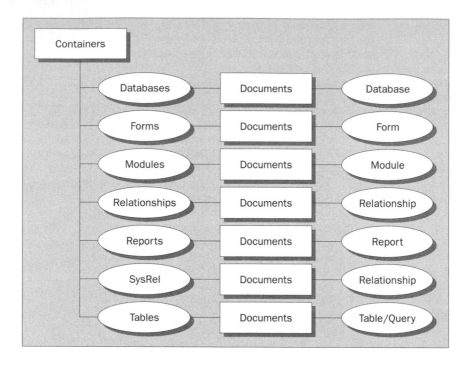

*There is one container shown on this diagram which we are not going to discuss: **SysRel**.
The **SysRel** container is used to store internal information about relationships within
Access 97 and is never used by the programmer. All the others contain the objects that you
use when creating your database.*

A point to note here is not to get confused by the objects under the **Containers** collection,
which are plural, and therefore might lead you to think that they are collections. In this case
this is not so, as the single container name is plural.

We'll now look at how you can view all the containers, and the documents they hold.

Try It Out—Containers

If you select Database Properties from the File menu, and then select the Contents page of the
dialog, you'll see a small database documentation utility. In order to examine containers in more
detail, we are going to create a similar utility.

1 Open **Whisky5.mdb** and create a new module. Then create a subroutine called
ListContainers and type in the following code:

```
Dim dbCurrent        As Database
Dim conTest          As Container

Set dbCurrent = DBEngine.Workspaces(0).Databases(0)
```

```
For Each conTest In dbCurrent.Containers
    Debug.Print "Container: "; conTest.Name
Next
```

2 Now open the Debug window and run the procedure by typing **ListContainers** and pressing *Enter*. You should see the following:

```
ListContainers
Container: Databases
Container: Forms
Container: Modules
Container: Relationships
Container: Reports
Container: Scripts
Container: SysRel
Container: Tables
```

Here you can see that the **Containers** collection contains objects of different types. Let's examine the code line by line to see how it works.

How It Works

```
Dim dbCurrent      As Database
Dim conTest        As Container
```

We started by defining two variables—one of type **Database** to point to the current database, and one of type **Container** to point to each element in the **Containers** collection. These are variable types that Access provides specially for these purposes.

```
Set dbCurrent = DBEngine.Workspaces(0).Databases(0)
```

We then set the **dbCurrent** variable to point to the currently active database. Since there is only one workspace and database active, this will be position 0 in the collection. Note that, when you are assigning objects, you must use the special keyword **Set**.

```
For Each conTest In dbCurrent.Containers
```

We then looped through all the containers using a **For Each...** loop. This is similar to the **For... Next** loop, but is designed specifically for collections. The format is easy enough to understand:

For Each *objectVariable* In *objectCollection*

> *The For Each... statement was new in Access 95. In previous versions of Access, you had to use the Count property of the collection to determine how many items it contained, and then loop through them. In the loop, you would set the object variable to the member of the collection. This new statement has greatly simplified this, making it much clearer and easier to read.*

```
    Debug.Print "Container: "; conTest.Name
Next
```

Finally, we printed the name and ended the loop.

That was fairly easy, so let's now have a look at the documents. To do this, we will add a second loop inside the first. As well as printing out the name of each container, we will loop through the documents and print their names.

Try It Out—Documents

1 Add another variable to the subroutine that you used in the last example to point to the document:

```
Dim dbCurrent      As Database
Dim conTest        As Container
Dim docTest        As Document
```

2 Now add the inner loop just after the line that prints the name of the container.

```
Set dbCurrent = DBEngine.Workspaces(0).Databases(0)
For Each conTest In dbCurrent.Containers
    Debug.Print "Container: "; conTest.Name
    For Each docTest In conTest.Documents
        Debug.Print "    Document: "; docTest.Name
    Next
Next
```

3 Run the procedure again and look at the results.

```
Container:    Databases
    Document:    AccessLayout
    Document:    MSysDb
    Document:    SummaryInfo
    Document:    UserDefined
Container:    Forms
    Document:    frmListMaintForms
    Document:    frmMaintBottling
    Document:    frmMaintCompany
    Document:    frmMaintCountry
    Document:    frmMaintLocation
    Document:    frmMaintPerson
    Document:    frmMaintRegion
    Document:    frmMaintWhisky
    Document:    frmPerson
Container:    Modules
    Document:    Chapter 3 Code
    Document:    Chapter 4 Code
    Document:    Chapter 5 Code
    Document:    Parse Name
Container:    Relationships
```

The output should look familiar, apart (perhaps) from the Databases container, which Access uses to store details about itself. AccessLayout contains the layout information, MSysDb the system information, SummaryInfo the summary information, and UserDefined any user-defined properties. You can easily see the SummaryInfo and UserDefined properties by looking at these pages on the Database Properties window, available from the File Menu.

The Forms Container

You have now seen how easy it is to see all of the documents and containers, but what's the use of this? Do you really need to see what's in your own database? You may think not, but it actually gives you great control over the database.

For example, the sample database has some tables for storing data that does not change very often—company details, etc.. These are called lookup tables, since they are mainly used to look up information. Even though this data is fairly static, you still need to be able to change it, and therefore each of these tables needs a form to allow editing. You also need a single form from which you can select the lookup details you wish to edit. You may think that the way to create this selector form is to hard-code the details, i.e. have one button for each lookup form. However, this isn't the best solution because, if you add another lookup table, you will have to alter your form. A better way is to name the forms consistently and use the **Forms** container to find them and put them in a list box. Now if you add another form for the new lookup table, it automatically appears in the list box. This is a little more work initially, but it pays off in the long run.

We'll implement this type of form in the next example.

Try It Out—Using the Forms Container

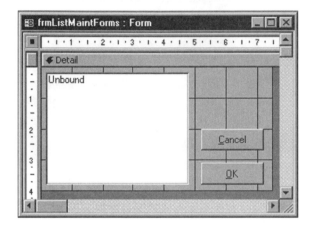

1 Create a new form called **frmListMaintForms**, and add a list box and two command buttons:

You can use the Command Button Wizard for the Cancel button since this is just going to close the form. We'll sort out the OK button later.

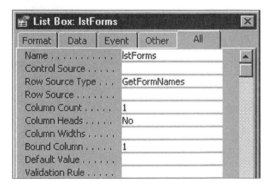

2 Examine the properties for the list box and change them to match the following:

You can see that the Row Source Type is not set to Table/Query as it is normally, but to GetFormNames. This is the name of the function that will fill the list box.

3 We can now create the function. Select <u>C</u>ode from the <u>V</u>iew menu and create a module level variable to hold the form names:

```
Private fastrFormNames() As String     'Array of maintenance form names
```

4 Now create a function, **GetMaintenanceForms**, to fill the above array with the form names:

```
Function GetMaintenanceForms()

    Dim dbCurr      As Database        ' Current database
    Dim docForm     As Document        ' Current form in collection
    Dim intCounter  As Integer         ' Count of forms

    ReDim fastrFormNames(0)

    Set dbCurr = CurrentDb()
    For Each docForm In dbCurr.Containers("Forms").Documents
        If Len(docForm.Name) > 8 Then
            If Left$(docForm.Name, 8) = "frmMaint" Then
                ReDim Preserve fastrFormNames(intCounter)
                fastrFormNames(intCounter) = Mid$(docForm.Name, 9)
                intCounter = intCounter + 1
            End If
        End If
    Next

    GetMaintenanceForms = intCounter

End Function
```

5 Now you need another procedure to fill the list box from the array:

```
Function GetFormNames(fld As Control, id As Variant, row As Variant, _
                col As Variant, code As Variant) As Variant

    Static intFormCount     As Integer

    Select Case code
        Case acLBInitialize
            intFormCount = GetMaintenanceForms()
            If intFormCount > 0 Then
                GetFormNames = True
            Else
                GetFormNames = False
            End If
        Case acLBOpen
            GetFormNames = Timer      ' Generate unique ID for control.
        Case acLBGetRowCount
            GetFormNames = intFormCount
        Case acLBGetColumnCount
            GetFormNames = 1
```

```
        Case acLBGetColumnWidth
            GetFormNames = -1          ' -1 forces use of default width.
        Case acLBGetValue
            GetFormNames = fastrFormNames(row)
    End Select
End Function
```

6 Now compile the code using the Compile Loaded Modules button to make sure that you have typed it correctly, save it and switch to Form view. The list box now contains the names of the forms:

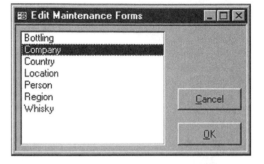

7 The only thing left to do now is to make the OK button do something. Switch back to Design mode and add the following code for the click event:

```
Dim strFormName As String

If Not IsNull(Me.lstForms) Then
    strFormName = Me.lstForms
    DoCmd.Close
    DoCmd.OpenForm "frmMaint" & strFormName
End If
```

8 Save the code and switch to Form view. You can now select a form and press OK to open it.

How It Works

The secret to creating this form is having the lookup tables all named in a similar fashion. In our database, they all start with **frmMaint**. We simply look through the **Forms** collection for any matches and add them to the list.

Let's examine the code in more detail:

```
    Private fastrFormNames() As String    'Array of maintenance form names
```

We started by declaring the array that holds the form names. This is a module-level variable as it is used in more than one function.

```
    Dim dbCurr      As Database        ' Current database
    Dim docForm     As Document        ' Current form in collection
    Dim intCounter  As Integer         ' Count of forms

    ReDim fastrFormNames(0)
```

We then defined a few variables and re-dimensioned the global array. This is because we don't know how many form names are going to be stored in the array, so we have to allocate a dynamic/flexible amount of storage space.

```
Set dbCurr = CurrentDb()
For Each docForm In dbCurr.Containers("Forms").Documents
```

Next, we opened the database using the function **CurrentDB** and started to loop through the form documents. Remember that we could have used **DBEngine.Workspaces(0).Databases(0)** to open the database. We used the above function because it is easier to read.

```
If Len(docForm.Name) > 8 Then
    If Left$(docForm.Name, 8) = "frmMaint" Then
```

Since all of our maintenance forms are more than eight characters, we first check the length, and then check that the first eight letters are **frmMaint**.

```
ReDim Preserve fastrFormNames(intCounter)
```

If the start of the form name matches, it needs to be added to the array, so the array itself needs to be re-dimensioned to allow for another entry.

```
fastrFormNames(intCounter) = Mid$(docForm.Name, 9)
```

The list box would not look very nice if the whole of the form name was included, so the **frmMaint** section is ignored and only the right-hand part of the name is added to the array. This is done with help of the **Mid$** function which is a close relation of the **Left$** and **Right$** functions that we encountered in Chapter 4. However, **Mid$** returns characters from the middle of the string; the part returned starts at the character number specified and continues to the end of the string, unless an optional value defining the length of the part to be returned is also provided.

```
            intCounter = intCounter + 1
        End If
    End If
Next
```

The counter is now increased, the **If** statements ended, and the loop ended.

```
GetMaintenanceForms = intCounter
```

Finally, the number of forms in the array is returned from the function.

How It Works—The GetFormNames Function

The **GetFormNames** function is no more complicated, although it does look it. The function can be named anything you like, as long it is the same name as that set in the RowSourceType property for the list box (or combo box).

```
Function GetFormNames(fld As Control, id As Variant, row As Variant, _
                col As Variant, code As Variant) As Variant
```

146

Similarly, the arguments can be named anyway you like, but they must be in the following order, and of the following type:

Argument	Type	Description
`fld`	`Control`	This refers to the list box or combo box which is being filled.
`Id`	`Variant`	This is a unique value which identifies the control being filled. It is really only used when you have more than one list box or combo box being filled by the same function, and you need to uniquely identify each control.
`Row`	`Variant`	This refers to the row currently being filled (starts at 0).
`Col`	`Variant`	This refers to the column currently being filled (starts at 0).
`Code`	`Variant`	This holds a value which determines what type of data the function should supply.

> ***GetFormNames*** *has to conform to a standard layout because Access supplies the arguments to the function—you have no control over this.*

Access will call this function several times—when the form first opens, and afterwards as the user manipulates the list box control by scrolling, etc.. Our task is to ensure that we return the correct information each time the function is called.

```
Static intFormCount        As Integer
```

The first real line of code declares a variable to hold the number of forms. This has to be a **Static** variable because the function is called several times and, otherwise, the value would be lost.

```
Select Case code
        Case acLBInitialize
            intFormCount = GetMaintenanceForms()
            if intFormCount = 0 Then
                GetFormNames = True
            Else
                GetFormNames = False
            End If
```

Now we get to the fun part, which revolves around the value held by the variable **code**. The variable is set to one of several values, each of which has an associated constant. Since there are many values, a **Select Case** statement is used.

The first entry is **acLBInitialize**. This occurs when the function is first called and the list box is to be initialized. Here, we want to fill our global array with the form names which we will then display in the list box. The first part is a check to see if there are any form names to be displayed in our list box. If **intFormCount** is greater than zero, then there are form names to be displayed and the value **True** is returned to tell Access that the function can fill the list. If **intFormCount** is zero, there are no form names and a **False** value is returned as the list cannot be filled.

```
Case acLBOpen
        GetFormNames = Timer        ' Generate unique ID for control.
```

The second entry is **acLBOpen**, which means that the list box is being opened. Here, we set a unique value for the control, in this case using the **Timer**. The **Timer** function simply returns the number of seconds that have elapsed since midnight. This is what you will use in most cases, as it generates a unique value. The value is passed back to the function as the argument **id** to identify which control was being filled.

```
Case acLBGetRowCount
        GetFormNames = intFormCount
```

The next value is **acLBGetRowCount**, which requests the number of rows being filled. We return the number of rows in the forms array.

```
Case acLBGetColumnCount
        GetFormNames = 1
```

Then comes **acLBGetColumnCount**, to request the number of columns in the list box. Since we only want to display one column, 1 is returned. This value must match the value on the property sheet, since otherwise it causes the list box to display the information incorrectly.

```
Case acLBGetColumnWidth
        GetFormNames = -1            ' -1 forces use of default width.
```

Next is **acLBGetColumnWidth**, to determine the width of the column. Using a value of -1 forces Access to use the default width.

```
Case acLBGetValue
        GetFormNames = fastrFormNames(row)
```

Finally comes **acLBGetValue**, which requests the actual string (form name) to be added to the list box. Each form name is taken from the global array and passed to **GetFormNames** in turn. We use the argument **row** to access the forms array. For each value of **row**, there is a different form name stored in the array. This then corresponds with each row displayed in the list box.

FYI

The two values that we haven't used in this example are **acLBGetFormat** and **acLBEnd**. The first—**acLBGetFormat**—is used to request the format string for the list entry, and **acLBEnd** is used when the form is closed.

So, although the function looks complicated, it actually follows a very simple method—Access calls it several times requesting different values. The number of times the function is called is also easy to work out:

 The function is called once for codes **acLBInitialize**, **acLBOpen**, **acLBGetRowCount** and **acLBGetColumnCount**. It initializes the list function, opens the query, and determines the number of rows and columns.

 The function is called twice for code **acLBGetColumnWidth**; once to calculate the total width of the list box and then a second time for the individual column width.

▶ For codes **acLBGetValue** and **acGetFormat**, the number of times the function is called depends upon the number of rows, whether the user is scrolling down the list, and other factors.

▶ For **acLBEnd**, the function is called when the form is closed or for each time the list box is queried.

Forms and Reports

There are two collections available which have not been mentioned so far because they are slightly different: **Forms** and **Reports**. You may be confused now because these appear in the section about containers. But remember what was said about containers—they store information about saved objects. The **Forms** and **Reports** collections store information about open objects. So, if you have nothing but the database window open, these two collections will be empty. However, as soon as you open a form, the **Forms** collection has one item.

Try It Out—The Forms Collection

1 Close the form from the last example and any other active forms.

2 Create a new module, open the Debug window, and type the following:

```
?Forms(0).Name
```

3 Press *Enter* and you should see the following error message:

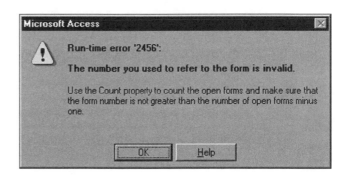

This shows that you are trying to access an invalid entry in the collection.

4 Now open a form and try again. This time you should see the name of the form.

```
?Forms(0).Name
frmMaintCompany
```

These two collections are very useful when you want to perform actions on forms or reports that are open. For example, imagine a form which gives the user the ability to change its details—perhaps from normal text to italic. This is very simple because a form just consists of controls. So each text box, label, etc, on the form is part of the **Controls** collection. We'll create a small subroutine to change text on all open forms to italic text.

Try It Out—Forms and Controls

1 Create a new subroutine, **FormsItalic**, in the module you created in the last example and add code to step first through the **Forms** collection, and then through each of the controls in the **Controls** collection for each form:

```
Dim frmCurrent      As Form         ' current form
Dim ctlControl      As Control      ' current control

For Each frmCurrent In Forms
    For Each ctlControl In frmCurrent.Controls
        ctlControl.FontItalic = True
    Next
Next
```

Within the inner loop, you are using the **FontItalic** property of the control, and setting this to **True**.

2 Open a form, for example, **frmMaintPerson**, and run the procedure from the debug window. The text on the form changes to italic, but you also get an error message.

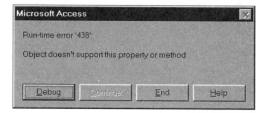

Microsoft Access

Run-time error '438':

Object doesn't support this property or method

[Debug]   [Continue]   [End]   [Help]

3 The reason for the error is that not every control on the form has a **FontItalic** property (the **PictureBox**, for example). There are two ways to prevent this error. The first, and probably the more correct, is to use the **TypeOf** statement to check the type of control.

FYI

The more hawk-eyed among you might have spotted that the command buttons didn't change to italic text, despite the fact that they do have **FontItalic** properties. The reason for this is that Access tries to change each property in turn, but when it encounters an error, the code stops without getting as far as the command buttons.

4 Replace the line that changes the property with the following code:

```
Dim frmCurrent      As Form         ' current form
Dim ctlControl      As Control      ' current control

For Each frmCurrent In Forms
    For Each ctlControl In frmCurrent.Controls
        If ctlControl.ControlType = acLine Then
            ' Do nothing
        Else
            ctlControl.FontItalic = True
        End If
    Next
Next
```

ControlType is a property that every control has that tells you the type of control it is, and **acLine** is an intrinsic constant that means this control is a line. There is a constant for each control type.

The procedure now works for this form, but what about forms that have other controls, such as **Rectangles** and **Page Breaks**, which do not have the **FontItalic** property either? There are two solutions here. The first is to use a **Select Case** statement.

```
Select Case ctlControl.ControlType
Case acCommandButton, acLabel, acListBox, acTabCtl, acTextBox,
acToggleButton
    ctlControl.FontItalic = True
Case Else
    ' Do nothing
End Select
```

Alternatively, you could put some error handling in so that you trap errors and ignore them if they mean that the control does not have the relevant property. This allows you to have a simple, easy to read section of code that caters for every control type. The following code, for example, uses this method:

```
On Error GoTo FormsItalic_Err

    For Each frmCurrent In Forms
        For Each ctlControl In frmCurrent.Controls
            ctlControl.FontItalic = True
        Next
    Next

FormsItalic_Exit:
    Exit Sub

FormsItalic_Err:
    If Err = 438 Then
        Resume Next
    Else
        MsgBox Error$
        Resume FormsItalic_Exit
    End If
```

One thing to bear in mind when using the **Forms** and **Reports** collections to change properties is that these are not saved when the form is closed. Try running the **FormsItalic** procedure on an open form, closing the form, and then opening it again. You will notice that it has reverted to the state before you ran the procedure. To make permanent changes to objects, you must do one of two things:

> Modify each form or report in the **Containers** collection. This involves opening the form or report in Design view, changing the properties and then closing it and saving the changes.

➧ The second option, which you might not have come across before, is to save the details of the change for your database in the Windows Registry, and then read this as each form is opened. This is clearly not a perfect choice since every form or report would have to check these details as it opened.

The Errors Collection

The **Errors** collection is used to store errors that occur within the data access objects (databases, tables, containers, etc.) and should not be confused with the **Err** object, which stores run-time errors generated by VBA, OLE objects, or the programmer.

> *The Errors collection was new in Access 95—there was no equivalent in previous versions.*

Any data access object can generate errors. These errors are placed in **Error** objects in the **Errors** collection. Any subsequent action by a data access object that generates an error will mean that the **Errors** collection is cleared and then filled with the new error details. This means that the **Errors** collection is not the same as other collections, where items are appended to the end. The **Errors** collection only ever holds details about a single error that has occurred. However, some errors, particularly ODBC databases, might generate more than one actual error as a single data access error can create errors in each layer of the ODBC driver. **Errors(0)** holds the lowest level error, **Errors(1)** the next lowest and so on. Generally when working with Access 97 databases, however, only one error code—in **Errors(0)**—will be generated.

Try It Out—The Errors Collection

In this example, we'll deliberately generate some errors to see the difference between the **Errors** collection and the **Err** object.

1 Create a new procedure called **ShowErrors** and add the following lines of code:

```
    Dim dbC         As Database
    Dim recR        As Recordset
    Dim errE        As Error

    On Error GoTo ShowErrors_Err

    Set dbC = CurrentDb()
    Set recR = dbC.OpenRecordset("AnyTable")
    recR.Close

ShowErrors_Exit:
    Exit Sub

ShowErrors_Err:
    ' The Err object
    Debug.Print "Err = "; Err; ": "; Error$
```

```
' The Errors collection
For Each errE In DBEngine.Errors
    Debug.Print "Errors:"; errE.Number; ": "; errE.Description
Next
Resume ShowErrors_Exit
```

This procedure opens the current database and then tries to open a **Recordset** for a table that does not exist. This will obviously generate an error. We print this error (**Err**) together with the error description (**Error$**), and then cycle through the **Errors** collection, printing the error number and description.

2 Run the procedure in the debug window. You'll see that two copies of the same error are printed:

```
ShowErrors
Err =  3078 : The Microsoft Jet database engine cannot find
    the input table or query 'AnyTable'.
    Make sure it exists and that its name is spelled correctly.
Errors: 3078 : The Microsoft Jet database engine cannot find
    the input table or query 'AnyTable'.
    Make sure it exists and that its name is spelled correctly.
```

3 Now try putting the following line before the **OpenRecordset** command:

```
Forms!frmPeople.Caption = "A new caption"
```

4 Run the procedure again. This time something different is printed:

```
ShowErrors
Err =  2450 : Microsoft Access can't find the form 'frmPeople'
    referred to in a macro expression or Visual Basic code.
    @* The form you referenced may be closed or may not exist in
    this database.
    * Microsoft Access may have encountered a compile error in a
    Visual Basic module for the form.@@1@211735@1
Errors: 3078 : The Microsoft Jet database engine cannot find
    the input table or query 'AnyTable'.
    Make sure it exists and that its name is spelled correctly.
```

How It Works

When you first ran the procedure, the data access error in the **Errors** collection was also reported in the **Err** object.

When you added the extra line, assigning a caption to a form, you still got two errors but this time they were not the same. The error reported in the **Err** object is not the same as that in the **Errors** collection. The error reported in the **Err** object explains that the form that you were trying to modify is not open. The second line, printed using the **Errors** collection, says that you could not open the table. But hang on a minute—the **OpenRecordset** has not been executed because the first error sent us to the error handling code. So how can the error still be generated? Well, the answer is quite simple—it is not generated. However, the **Errors** collection still contains the details of this error from the last time it occurred because another data access error has not occurred.

This shows that you should not rely solely on the **Errors** collection for your errors. It should be used in conjunction with the **Err** object. Errors are added to the **Errors** collection in the order in which they occur, so you should compare the error reported in the **Err** object with the last entry in the **Errors** collection.

The following screenshot shows the output from a failed ODBC query:

```
ODBCErr
Err = 3146 : ODBC--call failed.
Errors: 2627 : [Microsoft][ODBC SQL Server Driver][SQL Server]
               Violation of UNIQUE KEY constraint 'unqCase':
               Attempt to insert duplicate key in object 'tblCase'.
Errors: 3621 : [Microsoft][ODBC SQL Server Driver][SQL Server]
               Command has been aborted.
Errors: 3146 : ODBC--call failed.
```

This procedure attempted to write a record that already existed to a table in an ODBC data source. You can clearly see how the **Errors** collection is populated if more than one error is returned, and that the lowest level error is stored in **Errors(0)** as this is the first error generated by SQL Server. This error aborts the command, which adds another entry, this time in **Errors(1)**. Finally, Access recognizes that an error has occurred and fills in **Errors(2)** with the DAO error number. In this case you would have to check **Err** against **Errors(2).Number** to see if this was a DAO error.

Referring to Objects

So far, you have only used an index into the collection to reference the required item, but there are other ways to find the object you require. The first method we'll look at is probably the most common. It allows you to refer to an object explicitly as a member of a collection. For example, to set an object variable to the form **frmPeople** you can use:

```
Set frmP = Forms!frmPeople
```

You use the exclamation mark to separate the collection from the object. If the object has spaces in its name, you have to enclose it within square brackets:

```
Set frmP = Forms![frmPeople Form]
```

The second method is similar to using an index, but instead of a number you use the name of the object or a string variable:

```
Set frmP = Forms("frmPeople")
```

or

```
strFormName = "frmPeople"
Set frmP = Forms(strFormName)
```

And, of course, you can use a number to refer to an object in a collection just like you would with an array:

```
Set frmP = Forms(3)
```

This would set **frmP** to point to the fourth form in the collection (collection numbers start at 0). So, you can access a form either from its name or its position in the **Forms** collection. If you use **For Each...** to cycle through the collection, you use the numeric position in the collection. Using the name allows you to access single objects directly.

Special Objects

Although they are not really objects, there are some special properties that represent objects, and they can be extremely useful. For example, imagine you had some code in a module to change some properties on a form, but you only want to change the current form. The application is written in a way that allows the user to have any form open—so how does the code know which form is current? In this case, you can use the **ActiveForm** property of the Screen object. The table below shows these special properties and describes what they refer to:

Property	Applies to...	Refers to...
ActiveControl	Screen	The control that has the focus.
ActiveForm	Screen	The form that has the focus or contains the control with the focus.
ActiveReport	Screen	The report that has the focus or contains the control with the focus.
Form	Subform, form or the actual control	For a subform control, this is the subform. For a form, it is the form itself.
Me	Form or report	The form or report itself.
Module	Form or report	The form or report module.
Parent	Control	The form or report that contains the control.
PreviousControl	Screen	The control that had the focus directly before the control with the current focus.
RecordsetClone	Form	The recordset that underlies a form.
Report	Subreport, reports or the actual control	For a sub-report control, this is the sub-report. For a report, it is the report itself.
Section	Control	The section of a form or report where the control is.

Try It Out—The ActiveForm Property

1 Create a new procedure called **ShowActiveForm**, and add the following lines:

```
DoCmd.OpenForm "frmMaintPerson"
Debug.Print Screen.ActiveForm.Name
```

2 Run this from the Debug window. It will open the form and then print the name.

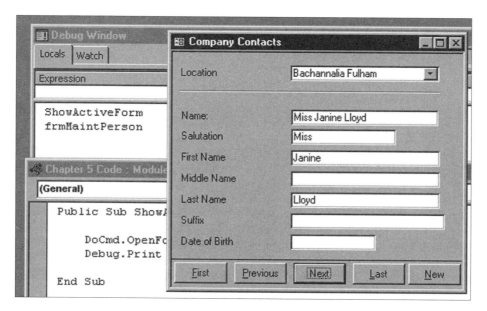

Imagine how this could be used with the earlier **FormsItalic** example. You could have a general procedure that changed some properties on whichever form happened to be active at the time, without the procedure knowing the form name. Why not try changing the first section of **FormsItalic** so that instead of all open forms, you just change the active one. To do this, we just remove the outer loop and use **Screen.ActiveForm** to refer to the currently active form:

```
For Each ctlControl In Screen.ActiveForm.Controls
   Select Case ctlControl.ControlType
   Case acCommandButton, acLabel, acListBox, acTabCtl, _
     acTextBox, acToggleButton
        ctlControl.FontItalic = True
   Case Else
        ' Do nothing
   End Select
Next
```

The major difference is that this cannot be called from the Debug window because, even if you have a form open, that form cannot be the active window—the Debug window is the active one because it has the current focus. This means that you have to call this procedure from a form module, or add a line that opens the form first (like we did in the previous Try It Out).

156

Instead, try creating a new button on any form and placing the **FormsItalic** procedure in the **On Click** event of the button. When clicked, it will run the **FormsItalic** procedure for that form.

The Me Property

The **Me** property is extremely useful since it refers to the object currently being executed. So, if you use **Me** in a form module, it refers to the form. We can modify the **FormsItalic** procedure once again to take an argument that is the name of the form on which it should work:

```
Public Sub FormsItalic (frmThis As Form)

    Dim ctlControl        As Control

    For Each ctlControl In frmThis.Controls
        Select Case ctlControl.ControlType
        Case acCommandButton, acLabel, acListBox, acTabCtl, _
          acTextBox, acToggleButton
            ctlControl.FontItalic = True
        Case Else
            ' Do nothing
        End Select
    Next

End Sub
```

The procedure would now be called in the following fashion:

```
Call FormsItalic (Me)
```

You can see that this is even more flexible since it allows the procedure to accept any form as an argument and then perform the changes on that form.

Default Collections

As objects can consist of one or more collections, Access defines one of these as a default. This allows you to refer to objects in that collection without mentioning the collection. For example, you can write:

```
Set dbCurrent = DBEngine(0)(0)
```

The default collection for **DBEngine** is **Workspaces**, and the default collection of a **Workspace** is **Databases**. Therefore, the code above is exactly the same as:

```
Set dbCurrent = DBEngine.Workspaces(0).Databases(0)
```

So what is the difference between the two? Not a lot, actually. The first method is marginally faster, but reduces clarity. Speed gains like this are really only crucial if you are setting object variables to reference collections in a loop.

The default collections for the Access 97 objects are shown below:

Object	Default Collection
Container	Documents
Database	TableDefs
DBEngine	Workspaces
Form	Controls
Group	Users
Index	Fields
QueryDef	Parameters
Recordset	Fields
Relation	Fields
Report	Controls
TableDef	Fields
Users	Groups
Workspace	Databases

The Object Browser

The Object Browser was new in Access 95. It is way of looking up information and shows all of the objects within the database—you can see what methods and properties are available to you. You may have seen it in Microsoft Excel. It is similar to the Expression Builder, but concentrates solely on objects. You can open the Object Browser when editing code by pressing *F2* or by using the Object Browser button.

This opens the Object Browser window:

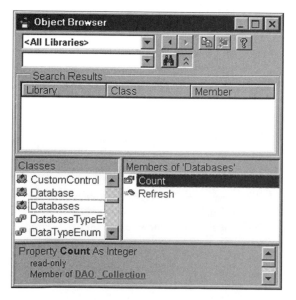

Let's have a look at these sections in more detail to see what they do.

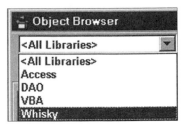

The combo box at the top lists all available libraries:

These are the four standard libraries of objects that are available:

▶ **Access** contains the objects, methods, properties, and constants that are available in the Access library

▶ **DAO** stands for the Jet Data Access Objects

▶ **VBA** is Visual Basic for Applications, which contains items that are implemented across all packages that use VBA

▶ **Whisky** is the current database

If you have another database open, its name would be shown here.

The buttons to the right of this allow you to move through the history of your selections, as well as copying the current selection to the clipboard, or jumping directly to the object code. The latter option only works for your own libraries.

The second combo in this section is for searching, and the middle section shows the search results. Finally there is the class section:

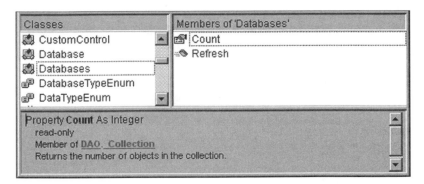

The pane on the left shows all of the classes, objects, collections, etc. and the pane on the right, the members of the selected object. Here you can see that Database is selected, and the members are Count and Refresh. Notice the difference between the icons. Count is a property of the Databases object, and Refresh is a method. The bottom pane gives the description of the selected item. Here you can see that Count is a property, of type integer. It is read-only, and a member of the DAO collection, and it returns the number of objects in the collection, in this case the number of databases.

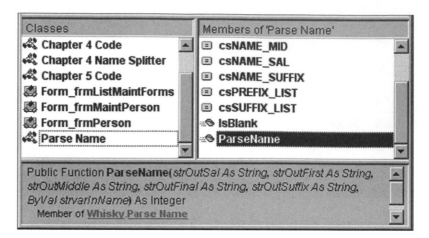

Select Whisky from the libraries combo and you see something else:

Here you have a list of forms (the reason these show up under forms is discussed in more detail in the Chapter 10), Modules and their members. The Parse Name class has some constants and some methods.

The Object Browser is an extremely important tool, especially when learning. It gives you a greater understanding of the objects within Access and what methods and properties are available. It really is worthwhile spending some time learning how to use it effectively. Just have a browse, wander around the classes. You'll be amazed at how many properties and methods you find that you didn't know existed.

> *One thing to beware of, though. If you add some references, by using the* ***References...*** *option from the* ***Tools*** *menu, and then copy your database to another machine, you may get spurious errors if the reference does not exist on the other machine.*

Summary

This chapter has described the basics of objects and how they are used within Access 97. The data access objects are a very important topic, so we have spent some time explaining these in detail. Almost everything you do in Access is based around one object or another, so you should make sure you feel comfortable with what they are, how they are collected together, and how you can use them. Later chapters will examine the other objects in more detail.

In brief, we have covered:

- The data access object hierarchy
- The different types of collection, such as containers and documents
- How to refer to objects and collections, including the **Me** property which refers to the object currently being executed
- The Object Browser as a reference to the object structure

The next chapter will look at how we go about using VBA to manipulate the data contained in Access, via the use of recordsets.

Exercises

1 In a similar fashion to the **FormsItalic** example, create a procedure that will let the user change the font on forms.

2 Think about how you could make this change permanent, so that the user selection is kept for the next time. Remember the difference between the Forms collection and the Documents collection.

3 Modify the documents Try It Out to include the owner and last modification date for the documents in your database. You can now use this to track changes to your database.

Working with Recordsets

The real power of a database is derived from the way you can organize, display and summarize information. We've explained how we put data into our database using VBA, now it's time to get some meaningful information out.

The process of normalization eliminates redundant information and inconsistencies within our database, but it also splits data up into separate tables that we might want to see as a whole. If we do want to view the information as a whole, we need to be able to manipulate both records and sets of records with VBA, in the same way that we've learned to manipulate forms.

In this chapter we look at:

> What a **Recordset** actually is

> The different types of **Recordset** in VBA

> How to open a **Recordset** in VBA

> Examining values in a **Recordset**

> Moving through records in a **Recordset**

> How to find a specific records in a **Recordset**

What is a Recordset?

Even if you do not know what a **Recordset** is, it is almost certain that you will already have used one. Put simply, a **Recordset** is just what it says—a set of records. When you open a table in Datasheet view, you are looking at a set of records. When you open a form, it will normally have a set of records behind it which supply the data for the form. Databases are all about sets of records, and you will find that you make extensive use of **Recordset** objects throughout your VBA code.

Let's start by looking at a procedure that illustrates exactly what a **Recordset** is. The following example displays the number of records in the table **Whisky**, which can be found in **Whisky6.mdb**. All of the code used in this chapter can be found in this database in the module Chapter 6 Code.

Try It Out—Recordsets

1 Open up **Whisky6.mdb** and create a new standard module. Insert a subprocedure called **OpeningARecordset**.

2 Add the following code to the subprocedure:

```
Private Sub OpeningARecordset()

Dim db As Database
Dim rec As Recordset
Dim intRecords As Integer

Set db = CurrentDb()
Set rec = db.OpenRecordset("Whisky")

intRecords = rec.RecordCount
MsgBox "There are " & intRecords & " records in the Whisky table"
rec.Close

End Sub
```

3 Now run the procedure. Remember, there are four ways to do this: you can hit *F5*, select Go/Continue from the Run menu, hit the Go/Continue button on the toolbar or type **OpeningARecordset** in the debug window and hit the *Return* key. You will get a message box telling you how many records there are in the table **Whisky**.

4 You can check that this is correct by opening the table in Datasheet view and having a look.

WhiskyID	WhiskyName	Distillery	RegionID	Label	Notes
3	Brora	Brora, Sutherland	Highland		The distillery was known as Clynelish until 1969. Sited just north of the A9 at
4	Caol Ila	Port Askaig, Islay, Argyll	Islay		Beautiful setting, overlooking the Paps of Jura, the name of the distillery is Gaelic for
5	Auchentoshan	Dalmuir, Dumbartonshire	Lowland		A most unusual whisky! Firstly, it is triple-distilled, rather than the more often
6	Glenkinchie	Glenkinchie,	Lowland		Now owned by United

Record: 1 of 49

How It Works

You should be getting a feel for the VBA code by now, so we won't explain every line that we write. Instead, we'll concentrate on the new or interesting parts.

In this example, we fill a variable with the data from the table **Whisky**,

```
Set rec = db.OpenRecordset("Whisky")
```

and then use the **MsgBox** function to display the count of the records in the **Recordset**:

```
intRecords = rec.RecordCount
MsgBox "There are " & intRecords & " records in the Whisky table"
```

Notice also that we close the **Recordset** at the end of the procedure:

```
rec.Close
```

Once a **Recordset** has been closed, you can't do anything else with it. This allows Access to free any resources associated with the **Recordset** and is particularly necessary in a multi-user environment or when you are dealing with attached tables (tables that are not stored in the currently open Access database, but that can be manipulated as such).

As we mentioned above, a **Recordset** is just that—a set of records. While a **Recordset** is open in your code (i.e. after it has been filled with records with the **OpenRecordset** method and before it is closed with the **Close** method), you can do what you like with the records in that **Recordset**—edit them, delete them or even add new records.

Different Types of Recordset

In VBA there is not one, but five, different types of **Recordset** object that you can use. Which one you use depends on a combination of factors, such as:

- Whether you want to update the records or just view them
- Whether the tables are in Access or some other type of database
- How many records there are in the recordset

We'll look in detail at when to use each of the five types of **Recordset** a little later, but first let's have a look at what they are. The five types of **Recordset** object are:

- Table-type **Recordset** objects
- Dynaset-type **Recordset** objects (normally just called dynasets)
- Snapshot-type **Recordset** objects (or just snapshots)
- Forward-only-type **Recordset** objects
- Dynamic-type **Recordset** objects

You open all five different types of **Recordset** object in the same way—using the **OpenRecordset** method against a **Database** object. Have another look at the portion of code that we used just now:

```
Dim db As Database
Dim rec As Recordset

Set db = CurrentDb()
Set rec = db.OpenRecordset("Whisky")
```

We create a **Database** object that corresponds to the database that we are currently in. Then we create a **Recordset** object within the current database and fill it with records from the table **Whisky**.

By default, this statement creates a table-type recordset. If we had wanted to be more explicit, we could have used the intrinsic constant, **dbOpenTable**, as a parameter to the **OpenRecordset** method just to make sure:

```
Set rec = db.OpenRecordset("Whisky", dbOpenTable)
```

If we had wanted a dynaset-type **Recordset** object, we would have used the **dbOpenDynaset** constant instead:

```
Set rec = db.OpenRecordset("Whisky", dbOpenDynaset)
```

And, not surprisingly, if we had wanted a snapshot-type **Recordset** object or a forward-only type **Recordset** object, we would have created them like this:

```
Set rec = db.OpenRecordset("Whisky", dbOpenSnapshot)
```

```
Set rec = db.OpenRecordset("Whisky", dbOpenForwardOnly)
```

Dynamic-type **Recordset** objects are somewhat different to the other four types as they are only used with ODBCDirect.

FYI

We shall say a little more about the new types of recordsets available in Access 97, the forward-only type and dynamic-type **Recordsets**, when we look at Multi-User Applications in Chapter 15. For the remainder of this chapter we will only deal with the first three types of recordset.

We can see from the above statements, then, that there are three things we need to think about when we are creating a **Recordset** object:

▶ Which database are the records in?
▶ Whereabouts in that database are those records?
▶ What type of **Recordset** object do you want?

There are, in fact, further optional levels of control we can apply when we open Recordset objects, but we'll look at those a little later in Chapter 15.

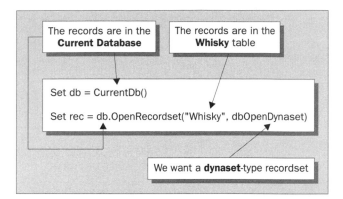

FYI

Access 97 now allows you to create a **Recordset** object in a single line of code, without having to create a **Database** object. So you could say:

```
Set rec = CurrentDB.OpenRecordset("Whisky", dbOpenDynaset)
```

However, the method we have used throughout this chapter, using an intermediate **Database** object, is the only method that works in Access 95. It is also preferable to use this two-step method if you are going to need to refer to the **Database** object elsewhere in your procedure.

Now we know how to create **Recordset** objects, which type should we use? Let's look at the different types in turn, and see to which situations they are best suited.

Table-type Recordset Objects

This is the default type for any **Recordset** objects opened against local or attached Access tables. In other words, if we try to create a **Recordset** object against an Access table and we do not specify the type of **Recordset** object we want to open, Access will create a table-type **Recordset** object:

```
Set rec = db.OpenRecordset("Whisky")
```

One of the main advantages of using a table-type **Recordset** object is that you can use indexes on the table to speed up the process of searching for specific records. By contrast, you cannot use indexes against the other **Recordset** objects.

Dynaset-type Recordset Objects

A dynaset-type **Recordset** object can contain either a local or attached table, or the result of a query. It contains a dynamic set of records that is not stored anywhere in the database. There are two key features of dynaset-type **Recordset** objects:

▶ You can edit a dynaset and the results will be reflected in the underlying tables.

▶ While a dynaset is open, Access will update the records in your dynaset to reflect the changes that other people are making in the underlying tables.

167

Access does this by storing the key values from a dynaset-type **Recordset** object whenever one is opened. Then, whenever you want to view the records in the **Recordset** object, Access fetches the latest version of those records from the database based on the key values it has stored. We will look at some of the implications of this behavior a little later. You should use dynaset-type **Recordset** objects when:

▶ You need to update the records in the **Recordset** object

▶ The **Recordset** object is very large

▶ The **Recordset** object contains OLE objects

Snapshot-type Recordset Objects

In contrast, snapshot-type **Recordset** objects are not updateable and do not reflect the changes that other users make to the records. In fact, just as the name suggests, you are taking a 'snapshot' of the data at a certain point in time. One of their advantages is that with modestly-sized **Recordset** objects, snapshots are generally faster to create than dynasets.

You would use a snapshot-type **Recordset** object in a situation where you don't wish to update the data and when the recordset isn't bigger than about 500 records.

> *The terms dynaset and snapshot were introduced in early versions of Access, but Microsoft now suggest that they should both be referred to just as recordsets. Throughout this chapter, if we mention dynasets and snapshots, we will be referring to dynaset-type* **Recordset** *objects and snapshot-type* **Recordset** *objects respectively.*

Opening Recordset Objects

We have already seen how **Recordset** objects can be created with the **OpenRecordset** method. The examples that we have looked at so far have all involved creating **Recordset** objects directly from tables. However, you can also create a **Recordset** object from a query. To do this, you simply substitute the query's name for the table name. For example, if you had a query called **qryTotalOrders** in your database, you could create a dynaset-type **Recordset** object that contained the records from the query like this:

```
Set db = CurrentDb
Set rec = db.OpenRecordset("qryTotalOrders", dbOpenDynaset)
```

or by entering a SQL **SELECT** statement directly:

```
Set db = CurrentDb
Set rec = db.OpenRecordset("SELECT * FROM Order", dbOpenDynaset)
```

Default Types

If you do not specify the type of **Recordset** object that you want to open, Access will choose what is normally the best-performing type of **Recordset** object available:

▶ If the **Recordset** object is based on a table in the current database, Access will return a table-type **Recordset** object.

⬤ If the **Recordset** object is based on a query or a SQL **SELECT** statement (or if it's from a table in a non-Access database), and if the underlying query or table can be updated, Access will return a dynaset-type **Recordset** object.

⬤ In other situations, Access will return a snapshot-type **Recordset** object.

However, there may be situations where you want to return a recordset of a different type than the one which Access would normally return. For example, dynaset-type recordsets are generally quicker to open than snapshots, if the recordset will contain over 100 records. So in the situation that Access would otherwise have created the recordset as a snapshot, you might want to explicitly create a dynaset instead.

Refreshing Data in Recordsets

If you want to make sure that the data in your **Recordset** is up-to-date, you can refresh it by executing the **Requery** method against the **Recordset** object:

```
rec.Requery
```

This re-executes the query on which the **Recordset** object is based, thus ensuring that the data is up-to-date. You can only do this, however, if the **Recordset** object supports requerying. In order to determine whether a **Recordset** object supports requerying, you should inspect its **Restartable** property. If the **Recordset** object's **Restartable** property is **True**, you can use the **Requery** method. You could test for this as follows:

```
If rec.Restartable = True Then rec.Requery
```

However, if the **Recordset** object's **Restartable** property is **False**, attempting to requery the recordset will generate an error.

Working with Recordsets

So far, we have only really looked at how to create **Recordset** objects and ensure that the data in them is up-to-date. But, of course, what we normally want to do is to look at the data itself.

To refer to individual fields within a **Recordset** object, you can use a variety of different methods. We'll create a subprocedure which opens a dynaset-type **Recordset** object based on the **tblCountries** table.

Try It Out—Looking at Values in a Recordset

1 In **Whisky6.mdb** and, in the module you created earlier in this chapter, insert a procedure called **OpenWhiskyRecordset**:

```
Sub OpenWhiskyRecordset()

Dim db As Database
Dim rec As Recordset
```

```
Set db = CurrentDb()
Set rec = db.OpenRecordset("Whisky")

rec.Close

End Sub
```

2 Now place a **Stop** command after the **OpenRecordset** command. This has the effect of suspending execution of the code.

```
Set rec = db.OpenRecordset("Whisky")
```

Stop

```
rec.Close
```

3 Now run the procedure, either by hitting *F5*, by selecting Go/Continue from the Run menu or by hitting the Go/Continue button on the toolbar. When the line containing the **Stop** command is reached, execution of the code should pause and the line should be highlighted. We can now use the Debug Window to inspect the records in the recordset.

4 Make sure the Debug Window is open by pressing *Ctrl+G*. The Locals pane of the Debug Window should look like this. (If you have named your module differently, you will see a reference to the name you have given the module, rather than to Chapter 6 Code).

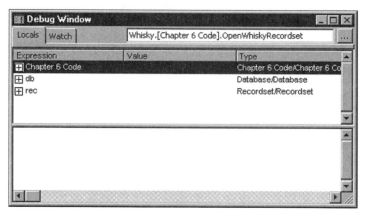

5 Now type the following in the lower half of the Debug Window:

?rec(0), rec(1), rec(2)

6 Hit the *Enter* key and the value of the first three fields for the first record in the **Whisky** table should be displayed:

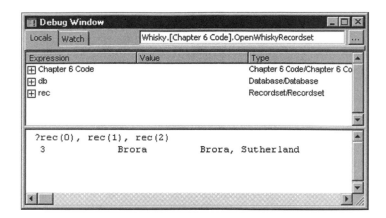

7 Finally, hit either *F5* or the Go/Continue button on the toolbar to allow the procedure to run to the end and close the **Recordset** object.

How It Works

Whenever you create a **Recordset** object, the first row of the recordset becomes the current record. As we created a table-type **Recordset** object, the records are ordered according to the Primary Key (**WhiskyID**) and so the current row is the record containing data for the whisky called **Brora**. We can then examine the value of any of the fields in this record. In this example we inspected the values of the first three fields of that record, the **WhiskyID**, **WhiskyName** and **Distillery** fields respectively.

At this point, you should note that the order of records in a query may not always be what you expect. If a query is based on a single table, the records in the query will normally be displayed in primary key order, unless you have explicitly chosen to sort the records in some other way when you designed the query.

However, if your query contains a criterion for a field that is not the primary key, the records will usually be displayed in insertion order (i.e. the order in which they were entered in the table). In fact, the rules for deciding in what order Access displays the records are even more complex, particularly when the query is based on more than one table. Suffice to say that you cannot rely on the records in a query being sorted in any particular order unless you have explicitly requested one.

If you want the records in a query to be sorted, you should specify a sort criterion (or an **ORDER BY** clause) when you design the query.

 If you have not specified any sort criteria, you should not rely on the records in the result set being in any particular order.

Examining Field Values

To look at the values of individual fields within the current record, we can use one of the same three conventions that we could with other objects. They are as follows:

```
RecordsetName!FieldName        e.g.  rec!Distillery
RecordsetName("FieldName")     e.g.  rec("Distillery")
RecordsetName(FieldIndex)      e.g.  rec(2)
```

> *When using the **RecordsetName(FieldIndex)** syntax to refer to fields in a **Recordset** object, you should remember that Access will always give the first field an index of **0** rather than **1**, irrespective of any **Option Base** setting you may have stated. So, **rec(2)** refers to the third field in the **Recordset** object, **rec**, not the second.*

Moving Through Recordsets

So far, however, things have been rather static. We are able to open a **Recordset** object and inspect all the values in the current record, but what if we want to move around the recordset? Suppose we wanted to move to the next record down and look at the values in that? Well, it's simple enough. If you applied the **MoveNext** method to the **Recordset** object in the last example by typing this in to the Debug Window,

```
rec.MoveNext
```

and then checked the value of **WhiskyName**, you would find that it was **Caol   Ila**:

```
?rec(0), rec(1), rec(2)
 3              Brora         Brora, Sutherland
rec.MoveNext
?rec("WhiskyName")
Caol Ila
```

Moving around a recordset is really very simple. The methods that you can use are:

Method	Description
MoveNext	Makes the next record the current record
MovePrevious	Makes the previous record the current record
MoveFirst	Makes the first record the current record
MoveLast	Makes the last record the current record
Move *n*	Makes the record *n* records away the current record

This is all very well, but we are still faced with the problem that we encountered back in the first couple of chapters. If we wanted to print the value of **WhiskyName** for every record in our recordset, we could keep on using the **MoveNext** method and then print the value of **WhiskyName**, but at some point we'll hit the last record. Access will let us try another **MoveNext**, but when we try to print the value of **WhiskyName**, we'll get a warning message telling us that there is no current record.

In Chapter 1, we had the same problem. We added code to the click events of the navigation buttons on the Company Contacts form to enable us to move to the first, next, last or previous buttons, but there was nothing to stop us trying to move beyond the last record, in which case we also got an error message:

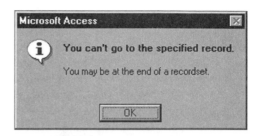

To make the form more user-friendly, we decided to disable certain buttons, depending on where we were in the recordset. In Chapter 2, we started to implement this feature and wrote code to disable the Next button when we were on the last record of the table. Well, it's taken a while to get here, but now we can look at the code that looks after *all* the buttons.

The Debug Window has highlighted the problem of moving through recordsets that we encountered in Chapter 2. Now we're in a position to deal with the problem for each button, because we have a set of methods at our disposal which allow us to test where we are in a recordset and actually move to the last record or first record in one straightforward action. Once we've executed these methods, we can then take appropriate action to disable the correct buttons, i.e. after we've pressed the First button and moved to the first record, we know we must disable the Previous button. So, without further ado, on to the code....

Try It Out—Creating Intelligent Navigation Buttons

1 Open up the Company Contacts form (**frmPerson**) in Design view.

2 Display the property sheet for the form, find its **On Current** event, and click the builder button to display the code that currently handles this event (this is the code you wrote in Chapter 2).

3 Replace the code that is there with the following:

```
Private Sub Form_Current()

Dim recClone As Recordset
Dim intNewRecord As Integer

'Make a clone of the recordset underlying the form so
'we can move around that without affecting the form's
'recordset
```

173

```
Set recClone = Me.RecordsetClone()

'If this is a new record then disable the <Next> and <New>
'buttons and enable the others. Then exit the procedure.
intNewRecord = IsNull(Me.PersonID)
If intNewRecord Then
    cmdFirst.enabled = True
    cmdNext.enabled = False
    cmdPrev.enabled = True
    cmdLast.enabled = True
    cmdNew.enabled = False
    Exit Sub
End If

'If we reach here, we know we are not in a new record
'so we can enable the <New> button
cmdNew.enabled = True

'But we need to check if there are no records. If so,
'we disable all buttons except for the <New> button

If recClone.RecordCount = 0 Then
    cmdFirst.enabled = False
    cmdNext.enabled = False
    cmdPrev.enabled = False
    cmdLast.enabled = False
Else
    'Synchronise the current pointer in the two recordsets
    recClone.Bookmark = Me.Bookmark

    'If there are records, see if we are on the first record
    'If so, we should disable the <First> and <Prev> buttons

    recClone.MovePrevious
    cmdFirst.Enabled = Not (recClone.BOF)
    cmdPrev.Enabled = Not (recClone.BOF)
    recClone.MoveNext

    'And then check whether we are on the last record
    'If so, we should disable the <Last> and <Next> buttons

    recClone.MoveNext
    cmdLast.Enabled = Not (recClone.EOF)
    cmdNext.Enabled = Not (recClone.EOF)
    recClone.MovePrevious
End If

'And finally close the cloned recordset
recClone.Close

End Sub
```

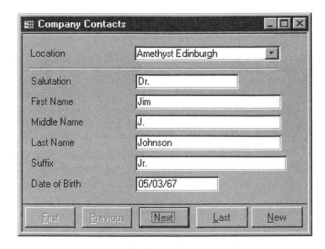

4 Now close down the module and switch to Form view. Try moving through the records—you'll see that you now have intelligent navigation buttons.

How It Works

The code is not complicated but there are a few new things, so let's have a look at it in detail.

```
Set recClone = Me.RecordsetClone()
```

The first thing we did was to create a duplicate copy of the form's **Recordset** object, using **RecordsetClone()**. This is an alternative to using the **OpenRecordset** method to create a **Recordset** object. Using the **RecordsetClone()** method against the form to create a **separate** copy of the recordset means that we can navigate or manipulate a form's records independently of the form itself. This is desirable, as we are going to want to move around the recordset behind the scenes and don't want our maneuvers to be reflected in the form's recordset. Instead, we are able to use a separate, cloned, read-only **Recordset** object that acts just as if it had been created using the **OpenRecordset** method.

```
intNewRecord = IsNull(Me.PersonID)
```

The first condition that we check for is whether or not we are in a new record. The simplest way to do this is to determine whether the **PersonID** field has a **Null** value. This works because the **PersonID** field is an **AutoNumber** field. **AutoNumber** fields are only assigned a value when the record is saved. Until then, they contain **Null**. Therefore, if the **PersonID** field is **Null**, we know that we are in a new record. If we are in a new record, we disable the Next and New buttons.

Note that although the **PersonID** field doesn't appear on the form, we can still refer to it because it is in the recordset behind the form.

```
If recClone.RecordCount = 0 Then
```

The next step is to check whether there are any records behind the form. It is often easy to forget to make this check but, if we try to move around a **Recordset** object with no records, Access will generate an error and cause our code to break. The easiest way to determine whether there are any records is to inspect the cloned **Recordset** object's **RecordCount** property. This will tell us the number of records in the recordset. If it is equal to zero, there are no records in the recordset and the only button that should be enabled is the New button.

FYI

It's worth mentioning here that the `RecordCount` property of some types of `Recordset` object is not always immediately available. You might need to move to the last record in the recordset to update it. However, here we've used a table-type `Recordset` object which doesn't suffer from this problem. You'll see more of this in a moment.

So, by now we have determined that we are not in a new record and that there is more than one record in the recordset. The next step is to work out where in the recordset we are—at the top, the bottom or somewhere in the middle?

Before we can do this, we need to make sure that the current record in our cloned **Recordset** object is the same as the current record in the form. Whenever you create a **Recordset** object, the first record in that **Recordset** object becomes the current record. However, our procedure is called from the form's **Current** event (i.e. not only when the form is opened, but also whenever the user moves to a different record). When a clone is created, it doesn't have a current record. So, we need some sort of mechanism to set the current record in the cloned **Recordset** object to match that on the form. We can do this with a **Bookmark**.

```
recClone.Bookmark = Me.Bookmark
```

A **Bookmark** is simply a way of identifying each individual row in a recordset. This is what Access uses in place of record numbers. A **Bookmark** consists of a **Byte** array. We shall be looking at them in a little more detail later on in this chapter when we discuss how we can find specific records in a recordset. For the moment, however, all we are concerned with is ensuring that the cloned **Recordset** object and the form are in sync. By assigning the **Bookmark** property of the cloned **Recordset** object the same value as the **Bookmark** property of the form, we ensure that the clone has the same current record as the one the user can see displayed on the form.

So now it is time to work out where the current record is in the recordset. If the current record is the first record, we must disable the First and Previous buttons. If the current record is the last record, we must disable the Last and Next buttons. To determine whether the current record is at either extremity of the recordset, we use the **BOF** and **EOF** properties. **BOF** stands for Beginning Of File and **EOF** stands for End Of File.

The **BOF** property of a **Recordset** object is **True** if the current record pointer is placed immediately before the first record, and the **EOF** property is **True** if the current record pointer is placed immediately after the last record. Consequently, if we attempt to move to the record previous to the current one and we find that the recordset's **BOF** property is **True**, we know that the current record is the first record in the recordset.

```
recClone.MovePrevious
cmdFirst.Enabled = Not (recClone.BOF)
cmdPrev.Enabled = Not (recClone.BOF)
recClone.MoveNext
```

176

If this code seems a little hard to fathom at first, just remember that the **BOF** and **EOF** properties return a **True** or **False** value. If **recClone.BOF** returns **True**, we're at the beginning of a recordset and we need to disable the **cmdFirst** button by setting its **Enabled** property to **False**. We use the **NOT** operator to simply reverse the Boolean value returned by the **recClone.BOF** expression. If **False** is returned, however, it means we're not at the beginning of a recordset, so we want the **cmdFirst** and **cmdPrev** buttons to be enabled by having a **True** value placed in their **Enabled** property. We could also have expressed this with an **If...Then** statement, but this method is more succinct.

Similarly, if we attempt to move to the record after the current record and we find that the **EOF** property of the cloned **Recordset** object is **True**, we know that the current record is the last record in the recordset.

```
recClone.MoveNext
cmdLast.Enabled = Not (recClone.EOF)
cmdNext.Enabled = Not (recClone.EOF)
recClone.MovePrevious
```

And that's about it. We just close the cloned recordset and the code is complete.

Counting Records in a Recordset

In the last example, we used the **RecordCount** property of a **Recordset** object to determine how many records it contained. The behavior of the **RecordCount** property is, in fact, a little more complex than we let on, and depends on the type of recordset in question.

Table-Type Recordsets

When you open a table-type recordset, Access knows the number of records in the table, and so the **RecordCount** property of the recordset is immediately set to that number.

Dynasets and Snapshots

In order to increase the performance of your code when creating dynaset-type **Recordset** objects and snapshot-type **Recordset** objects, Access executes the next line after an **OpenRecordset** as soon as the first row of data has been retrieved. Therefore, Access does not always immediately know the number of records in these types of **Recordset** object. In order to force Access to calculate the number of records in a dynaset-type **Recordset** object or in a snapshot-type **Recordset** object, you have to use the **MoveLast** method of the **Recordset** object.

```
Set rec = db.OpenRecordset("qryTotalOrders", dbOpenDynaset)
rec.MoveLast
Debug.Print rec.RecordCount
```

This forces Access to fetch all the rows in the recordset before continuing, and so enables it to determine the precise number of rows in the recordset.

FYI If you only want to know whether there are *any* records in the recordset, as opposed to finding out how many, you do not need to use a **MoveLast** method. When you use the **OpenRecordset** method and the recordset is not empty, Access waits until the first record has been returned before executing the next line of code. In other words, if the **RecordCount** property of a recordset is equal to zero, there are definitely no more rows to be returned.

If you add or delete records in a dynaset-type **Recordset** object, the **RecordCount** property of the object increases or decreases accordingly. However, if other users add or delete records in the underlying tables, these changes are not reflected until the **Recordset** object is requeried (using the **Requery** method). Again, you will need to use the **MoveLast** method after the **Recordset** object has been requeried, to ensure that the **RecordCount** property is accurate.

AbsolutePosition and PercentPosition

The record counting behavior has implications for two other recordset properties. The **AbsolutePosition** property returns the position of the current record in the recordset relative to 0. When using the **AbsolutePosition** property, bear these factors in mind:

▶ If there is no current record, the **AbsolutePosition** property returns -1

▶ It is by no means certain that records will always appear in the same order every time a recordset is opened unless a sort criterion (**ORDER BY** clause) has been specified

The **PercentPosition** property indicates the position of the current record as a percentage of the total number of records that is returned by the **RecordCount** property. With regard to accuracy of the values returned, the same considerations apply to the **PercentPosition** property as to the **RecordCount** property. In order to ensure that the **PercentPosition** property returns an accurate figure, you should use the **MoveLast** method after opening or requerying **Recordset** objects, and before inspecting the **PercentPosition** property.

Looking for Specific Records

So far, we have only concerned ourselves with moving through a **Recordset** object using the various **Move** methods. But there may be occasions when you know exactly which record you wish to find. In that situation, you will find that the **Seek** and **Find** methods are more suited to your task.

Finding Records in Table-Type Recordsets

The quickest way to find a record in a table-type **Recordset** object is to use the **Seek** method.

One of the important processes involved in designing a database is to determine how the tables within the database are to be indexed. If you search on an indexed field, Access is able to find records much more quickly. Also, Access can perform operations, such as joins and sorts, much faster if the fields which are being joined or sorted are indexed. One down-side of indexes is that they add an overhead to the length of time it takes Access to update records, so they should not be over-used.

178

As a programmer, you can take advantage of the extra speed provided by indexes if you use the **Seek** method. This allows you to perform a fast search on an indexed field. Using **Seek** is a two-step process:

▶ First select the indexed field that you wish to search on

▶ Then specify the criteria for finding the record

As an example, we'll search the **Bottling** table for bottles of malt whisky with a certain price.

Try It Out—Using the Seek Method

1 Open the **Bottling** table in design view and select the **Price** field.

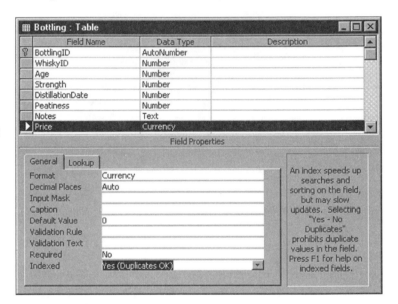

2 Add a non-unique index to the field by changing its Indexed property to Yes (Duplicates OK).

3 Now switch to Datasheet view, save the table design when prompted and sort the records by **Price**. This should be fast as the **Price** field is now indexed and, in any case, there are not too many records in the table.

4 Look for bottles of whisky which have the same price, such as Glengoyne 12yo, Glen Grant 10yo and Glen Ord 12yo in the example below. Make a note of the **Price** and **BottlingID** values. We shall be using these in a moment.

BottlingID	WhiskyID	Age	Strength	Distillation	Peatiness	Price
34	Tullibardine	10	40.0%		6	£14.49
35	Old Fettercairn	10	40.0%		4	£16.49
10	Tamdhu	10	40.0%		4	£17.39
11	Glen Moray	12	40.0%		3	£17.49
12	Aberlour	10	40.0%		4	£17.69
37	Glengoyne	12	40.0%		0	£18.99
13	Glen Grant	10	40.0%		4	£18.99
36	Glen Ord	12	40.0%		5	£18.99
17	Glen Keith		43.0%	1983	3	£19.99

Record: 6 of 60

179

5 Close down the table, saving your changes as you do so.

6 Now create a new procedure in the module you created earlier in the chapter and type in the following code:

```
Sub SeekPrice(curPrice As Currency)

Dim db As Database
Dim rec As Recordset
Dim strSQL As String
Dim strMsg As String

strSQL = "Bottling"

Set db = CurrentDb()
Set rec = db.OpenRecordset(strSQL)

rec.Index = "Price"
rec.Seek "=", curPrice

strMsg = "Bottling No. " & rec("BottlingID") & " costs " & _
        Format$ (rec("Price"), "Currency")

MsgBox strMsg

rec.Close

End Sub
```

7 Run the code by typing **SeekPrice(18.99)** in the Debug Window and hitting the *Enter* key.

8 A message box appears telling you the first of the bottles of malt whisky it has found with the price you specified.

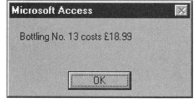

How Does It Work?

This example makes use of the **Index** property and **Seek** method to locate the required record in the table.

```
Set rec = db.OpenRecordset(strSQL)
```

The first thing we do is create a table-type **Recordset** object. Note that we did not need to explicitly request that the **Recordset** object should be a table-type **Recordset** object as it is based on a single local Access table and the default type for **Recordset** objects created from local Access tables is table-type.

```
rec.Index = "Price"
```

The next step is to specify the index that we want to use when seeking the required record. When setting the **Index** property of the **Recordset** object, you should use the name of the index as it appears in the Indexes window of the table in Design view (you can view this by pressing the Indexes button on the toolbar). If you try to set the **Index** property of a **Recordset** object to an index that does not exist, Access will generate a run-time error.

```
rec.Seek "=", curPrice
```

Once we have chosen an index, we are ready to look for the record we require. We do this using the **Seek** method. When using **Seek**, you need to specify two arguments. The first indicates the type of comparison you want to carry out and the second indicates the value you want to compare against the index.

In our example, we want to find records for which the value of the indexed field is equal to **18.99**, so the type of comparison is an equality comparison and the value we are comparing against the index is **18.99**. The following list shows the type of comparisons that can be carried out using the **Seek** method:

Comparison argument	Has this effect...
"="	Finds the first record whose indexed field is equal to the value specified.
">"	Finds the first record whose indexed field is greater than the value specified.
">="	Finds the first record whose indexed field is greater than or equal to the value specified.
"<"	Finds the first record whose indexed field is less than the value specified.
"<="	Finds the first record whose indexed field is less than or equal to the value specified.

Note that the comparison argument is enclosed in quotes. If you prefer, you can specify a string variable (or a variant variable of type 8, if you remember from our variant table) in place of the string literal. In other words, we could have written our code like this:

```
strComparison = "="
rec.Seek strComparison, curPrice
```

However, the important thing to remember is that the comparison argument must be a valid string expression.

```
strMsg = "Bottling No. " & rec("BottlingID") & " costs " & _
         Format$(rec("Price"), "Currency")
```

Once the **Seek** method has found a record matching the criterion we set, we display the result in a dialog box.

 Remember that there was more than one record that matched our criterion. The **Seek** method returns the first match it finds.

Try It Out—Allowing for No Matches

The above example assumes that **Seek** is going to be successful in finding a matching record. What happens, though, if this isn't the case?

1 Run the **SeekPrice()** procedure again, but this time pass it as an argument a value which you know will have no matching records, such as **3.64**. The result of this is that the code breaks and Access displays a dialog box telling you that there is no current record.

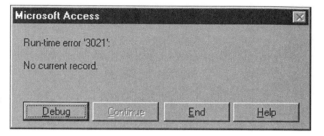

In order to work out how to solve this problem, we must first determine which line of our code caused the error to happen.

2 Hit the <u>D</u>ebug button. Access displays the code window with the offending line of code highlighted:

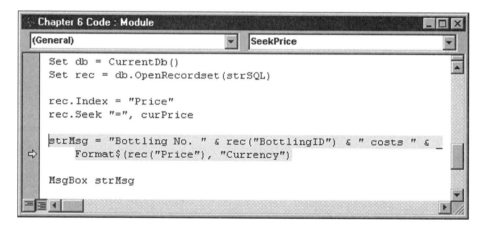

```
Set db = CurrentDb()
Set rec = db.OpenRecordset(strSQL)

rec.Index = "Price"
rec.Seek "=", curPrice

strMsg = "Bottling No. " & rec("BottlingID") & " costs " & _
    Format$(rec("Price"), "Currency")

MsgBox strMsg
```

As you can see, the line that caused the error to occur was the one in which we attempted to display the dialog box informing the user of the matching record. The code did not break simply because there was no record which matched. It broke because, when the **Seek** method fails to find a matching record, it doesn't know which record to make the current record and leaves the current record in an indeterminate state. So, when you subsequently try to perform an operation that requires the current record to be known, Access does not know which record is the current record and displays an error message.

What we need, therefore, is some mechanism that allows us to determine whether or not the **Seek** method found a record, so that we only attempt to display the result if we know it was successful.

3 Modify the **SeekPrice** procedure so that it now looks like this:

182

```
...
rec.Index = "Price"
rec.Seek "=", curPrice
```

```
If rec.NoMatch = True Then
    strMsg = "No bottlings cost " & Format$(curPrice, "Currency")
Else
    strMsg = "Bottling No. " & rec("BottlingID") & " costs " & _
        Format$(rec("Price"), "Currency")
End If
```

```
MsgBox strMsg
...
```

> The **NoMatch** property of a **Recordset** object is set to **True** when the **Seek** method (or any of the **Find** methods discussed below) fails to locate a record.

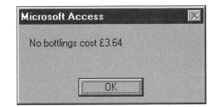

4 Run the procedure from the Debug Window, and pass **3.64** again. This time, you get a message box telling you what has happened:

This is a much more friendly way of doing things!

Finding Records in Dynasets and Snapshots

Using the **Seek** method is a very quick way of finding records, but it has two limitations:

▶ It can only be used on indexed columns, which means that...
▶ It can only be used against table-type recordsets

If we want to find records in dynaset- or snapshot-type **Recordset** objects, or in non-indexed fields of table-type **Recordset** objects, we must use one of the **Find** methods. There are four of these and their uses are described below:

This method...	Works like this...
FindFirst	Starts at the beginning of the recordset and searches downwards until it finds a record which matches the selected criteria and makes that record the current record.
FindLast	Starts at the end of the recordset and searches upwards until it finds a record which matches the selected criteria and makes that record the current record.
FindNext	Starts at the current record and searches downwards until it finds a record which matches the selected criteria and makes that record the current record.
FindPrevious	Starts at the current record and searches upwards until it finds a record which matches the selected criteria and makes that record the current record.

As with the **Seek** method, if any of the **Find** methods fails to find a record matching the specified criterion, the current record is left in an indeterminate state. This means that if you then try to perform any operation which requires the current record to be known, Access will generate a run-time error.

The syntax of the **Find** methods is somewhat different to that of the **Seek** method, as we need to specify the field we are searching on, as well as the value we are looking for. For example, if we had opened a snapshot-type **Recordset** object based on the **Order** table and wanted to use the **FindFirst** method to find the first record with an **OrderDate** after 1st January 1995, we would write this:

```
rec.FindFirst "OrderDate > #01-01-1995#"
```

 The argument we supply for a **Find** method is just the WHERE clause of a SQL statement, but without the WHERE in front.

It's quite intuitive really—the only thing you need to remember is that the criteria must be enclosed in quotes.

As with the **Seek** method, we could use a string variable to specify the criteria:

```
strCriterion = " OrderDate > #01-01-1995#"
rec.FindFirst strCriterion
```

Try It Out—Using the Find Methods

Let's try rewriting the last example using the **Find** methods.

1 Insert a new procedure and add the following code:

```
Sub FindBottleByPrice(curPrice As Currency)

Dim db As Database
Dim rec As Recordset
Dim strSQL As String
Dim strMatches As String
Dim intCounter As Integer

strSQL = "Bottling"

Set db = CurrentDb()
Set rec = db.OpenRecordset(strSQL, dbOpenSnapshot)

rec.FindFirst "Price = " & curPrice
Do While rec.NoMatch = False
    intCounter = intCounter + 1
    strMatches = strMatches & Chr$(10) & rec("BottlingID")
```

```
            rec.FindNext "Price = " & curPrice
    Loop

    Select Case intCounter
        Case 0
            MsgBox "No bottlings cost " & Format$(curPrice, "Currency")
        Case 1
            MsgBox "The following bottling cost " & _
                Format$(curPrice, "Currency") & " : " & _
                Chr$(10) & strMatches
        Case Else
            MsgBox "The following " & intCounter & " bottlings cost " & _
                Format$(curPrice, "Currency") & " : " & _
                Chr$(10) & strMatches
    End Select

    rec.Close

    End Sub
```

2 Open the Debug Window and run the procedure, using the price **3.64**. There are no matching records and the following dialog box is displayed:

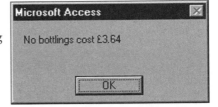

3 Now run it again, but this time pass as the argument **16.49**, for which there is one match.

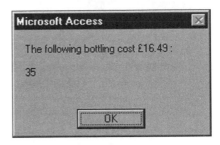

4 Finally, run the procedure again and pass a date for which there are several matches, e.g. **18.99**.

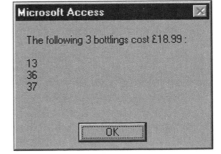

How It Works

The main difference in this portion of code is the method we use to find the matching records:

```
rec.FindFirst "Price = " & curPrice
```

We start by looking for the first record with a price matching the one entered.

```
Do While rec.NoMatch = False
    intCounter = intCounter + 1
    strMatches = strMatches & Chr$(10) & rec("BottlingID")
    rec.FindNext "Price = " & curPrice
Loop
```

If there is no order with this price,**rec.NoMatch** is **True** and so the subsequent **Do...Loop** structure is not entered. However, if a matching order is found, **rec.NoMatch** is **False** and we enter the loop.

Once inside the loop, three things happen. First we increment a counter to indicate how many matches have been made; then we build up a string using the linefeed character **Chr$(10)** (which causes a new line to be created) and the order number of the matching record; and finally we have a look to see if there is another record which matches our criterion.

If there is, we return to the start of the loop and, as **rec.NoMatch** is **False**, we run through the whole process again.

When there are no more matches found, **rec.NoMatch** is **True** and the loop terminates. Then, all that is left is to display the results in a message box.

```
Select Case intCounter
    Case 0
        MsgBox "No bottlings cost " & Format$(curPrice, "Currency")
    Case 1
        MsgBox "The following bottling cost " & _
            Format$(curPrice, "Currency") & " : " & _
            Chr$(10) & strMatches
    Case Else
        MsgBox "The following " & intCounter & " bottlings cost " & _
            Format$(curPrice, "Currency") & " : " & _
            Chr$(10) & strMatches
End Select
```

intCounter contains a count of the number of times we went through the loop, and, therefore, how many matches were found.

Notes on Formatting Dates in VBA

Among the most frequent types of data against which you search in **Recordset** objects are dates. For example, you may want to find orders placed on a certain day. If you do so, you need to be aware of how Access handles date formats in VBA, especially if you are working through this book somewhere other than in the United States.

Access will format date outputs according to the settings you make in the Short Date Style field of the Regional Settings section of the Control Panel. No problem there.

You may, for example, have your computer set up to display dates in the British format (so that 10-Nov-94 is displayed as **10/11/94**). This isn't a problem for Access when formatting date **output**—if you enter 10-Nov-94 and your Short Date Style is set to **dd/mm/yy**, Access will display the date as **10/11/94**. Just what you want.

However, Access is less than accommodating when requesting date **input**. Whenever you enter a date in a SQL statement in VBA, Access insists that it should be entered as **mm/dd/yy**, i.e. in US format. It completely ignores the fact that you have British format (**dd/mm/yy**) set in the Control Panel.

To avoid this problem, the safest solution is to explicitly convert all dates to US format before using them in SQL statements in VBA. To convert a date to US format, you would replace a statement like this,

```
rec.FindFirst "OrderDate = " & dtOrder
```

with one like this:

```
rec.FindFirst "OrderDate = #" & Format(dtOrder, "mm/dd/yy") & "#"
```

 FYI   The problem of non-US date formats only exists when you are dealing with dates in VBA and Visual Basic. In forms and queries, you can enter dates in your own local format, and Access will convert them for you.

When to Use Find and Seek

So far, we have looked at how to use the **Seek** and **Find** methods to locate records in a recordset. However, in all of the examples, our task could have been completed more quickly by opening a **Recordset** object based on an SQL string which defined our search criteria. Don't worry if you don't know much about SQL, the SQL in this example is very simple and we will be looking at SQL in more detail in the next chapter.

```
strSQL = "SELECT * FROM Bottling WHERE Price = " & curPrice
```

It simply assigns to the string **strSQL** an SQL statement which selects every field (using the ***** symbol) for each record of the **Bottling** table where the **Price** is equal to the price held in the variable **curPrice**. So, if we add this to our code, the **FindBottleByPrice()** procedure could be re-written like this:

```
Sub FindBottleByPrice2(curPrice As Currency)

Dim db As Database
Dim rec As Recordset
Dim strSQL As String
Dim strMatches As String
Dim intCounter As Integer
```

```
strSQL = "SELECT * FROM Bottling WHERE Price = " & curPrice

Set db = CurrentDb()
Set rec = db.OpenRecordset(strSQL, dbOpenSnapshot)

Do Until rec.EOF
    strMatches = strMatches & Chr$(10) & rec!BottlingID
    rec.MoveNext
Loop

intCounter = rec.RecordCount

Select Case intCounter
    Case 0
        MsgBox "No bottlings cost " & Format$(curPrice, "Currency")
    Case 1
        MsgBox "The following bottling cost " & _
            Format$(curPrice, "Currency") & " : " & _
            Chr$(10) & strMatches
    Case Else
        MsgBox "The following " & intCounter & " bottlings cost " & _
            Format$(curPrice, "Currency") & " : " & _
            Chr$(10) & strMatches
End Select

rec.Close

End Sub
```

The difference in speed between executing **FindBottleByPrice()** and
FindBottleByPrice2() could be particularly noticeable if you run the procedures against
attached ODBC tables over a Local Area Network or particularly over a Wide Area Network.
(We will look at ODBC tables in Chapter 15. Put simply, these are tables from another type of
external database, such as SQL Server.)

The reason for this difference in speed is that, in the first example, we are opening a
Recordset object which contains the entire contents of the **Whisky** table. All of these records
would have to be read from disk on the remote computer, sent across the network and then
read into cache locally; although, if it was a dynaset-type **Recordset** object, only the keys from
each row are cached. Then we would have to search through all of the records for the few
which meet our criteria.

In the second example, however, we are opening a **Recordset** object that contains only as
many rows as there are matching records. This will be much more efficient and will result in
considerably less network traffic, as only two or three rows will need to be retrieved.

Although the difference in speed might go unnoticed for relatively small tables, such as
Bottling, for others—such as **OrderLine**—the difference could be very great indeed.

For this reason, it is wiser to restrict the use of the **Find** methods to local tables, and to use
SQL **WHERE** clauses in queries against attached ODBC tables. If performance against local tables
is still a problem, check whether the field you are searching on is (or can be) indexed—and use
the **Seek** method instead.

We'll be looking at the whole area of optimizing performance against ODBC tables in Chapter 15.

Bookmarks

Earlier in the chapter, we used the **Bookmark** property to synchronize the current records in two **Recordset** objects which were clones of each other. The **Bookmark** property of a recordset is stored internally by Access as an array of bytes which uniquely identifies the current record. When you reference the **Bookmark** property in VBA code, however, you should always assign it to a **String** or **Variant** variable

```
Dim strBookmark As String
strBookmark = rec.Bookmark
```

or:

```
Dim varBookmark As Variant
varBookmark = rec.Bookmark
```

 Note that you can only use the **Bookmark** property to synchronize current records in **Recordset** objects which are clones of each other. If the **Recordset** objects have been created separately—even if they are based on the same query or SQL—the bookmarks of individual records may not match.

You can also use bookmarks to help you to return to records which you have already visited. This is done by storing the **Bookmark** property of the recordset in a variable when you are on a specific record, and then setting the **Bookmark** property of the recordset to that value when you want to return to that record. Don't forget that, as before, if you are using **Find** or **Seek** and a matching record cannot be found, the current record will be left in an indeterminate state.

Comparing Bookmarks

Sometimes, you may wish to compare two **Bookmark** properties. For example, you may want to check whether the current record is one that you visited earlier and whose **Bookmark** you had saved.

Although you can store a **Bookmark** as a **String** variable, you need to remember that a **Bookmark** is stored internally as an array of **Bytes**. For this reason, you should use **binary comparison** when comparing two bookmarks with each other.

If the **Option Compare Database** statement is present in a module, which it is by default, comparisons will be made according to the sort order determined by the locale of the database. In other words, when you compare two strings together in Access, the default is for the comparison to be case-insensitive. You can prove this by opening the debug window and evaluating the following expression:

```
?"aaa" = "AAA"
```

When you hit the *Enter* key, the result should be **True**, which means that string comparisons are not case-sensitive.

In contrast, when **binary comparison** is enabled, comparisons are made according to the internal binary representation of the characters, which is case-sensitive. Because lower case characters (e.g. **a**) are represented differently internally than upper case characters (e.g. **A**) a binary comparison of **"aaa"** and **"AAA"** should return **False**.

When you compare **Bookmark** properties, you want to make sure that the comparison is case-sensitive, otherwise you may find that the comparison returns **True** when the **Bookmarks** are not completely identical. There are two methods of ensuring that binary comparisons are made. Firstly, you can either replace the **Option Compare Database** statement with **Option Compare Binary** in the **Declarations** section of the module in which the procedure is located. This ensures that binary comparisons are made throughout the module. Better still, you could compare string variables with the **StrComp** function, which returns 0 if the two variables being compared are identical. This has an argument which allows you to choose what type of comparison you wish to perform:

- ▶ If the comparison argument is set to zero, it forces binary comparison of the two variables.

- ▶ If it is set to **1** it forces textual comparison.

- ▶ And if it is set to **2** or is omitted, the **Option Compare** setting determines the type of comparison used.

```
iResult=StrComp(strBkMk1, strBkMk2, 1)    'Textual comparison

iResult=StrComp(strBkMk1, strBkMk2, 0)    'Binary comparison
```

FYI Recordset objects based on native Access tables should all support bookmarks. However, Recordset objects based on linked tables from some databases, such as Paradox tables with no primary key, may not support bookmarks. Before you attempt to use bookmarks, you can test whether the Recordset object supports them by inspecting its **Bookmarkable** property. This will be **True** if the Recordset object supports bookmarks.

Editing Records in Recordsets

You now know how to find particular records within a **Recordset** object, but what if you want to edit them once you've found them? There are five main methods which can be used for manipulating data in recordsets. These are listed overleaf:

This method...	Has this effect...
Edit	Copies the current record to the copy buffer to allow editing.
AddNew	Creates a new record in the copy buffer with default values (if any).
Update	Saves any changes made to the record in the copy buffer.
CancelUpdate	Empties the copy buffer without saving any changes.
Delete	Deletes the current record.

From the table above you should be able to see that changes to records are made in the copy buffer rather than in the recordset itself. What this means in practice is that adding or amending a record is a three-part process:

▶ Copy the current record into the copy buffer with the **Edit** method, or place a new record in the copy buffer with the **AddNew** method

▶ Make any required changes to the fields in that record

▶ Save the changes from the copy buffer to disk with the **Update** method

FYI Note that if you try to make changes to a record without first copying it to the copy buffer (i.e. without using the **Edit** method), Access will generate a run-time error. And if you move to a new record without saving the changes to the current record in the copy buffer (using the **Update** method), those changes will be lost.

If you want to empty the copy buffer without moving to a new record, you can use the **CancelUpdate** method on the **Recordset**. This will undo any changes you may have made to the record in the copy buffer, but does not change the current record.

If you want to know whether any records have been copied into the copy buffer and not saved, you can inspect the **EditMode** property of the recordset. This can hold any of three values represented by the constants in the table below.

This constant...	Has this value...	And means this...
dbEditNone	0	There is no record in the copy buffer.
DbEditInProgress	1	The current record is in the copy buffer (the **Edit** method has been invoked).
DbEditAdd	2	The record in the copy buffer is a new record that hasn't been saved (the **AddNew** method has been invoked).

If you use the **Delete** method the deletion is immediate; you do not have to follow it with an **Update** method to make the deletion permanent. However, although the record is deleted, it is still regarded as the current record. You need to make a different record the current record before you perform any more operations that require a valid current record. Once you have moved away from a deleted record, you cannot make it current again.

We shall be looking at how Access locks records when editing and updating `Recordset` objects when we consider multi-user aspects of Access in Chapter 15.

Try It Out—Editing Records in VBA

1 Open the **Location** table and have a look at the place-names in the **Town** field. They should be in mixed case.

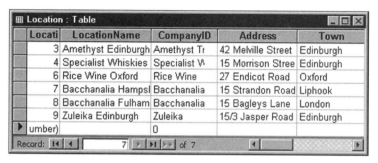

2 In a standard code module, add the **Capitalize** procedure:

```
Function Capitalize(strTable As String, strFld As String)

Dim db As Database
Dim rec As Recordset

Set db = CurrentDB()
Set rec = db.OpenRecordset(strTable)

'Start to loop through all records
Do

    'Copy the current record to the copy buffer
    rec.Edit

    'Make changes to the record in the copy buffer
    rec(strFld) = UCase$(rec(strFld))

    'Save the contents of the copy buffer to disk
    rec.Update

    'Make the next record the current record
    rec.MoveNext

'Keep on looping until we go beyond the last record
Loop Until rec.EOF

Capitalize = True

End Function
```

3 Now bring up the Debug Window by hitting *Ctrl-G*. In the Debug Window, type the following line of code.

```
?Capitalize ("Location", "Town")
```

When you hit the *Enter* key, if the **Capitalize** function executes correctly, it will convert all the names of the places in the **Town** field of the **Location** table to upper case and then return **True** to indicate success.

4 Open the **Location** table again and have a look at the names of the places in the **Town** field. They should now be in upper case.

Note that this example is simply an illustration of the sequence of events required when editing a record. In practice, using an **action query** would be considerably more efficient than stepping through all the records.

When a Recordset can't be Updated

We started the chapter by pointing out the differences between the various types of recordset. One of the most obvious differences between snapshot-type **Recordset** objects and dynaset-type **Recordset** objects is that snapshots are static images of the data and are never editable. So, if you try to use the **Edit**, **AddNew** or **Delete** methods against a snapshot-type **Recordset** object, Access will generate a run-time error. However, there are also several occasions when a dynaset-type **Recordset** cannot be edited, such as:

▶ When it is based on a crosstab query

▶ When it is based on a union query

▶ When you have not been granted permission to update the records in the table on which the recordset is based

In order to be sure that your **Recordset** object can be edited, you can inspect its **Updatable** property. This will be **True** if the recordset can be updated, and **False** otherwise.

```
If rec.Updatable = True Then
    rec.Edit
    ...
    ...
    ...
    rec.Update
End If
```

Summary

In this chapter, we have looked at one of the key features that differentiates VBA from macros—the ability to work with sets of records at the record level. With macros, you can only see the big picture—you can deal with sets of records as a whole but there is no mechanism for manipulating individual records. With VBA, however, you can go down to the record level and then work on individual fields within each record. You will find that creating and manipulating **Recordset** objects is one of the most frequent and useful operations that you will perform in Access with VBA. If you can master the use of the **Recordset** object you have won most of the battle.

The most common mistake you will make when you start to work with **Recordset** objects is that either you will forget to use the **Edit** method before you try to edit a record, or you will forget to use the **Update** method once you have finished editing the record. Don't worry, every one does to start with! The secret is practice.

This chapter has covered:

- When to use the different types of **Recordset** objects—particularly tables, dynasets and snapshots
- How to examine data in a **Recordset** using VBA
- Creating intelligent navigation buttons using the **Move** methods
- How to use **Find** and **Seek** to locate particular records
- The **Bookmark** property and what it is used for
- How to edit records in a **Recordset**

Once you feel happy with moving around **Recordset** objects and editing records in them, you can be a little more adventurous. Instead of just modifying a record, how about using VBA to modify the query's design? Instead of just moving around a table, how about using VBA to create a table from scratch? Sounds scary, huh? Well, they are just some of the many topics that we will look at in the next chapter and you'll see that they are nowhere near as daunting as they first appear.

Exercises

1 Earlier in this chapter we looked at the **AbsolutePosition** property of the recordset. See if you can use this to create a record indicator on the Company Contacts form (**frmPerson**). What are the limitations of this record indicator?

2 This chapter illustrated two methods for creating a recordset object:

```
Set rec = db.OpenRecordset(sSQL)
Set rec = forms!formname!RecordsetClone
```

There is also a third method:

```
Set rec = recOld.OpenRecordset
```

What do you think this is used for? Have a look at the **OpenRecordset** topic in the Access 97 online help to find out more about this method of creating a database. You can find a good example of this third method in the help file under the title 'Sort Property Example'.

Manipulating Objects

In the previous chapter, we looked at how recordsets are created and how we can move through records within a recordset one at a time, giving us a much finer degree of control than we have with macros. In this chapter, we will look at some of the other DAO objects and how, as developers, we are able to manipulate them to our best advantage.

This chapter takes as its theme the record selection functionality behind the View Order Details... button on the Switchboard form of the Malt Whisky Store application. We will be looking particularly at methods of creating queries and tables at run-time. This is a particularly handy way of allowing users to be as free as they like with the types of query they want to produce, without having to rely too much on the developer. The main topics that we will consider are:

- Creating queries at run-time
- Displaying records selected at run-time via one of three different methods
- Using the **WHERE** clause as a filter
- Modifying the form's record source
- Creating a table of matching records
- How to create a table using the DAO hierarchy

Creating Queries at Run-time

We will start this chapter by looking at how we can create and manipulate queries at run-time.

You may wonder why anyone would want to create a query at run-time. Why not just create the query at design-time? Well, it's true that you should try to create as many of your queries at design-time as possible—this has definite performance benefits, as we will see later. However, sometimes you just don't have enough information at design-time to allow you to build all the queries that will be necessary for your application to run. In this case, you have to enable the users to design queries while the application is running. In the Malt Whisky Store application, **frmCriteria** is a simple form which allows users to select orders based on a set of criteria which they specify themselves. We'll demonstrate how to use it now.

The Criteria Form

Open up the **Whisky7a.mdb** database, which is included on the accompanying CD. Open the Switchboard form, **frmSwitchboard**, if it is not already open and select the View Order Details option. This opens up **frmCriteria**.

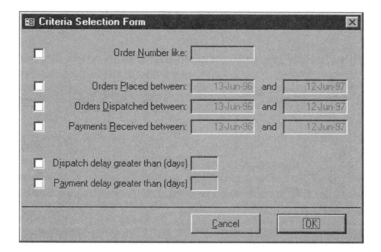

This form allows users to specify which orders they want to review—they just enter the relevant criteria and click OK. Once they have done that, a message box informs them how many, if any, records met the criteria they specified.

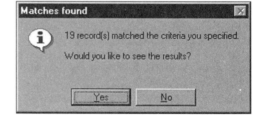

If they decide they wish to see those orders that matched their search criteria, they click the Yes button and two new forms are opened. The first is the Order Details form, **frmOrder**. This provides details of each order and the recordset behind this form consists of only those orders that meet the user's search criteria.

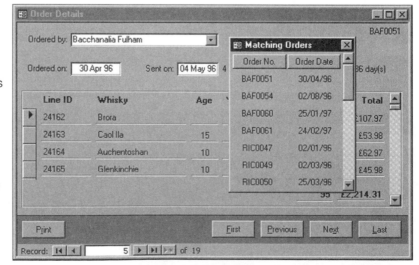

The second form that is opened is the Order Selection form, **frmMatchingOrders**. This is a small popup form that lists just the Order Number and Order Date of the matching orders. This can be used to navigate through the orders on **frmOrder**. The two buttons at the top of each column allow you to sort the orders on the Order Selection form by Order Date or Order Number, and clicking a record on the Order Selection form will take you to the appropriate record on the Order Details form.

Some of the things for which the Criteria Selection form can be used include getting the answers to the following questions:

▶ How many orders were made in July '94 for which we didn't receive the payment until October '94?

▶ How many times last year did we not ship orders within 3 days of receiving the order?

▶ Which orders did we dispatch on January 18th 1995?

We are going to spend a good part of this chapter looking at how we can code these forms to behave in the way described above—that is, how we can create a query at run-time from the criteria supplied by the user. You should already be able to see the advantages of this.

Flexibility

The form allows the users to find orders based on almost any combination of criteria. As the developer, we could try to work out every possible query that users might want to make, but the odds are that we wouldn't make a very good job. For a start, the application would soon be littered with hundreds of queries, making maintenance a nightmare. Secondly, you'll find that, with most applications, it is very difficult for users to predict every query they may require until they have used the application for a while—and sometimes not even then. (Obviously, you must be able to get a fairly good idea of the type of queries users will want to run, though— otherwise there would be no design to your application.)

Giving your app's users a way in which they can frame their own queries, instead of them having to rely on you, not only makes them happier, but also means that you will need to spend less time modifying the application to meet their requests for new queries.

Power at the Desktop

We all know of applications that don't do what they were meant to. The history of computing is littered with cases where users have asked for one thing and those responsible for developing the product have delivered something different. Most of the time, this comes down to a lack of communication. Either the users who specified the requirements didn't communicate them very well, or, just as likely, the developers who built the system didn't listen very well. Or perhaps the users didn't know what they needed—only what they wanted. One of the main reasons that so much documentation is produced during the lifetime of a computer project is that everyone involved realizes that communication may be suboptimal (i.e. lousy)—so they write down what was really said to cover themselves!

New methodologies, such as JAD (Joint Application Design), aim to remove some of these communication problems, but when it comes down to it, no-one knows better what users want from a system than the users themselves! So why not let the users write their own queries and cut out the communication problems altogether. It's all about empowerment. Give the people who need to analyze the data the tools to do so!

Using SQL

The **frmCriteria** form allows users to frame certain simple queries in a manner of their own choosing. It does this by converting the entries that the user makes on the form into an SQL statement and using that SQL statement to select the records that should be displayed.

SQL statements generally consist of three clauses:

```
SELECT OrderID, LocationID, OrderNumber, OrderDate
FROM Order
WHERE OrderNumber Like "SS*"
```

The **SELECT** clause indicates the columns or fields that will be displayed in the result set of the query. The **FROM** clause indicates the base tables from which the results are drawn and the **WHERE** clause indicates the criteria for determining which rows or records will be represented in the result set of the query.

Put another way, the **SELECT** clause is a form of vertical partitioning, and the **WHERE** clause a method of horizontal partitioning:

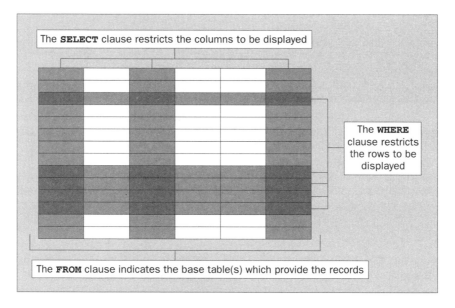

The **SELECT** clause restricts the columns to be displayed

The **WHERE** clause restricts the rows to be displayed

The **FROM** clause indicates the base table(s) which provide the records

In the case of the Malt Whisky Store, we know which fields we want displayed—the fields on **frmOrder** and **frmMatchingOrders** are fixed and don't change, irrespective of the criteria we select on **frmCriteria**. In other words, the **SELECT** clause will not change.

Similarly, we know that we are only dealing with the **Order** table. No other table is involved, so we know that the **FROM** clause will not change.

However, what certainly will change is the **WHERE** clause. What we are interested in is building up a SQL statement which will restrict the rows selected to those which meet our criteria. We can then use that **WHERE** clause in a variety of ways to restrict the number of records shown in **frmOrder**.

How frmCriteria Works—Building the SQL Statement

The first step, that of building the SQL statement is fairly mechanical, but deserves attention nonetheless. There is a procedure called **BuildSQLString** in the code module **Form_frmCriteria** that performs this function. It looks like this:

```
Sub BuildSQLString(strSQL As String)
'**********************************************************************
'Purpose:        To populate the string variable passed by reference with
a
'                SQL string reflecting the user's selections on the form
'Parameters:     strSQL - a string variable to be populated by this
function
'Returns:        Nothing
'Created By:     Robert Smith
'Created On:     11 Jun 97
'**********************************************************************

On Error GoTo BuildSQLString_Err

Dim strWhere As String

'Check for Order Number
If chkOrderNumber And Not IsNull(txtOrderNumber) Then
    strWhere = strWhere & " AND OrderNumber LIKE '" & _
               txtOrderNumber & "*'"
End If

'Check for Order Date
If chkOrdered Then
    If Not IsNull(txtOrderedFrom) Then
        strWhere = strWhere & " AND OrderDate >= #" & _
                   Format$(txtOrderedFrom, "mm/dd/yy") & "#"
    End If
    If Not IsNull(txtOrderedTo) Then
        strWhere = strWhere & " AND OrderDate <= #" & _
                   Format$(txtOrderedTo, "mm/dd/yy") & "#"
    End If
End If

'Check for Sent Date
If chkDispatched Then
    If Not IsNull(txtDispatchedFrom) Then
        strWhere = strWhere & " AND SentDate >= #" & _
                   Format$(txtDispatchedFrom, "mm/dd/yy") & "#"
    End If
    If Not IsNull(txtDispatchedTo) Then
        strWhere = strWhere & " AND SentDate <= #" & _
                   Format$(txtDispatchedTo, "mm/dd/yy") & "#"
    End If
End If
```

```
'Check for Paid Date
If chkReceived Then
    If Not IsNull(txtReceivedFrom) Then
        strWhere = strWhere & " AND PaidDate >= #" & _
                    Format$(txtReceivedFrom, "mm/dd/yy") & "#"
    End If
    If Not IsNull(txtReceivedTo) Then
        strWhere = strWhere & " AND PaidDate <= #" & _
                    Format$(txtReceivedTo, "mm/dd/yy") & "#"
    End If
End If

'Check for delay in sending order
If chkDispatchDelay And Not IsNull(txtDispatchDelay) Then
    strWhere = strWhere & " AND (SentDate-OrderDate) > " & _
            txtDispatchDelay
End If

'Check for delay in receiving payment
If chkPaymentDelay And Not IsNull(txtPaymentDelay) Then
    strWhere = strWhere & " AND (PaidDate - SentDate) > " & _
            txtPaymentDelay
End If

'Finally strip off the leading " AND "
If Len(strWhere) > 0 Then strSQL = Mid$(strWhere, 6)

BuildSQLString_Exit:
    Exit Sub

BuildSQLString_Err:
    MsgBox Err.Description
    Resume BuildSQLString_Exit

End Sub
```

The principle behind this procedure is simple enough, although it may look a bit daunting at first! The general idea is that a **String**-type variable, **strSQL**, is passed into the procedure and the procedure eventually puts into that variable a **WHERE** clause which reflects the criteria selected on **frmCriteria**.

To build the **WHERE** clause, we look at each of the text boxes in **frmCriteria** in turn. If the user has checked the check box for a criterion and has entered something in the relevant text box, we add that criterion to the **WHERE** clause. For example:

```
'Check for Order Number
If chkOrderNumber And Not IsNull(txtOrderNumber) Then
    strWhere = strWhere & " AND OrderNumber LIKE '" & _
            txtOrderNumber & "*'"
End If
```

Whenever we add a new section to the end of the **WHERE** clause, we also add an **AND** in front of it, to link the sections together. Therefore, if the user has selected any criteria, at the end of the procedure we are left with a spare **" AND "** in front that the first criterion and we need to strip it off. We do that with the **Mid$** function . The string **" AND "** is 5 characters long, so we use the **Mid$** function to return all the characters in **strSQL** from the 6th character onwards.

```
'Finally strip off the leading " AND "
If Len(strWhere) > 0 Then strSQL = Mid$(strWhere, 6)
```

We need to check the length of **strWhere** before removing the **AND** in case the user has not entered any criteria at all. If this was the case, and we didn't perform the check, Access would generate a run-time error when we tried to perform **Mid$(strWhere, 6)** on an empty **strWhere**.

Checking the WHERE Clause

You can check out the **WHERE** clause that is built up by **BuildSQLString** by adding the following line of code at the end of the procedure:

```
MsgBox strSQL
```

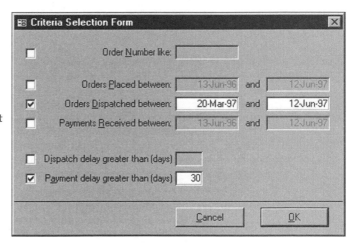

This will simply display the **WHERE** clause in a message box on screen at the end of the procedure. So, if the user fills in **frmCriteria** like this,

the **BuildSQLString** will produce this **WHERE** clause:

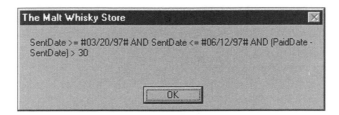

This technique is very useful for debugging purposes, but you should remember to comment out the line once you have finished.

An alternative method of displaying the value of the variable **strSQL** is to use the Debug Window, by adding the following line to our code:

```
Debug.Print strSQL
```

If the Debug Window is open, the value of **strSQL** will be displayed. If the Debug Window isn't open, as will be the case when the application runs normally, the line of code has no effect.

Displaying Selected Records at Run-time

Now that we have come up with a method for generating a **WHERE** clause, we need to apply that restriction to **frmOrder** (the form that displays the matching records). The whole point of allowing the user to specify criteria is so that we can restrict the records in **frmOrder** to meet those criteria. But how do we do this? Well, we'll look at three ways to implement this functionality. In ascending order of complexity they are:

▶ Using the **WHERE** clause as a filter

▶ Using the **WHERE** clause to modify the **RecordSource** of **frmOrder**

▶ Using the **WHERE** clause to build a table of matching orders

Let's look at each of these in turn.

Using the Where Clause as a Filter

This is the simplest method of filtering the records in **frmOrder**. It's slightly different from the way it has been done in **Whisky7a.mdb**, but it's the kind of thing that most of us will try when we start out. It works as follows:

▶ The user opens **frmOrder**, which initially displays all the records from **Order**.

▶ The user selects criteria by filling in the fields in **frmCriteria**.

▶ When the user hits the OK button, the **BuildSQLString** procedure generates a **WHERE** clause which is applied as a filter to **frmOrder**.

There is an example of this type of filtering in database **Whisky7b.mdb** which is on the accompanying CD. Let's look at how it works.

Try It Out—Modifying a Form's Filter Behavior

1 Open the **Whisky7b.mdb** database. Then open the Switchboard form and select View Order Details.

2 The Order Details form opens and displays every record from the table **Order**.

3 Now click the **Apply Filter...** toggle button which is in the lower left of the Order Details form. This should bring up the Criteria Selection form.

4 Specify on the Criteria Selection form that you are looking for orders dispatched between 20th March 1997 and 12th June 1997 where the Payment Delay was over 30 days and click the **OK** button.

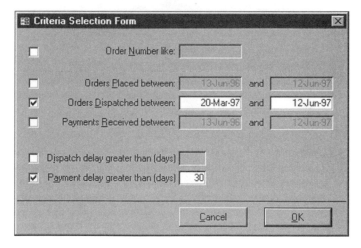

5 The Order Details should now only display those records that meet the criteria you entered on the Criteria Selection form. The navigation bar at the bottom of the form will also indicate that a filter has been applied.

How It Works

There are two procedures that make this whole thing work. The first of these is the `Click` event handler for the Apply Filter... toggle button on the Order Details form, `togFilter_Click()`:

```
Private Sub togFilter_Click()

If togFilter Then
    DoCmd.OpenForm "frmCriteria", , , , , acDialog, (Me.Name)
    If Me.FilterOn Then
        togFilter.Caption = "Filter Applied"
    Else
        togFilter = False
    End If
Else
    Me.FilterOn = False
    togFilter.Caption = "Apply Filter..."
End If

End Sub
```

The other procedure is the `Click` event handler for the OK button on the Criteria Selection form, `cmdOK_Click()`

```
Private Sub cmdOK_Click()

Dim strSQL As String
Dim frm As Form

BuildSQLString strSQL
Set frm = Forms(Me.OpenArgs)
```

```
    frm.Filter = strSQL
    frm.FilterOn = True

    DoCmd.Close acForm, Me.Name

    End Sub
```

Let's look at what these do. The first thing that we do is to click the Apply Filter… toggle button on the Order Details form. This causes **togFilter_Click()** to be executed and that procedure starts off by working out whether the user is clicking the filter on or off:

```
    If togFilter Then
```

Remember, an **If** statement works by evaluating the expression that follows it and determining whether it is **True**. The default property of a toggle button is the **Value** property and this is set to **True** when the toggle button is pressed in and **False** when it is not pressed in, so this line is asking whether the toggle button has been pressed in or not. If it has, the next line is executed:

```
    DoCmd.OpenForm "frmCriteria", , , , , acDialog, (Me.Name)
```

Note the parentheses around the final argument. Placing parentheses around an expression forces the expression to be evaluated. In this situation it means that Access evaluates the name of the form and passes it—as a string—to the **OpenForm** method of the **DoCmd** object. So this expression uses the value of the **Name** property of the form, rather than the **Name** property itself.

This opens the Criteria Selection form modally. That is to say that no other form or window in Access can have the focus while this form is open. Notice also that we are setting the **OpenArgs** property of the form we are opening to **(Me.Name)**. The **OpenArgs** property is a way of passing information to a form when you open it up. The information we are passing to the Criteria Selection form is the name of the form that is opening it. This will allow us to call the Criteria Selection form from a number of forms if we want to, without hard-coding any information about those forms into the Criteria Selection form itself.

> *Because, the Criteria Selection form has been opened modally, the **togFilter_Click()** procedure stops executing. It will only continue once the modal form has been closed.*

The next event occurs when the user clicks the OK button on the Criteria Selection form after entering any criteria. This initiates the **cmdOK_Click()** procedure. The first thing that this procedure does is to build up a SQL string using the **BuildSQLString** procedure that we looked at earlier.

```
    BuildSQLString strSQL
```

The **BuildSQLString** procedure fills the variable **strSQL** with a SQL string (actually the **WHERE** clause of a SQL string) corresponding to the criteria specified by the user. The next thing to do is to apply this to the Order Details form as a filter:

```
    Set frm = Forms(Me.OpenArgs)
    frm.Filter = strSQL
    frm.FilterOn = True
```

207

Remember, we passed the name of the Order Details form to the Criteria Selection form in the **OpenArgs** argument when we opened the form. We now interrogate the **OpenArgs** argument to find the name of the form, **frmOrder**, which opened this one and set the **Filter** property of the 'calling' form to the **WHERE** clause returned by the **BuildSQLString** procedure. This alone does not apply the filter to **frmOrder**. The filtration—for want of a better word—only occurs when the form's **FilterOn** property is set to **True**.

All that remains for the **cmdOK_Click()** procedure is to close the Criteria Selection form.

```
DoCmd.Close acForm, Me.Name
```

That's not quite the end of the story, however. Now that the Criteria Selection form has closed, the **togFilter_Click()** procedure can kick back into action again. Remember, execution in this procedure was suspended while the Criteria Selection form was open modally.

```
If Me.FilterOn Then
    togFilter.Caption = "Filter Applied"
Else
    togFilter = False
End If
```

The first line of code checks that the filter has been correctly applied to the Order Details form. The filter will not have been applied if the user clicked the Cancel button rather than the OK button on the Criteria Selection form. The Click event handler for the Cancel button simply closes the Criteria Selection form and redisplays the form that had caused the Criteria Selection form to be opened.

```
Private Sub cmdCancel_Click()

Forms(Me.OpenArgs).Visible = True
DoCmd.Close acForm, Me.Name

End Sub
```

It knows which form this is because we passed its name in to the Criteria Selection form's **OpenArgs** property when we opened it.

So if the filter has been applied, the caption of the toggle button is changed to Filter Applied. If the filter has not been applied—because the user clicked the Cancel button rather than the OK button on the Criteria Selection form, the toggle button is returned to its 'up' state.

The last few lines of the code take care of the situation when the user releases the toggle button:

```
Else
    Me.FilterOn = False
    togFilter.Caption = "Apply Filter..."
End If
```

The filter is removed from the form, and the caption is changed back to Apply Filter...

Modifying a Form's Record Source

So, using the **WHERE** clause as a filter is a simple way to make **frmCriteria** restrict the records that are displayed on the Order Details form. However, this method is not always suitable. If the **Order** table contained, say, 50,000 records and was located on a remote machine across a WAN or LAN, opening **frmOrder** without a filter would cause every record in that table to be pulled across the network to the users machine. This would:

▶ Take a significant amount of time

▶ Generate a lot of network traffic

▶ Get very tiresome...

Only after it had opened would the user be able to select the records they wanted.

However, if the user were somehow able to select the criteria before **frmOrder** were opened, it is likely that the number of records to be displayed would be significantly smaller. This would in turn mean that the form's opening time would be quicker and the network traffic (i.e. the number of rows that need to be fetched) would be reduced. So how can we do this?

Well, we could modify the **QueryDef** which is the **Recordsource** for the form **frmOrder**. In other words, we could have based **frmOrder** on a saved query, **qryfrmOrder**. When users changed the criteria on the **frmCriteria** form, we would use the **WHERE** clause generated by the **BuildSQLString** procedure to modify **qryfrmOrder** so that, when **frmOrder** was opened, it had the records that they selected.

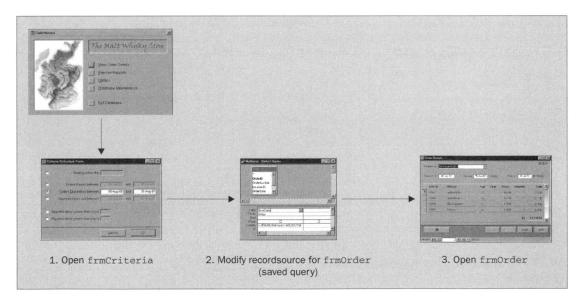

1. Open `frmCriteria`

2. Modify recordsource for `frmOrder`
   (saved query)

3. Open `frmOrder`

QueryDefs

You will probably remember from Chapter 5 that a **QueryDef** is the name given to a query object variable in VBA. Just as we can create a **String**-type variable to hold a piece of text, so we can create a **QueryDef** object to hold a query definition. Note that a **QueryDef** object holds the definition of a query, not the results. Query results, as we saw in the previous chapter, are held in **Recordset** objects. If you want, you can think of the **QueryDef** as being like a query in design view and a **Recordset** as representing a query in datasheet view.

The **QueryDefs** collection belongs to the **Database** object. This is fairly logical really—after all, a database can have multiple queries in it, but a query can only exist in one database.

To modify the query upon which **frmOrder** is based, we first need to know how to create and modify a **QueryDef** object. The following example demonstrates how this is done.

Try It Out—Creating and Modifying a QueryDef

1 Create a new standard code module or open an existing one and type in the following procedure.

You can find this procedure in the module called **Chapter 7 Code** on the CD that accompanies this book.

```
Function MakeQueryDef(strSQL As String) As Boolean

If strSQL = "" Then Exit Function

Dim qdf As QueryDef

Set qdf = CurrentDb.CreateQueryDef("MyQuery")
qdf.SQL = strSQL
qdf.Close
RefreshDatabaseWindow

MakeQueryDef = True

End Function
```

2 To run the procedure, open the Debug Window. Type in the following and hit *Enter*:

```
?MakeQueryDef("Select * from [Order] where SentDate > #1/1/97#")
```

The word **True** should appear in the Debug Window, indicating that the function completed successfully.

3 Press *F11* to view the database window and change to the Queries tab. You should see a query there called **MyQuery**.

4 Open **MyQuery** in design view. The design of the query should match the criteria that you passed as an argument to the **MakeQueryDef** function.

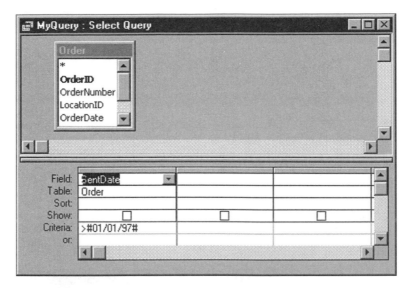

5 Now go back to the Module window and type in the following procedure:

```
Function ChangeQueryDef(strQuery As String, strSQL As String) As Boolean

If strQuery = "" Or strSQL = "" Then Exit Function

Dim qdf As QueryDef

Set qdf = CurrentDb.QueryDefs(strQuery)
qdf.SQL = strSQL
qdf.Close
RefreshDatabaseWindow

ChangeQueryDef = True

End Function
```

6 Run the procedure by typing the following in the Debug window and hitting *Enter*:

```
?ChangeQueryDef("MyQuery", "Select * from [Order] where PaidDate = #1/1/
97#")
```

The word **True** should appear in the Debug Window, indicating that the function completed successfully.

7 Press *F11* to view the database window and change to the Queries tab. Open **MyQuery** in design view. The design of the query should now have changed to match the new criteria you passed to the **ChangeQueryDef** function.

How It Works

Creating a **QueryDef** is very simple.

```
Dim qdf As QueryDef

Set qdf = CurrentDb.CreateQueryDef("MyQuery")
```

First, we create an empty **QueryDef** object. The **CreateQueryDef** method both creates a **QueryDef** object and assigns it the name that it will have when it is saved. If you don't intend to save it and will only use it in the current procedure, you can give it an empty string (**""**) as its name and it won't be saved. However, we want to save our **QueryDef**, so call it **MyQuery**.

```
qdf.SQL = strSQL
```

If you try to create a **QueryDef** object with a name that is the same as a saved query that already exists in the database, Access will generate a run-time error.

Next, we assign the **SQL** property of the **QueryDef** object. If you aren't too sure about how to write SQL, you can always try designing the query normally in the QBE grid and then switching the query to SQL view to see the SQL created. You can then copy the SQL to the clipboard and paste it into your procedure from there.

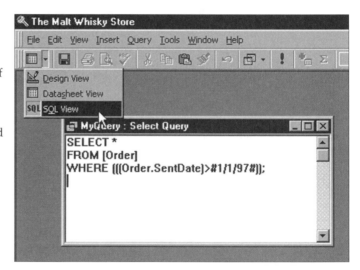

Finally, we close the **QueryDef**, with the following line:

```
qdf.Close
```

The act of closing the **QueryDef** saves changes to it in the database window.

FYI The **RefreshDatabaseWindow** method is new to Access 97. It causes any changes to database objects such as forms, reports and queries to be immediately reflected in the database window.

Modifying the **QueryDef** is just as simple. First you use a variable to reference the **QueryDef** called **MyQuery** in the current database.

```
Dim qdf As QueryDef

Set qdf = CurrentDb.QueryDefs(strQuery)
```

And then you modify its SQL property, save it and refresh the database window like we did in the previous function.

In previous versions of Access you could use the **OpenQueryDef** method to return a **QueryDef** object which referred to a saved query. This is no longer allowed in Access 97. Instead you should declare a **QueryDef** object and then use the **QueryDefs** collection of the **Database** object to return a reference to the saved query, just as we have in our example. The **QueryDefs** collection of a **Database** object contains one member for each saved query in the database.

You may now be able to see how we could use this method of modifying a **QueryDef** to display the selected records in **frmOrder**. If **frmOrder** were bound to a saved query, we could use the **Click** event handler for the OK button on the Criteria Selection form, **cmdOK_Click()**, to modify that query before we opened up the Order Details form. That way, the records displayed in **frmOrder** would only those be that meet the criteria specified in **frmCriteria**.

Creating a Table of Matching Records

We have looked at two methods of using **frmCriteria** to restrict the records displayed in **frmOrder**:

> Using the **WHERE** clause as a filter

> Basing **frmOrder** on a saved query and using the **WHERE** clause to modify the **QueryDef**

We'll now look at our third method. This is actually the way that it is implemented in **Whisky7a.mdb**. This method involves using the **WHERE** clause to build a table of matching orders.

Cast your mind back to the start of this chapter, where we looked at the way that the Search Criteria and Order Details form works in **Whisky7a.mdb**.

> We select the View Order Details option from the Switchboard form to open up **frmCriteria**

> We specify which orders we want to review and click OK

> A message box informs us how many, if any, records met our criteria

> We choose to see the orders that matched the criteria

> Two new forms are opened: the Order Details form and the Order Selection form

> We can also click the Print button on the Order Details form to print a report listing the matching orders

The important thing to notice about this process is that there are **two forms and a report** whose record source changes as a result of the criteria specified on **frmCriteria**. The forms are **frmMatchingOrders**, which displays a summary of each matching record, and **frmOrder**, which displays the details of the orders. There is also the report, **rptMatchingOrders**.

213

As we saw in the second example above, we could have based both forms and the report on saved queries and then used **QueryDef** objects to modify the **SQL** properties of these **QueryDef** objects at run-time. However, this method has a drawback in that it does not give optimum performance.

Compiled queries run faster than uncompiled queries. To compile a query in Access, you open the query in datasheet view and then close it. However, whenever you modify the **SQL** property of a query, in VBA or in the query's design view, you lose the compiled version. In other words, any queries created or modified in VBA aren't automatically compiled, as Access has to compile them when they first run. Therefore, execution is slower than with pre-compiled queries.

If we modified the queries on which **frmMatchingOrders**, **frmOrder** and **rptMatchingOrders** were based, all the queries would be uncompiled. This would mean that every time **frmMatchingOrders**, **frmOrder** and **rptMatchingOrders** were opened, they would need to recompile the query before retrieving their records.

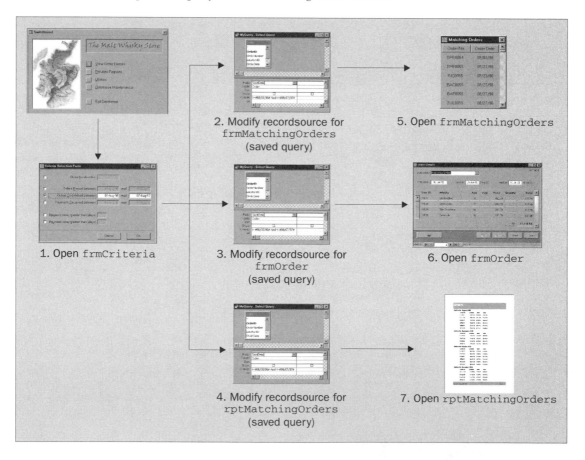

2. Modify recordsource for frmMatchingOrders (saved query)

5. Open frmMatchingOrders

1. Open frmCriteria

3. Modify recordsource for frmOrder (saved query)

6. Open frmOrder

4. Modify recordsource for rptMatchingOrders (saved query)

7. Open rptMatchingOrders

So, how can we get round this performance problem? Well, we could use **parameterized queries**. These are queries which contain placeholders for parameters that can change whenever the query is run. When a parameterized query is compiled, it stays compiled even if you change the values of the parameters when you next run it. So we could create a parameterized query, with one parameter for each element of the **WHERE** clause. In this case, however, that would be a little unwieldy as not only are there quite a few elements in the **WHERE** clause, but we do not know until run-time which of the parameters we will have values for. Parameterized queries are useful if you know that all of the parameters will be supplied by the user, but can be very complicated if you give the user the opportunity to supply some and leave others blank.

A better way to get round the performance problem is to create an indexed intermediate table, **CriteriaHits**, which is populated with the **OrderID** of any orders that meet the criteria specified by the user. This is done only once, for each time that the user clicks the OK button on **frmCriteria**, but it changes the membership of the recordsets for two forms and one report. As a result, we don't need to alter (and, therefore, cause recompilation of) the queries on which **frmMatchingOrders**, **frmOrder** and **rptMatchingOrders** are based—the intermediate table is used in the record source for the two forms and the report.

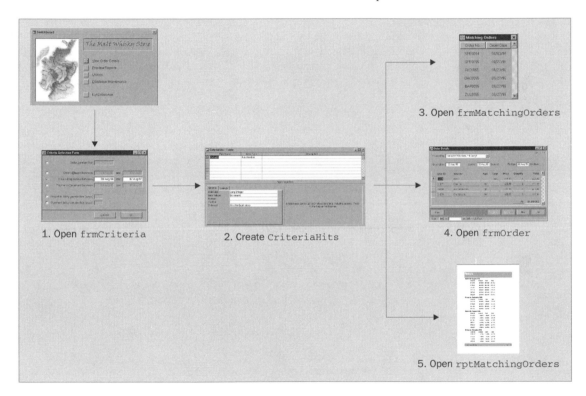

3. Open frmMatchingOrders

1. Open frmCriteria

2. Create CriteriaHits

4. Open frmOrder

5. Open rptMatchingOrders

Creating intermediate tables can be a useful way of increasing the performance (and reducing the complexity) of an application, when you find that you have a number of operations which need to be performed on a set of records with a fixed membership (i.e. the records which meet the criteria specified in **frmCriteria**). However, this also increases the size of your database file, since you are creating duplicates of certain records.

Bear in mind that the table **CriteriaHits** will be repopulated every time a user changes the criteria for selecting records. Two consequences follow from this:

▶ The table **CriteriaHits** will have to be a local table in each user's database

▶ We will need to start compacting the database more frequently, as the act of emptying and repopulating the **CriteriaHits** table will cause empty space to appear in the database

Implementing the Intermediate Table

Let's have a look at how this works in practice. Remember, the code that follows can be found in the database called **Whisky7a.mdb** on the accompanying CD. The following piece of code is executed when the user hits the <u>V</u>iew Order Details button on the Switchboard form:

```
Me.Visible = False
DoCmd.OpenForm "frmCriteria", acNormal, , , acFormEdit, acDialog, _
     (Me.Name)
```

Nothing too complex here. All we are doing is making the Switchboard form invisible and then opening the Criteria Selection form modally. Note that we are also supplying the name of the Switchboard form to the Criteria Selection form via the **OpenArgs** property. We use this to signal to the Criteria Selection form which form opened it up, so we can make the Switchboard form visible again once we have closed the Criteria Selection form.

Once we have made our selections, we hit the <u>O</u>K button on the Criteria Selection form and the following procedure is run:

```
Private Sub cmdOK_Click()

Dim strWhere As String
Dim qdf As QueryDef
Dim lngRecords As Long
Dim strMessage As String
Dim intResponse As Integer

BuildSQLString strWhere
If BuildOrderIDTable(vWhere:=strWhere, vRecordcount:=lngRecords, _
                 vMethod:="DDL", vIndexed:=True) Then

    Select Case lngRecords
        Case 0
            MsgBox "No records matched the criteria you specified", _
                vbExclamation, "No matches found"
        Case Else
            strMessage = lngRecords & " record(s) matched the criteria " _
                & "you specified." & vbCrLf & vbCrLf & _
                "Would you like to see the results?"
            intResponse = MsgBox(strMessage, _
                                 vbYesNo + vbDefaultButton1 + _
                                 vbInformation, "Matches found")
            If intResponse = vbYes Then
                DoCmd.OpenForm "frmMatchingOrders", , , , , , _
(Me.OpenArgs)
```

```
                         DoCmd.OpenForm "frmOrder", , , , , , (Me.OpenArgs)
                         DoCmd.Close acForm, Me.Name
                  End If

        End Select

   End If


   End Sub
```

By this stage you should be familiar with the first statement:

```
BuildSQLString strWhere
```

This populates **strWhere** with the SQL **WHERE** clause corresponding to the criteria we have specified. Then comes the new code:

```
If BuildOrderIDTable(vWhere:=strWhere, vRecordcount:=lngRecords, _
                     vMethod:="DDL", vIndexed:=True) Then
```

The **BuildOrderIDTable()** procedure is the one that takes the SQL **WHERE** clause and creates an indexed table full of **OrderID**s. It works in a similar fashion to the **MakeQueryDef()** procedure we wrote earlier. We'll look at the **BuildOrderIDTable()** function in more detail in just a moment. For the moment, however, we only need to know that it creates a table called **CriteriaHits** which contains a single indexed column, **OrderID**, populated with the **OrderID**s of all the orders which matched the criteria in the SQL **WHERE** clause, and that it then returns the number of records in the **CriteriaHits** table.

Armed with this information, we can display a message box indicating the number of records meeting our criteria, and asking whether the order details should be displayed.

```
strMessage = lngRecords & " record(s) matched the criteria " & _
             "you specified." & Chr$(10) & Chr$(10) & _
             "Would you like to see the results?"
intResponse = MsgBox(strMessage, _
             vbYesNo + vbDefaultButton1 + vbInformation, _
             "Matches found")
```

If the Yes button on the message box is clicked, it is simply a question of opening the Order Details form and the Order Selection form and closing the Criteria Selection form:

```
If intResponse = vbYes Then
    DoCmd.OpenForm "frmMatchingOrders", , , , , , (Me.OpenArgs)
    DoCmd.OpenForm "frmOrder", , , , , , (Me.OpenArgs)
    DoCmd.Close acForm, Me.Name
End If
```

Note that we pass the **OpenArgs** property of the Criteria Selection form to the two forms we are opening. This is then used when these forms are closed down to make visible the form that called the Criteria Selection form in the first place, i.e. the Switchboard form.

*The Order Details form and the Order Selection form do not simply have the table **Order** as their record source. Instead, the forms get their records from the **Order** table joined with **CriteriaHits** on the **OrderID** field. In other words, their recordset contains all of the values from the **Order** table, where the **OrderID** matches an **OrderID** in **CriteriaHits**.*

When a user changes the criteria for selecting records, all that changes is the membership of the **CriteriaHits** table (i.e. the **OrderIDs** it contains). There are no **QueryDefs** to change—and no uncompiled queries. It also means that by basing the report **rptMatchingOrders** on the **Order** table joined with **CriteriaHits** on the **OrderID** field, we can ensure that it will always be based on the same records as the Order Details form.

The BuildOrderIDTable Function

There was one step that we glossed over in the description above, and that was how the **BuildOrderIDTable()** function works. So here goes...

Here is the code listing for **BuildOrderIDTable()** in full:

```
Function BuildOrderIDTable(Optional vWhere As String, _
                           Optional vTableName = "CriteriaHits", _
                           Optional vRecordcount, _
                           Optional vTimeTaken, _
                           Optional vMethod = "DDL", _
                           Optional vIndexed = True) _
As Boolean
On Error GoTo BuildOrderIDTable_Err

Dim strSQL As String
Dim lngTime As Long
Dim intFromPos As Integer
Dim qdf As QueryDef

If Not IsMissing(vTimeTaken) Then lngTime = Now

Select Case vMethod
    Case "DDL"
        'State the table we want to get the IDs from
        strSQL = "SELECT OrderID FROM [Order]"

        'Add the restriction if one has been supplied
        If vWhere <> "" And Not IsMissing (vWhere) Then _
            strSQL = strSQL & " WHERE " & vWhere

        'Now turn the query into a make-table query
        intFromPos = InStr(strSQL, "FROM")
        strSQL = Left$(strSQL, intFromPos - 1) & "INTO " & _
            vTableName & Mid$(strSQL, intFromPos - 1)

        'Delete the table if it already exists
        CurrentDb.TableDefs.Delete vTableName
```

```
                    'Now run the make-table query to create the table
                    Set qdf = CurrentDb.CreateQueryDef("", strSQL)
                    qdf.Execute

                    'Return the number of records in the table if needed
                    If Not IsMissing(vRecordcount) Then _
                        vRecordcount = qdf.RecordsAffected

                    'Add an index if required
                    If vIndexed Then
                        qdf.SQL = "CREATE UNIQUE INDEX PrimaryKey ON " & _
                                    vTableName & " (OrderID ASC) WITH PRIMARY"
                        qdf.Execute
                    End If

                    'Close the querydef object
                    qdf.Close

            Case "DAO"
                    'We will put this in later

        End Select

        'Return the amount of time taken to run the procedure
        If Not IsMissing(vTimeTaken) Then _
            vTimeTaken = Now - lngTime

        'And finally, indicate success
        BuildOrderIDTable = True

    BuildOrderIDTable_Exit:
        Exit Function

    BuildOrderIDTable_Err:
        Select Case Err.Number
            Case 3265    'occurs if the table we are deleting doesn't exist
                Resume Next
            Case Else
                MsgBox Err.Description
                Resume BuildOrderIDTable_Exit
                Resume
        End Select

    End Function
```

First, let's look at the arguments that the function takes:

```
Function BuildOrderIDTable(Optional vWhere As String, Optional _
vTableName, Optional vRecordcount, Optional vTimeTaken, _
Optional vMethod, OptionalvIndexed) As Boolean
```

There are six arguments, all optional, and here's what they do:

This argument...	does this...
vWhere	supplies the SQL **WHERE** clause which was built up from the selections made on the Criteria Selection form. If **vWhere** is not supplied, the table is filled with all records from the **Order** table.
vTableName	supplies the name for the table to be created. If it is missing the table is called **CriteriaHits**.
vRecordCount	is used to return a number signifying the number of records placed into the new table.
vTimeTaken	is used to return the amount of time taken for the **BuildOrderIDTable()** procedure to execute.
vMethod	is used to specify what method will be used to build the new table. If this argumentis not supplied, the table will be created using a make-table query. (The alternative is to use DAO, and you will be writing that code later on as an exercise.)
vIndexed	is used to indicate whether the new table should be indexed on the **OrderID** field. If this argument is not supplied, the field will not be indexed.

You should be able to work out how the function works by reading the comments in the code. There are three things, however, that may be new to you:

▶ It is easy to turn a select query (which returns records) into a make-table query (which puts those records into a new table) by simply adding the words **INTO** *tablename* between the **SELECT** clause and the **FROM** clause of the query.

▶ The error handling (**Case 3265** etc.) allows the procedure to continue without an error if it cannot find an old version of **CriteriaHits** to delete.

▶ The **RecordsAffected** property of a **QueryDef** object returns the number of records affected when the query was run. This is how we tell how many records are inserted into the new table. (The **RecordsAffected** property only applies to **QueryDefs** which contain action queries).

Building a Table with the DAO Hierarchy

Occasions sometimes occurs when it makes sense to create a table in VBA code at run-time. We have seen one such example above—we used a temporary table when we were performing several operations with the same set of records, so that we didn't have to run the same query each time we wanted to fetch those records.

Temporary tables can also help speed up report production—fields in tables can be indexed, whereas fields in queries can't. Judicious use of indexes in tables can significantly improve the performance of any reports based on them.

In the example above, we created a table by building a make-table query. We'll now see how to build a table using the Data Access Object hierarchy. One of the advantages of using DAO to create the table is that it gives us more control over the way the table is constructed. When you use a make-table query to create a table, Access determines the datatypes for the fields in the tables. Also tables created from make-table queries don't have any indexes. In contrast, however, if we create a table using DAO, we can specify the datatypes of the fields in the table and add whatever indexes we want.

However, in order to do this, we must first understand exactly how tables are constructed. Aside from the data that is held in them, tables have two major constituents: **Fields** and **Indexes**.

> ▶ A **Field** is a column of data with a common data type and length. **Fields** may exhibit certain properties. For example, a **Field** has a **DefaultValue** property that, not surprisingly, indicates the default value that Access places there if the user doesn't supply one. Another property is the **Required** property which is **False** if a **Field** allows **Null** values and **True** if **Null** values aren't allowed.

> ▶ An **Index** is an object that holds information about the ordering and uniqueness of records in a field. Just as is it is faster to look up a page in a large book if it has an index at the back, so it is faster for Access to retrieve records from a large table if the table is indexed. As well as containing **Field**s, an **Index** object also has **Properties**. For example, the **Unique** property of an **Index** object indicates whether all values in the **Field** to which that **Index** applies should be unique.

We'll now take this opportunity to introduce another object that is very similar to the **QueryDef** object—the **TableDef** object. A **TableDef** object is an object that holds a complete table definition. Just as we saw with a **QueryDef** object, a **TableDef** object holds the definition of a table and not the actual data. If you want, you can think of the **TableDef** as being like a table in design view.

Access	VBA
Table (Design View)	**TableDef** object
Table (Datasheet View)	Table-type **Recordset** object
Query (Design View)	**QueryDef** object
Query (Datasheet View)	Dynaset-type, Snapshot-type or Forward-only-type **Recordset** object

The following diagram indicates how **TableDef** objects, **Field** objects and **Index** objects fit into the overall Data Access Object hierarchy. (Note that not all of the DAO hierarchy is displayed).

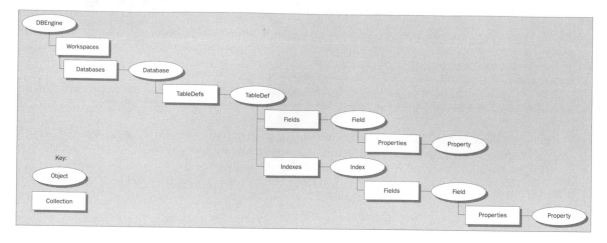

Once you understand the diagram above, creating tables in VBA is a relatively simple process. If you aren't sure you understand how objects and collections work, you should re-read Chapter 5 where they are described in detail. These are the fundamental building blocks of the Data Access Object hierarchy and you need to make sure that you are familiar with how they work.

The Ten Steps

To create a table using VBA, you will always carry out the following steps:

1 Create a **TableDef** object

2 Set any properties for the **TableDef**

3 Create one or more **Field** objects

4 Set any properties for the **Field** objects

5 Append the **Field** objects to the **Fields** collection of the **TableDef**

6 Create one or more **Index** objects

7 Set any properties for the **Index** objects

8 Append any **Field** objects to the **Fields** collection of the **Index**

9 Append the **Index** objects to the **Indexes** collection of the **TableDef**

10 Append the **TableDef** object to the **TableDefs** collection of the **Database**

Try It Out—Creating a Table Using the DAO

1 Create a new standard code module or open an existing one and type in the following subprocedure:

```
Sub MakeATable()

Dim db As Database
Dim tbl As TableDef
Dim fld As Field
Dim idx As Index

'Start by opening the database
Set db = CurrentDb()

'Create a tabledef object
Set tbl = db.CreateTableDef("Bottlers")

'Create a field; set its properties; add it to the tabledef
Set fld = tbl.CreateField("BottlerID", dbLong)

fld.OrdinalPosition = 1
fld.Attributes = dbAutoIncrField

tbl.Fields.Append fld

'Create another; set its properties; add it to the tabledef
Set fld = tbl.CreateField("BottlerName", dbText)

fld.OrdinalPosition = 2
fld.Size = 50
fld.Required = True
fld.AllowZeroLength = False

tbl.Fields.Append fld

'Create an index and set its properties
Set idx = tbl.CreateIndex("PrimaryKey")

idx.Primary = True
idx.Required = True
idx.Unique = True

'Add a field to the index
Set fld = idx.CreateField("BottlerID")
idx.Fields.Append fld

'Add the index to the tabledef
tbl.Indexes.Append idx
```

```
'Finally add table to the database
db.TableDefs.Append tbl

'And refresh the database window
RefreshDatabaseWindow

'Indicate creation was successful
MsgBox "The " & tbl.Name & " table was successfully created"

End Sub
```

2 Now run the procedure by hitting either *F5* or the Go/Continue button on the toolbar.

3 You should see a message box informing you that the table has been successfully created.

4 Press *F11* to go to the database window. The table that you have just created should be visible in the Tables pane. Open it in Design View and have a look at the two fields that you have created. Note the properties in the lower half of the window.

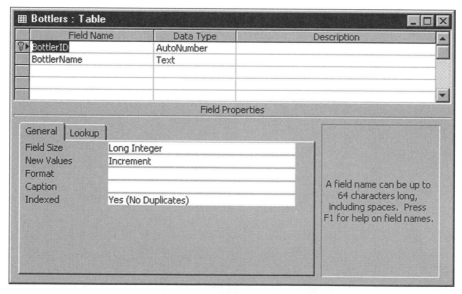

5 Now look at the indexes, either by clicking the Index button or by selecting Indexes from the View menu. Does everything look as you expected?

How It Works

Although the code may look a little tortuous, it's actually very easy to follow if you bear in mind the Data Access Object hierarchy and follow the steps listed above.

After opening the database, the first thing we must do is to create a new **TableDef** object:

```
Set tbl = db.CreateTableDef("Bottlers")
```

Creating any Data Access Object is a simple task. All you need do is to use the **CreateObject** method on the Data Access Object which is the next highest in the hierarchy. The **TableDefs** collection belongs to a **Database** object so, to create a **TableDef**, you use the **CreateTableDef** method on the **Database** object.

As with **QueryDefs**, when we create a **TableDef** object, we give it a name by which we can refer to it later and which will appear in the database window when it is saved.

We don't want to set any other properties for the **TableDef** (the next step in the process) and so move on and create a **Field** object:

```
Set fld = tbl.CreateField("BottlerID", dbLong)
```

Fields are a collection within the **TableDef** object, so we use the **CreateField** method on the **TableDef** object that will contain the **Field**, and give it a name by which we can refer to it later. We also need to specify the type of data that this **Field** will hold. We want the field to be an autonumber field, and as autonumber fields are long integers, we specify **dbLong** as the data type.

Next, we must set properties for the **Field**:

```
fld.OrdinalPosition = 1
fld.Attributes = dbAutoIncrField
```

The **OrdinalPosition** property indicates where a **Field** appears in a table. The leftmost **Field** in a table has an **OrdinalPosition** property of 1, the next has an **OrdinalPosition** property of 2, and so on. The **OrdinalPosition** property of the rightmost **Field** is equal to the number of **Fields** in the **TableDef**.

The **Attributes** property is used to specify how an object behaves. By setting the **Attributes** property of our **Field** to **dbAutoIncrField**, we are indicating that the field should behave like an autonumber field and increase by one every time a new record is added.

Now we must add the **Field** to the **Fields** collection of the **TableDef** using the **Append** method:

```
tbl.Fields.Append fld
```

We then repeat the process to create another **Field** and append it to our **TableDef** object.

Once all the **Field** objects have been added, we create an **Index** for the table and call it **PrimaryKey**:

```
Set idx = tbl.CreateIndex("PrimaryKey")
```

We then set its properties:

```
idx.Primary = True
idx.Required = True
idx.Unique = True
```

The **Primary** property indicates whether an **Index** is the primary key for the **TableDef** to which it is to be added. The **Required** property determines whether the **Index** can accept **Null** values—if it is **True**, **Nulls** will not be accepted. The **Unique** property determines whether duplicate values are allowed within the **Index**. We have set this to **True**, so duplicate values will not be allowed.

The next stage is to specify the **Field** which will be indexed:

```
Set fld = idx.CreateField("BottlerID")
idx.Fields.Append fld
```

Here, we use the familiar **CreateObject** syntax to create a **Field** object within the **Index** object. By setting the name of the **Field** object to **BottlerID**, we are indicating that the **Field** called **BottlerID,** which we created earlier in the procedure, is the one to be indexed. Next, we add the **Index** to the **TableDef**:

```
tbl.Indexes.Append idx
```

Finally, we add the **TableDef** to the Database:

```
db.TableDefs.Append tbl
```

And that's all there is to it!

If you cast your mind back to the **BuildOrderIDTable()** function, you may remember that we created the **CriteriaHits** table using a make-table query. It is left to you as an exercise at the end of this chapter to rewrite the procedure to allow the table to be created using the DAO hierarchy, but if you want to see how this is done, you can have a look at the **BuildOrderIDTable()** function in the finished version of the database.

226

Summary

In this chapter, we have spent a lot of time looking at the different methods that we can use to manipulate **TableDef** and **QueryDef** objects at run-time. The first part of the chapter was concerned with how to generate criteria to restrict the display of the records we needed. We used the user's input to create a **WHERE** clause using the **BuildSQLString()** procedure.

Once we had created the **WHERE** clause, we had several choices for displaying our record. We could:

▶ Use the **WHERE** clause as a filter against an Order form which already had all the records behind it

▶ Base the Order form on a saved query and modify the query before we opened the form—this enables the user to select the criteria before the form is created

▶ Create a table of matching records and use this in the record source for the Order form. This gives optimum performance

You should have realized by this stage that the key to the whole thing is the Data Access Object hierarchy. If you have a sound knowledge of how this fits together, you should have little problem putting into practice any of the techniques we have used in this chapter.

A knowledge of SQL is also important. Work at these two areas and you will find that you become more and more inventive with the things you attempt and the results you achieve.

Exercises

1 You can use the debug window to inspect the properties of data access objects. What line would you have to type in the lower pane of the debug window to determine how many fields there are in the **Location** table?

See if you can use the debug window to determine how many properties each of the fields in the **Location** table have. Why do some have more properties than others?

2 In this chapter, we used the **BuildIDTableFromSQL()** procedure to build up the **CriteriaHits** table from a given SQL string. We built the table by running a make-table query. See if you can rewrite the **BuildIDTableFromSQL()** procedure to build the table using the Data Access Object hierarchy instead. Once the table has been built using DAO, the procedure should populate it with an append query, e.g.

INSERT INTO CriteriaHits SELECT OrderID FROM [Order] WHERE...

Working With External Data

The major reason for buying a database is to store data. So far, you have seen how this data is stored in Access and how to manipulate it once it's in the database. You have yet to see how you can get data into and out of Access, or use data from other databases.

In this chapter, you're going to see how to:

- ▶ Import data into Access
- ▶ Export data from Access
- ▶ Send data via electronic mail
- ▶ Use data in external databases

Copying To or From Other Applications

There are, of course, thousands of applications that store data and with which it would be useful to be able to exchange data. However, since they store data in their own format, you would have to know that format to exchange data with them. Luckily, though, you don't need to know about every application—just a few basic ones. If you need to exchange data with a program that isn't in the list, you can usually pick a standard format that both your application and the other program can read.

Access can exchange data with four different types of application:

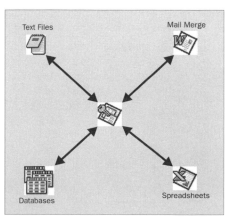

You will usually be dealing with old databases or spreadsheets, though, or proprietary legacy systems which you now wish to replace with Access. Whatever the case, you will find the import and export facilities extremely simple and flexible.

Databases

Databases vary from small desktop systems, including Access, through medium-sized server databases, to large mainframe databases. In Access, to transfer between databases you use the **TransferDatabase** method of the **DoCmd** object.

```
DoCmd.TransferDatabase [TransferType], DatabaseType, DatabaseName _
    [, ObjectType], Source, Destination [, StructureOnly] _
    [, SaveLoginID]
```

 The brackets indicate that an argument is optional.

Let's look at the arguments in more detail:

Argument	Description
TransferType	The action you wish to perform, which must be one of: **acImport** to import data **acExport** to export data **acLink** to link data If you leave this blank, **acImport** is taken as the default.
DatabaseType	The type of database that you wish to transfer from or to. It must be one of: Microsoft Access FoxPro 3.0 Paradox 3.X FoxPro DBC Paradox 4.X dBase III Paradox 5.X dBase IV FoxPro 2.0 dBase 5.0 FoxPro 2.5 Jet 2.x FoxPro 2.6 ODBC database
DatabaseName	The full name of the database involved, including the path.
ObjectType	The type of object involved, which must be one of: **acTable** **acQuery** **acForm** **acReport** **acMacro** **acModule** If the value is left out, **acTable** is taken as the default.
Source	The name of the object from which the data is coming.
Destination	The name of the object into which the data is being transferred.

Argument	Description
StructureOnly	This should be **True** if the object is a table and only the structure is to be transferred. Using **False** will also copy the data. **False** is the default.
SaveLoginID	This is only for ODBC datasources. If it's **True**, the login name and password will be stored for further connections. If it's **False**, you'll have to log in to the data source every time the source is accessed. **False** is the default.

Try It Out—The `TransferDatabase` Command

Like most shops, The Whisky Shop needs to print a brochure, and the publishers like the list of whiskies to be sent in database format. We'll create this database now.

1 Close any databases that you have open and pick New Database... from the File menu.

2 On the General Tab, select Blank Database and click OK. Name the new database **Brochure** and place it in the **BegVBA** directory (or wherever your sample databases are).

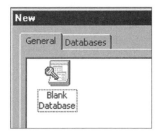

3 Now close this new database and open **Whisky8.mdb**. As we'll be performing this export on a regular basis, we'll create a form and set it up as a permanent feature.

4 Open up the Outside World screen, **frmOutsideWorld**, in form view. You'll see that there's already an option group there with the first entry created.

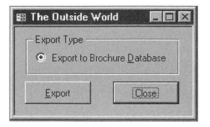

5 We need to activate the Export button so that, if it's clicked when the above option button is selected, the list of whiskies in the database is exported to **Brochure.mdb**. To do this, we need to add the **TransferDatabase** command to the button's click event handler. Switch to design view and go to the On Click event in the property sheet. Add the **TransferDatabase** command so it looks like the following:

```
Private Sub cmdExport_Click()

    Select Case fraExportType
    Case 1
        DoCmd.TransferDatabase acExport, "Microsoft Access", _
            "C:\BegVBA\Brochure.MDB", acTable, "Bottling", "The Whisky Shop"
```

```
        End Select

End Sub
```

We've used a **Select Case** statement to allow us to add other option buttons to the form in the future.

6 Close the module window and switch to Form view. Select the Export to Brochure Database option and press the Export button on the form. This will run the new procedure, causing the current list of whisky bottlings from **Bottling** to be exported into the new database, into a table called **The Whisky Shop**. If we were exporting to a database that existed previously and the table was already included, it would be replaced.

7 Close **Whisky8.mdb**, saving changes to the form, and open **Brochure.mdb**, which now contains the new table. Open this up to see the data.

⊞ The Whisky Shop : Table					
Bottl	**WhiskyID**	**Age**	**Strength**	**DistillationD**
4	3 ▼	22	58.7%	
5	4	15	43.0%	

FYI Notice that, because the **Bottling** table has a look-up field that references the **Whisky** table, only the ID is shown, not the whisky name. This is because the referenced table hasn't been transferred and therefore Access can not show you this information. You should bear this in mind when transferring tables between databases as the **TransferDatabase** command only transfers individual objects between databases, it does not transfer whole databases.

8 The table can still be viewed and edited, and you can change the **WhiskyID** field.

9 Close the Brochure database and open **Whisky8.mdb** once more. Edit the code you have just entered, changing **acTable** to **acQuery**, "Bottling" to "qryWhiskyAndPrices", and **"The Whisky Shop"** to **"qryWhiskyAndPrices"**. It should now look like this:

```
DoCmd.TransferDatabase acExport, "Microsoft Access", _
          "C:\BegVBA\Brochure.mdb", acQuery, "qryWhiskyAndPrices", _
          "qryWhiskyAndPrices"
```

10 Switch the form to Design view and hit the Export button again. Before opening **Brochure.mdb,** think about what you expect to see.

11 OK, in **Brochure.mdb** you now have a new query and not the data from the query. This is because the **TransferDatabase** command transfers database objects and not the underlying data. If you need to create a new table in another database with the data based upon a query, you should use a Make Table Query, and in this you can specify the target database and table name.

Although the **TransferDatabase** is very flexible, you'll probably find that you don't use it a great deal. It is often used to convert old database systems into new Access 97 ones, or to back up, in whole or in part, a database. For example, you could use this to implement an automated backup procedure. You could have a table that details which items are to be backed up and when, so the application could periodically check this table and run a **TransferDatabase** command on the objects to be backed up when their time arrives.

Spreadsheets

Transferring data to spreadsheets is one of the most frequently used transfer facilities. Access 97 is extremely good at querying data and producing reports, but when you want to analyze figures you really can't do better than to use a spreadsheet. You *can* do it in Access, but why bother when Microsoft Excel is so powerful and transferring the data is so easy? To transfer data to or from a spreadsheet you use the **TransferSpreadsheet** method of the **DoCmd** object:

```
DoCmd.TransferSpreadsheet [TransferType] [, SpreadsheetType], _
    TableName, FileName [, HasFieldNames] [, Range]
```

The arguments are very similar to the previous **TransferDatabase** command:

Argument	Description
TransferType	The action you wish to perform, which must be one of: **acImport** to import data **acExport** to export data **acLink** to link data If you leave this blank, **acImport** is taken as the default.
SpreadsheetType	A number representing the type of spreadsheet that you wish to transfer from or to. The constants you can use are as follows: **acSpreadsheetTypeExcel3** **acSpreadsheetTypeExcel4** **acSpreadsheetTypeExcel5** **acSpreadsheetTypeExcel7** **acSpreadsheetTypeExcel97** **acSpreadsheetTypeLotusWK1** **acSpreadsheetTypeLotusWK3** **acSpreadsheetTypeLotusWK4** **acSpreadsheetTypeLotusWJ2** (Japanese version only) Interestingly, the default is Excel3.
TableName	The name of the table or query involved.
FileName	The name of the spreadsheet file, including the path.
HasFieldNames	If you want to use the first row of the source table or spreadsheet as the field names in the destination table or spreadsheet, this should be **True**; if you want to treat the first row as normal data, this should be **False**. **False** is the default.
Range	This only applies to importing. It should contain the range of cells or range name to be imported. If it's left blank, the whole spreadsheet will be imported.

Try It Out—The `TransferSpreadsheet` *Command*

The accountants at The Whisky Shop use Microsoft Excel to help analyze the sales figures as it allows them to manipulate figures, examine budget and profits, and produce graphs. This next example will export data from **Whisky8.mdb** to an Excel spreadsheet.

1 Open up **Whisky8.mdb** and open the **frmOutsideWorld** form in Design view. Add another option button to the option group—it will have the value 2—and change the label as shown in the screenshot.

2 We now need to change the code behind the <u>E</u>xport button so that, if it is clicked when this new option button is selected, the sales data will be exported to an Excel spreadsheet. Add the following code to the **Select Case** statement created in the previous example:

```
Case 2
    DoCmd.TransferSpreadsheet acExport, 5, "qryMonthlySales", _
        "C:\BegVBA\WhiskySales.xls"
```

3 Switch to form view and select the second option button. Then, click <u>E</u>xport to produce the spreadsheet file. If you now open the file **C:\BegVBA\WhiskySales.xls**, you will see the data from **qryMonthlySales**.

Importing data from spreadsheets is just as simple. Many people tend to avoid databases because they think they are far too complex. However, at some point, the data becomes too complicated to be stored in a spreadsheet, and you will have to import it into a database, splitting the data into tables. In this case, you use the **TransferSpreadsheet** method in much the same way as above.

You will see other examples of sending data to Excel later in the book.

Text Files

There are two ways of importing and exporting textual data. The first uses delimited text files, in which a particular character determines where one field ends and another starts. The second way uses fixed width files which require that all fields and records be in set positions in the file—each record (and fields within it) has the same number of characters as all the other records.

Both forms use the **TransferText** method of the **DoCmd** object:

```
DoCmd.TransferText [TransferType] [, SpecificationName], _
    TableName, FileName [, HasFieldNames], [HTMLTableName]
```

Once again, the arguments are similar to the examples that you have already seen.

Argument	Description
TransferType	The action you wish to perform, which must be one of: **acExportDelim** **acExportFixed** **acExportHTML** **acExportMerge** **acImportDelim** **acImportFixed** **acImportHTML** **acLinkDelim** **acLinkFixed** **acLinkHTML** If you leave this blank, **acImportDelim** is taken as the default.
SpecificationName	The name of the import/export **specification**. This is required for fixed width files but isn't always necessary for delimited files. (Because there are many different 'settings' that you have to supply when handling text files, these are usually stored as a specification on disk and the name is then used as an argument to the **TransferText** method. Otherwise, you would have to supply values for many more arguments each time. We'll come to specifications in a moment.)
TableName	The name of the table you wish to import, export or link, or the name of the query whose results you wish to export.
FileName	The name of the text file, including the path.
HasFieldNames	This should be **True** if the first row of the text file contains field names, **False** otherwise. If left blank, **False** is taken as the default.
HTMLTableName	The name of the table or list in the HTML document that you wish to import or export. This option is ignored unless you have specified an HTML transfer (**acExportHTML** or **acImportHTML**). If you leave this empty then the first table or list is used. We will be looking at this more closely in the section on the Internet later in the book.

Delimited Text Files

Delimited text files use a special character to separate the fields. In most cases, this is a comma, so the text file would contain lines like:

```
field 1, field 2, field 3, field 4
```

Try It Out—The TransferText Command

The Whisky Shop recently took part in a survey for a magazine, which was trying to track the trends in whisky buying. They were particularly interested in which whiskies were bought and in which month. To help them a list will be sent in delimited text format.

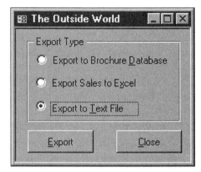

1 Add another option button to the option group on the Outside World screen. This will have the value 3. Label it as shown here:

2 Add the following code to the **Select Case** statement behind the Export button.

```
Case 3
    DoCmd.TransferText acExportDelim, , "qryMonthlyWhiskyCount", _
        "C:\BegVBA\Survey.txt", True
```

3 Switch the form to form view, select the third option button and click Export. Then, open up the file **c:\BegVBA\Survey.txt** in Notepad. It should look something like this:

```
"WhiskyName","Month","BottlesSold"
"Aberlour","April 1993",6
"Aberlour","April 1994",6
"Aberlour","April 1995",6
"Aberlour","April 1996",6
"Aberlour","April 1997",4
"Aberlour","August 1992",6
"Aberlour","August 1993",5
"Aberlour","August 1994",5
"Aberlour","August 1995",1
"Aberlour","August 1996",6
"Aberlour","December 1992",4
"Aberlour","December 1993",10
"Aberlour","December 1994",11
"Aberlour","December 1995",6
"Aberlour","December 1996",6
"Aberlour","February 1993",4
```

You can see that the default specification is a comma for the field separator and quotes around the text. This is often called a Comma Separated Value (or CSV) file and is usually the safest form of transfer as it's very widely used and recognized. Using quotes to surround text is sensible as it ensures that a comma in a text string isn't taken as a field separator. However, you should be aware of the problem with quotes within strings. For example, the apostrophe is a valid character to have in a string, and if a field contained an apostrophe, you wouldn't want the field terminated. You should be aware of what your data contains before you try this method, as the (mis)use of commas and quotes can have unpredictable results.

Fixed Width Text Files

The other method of transferring data via text files avoids any possible confusion over quotes, field separators, and field names. It requires the use of a specification to detail the field name, where the field starts, and how long it is. The easiest way to create these is through the Text Export Wizard.

Try It Out—Creating an Export Specification for a Fixed Width Text File

1 Go the Queries tab in the database window and open up qryMonthlyWhiskyCount in design view. Select the File menu and select the Save As/Export... option. Next, you must choose to save the query To an External File or Database and click OK.

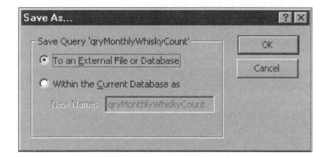

2 Make sure that the Save as type is set to Text Files. You can put in any file name you like as we are not actually going to save the data.

This has changed from Access 95 which allowed you to set the export format before giving a file name.

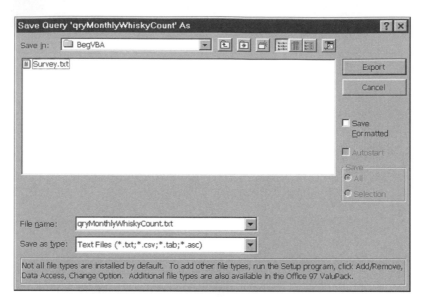

3 Press the Export button to begin the Export Text Wizard. Once the wizard has started up, select the Advanced option to get to the following dialog, and select Fixed Width for the File Format. Make sure you change the **Start** and **Width** columns for the fields so they are the same as the ones below.

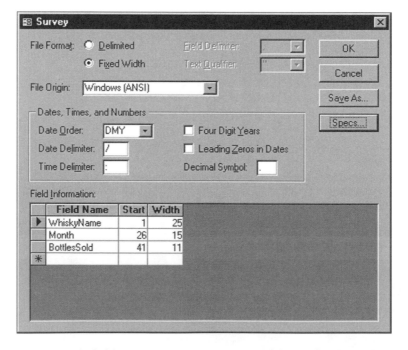

You can see that each field starts at a set position and has a fixed width.

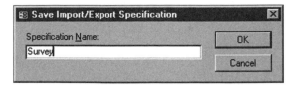

4 Select the Sa<u>v</u>e As option and save it as Survey.

5 Now click Cancel button twice to exit from the format specifications window and the wizard window. We can now use the Survey export specification that we have just created by modifying the code behind the export button as follows :

```
Case 3
DoCmd.TransferText acExportFixed, "Survey" , "qryMonthlyWhiskyCount", _
    "C:\BegVBA\SurveyFW.txt", True
```

6 Now when you run this, the export file looks slightly different:

```
SurveyFW - Notepad
File  Edit  Search  Help
"WhiskyName","Month","BottlesSold"
Aberlour              April 1993     6
Aberlour              April 1994     6
Aberlour              April 1995     6
Aberlour              April 1996     6
Aberlour              April 1997     4
Aberlour              August 1992    6
Aberlour              August 1993    5
Aberlour              August 1994    5
Aberlour              August 1995    1
Aberlour              August 1996    6
Aberlour              December 1992  4
Aberlour              December 1993  10
Aberlour              December 1994  11
Aberlour              December 1995  6
Aberlour              December 1996  6
Aberlour              February 1993  4
```

Here, you see a curious anomaly that has still not been fixed. Even though you have specified a fixed width file, this doesn't seem to apply if you opt to use the first row as column headings, since these use the CSV format. The other lines, however, obey the fixed width rule and are neatly aligned. This is documented, but not very clearly, and no reason is given for this behavior. We can only assume, either that, for some obscure reason, column headings must always use CSV format, or more likely—it was a bug in early versions, and Microsoft have decided it's easier to document than to fix!

Mail Merge

With the vast amount of data that is now stored in databases, it's important to be able to merge data into word processing documents. For example, this allows The Whisky Shop to send out mailings to all their customers, notifying them of special offers and promotions, as well as preparing the normal statements and invoices.

Try It Out—Creating a Mail Merge File

You can use the export facilities of Access 97 to create a Microsoft Word mail merge file.

1 Add another option button to the Outside World form, this time with a value of 4, and label it as shown here:

2 Add the following code to the **Select Case** statement:

```
Case 4
    DoCmd.TransferText acExportMerge, , "qryCompanyAddress", _
        "C:\BegVBA\Customers.DOC"
```

3 Now switch the form to Form view, select the mail merge option and click Export. This will create a Microsoft Word **Customers.DOC** file that can be used as the data source for a mail merge.

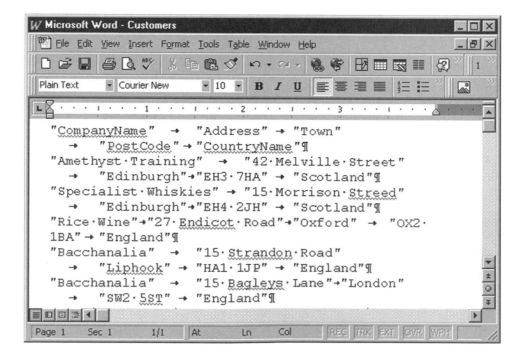

The arrows on the screenshot show that a Word mail merge file uses the tab character as the field separator. Text strings are enclosed in quotes.

You will see other examples of outputting data to Word later in the book.

Outputting Other Objects

So far, you have only seen how to export data from tables or as the results of running queries, but there will be many occasions when you'll want to output the data from other Access objects. In these cases, you can use the **OutputTo** method of the **DoCmd** object:

```
DoCmd.OutputTo ObjectType [, ObjectName] [, OutputFormat] _
     [, OutputFile] [, AutoStart], [TemplateFile]
```

The arguments are shown below:

Argument	Description
ObjectType	The object you wish to output. This must be one of: acOutputForm acOutputModule acOutputQuery acOutputReport acOutputTable
ObjectName	The name of the Access object.
OutputFormat	The format to output the object in. It must be one of: acFormatActiveXServer for Microsoft Active Server Pages acFormatHTML for an HTML document acFormatIIS for Microsoft Internet Information Server acFormatRTF for Rich Tech Format acFormatTXT for Notepad text acFormatXLS for Microsoft Excel format
OutputFile	The name of the file (including the path) to which the object is output.
AutoStart	Use **True** to automatically start the application associated with the output type, **False** otherwise. If left blank, **False** is taken as the default.
TemplateFile	The name of the template for HTML, HTX or ASP files. We will be looking at these in more detail in Chapter 17, The Internet.

Try It Out—The OutputTo Command

1 From the Report tab open **rptWhiskyTotal**. Notice that it has some formatted text. We are now going to output this to a Rich Text File.

2 Open the Outside World form and add a fifth option button to it. This will have a value of 5:

3 Then add the code to the **Select Case** statement:

```
Case 5
    DoCmd.OutputTo acOutputReport, "rptWhiskyTotal", _
        acFormatRTF, "C:\BegVBA\WhiskyTotal.RTF", True
```

4 When you open **frmOutsideWorld**, choose this option and click Export, and Word will automatically be started with this document

Note that the file name contains **RTF** as a suffix, so that Windows 95 or Windows NT can identify the type of file. **RTF** stands for Rich Text Format, which allows formatting to be contained in the text document, and is a Microsoft standard for formatting documents. Using this ensures that Word is started for you. Likewise, if you use the **acFormatXLS**, you should add **XLS** to the end of the filename. Even though Access 97 knows the type of file that you are creating, it doesn't add the suffix for you.

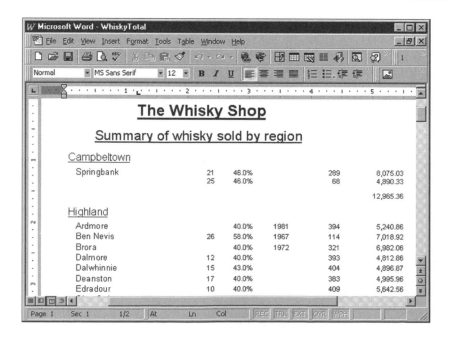

You can see that, because it is an **RTF** file, all of the formatting has been kept. However, notice that the line that was just above the region total is not transferred. Beware of this if you use graphics in your reports, since these are not saved in an RTF file. This option is useful if you need to distribute simple reports without having them printed out.

Electronic Mail

Another way of distributing data is via electronic mail. The great advantage of using e-mail is the ease with which you can send data, not only around local networks but also around the world. The increase in global networks (Microsoft Network, CompuServe, America On Line, the Internet, etc.) has decreased the time it takes for people to get the information they need—no longer do you have to print off a report, photocopy it five times and then post it to your branch offices. Instead, you just pick their names from your electronic address book and send the report in minutes.

You can send mail with a variety of mail clients, such as Microsoft Exchange and Outlook, Eudora, Pegasus, etc. I have used Microsoft Outlook in the examples since that is what I use at home, but other clients should work just as well.

The great beauty of Microsoft Outlook is that it can be used as a single mail client to many different types of networks and, because Outlook handles all the addressing, you don't need to know which type you are using. You just specify the addressee, and Outlook will manage the delivery of the mail.

Transferring data via Mail uses the **SendObject** method of the **DoCmd** object.

```
DoCmd.SendObject [ObjectType] [, ObjectName] [, OutputFormat] [, To] _
    [, CC] [, BCC] [, Subject] [, MessageText] [, EditMessage], _
        [TemplateFile]
```

Although there are more arguments than the previous examples, they are all very simple:

Argument	Description
ObjectType	The object you wish to output. It must be one of: acSendForm acSendModule acSendNoObject (for just sending a mail message) acSendQuery acSendReport acSendTable If you leave this item blank acSendNoObject is used.
ObjectName	The name of the Access object.
OutputFormat	The format to output the object in. This must be one of: acFormatXLS for Microsoft Excel format acFormatRTF for Microsoft Word rich text format acFormatTXT for Notepad text format acFormatHTML for HTML format If you leave this item blank Access will prompt you for the format.

Table Continued on Following Page

243

Argument	Description
To	A list of recipients for the mail. If there is more than one, they should be seperated with a semicolon (or with the List Separator shown on the Number tab of the Regional Settings properties sheet in the Windows control panel). Access prompts you for the recipients if you leave this item blank.
CC	A list of recipients for the **cc** line.
BCC	A list of recipients for the **bcc** line.
Subject	A string containing the subject line of the mail.
MessageText	A string containing the text for the message body. This is placed after the attached object.
EditMessage	To open the mail application immediately (to allow editing), you should use **True**. To send the message straight away, you should use **False**. If left blank, the default of **True** is assumed.
TemplateFile	The name of the file (including the path) for use as a template with HTML documents.

In the next example, a report is sent to several people, one of whom uses CompuServe, another Internet Mail, and another Microsoft Exchange. All you need do in Access, though, is to specify the name. There is no need to know what type of mail is being sent.

Try It Out—Electronic Mail

Obviously, to run this example, you will need to be connected to some form of mail system. However, even if you aren't, it's still worth following it through without actually implementing it, as it will show you just how easy it is to add this facility to your Access applications.

1 Add another option button to the group—this time it will have the value 6.

2 As this form is a fairly general export form, you don't want to clutter it up with mail details, so it's best to leave all the addresses blank. Therefore, add the following code to the **Select Case** statement:

```
Case 6
    DoCmd.SendObject acQuery, "qryWhiskyAndPrices", acFormatXLS, _
        , , , "Price List", "Here's our latest price list", True
```

Here we are sending the monthly sales query in Microsoft Excel format.

3 Run this bit of code by selecting the sixth option button in form view and clicking <u>E</u>xport. The **To**, **cc**, and **bcc** fields have been left blank, so the mail system will open as normal and allow us to select from the normal list of addressees who the object is to be sent to.

You can see that the **Subject** line has been filled in and the extra text has been placed after the object.

If you fill in the **To** line in the code, then set the **EditMessage** argument to **False**, the mail is delivered straight away and you aren't even aware of anything happening. It's as easy as that. So, if anyone tells you that communicating via Mail in Access is hard, just put them straight.

External Data

In the previous sections of this chapter, we have looked at how to get data into and out of Access, but there are occasions when you need to use data from elsewhere without importing it. Access can access (no pun intended) data from other sources, and they all appear as though they are Access tables, allowing you to store data in a variety of formats, but use it from within Access. If this is the case, you can **link** the data into your database. This works in a similar way to shortcuts in Windows 95—the data stays where it is, but you get a shortcut to it. If the data changes, you see those changes. If you change the data in your link, the original data changes.

So what's the use of having data elsewhere and just linking it into Access?

Well, for a start, Access is a great way to develop new systems, but you often have a large amount of existing data. Linking allows access to data in old databases or spreadsheets, while a new system is being developed. Alternatively, you may wish to use the superior querying and reporting facilities of Access, while keeping the existing application.

You may also want to separate the back end of your database from the front end. The back end is generally defined as the actual data, whilst the front end is the user interface. It includes the forms, reports, queries, macros and modules. This would split your application into two Access databases:

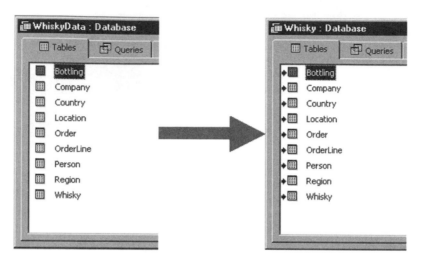

This is quite a common technique that allows you to update the front end without affecting the back end. Remember how hard it is to distribute applications to users? No sooner have you given them a copy of the latest database, than they want to make changes—but they have already started entering data. So, not only do you have to make the changes, but you also have to stop them all using the old database and copy the data to the new one. But if you split the front end from the back end, the database with the data never changes—you can replace the front end at will and just re-link the tables.

Should you decide to take this approach after you've already created an application, choose the Database Splitter subcommand on the Add-ins command on the Tools menu. The wizard attached to this command will guide you through the steps of separating your tables from the rest of the database objects.

Linking is also useful given the increasing popularity of client/server systems. Here, the back end of your database is usually a powerful database server, such as Microsoft SQL Server, giving you the advantage of all the features that a big relational database provides. You can have all your data on the server to make the most of its power, whilst still utilizing the features of Access, such as the forms, queries and reports.

In most cases, you can even move your queries to the server and execute them there rather than on your own machine. This can show a great speed improvement and also has the added advantage of minimizing network traffic. The only things that pass across the network are your instruction to start the query and the table of results coming back. This is part of client/server design, ensuring that the client and server (SQL Server, for example) do what they are best at—letting the server do the long queries, and using Access tables for quick access to information that does not change often. This is an area that is to large to cover here, and may not be relevant for many of you, but there are new books popping up all of the time on this topic if you wish to read more about it.

In version 2.0 of Access and earlier, linked tables were called attached tables.

Linked Tables

You may well have used linked tables before—they are easy to spot. Linked tables are marked in the Tables sheet of the database window with an arrow:

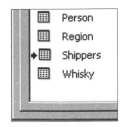

The figure shows a table in the sample **Northwind** database (supplied with Access) which has been linked to our **Whisky** application. You can delete a link at any time without deleting the actual table.

Try It Out—Linking an Object

In this example, we will use the **acLink** argument of the **TransferSpreadsheet** method of the **DoCmd** object. You can also use this argument with **TransferDatabase** and **TransferText**. We will link a spreadsheet into our application but, as we don't want to make this a permanent feature of the application, will do so using the debug window.

1 Open a new module and type the following code into the debug window:

```
DoCmd.TransferSpreadsheet acLink, 5, "WhiskySales", _
    "C:\BegVBA\WhiskySales.XLS"
```

This will link the spreadsheet that we created earlier. The second argument simply indicates that we are linking to an Excel version 5.0 or 7.0 file.

2 Now look at the Tables sheet of the database window. You should see a new linked object, which is really a spreadsheet (you may need to switch to another page and back before it appears):

This shows that not only do you see tables here, but you also see other sources of data. As long as Access can link to them, then they can be edited as though they are an Access table.

You can open **WhiskySales** as though it was a normal table. Any changes that you make to it will be reflected in the spreadsheet, but beware of columns that contain confusing data.

WhiskySales : Table		
F1	**F2**	**F3**
Month	Year	#Num!
Jan	1993	£9,491.25
Jan	1994	£5,961.47
Jan	1995	£6,682.48
Jan	1996	£8,331.49
Jan	1997	£5,163.81
Feb	1993	£5,265.97
Feb	1994	£11,749.09
Feb	1995	£7,405.72
Feb	1996	£5,593.75
Feb	1997	£9,785.32
Mar	1993	£8,166.95

Access has detected that the third column is full of numbers but the first row contains the column headings, which are text. If you intend to link spreadsheets this way you should ensure that the column headings are removed, or use the Range argument in the link to only include the correct data.

Try It Out—Refreshing the Link

If you do intend to split a database into a back and front end, you obviously need a way to refresh the link between the tables. This is useful, not only when you distribute a new copy of the front end database, but also if the back end database is installed in a different place from where Access expects to find it.

1 Create a new database (call it **BackEnd**) and click Create. To import the tables from the sample database, select the File/Get External Data menu and click the Import option. Next, select **Whisky8.mdb** in the Import dialog, click the Select All button and in the ensuing Import Objects dialog, click OK.

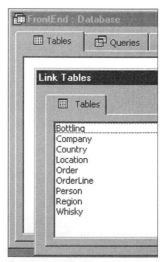

2 Close down this database, create another blank database (**FrontEnd**) and link the tables from the **BackEnd** database by selecting the Link Tables option from the File/Get External Data menu. Then repeat the above process.

3 Now rename the **BackEnd** database **NewBackEnd** and try to open one of the linked tables:

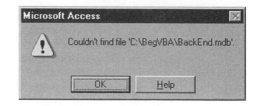

The tables here are just links. They don't actually exist in the **FrontEnd** database. Therefore, if you try accessing one when the back end database has moved, you'll get an error.

We'll now re-link the tables.

4 Create a new module and add a function called **RefreshTableLinks**. Add the following code:

```
Public Function RefreshTableLinks(strDB As String) As Integer

    Dim dbCurrent        As Database     ' current database
    Dim tblLinked        As TableDef     ' current table in collection

    On Error GoTo RefreshTableLinks_Err

    Set dbCurrent = CurrentDb()
    For Each tblLinked In dbCurrent.TableDefs
        If tblLinked.Connect <> "" Then
            tblLinked.Connect = ";DATABASE=" & strDB
            tblLinked.RefreshLink
        End If
    Next

    RefreshTableLinks = True

RefreshTableLinks_Exit:
    Exit Function

RefreshTableLinks_Err:
    MsgBox Error$
    RefreshTableLinks = False
    Resume RefreshTableLinks_Exit

End Function
```

5 Now open the debug window and call the function as follows:

```
RefreshTableLinks("C:\BegVBA\NewBackEnd.mdb")
```

6 Close down the module window and try opening a table again. This time, there should be no error message—you have re-linked the tables so Access has no problem finding the data.

How It Works

The function loops through the tables and modifies their **Connect property**. This property defines the connect string for a linked table. We then use the **RefreshLink** method to make sure that the link is refreshed. Let's have a look at the code in more detail:

```
Set dbCurrent = CurrentDb()
For Each tblLinked In dbCurrent.TableDefs
```

We start by opening the current database and cycling through the **TableDefs** collection.

```
If tblLinked.Connect <> "" Then
    tblLinked.Connect = ";DATABASE=" & strDB
```

We then check for a non-empty string in the **Connect** property. For local tables it will be empty—we don't want to update it for these. However, if it has a value, it needs to be updated with the new database name (passed to the function as **strDB**). The **Connect** property is the path and name of the database from which you are linking the tables. It takes the following form:

> **object.Connect = [databasetype;[parameters;]]**

We use the table that we've found in the loop, **tblLinked**, as the **object**. The **databasetype** argument is a string identifying the type of file—for Access this argument is left blank but we must still include the semicolon as the argument placeholder. If we wanted to connect to a Paradox table, the argument would be **"Paradox 5.x"** or similar. You'll find a full list of the identifiers in the Access Help file—search on Connect Property.

Finally, **parameters** is the full path and file name of the database preceded by **DATABASE=**, in our case **"DATABASE="** & **strDB**.

```
tblLinked.RefreshLink
    End If
Next
```

Now we end the loop by refreshing the link. We must do this because simply setting the **Connect** property doesn't cause the link to be re-established automatically. We use the **RefreshLink** method of the table object to do this.

You could, of course, extend this procedure and ask for the new name of the database, instead of accepting it as a parameter. This would add a greater degree of flexibility.

Differences between Linked and Local Tables

Linked tables have several advantages over local ones but, as with everything, there is a certain price to pay:

▶ As linked tables aren't part of your database, and the records have to be retrieved from another file every time you access them, you might experience speed problems—especially if the linked table is on another machine on the network.

▶ Linked tables must be opened as dynaset- or snapshot-type recordsets and, therefore, they don't support the **Seek** method which is only applicable to table-type recordsets.

▶ You must be careful when joining tables from different places (e.g. one local and one remote) as the field types may not be completely compatible. For example, you could have problems if you joined two date fields when one is held in US format and the other is British format.

▶ You must be careful when joining large linked tables to small local tables. If both tables are local, Access can optimize the join but, if a large table is linked, all the data must be brought across before the join can take place. And, of course, you still have to take into account the overhead of transferring the data again as the query is executed.

However, do not let the above put you off trying this. The back end/front end solution is extremely useful for a lot of business where a database application is being constantly changed, or delivered in stages.

ODBC

ODBC stands for **Open DataBase Connectivity** which is just another way of accessing external data. All databases store their data in different formats and use different methods of accessing it. As you have seen, you can link tables from various different types of database to your Access database. However, this only tends to include the desktop systems such as dBase and Paradox types.

To allow all database systems to exchange data more freely requires a common method of accessing them—using suitable software **drivers** which sit between the database engine and the other system's data. ODBC is the computer industry method of achieving this—a single system with a widely published interface that other database manufacturers have supported by producing their own drivers. Microsoft started this off several years ago, but international standards groups now control it and almost every database supports ODBC, including Oracle, IBM DB/2, Ingres and Informix. The great advantage is that programs can be written using the standard ODBC interface and they will work with any database for which drivers are available. The following figure shows how the different components fit together:

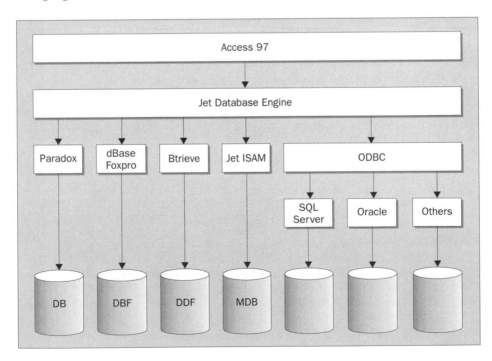

You can see that the Jet database engine supports a few common desktop database formats directly through drivers that are included in Access, and then ODBC as a separate entity in the driver 'layer'. The ODBC manager can then support as many databases as it likes, each through its own driver layer. Most major databases, such as Oracle, DB2 and other mainframe and mini-based systems, support ODBC giving a great deal of flexibility. If your needs change, so can your database.

Linking a Table using ODBC

ODBC databases are accessed by creating a data source. This is done using the Windows 95 Control Panel:

Selecting the 32-bit ODBC icon allows you to set up your ODBC data source:

ODBC

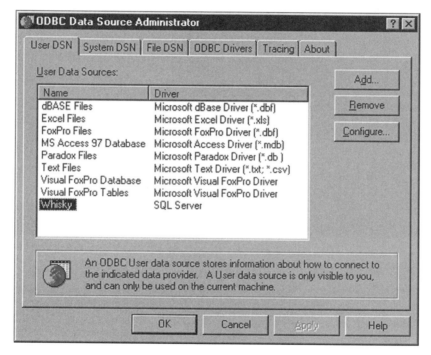

In this case, the data source Whisky is set as a Microsoft SQL Server database.

Once you have an ODBC data source set up, you can link tables in the usual way:

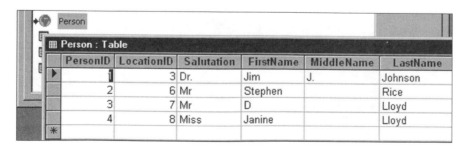

Even though this is a Microsoft SQL Server table, because it is linked it behaves just like any other linked table.

Using ODBC with Pass-through Queries

You can also access ODBC data sources without linking them into Access as we did earlier. This method is used more in Microsoft Visual Basic than in Access' VBA language, but it does give speed improvements. Have another look at the database diagram, this time with the connection to ODBC amended:

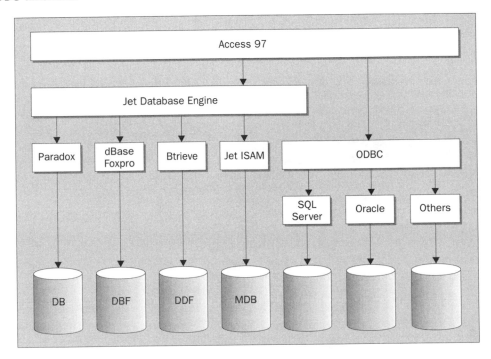

Here you can see that the Jet database engine is being bypassed altogether. We access the ODBC driver directly from Access. To do this we use a **pass-through query**, a special kind that is selected from the Queries menu. It is created as an SQL statement, in the language of the server database rather than Access' own SQL syntax.

Access' version of SQL is non-standard in many respects, and will almost definitely be different to the language used by the server—especially with regard to data types.

This method is known as pass-through because queries can be passed directly through to the ODBC layer, and then on to a remote database server. The advantage is that, because Jet has no part to play, there is one less stage to go through and thus it is faster. And, of course, because the query is executed on the server, only the initial SQL string and the returned records have to be passed between the machines.

There are, however, a couple of points that you must watch for when doing this:

▶ Linked tables are not possible using this method—instead we are accessing the tables *directly on the server*. This means that you can't create updatable (dynaset-type) recordsets based on these tables. Any recordset that you create is automatically a snapshot-type, so any updating has to be done with queries and the Data Description Language.

▶ When you use pass-through queries, however, queries are sent directly to the server. This means that SQL statements must be in the format used by the server that you are connecting to. (When you use linked tables with ODBC, as in the previous section, queries are first processed by the Jet database engine and then converted into a SQL statement that the server understands.)

Pass-through is extremely fast, but the cost is flexibility. You will have to do more things manually if you use this method, but the benefits can be worth it. Not only can a large database server store the data more easily, but it is likely to be faster when processing it—so all of your queries can be run on the database server as well.

This has only been a brief look at ODBC, showing a few similarities with linked tables and the sort of benefits that you can expect when using it. Whole books have been written on ODBC and client/server development techniques, and they are really beyond the scope of this book.

Summary

This chapter has shown you that Access 97 doesn't stand alone as a database. With just a few commands you can get access to information held in a wide variety of formats. Not only can you copy this data into Access 97 tables, but you can also link it and use it without requiring the original application. This makes Access 97 useful for providing a new look to an old application.

The ability to retrieve data from Access 97 is just as important as getting it in, and the same commands provide this. Many people find that Access 97 is a great repository for information but, being used to spreadsheets, they often want to analyze their data there, so the need to provide your applications with an interface to the outside world is extremely important.

This chapter has covered:

▶ Using the **Transfer** method of the **DoCmd** object

▶ Exporting data to database, spreadsheet, text and mail merge files

▶ Linking tables to other applications

▶ Refreshing links between tables

▶ A brief overview of ODBC

Later in the book, you will see other ways of exchanging information with Microsoft Word and Excel, which give you an even greater degree of flexibility and power.

Exercises

1   Use the Database Splitter to create a back-end and front-end database. Are there any changes you need to make to the font end to make sure that it still works correctly?

2   If you are connected to a mail system create a form to allow users to fill in Bug Reports and Enhancement requests, and use the **SendObject** method to let the user send them to you.

Reports

Reports, like forms, are one of the most visible aspects of Access 97. The users see them, managers see them and customers see them. Therefore, they have to look good. A clear, concise report can say much about your organization. Fortunately, creating great-looking reports is extremely simple in Access 97, and the use of code can further tweak them to add that final touch. Most of the code used in reports will be very short, sometimes only one line, but the effect it can bring can make all the difference.

In this chapter, you will be looking at:

- ▶ How to use expressions
- ▶ Using the **IIf** function
- ▶ Adding and summarizing data to provide totals
- ▶ Using print events in a report

Expressions

You have come across plenty of expressions in previous chapters, though you might not have realized it. An expression is simply something that returns a value, for example:

```
Total = Cost * Quantity
```

In reports, you use expressions to combine values. The following example demonstrates this.

Try It Out—Expressions

Next month the auditors are visiting The Whisky Shop and have asked for a complete list of orders to be ready for their inspection. There is a report similar to the one we want, but it needs a few additions.

1 Open **Whisky9.mdb** and open the report **rptFullOrderDetails** in Preview mode:

> **rptFullOrderDetails : Report**
>
> ## Full Order Details
>
> Amethyst Training   Amethyst Edinburgh   Scotland
>
> **Order Number: AME0010**   Order Date: 29/11/92
>
> | Whisky Name | Bottling Details | Quantity | Price |
> |---|---|---|---|
> | Glen Moray | 17 years old, 43.00%, distilled in | 1 | £22.69 |
> | Glenturret | 12 years old, 40.00%, distilled in | 1 | £23.49 |
> | Glengoyne | 12 years old, 40.00%, distilled in | 1 | £18.99 |
>
> **Order Number: AME0011**   Order Date: 28/12/92
>
> | Whisky Name | Bottling Details | Quantity | Price |
> |---|---|---|---|
> | Glendronach | 12 years old, 40.00%, distilled in | 1 | £20.99 |
> | Oban | 14 years old, 43.00%, distilled in | 1 | £22.99 |

This report might look fine at first glance, but it's missing some important information. There is no line total, order total, page numbers, and the Bottling Details column is not finished correctly.

2 Now open the report in Design view and add an unbound text box to the right of the Cost field in the detail section. Cut and paste the label into the header section and change its caption to Line Total.

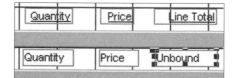

3 To calculate the line total, you need to use an expression placed in the Control Source property. The expression is very simple:

```
=[Quantity]*[Price]
```

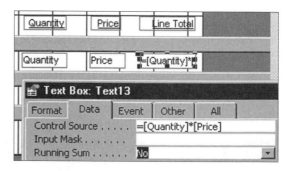

Notice that there is an equals sign at the beginning, which tells Access that it's an expression.

4 Change the Format property (on the Format tab) of the text box to Currency and switch to Preview mode to see the results. You might have to page down a little to find an order line with a quantity greater than one. Unfortunately, not many people buy more than one bottle of the same type at a time!

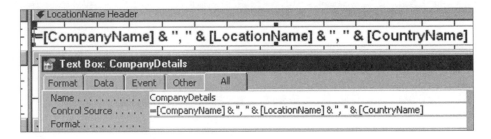

We could also tidy up the line with the company details. This still looks a bit messy, as there are three separate fields and, if one field is short, there could be a large empty gap.

5 To tidy this up, we'll join the fields together using what is called **concatenation**. Delete them from the report and add an unbound field in their place. Then change the field's Control Source property to the expression:

```
=[CompanyName] & ", " & [LocationName] & ", " & [CountryName]
```

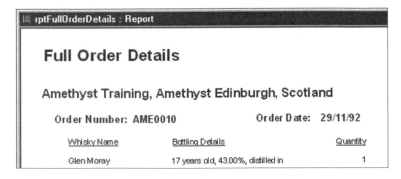

Here, we use the string concatenation character (the ampersand) to join the three strings together. There is also a comma and a space between each field.

6 Now switch to Preview mode:

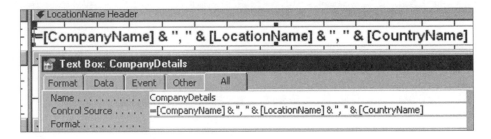

You can see that using expressions on reports is extremely simple. For the line total and the company and location details, you would probably be better putting them into the query upon which the report is based. For example, the line total could be added to the query as:

Quantity	Price	LineTotal: [Quantity]*[Price]
OrderLine	Bottling	
☑	☑	☑

This is better because the expression becomes a new field in the resulting recordset, and can, therefore, be used by other reports based on the query.

Page Numbers

Page numbers are extremely important on reports. You should show the total number of pages, as well as the current page number. Then, if you are looking at a report which says 'Page 1 of 10' and you only have 8 pages, you know that something is wrong.

Try It Out—Page Numbers

1 We need to add yet another unbound text box to the report, but this time you can save some time. Select the Page Numbers... option from the Insert menu:

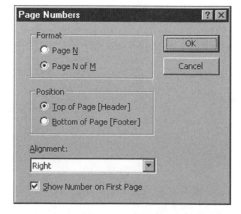

2 Then select the following options from the dialog that appears and click OK.

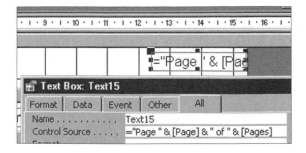

This will automatically add a field with the expression you need. You might like to increase the size a little.

3 Another item that is useful on a report is the current date, to show when the data was produced. There is nothing worse than having a report full of figures and not knowing how up-to-date they are. Again, you can use an option from the Insert menu:

4 Select the following options from the dialog:

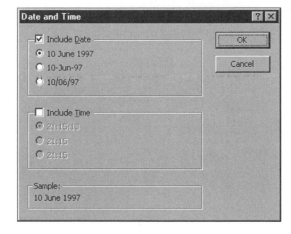

5 Click OK and Access will place the field in the detail section of your report. It is a good idea to move this to the page footer:

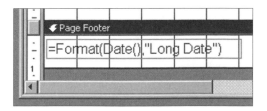

Yes/No Values

Yes and No values can be represented on reports in the same way as on forms: by using tick boxes, check boxes or radio buttons.

The Whisky Shop has a target of sending an order out within two working days of receiving it. To see whether the target has been met would involve adding the `SentDate` column from the query to the report, and then calculating the difference between the two dates. Not a difficult task, but a Yes/No value would be easier to understand at a glance than a column of figures.

Try It Out—Yes/No Values

1 In the OrderNumber Header section add a check box to the right of the OrderDate field—you might have to move the OrderDate to the left a little for this. Change its Caption to Target Met, and move the caption to the left. It's also a good idea to format it the same as the other fields in this section so that it stands out.

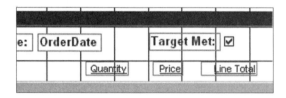

2 Now modify the Control Source so that it checks for a value in the Sent date field:

Here we need to check whether the difference between the date the order was sent and the date it was placed is less than two. When subtracting one date from another the difference is the number of days, so we can just compare that to our target figure. Notice that we have used parenthesis to force the operator precedence, making sure that the difference is calculated before being compared to a value of two. The whole expression will return **True** if it is less than two days, and **False** if not, so the check box gets set accordingly.

3 Run the report to see the results. On the first few orders the target was not met, but later on it was.

Order Number: AME0010	Order Date: 29/11/92			Target Met: ☐	
Whisky Name	Bottling Details		Quantity	Price	Line Total
Glen Moray	17 years old, 43.00%, distilled in		1	£22.69	£22.69
Glengoyne	12 years old, 40.00%, distilled in		1	£18.99	£18.99
Glenturret	12 years old, 40.00%, distilled in		1	£23.49	£23.49

Order Number: AME0023	Order Date: 31/12/93		Target Met: ☑	
Whisky Name	Bottling Details	Quantity	Price	Line Total
Glen Grant	10 years old, 40.00%, distilled in	1	£18.99	£18.99
Glenfiddich	years old, 40.00%, distilled in	1	£19.99	£19.99

This is much easier to see than adding the date sent to the report and working out the difference for yourself.

IIf

We first met the **IIf** function in Chapter 4, and, despite our warnings, it is very useful when it comes to creating reports as it gives decision-making ability within one line. This often fits well within the Control Source property of a control.

One of the most common uses of **IIf** is in conjunction with the **IsNull** function. It allows you to test whether a value in a field is null and then return one of two values, depending on the result of the test.

Try It Out—The IIf function

	The Glenlivet 12 years old, 40.00%, distilled in
	Glen Keith years old, 43.00%, distilled in 1983
Have a look at the bottling details column.	Aberlour 10 years old, 40.00%, distilled in
	Glen Moray 12 years old, 40.00%, distilled in
	Brora years old, 40.00%, distilled in 1972
	Oban 14 years old, 43.00%, distilled in

You can see that this is messy because not every bottling of whisky has a specific year or distillation date. What is really needed is to only show them if they exist.

1 Edit the Control Source for this field. You need to replace the first section that shows the age

```
[Age] & " years old, "
```

with the following **IIf** statement:

```
IIf(IsNull([Age]), "", [Age] & " years old,")
```

This line simply checks whether **Age** is null and, if it is, returns an empty string (denoted by **""**). If it isn't null the value and the string after it are returned. Remember that **IIf** accepts three arguments: the first is the item we want to test, the second is the value to return if the test is true and the third is the value to return if the test is false.

The Glenlivet	12 year old,40.00%, distilled in
Glen Keith	43.00%, distilled in 1983
Aberlour	10 year old,40.00%, distilled in
Glen Moray	12 year old,40.00%, distilled in
Brora	40.00%, distilled in 1972
Oban	14 year old,43.00%, distilled in

2 Now run the report. You should see that the first part is now tidy.

3 The distillation date needs looking at now, so replace

```
", distilled in " & [DistillationDate]
```

with the following:

```
IIf(IsNull([DistillationDate]), "", ", distilled in " &
[DistillationDate])
```

As with above this checks the **DistillationDate** and, if it is null, just uses an empty string.

The Glenlivet	12 year old,40.00%
Glen Keith	43.00%, distilled in 1983
Aberlour	10 year old,40.00%
Glen Moray	12 year old,40.00%
Brora	40.00%, distilled in 1972
Oban	14 year old,43.00%

4 Try running the report now and it should look much better.

Totals

The one thing missing from this report is totals. Again, these are extremely easy to add. The grouping facility on reports gives you the ability to add totals at any level with one simple action.

Try It Out—Adding Totals

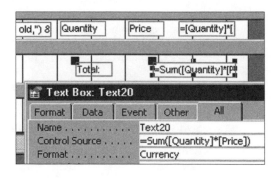

1 Switch back to Design view and add a text box in the OrderNumber Footer. Set the Control Source property to perform the totaling for you:

That is all you have to do! When you use the **Sum** function in a group footer, it sums all of the values for that particular group. Notice that because the line total field is calculated on the report, you also have to do this for the group total. This is another good reason for adding the line total to the query—then you can just sum the line total column and the information can be included in other reports.

2 Switch to Preview mode to see how this works:

The Glenlivet	12 year old, 40.00%	1	£19.99	£19.99
Glen Keith	43.00%, distilled in 1983	1	£19.99	£19.99
Aberlour	10 year old, 40.00%	1	£17.69	£17.69
Glen Moray	12 year old, 40.00%	1	£17.49	£17.49
Brora	40.00%, distilled in 1972	1	£35.99	£35.99
Oban	14 year old, 43.00%	1	£22.99	£22.99
		Total:		£226.90

Remember, if you place the **Sum** function in a control in the page or report footer, it will sum the values over the whole page or report, rather than over the group.

Print Events

The above examples have illustrated how you can use simple expressions to enhance your reports. What you may not realize, however, is that reports also respond to events, just like forms. For example, opening and closing a report generates events and you can add code to respond to these just as you would with the events in a form.

To add event procedures to your report, you can do one of two things. You can press the right mouse button when you have a section highlighted and select Build Event....

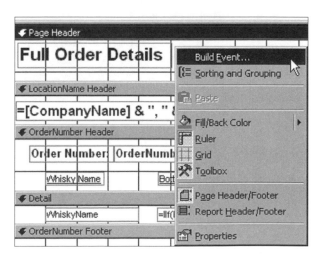

Or you can use the Event page on the property sheet and click the builder button against the event you wish to create a procedure for:

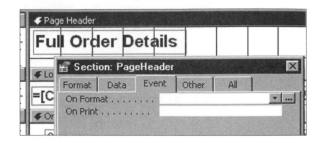

This will open up the module window.

FYI Report modules are just like form modules and follow exactly the same rules. The module window is exactly the same, the only difference being the objects available and the events to which they respond. Just like forms, you can create general procedures that are only applicable, and available, to the report.

Let's have a look at the events in detail.

Open

The Open event is generated when a report is opened, before any printing takes place. You could use this event to warn users that a report may take a long time, or even to password protect sensitive reports. Have a look at the following code:

```
Private Sub Report_Open(Cancel As Integer)

    Dim strPwd As String

    strPwd = InputBox("Please enter the report password", "Password")
    If strPwd <> "OpenTheReportHAL" Then
        MsgBox "I'm afraid I can't do that Dave!"
        Cancel = True
    End If

End Sub
```

In this case, when the report is opened, an input box will be displayed requesting the password.

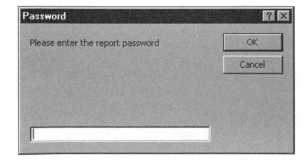

If the correct password (which in this case is case sensitive) is not supplied, the **Cancel** argument will be set to **True**. This cancels the Open event and, because the Open event is triggered before the report becomes visible, the report does not open.

Activate

The Activate event is generated when a report that has been opened becomes the active window. Therefore, it occurs after the open event. It can be used in much the same way as for forms—for example, to display a custom menu or toolbar:

```
Private Sub Report_Activate()

    DoCmd.ShowToolbar "FullOrder", acToolbarYes

End Sub
```

Deactivate

The Deactivate event is triggered when a report window stops being the active window, but before another Access window becomes active. It only occurs before another *Access* window becomes active—not before another application becomes the active window. It can be used to reverse the actions of the activate event—for example, to remove a toolbar:

```
Private Sub Report_Deactivate()

    DoCmd.ShowToolbar "FullOrder", acToolbarNo

End Sub
```

Close

The Close event occurs when a report is closed and removed from the screen. If, for example, you had kept a table containing usage details for all forms and reports, you could use this event to log who was using the report. In the example below, we use a procedure we've written called **LogUsage** to do this. It accepts two arguments—the first is the name of the report, the second the name of the user opening the report.

```
Private Sub Report_Close ()

    Call LogUsage (Me, CurrentUser)

End Sub
```

Error

The Error event occurs when an error is generated within a report. This includes database errors, but not VBA run-time errors. When this event occurs, two arguments are passed into the procedure. The first, **DataErr**, is the error number, as set by **Err**. The second, **Response**, determines whether or not error messages should be displayed and takes one of two values (defined as intrinsic constants):

Value	Meaning
`acDataErrContinue`	The error should be ignored and the Access error message will not be displayed.
`acDataErrDisplay`	The default Access error message should be displayed. This is the default.

If you use `acDataErrContinue`, you should supply an error message of your own, otherwise the error will be completely ignored. Alternatively, you could log the error and continue:

```
Private Sub Report_Error (DataErr as Integer, Response as Integer)

    Response = acDataErrContinue
    LogError (Me, DataErr)

End Sub
```

Here, we've canceled the display of the error by setting the **Response** argument to **acDataErrContinue**. Then, we execute another procedure called **LogError** (not shown) which records details of the error in a log file.

Format

The Format event is quite useful, since it is generated when Access knows what data is going to be placed in a section, but before it is formatted. This means that you should use it when your event procedure will change the layout of a section. One of its main uses is to make fields visible or invisible, depending upon certain criteria.

Try It Out—The Format Event

Suppose you want to display information regarding a new discount scheme on your invoices, but only want it for orders over a certain amount.

1 Open the invoice report, **rptInvoice**, in Design mode and add a label in the OrderNumber Footer. Type in the caption as shown in the screenshot and name the label lblAccount.

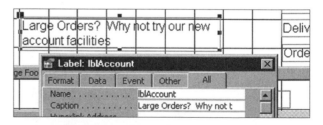

2 Now click on the OrderNumber Footer bar or on a blank area of the footer. Select the Event tab, click the builder button next to the On Format event and select Code Builder. You can now amend the subroutine so that it looks like this:

```
Private Sub GroupFooter2_Format(Cancel As Integer, _
        FormatCount As Integer)
```

```
    If txtTotal > 1000 Then
        lblAccount.Visible = True
    Else
        lblAccount.Visible = False
    End If

End Sub
```

This makes the label visible if the order value is over 1000, otherwise it is hidden.

3 Now switch to Preview mode and see how the label does not appear for the smaller orders, but does for those over 1000.

Large Orders? Why not try our new account facilities

Sub Total:	£1,854.24
Delivery:	£10.00
Order Total:	£1,864.24

You will notice that this event takes two arguments. The first, **Cancel**, works the same as the open event. If you set **Cancel** to **True**, the event is canceled, the section is not formatted and printing moves on to the next section. The second argument, **FormatCount**, determines how many times the section has been formatted. For example, imagine you had a detail section that spanned two lines and you have the KeepTogether property set to Yes. If, when printing, the records do not fit on a page, they are *both* moved to the next one and formatted again, with the result that **FormatCount** is now **2**.

So what's the point of this? Well, for a start you can use it to ensure that any code that you put in the format event is not executed more that once. Imagine that you needed to keep some totals throughout the report, but were unable to use the **Sum** function. By checking **FormatCount**, you can ensure that the totals were not added up more than once.

You could also use this argument to prevent time-consuming procedures being executed more than once within the event procedure.

Try It Out—The FormatCount Property

The Whisky List report, **rptWhiskyTotal**, is a total list of the whiskies sold by whisky and region. If you wanted to total the number of whiskies less than 15 years old and those more than 15 years old for each region you would not be able to use the **Sum** function. The **Sum** function applies to all records, and you need a subset of these records.

1 Open the **rptWhiskyTotal** report in Design view and select Code from the View menu.

2 Add the following variables to the **(General)(Declarations)** section, to declare the global variables which will hold the numbers found:

```
Private intLessThan15 As Integer
Private intMoreThan15 As Integer
```

3 Add the following line to the **GroupHeader0 Format** (the RegionName Header) event which occurs when the *header* section of each group is printed:

```
intLessThan15 = 0
intMoreThan15 = 0
```

This make sure that the total is initialized to zero for each region.

4 Add the following lines to the Format event for the detail section. This event occurs once for every record in this detail section:

```
Select Case Age
    Case Is <= 15
        intLessThan15 = intLessThan15 + 1
    Case Is > 15
        intMoreThan15 = intMoreThan15 + 1
    Case Else
        ' do nothing - ignore whiskies with no explicit age
End Select
```

This checks for the age and increments the appropriate total. Notice that we need to ignore those whiskies with no explicit age.

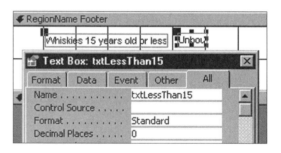

5 Before you can set the total, you need to add two text boxes to the footer for the region. Make their names txtLessThan15 and txtMoreThan15.

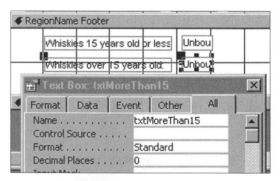

6 Now you need to set the total, so add this to the **GroupFooter1 Format** (the RegionName Footer) event which occurs when the *footer* section of each group is printed:

```
txtLessThan15 = intLessThan15
txtMoreThan15 = intMoreThan15
```

7 To begin with we want to see what happens when all of the whiskies for a region fit on a page, so you'll have to play around with the report a bit. Make the Detail section as small as it will go, with no space above or below the whisky name:

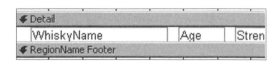

8 Now switch to Preview mode and look at the Islay region.

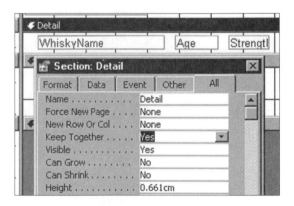

The count is correct.

9 Now increase the size of the Detail section so that some of the whiskies for this region fall over the page. You might have to experiment with this to get the required result. A Height of 0.661cm for the section works on my machine, but your paper size may be different.

10 Now switch to Preview mode to see the results. Some of the whiskies are on the first page, but others have moved to the next page.

The count for the whiskies over 15 years is three instead of two. This is because the first entry on this page, Lagavulin, has been formatted twice—once at the bottom of the previous page and once at the top of this one. Therefore, the code in the Format event occurred twice for this entry. Depending upon which whisky was formatted twice you might find your figures are 7 and 2 rather than 6 and 3. To avoid this, you need to modify your code in the **Detail_Format** method.

8 Change the code in this event to the following:

```
If FormatCount = 1 Then
    Select Case Age
    Case Is <= 15
        intLessThan15 = intLessThan15 + 1
    Case Is > 15
        intMoreThan15 = intMoreThan15 + 1
    Case Else
        ' do nothing - ignore whiskies with no explicit age
    End Select
End If
```

This uses the **FormatCount** argument that Access supplies to this function. When the event is triggered for the whisky on the first page, **FormatCount** is 1 and the totals are incremented. When formatted on the second page, **FormatCount** is 2 and the totals are not incremented. If you switch the report back to Preview mode the totals will now be correct.

FYI   If your page setup is not the same as ours, you may not see an error here. Remember, it only happens if Access formats a section on one page, then finds that it won't fit and has to format it again at the top of the next page.

Print

The Print event is generated after a section has been formatted, but before it is printed. You should use this for performing tasks that are not going to affect the layout of the report, such as totals. But hang on a minute, isn't that what just happened in the format event procedure? Correct, but when using the print event for totals, watch out because the event is only triggered just before the section is printed. So, if a page is skipped, no event gets fired. Imagine you have a report that is performing calculations, creating totals in the print event procedure and then displaying them on a summary page at the end of the report. Now, think about what would happen if the report was opened in Preview mode and the user skipped straight to the last page. The only time the print event would be generated is on the first page, which is always shown, and on the last page. Your totals would not be correct because the event procedure for the intervening pages would not be run.

Retreat

The retreat event is triggered when Access returns to a previous section during formatting. When Access has a section with the Keep Together property set to either Whole Group or With first detail, it must format the section before deciding whether the section fits on the page. Once it has made the decision, it will retreat back up over the section and format it again, either on the current page or on the next page. In this case, the **FormatCount** property is not increased.

Try It Out—The Retreat Event

This is quite a tricky concept to get across, and the best way to understand it is to see exactly when the event is triggered.

1 Switch the report back into Design view and open the Sorting and Grouping window for the RegionName section. You can do this by right mouse clicking on the section bar to get the menu.

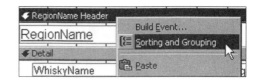

You will then get the following window.

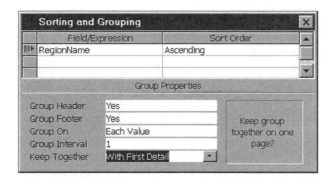

Make sure that the Keep Together property is set as shown, so that the header section is always accompanied by the first detail line (the whisky name). If the header fits at the bottom of a page but the detail line does not, then the header is not printed until the next page.

2 Now view the code and select the **Format** event for the **GroupHeader0** object and add the following line of code, just above your other code:

```
Debug.Print "Group: Format: "; RegionName; " "; FormatCount
```

This will print a message in the Debug window showing the event being processed, the region name (**GroupHeader0** is the Region header) and the value of the **FormatCount** property.

3 Now move to the retreat event for this object and add the following line:

```
Debug.Print "Group: Retreat: "; RegionName
```

Again, this shows the event as it is executed.

4 Select the format event for the detail section and add another line, just above the rest of your code:

```
Debug.Print "Detail: Format: "; WhiskyName; " "; Age; " "; FormatCount
```

This will show the event as it occurs, along with the whisky name, age and value of the **FormatCount** property.

5 Minimize the code window and switch the report to Preview mode, and you will see the report as it was before. Nothing has changed here.

6 Now you need to open the Debug window. You can do easily by pressing *Ctrl-G*, or by displaying the code and pressing the code window button.

```
Group: Format: Campbeltown  1
Detail: Format: Springbank  21    1
Detail: Format: Springbank  25    1
Group: Format: Highland  1
Detail: Format: Ardmore Null  1
Group: Retreat Highland
Group: Format: Highland  1
Detail: Format: Ardmore Null  1
Detail: Format: Ben Nevis  26    1
Detail: Format: Brora Null  1
Detail: Format: Dalmore  12    1
```

7 Click in the Debug window and move the vertical scroll bar to the top so that you can see the first items that were printed.

Let's examine these in a little more detail:

```
Group: Format: Campbeltown  1
Detail: Format: Springbank  21    1
Detail: Format: Springbank  25    1
```

This shows the formatting for the first group and the detail items within that group. The first group is the Campbeltown region, and the whiskies are the 21 and 25 year old Springbanks. When With first detail is used, Access must check that the first record fits on the page, along with the header. The very first record, however, does not need to be checked as this will always be printed on the first page—even if it does not fit. The logic behind this is that if it does not fit on the first page, it will not fit on the others, and so it might as well be printed on the first one anyway.

The next section is for the next group and its detail lines:

```
Group: Format: Highland  1
Detail: Format: Ardmore Null  1
Group: Retreat Highland
Group: Format: Highland  1
```

```
Detail: Format: Ardmore Null  1
Detail: Format: Ben Nevis  26    1
Detail: Format: Brora Null  1
Detail: Format: Dalmore  12    1
Detail: Format: Dalwhinnie  15    1
Detail: Format: Deanston  17    1
Detail: Format: Edradour  10    1
```

The order of events here is different from the first group. First, the group header is formatted, followed by the first item in the group. Access now knows that the first item fits on the same page as the header, so it backs up (retreats) over the group header, and repeats the formatting for this page.

You will notice that the **FormatCount** property stays at 1, even though the Format event has been executed more than once. This is why the retreat event is important, because it allows you to undo any changes you made in the group header that could be made twice.

An example of where this can come into play is in totals. Remember, in the previous example we corrected the problem with the total by adding an extra condition to the If statement used to check the year:

If FormatCount = 1...

If the KeepTogether property had been set to Whole group, Access would have formatted all of the detail items for the group before executing the retreat event.

NoData

As its name implies, the NoData event is triggered when the report has no data to print. This could happen, for example, when a report is based on user-defined criteria and no rows are returned in the underlying query. In this case, you could display a message and cancel the opening of the report.

```
Private Sub Report_NoData(Cancel As Integer)

    MsgBox ("Your selection criteria did not find any data")
    Cancel = True

End Sub
```

Like some of the other report events, if you set **Cancel** to **True**, the event is canceled. In this case, setting the **Cancel** argument to **True** tells Access that the report is not to be opened, just as it did for the report **Open** event. This means that the message box will be displayed, but no report. If, however, you set **Cancel** to **False**, then the report will be displayed, but won't show any records, since there is no data for it to show.

The NoData event was new in Access 95.

Page

The Page event is triggered after a page is formatted, but before it is printed. You can use this to add graphics to the report as a whole, rather than just to a section. For example, the following line of code will draw a border round the report:

```
Me.Line(0, 0)-(Me.ScaleWidth, Me.ScaleHeight), , B
```

This type of graphic can't be achieved as easily by adding lines to the various report sections. Refer to the Access help file for more information on the `Line` method.

The Page event was new in Access 95.

When To Use the Different Events

As the format, print and retreat events are not used very often, deciding when to use which type of event can often be the hardest part of report design. Here are a few guidelines to help you:

Format

You should use this when your procedure could affect the layout of the page, for example, for making controls invisible. Access will actually lay out (format) the section after your procedure has run.

You could also use this in conjunction with a hidden section. If you need to perform some totaling for a section which is not visible, you can't use the print event procedure since this will never be generated. In this case, you have to use the format event procedure.

Print

This should be used when your procedure does not modify the layout of the report, or when the procedure depends upon the page the records are printed on. It only affects sections that print, so, if you only print the last page of a report, the print event is not generated for the other pages. This is particularly important if you are using the event to calculate running totals.

Retreat

This is best used in conjunction with the format event. For example, if you have a format event procedure that is calculating totals, you may wish to undo some of them if you are backing up (retreating) over previously formatted sections.

The FormatCount and PrintCount Properties

You should use these to ensure that actions within the format and print event procedures are only executed once. These properties increment each time a record is formatted or printed, including occasions where a record does not fit on a page.

You will probably perform most of your totals by using the `Sum` command in the footer sections of the report, but the format and print event procedures provide a flexible way of adding totals which are not based on a grouping. However, do bear in mind the problems you can experience if you don't check these, as seen in the above examples.

Summary

In this chapter we have looked at some of the reports supplied with the sample application, and seen how we can use simple expressions to help users analyze the information—displaying line totals, showing how many days the payment is overdue, providing simple yes/no values etc.. We have also seen how to format a report with page numbers and the current date.

The second half of the chapter dealt with the different events that are generated for a report and how they can be used to control report output. We looked at the following events:

▶ Open
▶ Activate
▶ Deactivate
▶ Close
▶ Error
▶ Format
▶ Print
▶ Retreat
▶ NoData
▶ Page

Exercises

1 Create a report that shows the whiskies and total sales so far. Now add a form that allows selection of a region, and call this from the open event of the report. Use the region selected as a filter for the report, so that only the user selection is shown.

2 Add a field to this report that is only visible when a selection is in place, so that users don't mistake this as a full report.

Advanced Programming Techniques

At this stage of the book, we have covered most of the fundamentals of programming with Visual Basic in Access 97. We will now take a look at some of the more sophisticated features of VBA. As such, this chapter is a mixed bag of ideas and techniques that have been either too complex to tackle until now, or required knowledge of other features before you could learn about them. We will also discuss in more detail a few items that we've already snuck into some of the earlier chapters. In effect, we are going to be looking at four separate subject areas under the broad umbrella of advanced programming.

First, we will take another look at arrays, because there is much that we haven't yet considered, such as how Access distinguishes arrays from variables. Then we'll have a look at some of the more interesting ways that we can pass arguments between VBA procedures. After that, we will be investigating how we can extend the functionality of VBA by using code from DLLs. Finally, we'll look at how we can extend Data Access Objects by adding our own properties to them.

So then, the main topics of discussion are:

- Getting more out of arrays
- Passing parameters by reference and by value
- Using DLLs
- Creating custom properties for Data Access Objects

Arrays

We first encountered arrays in Chapter 4 where we looked at what an array is and the difference between static and dynamic arrays. You will remember that an array is simply a group of variables, all with the same name and data type, differentiated by their index. You declare an array simply by placing parentheses after the variable name:

```
Dim intarray() As Integer        'declares an array of integers
```

Detecting Arrays

There are three ways in which you can determine whether a variable is a single variable or an array. These involve using one of the following functions:

- IsArray()
- VarType()
- TypeName()

The IsArray() Function

This function returns **True** if the variable passed to it is an array, and **False** if it is not. Have a look at the following procedure:

```
Sub ArrayTest()

    Dim intNum1 As Integer
    Dim intNum(1 To 10) As Integer

    Debug.Print "intnum1: " & IsArray(intNum1)
    Debug.Print "intnum: " & IsArray(intNum)

End Sub
```

You can run this procedure by typing **ArrayTest** in the Debug window, or by hitting *F5* when you are in the procedure in the module window. Either way, you should see the words **False** and **True** appear in the Debug window:

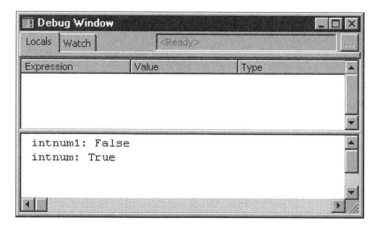

This is because **IsArray(intNum1)** is **False** and **IsArray(intNum)** is **True**. In other words **intNum1** is not an array, whereas **intNum** is.

The VarType Function

Another method for determining whether or not a variable is an array is to use the **VarType** function. This function indicates what the variable's type is, as well as whether it is an array. Have a look at this procedure:

```
Sub ArrayTest2()

    Dim intNum1 As Integer
    Dim intNum(1 To 10) As Integer

    Debug.Print "intnum1: " & VarType(intNum1)
    Debug.Print "intnum: " & VarType(intNum)

End Sub
```

If you run **ArrayTest2** by hitting *F5*, you should see the values 2 and 8194 when you open the Debug window:

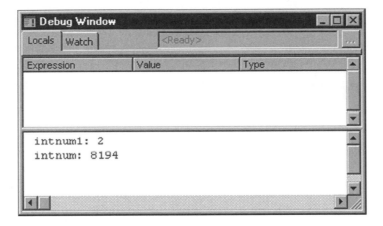

The return value of the **VarType** function is normally a number from 0 to 17, excluding the values 15 and 16, indicating the variable type (for example, 2 corresponds to integer). However, if the variable passed to **VarType** is an array, 8192 is added to the return value. So, in our example, both variables are of integer type (2), and the second one is an array (8192) of integers, giving a total of 8194.

FYI The **VarType** function is described in Chapter 3. You can also consult the Help files for a full list of its possible return values.

The number 8192 can be represented by the intrinsic constant **vbArray**. We can, therefore, modify the procedure to make the results a little more readable:

```
Sub ArrayTest3()

    Dim intNum1 As Integer
    Dim intNum(1 To 10) As Integer

    Debug.Print "Array: " & (VarType(intNum1) > vbArray),
    Debug.Print "Type: " & (VarType(intNum1) And Not vbArray)
    Debug.Print "Array: " & (VarType(intNum) > vbArray),
    Debug.Print "Type: " & (VarType(intNum) And Not vbArray)

End Sub
```

If you run this procedure, you should get the results shown below:

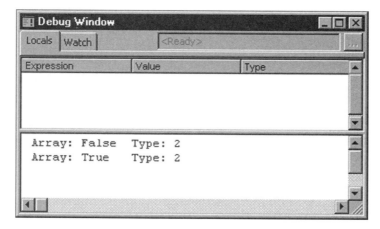

The code looks a little more complex, but isn't that hard to follow. The first thing to remember is that putting parentheses around an expression in VBA forces the expression to be evaluated. You will probably have come across this before in mathematics. The expression 6+(3*4) is equal to 18, because the parentheses around (3*4) force that part of the expression to be evaluated first, leaving us with 6+12. In the same way, the parentheses around

```
(VarType(intNum1) > vbArray)
```

force that expression to be evaluated first. The result of the expression is true because **VarType(intNum1)** is indeed greater than **vbArray**.

The next step is to determine the data type of each variable. We do that with this expression:

```
(VarType(intNum1) And Not vbArray)
```

The parentheses again cause the expression to be evaluated. But what exactly is being evaluated? To understand the logical expression **And Not** we need to start thinking in binary again. If you remember, in Chapter 4 we looked at how an integer variable could be used as a set of flags. Well, that's how the **vbArray** constant is used.

To see how this works, let's look at what **VarType(intNum1)** and **vbArray** look like in binary. We know from the previous procedure, **ArrayTest2()**, that the value of **VarType(intNum1)** is 8194 and that **vbArray** is 8192. In binary those are 10000000000010 and 10000000000000 respectively.

		Array bit						
	16384	8192	4096	2048	1024	512	256	128
Data type	0	0	0	0	0	0	0	0
Array flag	0	1	0	0	0	0	0	0
Total	0	**1**	0	0	0	0	0	0

		Datatype bits						
64	32	16	8	4	2	1	Total	
0	0	0	0	0	1	0	2	
0	0	0	0	0	0	0	8192	
0	0	0	0	0	1	0	**8194**	

The rightmost five binary digits are used to indicate the data type of the variable. The 14th binary digit from the right, whose value is 8192, is used to flag whether the variable is an array or not. If it is an array, this flag is set to 1, increasing the value of the **VarType** by 8192.

What we want to do is to determine the value of the digits without the influence of the 14th digit, i.e. the **vbArray** digit. To do this we use the logical operator **And** against **Not vbArray**. **Not vbArray** is the reverse of **vbArray**. In other words, the 0s become 1s and the 1s become 0s. The result of an **And** operation is that bit flags in the result are set to 1 only if the bit was 1 in both the numbers being compared. So using an **And** with **Not vbArray** has the result of leaving 15 of the bits in the result the same as they were in the original number, whilst ensuring that the 14th bit is set to 0.

	32768	16384	Array bit 8192	4096	2048	1024	512
VarType (intNum1)	0	0	1	0	0	0	0
Not vbArray	1	1	0	1	1	1	1
Result	0	0	0	0	0	0	0

256	128	64	32	16	8	Datatype bits 4	2	1
0	0	0	0	0	0	0	1	0
1	1	1	1	1	1	1	1	1
0	0	0	0	0	0	0	1	0

The TypeName Function

The **TypeName** function does much the same as the **VarType** function, except that it returns its result in plainer terms.

For example, the following procedure,

```
Sub ArrayTest4()

    Dim intNum1 As Integer
    Dim intNum(1 To 10) As Integer

    Debug.Print "intnum1: " & TypeName(intNum1)
    Debug.Print "intnum: " & TypeName(intNum)

End Sub
```

will give these results:

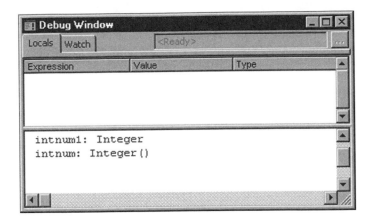

As you can see, the return value of the **TypeName** function is a whole lot easier to understand. It returns the type of the variable in plainer terms, **Integer**, and adds a pair of empty parentheses if the variable is an array, **Integer()**.

Multi-dimensional Arrays

So far, all the arrays that we have been using have been one-dimensional. However, you might wish to store data that relates to a position on a grid, map or mathematical settings. Arrays can have two, three or even more dimensions and can store information in this way. For instance, you could store the **BottlingID** and **WhiskyID** of a number of bottlings in an array like this:

BottlingID	WhiskyID
65	56
59	51
8	5

To declare a multi-dimensional array, like the one above, simply specify the bounds of each dimension separated by commas. For example, to specify a dynamic array of 2 x 3 (i.e. 6) elements whose dimensions start at 1, use the following syntax:

```
Dim iNum(1 To 2, 1 To 3) As Integer
```

Alternatively, for an array of the same size, but whose dimensions start at 0 (assuming there is no **Option Base 1** statement), you could use:

```
Dim iNum(1, 2) As Integer
```

Dynamic Multi-dimensional Arrays

As with normal one-dimensional arrays, there is the option to make the arrays dynamic and resizable, according to your needs. To declare a dynamic, multi-dimensional array, you would use the following syntax:

```
Dim iNum() As Integer

Redim iNum(1 To 2, 1 to 3)
```

Or, alternatively, for a dynamic array whose dimensions start at 0 (assuming there is no **Option Base 1** statement), you could use:

```
Dim iNum(1, 2) As Integer

Redim iNum(1, 2)
```

Referencing Elements in a Multi-dimensional Array

To reference elements in a multi-dimensional array, you simply specify the appropriate number of indexes to the array.

```
Sub MultiDimArray()

    Dim i As Integer
    Dim j As Integer
    Dim intNum() As Integer                       'Create a dynamic array

    ReDim intNum(2 To 3, 3 To 5)                  'Resize the array

    For i = 2 To 3                                'Populate the array
        For j = 3 To 5
            intNum(i, j) = i ^ j
        Next
    Next

    For i = 2 To 3                                'Print the contents...
        For j = 3 To 5                            '...of the array
            Debug.Print i & "^" & j & "=" & intNum(i, j)
        Next
    Next

End Sub
```

This procedure produces the following results:

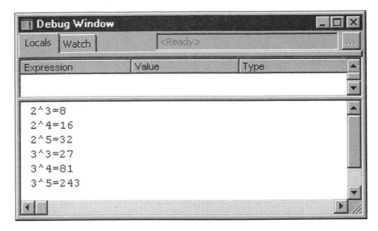

As you can see, the procedure has two parts: the calculation and then printing the results. Each part has two loops, one nested inside the other. The inside loop is executed three times (**For j = 3 to 5**) for each value of **i** in the outer loop, which is executed twice (**For i = 2 to 3**).

The number of elements in a multi-dimensional array (i.e. the number of separate values that it can hold) is calculated by multiplying together the number of elements in each dimension of the array. For example, the array in the procedure above would be able to hold 2 x 3 = 6 values.

Similarly, the following declaration,

```
Dim intNum() As Integer

ReDim intNum(9, 19, 29)
```

would produce an array of 10 x 20 x 30 = 6,000 elements (again, assuming there is no **Option Base 1** statement in the module).

Memory Considerations

We mentioned in Chapter 3 that it's important to select the right data type for your variables. This helps to avoid errors, but it's also important because the different data types take up different amounts of memory. For example, a long integer takes up more memory than an integer.

Arrays require twenty bytes of memory, plus four bytes for each array dimension, plus the number of bytes occupied by the data itself. The memory occupied by the data can be calculated by multiplying the number of data elements by the size of each element.

Therefore, to calculate the memory that the array **intNum(9, 19, 29)** would take up, we multiply the number of elements in the array by the size of each of the elements,

> 10 x 20 x 30 = 6,000 elements
> 6000 x 2 bytes for an integer = 12,000 bytes

and then add the overhead,

20 bytes + (3 x 4 bytes) = 32 bytes

giving a total of 12,032 bytes.

If we compare this to the amount of memory that the array would have taken up if it had been declared as a **Variant**, you'll see just why it is important to choose your data type carefully.

```
Dim varName As Variant

ReDim varName(9, 19, 29)
```

Variant type variables containing strings require (22 + the string length) bytes of memory per element. So, the memory requirements would have been,

10 x 20 x 30 = 6,000 elements
6000 x 22 bytes (minimum) for a **Variant** = 132,000 bytes

plus the overhead,

20 bytes + (3 x 4 bytes) = 32 bytes

giving a total of at least 132,032 bytes—around 128 K.

It is clear that the more dimensions you have in your array and the larger the data type, the easier it is to consume vast amounts of memory.

In theory, the maximum number of dimensions that you can declare in an array is 60. In practice, though, you will probably find it very hard to keep track of what is happening in arrays of more than three, or perhaps four, dimensions.

Erasing Arrays

When you have finished with a *dynamic* array, you can re-claim the memory that it took up by using the **Erase** statement:

```
Erase intNum
```

Using the **Erase** statement on a *static* array will reinitialize the array, but will not reclaim the memory that it takes up. So, if you only need to use an array for part of the time—especially if it's declared as a global array—you should consider declaring it as a dynamic array.

Parameter Arrays

Access also allows you to pass parameter arrays to functions and subprocedures. A parameter array, as its name suggests, is an array of parameters. In other words, it allows you to pass a variable number of arguments to a procedure. This can be useful if, at design-time, you don't know how many arguments you will want to pass to a procedure. Have a look at the following code:

```
Function Avge(ParamArray aValues()) As Double

    Dim Value
    Dim dblTotal As Double

    For Each Value In aValues
        dblTotal = dblTotal + Value
    Next

    Avge = dblTotal / (UBound(aValues) + 1)

End Function
```

This function returns the average value of a series of numbers. If you type the following line in the Debug window,

```
?Avge (1,2,3,5,5,8)
```

you should get 4 when you hit the *Enter* key.

In the above example, **aValues()** is a parameter array. To declare an argument as a parameter array, you just prefix it with the keyword **ParamArray**. There are two important things to remember when declaring parameter arrays:

▶ A **ParamArray** argument can only appear as the final argument passed to a **Sub** or **Function**

▶ **ParamArray** arguments are always of type **Variant**

In the **Avge** function, we loop through each of the elements in the **aValues()** array and add it to a running total, **dblTotal**.

```
For Each Value In aValues
    dblTotal = dblTotal + Value
Next
```

We then divide the total by the number of elements in the array.

```
Avge = dblTotal / (UBound(aValues) + 1)
```

We've used the **UBound** function which, if you remember from Chapter 4, returns the value of the highest index in the array. Note that, here, we calculate the number of elements as **UBound(aValues) + 1**. This is because parameter arrays always start at element 0—*even* if you have specified **Option Base 1** in the **Declarations** section of the module containing the procedure.

> *That last sentence is important—if it didn't sink in just now, read it again. This is guaranteed to catch you out one day!*

289

The GetRows Method

Another way to create an array is to use the **GetRows** method of the **Recordset** object. This is used to copy a number of rows from a **Recordset** object into an array. The technique is very useful because it allows the **Recordset** object to be closed, minimizing potential locking conflicts, but still giving you access to the values in the records. In addition, it can be faster to perform operations on the values stored in the array than reading the records from the **Recordset** object, because the array does not have the overhead of the sophisticated cursor functionality which Access provides via **Recordset** objects. Note, however, that any changes made to the values in the array will not be reflected in the recordset from which you copied them.

We'll now demonstrate with an example where we'll create an array which takes data from the first two rows of the **Order** table.

Try It Out—GetRows

1 Open a code module in **Whisky10.mdb** and type in the following code:

```
Sub TestGetRows()

    Dim varValues As Variant
    Dim rs As Recordset
    Dim varRow As Variant
    Dim intRowCount As Integer
    Dim intFieldCount As Integer
    Dim i As Integer
    Dim j As Integer

    Set rs = CurrentDb().OpenRecordset("Order")
    varValues = rs.GetRows(2)
    rs.Close

    intFieldCount = UBound(varValues, 1)
    intRowCount = UBound(varValues, 2)

    For j = 0 To intRowCount
        For i = 0 To intFieldCount
            Debug.Print "Row " & j & ", Field " & i & ": ";
            Debug.Print varValues(i, j)
        Next
    Next

End Sub
```

2 Open the Debug window and run **TestGetRows**. You should get a list of the contents of each field in each of the first two rows of the table **Order**.

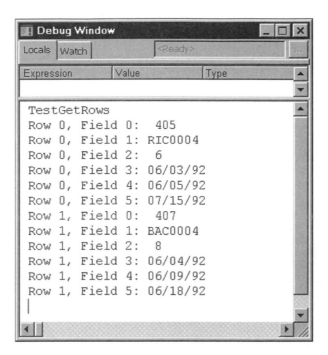

How It Works

The **GetRows** method takes, as an argument, the number of rows that we want to copy into the array:

```
varValues = rs.GetRows(2)
```

Here, we copy the first two rows. The rows that are copied are relative to the current record. As the recordset has just been opened, the current record is the first row in the recordset, so the first two rows will be copied. If the number of rows requested is greater than the number of rows between the current record and the last record in the recordset, **GetRows** will return all the available rows.

After the **GetRows** method has been applied, the current row will be the one after those that have been copied. This is useful because it allows us to copy one block of records (say the first 50) into our array and process them. Then, when we have finished with them, we can read the next block.

Note that the rows are copied into a **Variant** variable, rather than into an array declared with the usual syntax.

```
Dim varValues As Variant
  .
  .
  .
varValues = rs.GetRows(2)
```

Variants can hold arrays just as easily as they can hold single variables. What is more, they do not need to be declared as arrays in order to do so. The only arrays they can't hold are arrays either of user-defined types or fixed-length strings.

The array created by the **GetRows** method is two-dimensional. The first element corresponds to the field index, the second to the row index. To inspect the index of the last field returned, inspect the value of the highest index in the first dimension of the array:

```
intFieldCount = UBound(varValues, 1)
```

 When using UBound with a multi-dimensional array, you should specify which dimension you want to find the highest index. Specify it as a number following the array name.

To find the index of the last row returned, inspect the value of the highest index in the second dimension of the array returned:

```
intRowCount = UBound(varValues, 2)
```

> *Note that the array returned by **GetRows** is zero-based. This means that the number of fields is **intFieldCount+1** and the number of rows is **intRowCount+1**.*

Once we have determined the number of elements in each dimension of the array, we loop through each dimension, printing the results.

```
For j = 0 To intRowCount
    For i = 0 To intFieldCount
        Debug.Print "Row " & j & ", Field " & i & ": ";
        Debug.Print varValues(i, j)
    Next
Next
```

 Placing a semicolon at the end of the Debug.Print line means that there will be no carriage return before the next line is printed. In other words, in the Debug window, the output of the two code lines will be printed together on one line.

This concludes our look at arrays. Hopefully, splitting the discussion over two separate chapters hasn't confused you. This was necessary as we needed to discuss the fundamentals of what static and dynamic arrays were early in the book before we could move on to more unusual topics such as multi-dimensional arrays and using the **GetRows** method to create an array. The next topic is unrelated to arrays, but is a continuation of another concept learned earlier in the book: passing arguments.

Arguments

Normally, when an argument is passed to a function, it is passed by **reference**. In other words, the procedure receiving the argument is passed a reference, or pointer, which indicates where in memory the variable is stored. It *doesn't* receive the actual **value** of the variable.

Passing variables by reference has two effects. The advantage is that it's faster—Access doesn't need to make a copy of the value in another location ready for the procedure to read. However, because the procedure has access to the original variable (it knows where it is stored in memory), it can change the value of this variable. When the procedure ends, the code that called the procedure will see and work with the new value.

This is useful if you *want* the procedure to change the value, but it can create unexpected results.

Passing Arguments By Value

The other alternative is to pass arguments by value. This is where VBA just makes a copy of the data and passes that copy to the procedure. In this way, if the value of the copy is changed, the original value remains the same.

Let's compare the two methods by using each of them to calculate the cube root of 8.

Try It Out—Passing Arguments By Value

1 Open an existing code module or create a new one.

2 Create the **CubeRoot** subprocedure by typing in the following code:

```
Sub CubeRoot(dblNumber As Double)

    dblNumber = dblNumber ^ (1 / 3)

End Sub
```

3 Now create a 'wrapper' procedure which will call the **CubeRoot** procedure:

```
Sub CubeRootWrapper()

    Dim dblVariable As Double
    dblVariable = 8

    Debug.Print "Before: " & dblVariable
    CubeRoot dblVariable
    Debug.Print "After: " & dblVariable

End Sub
```

4 Run the **CubeRootWrapper** procedure by hitting *F5*. You should then see the following in the Debug window:

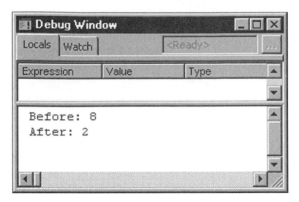

5 Now modify the **CubeRoot** subprocedure by inserting the keyword **ByVal** before the argument, like this:

```
Sub CubeRoot(ByVal dblNumber As Double)

    dblNumber = dblNumber ^ (1 / 3)

End Sub
```

6 Run the **CubeRootWrapper** procedure again. The output should now look like this:

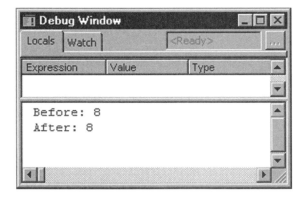

How It Works

The **CubeRoot** subprocedure simply calculates the cube root of a number (no surprises there). The main procedure then prints the number twice—once before the function is run and once after.

By default, Access passes variables by reference. Therefore, the first time we run the **CubeRootWrapper** procedure, we pass the variable **dblVariable** to the **CubeRoot** procedure by reference. In other words, the **CubeRootWrapper** procedure passes a pointer to the place where **dblVariable** is stored in memory.

```
    CubeRoot dblVariable
```

The **CubeRoot** procedure labels what it finds at this location as **dblNumber** and then modifies the contents of that memory location.

```
    dblNumber = dblNumber ^ (1 / 3)
```

Consequently, when the **CubeRootWrapper** inspects what is at that location, it finds that its contents have changed.

```
    Debug.Print "After: " & dblVariable
```

We then change the code in **CubeRootWrapper**. Placing the **ByVal** keyword before the argument means that it will be passed by **value** instead of by reference—the actual value of the variable will be passed, as opposed to just a pointer to its memory address.

```
    Sub CubeRoot(ByVal dblNumber As Double)
```

This time, the **CubeRoot** procedure has no idea where the original variable **dblVariable** in the calling procedure is located in memory—all it has got is its value. The variables **dblNumber** and **dblVariable** are now quite distinct from each other. It quite happily changes the value of **dblNumber**, but **dblVariable** is not modified.

FYI   Even if a procedure is expecting a variable to be passed by reference, you can pass a variable by value. To do this, you would simply enclose the variable in parentheses when passing it into a procedure, e.g. CubeRoot (dblVariable). As we saw earlier, parentheses cause VBA to evaluate the expression within them. Consequently, what gets passed to CubeRoot is not dblVariable, but just the number which is the result of evaluating dblVariable.

Passing arguments by reference is quicker than passing by value, as we noted earlier, but you should consider passing arguments by value in the following circumstances:

▶   When you do not want the contents of a variable to change, but you need to pass it to a procedure that someone else has written and you don't know how it works. After all, you've no idea what the procedure you are calling might do to your variable!

▶   When passing variables to procedures in DLLs.

If you have no idea what that last point means, don't worry. That's what we are going to look at now—how to extend the functionality of VBA through using DLLs.

Dynamic-Link Libraries (DLLs)

Even if you have not done any VBA or C coding before, you may well have come across DLLs. Just have a look in the System or System32 subdirectories of the Windows directory on your computer and you will find tens, if not hundreds or even thousands of them. But what exactly are DLLs?

Well, clearly they are files. In fact, they are code files, similar to the modules that you get in Access. DLL stands for **dynamic-link library** and if we look at what the name means, we begin to understand a little better how they work. They are called **libraries** because they contain a number of procedures that can be read and used. A library in real life is a place where lots of books have been collected. People can access the library and borrow a book whenever they want. This means that they don't need to buy their own copy of the book, saving them the expense and shelf-space.

So, in programming parlance, a library is a place where lots of procedures have been collected. Other programs can access (or **link** to) the library to use a procedure whenever they want. This means that the other programs don't need to contain their own copy of the procedure, saving the programmer's expense and the user's disk-space

The **dynamic** part of the name comes from the fact that the DLL itself isn't loaded into memory until a procedure within that DLL is first called by an application. It's the same as saying that a book is only borrowed from a real library when someone wants to read it. Actually, there is no real limit on the number of applications that can link to a DLL at the same time. Windows keeps track of when the DLL needs to be loaded into memory, and when applications have finished with the DLL it can be unloaded from memory.

Some DLLs contain functions with fairly limited appeal. Others, such as **Kernel32.dll**, **User32.dll** and **Gdi32.dll** are used by every Windows application to provide their basic operations. As a Windows application, our VBA code can also use the functions in these DLLs to achieve things that aren't otherwise supported in Access. There are literally hundreds of functions in these three DLLs, so we have plenty of scope! Of course, we can make use of functions in other DLLs as well and, if none provide the function we need, we can even build our own DLL if we have tools like Visual Basic or Visual C++ and know how to use them.

So let's move on and see how we use DLLs in VBA.

Declaring a DLL in Code

Before we can use a procedure in a DLL, we must tell Access where it is—both the name of the DLL itself, and which procedure in that DLL we want to use. Access can then dynamically link to that routine, as required, while the application is running. Access doesn't automatically check that the procedure exists, either when you compile or start the application. If it can't be accessed, you will only find this out when an error message appears as you make the call to the function.

One very useful DLL function we can use is **timeGetTime** which can be found in **Winmm.dll**. This function returns the number of milliseconds that have elapsed since Windows started. It is useful because we can execute this function twice, once before and once after executing a portion of code and, by subtracting one from another, we can determine how long the code took to execute. This is a typical example of using a procedure in a DLL to enhance standard Access functionality—the **Timer** function in Access is only accurate to a whole second. Another function, **GetTickCount** in **Kernel32.dll** can also be used to return the number of milliseconds that have elapsed since Windows started, but the accuracy of **GetTickCount** varies between different operating systems and processors.

The process of calling a procedure in a DLL is also referred to as 'making an API call'. API **stands for** Application Programming Interface—the published set of routines that a particular application or operating system provides for the programmer to use.

In order to declare the **timeGetTime** function, we place the following statement in the **Declarations** section of a module:

```
Declare Function timeGetTime Lib "WINMM" () As Long
```

This indicates that the function is called **timeGetTime** and that it returns a **Long** type value. It is in the **WINMM** library (**Winmm.dll**) and it takes no parameters, hence the empty brackets towards the end of the function declaration.

> *Make sure that you type the function declaration exactly as it appears above. Function declarations in 32-bit versions of Windows (i.e. Windows 95 and Windows NT) are case-sensitive. If you do not capitalize the name of the function correctly Access will generate an error message and the code will not execute correctly.*

Once a function has been declared in this manner, all we have to do is execute it. If you type the above declaration in a module, and then enter the following in the Debug window,

```
?timeGetTime()
```

the number of milliseconds since Windows was started will be returned.

Did you know that there is also an API call (i.e. DLL procedure) that can tell you whether or not the user of the computer is left-handed? To declare it, we place the following statement in the **declarations** section of a module:

```
Declare Function GetSystemMetrics Lib "user32" (ByVal nIndex As Long) _
        As Long
```

The function is called **GetSystemMetrics** and is in the **User32.DLL** library.

> *We haven't specified a path in front of the library name, so the default system path, then the* **\Windows** *folder, and finally the* **\Windows\System** *subfolder are searched to find the DLL. If it can't be found, a run-time error will be generated. If you want to use a DLL that resides anywhere else but these three locations, you need to qualify it with a full path.*

The **GetSystemMetrics** function takes an argument **nIndex** of type **Long** and returns a **Long**. The function actually returns information about the layout of the user interface (e.g. the height of window title bars, the width of scroll bars) as well as other juicy tidbits such as whether the user has swapped the left and right mouse buttons (via the Control Panel). The argument **nIndex** is used to specify a constant indicating the type of information we want. In our case, we want to know whether the mouse buttons have been swapped. So we need to declare the following constant and pass it as an argument to the function:

```
Public Const SM_SWAPBUTTON = 23
```

In fact, you can try it out for yourself!

Try It Out—Using a Function in a DLL

1 Open an existing module or create a new one.

2 In the **Declarations** section, type the following function declaration:

```
Declare Function GetSystemMetrics Lib "user32" (ByVal nIndex As Long)
        As Long
```

3 Now declare the following constant, again in the **Declarations** section:

```
Public Const SM_SWAPBUTTON = 23
```

4 Create the **ShowHands** procedure by typing the following code into the module:

```
Sub ShowHands()

    If GetSystemMetrics(SM_SWAPBUTTON) = False Then
        MsgBox "Your mouse is right-handed!"
    Else
        MsgBox "Your mouse is left-handed!"
    End If

End Sub
```

5 Run the **ShowHands** procedure and a dialog box should appear which indicates whether your mouse is configured for right- or left-handed use.

6 Now swap the left and right mouse buttons by altering the button configuration. You can do this by opening the Control Panel, selecting Mouse and changing the Button configuration option on the Buttons tab of the dialog box which appears.

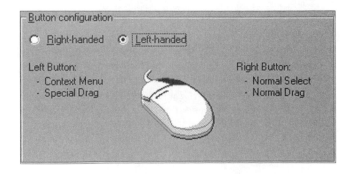

7 Hit the OK button to close the Mouse Properties dialog box and go back to the module that you have just created.

8 Run the **ShowHands** procedure again. This time, the message box which appears should indicate that the mouse buttons have been swapped. Click the OK button to close the message box:

If you're still sitting there wondering why you can't seem to click OK button, remember that you have swapped the mouse buttons round and you should be clicking the *other* button!

9 Finish up by changing the mouse buttons back to their original settings (and get even more annoyed on the way because you keep bringing up context-sensitive menus when you just want to click things!).

How It Works

As we explained just before the example, the **GetSystemMetrics** function returns information about the screen layout. The actual information that is returned depends on the argument we pass to the function. We passed it the **SM_SWAPBUTTON** constant. But how did we know that was the constant to use? And how did we know that this was the declaration for the constant?

```
Public Const SM_SWAPBUTTON = 23
```

Come to think of it, how did we even know about the **GetSystemMetrics** function?

Well, in the real world, the most popular libraries have good indexes, and it's the same in the programming world. For OLE libraries and Access library databases, such an index is provided by the Object Browser. However, for DLLs, we rely on the vendor's documentation for information about the functions within the DLL—what arguments they take, what values they return and so on.

Because **User32.dll** is such a vital and frequently used component of Windows, it is very well documented. The authoritative source of such information is the *Microsoft Win32 Software Development Kit* but you may find it easier to find the information by searching the Microsoft Developer Network or Microsoft TechNet CDs. Alternatively, if you only want the function declaration and any constant or type declarations, you can use the Win32 API Viewer, which comes with Microsoft Office 97 Developer Edition.

If you do look up the documentation, you will see that when **GetSystemMetrics** is called with the **SM_SWAPBUTTON** constant, it returns a non-zero value if the buttons have been swapped and **False** if they have not. It's as simple as that!

Aliases

Once you have declared your function, you can call it by name from within VBA, as if it were a native VBA function. However, there may be occasions when you want to change the name of the DLL function. For example, VBA has a **SetFocus** method that applies to forms and controls. If you wanted to use the **SetFocus** API call (i.e. the **SetFocus** function in the **User32.dll** library) and declare it in the normal manner, it might cause confusion:

```
Declare Function SetFocus Lib "user32" (ByVal hwnd As Long) As Long
```

Now you would have a **SetFocus** method and a **SetFocus** API call. To make things clearer, you can create an **Alias** for the API call. In other words, you can rename it. So, for example, you can declare the **SetFocus** API call, but rename it as **Win32SetFocus**:

```
Declare Function Win32SetFocus Lib "user32" Alias "SetFocus" _
   (ByVal hwnd As Long) As Long
```

The **Alias** keyword is also useful if the name of the DLL function isn't legal in VBA or Visual Basic. The API functions **_lopen**, **_lread** and **_lwrite** can't be declared directly because the use of an underscore at the beginning of a function name is illegal in Access. However, they can be declared if they are aliased to a legal name such as **LOpen**.

FYI You do not have to use aliases for your functions, but it is often a good idea, if only to avoid confusion. For example, you might want to give functions aliases which begin with the prefix api_, such as api_SetFocus. This makes it easier for people reading your code to see when you are using native Access functions and when you are calling functions in other DLLs and this, in turn, can make the code easier to debug.

Parameters and Return Values

Using the ByVal Keyword

We saw earlier that, by default, Access passes arguments to a procedure by reference. In other words, Access passes a pointer to the memory address of the variable that is being passed, rather than the actual value of the variable. However, many functions in DLLs expect to receive the value of the variable, rather than a pointer to its memory address. If this is the case, you need to pass the argument by value by placing the **ByVal** keyword in front of the argument when you declare the function:

```
Declare Function GetSystemMetrics Lib "user32" (ByVal nIndex As Long) _
      As Long
```

Passing Strings

The functions in most DLLs expect any strings which are passed to them to be **null-terminated** strings. A null-terminated string uses a null character (ASCII value 0) to indicate the end of the string. VBA, however, doesn't use null-terminated strings. Therefore, if you pass a string from VBA to a function in a DLL, you will need to convert it. This can also be done with the **ByVal** keyword.

300

When the **ByVal** keyword is used with a string argument, VBA converts the string variable into a null-terminated string. It then passes a pointer to the memory address of the null-terminated string to the DLL function (i.e. it passes the null-terminated string **by reference**). Yes, this is the opposite of what we said earlier about using the **ByVal** keyword—but it only applies with VBA and VB strings.

Because the string is passed to the DLL function by reference, the DLL can modify it. This presents a problem. If the DLL attempts to modify the value of a null-terminated string and the new value is longer than the original one, the function doesn't increase the length of the string. Instead, it simply carries on writing the remainder of the string into the memory location adjacent to that of the null-terminated string. This is not good! In fact, if it happens, your application will probably crash.

To prevent this, you should make sure that the string you pass to the function is large enough to accept any value that the function may place in it. You do this by passing a **fixed-length** string of a suitably large size:

```
Dim strFilename As String*255
```

 You should consult the documentation for the DLL function to determine the maximum size, but 255 characters is usually sufficient.

Passing Arrays to a DLL

To pass an array of numeric values to a procedure in a DLL, you simply pass the first element of the array. You can do this because all the elements of a numeric array are laid out sequentially in contiguous memory space. After you have passed the first element of the array, the function is then able to retrieve the remaining elements by itself. However, you *can't* pass string arrays this way—attempting to do so may cause your application to crash!

Type Conversion

Because most DLLs are written in C or C++, the data types used by the arguments to the procedures within the DLL aren't identical to the data types used by VBA. However, it's not difficult to map the C data types to the Visual Basic data types if you consult the following table:

C Data type	Description	VBA Equivalent
BOOL	Boolean	ByVal b As Boolean
DWORD, LONG	Long	ByVal l As Long
HWND	Handle	ByVal l As Long
INT, UINT, WORD	Integer	ByVal i As Integer
LPDWORD	Pointer to a long integer	l As Long
LPINT	Pointer to an integer	i As Integer

Table Continued on Following Page

C Data type	Description	VBA Equivalent
`LPSTR`	Pointer to a string	`ByVal s As String`
`LPRECT` (for example)	Pointer to a type	See below
`NULL`	Null	See below
`VOID`	Void	Use a subprocedure

User-defined Data Types

Often, procedures in DLLs use **structures** as their arguments. A structure is the C-language equivalent of a user-defined type in VBA, i.e. a type that you have defined yourself. If a procedure expects a structure, we can pass it a user-defined type so long as we pass it **by reference**.

 FYI User-defined types allow you to place several different data types together in one type, allowing you to group together related variables. For example, in an Accounting system you might wish to create a type for a Customer which includes the name, account number, credit limit etc..

One of the more frequently used structures in DLL functions is the **RECT** structure. This is a representation of a rectangular area and is composed of four elements representing the left, top, bottom and right coordinates of the rectangle.

The **RECT** structure can be represented by the following user-defined type in VBA:

```
Type RECT
    Left As Long
    Top As Long
    Right As Long
    Bottom As Long
End Type
```

It's typically used to represent a rectangular area on the screen. You can see from the diagram below that the coordinates for the four elements are measured from the top left corner of the screen:

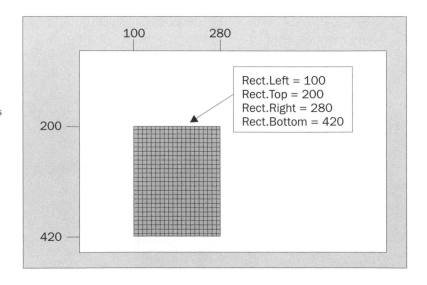

An example of a DLL procedure which uses this structure is the **ClipCursor** function. When this is passed a **RECT** structure, it confines the mouse pointer to a rectangular area on the screen defined by the coordinates of the structure.

```
Type RECT
    Left As Long
    Top As Long
    Right As Long
    Bottom As Long
End Type

Declare Function ClipCursor Lib "user32" (lpRect As RECT) As Long
```

```
Sub Foo()

    Dim rectClipArea As RECT
    Dim lngRetVal As Long

    rectClipArea.Top = 200
    rectClipArea.Left = 100
    rectClipArea.Bottom = 420
    rectClipArea.Right = 280

    lngRetVal = ClipCursor(rectClipArea)

End Sub
```

Null Pointers

Sometimes a procedure in a DLL expects to be passed a **null pointer**. If you have confined the mouse pointer with the **ClipCursor** function, you can free it by passing a null pointer to the **ClipCursor** function. In VBA, the equivalent to a null pointer is just the value zero, usually written as:

```
ByVal 0&
```

The **&** is a type-declaration character which indicates that the pointer is a **Long** (i.e. 32-bit pointer). Note that the null pointer *must* be passed by value. If the **ByVal** had been omitted, we would have found ourselves passing a pointer to **0&** rather than a null pointer.

However, we told Access in our function declaration that the argument is of type **RECT**, so it will generate its own error if we try and pass anything else—like a null pointer—to the function. The answer is to declare the argument with a type of **Any**:

```
Declare Function ClipCursor Lib "user32" (lpRect As Any) As Long
```

This turns off Access' type checking and allows any data type to be passed to the function. So the call to free the mouse pointer would look like this:

```
lngRetVal = ClipCursor(ByVal 0&)
```

Let's try this out, just to prove that it works.

303

Try It Out—Clipping and Unclipping the Cursor

1 First, create a new module or open an existing one and add the type declaration and function declaration to the **Declarations** section.

```
Type RECT
    Left As Long
    Top As Long
    Right As Long
    Bottom As Long
End Type

Declare Function ClipCursor Lib "user32" (lpRect As Any) As Long
```

2 Create a new form and add two command buttons.

3 Rename the buttons **cmdClip** and **cmdUnclip** and change the captions on the button to read Clip and Unclip.

4 Place the code to clip the cursor in the click event of the Clip button.

```
Private Sub cmdClip_Click()

    Dim rectClipArea As RECT
    Dim lngRetVal As Long

    rectClipArea.Top = 200
    rectClipArea.Left = 100
    rectClipArea.Bottom = 420
    rectClipArea.Right = 280

    lngRetVal = ClipCursor(rectClipArea)

End Sub
```

5 The second procedure simply passes the null value to turn off the clipping. Place this in the click event of the Unclip button.

```
Private Sub cmdUnclip_Click()
```

```
        Dim lngRetVal As Long

        lngRetVal = ClipCursor(ByVal 0&)

    End Sub
```

6 Now run the form and click on the Clip button. Your cursor will be restricted to the defined rectangle. Annoying isn't it?

7 To cancel the clipping, click on the Unclip button. If you have placed the Unclip button outside the cursor area, don't panic! Just press *Tab* to move the button and then hit the *Spacebar* key. The **ClipCursor** function only affects the operation of the mouse, not the keyboard.

The Dangers of Using DLLs

Bear in mind when you use DLL functions that, as soon as execution passes into the DLL, you lose all the cozy protection that Visual Basic offers. Although Windows API functions themselves, and all good third-party DLLs, are designed to trap their own errors and exit gracefully, they will not always do this if you supply the wrong parameter types or values.

Each time your code calls *any* procedure—either another VBA routine or a DLL—the data type of each argument is checked against those declared in the procedure. If you try to pass a wrong data type to any function or subroutine you get a Type Mismatch error. When you declare a DLL procedure in VBA, you can take advantage of the built-in type checking that occurs. That way, if you pass a wrong data type, you'll get a friendly VBA error message rather than a system crash.

You could, of course, declare all the arguments as type **Any**, and Access would allow you to pass any data type you wanted. Almost without exception, your next step would then be *Ctrl-Alt-Del* because the format of the arguments doesn't match those required by the DLL. It's not that the DLL has caused the error directly, but simply that it can't make head nor tail of what you've sent it!

So, to minimize errors, you should always place as tight a definition on your DLL data types as possible when you declare them. Of course, there are times, such as with the **ClipCursor** function you saw, that you can declare a function in two different ways. In this situation, one step you can take to make your declarations safer is to use an **Alias** to rename one or more of them:

```
Declare Function ClipCursorRect Lib "user32" Alias "ClipCursor" _
                                    (lpRect As RECT) As Long
```

```
Declare Function ClipCursorAny Lib "user32" Alias "ClipCursor" _
                                    (lpRect As Any) As Long
```

Both can coexist in your code together and you can call the correct forms of the function as you need them.

FYI When you use DLL or API functions you should *always* save your work regularly and back up any databases before you modify them. If you are using Windows 95, you should also ensure that no other applications (outside Access) have unsaved data in case you freeze Windows 95 completely.

Well, that's three of our topics down and one to go. This final topic, like the one we have just covered, is also concerned with extending the functionality of Access. It's all about extending Data Access Objects by adding user-defined or custom properties.

Custom DAO Properties

As you know, a property is a characteristic or attribute of an object. For example, all forms have a **Caption** property, which defines the text appearing in its title bar. This property can be read and written to both at design- and at run-time. Reading the property allows its value to be stored in a variable. Writing to the property allows it to be changed.

Other properties are read-only. For example, the **DBEngine** object has a **Version** property which indicates the version number of the Microsoft Jet database engine. This can be inspected but not changed.

With other properties, whether you can read or write to them depends on whether the object is in Design view, or whether it is being run. For example, the **AutoResize** property of a form can be read or written to at design-time, but is read-only at run-time.

A great deal of the time that you spend writing VBA will be spent modifying the in-built properties of Data Access Objects and other objects. But, even with all the versatility provided by these in-built properties, there are times when you would like that little bit more control. This is when you can take advantage of the custom properties which Access exposes.

The simplest way to create a custom property for a Data Access Object is to use the **CreateProperty** method. We are going to add a custom property to the **CriteriaHits** table which we created in Chapter 7, and we are going to use the property to store the criteria which were used in the creation of the table.

Try It Out—Creating Custom DAO properties

1 If you haven't already done so, open the database called **Whisky10.mdb** from the accompanying CD.

2 Open the code module for the Criteria Selection form, **frmCriteria** and find the **cmdOK_Click()** subroutine. Change the value of **vMethod** to **"DAO"**, so that we can create a custom DAO property in the **BuildOrderIDTable** method:

```
Private Sub cmdOK_Click()

Dim strWhere As String
Dim qdf As QueryDef
```

```
Dim lngRecords As Long
Dim strMessage As String
Dim intResponse As Integer

BuildSQLString strWhere
If BuildOrderIDTable(vWhere:=strWhere, vRecordcount:=lngRecords, _
                    vMethod:="DAO", vIndexed:=True) Then

    Select Case lngRecords
```

3 Now find the **BuildOrderIDTable()** procedure. This procedure builds a table of **OrderIDs** based on the selection made by the user on the form.

Add the following declaration to the list of variable declarations at the top of the **BuildOrderIDTable()** procedure.

```
Dim prpCriteria As Property
```

4 Now insert the following lines of code near the end of the procedure:

```
        .
        .
        .
'Return the amount of time taken to run the procedure
If Not IsMissing(vTimeTaken) Then _
    vTimeTaken = Now - lngTime
```

```
'Now add a custom property to the table to hold the criteria
Set tbl = db.TableDefs(vTableName)
Set prpCriteria = tbl.CreateProperty("Criteria")
prpCriteria.Type = dbText
If vWhere = "" Or IsMissing(vWhere) Then
    prpCriteria.Value = "All Records"
Else
    prpCriteria.Value = vWhere
End If

tbl.Properties.Append prpCriteria
```

```
'And finally, indicate success
BuildOrderIDTable = True
        .
        .
        .
```

5 Now compile the code and close the form, saving the changes you have made.

6 Open the Switchboard form and select the <u>V</u>iew Order Details option.

7 When the Criteria Selection form opens, specify that you are looking for orders dispatched between 20th March, 1997 and 12th June 1997 where the Payment Delay was over 30 days and then click the <u>O</u>K button. This will cause the new **CriteriaHits** table to be selected.

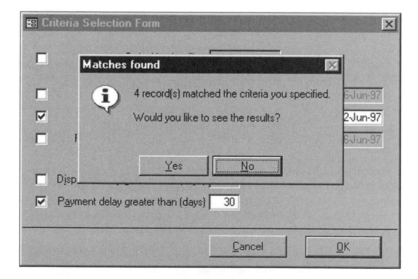

8 When a message box appears, asking you whether you want to see the results, hit the <u>N</u>o button.

9 Now close the Criteria Selection form and the Switchboard form when it appears. Open the Debug window, by hitting *Ctrl+G*, and evaluate the following statement:

```
?currentdb.TableDefs("CriteriaHits").Properties("Criteria")
```

10 The criteria you specified on the Criteria Selection form should now be displayed in the Debug window:

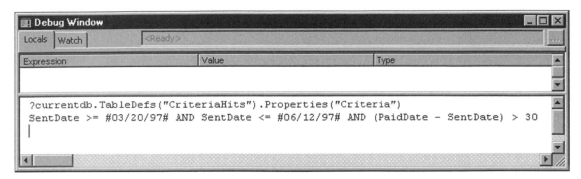

How It Works

We created a new property called **Criteria** for the new table, and used it to store the criteria which was used to generate the table. Let's look at how we did it in a bit more detail.

First, we declare a variable having the data type **Property**.

```
Dim prpCriteria As Property
```

Next, we create a reference to the table we have just created.

```
Set tbl = db.TableDefs(vTableName)
```

Then we create a new property for that object. When we create the property, we need to give it a name. We have called it **Criteria**.

```
Set prpCriteria = tbl.CreateProperty("Criteria")
```

The next step is to specify the type of value that the property can hold. We want the new **Criteria** property to hold a textual value, so we specify the intrinsic constant **dbText** as the property's type.

```
prpCriteria.Type = dbText
```

Then, we assign a value to the property. If an empty SQL string—or no string at all—was passed to the **BuildOrderIDTable()** procedure, we set the value of the property to **"All Records"**, otherwise we set it to the SQL string that was passed in.

```
If vWhere = "" Or IsMissing(vWhere) Then
    prpCriteria.Value = "All Records"
Else
    prpCriteria.Value = vWhere
End If
```

Finally, we need to make the property persistent. In other words, we need to save it to disk, so it is preserved even when the application is closed. We do this by appending it to the **Properties** collection of the **TableDef** object for the table to which it belongs:

```
tbl.Properties.Append prpCriteria
```

The property can be inspected and set in the same way as any of the in-built properties, either in a procedure or in the Debug window. So you can display the current value of the table's **Criteria** property by typing the following in the Debug window:

```
?CurrentDB()("tblCriteriaHits").Properties("Criteria").Value
```

In the case where no criteria have been specified, **"All records"** will be returned.

Database Properties

Of course, tables aren't the only Data Access Objects which can have custom properties. Some of the most useful applications of custom properties concern the **Database** object. To start with, let's have a look at how many properties a **Database** object has by default.

Try It Out—Custom Database properties

1 Create a new Access database and call it **DBProperties.mdb**.

2 Open a new standard code module, and type in the following procedure:

```
Sub EnumDBProperties()

    Dim pty As Property

    On Error Resume Next

    For Each pty In CurrentDb.Properties
        Debug.Print pty.Name & ": " & pty.Value
    Next

End Sub
```

3 Run the procedure by hitting the *F5* button. When you open up the Debug window, you should see a list of 12 properties, 9 of which have values displayed.

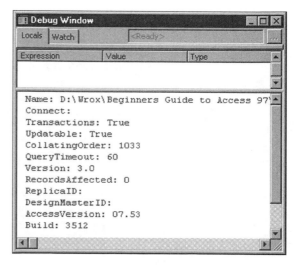

4 Now switch to the Database Window and open up the Startup... dialog from the Tools menu. Give your application a name of 'My New Database' and hit the OK button.

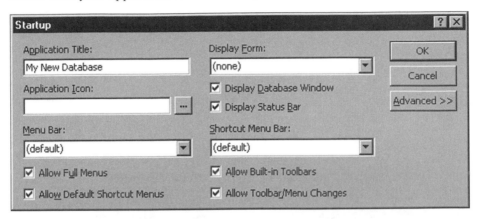

5 Now go back to the module window and delete everything from the Debug window. Then run the **EnumDBProperties** procedure again. Things should look quite a bit different!

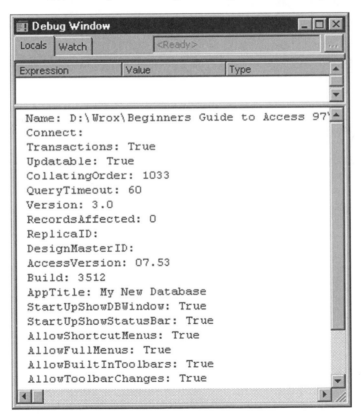

How It Works

The **EnumDBProperties** procedure displays the properties of the current database. In fact, what we are doing here is looping through the **Properties** collection of the current **Database** object and for every **Property** object in that collection, we are displaying its **Name** and **Value**.

```
For Each pty In CurrentDb.Properties
    Debug.Print pty.Name & ": " & pty.Value
Next
```

You may have wondered why we put in the error handling line.

```
On Error Resume Next
```

The reason for this is that, whereas all **Property** objects have a **Name** property, not all have a **Value** property. Of the 13 standard properties of the **Database** object, one of them—the **Connection** property—does not have a **Value**. If we try to print the **Value** of a **Property** which doesn't have one, Access would normally generate a run-time error. By inserting the statement **On Error Resume Next**, we are telling Access to ignore any statements that cause errors and simply resume execution on the next line. This is why there is no line printed in the Debug window for the **Connection** property. So, there are 13 standard properties of a **Database** object and the Debug window contains the names and values of 12 of them.

But once we make a change in the Startup... dialog from the Tools menu, we suddenly find that there are nine new properties. Where did these come from? The answer is that these are **application-defined properties**. In other words, they are not standard properties that exist in every new database, but are added by Access as needed.

You should also be aware that not all database properties can be accessed using the **db.*propertyname*** notation. So although we can do this in the debug window:

```
?Currentdb.Version
3.0
```

You can't do this:

```
?Currentdb.AppTitle
```

In order to determine the value of these non-standard properties, we have to get in through the **Properties** collection of the **Database** object. So to find the value of the **AppTitle** property, we would do this:

```
?Currentdb.Properties("AppTitle").Value
My New Database
```

This also means that we need to exercise a little care when setting the value of these properties. We need to check that the property exists before we set its value, and if it doesn't exist, we need to create it using the DAO hierarchy as we did earlier. So, if we wanted to programmatically prevent the user from bypassing the **Autoexec** macro or Startup... dialog options, we would set the **AllowBypassKey** property of the database to **False** like this:

```
Sub KeepEmOut()

    Dim db As Database
    Dim pty As Property

    On Error GoTo KeepEmOut_Err

    Set db = CurrentDb
    db.Properties("AllowBypassKey").Value = False

KeepEmOut_Exit:
    Exit Sub

KeepEmOut_Err:
    If Err.Number = 3270 Then        'Error code for "Property not found"
        '...so we'll create it ourselves
        Set pty = db.CreateProperty("AllowBypassKey", dbBoolean, False)
        db.Properties.Append pty
    Else
        MsgBox Err.Description
        Resume KeepEmOut_Exit
    End If

End Sub
```

Summary

If you look back over this chapter, you'll see that we have covered a quite a few topics. We have looked at:

▶ Using functions to determine variables and arrays

▶ Multi-dimensional arrays

▶ Transferring recordsets into arrays using the **GetRows** method.

▶ Passing arguments by reference and by value, and the advantages of each method

▶ Enhancing the functionality of Access through use of DLLs

▶ User-defined and application-defined DAO properties

We are now getting to the stage where our code is getting a little complex. In one or two of the procedures in this chapter, we came into situations where the things we were trying to do might have caused errors to occur, so we had to put in some code to handle those situations. In fact, you will find out that even seemingly innocuous lines of code can sometimes cause errors to occur.

Now is probably the time to stop for a moment and spend some time looking at how we can make our VBA code more robust. That is why the next chapter will look at how we can ensure our code and applications work in the way they were intended to, by using sound debugging and error-handling techniques.

Exercises

1 The **Nz** function is used to return a given value if the variable passed to the function is null. So the function **Nz(varAny, 0)** returns **varAny** if **varAny** isn't null, and **0** if **varAny** is null.

See if you can write a function that accepts a variable passed by reference and—if that variable is null—converts to it to **0** and returns **True**.

2 The **Kernel32** dynamic link library contains a function called **GetWindowsDirectory** which returns the path to the Windows directory. You can declare the function like this in VBA:

```
Private Declare Function GetWindowsDirectoryA Lib "kernel32" _
(ByVal strBuffer As String, ByVal lngSize As Long) As Long
```

The first argument should be passed as a fixed-length string and will be populated by the function with a string representing the path to the Windows directory. You should populate the second variable (**lngSize**) with the length of **strBuffer** before you call the **GetWindowsDirectory** function.

Use this function to create a VBA procedure called **GetWinDir** that accepts no arguments and simply returns the path to the Windows directory.

.

Error Handling, Debugging and Testing

You have learnt a lot about programming in Access 97, and how to make great applications. What you haven't learnt is how to stop problems from occurring, and how to find problems when (and I mean *when*, not *if*) they occur.

The term **debug** means 'to remove errors from'. No one writes bug-free programs first time, as there's always something you haven't thought of. Therefore, you should be aware of how you can prevent errors, and what to do when they inevitably creep in.

In this chapter you will learn

- How to prevent errors
- The different types of error
- Methods of handling errors
- How to use the error events

Planning for Errors

One of Murphy's laws states that 'If you perceive six possible ways for something to go wrong and circumvent them, then a seventh one, unplanned for, will promptly develop'. Another states that 'It's impossible to make anything foolproof because fools are so ingenious'. Nevertheless, despite the truth of these observations, planning for errors is possible.

Users don't care how great your code is. They don't care if you have just invented the greatest and fastest algorithm for calculating Pi. All they want is an application that looks good and that works. But, and it's a very big but, you should never use this reason to cut corners in your code. Finding and fixing an error is almost always more time-consuming, and therefore more expensive, than a little advance planning.

The Design

If you have just said, 'Design—what design?' then you should go directly to jail, without passing Go, or collecting $200. The design is the most fundamental part of your application—the foundation upon which everything else rests. The design stage should be where you work out exactly what the application needs to do. One of the most common causes of errors is change. Applications are often delivered which do not meet the user's requirements and need changing. So you start adding bits of code here and there, and gradually errors creep in. Think ahead—spend time talking to the users to try to find out everything they will need. But don't be surprised when, after weeks of exhaustive analysis of user requirements, you finally deliver the application and the user says 'Great, but can you just add...?'. This is bound to happen because users are often unsure of what they want until they have seen something. Do not, however, be tempted to just dive in and do the fix. Plan it, and any implications it may have, first. This will save a lot of wasted time and effort later.

If you are aware of these principles in advance, you have a better chance of producing an application that can be modified more easily. This, in turn, should reduce the number of errors. Below are a few general concepts to think about before you begin coding.

Tables

You are probably getting bored with this now, but plan ahead. Try to think of the fields that might be required but that the user hasn't thought of. The users may just request an address for a company table, but what happens if you need to sort your companies by area, or even sales region. You will need more than one field—Town, State, etc.. We encountered this problem right back at the start of the book and looked at how to break a name down into its constituent parts.

Queries

For each table, you should create a query that simply shows all of the fields in the following fashion:

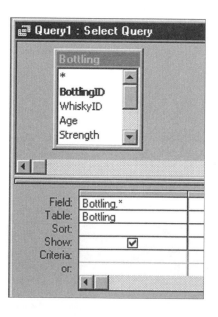

It is preferable to use the asterisk form shown, rather than explicitly specifying each field, as it allows you to add fields to the table without changing the query. You should base all your forms and reports on these queries, rather than on the tables themselves. The advantage of this is that it allows the table details to change without affecting the form or report, except, of course, that the new fields will not automatically show up on the form or report. For example, if you need to rename a field in the table, you can just create an alias for it in the query. Any forms based on the query will not need changing.

Forms and Reports

The principle idea here is to keep it simple. You may love creating forms that do great things, but are they really needed? Do they make the application better? Do they help people use the application? Your application should help the user do his or her job better. If what you add to the interface doesn't do that, then strip it out.

It's said that 80% of the people use 20% of the functionality of an application. Bear this in mind, and do not overload your forms with too much information. If you only want one form, but have a lot of data to display, then try to use the Tab Control, which allows you to split the fields into logical pages.

Function Grouping

Function grouping simply means keeping like things together. If you are writing a series of string-handling routines, put them all together in one module. This ensures that you will not duplicate any procedures, since all routines of a similar type are together. Also, once the procedures in a module have been fully debugged, you can import these modules into other databases when you want to use the routines again, without the worry of having to debug them.

Object-Oriented Techniques for Preventing Errors

You can use some of the techniques of object orientation to help you in the battle to make your application error free.

Encapsulation

Encapsulation is often called 'data hiding', as this is exactly what it does. The idea is that, instead of having public variables that can be accessed from any function, you use private variables and create public procedures to access them. This ensures that you have greater control over the data and allows you to change the actual implementation of the code and its variables, without affecting other routines. Every object should know everything about itself and should not break if you move it into another environment.

The new feature of class modules in Access 97, and the **Property Get** and **Let** procedures that were introduced in Access 95, as described in the previous chapter, have brought another degree of encapsulation to Access. They allow all of a form's or module's data to be private, but allow public access by selected routines. This also allows you to change the underlying code, as long as you keep the interface the same. You can also add to the interface by the use of Optional arguments—any new calls could use these, and, since they are optional, the old calls would still work.

Re-use

Re-use goes very well with encapsulation and can be summed up with the phrase 'Don't re-invent the wheel'. If you have a piece of code that meets your needs, use it again. Not only does this save time but, if the code is error free, you won't have to worry about debugging it. Don't be afraid of using another person's code, as long as you can guarantee it works well, and as long as you don't break any copyright laws. Re-use is not the same as stealing.

When creating functions, you should always think about whether they should be implemented as generic functions. For example, if you have common code that is used in each form, create a new module and move the code there. If the procedure refers to the form, you can pass the form object into the procedure using the **Me** object. Any changes that have to be made to this routine can then be done in just one place, rather than several times in each form. Of course, this does have the disadvantage that an error in the procedure will affect several areas. But if you test well, and make each code section stand-alone, you can move them between projects without fear.

Several large companies have a policy of paying programmers a bonus each time their code is re-used. This is a good incentive as it encourages you to plan ahead and think of other areas where your code could be used.

Option Explicit

The **Option Explicit** command was first mentioned in Chapter 2. This is extremely useful and should be the default for all of your code modules. You can set it from within the Module pane of the Options... dialog that is accessed from the Tools menu:

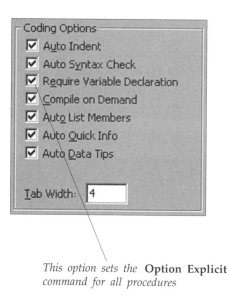

This option sets the **Option Explicit** *command for all procedures*

When this option is set, any new code modules you create automatically have the statement **Option Explicit** added to them, with the result that all the variables you use must be explicitly declared. This means that you can avoid hard-to-find errors that are caused by typing mistakes. For example, consider the following:

```
Public Function Circumference (dblRadius As Double)

    Circumfrence = 2 * 3.1415926 * dblRadius

End Function
```

Did you spot the mistake? The function name has been typed incorrectly when calculating the return value, and therefore the correct answer will never be returned. Although this procedure only contains one line, the error could take a long time to put right since the value from this function might be used elsewhere. The use of **Option Explicit** ensures that this type of error never happens. With **Option Explicit** declared**, "Circumfrence"** will be flagged as an undeclared variable at compile time, forcing you to correct the typographical error.

Syntax Checking

The Module page of the Options dialog also provides the option Auto Syntax Check. When this is set, Access checks the syntax of your code as you type in the lines, as well as when it is compiled, and displays an error if the line is incorrect. If you do not have this option set, the incorrect line turns a different color (set from the Tools, Options menu), and your code is checked when it is compiled. The Auto Syntax Check is especially important if you don't compile your code before giving it to the users, as syntax errors could be generated when they run it.

Sometimes you may find this option frustrating (I do), but it is worth leaving it set. The benefits outweigh any disadvantages it may have. If you can't live with it turned on, make sure you select Compile All Modules from the Debug menu (when you have a module window open) each time you complete an editing session.

Comments

This is actually a bit of a dilemma. There are people who put no comments in their code at all ('If it was hard to write, it should be hard to read'), and there are others who comment every line. Both are wrong. You need to strike a happy medium. Listed below are some guidelines that you should consider:

▶ Put a comment at the top of each procedure describing what it does, what arguments it takes, and what value it returns. For example:

```
Public Function Circumference(dblRadius As Double) As Double
'
' Purpose:      To calculate the circumference of a circle
' Arguments:    dblRadius       The circle radius
' Returns:      The circumference
' Author:       David Sussman
' Date:         11 June 1997

    Circumfrence = 2 * 3.1415926 * dblRadius

End Function
```

▶ Comment variables, describing what they are used for

▶ Place comments on their own lines, except where you are describing a variable, in which case the comment should be on the same line as the declaration

▶ Comment sections of code—functionality, rather than each line

▶ Do not comment the obvious. If you are assigning a value to a variable, do not put in a comment that says 'set value to...'. Only comment these if there is a reason to describe why you are doing it, such as setting a value to **Empty** or **Null** where later on in your code you check for it explicitly.

▶ Debug the code, not the comments. Do not rely on the comments, since they are often not changed when code is updated. You should make sure that any changes *you* make are always reflected in the comments.

The most important thing to remember is consistency. As with the rest of your application, pick a style you feel comfortable with and stick to it.

Testing

Many large organizations have teams devoted to just testing. Others like to let the users do the testing (that's what beta products are *really* for!). However, no matter how experienced you are, or how long you have been programming, you should never be above testing your own code. Every programmer should take responsibility for the code they produce. After all, you are the one who is going to have to fix any errors that are found.

Testing can take several forms and you should allow time in your schedule for all of them. You should think of this part of the process as being as important as the code creation itself. We'll look at the different stages of testing now.

Functional Testing

Functional testing can involve checking that the whole application, or just a part of it, does what it is supposed to do. There are three ways to achieve this and they should be used in the correct order:

▶ Test it yourself, as you understand how it is supposed to work

▶ Give it to the users. After all, they are the ones who know what it should do

▶ Give it to a third party, along with the specification. If they know nothing about it, apart from what is written, they will not make any assumptions. They also will not worry about upsetting you if it does not come up to scratch.

Usability Testing

This is the next stage after you have decided that the application meets its requirements. Usability testing really applies to the visible portions of the application. You need to know whether it is easy to use. Does it confuse the users? Does it follow the usual conventions? After all, if the users don't like the application, it doesn't matter how well it meets their requirements. You may have your own ideas about what is good but, at the end of the day, you must supply something that the user will be happy with. You may also wish to include the time it takes to accomplish a task as 'usability'. You may have to re-design your code if a particular function takes longer than is acceptable to execute.

Destructive Testing

This is a fun stage. Give it to someone and ask him or her to break it. Tell them to try the unconventional. Search for that unplanned seventh problem. If you are testing a form, then let someone who does not use forms, or even computers, play around. If you are testing some code, then give it to another programmer. They will love the chance to break your code. And you can be sure that once they have found a few glaring bugs to gloat over, you'll soon start to tighten up your own checking. It may hurt your pride initially, but in the long run you'll become a better programmer! (And you'll always get a chance for revenge when they ask you to test their code.)

Maintenance

It is said that 60% of a programmer's time is spent maintaining old programs (it's also said that 85% of statistics are made up, but that's another story). When making changes to code, whether it is an old program or a new one, there are some important things to consider:

▶ Will the change you are making impact on anyone else? If it is a library routine then check with other people who are using your routine before making any changes. If there is an error in the code, other people might have coded around the error, so if you correct your code, theirs might stop working.

▶ Keep focused on correcting the problem you are looking for.

Only do one change at a time. Imagine correcting what you think are several problems, but when you run the code you get new errors. Which one of your changes caused this? If you track down problems one at a time, and test them one at a time, your overall maintenance time could be reduced.

▶ Don't get distracted into 'tidying up' or improving code, unless that's the explicit reason you are modifying it.

The above are really common sense, but you'd be surprised how often common sense flies out of the window when we have our heads stuck into code.

Types of Errors

You can (and should) follow all the above guidelines for error prevention, but, unfortunately, it's a fact of life that you'll still get errors in your code. Errors occur in many guises, and it is important to know what type of error you are dealing with, so that you can choose the best method to cure it. We mentioned in Chapter 2 that there are three types of error:

▶ Syntax errors

▶ Run-time errors

▶ Semantic or logic errors

We'll now have a closer look at these and see what can be done to put them right.

At this early stage it's important to understand the distinction between Errors and bugs. An error can be a useful event, such as Data Access Errors, which allow you to run some code when a table error occurs. For example, if a table does not allow null values in a certain field, you could show a custom dialog box describing the error, and where to go for help if the user still has problems. This is a trappable error that can be handled by the programmer. A bug is an unhandled error that the programmer has not seen in advance.

Syntax Errors

This is the simplest form of error, and is often caused by typing mistakes. Those of you who have graduated beyond two fingers may find less of these but, as we've mentioned, there is an easy way to find them—let Access do it for you. If you turn on syntax checking and ensure that all variables must be declared, Access will alert you when you misspell statements. However, you'll also meet cases where you have used the wrong construction. Again, Access will pick these up for you.

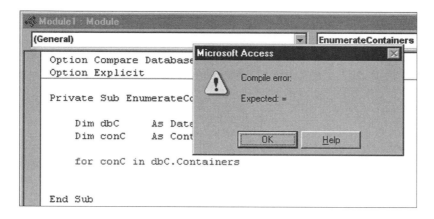

Here you can see that the syntax used with the **For...Next** and **For...Each** statements has been confused. Access has not found an **Each** statement and so expects the equals sign. This isn't there, so when you press *Return*, the line is highlighted and an error message displayed. You can click the OK button to cancel the warning and then either correct the error or come back to it later. If you don't fix it, the error will be found again when you compile the module.

Another type of syntax error cannot be found immediately. Have a look at the following:

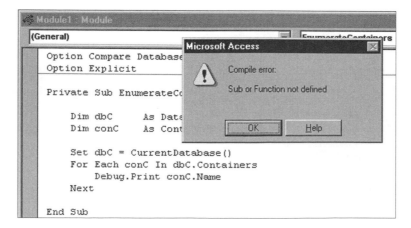

When you press the OK button the **CurrentDatabase** function is highlighted, either because you have mistakenly typed it instead of **CurrentDB**, or because it is a function of your own that does not exist, or cannot be seen. This could happen if you create a **Private** procedure in another module when you meant to create a **Public** one.

Run-time Errors

Run-time errors, as the name suggests, will only be found when the code is run. A run-time error is one that causes the code to fall over when executed, despite the fact that the syntax of the language is correct and code can be compiled. In fact, successful compilation only indicates that the statements in your code are in the correct order and no undefined functions are used. There can be plenty of other kinds of error lurking in the background.

The extensive use of Auto Tips has eased many of the common run-time errors because Access helps with procedure parameters and object properties and methods. However, it is still easy to miss many.

One of the most common of these is the ubiquitous Type Mismatch error. This is where you assign a value of one type to a variable of a different (and incompatible) type. When this occurs you see the following message:

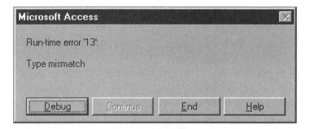

In this case, you can pause the code and highlight the offending line by pressing the Debug button. Here, a variable of the type **Integer** has been assigned a text value—which is clearly wrong:

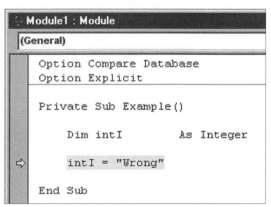

This shows the importance of testing and a decent, consistent naming convention, since this error is not easy to spot just by looking at the code. Even experienced programmers would not always spot this first time.

Semantic Errors

There was a press report recently about a small British company that has developed a method of writing software that is guaranteed to be error free. This has yet to be proved, but if true, then the owners of this company are likely to be very rich indeed. Bill Gates, watch out!

Semantic errors are the hardest type of error to find, since they represent errors in the logic of the program, and even Microsoft ship products with these errors, so you can see why they are so important. Sometimes, these may produce run-time errors, in which case you get the run-time error dialog box, as shown above, which will allow you to identify the line. Beware of taking this too literally, though, as the line which generates the error may not always be the cause of the problem. This is especially true if the line contains several variables. For example, if one of the variables has an incorrect value, you have to find out where this value was set. If you have written well-structured modular code, you may be three or four functions deep (that is, where one function has called a different one, and that in turn has called another), so you need to work back through the procedures to find the root of the problem. You will see how to do this later in the chapter.

The testing of semantic errors is also the hardest to do, as you tend to test what you think the code *ought* to be doing and not what it *is* doing. This is not as odd as it seems, because we programmers tend to be fairly focused people. We look at a piece of code and think 'OK, this is doing…—I know that' and skim over the code. Don't get into this habit. When testing and debugging you have to throw away your perceptions of the problem and start from scratch. At times it's difficult to avoid, but you have to try.

Let's take a look at an example of a run-time failure that was caused by a semantic error. This particular example demonstrates how an error message may not actually indicate the cause of the error.

Try It Out—Run-time and Semantic Errors

1 Create a new module, and add the following procedure:

```
Public Function DivideNumbers (dblNum1 As Double, dblNum2 As Double) _
        As Double

    DivideNumbers = dblNum1 / dblNum2

End Function
```

This simply divides one number by another.

2 Compile the code by clicking the Compile Loaded Modules button and save the module.

3 Next create a new blank form with three unbound text controls and a command button. Change the captions as shown here and change the Name properties of the text boxes to **txtNumber1**, **txtNumber2** and **txtResult**, and the command button to **cmdDivide**.

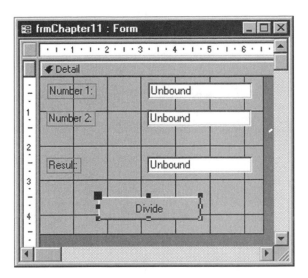

4 Now add the following line of code to the On Click event procedure for the command button:

```
txtResult = DivideNumbers (txtNumber1, txtNumber2)
```

5 Switch the form to Form view and try the following numbers:

Exactly what you expected.

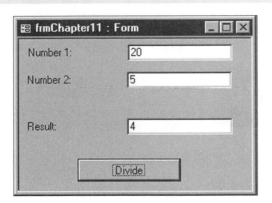

6 Now try it again and input 0 for number 2.

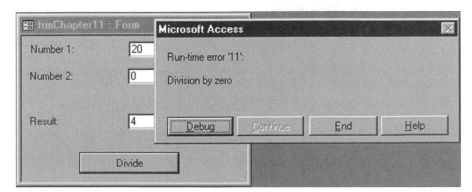

The good old Division by zero error rears its ugly head.

7 Press the <u>D</u>ebug button and you're taken to the line of code in the **DivideNumbers** function where the error occurred.

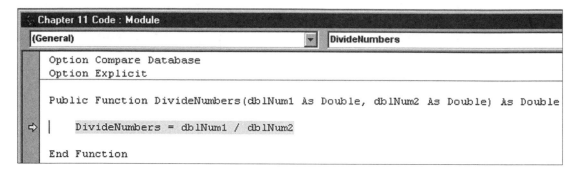

```
Chapter 11 Code : Module
(General)                                          DivideNumbers

    Option Compare Database
    Option Explicit

    Public Function DivideNumbers(dblNum1 As Double, dblNum2 As Double) As Double

⇨ |    DivideNumbers = dblNum1 / dblNum2

    End Function
```

You now have to decide if this is really the line with the problem. The problem lies in the number that the user typed in—we obviously need to check somewhere that the number they typed is not 0.

The data was passed in from another procedure, so should we check the user's input in that procedure or in this one? In this case, the **DivideNumbers** function should do the checking. A function should be completely self-contained—if every procedure that needed to call this one had to check the values, the code would become very cumbersome. Therefore, we should add a check here.

FYI To get out of debug mode you need to select the **End** button on the toolbar. You need to do this to be able to execute the code again or use the form in form view.

8 Add the following lines to the **DivideNumbers** function. Don't forget to save your code after you have made the changes.

```
Public Function DivideNumbers(dblNum1 As Double, dblNum2 As Double) _
      As Double

    If dblNum2 <> 0 Then
        DivideNumbers = dblNum1 / dblNum2
    End If

End Function
```

9 Switch back to the form and try the example again. This time there's no error message. The function doesn't attempt to divide by 0. However, you can't pat yourself on the back just yet. The mathematicians among you will have noticed that although you don't get an error message, you don't get the right answer either. The result of a number divided by 0 is not 0. Neither have we provided for all the possible erroneous entries that a user could make. What happens when a user enters a letter, for example? You'll get another error message, this time a Run-Time Error 13, Type Mismatch. This tells you that you have your variable types confused, and are trying to divide by a letter or string.

What we need to do is to use a function that defends itself, thus ensuring that a run-time error is not generated.

10 Change the **DivideNumbers** function to the following:

```
Public Function DivideNumbers(dblNum1 As Variant, _
                   dblNum2 As Variant, dblRV as Double) As Boolean

    On Error GoTo DivideNumbers_Err

    dblRV = dblNum1 / dblNum2
    DivideNumbers = True

DivideNumbers_OK:
    Exit Function

DivideNumbers_Err:
    DivideNumbers = False
    Resume DivideNumbers_OK

End Function
```

11 Next, change the command button's On Click event handler to:

```
Dim bolErrorCheck    As Boolean
Dim dblCalcResult    As Double

bolErrorCheck = DivideNumbers(txtNumber1, txtNumber2, dblCalcResult)

If bolErrorCheck = True Then
    txtResult = dblCalcResult
Else
    txtResult = "Semantic Error"
End If
```

12 Now run the example again. This time there shouldn't be any errors, no matter what you type in.

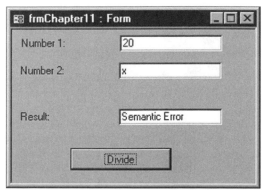

How It Works

At the end of the Try It Out the function accepts three arguments. The first two are as before—they pass the two numbers to be divided into the function. The third is used to hold the result of the division and will pass this back to the form if the calculation is completed successfully. As the number of parameters that the function accepted changed, so the number of parameters with which the function was called has been amended accordingly.

The result of whether the calculation has been completed is transmitted to the Boolean variable **bolErrorCheck**. It takes its value from the value that the function returns. If it is **True**, the result of the calculation result is displayed; if it is **False**, the message Semantic Error is displayed.

If there is any error at all in the division operation, the error trap, which we enabled with **On Error GoTo DivideNumbers_Err**, re-directs execution to the **DivideNumbers_Err** label. Here the return value of the function is set to **False**, and we exit the function via the **DivideNumbers_OK** label. Of course, if there is no error, the return value of the function is set to **True**.

This now puts the onus back on the calling procedure to check whether or not it worked. You would probably never have a function just to divide two numbers, but you can see the principles involved. The procedure should be able to defend itself against incorrect data, but it should never hide errors, although it can handle them, as long as error code information is made available.

Locating Errors

One thing to remember when tracking down errors is that Access is event-driven and code can be activated in unexpected areas. Consider opening a form. What event(s) do you think are generated? There are, in fact, five events:

Open → Load → Resize → Activate → Current

Closing a form generates three events:

Unload → Deactivate → Close

So, if opening a form seems to be causing a problem, don't forget to check the other events. A good way to check for all of the procedures in a module is to set the Full Module View option on the Module page of the Options window on the Tools menu.

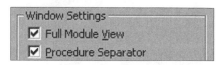

Or by using the button in the bottom-left corner of the module window.

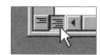

This will show all of the modules together in the module window, using (if the Procedure Separator option is selected) a line to separate each procedure. If you do not have this set, you can use the *Ctrl* key in conjunction with the up and down arrows to move between procedures.

Other Errors

This is the pic'n'mix bag, where we look at just about anything else that can generate an error. Of course, the number of errors that occur is always in proportion to the importance of the application, and in inverse proportion to the time you have to fix it!

One cause of these 'other' errors can be the use of external applications, such as dynamic link libraries (DLLs) or custom controls. If the programmers who wrote these have done their testing well, you shouldn't see failures, but bugs can occur.

Other problems, such as lack of memory or a corrupt registration database, can cause some very odd things to happen. Running out of memory (yes it can happen, even in Windows 95) can mean that Access doesn't have enough resources to display the screen properly.

Although there's usually nothing you can do in these situations, it's useful to know what sort of problems can create unexplained errors. If you're stuck for an answer, try the following steps:

▶ Check your code thoroughly

▶ Try running the application on another machine

▶ If that works, examine the differences between the two machines. There have been noted cases where an error such as this was caused by an out-of-date DLL residing on one machine, when the correct version was on the other.

▶ Get someone else to check your code, or even dry-run through your code explaining it to someone else. It's amazing how often you will spot an error when you have to explain to someone exactly what you are supposed to be doing.

▶ Panic!

You should never reach the last stage as there is always somewhere or someone you can find the answer from. If you can, use the Microsoft Developer Network, or online services such as the Microsoft Network, CompuServe and the Internet. There is a big wide world out there with lots of people and all of them (well, most, anyway) are willing to help.

Debugging

Now that you have seen ways to prevent errors, and the type of errors that you can encounter, you need to know how to track them down. As you become more experienced, you will find your instinct becomes fairly well honed and your intuition will start to tell you where the error lies. Until then, we'll try and point you in the right direction.

Program Execution

Access provides a number of ways to help you navigate through your code whilst it is running. This enables you to start from a place where you know the code works, even if that is the beginning, and gradually narrow down to the area with the error.

There are two places which contain all of the useful facilities for debugging. The first is the Visual Basic toolbar:

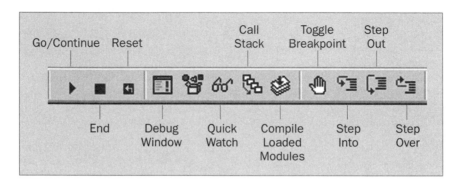

The second is the Debug menu:

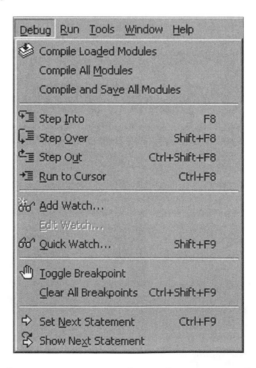

A combination of these gives you great control over how your program executes. The following sections explain what each button does and how it can be used, and then we'll try them out.

Breakpoints

Breakpoints are at the heart of debugging as they allow you to mark the lines at which you want the program execution to be temporarily suspended. You can set breakpoints in any of four ways:

> ▶ Clicking the Toggle Breakpoint button
> ▶ Selecting the Toggle Breakpoint option on the <u>D</u>ebug menu
> ▶ Pressing *F9*
> ▶ Clicking in the border at the left of the module window

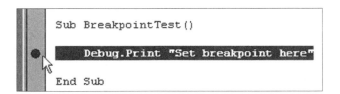

All of these act as a toggle, so they will set a breakpoint where one does not exist and remove one where it does. There is no limit to the number of breakpoints that you can have at any one time.

When Access encounters a line with a breakpoint, the program is halted, the code window displayed, and the line with the breakpoint highlighted. You can then use the debug window to inspect or set variables, or even change the code in the module window. The program will remain active unless you stop it.

Program execution can also be halted by pressing *Ctrl+Break* whilst it is running. This has the same effect as a breakpoint, including allowing you to inspect variables, and even change the code.

Continuing Execution

You can use the Go/Continue button to continue the execution of a halted program. Execution will resume at the current line and continue until user input is required or another breakpoint is reached.

Stopping Execution

You can use the End button at any time to stop execution of the program.

The Reset button stops execution and re-initializes all of the variables in your program. This is most useful when you are using static variables that retain their values. You also need to use this button when you are debugging form or report modules. When execution halts in one of these, you cannot access the form or report until you either Continue or Reset the code.

Stepping Through Code

Stopping at a breakpoint is all very well, but what happens when you want to examine lines as they are executed? Setting breakpoints at each line would be extremely tedious, and this is where stepping comes in. Stepping through the code means running lines one at a time, and is done in conjunction with breakpoints. When a program has been halted, you can run one line at a time, allowing you to find out which lines are correct. There are several ways of stepping through the code:

➤ The **Step Into** button runs only the line that the cursor is placed on. If that line happens to contain a procedure, it will step into the procedure and continue the single stepping through the code within the procedure.

➤ The **Step Over** button also only runs the line that the cursor is placed on. However, if that line contains a procedure, the code in it is run normally—without single-stepping. Then, on return from the procedure, single-stepping resumes automatically.

➤ The **Step Out** button continues execution in the current procedure and then halts execution at the line after the calling procedure. This is a bit like combining **Step Into** and **Step Over**.

If you want even more flexibility, you can use the <u>R</u>un To Cursor option from the <u>D</u>ebug menu. Just place the cursor on the line you want execution to halt at, and then select <u>R</u>un To Cursor. All of the lines in between will be run without stepping, as though a temporary breakpoint had been placed upon this line.

The advantage of the **Step Into** method is that you can check every line in every procedure that is encountered. However, this is also its disadvantage since it can be very time consuming, especially if a procedure contains loops. **Step Over** allows you to run a procedure quickly, which is useful if you know it is correct. And, of course, if you are using procedures that have already been fully tested and debugged, you can step over them and concentrate more easily on the new code, where the errors are expected to lie.

The **Run To Cursor** option is extremely useful when you have loops, as it enables you to quickly jump to the statement after the loop, thus saving time.

Rerunning Lines of Code

The ability to rerun lines of code was introduced in Access 95, but it has been made much simpler in Access 97. This can be of real benefit when you have stopped at a breakpoint, and notice that a line that has already been executed is wrong. Now you can just skip back and rerun it. You can do this by grabbing the arrow in the module window border and dragging it to its new location. Click the mouse button on the line the code is stopped at, and then, while holding the mouse button down, move it to another line:

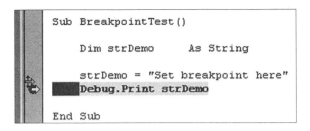

You notice that the cursor changes to an arrow pointing at the new line. When you are on the next line you can drop it, by letting the left mouse button go:

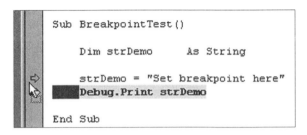

Now, when you continue running the program, it will start from the new line. You can also do this by placing the cursor on the new line and pressing *Ctrl + F9*.

Skipping Lines of Code

Skipping lines of code can be useful but it should be done with care. By placing the cursor on a line that has not yet been executed, you can use the Set Next Statement option from the Debug menu to tell Access that this is the line you want executed next. All lines in between are ignored.

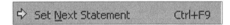

This might be useful if you need to skip a few lines that you suspect are causing problems. But remember that any code in these lines is not executed. This means that things that you may have expected to happen don't, which could lead to further errors. This is especially true if the skipped lines contain other procedure calls, since you may miss more code than you think. You can also use this method to re-execute lines of code in the same way that the previous example works.

The Show Next Statement option will tell you which line will be run next. This is quite useful if you have been examining other procedures and have lost your position in the code window.

Changing Code

Access allows you to change code whilst the program is stopped, so you can correct errors as they occur. You can then press the Continue button to continue execution from the newly corrected line. In fact, you can rewrite whole sections of code and still continue with the program. However, Access will not allow you to modify a declaration statement. Doing so means that the whole structure of the code could change (rather than just a few lines) and you get a message asking whether you wish to abandon the changes or to reset the program. Selecting reset is the same as clicking the Reset button—it stops your code executing, resets all the variables and moves the next execution point back to the first line of your code, ready to re-start.

If you do need to change some variables, but do not wish to reset the program you could step out of the procedure, then change the local variables, and then set the next statement so that the procedure is run again.

The Call Stack

When you are debugging large or complex programs, or those which are well modularized, you can often lose track of where you are in the program. By pressing the Call Stack button, you will see a list of procedures that are currently active:

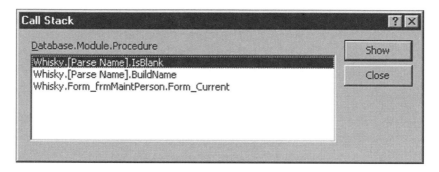

Note that this is not the procedures that have *been* run, but those that are running at the moment. So, for example, if procedure A calls B and B calls C and you halt execution in C, pressing the Calls button will show C, B, A, i.e. the currently executing procedure and those that called it. If you had finished executing C and then continued from B, only B and A would be shown.

This is a good time to use Show Next Statement, as you can often forget where you were when you starting moving around procedures in the middle of debugging.

The Debug Window

You have already seen many examples of using the debug window to type in commands which are executed immediately—and, in earlier versions of Access, it was called the immediate window. However, it is used most often in debugging. You can output data to it, run code from it, and also use it to examine variables.

You can also use the debug window to change the contents of variables, which is useful for correcting values that may be causing errors. If you suspect that a certain value is causing problems later in your code, you can change the value and continue. This is also quite useful during testing since it allows you to force bad values into variables to test the rigidity of your procedures.

If you have used previous versions of Access you will have noticed that this has changed considerably, so let's have a look at the window itself:

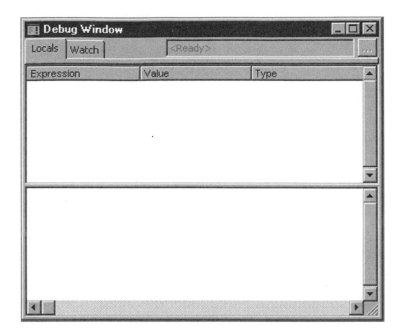

The Locals pane shows the variables and their contents that are in the currently active procedure. The Watch pane shows variables that you want specifically to watch. To the right, a text box shows the state of the procedure, and the builder button to the right of that displays the Call Stack window. The pane at the very bottom is the Immediate Pane, and it is this that you have used so far for calling procedures.

Instant Watches 👓

The Instant Watch button allows you to set a watch on variables or expressions. You can also use the watches as conditional breakpoints. If you specify a watch with the Break When Expression Is True, or Break When Expression has Changed options, the code will stop allowing you to examine both it and the values in the variables.

This is really useful when you have a variable that is causing problems but you are not sure where the value is being set. In this case, you can add a break option for the watch, and execution will halt as soon as the value is true or just changes. Using this form of breakpoint does slow down execution of the program, but generally this is not a problem when you are debugging.

Try It Out—Debugging Code

For this example you need to open the Chapter 11 Debugging module from **Whisky11.mdb** in design view. The module contains the following three procedures:

▶ **DisplayWhisky**, which shows all of the whiskies for a region name

▶ **GetWhisky**, which loads the whiskies for the region into a global array

▶ **DisplayWhiskies**, which displays the contents of the global array

337

DisplayWhisky accepts an array of region names **astrRegions()** and calls the **GetWhisky** function once for each region in the array. It then calls **DisplayWhiskies** to display the values held in the global array in the debug window. **GetWhiskies** creates an SQL statement to retrieve all the records for the region selected, and, for each whisky, adds it to the array. There is an optional argument that will allow the price of the whisky to be included or excluded, as we deem fit.

We will experiment with each of these functions and look at how we debug them when we find an error, as well as examining the variables they contain. You will be controlling execution of the functions from the debug window, so that needs to be open as well.

1   The first thing to do is to set a breakpoint and, since you want to step through the code, put it on the first executable line in the **DisplayWhisky** function:

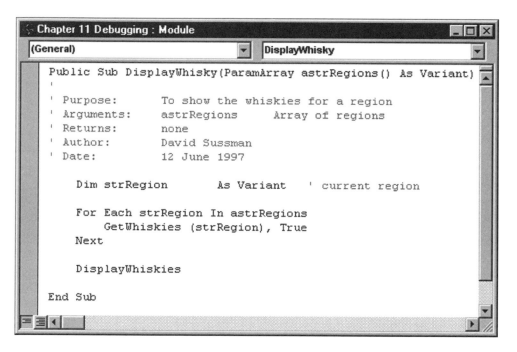

```
Public Sub DisplayWhisky(ParamArray astrRegions() As Variant)
'
'  Purpose:       To show the whiskies for a region
'  Arguments:     astrRegions     Array of regions
'  Returns:       none
'  Author:        David Sussman
'  Date:          12 June 1997

     Dim strRegion        As Variant    ' current region

     For Each strRegion In astrRegions
         GetWhiskies (strRegion), True
     Next

     DisplayWhiskies

End Sub
```

2   Now call the procedure from the debug window by typing the following:

```
DisplayWhisky "Islay", "Highland"
```

You should see that the code has been halted. Click on the Debug Window to bring it to the front:

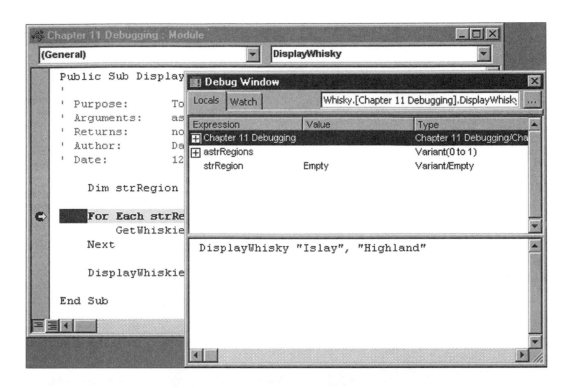

 FYI   Notice that the line under the title in the debug window shows the function that is currently being executed.

3   Let's examine the Locals pane in more detail:

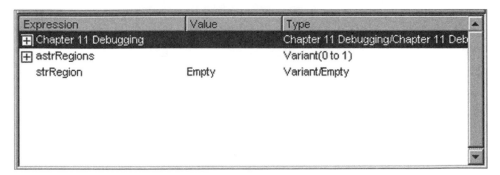

You can see that this shows all of the variables that are currently active, or in scope. The first line is for the module itself, and the plus sign shows that there are items underneath this. The second line shows **astrRegions**, a local array with no value yet assigned. The third line shows **strRegion**, a local variable with a value of **Empty**, which is the value that variants are assigned when they are created.

4 Click on the plus symbol (or double click the line) to expand the Chapter 11 Debugging line:

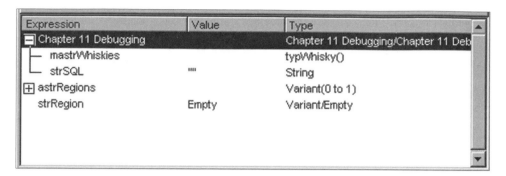

This shows the two global variables, along with their values and types. You can see that **mastrWhiskies** is an array of type **typWhisky**, and that **strSQL** is a **string**. Expand **astrRegions** to see what it contains:

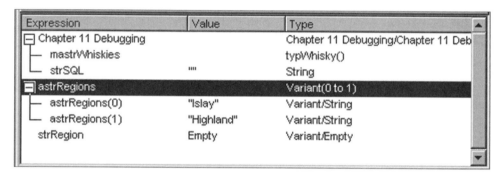

As **astrRegions** is an array, each element of the array is shown, along with its contents.

5 Let's look at another way you can examine variables. You can also type a question mark in the debug pane, followed by the variable name:

```
DisplayWhisky "Islay", "Highland"

?astrRegions(0)
Islay
```

Displayed is the name of the region that you passed to the procedure as the first argument. You can also look at **strRegion**, but this will be empty because this line has not yet been run and has, therefore, not been set to anything.

6 Now press the Step Into button to step through this line of code. Hold the cursor over **strRegion** on the line in the loop, to see yet another way to examine variables.

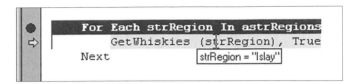

You get a little tooltip that pops up and shows you the value.

7   The breakpoint is still on the **For Each** line, but the current line is the one after, as indicated by the highlight. Now we can see the last method of examining variables, the Quick Watch. Place the cursor over **strRegion** and press the Quick Watch button (or use *Shift-F9*):

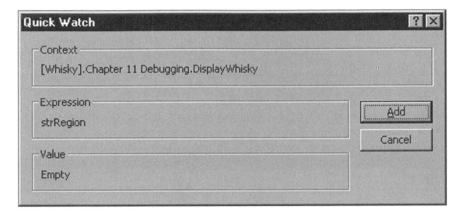

This shows the same information as the Locals pane but in a different format. You also have the option to add this Watch to the Watch list. We'll have a look at this in a minute, but for now press the Cancel button and carry on.

8   Use the Step Into button to move into the **GetWhiskies** procedure, and click on the Debug Window to bring it to the front:

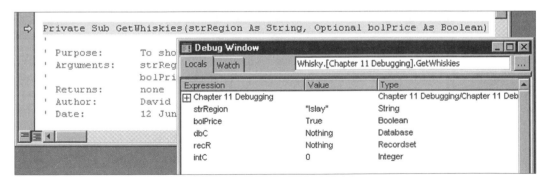

Notice that the variables for the **GetWhiskies** procedure are now shown in the Locals window. The arguments have values, but the local variables don't, as we have not yet set them to anything.

9 This is a good time to examine the procedure stack so press the Calls button to see where you are:

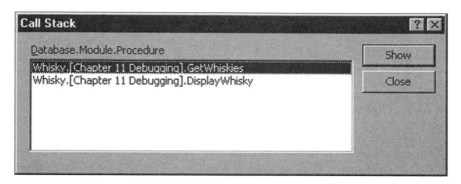

This shows the order in which you have executed the procedures. The most current procedure (the one that is currently active) can be seen at the top, with the procedure that called it below. The first procedure is at the bottom of the list. Although this is a simple example, you can imagine how useful it can be once your programs become larger.

 FYI   The **Show** button allows you to jump to any procedure that you highlight in the window, giving you a quick way to move around the currently active procedures.

10 Now imagine that you wished to step through the code until you are on the line that reads the next record from the recordset. Simply place the cursor on the line

```
recR.MoveNext
```

and pick the <u>R</u>un To Cursor option from the <u>D</u>ebug menu. Execution continues until the selected line. You have now filled a member of the array and execution has halted on your selected line, so switch to the Debug Pane. Firstly expand **recR** to see the recordset:

Expression	Value	Type
⊞ Chapter 11 Debugging		Chapter 11 Debugging/Chapter 11 Debug
strRegion	"Islay"	String
bolPrice	True	Boolean
⊞ dbC		Database/Database
⊟ recR		Recordset/Recordset
— AbsolutePosition	0	Long
— BatchCollisionCount	<Operation is not	Long
— BatchCollisions	<Operation is not	Variant
— BatchSize	<Operation is not	Long
— BOF	False	Boolean
⊞ Bookmark		Byte(0 to 3)
— Bookmarkable	True	Boolean
— CacheSize	0	Long

Notice that all of the properties for the recordset are available. Some do not have values, or are not applicable to this type of recordset, but everything is instantly in view. Scroll down and have a look. The collections of the recordset are also shown:

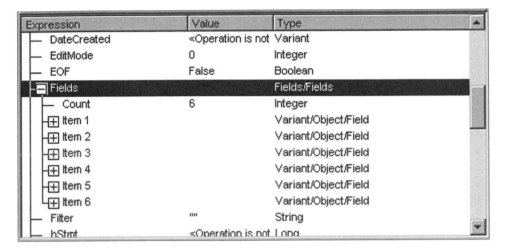

Expression	Value	Type
— DateCreated	<Operation is not	Variant
— EditMode	0	Integer
— EOF	False	Boolean
□ Fields		Fields/Fields
— Count	6	Integer
⊞ Item 1		Variant/Object/Field
⊞ Item 2		Variant/Object/Field
⊞ Item 3		Variant/Object/Field
⊞ Item 4		Variant/Object/Field
⊞ Item 5		Variant/Object/Field
⊞ Item 6		Variant/Object/Field
— Filter	""	String
— hStmt	<Operation is not	Long

Notice that this recordset has six fields in it, and you can expand on these too, to examine their details. You might like to have a more detailed look at this later, but for now carry on.

11 Scroll back to the top and expand the Module 11 Debugging line and expand **mastrWhiskies**:

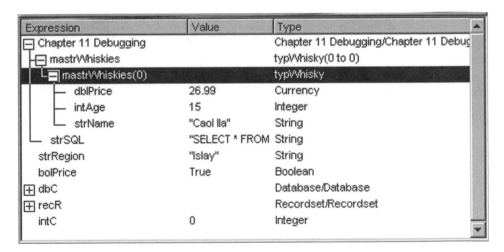

Expression	Value	Type
□ Chapter 11 Debugging		Chapter 11 Debugging/Chapter 11 Debug
□ mastrWhiskies		typWhisky(0 to 0)
□ mastrWhiskies(0)		typWhisky
— dblPrice	26.99	Currency
— intAge	15	Integer
— strName	"Caol Ila"	String
— strSQL	"SELECT * FROM	String
strRegion	"Islay"	String
bolPrice	True	Boolean
⊞ dbC		Database/Database
⊞ recR		Recordset/Recordset
intC	0	Integer

Notice that, as this is the first time through, only the first member of the array has been created, and that the three elements have their correct values. This is far easier than the old method of typing in each element in the debug pane to see its contents.

12 Put the cursor on the **recR.Close** line, and select Run To Cursor. Execution of the code will continue until the requested line. You can see how useful this is when debugging code with loops since you can place the cursor on the statement after the loop and then just skip to it without having to set a breakpoint.

343

13 Press the Step Into button a couple of times, and you return to **DisplayWhisky**, the calling function. Step through a few more times until you reach the following line in the **GetWhiskies** procedure:

```
.strName = recR("WhiskyName")
```

You are once again in the loop where the global array is filled. We want to see the whisky name without printing it to the debug window or flipping to the Locals pane—so we will set a Watch on this variable so we can always see it.

14 Highlight **recR("WhiskyName")** and press the Quick Watch button. The Quick Watch window appears showing the variable and its contents. This time click Add. You are switched to the Watch pane with your variable showing:

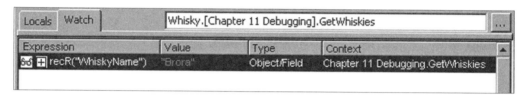

This shows exactly the same information as the Locals pane, but only for variables you are interested in. Since you can have variables from many procedures the context is also shown. In this case the context is for the current module.

15 Position the windows so that you can see the watched variable and the code, and step through until **recR.MoveNext**. Keep an eye on your watched variable as you step through and you can see its value change.

16 You can also add more watches by right clicking in the watch window and selecting Add Watch.... The following dialog appears:

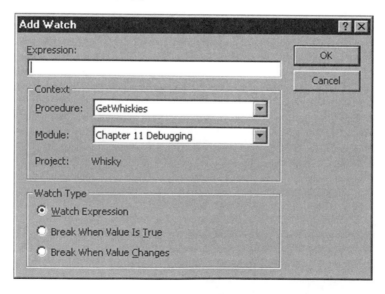

17 Now you can choose not only what to watch, but how you want to watch it too. A Watch Type of Watch Expression is like the one you have already seen. It shows the value of the expression you are watching. Break When Value Is True will add a watch expression and halt execution when the value of that expression is true. Break When Value Changes will halt execution when the value changes. This can be extremely useful when you have a global variable that is being changed by another procedure, but you are not sure where it is being changed. In this case you can just set a watch in place and run the program as normal, and every time the expression changes, the code will be halted.

18 Let's try a Break When Value Is True, to break when the price of a whisky exceeds £30:

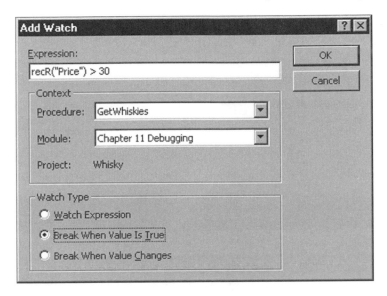

Click OK and notice how the watch has been added:

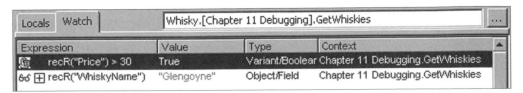

The current value is False.

19 Press the Go/Continue button and the Watch window will pop to the front showing that the expression is now true:

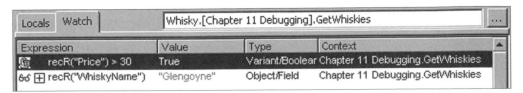

The program continued executing until it found a price of above £30. You can confirm this by examining the details in the Locals window, or in the Debug Pane:

```
ShowWhisky "Islay", "Highland"

?recR("Price")
 32.99
```

20 Let's assume that this price is incorrect. You cannot change the value in `recR("Price")` without performing a `recR.Edit` and `recR.Update`, but you can change the value in the array. So in the Debug Pane, just set the new value and press *Return*:

```
mastrWhiskies(intC).dblPrice = 100
```

This is just like setting a variable in code.

21 Now press the Continue button to continue execution without stepping. The procedure will finish and the details will be printed. Scroll up the window a little to find the 12-year old Glengoyne, the value you changed.

```
Glen Ord
 12
 18.99
Glengoyne
 12
 100
Glengoyne
```

You can see that the new Locals pane is a great boon to the developer. It's also quite useful as a learning tool, for examining the properties of objects as they are being used. It's worthwhile spending some time getting used to this as it can save a great deal of time.

Using Help

Single stepping is useful for finding errors, but don't go straight there. One of the first places that you should look is the help file, as it contains a list of the most common types of errors and descriptions of what you are doing wrong. There is generally a Help button on the error message dialogs that appear so annoyingly while you are trying to debug your code. If you place the cursor on a keyword in the code window and press *F1*, you get context-sensitive help for that keyword. Otherwise, you can always select Contents and Index from the main Help menu to find help on any particular topic—and of course Access supports Answer Wizard (same menu) which allows you to enter a natural language question. You can also use the new Office Assistant to help you answer your queries:

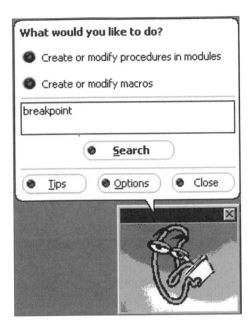

Press the search button and Clipit will give you a list of topics:

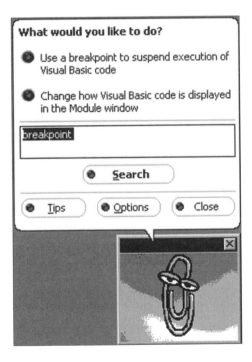

We are going to look at some other ways in which the Office Assistant can be used later on in the book.

The help file is really useful for those occasions when the error message does not really describe what is wrong. Consider the **ErrorHelp** procedure, in the Chapter 11 Debugging module:

```
Public Sub ErrorHelp(strColumn As String)
' Purpose:        Demonstrate a naff error message, but useful help
'                 when searching a recordset for a column
' Arguments:      strColumn   The column to search for
' Returns:        none
' Author:         David Sussman
' Date:           11 June 1997

    Dim dbCurrent    As Database    ' The current database
    Dim recBottling As Recordset    ' Snapshot on bottling table
    Dim strSQL       As String      ' SQL string

    ' build a SQL string and open the recordset
    strSQL = "SELECT " & strColumn & " FROM Bottling"
    Set dbCurrent = CurrentDb()
    Set recBottling = dbCurrent.OpenRecordset(strSQL, dbOpenSnapshot)

    ' run through the recordset printing out the column
    While Not recBottling.EOF
        Debug.Print recBottling(strColumn)
        recBottling.MoveNext
    Wend
    recBottling.Close

End Sub
```

This accepts a string, which it uses to select the right field from the Bottling table. Try running it with the following,

```
Call ErrorHelp ("DistillationDate")
```

and you will receive a list of all of the distillation dates for the bottling. However, try it with the following,

```
Call ErrorHelp ("DateDistilled")
```

and you will receive this error message:

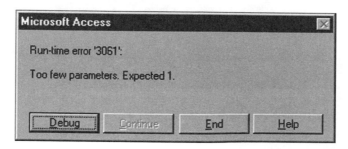

Yeah, right. Very helpful. But press the Help button and you'll get something that makes much more sense:

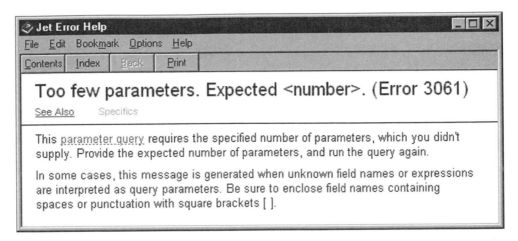

The second paragraph is the important one here, telling you that you are trying to select an unknown field name.

Error Handling

Now that you know how to prevent mistakes, and how to find the ones you did not prevent, you really need to know how to handle errors gracefully. Notice that *mistakes* and *errors* are not the same thing. Good design, proper testing and debugging, should have removed all the mistakes from your code. But that doesn't mean that errors will not occur.

For example, imagine your code accesses a particular file on disk—say a linked file. You know the code has no mistakes in it and will always access the file correctly and manipulate the data without a problem. But errors can still occur—if someone moves the file to another location or deletes it altogether, you'll get an error no matter what.

There are occasions when you may want to ignore a certain error, or when you want to do something different from Access 97 when it encounters the error. In this case, you need to prevent Access grinding to a halt and displaying the standard error message—you need to **handle** the errors yourself as they arise.

Visual Basic Errors

You have probably seen examples of error handling code, especially if you have used the Command Button Wizard when creating forms. If you don't include an error handling routine, Access uses a default routine that displays an error message and stops execution of the code. By using the **On Error** statement, you tell Access that you are going to use your own routine to display errors. For example, look at the following:

```
Private Sub ErrorHandling()
```

```
        On Error Goto ErrorHandling_Err:
        ' Some code goes here

ErrorHandling_Exit:
    Exit Sub

ErrorHandling_Err:
    ' Error handling code goes here

End Sub
```

This is the recommended layout for most routines.

The **On Error** statement specifies a label to jump to when an error occurs. Labels are just markers in your code and follow the same naming conventions as variables, except that they must have a colon on the end. By convention, you should use the procedure name and append **_Err** to it for an error label.

You use the **Resume** command to tell Access that the error handling is over and that it should resume execution in the main routine. When the error routine code has been processed, you should do one of several things:

▶ Try the statement that produced the error again, using **Resume**. This tells Access that it should return to the statement that caused the error and run it again. However, you should only use this when you are sure that the error will not continually reappear. It is often used in conjunction with a message box asking the user if they wish to try something again.

▶ Continue with the next line of the main procedure if the error can be handled without the routine stopping. In this case, you use **Resume Next** and the routine continues from the line after the one on which the error occurred. You should only use this when the error will not cause problems later in your code.

▶ Exit the procedure if the routine cannot continue. In this case, you should use **Resume ErrorHandling_Exit** to tell the routine to jump to the exit.

▶ Exit the program, using **End**, if the error was serious enough to stop the execution of the whole program.

OK, we're ready to have a go at creating our own error handler. We'll just use the simple example of an input box which asks the user for a number and then divides 10 by the number the user supplied.

Try It Out—Creating an Error Handler

1 Create the following **ErrorHandling** subroutine:

```
Public Sub ErrorHandling()

    Dim dblResult    As Double
```

```
    dblResult = 10 / InputBox("Enter a number:")

    MsgBox "The result is " & str$(dblResult)

End Sub
```

2 Run it in the Debug window. The procedure simply displays a message on the screen requesting a number to be entered. It sets **dblResult** to 10 divided by the entered number, and then displays the result. Enter a few values to try it out.

3 Enter 0—you'll receive a Divide By Zero error. Then leave the entry box blank—you'll get a Type mismatch error.

The Type mismatch error occurs because a string is returned—**InputBox** returns an empty string if no value is entered. Therefore, when Access tries to divide 10 by this, it realizes that the variable types do not match. What we need is an error-handling routine.

4 Change the code to the following, and try running it again:

```
Public Sub ErrorHandling()

    Dim dblResult    As Double

    On Error GoTo ErrorHandling_Err

    dblResult = 10 / InputBox("Enter a number:")

    MsgBox "The result is " & str$(dblResult)

ErrorHandling_Exit:
    Exit Sub

ErrorHandling_Err:
    MsgBox Err.Description & " - " & Err.Number
    Resume ErrorHandling_Exit

End Sub
```

In a previous Try It Out, we filtered out errors using Boolean variables, but we didn't distinguish between the different types of error, we just dubbed them semantic errors. This error handling routine displays the error message and the error number and then jumps to the exit. In some circumstances, this may be better than the default error message, and it does allow you to customize the message if you want to. What we want to do now, though, is to trap two particular errors and then do something different.

The Err object was new in Access 95. You can continue to use Error$ and Err for the error description and number if you like, but the new object contains more information and is much clearer. You should really use the Err object in all new code.

5 Change the error handling code again so that it now adds a little intelligence:

```
ErrorHandling_Err:
    Select Case Err.Number
    Case 13 ' Type mismatch - empty entry
        Resume
    Case 11 ' Divide by zero
        dblResult = 0
        Resume Next
    Case Else
        MsgBox Err.Description & " - " & Err.Number
        Resume ErrorHandling_Exit
    End Select
```

6 Try entering either 0 or a letter and see what happens. If you wish to get out of this procedure, just type in a number that isn't 0.

How It Works

Instead of Access just displaying a standard message, you can now be very specific about what you want to happen.

```
Select Case Err.Number
```

First, **Err.Number** is checked as this contains the error number.

```
Case 13 ' Type mismatch - empty entry
    Resume
```

Error 13 indicates a type mismatch, so either the box was left blank or text other than a number was entered. In this case, the box is redisplayed—the **Resume** statement instructs Access to return to the line that caused the error. This, in fact, shows a flaw in the error routine that I have deliberately left in. If you tried pressing the **Escape** button, you would have found that there is no escape. Ditto for the Cancel button on the input box. **InputBox** returns an empty string if no value is entered, so the same error is generated. This is one good reason not to use the results of a function such as **InputBox** directly in numerical expressions without first checking their contents.

```
Case 11 ' Divide by zero
    dblResult = 0
    Resume Next
```

Error 11 means that 0 has been entered, in which case we can just ignore the error. So set the result to 0, and issue the **Resume Next**, which tells Access to continue from the line after the one which generated the error. This is the line with **MsgBox** on it.

```
Case Else
    MsgBox Err.Description & " - " & Err.Number
    Resume ErrorHandling_Exit
```

No other errors are expected, but it's as well to allow for them anyway. A message is displayed and the procedure exits.

The real problem with this example is that we now return 0 for a division by 0 error, with no error being displayed. Remember that we mentioned this earlier in the chapter. You should really arrange your code so that an error is returned, or at least displayed, since this is clearly wrong, and could indicate an error earlier in the program.

Although this is a very simple example, you can see how easy it is to customize the error routine, giving a great deal of flexibility.

Using Exit Function and Exit Sub in your Error Handling Routines

You can also take advantage of two other Access statements in your error handling routines—Exit Function and Exit Sub. These allow you to omit the labels and generally make the routines easier to read and debug. For example, we could re-write the **ErrorHandling** function as:

```
Public Sub ErrorHandling()

    Dim dblResult    As Double

    On Error GoTo ErrorHandling_Err

    dblResult = 10 / InputBox("Enter a number:")
    MsgBox "The result is " & str$(dblResult)

    Exit Sub

ErrorHandling_Err:
    Select Case Err.Number
    Case 13 ' Type mismatch - empty entry
        Exit Sub
    Case 11 ' Divide by zero
        dblResult = 0
        Resume Next
    Case Else
        MsgBox Err.Description & " - " & Err.Number
        Exit Sub
    End Select

End Sub
```

This method also gives us a way to handle the Cancel button that didn't work earlier on. We just **Exit Sub** when an error number of 13 is detected. Although this might seem easier, with fewer labels, I recommend the first form for one very important reason—you only have one exit point from the procedure. This means that you can enter code before the exit procedure and you know it will always be run, which might not be the case if **Exit Sub**s were scattered throughout the code.

Form and Report Errors

In Access, there are errors that are associated with forms—forms have an **Error** event. Normally, this is blank and the default error routine is executed, but, just as in normal procedures, you can add your own error code. The error event takes two arguments:

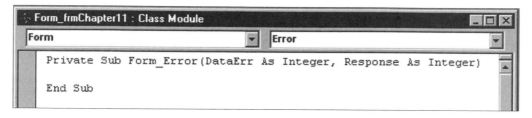

```
Private Sub Form_Error(DataErr As Integer, Response As Integer)

End Sub
```

The first argument, **DataErr**, is the error number and is used in the same way as **Err** in the examples above.

The second argument, **Response**, defines whether or not you want a default message displayed. If you set this to **acDataErrContinue**, Access will ignore the error and continue with your code—which allows you to display your own error message. If you set it to **acDataErrDisplay**, which is the default, the default error message is displayed. Let's have a look at the way this has been implemented in the database, and alter the message that is displayed when a particular error occurs.

Try It Out—The *Form_Error* Event

1   Open the form **frmChapter11ErrorHandling**. This shows the table **Whisky** in datasheet mode. Try adding a record without selecting a region—you get the following error:

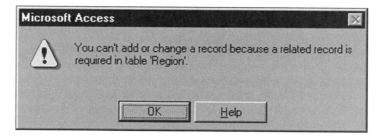

Once again, this is not the easiest message to understand. What it means is that because the Maintain Referential Integrity option (this is set on the Relationships... option on the Tools menu) is set for the link between the tables, you cannot add a whisky without it belonging to a region. Let's make this the error message instead.

2   Close the form down in Datasheet view (you can cancel the new record by pressing *Escape*), switch the form to Design view and select the **Error** event for the form. Add the following code to the event procedure:

```
Select Case DataErr
    Case 3201
```

```
        MsgBox "You must select a region"
        Response = acDataErrContinue
End Select
```

Error number 3201 means that you are trying to add a record that will violate the referential integrity of the data in the table. So, in this case, you can add your own error message and tell Access 97 to ignore its default one. If the error number is something else, you let Access handle it.

3 Try adding another whisky without the region. This time you get a more meaningful message box.

If you wanted to add this sort of routine to several forms, it would be sensible to create some public constants for the error numbers in a module. Then you can refer to them without having to look them up first, or force the error to read the value. A good example would be:

```
Const ERR_REFINTEGRITY = 3201
```

Then, in place of Case 3201, you would have a more easily readable entry.

```
Case ERR_REFINTEGRITY
    MsgBox "You must select a region"
...
```

DAO Errors

As mentioned in Chapter 5, the **Errors** collection (introduced in Access 95) contains all of the errors about a single data access error. If you think that your error came from a data access object, you should make sure that you check the collection for error messages, as well as checking the error object.

User-defined Errors

Much has been said about Access errors, but you can also define your own errors. This is very useful because it allows you to create a specific error in your procedure if something happens, then handle it in the same way as built-in errors. It also allows you to trigger the default error routines yourself without actually having an error occur.

Using the **Raise** method of the **Err** object generates user-defined errors. All this does is cause the object to report an error in the normal way. The difference is that you must supply an error number. This can be a VBA standard error number, such as 13 for Type Mismatch, or one of your own that is outside the range VBA uses. The highest number is 65535, but VBA doesn't itself use anything above 32000 so you have plenty to choose from.

If you want to see what the error numbers are, there is a routine in the module Chapter 11 Code Debugging called **AccessAndJetErrorsTable**, which will create a table of the error numbers and descriptions for you.

355

Try It Out—Raising Errors

We'll create an error and see how it's handled.

1 Open the **ErrorHandling** procedure that you were looking at earlier and modify the code to read as follows:

```
Public Sub ErrorHandling()

    Dim dblResult    As Double
    Dim VarNumber    As Variant

    On Error GoTo ErrorHandling_Err

    VarNumber = InputBox("Enter a number:")
    If Not IsNumeric(VarNumber) Then
        Err.Raise 32000
    End If
    dblResult = 10 / VarNumber
    MsgBox "The result is "& str$(dblResult)

ErrorHandling_Exit:
    Exit Sub

ErrorHandling_Err:
    Select Case Err.Number
    Case 13 ' Type mismatch - empty entry
        Resume
    Case 11 ' Divide by zero
        dblResult = 0
        Resume Next
    Case Else
        MsgBox Err.Description & " - " & Err.Number
        Resume ErrorHandling_Exit
    End Select

End Sub
```

Now, if the entry is not numeric, the error routine is called with an error number of 32000. However, to prevent conflicts with Access, make sure that you always use numbers 32000 and above for your code.

2 Now modify the error handling routine so that it has an extra selection:

```
    Case 32000
        MsgBox "Must be a number"
        Resume ErrorHandling_Exit
```

3 Run the procedure and enter a letter. The new error handler processes the error number 32000 in exactly the same way as other errors. So now the function displays our own message.

If you don't explicitly handle your user-defined errors, but simply use a message box to display the standard error text, you'll get the message Application-defined or object-defined error.

```
MsgBox Err.Description & " - " & Err.Number
```

For example, this would display the message Application-defined or object-defined error - 32000, if used in the previous procedure.

The Error Stack

Because Access is event-driven, it is constantly running small pieces of code which correspond to events. As each procedure is entered, the error handler is reset and so any error is treated as the only error. Access does not have to keep a stack of errors, but responds to them as they occur. This is fairly sensible, but you have to watch out for where Access looks for the error-handling code.

When an error occurs, Access backtracks through its currently active procedures looking for an error-handling routine and executes the first one it finds. If it does not find one, the default error handler routine is called.

For example, let's imagine that you have three procedures, A, B and C. A calls B, and B in turn calls C. If C generates an error, Access will backtrack through B to A looking for an error routine. If it does not find one in B or A, it calls the default routine.

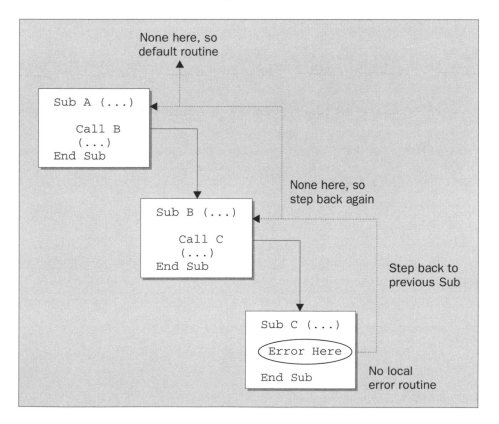

Note that this does not affect the flow of control in the program, as procedure C is still currently active. The backward arrows just show what Access does when searching for an error routine.

Now suppose that you need to add a little more meaning to this default error routine so you decide to create your own. Do you put a routine in each of A, B and C, or do you make use of the backtracking feature and just put it in A? Clearly, if you are dealing with similar errors, it makes sense to have one error routine and, because of the backtracking, it is also sensible to put it at the highest level.

Now imagine that you have the following error-handling code in procedure A, and none in the other procedure:

```
A_Err:
    Select Case Err.Number
    Case w ' Dangerous, so quit
        Resume A_Exit
    Case x ' Safe to carry on to next line
        Resume Next
    Case y ' Retry again
        Resume
    Case z ' A default error, let Access 97 handle it
        Err.Raise q
    End Select
```

This seems straightforward but there is one serious drawback. This can change the program flow. Both **Resume** and **Resume Next** do not continue execution in procedure C as you would think, but at the current line in the procedure that handles the error.

So **Resume** will resume execution at the line that called procedure B—this is the current line in procedure A.

Likewise, **Resume Next** will continue on the line after the call to procedure B. Notice that neither method will return execution to procedure C. Have a look at this diagram to see what happens:

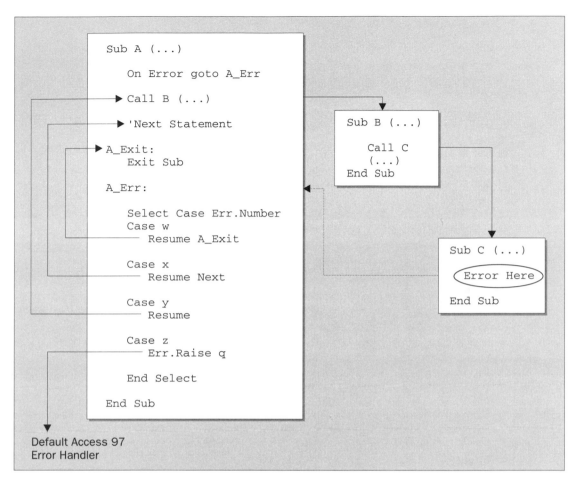

```
Sub A (...)

    On Error goto A_Err

    Call B (...)

    'Next Statement

    A_Exit:
        Exit Sub

    A_Err:

        Select Case Err.Number
        Case w
            Resume A_Exit

        Case x
            Resume Next

        Case y
            Resume

        Case z
            Err.Raise q

        End Select

    End Sub
```

```
Sub B (...)

    Call C
    (...)
    End Sub
```

```
Sub C (...)

    Error Here

    End Sub
```

Default Access 97
Error Handler

This clearly shows the danger of using a single routine for errors. However, it can also be useful—the thing to do is to be aware of this and plan accordingly. You can, for example, have a single error routine in A, and then another in C. The one in C would handle errors generated there, allowing continuation in non-fatal circumstances, whereas the one in A could be used to cope with errors from A and B. You could also use **Err.Raise** in C to force Access to move the error handler up to the next level. For example, look at the following code:

```
Sub c()

    On Error GoTo c_Err
```

```
        Dim intOne       As Integer

        intOne = 123456789
        intOne = "wrong"

    c_Exit:
        Exit Sub

    c_Err:
        Select Case Err.Number
        Case 13
            MsgBox "c: Error " & Err.Number & ": " & Err.Description
        Case Else
            Err.Raise Err.Number, "c", Err.Description
        End Select
        Resume c_Exit

    End Sub
```

This procedure has an error handler that checks the error number. If it is error 13 (Type Mismatch), then the error is displayed here, but any other error is handled by sending the error back up the call tree. This is done by using the **Raise** method of the **Err** object, which in effect fires the error off again. The three arguments are the error number, the source (in this case the procedure 'c'), and the description. The actual code of the procedure only consists of two lines, both of which generate errors. The first sets an integer variable to a very large value, which will cause an overflow—this is not error 13, and so will raise the error again. The second line is error 13, and so would be handled here. In this example, however, you would have to comment out setting the variable to the large value before you could generate this error, as they can't both happen. Let's look at a procedure that calls this one:

```
    Sub b()

        Dim intI        As Integer

        Debug.Print "In b"

        Call c

        Debug.Print "In b: setting intI to 123456789"

        intI = 123456789

    End Sub
```

This procedure just calls procedure **c** and then generates its own error—an overflow. It has no error handling of its own, so Access will search back through the call tree to find an error handler, and in this example it's in procedure **a**:

```
    Sub a()

        On Error GoTo a_Err
```

```
        Debug.Print "In a"

        Call b

        Debug.Print "In a: 2 / 0 = " & 2 / 0

    a_Exit:
        Exit Sub

    a_Err:
        MsgBox "a (" & Err.Source & "): Error " & Err.Number & ": " & _
            Err.Description
        Resume a_Exit

    End Sub
```

This does have an error handler, which displays the source of the error, the number and the description. Let's review the procedures:

- **a** calls **b**, which calls **c**
- **c** has its own error handler, but this only handles error 13—all others are sent back to **b**
- **b** does not have its own error handler, so it sends the error back to **a**
- The handler in a displays the error message

This shows you can handle some errors locally, but still have a general error handler to cope with the others. The **Source** property of the **Err** object allows you to identify where the error was generated.

Debugging your Debugging Code

There may be times when you have added some error-handling routines but these themselves have errors in them. What you do in these circumstances is go to the Tools menu, pick Options, and then select the Advanced pane. Among the Coding Options group is Break on All Errors:

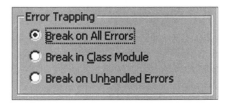

If you turn on this option, Access will ignore your error-handling routines and always use the default. This allows you to code error routines as you create your application, but have the option to turn your error routines off for debugging purposes.

Version Control

You may be wondering what a section about version control is doing in a VBA book, let alone in a section on debugging and testing. Some of you may even be wondering what version control is. For those who don't know, version control is the ability to mark changes as separate versions. This gives you the ability to keep a history of changes, each with a version number, examine the differences between subsequent versions, and even reverse out changes.

So what good is that then, I hear you ask? Well it's this very control which is so important. As a developer you often have to make many changes to code; bug fixes, enhancements, and even the "Hmmm—I'll just see if this works" type of change. In the bad old days there was no way to identify what was changed, apart from comments, and we all know how unreliable those can be. Then along came version control, and lo, our lives were free and easy once more. OK, I exaggerate a little, but you get the picture. This is where it fits into this chapter.

If you're not convinced yet, then bear with me a while longer. Imagine a typical work situation. You've shipped a database and it's been well received by the users. However, as part of an upgrade process you are going to have to do more work, and deliver three or four more phases, as well as correcting bugs. What would you do now? Maybe you'd have a copy of the database for each phase. Or perhaps code that only included the correct functionality depending upon the phase. What about bug fixes? How do you differentiate one fix from another? And what happens if you implement a fix, but then you need to remove it? Can you remember exactly what you changed? This happens every day in many workplaces (not just in programming) and applies not just to IT departments, but to single developers too.

One of the most requested features for the new version of Access was Version Control. Many people had been pushing for it in Access 95, but it just didn't make it. Now, at last, this facility is available.

Let's look at the new version control features in Access 97 and see how they can improve your development.

Version Control in Access 97

Let me start by saying that version control is not an automatic feature in Access, nor is it a facility you get for free. To use version control you need the Office Developer Edition Tools and Microsoft Visual SourceSafe.

▶ Visual SourceSafe is the product the actually does the version control. It has been around for several years and has mainly been used by Visual Basic programmers.

▶ The Office Developer Edition Tools give you, amongst other tools, the Add-In that connects Access to Visual SourceSafe.

Both of these are addition items you must buy, but consider them an investment. They will save time. Guaranteed.

Visual SourceSafe

Visual SourceSafe performs version control for any file type: Visual Basic files, documents, binary files, etc.. It is project oriented and allows the organization and sharing of code, as well as control over editing. Let's have a look at the main screen:

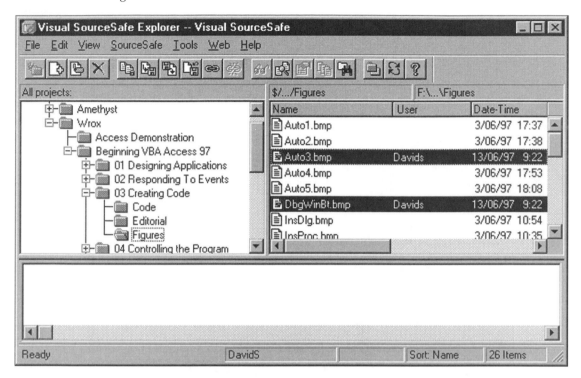

The first thing you notice is that it's very Explorer like. It the left pane you see a list of projects. $/ is used as the root, much like `c:\` is the root of your disk drive. Underneath that is a list of projects and under them, sub-projects. You can see I have kept this book under it, including the database, Word documents, and pictures. The right hand pane shows a list of files associated with a project, user name, and date they were last modified.

So what does Visual SourceSafe do? The easiest thing is to think of it as a librarian. You can check out all of the books it has, that your name is stamped against them, and when you have made your changes you can check them back in again. You can see from above that I had two files checked out. Every change you make to a file gets added as a separate version.

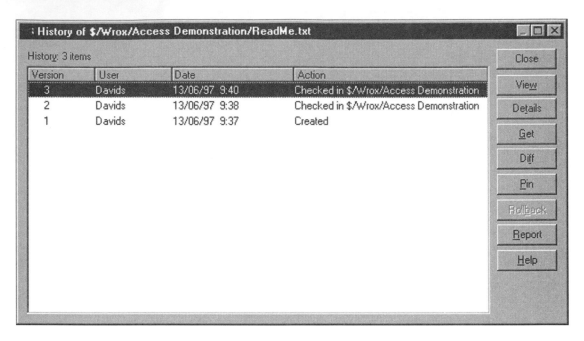

Here there are three versions of the **ReadMe.txt** file. You can see who checked it in and when. One of the great features of Visual SourceSafe is that you can see the changes that have taken place between different versions.

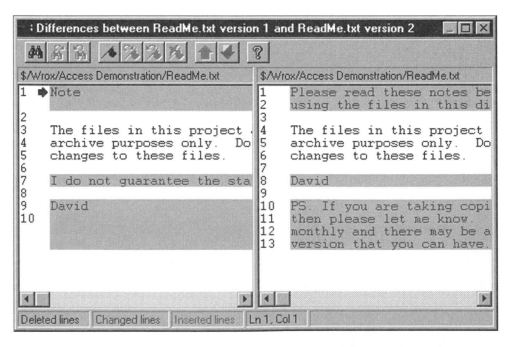

Visual SourceSafe very cleverly highlights deleted lines, changed lines, and new lines, so you can see exactly what has changed. This is extremely useful when you can't quite remember what you changed, or when you are working in teams and you need to see what someone else has done.

Access SourceSafe Add-In

The Access component of Visual SourceSafe comes as an Add-In, which gets added to the Tools menu.

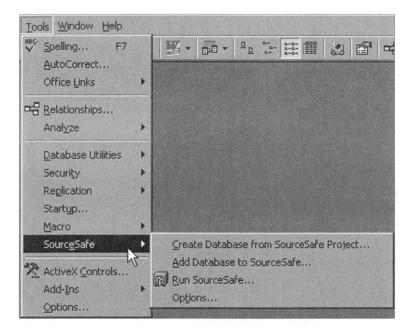

When you add a database to Visual SourceSafe each item is locked, disallowing any changes to it.

You can see how the icon has changed, indicating that it is locked. To Check Out a file you simply press the right mouse button and select Check Out.

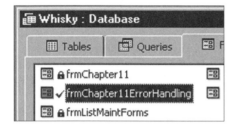

This will then place an editable copy of the object in the database. Again, the icon changes so you can see what state the object is in.

You can now edit your object, and when finished, check in back in again, safe in the knowledge that everything you have just changed is kept separate from every other change. Also, since notes about your change can be added when you check files back in, you can use Visual SourceSafe to produce release notes and a list of changes.

This has been a very brief look at Visual SourceSafe and how it is used in Access, and although they are not standard components, they really are worth the investment. I once spent three days tracking down a very obscure bug in a large project. If version control had been available, I could probably have found the bug in several hours. I think being able to control changes is an important part of development, so put the book down and go and buy it now.

Summary

If you've been reading between the lines, you may have realized that the underlying message in this chapter is planning. A huge amount of effort goes into tracking down problems in software, when even just a little planning would reduce this wasted time—it always pays off in the end.

As well as planning your application well, you should also try to pre-empt the user. Try to think of the things that they will do, so that you make your program fun to use (or at the very least easy). You should never put a user in a position where an error message leads them to think they have done something wrong, as they then become resentful of the software and may even stop using it. Alan Cooper, the inventor of Visual Basic, says "We spend so much time working with computers we forget that although it's fine to humiliate a computer, you can't afford to humiliate a user."

This chapter has covered:

- How to design your application to minimize errors
- The object-oriented techniques that can be used in error prevention
- The tests you should carry out on any new application
- The different types of error and how to correct them
- How to debug your code by stepping through it using breakpoints and watches
- How to write your own error handling routines
- A brief look at version control

Preventing errors and tracking them down once they've occurred will undoubtedly improve the performance of any application you program. However, you can also improve performance in error-free applications. This is known as optimization and we will deal with this in the next chapter.

Exercises

1 Examine the forms in the sample database. Do you think that any error routines could be removed and a global error routine used instead? What would be the disadvantages of this?

2 Using a global or static array, implement a generic error routine that shows the name of the procedure in which the error was generated. Hint—instead of passing the name into the function, add an item to the array at the beginning of a procedure and remove it at the end.

Class Modules

Back in Chapter 5, we introduced the concepts of objects and object-oriented programming. Since then we have looked at the Data Access Object hierarchy and how working with these different Access objects is really at the heart of programming in Access. In this chapter, we are going to look at how we can create our own objects and how we can use some of the new object-oriented aspects of Access 97 to fill in some of the gaps.

For many people, the idea of object-orientation seems a bit scary. There are all those long words like instantiation, encapsulation, inheritance and (my favorite) polymorphism. And don't you need to know all about callback functions and inproc servers and all that malarkey? Well, not really. The implementation of class modules and user-defined objects in Access 97 is actually fairly simple. It may not give you the flexibility of tools such as Visual C++, but what that means in turn is that it is very easy to pick up. Hopefully, this chapter will show you just how easy it is, and by the time you finish you should have added a very powerful tool to your programming armory.

We'll be looking at the following topics in this chapter:

- What objects are
- The benefits of object-based programming
- Building and instantiating custom objects
- Building object hierarchies through collections
- Custom properties and methods for forms
- Creating multiple instances of a form

Class Modules and Custom Objects

If you can remember that far back, in Chapter 5 we started to look at how Access implements an object hierarchy—the Data Access Object hierarchy—to allow developers to access the data in tables programmatically and to manipulate the building blocks that make up an Access database—tables, queries, forms and reports. We looked then at the concepts of objects, methods and properties. We are going to spend a little time now reviewing those concepts in a little more detail, before we examine how Access 97 provides developers with the capability to create their own custom objects through the use of class modules.

What are Objects?

Object-oriented development has been a hot topic for quite a few years now, but for many people the topic is one still shrouded in mystery. The obscure jargon used, the seemingly acrobatic mental leaps and steep learning curve required for the tools used to implement object-oriented development have all contributed towards the belief that it is a black art to be attempted only by the bravest. And that is a bit of a shame, because the principles behind object-orientation are really fairly straightforward, once you get beyond the jargon.

So let's start with the basics and find out what objects really are. There are many definitions of what an object is, but we'll use a simple one to start with and say this:

> An **object** is a self-contained entity that is characterized by a recognizable set of attributes and behaviors.

For example, think of a dog as an object. Dogs are certainly recognizable by their characteristics and their behavior. If we were to put some of these down on paper we might come up with a list like this:

Characteristics	Behaviors
They are hairy	They bark
They have four legs	They bite mailmen
They have a tail	They sniff things

Now, if you were to ask anyone what is hairy, has four legs and a tail and barks, bites and sniffs things, there aren't many people who wouldn't instantly know that you were talking about a dog—you would have described to them quite succinctly the characteristics and behavior of a dog.

In fact, what you would be describing was not any single dog. Rather, you were describing the characteristics and behavior of all dogs. In one sense, what makes a dog a dog is that it is like all other dogs. Sure, there are some minor differences, in size, color (and smell), but all dogs have a certain dogginess. Now, before you start to think that you are reading a book on canine philosophy, let's apply that to the world of software. An object-oriented programmer would have summarized those last couple of paragraphs like this:

- There exists a **class** called **Dog**
- **Instances** of this **Dog class** have the following **properties**: **Hairiness**, **Four-Leggedness**, **Tailedness**, **Size**, **Color**, **Smelliness**
- **Instances** of this **Dog** class expose the following **methods**: **Bark**, **Bite**, **Sniff**

OK, so let's look at some of that jargon. First of all—**classes**. A **class** is a type of blueprint or mould. In the case of animals, that blueprint is genetic. If the object we were talking about were candles, the blueprint would be the mould into which the wax is poured.

Dogs and candles are **instances** of their particular class, and as such they inherit the characteristics of the class to which they belong. Dogs bark because that is a characteristic of the **Dog** class. So we can now define a class.

> *A **class** is a blueprint or template which defines the methods and properties of a particular type of object.*

Now, let's have a look at an object in Access with which we are already familiar—the **Recordset** object—and see how it fits into our model. First of all we can say that all **Recordset** objects have the same properties and methods. The properties include things like the **RecordCount** property, which is the number of records in the **Recordset** object, and the **Updatable** property, which determines whether, or not, the **Recordset** object can be updated. The methods include the **GetRows** method, which takes a given number of records and places them into an array. All **Recordset** objects possess the same objects and properties, because they are all derived from the same class. As Access developers we cannot see the class itself—all we see are the objects derived from that class. The class itself (**CdaoRecordset**) was defined using Visual C++. What we see in VBA are instances of that class.

Why Use Objects?

Now we are getting a feel for what objects and classes are, we can start to think about some of the benefits of using them. Hopefully, this section will blow away some of the mystique that surrounds the long words that bedevil object orientation. Three big benefits of using objects in Access come from abstraction, encapsulation and polymorphism…

Abstraction

One of the most immediate advantages is something called **abstraction**. What that means is simply that users of the object shouldn't have to know the nitty-gritty of how the object does what it does. In other words, the user doesn't need to worry about technicalities. It is a bit like turning an electric light on. People don't need to know anything about voltage, current and resistance. All they need to know is how to flick a switch. They are removed from the physics that results in the bulb lighting and the room getting brighter.

We can see this with the **Recordset** object. All we need to do is to use the **Requery** method and somehow the **Recordset** object is repopulated with a more recent set of data. How does it do it? Who cares! All we need to know is that it works. And that is rather good, because it means that we can spend more time developing our application rather than worrying about the low-level details of things like cursor functionality.

> *Abstraction means we can use objects without having to know the software details of how the object does what it does. This is one of the key advantages of using custom objects in Access.*

Encapsulation

Closely related to abstraction is the idea of **encapsulation**. Objects should encapsulate within them everything they need to allow them to do what they do. That means that they should contain their own methods, properties and data—and it means that they don't need to rely on other objects to allow them to exist or to perform their own actions.

As we saw in Chapter 5, **Forms** and **Reports** are types of objects. They illustrate encapsulation quite well—if you use VBA for your event procedures you can import a form into another database and all the controls on the form and the code in its module go over with it. It's all encapsulated in the form.

Another good example of encapsulation is an ActiveX control such as the Calendar control. The Calendar control carries with it—or encapsulates—its own methods and properties, which are immediately accessible to you when you place it on a form.

> *Encapsulation means that because an object contains all its own data, properties and methods, it can be quickly and easily reused elsewhere. This is another benefit of using custom objects in Access—if you do it right!*

Polymorphism

What a great word! The concept is pretty cool—it just means that you can have a whole load of disparate objects, but you can tell them all to do the same thing and they'll all know how to do it. Put another way, it means that objects can share the same methods and properties, but have different content behind the methods and properties to implement their behavior. For example, controls, forms and pages in Access all have a **SetFocus** method. In all these cases, invoking the method shifts focus to the selected object, but the way they do it 'under the hood' is different in each case.

> *The advantage of polymorphism is that you can present a familiar, consistent interface to the user of the object, whilst hiding the differences in implementation. If you want to implement polymorphism using Access custom objects, you have to do it yourself.*

Inheritance

Inheritance is mentioned here as it is a fairly key concept of object-oriented design. What it means is that you can use a class to create a subclass which inherits all of the class' methods and properties. In the analogy we have been using, we could say that the **Dog** class is a subclass of the **Mammal** class. It therefore inherits the properties and methods of that class. Properties such as **hairiness** and methods such as **suckling** are inherited from the **Mammal** class.

> *Inheritance makes it easier to create new classes, as you are often able to simply sub-class an existing class and then add some specialization. However, there is not much opportunity for this when using custom objects in Access.*

What are Custom Objects?

OK, so enough of the theory. How does all of this help us with our VBA? Well, we have seen so far in this book that Access gives us a whole raft of objects we can use in VBA code. We have got **Recordset** objects, **QueryDef** objects and all the other objects in the Data Access Object hierarchy. We have got the objects within Access itself, such as **Form** and **Report** objects. And we'll see later on that by using OLE Automation, we can even use ActiveX objects from within other applications, such as the **Chart** object from Excel.

What is new in Access 97 is the ability to create your own objects. If you are new to VBA programming, you may not realize just what a benefit it is to be able to create your own objects. It's often the way when a new feature is introduced, that people think "Cool feature... if only I had a reason to use it!"

Well, wouldn't it be good to have a **MyComputer** object? You know, an object that lets you know what sort of computer your program was running on. Then you would be able to do this...

```
Dim computer As New MyComputer

If computer.CPULevel <= 486
    MsgBox "This is gonna be slow. Sure you want to do it?"
End If

computer.ScreenResolution = "800x600"
```

Sure, but how? Access doesn't provide us with a **MyComputer** object. Well, it's time to have a go at building our own.

Designing Custom Objects

The aim of this first section is to create an object, accessible through VBA code, which exposes to us various bits of information about the computer on which the application is running.

Designing the Interface

The first task is to determine exactly what we want to provide to users of our object. We need to think about just what information we will want to show about the computer. In other words, we need to define what will be the properties of the **MyComputer** object. Listed below are some of the properties that we might want to implement.

Property	Description
MyComputer.**AccessDir**	Returns a **String** indicating the location of the directory on the current machine where **msaccess.exe** is located.
MyComputer.**ButtonsSwapped**	Returns a **Boolean** value indicating whether or not the user has swapped the mouse buttons to a left-handed configuration.
MyComputer.**ComputerName**	Returns a **String** containing the computer name.
MyComputer.**CPUArchitecture**	Returns a **String** identifying the architecture of the computer's CPU.
MyComputer.**CPULevel**	Returns a **String** identifying the level of the computer's CPU.
MyComputer.**FreeDiskSpace**	Returns a **Long** representing the number of bytes free on the user's hard disk.
MyComputer.**OSName**	Returns a **String** identifying the name of the operating system currently in use.
MyComputer.**OSVersion**	Returns a **String** identifying the version of operating system currently in use.

Table Continued on Following Page

Property	Description
MyComputer.**OSBuild**	Returns a **String** identifying the build of the operating system currently in use.
MyComputer.**ScreenResolution**	Returns a **String** identifying the current screen resolution.
MyComputer.**UserName**	Returns a **String** containing the name of the currently logged on user.
MyComputer.**WinStarted**	Returns a Date/Time indicating when Windows was last started.

Objects can also exhibit behavior through methods. We could use methods of the **MyComputer** object to affect the behavior of the computer we are using. One of the methods we might choose to implement could be:

MyComputer.**SwapButtons**   Sets the mouse buttons to either a right-handed or left-handed configuration

Designing the Implementation

Obviously, we also need to know how we are going to get the information that we will present through the object. After all, how can we present information to the user, if we don't know how to get hold of it in the first place?

Sometimes, a property or method may simply be implemented by calling a native VBA function. An example might be the **AccessDir** property of the **MyComputer** object. We can determine the location of the Access directory by using the Access **SysCmd** function.

At other times, there is no single VBA function corresponding to the property or method we want to implement, so instead we have to call a function or procedure that we have specially written in order to implement the functionality of the method or property.
But sometimes there are situations where more complex functionality is required than can be implemented either through the use of native VBA functions or user-defined functions and procedures that we have written. An example of this would be the **WinStarted** property of the **MyComputer** object. There is neither a native VBA function that returns this value, nor is there a method to determine this by writing a simple VBA procedure. However, we can determine how long a session of Windows has been running by nipping out of VBA and using the **timeGetTime** API call, which returns the number of milliseconds since Windows was started.

By taking complex operations such as making API calls and wrapping them up as simple properties of objects we can make life much easier for ourselves and for other developers in the future. Once the **MyComputer** class has been built, it will be a lot easier to determine when Windows was started by creating a **MyComputer** object and inspecting the value of its **WinStarted** property than to remember the exact syntax of the API function declaration for the **timeGetTime** API and write the necessary code to use the API function to determine when Windows was started.

Building and Instantiating objects

We build classes using the class modules that have been introduced in Access 97. In fact, what we will be doing with the class modules is design a template, or class, which contains all of the required methods, properties and data. Then, once the class has been designed we will be able to use it in VBA to create instances of objects based on that class.

Let's have a go...

Try It Out—Creating an Object

1 Turn to the Module page of the database window and select Class Module from the Insert menu.

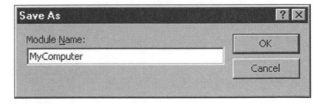

2 A new class module will be opened. Change its name to **MyComputer** by hitting *Ctrl+S* to save it and typing **MyComputer** in the Save As dialog which appears.

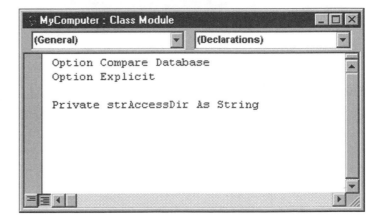

3 In the **Declarations** section of the class module, declare a private string variable called **strAccessDir**.

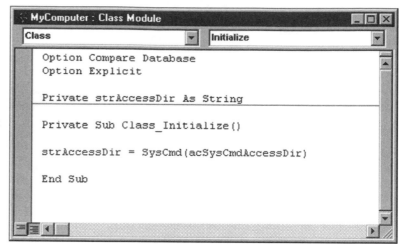

4 Now bring up the **Class_Initialize()** subprocedure, by selecting Class from the Object combo box and Initialize from the Procedure combo box and then type in the following code.

5 Now create a new property procedure by typing the following code at the end of the class module.

```
Public Property Get AccessDir() As String

    AccessDir = strAccessDir

End Property
```

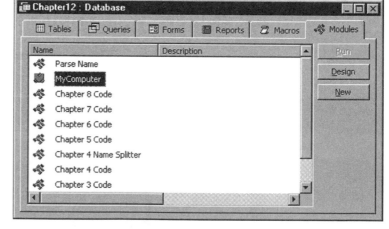

6 Close the class module, saving changes when prompted to do so. There should now be an icon for the **MyComputer** class module in the database window.

7 Now open a new standard code module and insert a subprocedure called **ShowAccessDir()**.

```
Sub ShowAccessDir()

    Dim MyComp As New MyComputer

    MsgBox MyComp.AccessDir
```

```
    Set MyComp = Nothing

End Sub
```

8 Finally, run the **ShowAccessDir()** procedure by hitting *F5*. If everything works correctly, you will see a dialog box like telling you where Access is installed on your computer.

Congratulations! In about five minutes, you have built your first class module and created your first instance of the **MyComputer** object!

How It Works

There was quite a lot going on there, so we will go through it one step at a time. The first thing we did was to create a new class module. Class modules are almost identical in appearance to standard code modules. One key difference, however, is the fact that class modules can contain two extra procedures, the **Class_Initialize()** and the **Class_Terminate()** procedures.

The **Class_Initialize()** procedure is executed whenever a new instance of an object is created from a class module. It therefore contains, not unnaturally, initialization routines that carry such tasks as establishing default values for the object's properties. The **Class_Terminate()** procedure is created whenever an instance of an object based on the class module is destroyed, either by being set to **Nothing** or by going out of scope. Note that you don't *have* to put any code into these two procedures. But if you do want code to execute whenever an instance of an object is either created or destroyed, this is where it would go.

In the **Class_Initialize()** procedure, we ascertained the location of the directory in which Access is installed by using the **SysCmd** function. The **SysCmd** function can be used to do a number of very different things. However, if you pass it the intrinsic constant **acSysCmdAccessDir** it returns a string indicating the directory that contains **Msaccess.exe**.

Notice that we assigned the return value of the **SysCmd** function to a **Private** variable. Because the variable was declared using the keyword **Private**, it is visible only within the **MyComputer** procedure. It is important to declare variables within class modules as **Private** variables, if you want to ensure that the variables you create cannot be seen (and therefore modified) by procedures outside the class in which they exist.

So far, then, we have a class module which, when an instance of it is created, gets the name of the Access directory and puts it into a **Private** variable. What we need to do now is to expose that value to the outside world as a property, so we can use the **MyComputer.AccessDir** syntax to reference it. To do this, you create properties with the **Public Property Get** procedures.

Our property procedure started like this:

```
Public Property Get AccessDir() As String
```

This opening line tells us a lot:

➧ The **Public** keyword tells us that this property is public—and can therefore be read by procedures outside the class module as well as by those within it

➧ The keyword **Get** indicates that this procedure defines what should happen when something outside this code module wants to **Get** (i.e. inspect) the value of this property

➧ The identifier **AccessDir** tells us the name of the property

➧ The keyword **String** tells us the datatype of the property

In other words, this procedure creates a property called **AccessDir**, which returns a **String** and is publicly visible.

Whenever something attempts to inspect the value of the **AccessDir** property of the **MyComputer** object, the **Property Get AccessDir()** procedure is run. By inserting the line

```
AccessDir = strAccessDir
```

we are telling the class module to assign the value of the **Private** variable **strAccessDir** to the **Public** property **AccessDir** so it can be viewed from the outside world.

Note that the location of the Access directory is determined once only—in the **Class_Initialize()** event—when the object is **instantiated**, i.e. when a new instance of the object is created. If we had wanted, we could have placed the **SysCmd** function inside the **Property Get** procedure, which would redetermine the Access directory whenever the property was inspected. Given that the location of the Access directory will not change during the lifetime of the **MyComputer** object, it makes more sense to determine it once, when the object is instantiated. However, if the property value were more dynamic—such as the **MyComputer.FreeDiskSpace** property—you would determine its value whenever the property were inspected by placing the code in the **Property Get** procedure

Creating Object Instances

We can see how this all works when we go to instantiate an object from this class. If you have the Auto Quick Info option checked, then in the **ShowAccessDir** procedure, as soon as we have typed

```
Dim MyComp As New
```

Access displays a list of valid object classes including the new **MyComputer** class.

```
Sub ShowAccessDir()

Dim MyComp As New My

End Sub
```

MyComputer
Node
Nodes
ObjectFrame
OptionButton
OptionGroup
OrderSearch

Similarly, when we type:

```
MsgBox MyComp.
```

Access displays a list of the valid properties and methods that exist for the **MyComp** object.

```
MsgBox MyComp.
    AccessDir
```

> *Once we create an object using a class module, all of its methods and properties are exposed just as if it were a built-in Access object such as a **Recordset** or **QueryDef** object.*

We prepare the creation of a new instance of the **MyComputer** object with the following line:

```
Dim MyComp As New MyComputer
```

In fact, this does not create a new instance straight away. Rather it allocates resources in preparation for a new instance of the object to be created. The new instance is actually created the first time that the object is subsequently referenced in code. This occurs on the next line when the object's **AccessDir** property is inspected.

```
MsgBox MyComp.AccessDir
```

In other words, it is the line containing the **MsgBox** statement which triggers the **Class_Initalize()** event. If we had wanted, we could have used a different syntax:

```
Dim MyComp As MyComputer

Set MyComp = New MyComputer
```

In this situation, the **Dim** statement allocates space for the creation of an object, and the **Set** statement causes the object to be instantiated and the **Class_Initialize()** event to be triggered.

Notice also that we set the **MyComp** object variable to **Nothing** at the end of the **ShowAccessDir** procedure. This is good programming practice as it allows any resources used by the object variable to be released.

Data Hiding

You will have noticed that, with the exception of the properties themselves, everything that we declared in the **MyComputer** object was declared privately. This is the principle of **data hiding**, which is very important in object-oriented programming. What it means is that you should never expose the implementation details of a class to the outside world. The only parts of a class that should be visible are the properties and methods—also known as the interface, or type—of the class.

Why do we implement data hiding? Because it allows us to change the internal structure of a class, when needed, without affecting the outside world at all. If we allow access to the internals of a class, then every user of the class could be affected by the changes. Every routine that uses objects of the modified class would need to be checked to ensure that they do not break when the class is changed. This would be a nightmare. What we want to do is to be able to modify a class definition without changing any of the code that uses objects of that class. The way to do that is to keep the implementation hidden and only expose the interface.

Making Properties Writable

To recap, we have seen how easy it is to create our own classes and objects using VBA in Access 97. The object we have created is the **MyComputer** object, which has a single read-only property called **AccessDir**, which tells us in which directory Access is installed. But what if we want to make a property whose value we can set? After all, when we use Data Access Objects, we don't just read properties, we set them as well. How can we do that with our objects? The answer is that, instead of **Property Get**, we use the **Property Let** procedure.

> *Those of you who used versions of Basic some years ago may remember that **Let** was used to assign a value to a variable, e.g. **Let x = 42**. In fact you can still use **Let** for assigning values to variables but it is now accepted as good practice to omit the **Let** keyword in normal assignation statements. However, it cannot be omitted in **Property Let** procedures.*

The easiest way to see a **Property Let** procedure in action is to try it out for ourselves. We are going to add a new property to the **MyComputer** object, which will tell us whether or not the user has swapped over the mouse buttons for left-handed use. We will call the property **ButtonsSwapped** and it will return **True** or **False**. We will also make the property writable, so it can easily be used to swap the use of the left and right mouse buttons.

Try It Out—Swapping Mouse Buttons

1 Open in Design view the **MyComputer** class module that we created earlier in this chapter.

2 In the **Declarations** section of the module type the following function and constant declarations:

```
'Windows API function declarations
Private Declare Function SwapMouseButton Lib "user32" (ByVal bSwap _
    As Long) As Long
Private Declare Function GetSystemMetrics Lib "user32" (ByVal nIndex _
    As Long) As Long

'Windows constant declarations
Private Const SM_SWAPBUTTON = 23
```

3 Now add a **Property Get** procedure with the following code:

```
Public Property Get ButtonsSwapped() As Boolean

    ButtonsSwapped = GetSystemMetrics(SM_SWAPBUTTON)

End Property
```

4 And then add a **Property Let** procedure like this:

```
Public Property Let ButtonsSwapped(bSwap As Boolean)

    Dim lngSwap as Long

    lngSwap  =  CLng(bSwap)
    Call SwapMouseButton (lngSwap)

End Property
```

5 Now compile the class module and close it, saving changes to it when prompted.

6 Open a standard code module and add the following procedure to it:

```
Sub SwapMouseButtons()

    Dim MyComp As MyComputer
    Dim bSwapped As Boolean

    Set MyComp = New MyComputer

    bSwapped = MyComp.ButtonsSwapped

    If bSwapped = True Then
        MsgBox "The mouse is set up for left-handed use"
    Else
        MsgBox "The mouse is set up for right-handed use"
    End If

    MyComp.ButtonsSwapped = Not (bSwapped)

    bSwapped = MyComp.ButtonsSwapped

    If bSwapped Then
        MsgBox "The mouse is now set up for left-handed use"
    Else
        MsgBox "The mouse is now set up for right-handed use"
    End If

    Set MyComp = Nothing

End Sub
```

7 Compile the code module and run the **SwapMouseButtons** procedure. When you do so a dialog will appear, telling you how your mouse buttons are currently configured.

381

When you hit the OK button, a second dialog will appear to inform you that your mouse buttons have been reconfigured.

To change the mouse buttons back to their original configuration, simply run the procedure for a second time.

How It Works

The first thing we did here was to declare a couple of functions from the **User32.dll**.

```
Private Declare Function SwapMouseButton Lib "user32" (ByVal bSwap _
    As Long) As Long
Private Declare Function GetSystemMetrics Lib "user32" (ByVal nIndex _
    As Long) As Long

'Windows constant declarations
Private Const SM_SWAPBUTTON = 23
```

We looked at the **GetSystemMetrics** function in Chapter 10, where we saw that it returns a **Boolean** value indicating whether the user swapped the functionality of the mouse buttons. If you do not understand how we use functions from DLLs, you should review Chapter 10.

You might have noticed that we have declared these functions and constants privately (i.e. **Private Declare...**). This is consistent with the concept of **data hiding**, which we described in the section above. In fact, you are not allowed to declare functions, subprocedures or constants publicly within class modules and attempting to do so will generate a compile error.

In order to expose the **ButtonsSwapped** property, we use the **Property Get** procedure.

```
Public Property Get ButtonsSwapped() As Boolean

    ButtonsSwapped = GetSystemMetrics(SM_SWAPBUTTON)

End Property
```

If you remember from Chapter 10, when we pass the **SM_SWAPBUTTON** constant to the **GetSystemMetrics** procedure, 0 is returned if the mouse buttons are not swapped and a non-zero value is returned otherwise. So, the **ButtonsSwapped** property of the **MyComputer** object is **False** if the mouse buttons are set up for right-handed use and **True** if the mouse buttons are set up for left-handed use.

To make the **ButtonsSwapped** property writable, we use a **Property Let** procedure.

```
Public Property Let ButtonsSwapped(bSwap As Boolean)
```

```
    Dim lngSwap As Long

    Call SwapMouseButton (lngSwap)
    SwapMouseButton bSwap

End Property
```

The opening line of this procedure declares the **ButtonsSwapped** publicly, to expose it to the outside world. The argument to this procedure—**bSwap As Boolean**—has to be the same datatype as was used in the **Property Get** procedure. This variable holds the value that is passed to the **Property Let** procedure from the right hand side of the equals sign when the property is set by a calling procedure. So, if a procedure includes this line:

```
MyComp.ButtonsSwapped = False
```

then the value of **bSwap** in the **Property Let** procedure will be **False**.

This value is then passed to the **SwapMouseButton** function. This is a function from **User32.dll** and it sets the mouse buttons to a left-handed configuration if passed a non-zero value and a default right-handed configuration if passed **0**. It also returns a non-zero value if the mouse buttons were already swapped, or **0** if the mouse buttons were originally set up for a right-handed person.

> *Note how we convert the **Boolean** value **bSwap** to a **Long** before the value is passed to the DLL function. Although not strictly necessary in this instance—passing a **Boolean** to this function won't cause an error—it is prudent to get into the habit of passing exactly the right data types to API calls.*

Setting the **ButtonsSwapped** property of the **MyComputer** object to **False** will cause the mouse buttons to revert to their default setup, while setting it to **True** will swap their functionality.

If you have got this far, the **SwapMouseButtons()** procedure should be fairly self-explanatory at this stage. First, it interrogates the **ButtonsSwapped** property of the **MyComputer** object and displays a dialog appropriately.

```
bSwapped = MyComp.ButtonsSwapped

If bSwapped Then
    MsgBox "The mouse is set up for left-handed use"
Else
    MsgBox "The mouse is set up for right-handed use"
End If
```

And then it reverses the mouse configuration, by setting the **ButtonsSwapped** property to the opposite of what it was originally.

```
MyComp.ButtonsSwapped = Not (bSwapped)
```

That just about wraps up properties! But we are not done with objects yet. There's another very important part of the interface exposed by objects to the outside world, and we are going to look at that now.

Methods

Methods are easy! They are simply public procedures. If we want to implement a **SwapButtons** method of the **MyComputer** object, we need only create a public procedure within the class module like this:

```
Public Sub SwapButtons(bSwap As Boolean)

    SwapMouseButton bSwap

End Sub
```

This allows us to swap or unswap the mouse buttons by invoking the **SwapButtons** method of **MyComputer** like this:

```
MyComputer.SwapButtons True
```

Note that the procedure is exposed via the **Public** keyword. In fact, the default scope for procedures inside class modules (and standard modules) is **Public**, but it does no harm to explicitly declare the procedure as **Public** and this makes the scope clearer to anyone looking through our code.

It is not just subprocedures that we can use to create methods. We can use public functions too, if we want the method to return a value. For example, we could have implemented a **SwapButtonChanged** method, which would not only allow us to specify whether we want the mouse to be set left- or right-handed, but also indicated whether or not this involved changing the mouse configuration from its original state.

```
Public Function SwapButtonChanged(bSwap As Boolean) As Boolean

    Dim bNewState As Boolean

    bNewState = SwapMouseButton(bSwap)
    If bNewState = bSwap Then
        SwapButtonChanged = False
    Else
        SwapButtonChanged = True
    End If

End Function
```

You would invoke this method like this:

```
bChanged = MyComp.SwapButtonChanged(True)
```

This would set the mouse to a left-handed configuration and return **True** if the mouse had originally been right-handed, and **False** if the mouse was already left-handed.

When a public function is used to expose a method of a class module, it can return any standard datatype, including objects. This is particularly useful if you want to implement methods to create other objects and then return references to them. This is just like the

Create... methods of Data Access Objects. For example, the **CreateTableDef** method of the database object accepts a table name, creates a **TableDef** object and returns a reference to it.

```
Set tdfNew = dbsNorthwind.CreateTableDef("Contacts")
```

Instantiation

So far, we have seen how to create class modules, their methods and their properties, and we've also had a quick look at how we instantiate objects based on those classes. We'll just spend a little more time on instantiation before we look further at what you can do with objects.

The first thing to say is that there is a difference between creating an object variable and creating an object. We touched on this a little earlier but it is perhaps worth reiterating. Let us look at the line of code below:

```
Dim MyComp As New MyComputer
```

All this does is to allocate resources in readiness for the creation of a new **MyComputer** object. The object is not created until it, or one of its properties or methods is first referenced in code.

An alternative is to use the following syntax:

```
Dim MyComp As MyComputer

Set MyComp = New MyComputer
```

In this situation, the **Dim** statement again allocates resources to allow a new **MyComputer** object to be created (or an existing **MyComputer** object to be referenced). But the **Set** statement actually instantiates the object and returns a reference to it. This manner of instantiating objects is quicker and therefore you may prefer to use it. It is also easier with this method of instantiation to see exactly when the object comes into existence. With the first method, we need to look through the code to find where the object is first referenced to determine just when it is instantiated.

We can, of course, also have multiple objects in existence at the same time, all derived from the same class. Indeed, this is one of the advantages of using objects. Because each object is encapsulated—that is to say, all the data they contain is 'on the inside'—these objects should be interoperable without interfering with each other.

Object Lifetimes

Another situation which can arise is where we have one object in existence, but have multiple object variables referring to it. An important consideration when using multiple object variables, all referencing a single object, is that we cannot destroy the object until we have removed all references to it. References to an object are removed either when the object variable goes out of scope or if it is explicitly set to **Nothing**.

```
Set  MyComputer  =  Nothing
```

However, the resources used by this object are not freed up until the last reference to it is removed.

Forms as Class Modules

We mentioned earlier in the book that although class modules could not be used on their own in versions of Access prior to Access 97, the idea of forms and reports as class modules was introduced in Access 95. What this means is that you can create your forms in the manner we have been describing above.

> *In fact, in Access 97 forms and reports do not have associated class modules by default. The class module is only generated when you first attempt to view or enter code in the form's class module. Forms and reports in Access 97 now have a **HasModule** property which returns **True** or **False** to indicate whether the object has an associated module. This property is read-only at run-time but can be written to at design time.*

Creating Custom Properties for Forms

We create custom properties for forms in just the same manner as we do for other classes. The easiest way to see this is to try it out for yourself—so let's do it! In the following example, we will create a **Maximized** property for the form **frmOrder** and define what happens when the property is set.

Try It Out—Creating a Custom Form Property

1 Create a new standard code module or open an existing one and type the following declaration in the **Declarations** section:

```
Public Declare Function IsZoomed Lib "User32" (ByVal hWnd As Long) As
Integer
```

2 Now open the code module for the form **frmOrder** and type in the two new procedures listed below:

```
Public Property Get Maximized() As Boolean

    If IsZoomed(Me.hWnd) Then
        Maximized = True
    Else
        Maximized = False
    End If

End Property
```

```
Public Property Let Maximized(bMax As Boolean)

    If bMax Then
        Me.SetFocus
        DoCmd.Maximize
    Else
```

```
        Me.SetFocus
        DoCmd.Restore
    End If

End Property
```

3 Close **frmOrder**, saving the changes that you have made. Then open it up in Form view. Make sure it isn't maximized and it should look something like this:

The important thing to notice on this form is that the control buttons in the top right corner indicate that the form is not maximized.

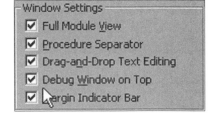

4 Now select the Options... dialog from the Tools menu. Switch to the Module tab and make sure that Debug Window on Top is checked.

5 Now open the Debug window by hitting *Ctrl+G*.

6 Inspect the form's **Maximized** property by typing the following in the Debug window and hitting the *Enter* key.

```
?forms("frmOrder").Maximized
```

It should return **False**, indicating that the form is not maximized.

7 Now maximize **frmOrder** and inspect its property again in the Debug window. This time it should return **True**, indicating that the form is maximized.

8 Finally set the form's **Maximized** property to **False** in the Debug window with the following statement.

```
forms("frmOrder").Maximized=False
```

You should see the form return its normal non-maximized state when you hit the *Enter* key.

How Does It Work?

In order to create a custom form property, we use the now familiar **Property Let** and **Property Get** procedures. The **Property Let** procedure allows us to set the property's value and the **Property Get** procedure allows us to interrogate its value. The first procedure we wrote was the **Property Get** procedure.

```
Public Property Get Maximized() As Boolean
```

The procedure creates a property called **Maximized**, which can be either **True** or **False** and which is visible to all procedures.

```
If IsZoomed(Me.hWnd) Then
    Maximized = True
Else
    Maximized = False
End If
```

These next lines are responsible for determining the value returned to anyone interrogating the value of the **Maximized** property. If **IsZoomed(Me.hWnd)** is true, then the **Maximized** property is **True**, otherwise it is **False**. **IsZoomed()** is simply an API function, a procedure in an external DLL. The DLL, **User32**, contains procedures that handle interaction of Windows programs with user interfaces, and so is responsible for tasks such as window management.

The **IsZoomed()** procedure takes the handle of a Window as an argument. It returns **False** if the window is not maximized and a non-zero value if it is maximized. A handle is simply a unique long integer identifier generated by Windows and used to allow it to keep track of individual windows and controls. We get the handle of the form's window by using the form's **hWnd** property. You probably won't come across this property very much, and when you do it will almost invariably be when you want to pass the handle to an API function.

To set the property we use the **Property Let** statement.

```
Public Property Let Maximized(bMax As Boolean)
```

Again, we can see from the opening line of this procedure that the property's name is **Maximized** and that has a **Boolean** datatype.

As for the rest of the procedure, it is fairly straightforward.

```
If bMax Then
    Me.SetFocus
    DoCmd.Maximize
Else
    Me.SetFocus
    DoCmd.Restore
End If
```

If the value to which **Maximized** is being set is not **False**, we need to maximize the form. If the value is being set to **False**, we need to restore the form.

As you can see, creating form properties is a fairly simple task once you have got your mind around the syntax of the **Property Let** and **Property Get** statements. There will be a chance for you to practice this some more in the exercises at the end of this chapter.

Custom Form Methods

As well as custom form properties, you can also create custom form methods. To create a custom method, you simply write a procedure within the form module and expose it outside the form by making it **Public**.

So, to create a **Maximize** method that reduces the size of the form as described above, simply type this code into the form module of **frmOrder**:

```
Public Sub Maximize()

    Me.Maximized = True

End Sub
```

Because this procedure has been made **Public**, it can be invoked from outside the form in the following manner.

```
forms!frmOrder.Maximize
```

And there you have a custom form method! Now that wasn't too hard, was it?

Creating Multiple Instances of Objects

Now we'll move on to another feature that is exposed to us through Access' object-oriented nature—the ability to create multiple instances of a single form. When you open a form, you are creating an **instance** of that form. The first instance is called the **default instance**. Most of the time, that is the only instance you will need, but there may be occasions when you want to have multiple instances of the same form open at the same time.

Typically, you will create multiple instances of forms when you want to view two records alongside each other. Have a look at the example in the Malt Whisky Store database. If you open the **frmOrder** form and double-click the name of the bottlings which makes up the order lines subform, a new form **frmBottlingDetails** will appear in the center of the screen, displaying details of the bottling you selected.

389

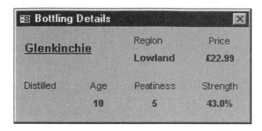

Now move the Bottling Details form out of the way
and double-click another bottling in the lower half of
the order form. A second instance of
frmBottlingDetails should appear in the center
of the screen, this time showing details of the second
whisky you selected.

So how is this done? Well, the following lines of code do it all. These are in the **DblClick**
event handler for the **WhiskyName** control on **frmsubOrderLine**:

```
Private Sub txtWhiskyName_DblClick(Cancel As Integer)

    Dim frm As Form_frmBottlingDetails

    'Instantiate a new frmBottlingDetails
    Set frm = New Form_frmBottlingDetails

    'Show the form
    frm.Visible = True

    'Add the new instance to a form-level collection
    'so that it does not perish when the procedure closes
    colfrmBottlingDetails.Add frm

End Sub
```

Again, it's not as bad as it looks. We'll examine it bit by bit.

```
Dim frm As Form_frmBottlingDetails
```

The first thing we do is to create a variable of type **Form_frmBottlingDetails**. As was
mentioned above, if there is any code behind a form—or if there is no code, but you have
explicitly set the **HasModule** property of the form to **True**—then the form is saved as a class
module and we can create an object variable based on that class. (The corollary is that if there is
no code behind the form—and you have not set the **HasModule** property of the form **True**—
there will be no class module so you will not be able to create multiple instances of the form.)

The next stage is to instantiate a new **frmBottlingDetails**.

```
Set frm = New Form_frmBottlingDetails
frm.Visible = True
```

This is done by simply setting the variable **frm** to a new instance of the form **frmBottlingDetails** using the **New** keyword, and then making it visible.

However, if we simply left the procedure like this, it would be incomplete. Form instances perish when the variables referencing them go out of scope. The variable **frm** was declared at the procedure level, and so will go out of scope when the procedure exits. In other words, the procedure creates a form instance that dies almost immediately as the procedure ends.

In order to prolong the lifetime of the form instance, we add it to a collection that was declared at the form level (i.e. in the **Declarations** section of the form module for **frmsubOrderLine**).

```
Option Compare Database
Option Explicit

Dim colfrmBottlingDetails As New Collection
```

We can then add the form instance to the collection.

```
colfrmBottlingDetails.Add frm
```

This variable will only go out of scope when the form **frmsubOrderLine** is closed. Any form instances that are added to the collection survive beyond the end of the procedure that created them, but perish when **frmsubOrderLines** is closed because, at that point, the collection variable **colfrmBottlingDetails** goes out of scope. Note also that the form instance would perish if it were removed explicitly from the collection and there were no other references to it.

Collections—Creating a Hierarchy

In fact, you can use collections to create an object hierarchy, just like the Data Access Object hierarchy. In our **MyComputer** object, we could have implemented a **FreeSpace** property to indicate how much disk space was free. However, computers frequently have more than one drive, so a more appropriate model would have a **MyComputer** object with a collection of **Drive** objects. And it should be the **Drive** object that has a **FreeSpace** property.

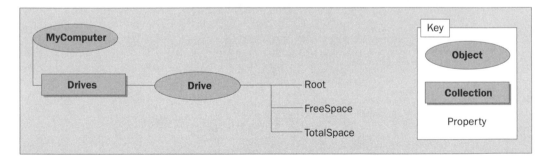

This is how the **MyComputer** class in the final version of the database on the accompanying CD is designed. The portion of code below comes from the **Class_Initialize()** property of the **MyComputer** object, and shows how the **Drives** collection is populated with **Drive** objects.

```
'Get details of drives
strDriveString = Space$(255)
```

```
    lngBuffSize = Len(strDriveString)
    intDriveLength = GetLogicalDriveStrings(lngBuffSize, strDriveString)
    intPos = InStr(1, strDriveString, "\")

    Do While intPos <> 0
        ReDim Preserve strDrive(intDriveCount)
        strDrive(intDriveCount) = Mid$(strDriveString, intPos - 2, 3)
        intDriveCount = intDriveCount + 1
        intPos = InStr(intPos + 1, strDriveString, "\")
    Loop

    For intCounter = 0 To intDriveCount - 1
        Set typDrive = New Drive
        typDrive.Root = strDrive(intCounter)
        Drives.Add typDrive
        Set typDrive = Nothing
    Next
```

The first four lines of code in this procedure are responsible for determining the number of logical drives in the computer by using the **GetLogicalDriveStrings** API call. This populates the **strDriveString** variable with a null-terminated string, which in turn contains a null-terminated string for each logical drive indicating its root directory. So, if the computer had four logical drives called **A:**, **C:**, **D:** and **E:** then the string returned would look like this:

"A:*NULL***C:***NULL***D:***NULL***E:***NULLNULL***"**

The **Do...Loop** then reads the string, looking for the backslash character (**"\"**). The backslash is taken, with the two preceding characters, and placed in the **strDrive** array. At the end of the loop, the array looks like this.

strDrive(0)	**A:**
strDrive(1)	**C:**
strDrive(2)	**D:**
strDrive(3)	**E:**

A **For...Next** loop then creates a **Drive** object for each element of the array and references it with the variable **typDrive**.

```
    Set typDrive = New Drive
```

The next step is to set the **Root** property of the new **Drive** object. This is a readable and writeable property and describes the root directory of the drive to which the object refers.

```
    typDrive.Root = strDrive(intCounter)
```

Next, the **Drive** object is added to the **Drives** collection of the **MyComputer** object.

```
    Drives.Add typDrive
```

Drives is a collection which was declared publicly in the **Declarations** section of the **MyComputer** class module.

```
Public Drives As New Collection
```

Remember, when you are using the **New** keyword, it is not the declaration of the object that causes it to be created. Rather, the object is only instantiated when it is first referenced thereafter. So, in our procedure the **Collection** object is created when we try to add the first **Drive** object to the collection.

Because the collection was declared in the **Declarations** section of the **MyComputer** class module, it will exist so long as the **MyComputer** exists. Furthermore, any **Drive** objects added to the collection will have the same lifetime. So we can remove our reference to the variable in the **Class_Initialize()** procedure, safe in the knowledge that the **Drive** object we have created will still exist, because it is still referenced by the **Drives** collection.

```
Set typDrive = Nothing
```

As well as the **Root** property, the **Drive** class module has two other properties, both read-only, the **TotalSpace** and **FreeSpace** properties, which return the total space available on the drive and the amount of free space available on the drive.

Going back to the **MyComputer** object, the **Drives** collection was declared publicly, which means that it is exposed to the outside world. This allows other procedures to access objects in the collection like this:

```
Dim mc As New MyComputer
Dim drv As Drive

For Each drv In mc.Drives
    Debug.Print drv.Root, "Total: " & drv.TotalSpace, "Free: " &
drv.FreeSpace
Next

Set mc = Nothing
```

Getting the Most from Class Modules

To finish with, here are five closing thoughts to help you on your way when using objects and collections. It really is worthwhile getting to grips with class modules. They are a key part of Microsoft's programming strategy across all their development products and you can be sure that the limited implementation in Access 97 will be expanded and improved in later versions.

Hide Your Data

Make sure that you declare everything privately unless you really want to expose it as a method or property of the class. If you expose something you shouldn't, then one of three things could happen:

> **Code outside your object may accidentally alter data within your object.**
>
> This could cause your object to behave in a way other than it should and can be a beast of a bug to track down.

> ◆ **Procedures that use your objects may rely on those wrongly-exposed properties for their functionality**.

> This makes maintenance a nightmare. You expect to have to check procedures that access your object when you modify your class's interface, but you don't want to have to check that they will still work whenever you modify the implementation as well.

> ◆ **Variable names within your objects may clash with variable names in procedures that use your objects.**

> This kind of thing doesn't make you too popular...

Don't Overdo It

Although objects are useful in some situations, that's no excuse for using them everywhere. Creating an instance of an object and invoking a method of that object not only consumes more memory than calling the function in a standard module, but is also more time-consuming. So use class modules judiciously.

Avoid Get and Set Methods

It is not good practice to create objects with lots of methods whose names begin with **Get** and **Set**. For example, we could have implemented a **GetButtonState** and **SetButtonState** to inspect and change the mouse button configuration in the **MyComputer** object. But if you want users of your objects to 'get' some form of information about of your object, then you should formally expose that information as a property. And if you want users to alter your object, then make the property writeable.

Get the Object Model Right

It is easy to just wade in and create models without thinking through exactly what your object model should look like. But the same caveat applies to designing objects that applies to designing databases: design time is the best time to design! If you have to redesign your object model half-way through the build process, the chances are that you will then have to change all the code that uses those objects. That's seldom cheap and it's never, ever fun.

Make it Look Easy

We mentioned earlier that one great advantage of using objects is that they offer the possibility of abstraction. In other words, the code inside the object might be quite complex, but the interface the object presents to users is very straightforward. On the CD that accompanies this book, there is a slightly fuller version of the **MyComputer** and **Drive** classes that make extensive use of API calls. But the key point is that you don't need to know anything about DLLs or API calls to use them. The implementation might be complex, but the interface is easy.

Summary

That's pretty good going! In just over thirty pages you've got to grips with object-oriented programming! Obviously this chapter doesn't cover everything to do with OOP in Access 97, but we have covered a good deal of material and certainly enough to get you started.

If you are coming to this from a traditional programming background, you might find it takes a little time to feel totally comfortable with the way it works. But don't worry, just read the chapter again, try the exercises and don't be afraid to experiment. After all it's often only when you get down to cutting code for yourself that you really understand how it all fits together.

The good thing about the way that Access 97 implements classes is that it's a fairly limited implementation. Visual Basic 5.0, for example, has a much richer implementation of object orientation and so it has a somewhat steeper learning curve. You may not be able to do as much in Access 97 as in VB5, but you should find it easier to get started.

Anyway, that's enough creativity for one day! In the next chapter we won't be looking at any new ways of adding functionality to our database. Instead we'll spend the chapter looking at something that's very important, though often neglected—how to optimize our database.

Exercises

1 We looked in this chapter at how to create custom objects through the new class modules in Access 97. See if you can create a **Stats** class with a **LoadData** method and three properties: **Sum**, **Count** and **Average**. The object should accept an array of **Double**s and calculate the sum, count and average of the numbers passed in the array. To help you start, here is the code that you would use to test the class.

```
Sub TestStats()

    Dim MyStatsObject As Stats
    Dim dblMyNumbers(1 To 5) As Double

    dblMyNumbers(1) = 10.34
    dblMyNumbers(2) = 24.48
    dblMyNumbers(3) = 13.26
    dblMyNumbers(4) = 93.23
    dblMyNumbers(5) = 62.65

    Set MyStatsObject = New Stats

    MyStatsObject.LoadData dblMyNumbers()

    Debug.Print "Count = " & MyStatsObject.Count        'Should be 5
    Debug.Print "Sum = " & MyStatsObject.Sum            'Should be 203.96
    Debug.Print "Average = " & MyStatsObject.Average    'Should be 40.792

    Set MyStatsObject = Nothing

End Sub
```

2 Now see if you can make the **Stats** object display a message box when it is destroyed, displaying the number of times that the **Sum** property was inspected!

Optimizing the Database

Chambers 20th Century English Dictionary defines optimization as:

Preparing or revising a computer system or program so as to achieve the greatest possible efficiency.

This is the focus of this chapter. We shall be looking at the different methods available to you as a developer to ensure that your database application operates as efficiently as possible.

In particular, we will cover:

- What makes a piece of code efficient
- How to measure the speed of a program
- Some coding tips for creating faster programs
- What to bear in mind when writing networked applications

Efficiency

The Performance Analyzer (which you can access from the menu bar by clicking Tools/Analyze and then selecting Performance) can help you to a large degree and it is always useful to run it against a poorly performing database application. However, the Performance Analyzer doesn't help you with several other factors that you should consider, one of these being optimization of your VBA code.

If our aim is to achieve maximum efficiency, the key question is, of course, "What constitutes efficiency?" This is a more complex question than it may at first appear. Listed below are four of the most frequently cited benchmarks for evaluating the efficiency of a database application:

- Real execution speed
- Apparent speed
- Memory footprint (i.e. size)
- Network traffic

It is nearly always possible to optimize your application with respect to one of these benchmarks, but how do you optimize with respect to them all? The simple answer is that you can't—and you shouldn't try to.

One of the key tasks at the start of a development project is to devise a list of coding priorities. Which of the six factors listed above are most important for the successful implementation of the application? Which would it be nice to have? And which are irrelevant?

To the four factors listed above, you can add another four:

- Portability
- Robustness
- Maintainability
- Re-usability

None of these will necessarily help to increase the efficiency of the application—optimizing a piece of code for portability or robustness may well cause the code to run slower or consume more memory than before.

In fact, these eight factors can all pull in separate directions. Consider these two bits of code:

```
If (bool1 = True And bool2 = True) Or (bool1 = False And bool2 = False)
Then
     boolResult = False
Else
     boolResult = True
End If
```

```
boolResult = (bool1 Xor bool2)
```

Both of these examples produce the same result. However, the first can take approximately four times as long to execute as the second. If you were optimizing for speed, you would go for the latter.

On the other hand, many developers, especially inexperienced ones, would find the first example easier to follow. If you were optimizing for maintainability, you would probably choose this one (especially given that, on a typical machine, both examples execute in a fraction of a second).

This chapter, then, is not going to tell you the optimal way to write your code. That will depend on the coding priorities that you determine for your application. What this chapter will do is to indicate the impact, in terms of the four most frequently cited coding priorities, shown above.

Reducing Memory Overhead

A modern desktop computer running Access 97 will typically have between 16 and 64 Mb of memory (RAM). This is where all of your application's code is executed. The more memory your computer has, the less frequently your machine will need to read from and write to the disk (a relatively slow process) and, therefore, the faster the program will run.

As a general rule, more memory equals better performance. In the dim and distant past, computers were limited to around 32 or 64 **kilobytes** of memory. To put this in perspective, that is about 2000 times less than the amount in the machine that I am using to produce this chapter. Even if you had an operating system or program able to use 96 Mb of RAM in those days—and that is much more than was utilized in many mainframes—the sheer cost of the memory would have torn your scheme to shreds.

It's not surprising, therefore, that with such limited memory available, programmers spent a great deal of time shoe-horning their quart of code into the pint pot that was their computer. The key phrase was 'disciplined programming'; the language was typically assembler or machine code (almost impenetrable to the layman) and the results produced were a testimony to the ingenuity and patience of the programmers involved.

But these days we live on easy street... if a program is running slowly, just spend $100 on another 16 Mb of RAM for your machine! This isn't a completely heinous attitude—after all, it might cost $40,000 in man-days to re-code the program so that it runs as quickly on a computer with 12Mb of memory as the old version of the program did on a computer with 24 Mb of memory!

However, that is not to say that we should let this newfound freedom allow us to churn out sloppy code. Memory, although relatively cheap, is still precious. The less memory your program takes up, the faster it, and all the other programs running simultaneously, should perform.

Additionally, if you are writing an application that will be used by a thousand users, then every extra megabyte of memory required by your application equates to 1000 Mb of memory across all those machines.

In other words, for most projects, producing an application with a small memory footprint is still a very real coding priority.

You should, therefore, bear the following guidelines in mind when developing any application:

- Use the right data type
- Group procedures into modules
- Strip out comments and unused code
- Reclaim memory where possible
- Don't load unnecessary modules/libraries
- Save the database as an MDE file

Use the Right Data Type

Different types of variable take up different amounts of memory. The size of the memory taken up by each of the data types is shown in the table below:

Data type	Storage size	Range
Byte	1 byte	0 to 255
Boolean	2 bytes	**True** or **False**
Integer	2 bytes	-32,768 to 32,767
Long	4 bytes	-2,147,483,648 to 2,147,483,647.
Single	4 bytes	-3.403E38 to -1.401E-45; 0; 1.401E-45 to 3.403E38
Double	8 bytes	-1.798E308 to -4.941E-324; 0; 4.941E-324 to 1.798E308
Currency	8 bytes	-922,337,203,685,477.5808 to 922,337,203,685,477.5807.
Decimal	14 bytes	-7.923E28 to 7.923E28 (varies with number of decimal places in number stored)
Date	8 bytes	January 1, 100 to December 31, 9999
Object	4 bytes	A reference to any object
Fixed String	1 byte per character	Up to approx. 65,400 characters
Variable Length String	10 bytes + 1 byte per character	Up to approx. 2 billion characters
Variant (numeric)	16 bytes	As double
Variant (string)	22 bytes + 1 byte per character	As variable length string

As you can see, variables of type double take up four times as much memory as variables of type integer. But then again, optimization is a question of compromise—double and single variables can hold a wider range of values than integer variables.

The problem of memory usage becomes even more marked when dealing with arrays. This line:

```
ReDim adbl(9, 9) As Double
```

takes up approximately 800 bytes of memory, compared to the 200 or so bytes taken up by this one:

```
ReDim aint(9, 9) As Integer
```

 For more detailed information on calculating the memory requirements of arrays, refer back to the Memory Considerations section in Chapter 10.

As a rule, if memory footprint size is a coding priority—as it nearly always is—you should choose the smallest variable that can hold the values that you will be dealing with. To remind you to explicitly assign types to variables, you should tick the Require Variable Declaration option in the Tools/Options... dialog.

And it has been said before—but I make no apology for saying it again—always, always be wary of the variant data type.

Group Procedures into Modules

VBA only loads modules when a procedure in that module is called. This is called loading on demand. Therefore, if you have a routine that calls three procedures and they are all in separate modules, all three modules will be loaded into memory. By judiciously grouping related procedures into the same module, you can minimize the number of modules loaded into memory at any one time.

Strip Out Comments and Unused Code

As we have said before, it is a good idea to always comment your code. Even if you understand what your code is doing when you write it, you can guarantee that when you come back to it in six months time you won't! And, of course, commenting code also makes it easier for other people to understand what you are doing. Putting comments in takes virtually no time at all if you do it as you go along and can save hours of frustration in the future. But, of course, there is a price.

Every comment in your code is loaded into memory with your procedure. To reduce the memory overhead of your application, you may consider copying your original database file and stripping all the comments out of the copy which you distribute. In this way, you will have a really lean version which you can use and distribute, and a commented version that you can refer to when you need to change something in the future. Better still, save the database as an MDE file. This process strips out the comments and compiles the code automatically. We'll be looking at MDE files in Chapter 18.

Whatever you do, though, don't use the 'I have no memory' argument as a reason for not commenting your code when, in fact, the real reason is that you don't want to. Don't be lazy!

The same applies to unused procedures, or so-called 'dead code'. The development process is necessarily one of constant experimentation and you'll often find that an application becomes littered with the corpses of now defunct procedures, or with those procedures that "I'm-not-actually-using-at-the-moment-but-I-don't-want-to-delete-because-it'll-be-really-cool-once-I've-figured-out-how-to-fix-the-overflow-problem". Again, strip them out of the production version of your application.

Reclaim Memory Where Possible

You can use the **Erase** statement to reclaim the memory used by a dynamic array. When you have finished with the array, using the **Erase** statement will discard the data in the array and free up the memory that it had been using.

The **Erase** statement doesn't reclaim space from static (i.e. fixed-size) arrays. However, it does re-initialize them. For more information on re-initializing arrays, refer back to Chapter 4.

You can also reclaim the memory used by object variables when you have finished with them. You do this by setting them to a special value called **Nothing**.

```
Set objExcel = Nothing
```

Remember, however, that the memory used by an object cannot be reclaimed if there is another reference to the object elsewhere in code. We used this to our advantage in the previous chapter where we prevented an instance of a popup form from being destroyed by placing a reference to it in a collection declared at the module level of another form. This ensured that the popup form was not destroyed until the second form was closed and the collection went out of scope.

Don't Load Unnecessary Libraries

We'll see in the next chapter that library databases can be a useful way to store and re-use frequently needed procedures. They can also be used to house wizards and add-ins, such as the control and form-design wizards that ship with Access. However, each of these library databases needs to be loaded into memory when used and that can have a significant hit on the amount of memory that is being used. So, to reduce the memory footprint of your installation, you should unload any library databases or add-ins that are not essential.

Save as an MDE

Towards the end of the book, we'll look at the final touches that you should apply to your application before you give it to the end users of the databases. One of those things is converting your database into an MDE file. This conversion compiles any modules within the database and then strips out the original source code. This in turn has the twin advantages of making your database more secure and reducing the memory footprint of your application.

> *Bear in mind that you cannot modify the design of MDE files and that you should always keep an original source version of your database in MDB format.*

A Final Recommendation—Buy More Memory!

No, it's not cheating! Access 97 is quoted as needing a minimum of 12 Mb of RAM on Windows 95 and 16Mb on Windows NT Workstation. I've tested it with 12 Mb, 16 Mb, 24 Mb and 32Mb and would say that 16 Mb is the realistic minimum if you want to get acceptable performance with Access 97 running on its own on Windows 95 and 24Mb on Windows NT.

If you are running on a network, or using other Windows applications at the same time, you will find that the extra $50 it will cost to buy another 8 Mb will be well worth it.

Increasing Execution Speed

Reducing the amount of memory that your Access database and its code occupies may result in both it and other Windows applications running faster. But, if fast execution is a real coding priority, there are other methods you can consider:

- ▶ Use constants
- ▶ Use specific object types (early binding)

- Use transactions where appropriate
- Use variables, not properties
- Avoid slow structures
- Use string functions
- Beware of **IIf**
- Use integer arithmetic where possible
- Use in-line code
- Use **DoEvents** judiciously
- Use **For Each...** loops
- Use the **Requery** method not the **Requery** action
- Use **Me**
- Base forms on saved queries
- Speed up database operations

We'll look at these in more detail and provide some code samples that prove the point. The code samples have been included so that you can gauge the impact of these techniques for yourself. After all, computers differ greatly in terms of the amount of RAM, processor speed, cache size, disk speed, etc.. And these differences are reflected in the performance of VBA on those machines. Don't take my word for it, try out these examples for yourself!

Looking at the results below, you might be forgiven for wondering whether it is worth bothering with some of the improvements. After all, if it only takes three milliseconds to perform an operation, why bother going to the effort of optimizing your code so that it only takes one millisecond. After all, who's going to notice? Well, although it's fair to say that the difference may not be noticeable in a single line of code, it might be if that code is executed many times. For example, you may be looping through all the controls on a form to check for a certain condition. Or you might be looping through all the records in a recordset. Get into the habit of coding efficiently all the time—then it won't be a struggle to do it when it really matters.

Timing the Code Samples

There are several options available to you for testing how quickly a piece of code executes. A very simple method is to use the **Timer** function. For example, we could use the following sample of code to time how long it takes for a **For... Next...** structure to loop through 32,000 values.

```
Option Compare Database
Option Explicit


Dim lngStart As Long
Dim lngEnd As Long


Sub ShowTime()
    MsgBox lngEnd - lngStart & " secs."
End Sub
```

```
Function UseTimer()

    Dim i As Integer
    lngStart = Timer
    For i = 0 To 32000
    Next i
    lngEnd = Timer
    ShowTime


End Function
```

The **Timer** function returns the number of seconds elapsed since midnight. In the example above, we save the value of **Timer** in the variable **lngStart** before the loop commences:

```
lngStart = Timer
```

and then save the value of **Timer** in the variable **lngEnd** when the loop has finished:

```
lngEnd = Timer
```

By subtracting one from the other, we can determine how long it took for the loop to execute:

```
MsgBox lngEnd - lngStart & " secs."
```

However, if you try this example for yourself, you will soon note the obvious limitation. Because the **Timer** function is only accurate to the nearest second, you will probably see the following message box when you run the code detailed above.

Not too useful if you are testing code that takes less than a second to execute! An alternative is to use an API call to do the timing for you. The **winmm.dll** library contains a function called **timeGetTime** which returns the number of milliseconds since Windows was started. We looked at this in the chapter dealing with advanced programming techniques. Since the value this returns is accurate to a millisecond (1/1000 of a second), it is much more useful when timing code execution. It is a very simple function to implement. The next code sample shows you how to declare the function and use it to time the same code as above:

```
Option Compare Database
Option Explicit

Declare Function TimeIt Lib "winmm.dll" Alias "timeGetTime" () As Long

Dim lngStart As Long
Dim lngEnd As Long

Sub ShowTime()
    MsgBox (lngEnd - lngStart) & " milliseconds"
End Sub
```

```
Function UseTimeIt()

    Dim i As Integer
    lngStart = TimeIt
    For i = 0 To 32000
    Next i
    lngEnd = TimeIt
    ShowTime

End Function
```

The significant change here is the addition of the declaration of the **timeGetTime** function which allows us to call it directly from Access as the **TimeIt** function:

```
Declare Function TimeIt Lib "winmm.dll" Alias "timeGetTime" () As Long
```

 FYI   For more information on using API calls, have a look at Chapter 10.

The result this time will be something more along the lines of:

We will be using the **timeGetTime** function to time code examples throughout this chapter. In fact, there is a class module in the **Whisky14.mdb** database that acts as a wrapper for the **timeGetTime** function. We will use this to create a **StopWatch** object with which to time our code. The **StopWatch** object has the following methods:

Method	Description
StartTiming	Resets all counters to zero and deletes all lap times
SaveLapTime	Adds an entry to the **LapTimes** collection recording an intermediate measurement of the number of milliseconds since **StartTiming** was invoked
StopTiming	Sets the value of the **StopTime** property to the number of milliseconds since **StartTiming** was invoked

The following portion of code illustrates how you could use the **StopWatch** object to time the execution of your code.

```
Dim lngIterations As Long
Dim sw As StopWatch
Set sw = New StopWatch

'Start Stopwatch object
sw.StartTiming
```

```
'Determine time taken for method 1
For lngIterations = 1 To 100000
...Call SlowProc
Next
sw.SaveLapTime

'Determine time taken for method 2
For lngIterations = 1 To 100000
    CallFastProc
Next
sw.StopTiming

'Show results
Debug.Print "SlowProc (ms.): " & sw.LapTimes(1)
Debug.Print "LongProc (ms.): " & sw.StopTime - sw.LapTimes(1)

'Destroy Stopwatch object
Set sw = Nothing

End Sub
```

You will notice that the code we test is in a **For... Next...** loop which iterates many times. We need to do this because, although **timeGetTime** is very accurate, each line of code executes extremely quickly and so executing many iterations of the code increases the accuracy of our measurement. It also helps to minimize the very small overhead of calling the **Stopwatch** object.

For greater accuracy, you should also measure the impact of the **For... Next...** loop itself on the results. Although this overhead is small—typically about 50 milliseconds for 100,000 iterations—and can be safely ignored when testing lengthy operations, it can seriously skew tests on simple lines of code.

For this reason, the **Stopwatch** object has two extra methods, the **StartCorrection** and **SaveCorrection** methods. These can be used to time an empty loop. The time taken is stored in the **Correction** property and this can be subtracted from the **LapTimes** and **TotalTime** for more accurate results. Using this technique, our test harness would look like this.

```
Sub TestHarness()

Dim lngIterations As Long
Dim sw As StopWatch
Dim sResult As String

Set sw = New StopWatch

'Determine overhead of looping
sw.StartCorrection
For lngIterations = 1 To 100000
Next
sw.SaveCorrection
```

```
'Restart Stopwatch object and test first code
sw.StartTiming
For lngIterations = 1 To 1000000
    ←----------------------------'Insert first code to be tested here
Next
sw.SaveLapTime

'And now test speed of next code
For lngIterations = 1 To 1000000
    ←----------------------------'Insert next code to be tested here
Next
sw.StopTiming

'Show results
sResult = "Overhead of loop: " & sw.Correction & "ms." & Chr$(10) &
Chr$(10)
sResult = sResult & "First code: " & sw.LapTimes(1) & " ms." & _
            " <" & sw.LapTimes(1) - sw.Correction & " ms.>" & Chr$(10)
sResult = sResult & "Second code: " & sw.TotalTime - sw.LapTimes(1) & _
            " ms." & _ " <" & sw.TotalTime - sw.LapTimes(1) - _
            sw.Correction & " ms.>"

MsgBox sResult

'Destroy Stopwatch object
Set sw = Nothing

End Sub
```

This code and all of the code samples that follow can be found in the **Chapter 13 Code** module of the **Whisky14.mdb** database on the CD that accompanies this book. You will probably want to run the tests to see how they perform on your machine. The sample timings shown in this chapter were produced on a 100MHz Pentium machine with 2 x 1Gb IDE disks (10ms access) and 96Mb RAM (I never believe minimum specs!). These timings can also be found in the **Timings.xls** spreadsheet on the CD.

When testing the execution speed of your code, you should make the test conditions as realistic as possible. In other words, test the application on the same specification of computer that will be used in production, load up any other applications which the users will be running, and use realistic volumes of data. Also, run your tests three or four times to see if performance varies from run to run. You might find that the first run of the following examples will give varying results as the code and any data has to be loaded into memory before it can be run. On subsequent runs the code and data should already be in memory so the speed will improve and the results will be more consistent.

Use Constants

If you use values in your code that do not change, then you should consider assigning them to constants rather than to variables. When a variable is encountered in a line of VBA code, Access needs to access the memory location that contains the variable in order to determine the value of the variable. In contrast, the value of a constant is resolved and written into the code at compile time. Because the constant value is closer at hand, reading values from constants generally works out slightly quicker than reading values from variables.

Procedure	Comments	Iterations	Results (ms.) Total	Per iteration
VarsAndConstants (Part 1)	Using local variables	100000	67.8	0.0007
VarsAndConstants (Part 2)	Using local constants	100000	50.0	0.0005

Don't be Vague!

Use Specific Object Types (Early Binding)

In earlier versions of Access, it was common to see lines of code like this:

```
Dim frm As Object
Set frm = forms!frmSwitchboard
```

Although this code will run, it is not very efficient. Because the object variable **frm** has been declared **As Object**, Access does not know what type of object it is. This in turn means that whenever we try to inspect or set a property value, or invoke a method against that object at run-time, Access must first check whether or not that property or method is appropriate for the object. This is what is known as **late binding**. A better way to write this code would be like this:

```
Dim frm As Form_frmSwitchboard
Set frm = Forms!frmSwitchboard
```

This time round, Access knows what type of object **frm** is. This means that it can determine at compile time which properties and methods are appropriate to it. This is therefore known as **early binding**. Because Access only has to perform this check once, and it does it prior to run-time, the difference in execution speed at run time between code using the two methods can be very significant.

A secondary advantage of early binding is that because Access can determine which properties and methods are appropriate at compile time. Any errors in your code, which result from misspelling property or method names, are caught at compile time rather than appearing as run-time errors.

Procedure	Comments	Iterations	Results (ms.) Total	Per iteration
`SpecificObjects` (Part 1)	Using `As Object` syntax	100000	35796.5	0.3580
`SpecificObjects` (Part 2)	Using specific object variable	100000	7507.1	0.0751

Use Variables, Not Properties

You can realize similar performance benefits if you use variables to refer to forms, controls and properties. If you are going to refer to a form, report or control more than once in a procedure, you should create an object variable for the object and then refer to that instead of the object itself.

```
Dim frm as Form_frmSwitchboard
Dim ctl As Image
Set frm = Forms!frmSwitchboard
Set ctl = frm!imgLogo

sTemp1 = ctl.Picture
sTemp2 = ctl.PictureAlignment
sTemp3 = ctl.SizeMode
```

Alternatively, you can use the **With** structure.

```
With ctl
    sTemp1 = .Picture
    sTemp2 = .PictureAlignment
    sTemp3 = .SizeMode
End With
```

Code written using either of these two syntaxes will execute considerably faster than code which uses the long-hand syntax.

```
sTemp1 = Forms!frmSwitchboard!imgLogo.Picture
sTemp2 = Forms!frmSwitchboard!imgLogo.PictureAlignment
sTemp3 = Forms!frmSwitchboard!imgLogo.SizeMode
```

In this situation the **With... End With** syntax takes fractionally longer than the first method which simply uses object variables. This is because of the overhead involved in setting up the **With** structure. However, you would find that if you were to add more and more references to the specified object between the **With** and **End With** statements, then this structure would become more efficient.

A further advantage of using object variables, as we have in the first two syntaxes, is that it involves early binding, and so makes it easier to detect errors prior to run-time.

Procedure	Comments	Iterations	Results (ms.) Total	Per iteration
`VariableSubstitution` (Part 1)	Using long-hand references	10000	16282.3	1.6282
`VariableSubstitution` (Part 2)	Using object variables	10000	1875.1	0.1875
`VariableSubstitution` (Part 3)	Using object variables and `With`	10000	1914.1	0.1914

Use String Functions

Another area where vagueness can creep in is when using string functions. Most string functions have variant alternatives. For example, the `Format` function returns a `Variant` in a certain format.

```
varTemp = Format("abcdef", ">")
```

By contrast, the `Format$` returns a formatted `String`.

```
strTemp = Format$("abcdef", ">")
```

In fact, any function which is suffixed with a `$` will return a `String`. If you are formatting a variable or literal that will then be assigned to a `String` variable, you will get better performance if you use the string version of the function, rather than the variant version.

Procedure	Comments	Iterations	Results (ms.) Total	Per iteration
`StringFunctions` (Part 1)	Using `Format`	100000	7141.3	0.0714
`StringFunctions` (Part 2)	Using `Format$`	100000	6749.9	0.0675

Avoid Slow Structures

Another way to make your VBA code run faster is to avoid using slow structures. What does this mean? Well, most languages offer the programmer several different methods of performing a single task. If real execution speed is a coding priority, you should test each of these different methods for speed and decide which to use accordingly. In practice, you may find that the faster method conflicts with another of the project's coding priorities, so you may have to compromise. Even if this is the case, though, the time spent timing the code will not have been wasted as you will be able to use this knowledge in future projects.

Immediate If (IIf)

The Immediate If (`IIf`) function is often viewed as a quick and easy way to return one of two values depending on whether an expression evaluates to `True`. We looked at this function in Chapter 4. Its syntax is:

```
value = IIf(Expression, TruePart, FalsePart)
```

TruePart is returned if **Expression** is **True** and **FalsePart** is returned if **Expression** is **False**. This is the same as writing:

```
If Expression Then
    value = TruePart
Else
    value = Falsepart
EndIf
```

However, the key difference between the two formats is that the **IIf** function will always evaluate both **TruePart** and **FalsePart**, whereas the normal **If** structure will only evaluate the part which is returned. To see the implications of this, consider these two portions of code:

```
If lngNumber = 5 Then
    lngRetVal = 10
Else
    lngRetVal = DLast("OrderID", "Order", "OrderDate < #01-01-96#")
End If
```

```
lngRetVal = IIf(lngNumber = 5, 10, _
                DLast("OrderID", "Order", "OrderDate < #01-01-96#"))
```

Both of these procedures do the same thing. They evaluate the variable **lngNumber** and if it is equal to **5**, the procedure sets the value of **lngRetVal** to **10**. If it isn't, the procedure sets the value of **lngRetVal** to a value that it looks up in the **Order** table.

The difference between the procedures is that the second one will always look up the record from **Order** whether it's required or not. So whenever these procedures are called with **lngNumber** equal to **5**, the second one will be considerably slower.

Procedure	Comments	Iterations	Results (ms.) Total	Per iteration
IfAndIIf (Part 1)	**IIf** where **lngNumber** = **5**	100	4918.5	49.1850
IfAndIIf (Part 2)	**If** where **lngNumber** = **5**	100	1.0	0.01
IfAndIIf (Part 1)	**IIf** where **lngNumber** = **10**	100	4634.3	46.3425
IfAndIIf (Part 2)	**If** where **lngNumber** = **10**	100	4596.4	45.9638

Use Integer Arithmetic Where Possible

The speed with which arithmetic calculations are performed depends on the data type of the variables concerned and the type of operation being performed.

In general, however, **Integer** and **Long** variables are faster than **Single** and **Double** variables. These, in turn, are faster than **Currency** variables. **Variant** variables are considerably slower, with most operations taking typically twice as long as with other data types.

 You can carry out tests to verify this by running the **TestTypes** procedure from the **Whisky14.mdb** database.

Although the difference in execution times for a single operation is very small, it will become more noticeable for repeated operations (such as within large loops).

Use In-Line Code

Earlier on, we noted that variables could be passed as arguments to procedures by reference or by value. When a variable is passed by reference (the default), the procedure that is called is passed a pointer to the memory location of the variable being passed. In contrast, when a variable is passed by value, a copy of the variable is made and is passed to the procedure. Although passing variables by value has its uses, it is fractionally slower than passing by reference.

Both of these methods are slower, however, than placing the code in-line and not calling a procedure at all. The downside of in-line code is that it is more difficult to maintain if you have the same code appearing in-line in multiple procedures. But if your chief coding priority is execution speed, you should seriously consider using in-line code.

The following procedures can be used to illustrate the difference between the three methods described above:

```vba
Sub TestPassing()

Dim dbl1 As Double
Dim dbl2 As Double

dbl1 = 1234

'Passing by value
dbl2 = FourthPowerByVal(dbl1)

'Passing by reference
dbl2 = FourthPower(dbl1)

'Inline coding
dbl2 = dbl1 ^ 4

End Sub
```

```vba
Function FourthPower(dblNumber As Double) As Double

FourthPower = dblNumber ^ 4

End Function
```

```
Function FourthPowerByVal(ByVal dblNumber As Double) As Double

FourthPowerByVal = dblNumber ^ 4

End Function
```

Procedure	Comments	Iterations	Results (ms.) Total	Per iteration
TestPassing (Part 1)	Passing by value	100000	1161.4	0.0116
TestPassing (Part 2)	Passing by reference	100000	1054.3	0.0105
TestPassing (Part 3)	Inline coding	100000	771.4	0.0077

Use For Each...

Visual Basic has a looping structure called the **For Each... Next...** loop which allows us to loop through each of the elements of an array or collection in turn.

```
For Each qdf In CurrentDb.QueryDefs
    sTemp = qdf.SQL
    qdf.Close
Next
```

Prior to the introduction of VBA, it was standard practice to determine the number of elements in the collection or array and then use a **For... Next...** loop to inspect each element using the loop counter as an index to the collection.

```
For iCounter = 0 To CurrentDb.QueryDefs.Count - 1
    Set qdf = CurrentDb.QueryDefs(iCounter)
    sTemp = qdf.SQL
    qdf.Close
Next
```

Wherever you can, you should use the first structure. Using a **For Each... Next...** loop is often significantly faster than attempting the same operation using a traditional loop using the loop counter as an index to the collection or array.

Procedure	Comments	Iterations	Results (ms.) Total	Per iteration
ForEach (Part 2)	Using traditional loop	10	592.3	59.2250
ForEach (Part 1)	Using **For Each...** structure	10	237.8	23.7750

Use DoEvents Judiciously

When a VBA procedure is running, it will act very selfishly and hog the Access limelight unless you tell it otherwise. For example, if you were to run the following portion of code, you would find that Access was locked up until the code finished running.

413

```
For lngCounter = 1 to 1000000
    i = Rnd*12
Next lngCounter
```

FYI Under Windows 3.11 this would have locked up the whole Windows system. With the multi-threading capabilities of Windows 95 and Windows NT, only Access will be locked.

This routine takes approximately 2.8 seconds to execute on my computer. But it is considered good etiquette (and common sense) to yield control to Windows every so often. For example, whilst your routine is running you may wish to cancel it, pause it for a moment or do something else. If your routine ignored all your requests then you wouldn't be very happy. What you need is a way to allow other events to be processed while your routine runs.

This can be achieved with the **DoEvents** statement. This instructs Windows to process any messages or keystrokes that are currently queued. In the following portion of code, whenever the loop reaches the **DoEvents** statement, control passes to Windows which checks to see whether any other application has any messages or keystrokes waiting to be processed. It then passes control back to the procedure.

```
For lngCounter = 1 to 1000000
    i = Rnd*12
    DoEvents
Next lngCounter
```

Although this is good practice, it does take up time. In fact, the routine, which checks for events every time the loop is passed through, takes *over 55 minutes* to run! If you want to use the **DoEvents** statement, do so sparingly. The portion of code shown above can be rewritten like this:

```
For lngCounter = 1 to 1000000
    i = Rnd*12
    If lngCounter Mod 50000 = 0 Then DoEvents
Next lngCounter
```

Now, control passes to Windows every 50,000 loops. This means 20 times in the 4.13 seconds or so that the loop now takes to finish, which leaves you with a well-behaved and yet fast bit of code. The **DoEvents** adds only 1.34 seconds to the execution time of this code.

Typical results for the three code samples on a Pentium-class machine above are shown in the table below. You can test them for yourself with the **DoEventsTest** procedure in the **Whisky14.mdb** database on the CD accompanying this book, but be careful to remember that running the test with a **DoEvents** on every loop will be very slow.

Procedure	Comments	Iterations	Results (ms.)	
			Total	Per iteration
`DoEventsTest` (Part 1)	No `DoEvents`	100000	2785.0	0.0279
`DoEventsTest` (Part 2)	20 `DoEvents`	100000	4127.0	0.0413
`DoEventsTest` (Part 3)	100000 `DoEvents`	100000	3348986.0	33.4899

FYI Whenever you yield control to the processor from within an procedure, you should always make sure the procedure is not executed again from a different part of your code before the first call returns. If it does—this is called re-entrancy—your code will probably not work the way you intended it to and the application may either hang or crash.

Use the Requery Method, not the Requery Action

Another method of speeding up your procedures is to avoid using the **Requery** action to display up-to-date values in a form or control. Use the **Requery** method instead. This is quicker as it simply re-runs the query behind the form or control instead of closing it, re-opening it and then re-running it, as the **Requery** action does.

```
DoCmd Requery ctlText.Name      'This is slow

ctlText.Requery                 'This is much quicker
```

*Be aware, however, that in some situations the **Requery** method and the **Requery** action may produce different results. The **Requery** method simply fetches up-to-date non-key values into the form's recordset, based on the existing keyset, or set of key values. By contrast, the **Requery** action rebuilds the keyset and then fetches the non-key values.*

Use Me

When you use the **Me** keyword to refer to a form within an event procedure, Access only searches in the local name space for the form. This means that the form is found more quickly than if the full reference to the form is specified.

```
Forms!frmFoo.BackColor = QBColor(9)      'This is slow

Me.BackColor = QBColor(9)                'This is quicker
```

Speed Up Database Operations

Whereas the optimizations you can realize through changing the syntax of your VBA are sometimes marginal, optimizing your database calls almost always leads to substantial performance benefits. The reason for that is simple. Database calls generally take longer to execute than normal VBA statements, so a 10% improvement in performance in both will be more noticeable in the case of the database call. We'll look below at some of the ways you can improve the way that VBA code interacts with your database.

Use Indexes

Adding an index to a field can be an excellent way of improving the performance of searches on that field. Although adding indexes slows updates and increases locking contention, very often this overhead is more than offset by the performance benefits gained if the fields are frequently used to search on in queries. You can see the performance benefits for yourself by running the **UsingIndexes** procedure. You'll find it in the **Chapter 13 Code** module in **Whisky14.mdb** on the CD accompanying this book. This procedure opens a recordset twice using the following code:

```
Set rec = CurrentDb.OpenRecordset _
        ("SELECT OrderID FROM [Order] WHERE OrderDate < #1/1/96#", _
            bOpenDynaset)
    rec.MoveLast
    lngRetVal = rec(0)
    rec.Close
```

The first time it opens the recordset, the **OrderDate** field is not indexed; the second time it is indexed. The table below shows sample timings for this function, but you may want to test them out for yourself.

Procedure	Comments	Iterations	Results (ms.) Total	Per iteration
UsingIndexes (Part 1)	**OrderDate** not indexed	100	4653.0	46.5300
UsingIndexes (Part 2)	**OrderDate** indexed	100	2163.0	21.6300

Avoid Domain Aggregate Functions

Consider the following line of code:

```
lngRetVal = DLast ("OrderID", "Order", "OrderDate < #01-01-96#")
```

This performs the same function as the lines of code we have just looked at in the **UsingIndexes** section. And yet, when we look at the relative performance, we see that the domain function takes considerably longer.

Domain aggregate functions are sloooowwww! They may be fine when you are knocking together a prototype, but if you want fast database access in your VBA code, then you should be wary of using them.

Procedure	Comments	Iterations	Results (ms.) Total	Per iteration
`DomainFunction`	Using `DLast`	100	5047.3	50.4725

Use Forward-Only and Read-Only Recordsets

Another way of increasing the performance of data access in code is to use forward-only recordsets.

```
Set rec = CurrentDb.OpenRecordset _
    ("SELECT OrderID FROM [Order] WHERE OrderDate < #1/1/96#", _
        dbOpenForwardOnly)
```

These only allow you to scroll downwards through a recordset and you cannot use certain methods (e.g. `MoveLast`) against recordsets created like this. Although this means that you cannot use forward-only recordsets in all situations, the fact that they do not need a complicated cursoring mechanism means that they will often outperform conventional recordsets.

The same applies for read-only recordsets:

```
Set rec = CurrentDb.OpenRecordset _
    ("SELECT OrderID FROM [Order] WHERE OrderDate < #1/1/96#", _
        dbOpenDynaset, _ dbReadOnly)
```

Although not always appropriate, they will often perform better than updateable recordsets because they do not need as complicated a cursor mechanism.

The table below shows sample timings for opening the recordset shown above, using different types of recordset each time. If you want to test them out for yourself, you should run the `RecordsetTypes` procedure which you can find with all the other test procedures for this chapter in the **Chapter 13 Code** module in the **Whisky14.mdb** database accompanying this book.

Procedure	Comments	Iterations	Results (ms.) Total	Per iteration
`RecordsetTypes` (Part 1)	Standard dynaset	100	1977.9	19.7788
`RecordsetTypes` (Part 2)	Read-only recordset	100	1960.4	19.6038
`RecordsetTypes` (Part 3)	Forward-only recordset	100	1790.0	17.9000
`RecordsetTypes` (Part 4)	Forward-only, read-only recordset	100	1791.3	17.9125

The performance of each of the examples in this section is highly dependent on the size of the base table, the restrictiveness of the criteria and which fields are indexed. In short, there is no substitute for performance testing on your database when you are completing the application. And when you run the performance testing, replicate both the expected data volumes and the conditions of the production environment as closely as you can.

Use Bookmarks

Each record in a recordset is automatically assigned a **Bookmark** when the recordset is opened If you are in a recordset and know that you will want to move back to the record that you are currently on, you should save the record's **Bookmark** to a variable. By setting the **Bookmark** property of the **Recordset** object to the value you saved in the variable, you will be able to return to the record far more quickly than you would be able to if you used any of the **Find** or **Seek** methods.

*   **Bookmarks** *are stored as arrays of byte data and so should be saved as byte arrays rather than strings. Although you can save a* **Bookmark** *to a string variable, comparing a record's* **Bookmark** *to a* **Bookmark** *stored in a string variable will not yield correct results, unless the comparison is performed as a binary comparison. For more information on* **Bookmarks** *and binary comparison, refer to Chapter 6.*

Base Forms on Saved Queries

Saved queries run more quickly than dynamically created SQL, because they have already been compiled. Therefore, a form based on a saved query will open faster than one which has an SQL statement as its **RecordSource**.

The downside to this is a maintenance overhead. If you export a form based on a saved query to another database, you must remember to export the correct query as well. If, in contrast, the form has an SQL statement as its **RecordSource**, only the form needs to be exported.

Increasing Apparent Speed

Although you may be able to do much to increase the real execution speed of your VBA code and your database calls, there is only so far you can go. So what happens if you have optimized your application for real execution speed and it still appears sluggish? One option is to increase the application's **apparent** speed. This is how fast the user *thinks* the application is, rather than how fast it really is.

FYI Users of an application do not get upset when the application is slow. They get upset when they notice that it is slow! There is a big difference.

Consider the following ways of making an application appear more quickly:

  Using a startup form

- ◗ Using gauges
- ◗ Removing code from form modules
- ◗ Pre-loading and hiding forms
- ◗ Caching data locally

Simple Startup Form

One trusted method of distracting users from the fact that an application is taking a long time to perform some task is to distract them with some fancy graphics. After all, Microsoft do it all the time. What happens when you start up Access, Word or Excel? You see a startup form or splash screen:

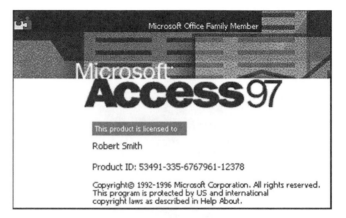

"Gosh! That's pretty. I wish my application looked so professional!" you think to yourself. And by the time you have snapped out of your reverie, the application has loaded.

If there had been no splash screen you would have probably thought to yourself, "What on earth is happening! Why does it take so long for this application to start?" Splash screens really do work.

The really good news is that it takes next to no effort to implement a splash screen in Access 97. Simply create a form and specify its name in the Display Form box on the Tools/Startup... dialog.

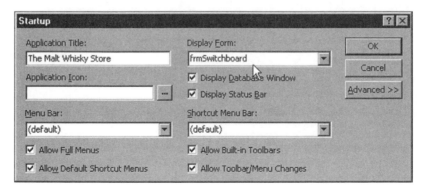

A word of warning—don't overload your startup form with too many controls or complex **Load** event code or else it will take ages for the splash screen to appear and you will have defeated the object of the exercise!

Use Gauges

Another way that you can distract users—and re-assure them that *something* is happening—is to show a meter displaying the progress of operations which are being performed. The **SysCmd** function provides a simple way of doing this. There are three steps involved in displaying a progress meter in the status bar of your application:

> Initialize the meter and specify its maximum value and text to be displayed

> Repeatedly update the meter to show progress

> Remove the meter

The following code illustrates one way of displaying a progress meter:

```
Sub ShowProgress()

Dim varRetVal As Variant
Dim i As Integer
Dim j As Integer
Dim intRnd As Integer

'Initialise Progress Meter and set Maximum to 300
varRetVal = SysCmd(acSysCmdInitMeter, "Testing...", 300)

For i = 0 To 300
    'Perform some processing or other...
    For j = 0 To 1000
        intRnd = Rnd * 10 + 1
    Next j

    'Update Meter to Show Progress
    varRetVal = SysCmd(acSysCmdUpdateMeter, i)
Next i

'Remove Meter from Status Bar
varRetVal = SysCmd(acSysCmdRemoveMeter)

End Sub
```

This procedure causes a gradually filling progress meter to be displayed with the text "Testing..."

Of course, you do not need to set up a loop to update your progress meter. Instead you could structure your procedure like this:

```
Sub ShowProgress()

Dim varRetVal As Variant
```

```
'Initialise Progress Meter and set Maximum to 300
varRetVal = SysCmd(acSysCmdInitMeter, "Testing...", 300)

'Perform some processing or other...
....
'Update Meter to Show Progress
varRetVal = SysCmd(acSysCmdUpdateMeter, 5)

'Perform more processing...
....
'Update Meter to Show Progress
varRetVal = SysCmd(acSysCmdUpdateMeter, 10)

'And yet more...
....
'Update Meter to Show Progress
varRetVal = SysCmd(acSysCmdUpdateMeter, 15)

    .
    .
    .


'Remove Meter from Status Bar
varRetVal = SysCmd(acSysCmdRemoveMeter)

End Sub
```

The three constants **acSysCmdInitMeter**, **acSysCmdUpdateMeter** and **acSysCmdRemoveMeter**, which are used to initialize, update and remove the status bar, are intrinsic to Access. In other words, they are built into the language and do not need to be declared anywhere.

Note that the progress meter will only be shown if the status bar is visible in your database. To make it visible in the Whisky database, select **Startup** from the **Tools** menu option (available when the database window is active) and tick the **Display Status Bar** option. You will have to reopen the database for this to take effect.

Remove Code from Form Modules

Users are likely to get irritated if they click a button to open a form and it then seems to take ages for the form to appear. This usually happens when a form has substantial amounts of code in its module which delays the form's loading. In this situation, you might consider removing the code from the form module and placing it in a standard code module. This will cause the form to load more quickly, as code will only be loaded on demand after the form was open.

Pre-Load and Hide Forms

Alternatively, if you find that you use a form frequently and it takes a long time to load and unload, you might choose to load the form during the application's startup and then make it visible and invisible instead of loading and unloading it.

This technique will slow down the startup of your application but will appear to increase its subsequent performance. You can even delay the loading of the form until after the main form has already appeared. While the user is looking at the main form it can be loading in the background.

This method works well if apparent speed is a coding priority, but you should bear in mind that having several forms loaded concurrently will increase the application's memory usage.

Cache Data Locally

A **cache** is just an area of memory (or hard disk space) which is used to hold values that have been retrieved from somewhere else, ready to be used again. For example Windows 95 places the data that comes from your hard disk into a cache made up of an area of memory. Often a program uses the same data over and over again. This way it can just read it from the cache the next time instead of having to fetch it from the hard disk again. And of course reading from memory is much quicker and more efficient that reading from a hard disk.

So you can increase an application's performance by caching data in one form or another. In decreasing order of speed (i.e. fastest first), the three methods of data retrieval are:

- Reading data from memory (e.g. variables, arrays)
- Reading data from local tables
- Reading data from tables across the network

If you want to increase the perceived speed of your application, think about how you can cache data to 'move it up' a level.

If you keep frequently accessed, non-volatile data (i.e. data that doesn't change much) in a table on a network server, you might consider copying that data to the local client machine to make the application run faster. However, you will need to make sure that whenever data is updated on the server, it is also updated on all client machines as well (and vice versa).

Similarly, if you have data in a lookup table (e.g. **Region**) which you frequently access in VBA code, you could create an array to hold that data with the **GetRows** method. This could make retrieving the data substantially faster. However, it will also increase the memory usage of your application.

FYI

Both these methods increase the apparent speed of your application. They may not increase the actual speed, because there will be a performance overhead involved in the process of caching the data in the first place. Remember that caching only works well if you need to read the data several times. If you only read it once, caching will slow your application down.

Network Considerations

So far, we have concentrated on writing code that fits into as small an amount of memory, and can be executed as quickly as possible—or at least appears to do so. But that is only part of the story. One of the major reasons why Access database applications run slowly has nothing to do with memory footprints or code execution speed. Instead, the albatross around the neck of many applications is the vast amount of data which needs to be read from disk and passed across a network.

A network has two major drawbacks. Firstly, performance across a network—particularly a slow one—can be worse than performance against local tables. Secondly, you might find that your application generates a lot of network traffic. This will not make you popular with other users of the network, who find that their applications have slowed down considerably because of the log-jam. If either of these causes you a problem, consider:

- Searching on indexed fields in attached tables
- Putting non-table objects on the local machine
- Disabling **AutoExpand**

Search on Indexed Fields in Attached Tables

One method of minimizing the amount of data that an application has to read from disk is to ensure that fields used in the queries are indexed. If you run a query with a criterion against a field which is indexed, Access will be able to determine the exact data pages which contain the records it needs to retrieve in order to run the query. It will retrieve only the data pages that contain those records.

However, if you are running a query which uses a criterion against a field which is not indexed, Access will need to read into memory every single record in the underlying table, to see whether it meets the criterion. If the table is large and is on a network server, this will result in large amounts of network traffic and a very slow and frustrating query.

To look at an example of this in a little more detail, consider the following query:

```
SELECT DISTINCTROW OrderNumber, OrderDate
FROM [Order]
WHERE LocationID=4
```

If the **LocationID** field in **Order** is indexed, then the Jet engine knows that it will only need to retrieve the pages containing records with a **LocationID** of **4** from the **Order** table.

However, if the **LocationID** field is not indexed, then Jet will have to read the whole of the **Order** table from disk and transfer it into the memory of the PC running the query. If the **Order** table is on a network server, this means that the whole table will need to be transferred across the network. Once it is in local memory, Jet can determine which records match the criterion by going through each record in turn and checking whether the **LocationID** field is equal to **4**. This is known as a table scan and is slow.

Imagine if the **Order** table contained half a million records, each approximately 50 bytes long. A table scan on an attached table would mean reading (50 x 500,000 bytes =) 25 Mb across the network and trying to fit them into local memory....

As a rule, therefore, always use indexes on fields which are involved in joins or which have criteria applied to them in queries.

Put Non-Table Objects on the Local Machine

Another way to minimize the amount of network traffic that a networked application generates is to place tables on the network server but to place other objects into a local copy of the database. Then the data in the tables can be shared by all users, but all other objects (i.e. queries, forms, reports, macros and modules) will reside on the local computer. Consequently, when that object is activated—say, when a form is opened—the computer only needs to read it into memory from its local disk. This will generally be quicker than loading them over the network and will also mean a noticeable reduction in network traffic.

The downside of this strategy is that you will have to distribute a new copy of the database to each user whenever you revise the code or any of the objects in it. Despite this, most applications benefit from this sort of segmentation.

Disable AutoExpand

The **AutoExpand** property of a combo box forces Access to fill it automatically with a value that matches the text you have typed. Although this is a neat feature and can make the process of filling in forms less of a chore, it comes at a price—the table that supplies the values has to be queried as the user types in text. If the table on which the combo box is based resides across the network the result may be a substantial increase in network traffic, especially if the combo box contains many values.

Finishing Touches

All of the tips so far have been aimed at specific coding priorities. Some increased real execution speed, others reduced network traffic, still others reduced the memory footprint of the database application.

In some cases, a single optimization may bring many benefits. For example, changing a variable's data type from variant to integer will reduce memory demands *and* increase execution speed.

However, in other cases an optimization may have an antagonistic effect. It may bring a benefit *and* incur a cost. For example, loading forms and hiding them will increase the apparent execution speed of your application, but it will also increase your application's memory footprint. In that situation you must decide what your priorities are and act accordingly.

The final section of this chapter concentrates on the things that you can do which will always benefit your application—irrespective of your coding priorities.

These include:

▶ Compacting the database

▶ Compiling all modules

▶ Opening databases exclusively

Compact the Database

Over a period of time you may find that the performance of your database slowly degenerates. This may be because the database has become fragmented.

Fragmentation occurs when objects are deleted from a database, but the space used by those objects isn't reclaimed. The database becomes like a Swiss cheese—full of little holes. As pretty a simile as that may be, it also means that your database slows down. It's not damaged in any way, but performance suffers. This is because it is physically slower to read non-contiguous (i.e. fragmented) data from a disk than it is to read contiguous data.

Compacting a database removes any unused space (i.e. the holes in the cheese!) and makes all the data pages in the database contiguous. This has two benefits:

▶ Database performance improves

▶ The size of the database file is reduced

 Note that you should always back up a database which you are about to compact just in case something goes wrong with the compacting process.

As well as compacting a database from the menu bar, you can also compact a database from VBA, using the **CompactDatabase** method of the **DBEngine** object:

```
DBEngine.CompactDatabase "c:\myold.mdb","c:\mynew.mdb"
```

For optimal performance, you should occasionally use a disk defragmentation program (such as the Disk Defragmenter supplied with Windows 95) before compacting your database.

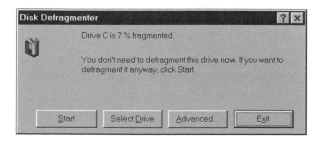

Compile All Modules

You have been working feverishly all weekend to get that database application finished for Monday's demonstration to the board. You tested the application last night—making sure you tested it in a production environment—and it was really zippy. There's an hour to go and you think you might as well run that little library routine of yours to add fancy headers to the procedures. It only takes a couple of minutes to run and you've done it so often you know that it's bug free.

The time comes, the board members sit down and you hit the icon to start your application... and wait... and wait... and wait....

"Whaaaaat!" you scream, inwardly of course, "What's happened to my speedy app???" It's suddenly performing like a three-legged dog... in a coma. Looks like you forgot to re-compile your application!

When you make any changes to code in a standard code module or a class module (including form and report modules), the module has to be re-compiled before it can be run. To compile the code in all the modules in your database, choose Compile and Save All Modules from the Debug menu.

If you don't explicitly compile your code in this manner, Access compiles your code at run-time. This can cause a significant delay, especially if there is a lot of code in the module being compiled. This delay is reduced, however, if you have ticked the Compile On Demand box on the Module page of the Tools/Options... dialog. In this case, Access only compiles the parts of the code that are called by the procedure that is executing—the call tree—rather than all of it. So there is less delay. However, to be safe, you should always compile all your code before delivery. After all, compilation will also detect compile-time errors such as a **For...** statement without a corresponding **Next** statement.

You can increase performance further still by saving your database as an MDE file. We will be looking at MDE files—and the whole area of compilation—in more detail in Chapter 18, on Finishing Touches.

Open Databases Exclusively

If you are the only person who will be using the database at any one time, you should open the database **exclusively**. This means that your application will perform better because Access will not have to spend time monitoring whether other users want to lock records. You can ensure that databases are opened exclusively by default by selecting Exclusive as the Default Open Mode on the Advanced page of the Tools/Options... dialog.

To open a single database in exclusive mode when shared mode is the default, you click on the Exclusive tick box on the Open Database dialog.

If you use a command line to start your application, you can use the **/Excl** switch to achieve the same result.

```
c:\access\msaccess.exe c:\abwrox\code\wrox.mdb /Excl
```

And if you are opening the database in VBA, set the **Exclusive** argument to **True** when using the **OpenDatabase** method:

```
Set db = DBEngine(0).OpenDatabase("c:\abwrox\code\wrox.mdb", True)
```

Summary

Producing an application is one thing. Producing an application that runs (or at the very least, appears to run) quickly and doesn't hog the whole of your computer's memory is quite another—but this is what will make or break your application. Users are impatient beings, and to them there is nothing worse than an inefficient program.

This chapter has covered several tips and tricks for improving the general speed of your code. Before you start to put your application together, you should decide what your coding priorities are, and then follow the guidelines drawn up here to achieve them. Remember that optimizing for one priority, such as maintainability, may adversely affect a secondary aim, such as the speed of your code—it is up to you to decide which is more important.

We have covered:

> How to reduce memory overhead by choosing the right data types, reclaiming memory and not overloading your code with comments

> Which coding techniques to employ to increase execution speed

> Tricks, such as using a startup screen and progress gauges, to distract the user and make it appear that an application is running quicker

> How to make a networked app more efficient

In the next chapter we will be concentrating on the benefits of using re-usable code, looking at how you can use code libraries and add-ins to reduce development and testing time.

Exercises

1 We can write a procedure in a number of ways according to our coding priorities. Try to write a procedure that tells you the date of Beaujolais Day (the third Thursday in November) for a given year. Now re-write the procedure so that it is optimized for:

> Real execution speed

> Maintainability

> Re-usability

2 Create a form and place a button on it. Now write a procedure that prints to the debug window the number of fields and records in each table in the database when the button is clicked. Now add a gauge to the status bar to display the progress of this operation.

Libraries and Add-Ins

This chapter is all about code libraries. The library with which most people are familiar is the type that contains books. People can go to the library—once they have found out where it is—and borrow those books. Libraries are typically public buildings, which means that anyone can use them, albeit after going through some registration procedure. And, of course, you can use as many libraries as you like; you aren't limited to just one.

The features that affect the popularity of the library—how much it's used—are the quality of its contents and its indexing structure. Not only are the books grouped together into sections (e.g. Fiction, Reference, Natural History), but there's a readily accessible index which allows a newcomer to quickly locate the book they are looking for.

Every feature described above applies just as well to code libraries as it does to book libraries. A code library contains a number of procedures (and possibly objects such as forms and tables) which other people can borrow. Anyone can use a code library provided they follow the correct registration procedure. You can use procedures from many libraries at the same time, and, as with book libraries, code libraries need to formally publish their contents so that other people can use them.

The advantage of using libraries is a topic that should be familiar to you—reusability. A procedure in a library needs to be written (and tested) only once, and can then be re-used and re-used—which brings significant benefits by reducing both the time required to build an application and the number of bugs appearing in the application's code.

In this chapter, we will be looking at the following types of library:

- Creating a library database
- Referencing library databases
- Using class libraries
- Adding add-ins to Access 97 using the Add-In Manager
- Add-ins in action
- Creating your own add-ins

Library Databases

All the code we have written so far only works in the database in which it was written. Similarly, the other objects—the forms, tables, reports etc.—are only accessible from within the database where they reside, unless of course, you are using linked tables. This can cause you problems. For example, you might want to use a password form in more than one database. Or there might be a useful procedure that you feel you may need to use over and over again.

Think over all you have learnt about class modules. The object-oriented features really promote re-use. Wouldn't it be good if you could just tap into the database and borrow that form, procedure or class whenever you wanted to? Well, the good news is that you can—if you place them in a library database.

Creating a Library Database

Let's have a go a creating a library database. One of the underlying themes throughout this book has been re-use, so let's add some functions that will be useful in many applications.

One very useful function in VBA is **InStr**, which finds the contents of one string in another. But how often have you wanted to find the last occurrence of a string in another string? In fact when dealing with filenames you often want to find the last occurrence of a string, perhaps the final \ so you can split the actual filename from the path. Or the . (dot) to split the filename from the suffix. We are going to create a function that does this.

Try It Out—Creating a Library Database

1 Start Access and create a new database. Pick the General tab from the New database dialog, select Blank Database and press OK.

2 Enter **GeneralUtilities** as the database name, and make sure the Save as type is set to Add-ins.

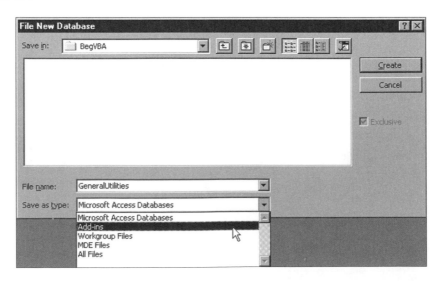

3 Create a new module and create a new function called **InStrR**, with two arguments:

```
Public Function InStrR(ByVal strString As String, _
                       ByVal strItem As String) As Integer
```

The first argument, **strString**, is the string to be searched, and the second, **strItem**, is the item to search for.

4 Add the following code to the function:

```
Dim intPos       As Integer       ' current position of item
Dim intLP        As Integer       ' last position of item

intPos = InStr(strString, strItem)
While intPos <> 0
    intLP = intPos
    intPos = InStr(intPos + 1, strString, strItem)
Wend

InStrR = intLP
```

Since we already have a function that searches for strings, we are using that. **InStr** finds the next occurrence, so we are going to keep looking for the next occurrence until **InStr** does not find another one. We can then use the last one found as the position we need.

That's it. A very simple function, but quite useful. You might like to try it from the Debug Window, just to check it works.

```
?instrr("C:\BegVBA\Temp\File.Ext", "\")
 15
```

That's all on the library for the moment—let's see about using it from another database. So, save the module and exit the database. It doesn't matter what name you give the module in the library database as this will not be used elsewhere—it's the procedure name that is important.

Using a Library Database

To use a library database from another database you need to set a reference to it. You've seen this with the object libraries for ActiveX controls, but this is slightly different, so let's try it out.

Try It Out—Calling a Function in a Library Database

1 Create a new database and call it **Test.mdb**.

2 Create a new module, and select References... from the Tools menu.

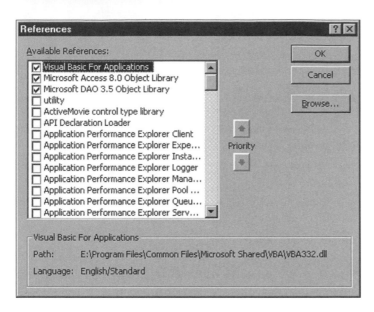

You've seen this dialog plenty of times, but this time you need to press the Browse... button.

3 Now select the directory where you created your library database, and make sure the Files of type is set to Add-ins.

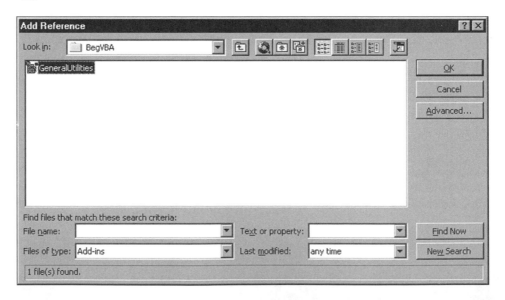

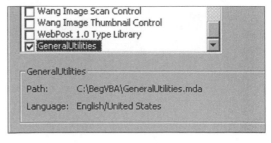

4 Select the `GeneralUtilities` add-in and click OK. This will display your add-in alongside all of the others.

5 Click OK to close the References dialog box.

6 Switch to the Debug Window and try the function, as you did earlier. It works just as it did before, but this time the code isn't in your current database. Now you can add these general utilities to every database you use.

Considerations

One thing to bear in mind when creating library routines is the possible overlap of function names. You can have functions in different databases with the same name. If Access finds the function locally, then it will use that copy, which is not what you might have intended. There are two ways around this.

The first is to prefix the function with the library name:

```
[GeneralUtilities].InStrR(...)
```

This also works in the Debug Window—try it, and you'll see that Quick Tips appear just as normal. This is rather cumbersome, so a better solution is to prefix all library routines, with **lib** or perhaps your, or your company's, initials.

```
Public Function wroxInStrR (...)
```

This is more likely to guarantee uniqueness, and is less confusing.

Class Libraries

As was explained in an earlier chapter, class modules are a great way to hide DLL calls by providing a nice easy wrapper. Classes also promote re-use, and this goes hand in hand with libraries, so why not create classes, and then add them to a library. That way you get the best of both worlds.

However, Access does not give you this facility as you would really like it. Classes are only available in the database in which they are created, which does tend to negate some of the reasons for creating them in the first place. In my opinion, Microsoft has really let us Access programmers down here. But look on the bright side—there is a way of achieving what we want, even though it is a bit of a kludge. What you have to do is create a normal module in the same database as the class module, and let procedures in this module handle the classes. Sounds horrid, but it's not too bad, and quite easy to code.

Let's give this a try by moving the **MyComputer** and **Drive** classes into your new library module, and seeing how they can be made accessible from other databases.

Try It Out—Class Libraries

1 Open the **GeneralUtilities** Add-In database that you created earlier.

2 From the File menu select Get External Data and select Import.

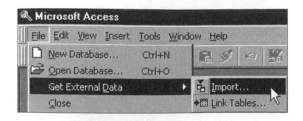

3 Now select the **Whisky13** database, in which you created the class modules, to see the import screen.

4 Select the **Drive** and **MyComputer** classes (you can use the *Shift* or *Control* key as you select them, which will allow you to select them both at once) and press the OK button. This will import these two modules into your library.

5 Create a new module, called **NewMyComputer**.

6 Add the following variable to the **Declarations** section:

```
Private colMyComp       As New Collection
```

7 Now a couple of procedures. This first will create an instance of the class object for us.

```
Public Function CreateMyComputer() As MyComputer

    Dim objMC       As MyComputer

    Set objMC = New MyComputer
    colMyComp.Add objMC, "I" & objMC.ID
    Set CreateMyComputer = colMyComp(colMyComp.Count)

    Set objMC = Nothing

End Function
```

The second destroys the instance:

```
Public Sub DestroyMyComputer(objMC As MyComputer)

    Dim objO        As MyComputer
```

```
        For Each objO In colMyComp
            If objO.ID = objMC.ID Then
                colMyComp.Remove ("I" & objO.ID)
                Exit For
            End If
        Next


        Set objMC = Nothing
        Set objO = Nothing

    End Sub
```

8 Compile the module and save the changes.

9 Close the database and switch to the database you created in the previous Try It Out, `Test.mdb`.

10 Create a new module and enter the following into a new procedure called `testMyComputer`.

```
Dim objDrive          As Object
Dim objMyComputer     As Object

Set objMyComputer = CreateMyComputer
Debug.Print objMyComputer.OSName & " " & objMyComputer.OSVersion

Debug.Print objMyComputer.ComputerName
Debug.Print objMyComputer.UserName
Debug.Print objMyComputer.CPUArchitecture
Debug.Print objMyComputer.CPULevel
Debug.Print objMyComputer.OSName
Debug.Print objMyComputer.OSVersion
Debug.Print objMyComputer.OSBuild
Debug.Print objMyComputer.WinStarted
Debug.Print objMyComputer.ScreenResolution

For Each objDrive In objMyComputer.Drives
    Debug.Print objDrive.Root, "Total: " & _
                objDrive.TotalSpace, "Free: " & objDrive.FreeSpace
Next

Call DestroyMyComputer(objMyComputer)
```

11 Switch to the Debug Window and enter `testMyComputer`:

```
testMyComputer
Windows NT 4.0
|
```

This displays the details of your computer, even though the **MyComputer** class is not in your current database. Let's see how this works.

How It Works

Let's look at the code in the **NewMyComputer** module in the **GeneralUtilities** database.

First, we create a private module level variable:

```
Private colMyComp      As New Collection
```

This is a collection and will be used to store the instances of **MyComputer** as they are created. Because the intention is to let this be used in a library database, called from another database, you cannot just create a **New** instance as with normal classes or objects. As Microsoft have limited instantiating a class to the current database, you have to use another method, and that also means having somewhere to store those instances. The **colMycomp** collection will be that store, and the method is a wrapper for the class. So, instead of saying **New MyComputer**, we now call the new module function to do it for us, and it will store instances of the class in its collection.

Next we create a function to instantiate the class:

```
Public Function CreateMyComputer() As MyComputer
```

This is a normal function, which returns an object of type **MyComputer**.

```
Dim objMC As MyComputer

Set objMC = New MyComputer
```

Next we create an object variable to hold the instance of **MyComputer**—as normal. We could just pass this back to the calling function, but remember about variable scope. This instance will die when the function ends. So, why not store it as a global variable? Good question, and the answer is that we could have done. The only problem then is that we could only ever create one instance. That's where the next bit comes in.

```
colMyComp.Add objMC, "I" & objMC.ID
```

Here we add the new instance to the collection. Remember a collection is just like an array, but for storing any kind of object. We use the **Add** method to add a new item to the collection, and pass in the instance of **MyComputer** we have just created. The second argument may look a little confusing, but it just sets the **Key** for the item in the collection. Every item in a collection can have a key to uniquely identify it, and these are generally strings. So we take the **ID** property of the object (this is unique) and add an **I** in front of it. It could be anything, just so long as it's a string, but we are using the **ID**, as we will use it again later. The collection now has a new object in it, with a unique key.

```
Set CreateMyComputer = colMyComp(colMyComp.Count)
```

Now we set the return value for the function. We want to pass back the object we have just added to the collection. This will be the last one in the collection, so we can use the **Count** property to find the last one (the **Count** for collections starts at 1) and use this to index into the collection. Note that because this function returns an object, we must use the **Set** statement to set the return value:

```
Set objMC = Nothing
```

We then set the local object to **Nothing**, as the **MyComputer** object is not in the collection.

Now let's look at the code to destroy the object. First the procedure declaration:

```
Public Sub DestroyMyComputer(objMC As MyComputer)
```

Notice that the argument is a **MyComputer** object. This is because we are going to pass into this function the instance of the object we wish to destroy:

```
Dim objO        As MyComputer
```

Now we create a variable—this will be used to loop through the collection.

```
For Each objO In colMyComp
    If objO.ID = objMC.ID Then
        colMyComp.Remove ("I" & objO.ID)
        Exit For
    End If
Next
```

Now we can loop through the collection. For each object in the collection we check the **ID** to see if it is the same as the **ID** of the object passed in. If so we use the **Remove** method for the collection to remove this object. Notice that this is where the key is used—you have to use a key to remove objects from a collection.

```
Set objMC = Nothing
Set objO = Nothing
```

Finally, we destroy the memory associated with the object:

This may seem complex but it's actually very simple. All we have done is create a new instance of an object, added this to a collection, and then returned the item in the collection. So to call this routine, you would use:

```
Dim objMC As Object
Set objMC = CreateMyComputer
```

This differs only slightly from the normal method of using the **New** keyword, but has the same effect. The only downside is that you have to use late-binding, by declaring the object as **Object**. This is because the actual class is not visible to you—only the creation function is. To destroy the function you use:

```
Call DestroyMyComputer (objMC)
```

This calls into the destroy routine the object created earlier.

Using a collection like this does complicate your code marginally, but you can see it is only a few lines of code, and gives the flexibility of being able to create any number of instances of the **MyComputer** object. Of course, if Microsoft had allowed classes to be visible from outside of library databases, then none of this would have been necessary. Still this does show that there's usually a way around most problems.

Add-Ins

Add-ins are another form of library and, although they contain objects such as code modules, tables and forms, they generally consist of complete tools, rather than small routines.

There are three types of add-ins, and which you use will depend upon the task you wish to perform. If your add-in is used during the creation of objects, or depends on an object, it will probably be a wizard or a builder. If it is more general, it will be a menu add-in. Let's look at these in more detail.

Wizards

You have already seen several wizards in Access 97 and you will have realized that they generally consist of several forms to aid the step-by-step process of object creation. The most common of these are the form and report wizards which can be used to create forms and reports that are similar in style, whilst hiding the complexities of this creation from the user.

You will notice that each wizard is designed for one type of object only. For example, the wizards for adding controls to forms are all very similar in style but are only used for one small task—that of aiding the creation of controls. Everything that they do can be done manually and, for the experienced user, this can often be quicker, but they can add a degree of consistency to the control creation.

Builders

Builders generally consist of just one or two dialogs and are usually much simpler to use than wizards. They are often useful when you are creating a single element of data, such as an expression, because they are quick and easy to handle. The Expression Builder is a very good example of this, consisting of only one form, with a single task to perform.

Menu Add-ins

Menu add-ins tend to be more general purpose utilities and usually apply to more than one object, though there is no reason why they can't apply to just one. Access 97 supplies several menu add-ins, available from the Add-Ins option on the Tools menu.

On the CD accompanying the book we've included three of our own add-ins—**Wrapper.mda**, **Schemes.mda** and **Language.mda**. We'll be using these in the rest of the examples in this chapter.

FYI Notice that the suffix for these is mda, not mdb as with normal databases. There is no difference between the two, and you can create add-ins as normal databases and rename them when they are ready for distribution.

Try It Out—The Procedure Wrapper Add-in

The Procedure Wrapper add-in only applies to one object type—modules—but can't be classed as a wizard or builder, because it doesn't guide you through the creation of objects, nor does it build anything. It must, therefore, be considered as an add-in, even though it isn't a menu-based one. What it does is add header comments and error-handling to code modules.

1 The first thing to do is to add this as an Add-In so it can be used in your database.

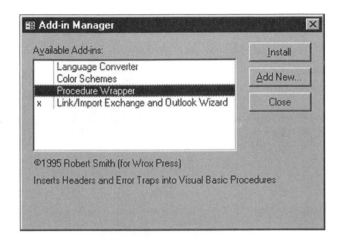

2 From the Add-Ins option on the Tools menu select Add-In Manager, to get the following screen:

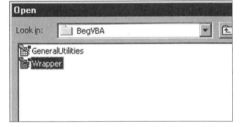

This shows a list of add-ins available—your screen may differ slightly, depending upon which add-ins you have previously loaded. To add a new one, such as the procedure wrapper, click the Add New... button to display the familiar Open dialog.

Select Wrapper, and press the Open button. This returns you to the Add-In Manager screen, with the new add-in selected. Now you are ready to use it.

3 From the Add-Ins option on the Tools menu select Procedure Wrapper, and you will see the Wrapper options dialog.

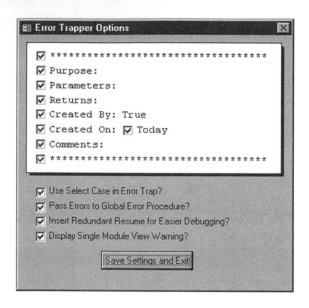

The top section shows how the header comment will look, and ticking each item will include it in the header. There is a text box to the side of the Created By option (where True is shown) that allows you to type your own name in, and ticking Today will enter today's date as the creation date.

The bottom section shows the options for error handling and warnings. First you can select whether a **Select Case** statement is used to decide the action for the error number. Secondly you can have a call to a global error handling procedure, and next you can have an extra **Resume** statement added to help with debugging. Finally you have an option to show a warning about being in single module view—this is necessary for the procedure wrapper to work correctly. We'll examine why later.

4 Make sure all of the options are selected to start with, and press the Save Settings and Exit button.

5 Now open a module and create a new procedure. Run the Procedure Wrapper from the Add-Ins menu, and you will be greeting with the warning dialog.

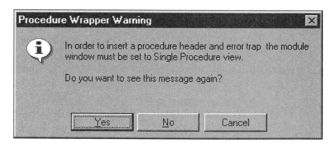

The Procedure Wrapper needs you to be in Procedure view for the code to work (we'll see why in a little while).

If you're not in Procedure view you can press Cancel to cancel the insert. If you are in Procedure view, you can press Yes or No to insert the wrapper—Yes will show the dialog next time the wrapper is run, whereas No skips the dialog.

6 If you aren't using Procedure view then cancel the dialog and switch modes. You can do this by clicking the Procedure View button on the bottom left corner of the module window, or from the Tools menu, by selecting Options, then on the Module tab unclick the Full Module View option. Move to your new procedure and run the add-in again, this time selecting Yes or No, and watch what happens.

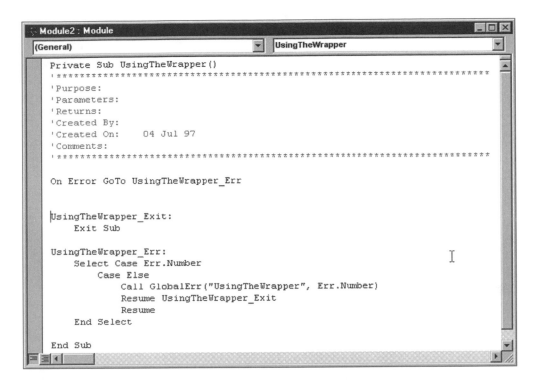

```
Module2 : Module                                                    _ □ ×
(General)                        ▼   UsingTheWrapper                       ▼
    Private Sub UsingTheWrapper()
    '***********************************************************************
    'Purpose:
    'Parameters:
    'Returns:
    'Created By:
    'Created On:     04 Jul 97
    'Comments:
    '***********************************************************************

    On Error GoTo UsingTheWrapper_Err


UsingTheWrapper_Exit:
        Exit Sub

UsingTheWrapper_Err:
        Select Case Err.Number
            Case Else
                Call GlobalErr("UsingTheWrapper", Err.Number)
                Resume UsingTheWrapper_Exit
                Resume
        End Select

    End Sub
```

Notice how the header comment reflects what was shown on the dialog. A **Select Case** statement has been used for the error number, a global error handling routine is called, which takes two arguments: the name of the procedure that called it and the error number. Finally, the redundant **Resume** is added. This is useful for debugging—imagine the error-handling routine being called whilst you are stepping through some code. You correct the error, and simply use the **Resume** to retry the statement again.

7 This is quite a useful facility, but having to use the menus every time is a bit cumbersome, so let's make this work from a keystroke. First you must add a reference to **Wrapper.mda**. You can do this by opening a module (any one will do) and selecting References from the Tools menu, and then pressing the Browse button. This shows the open dialog where you can select **Wrapper.mda** as you did when using the Add-In Manager. Don't forget to change the file type to Add-Ins on this dialog, otherwise you won't see the correct files.

8 Now edit (or create it if it doesn't exist) a macro called **Autokeys**. For the macro name you want the keystroke, and the action is going to run some code. It should look like this:

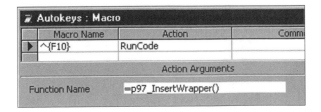

This set of keys corresponds to *Ctrl-F10*—to find out more about the key combinations search help for **Autokeys**. The action is to run some code, and the function name is the procedure in **Wrapper.mda** that starts the add-in. That's it. Now you can use *Ctrl-F10* to start the wrapper.

How It Works

Let's have a look at how this wrapper works, and explain some of the reasons why it has been written as it has. We are not going to examine it in close detail, but we'll look at the principles and some of the methods used. You might like to follow this through, examining the code as it's explained.

Close the current database and open **Wrapper.mda**. There is only one form, the options form, but we are not going to look at that, as the code is very simple. All it does is use the **SaveSetting** and **GetSetting** functions to store and retrieve entries from the Registry. These procedures are covered in more detail at the end of the book.

Switch to the Module tab, and open the API Calls module. The first thing you notice is a lot of API declarations. These give us some extra functionality that Access doesn't possess. For any of you that have been delving through the help files, you may have noticed that there are several new functions relating to the **Modules** object, that allow text to be entered, and procedures to be created. So why are we using API calls instead of these? Well, the simple reason is that all of these add text at a certain line number. There is no way (well, we haven't found one) to enter text at the current cursor or at the first line in the current procedure, or even to find out the current line number. This means that we cannot enter text at the current cursor position, so we have had to resort to other methods.

Let's have a look at the functions in this module. The first is just an error routine, so we will ignore that. Next is **WindowIsModule**, which identifies the currently active window. This allows us to pop up the options dialog box if the current window is not a module, or insert the wrapper if it is. So how does this work? Access is an MDI application (Multiple Document Interface), which means there is one main window, and all of the others (Database, Forms, Modules, etc) are held within it. The main window is termed the **parent** and the other windows are **children**. Each window also has a **class**—this is the internal name. For the Access parent this is **OMain**, so we first get the active window and check to see if it is **OMain**. This allows us to check whether the currently active window is, in fact, Access.

Now we need to look at all of the child windows, and there are different types of these. The status bar, for example is one of these. The type we are interested in is an **MDIChild** window, as this is what all the other main window types are. We can then find the topmost one, that is, the one that is currently active. If this has a class of **OModule** then it is the module window.

This may sound a bit complicated, but it's fairly easy to imagine. Just think of Access in 3D. The main window is at the back, and all of the other windows sit in front. We want to find the one at the very front. The code looks a little complex, but all it is doing is searching through the windows until it finds the front one. It uses **GetWindow** to find the window **handle**—this is a unique identifier for the window. You can liken this to a unique key for a record. **GetClassName** is then used to find out what the window is called.

The next function, **GetClipboardText**, is used to fetch some data from the clipboard. The clipboard is the mechanism by which we get text from the module window into a string. This has some nasty sounding functions, but is again quite simple. The first thing to do is find out where the clipboard stores its data—it's in memory somewhere, but where? We use **GetClipboardData** to give us a **handle** to the memory area. If this confuses you, just think of a string. You declare a string with a certain name, and copy some data into it. Access allocates some memory—you don't know (or care) where this is, because you use the name to get to the data it holds. Think of the variable name as the name as the **handle**. So we now have a way to get to the data that the clipboard holds. We then have to lock the memory in place, so that we can get hold of it. This stops Windows moving the memory around whilst we are using it—there's nothing worse than things not being where you put them! Then we use **lstrcpy** to copy the data from this area of memory into a string, and once that's done we can unlock the memory.

That's it for this module. Now open the **Error Insertion Procedures** module. Notice that there are some constants that contain the header text that will be written to the procedure when the add-in is run. Let's firstly look at **p97_InsertWrapper**, as this is the entry point into the add-in. The first thing done is to check whether we are in a module window or not, using **WindowIsModule**, the function described earlier. If we are not in a module we can pop up the options form. If we are in a module, a warning box is displayed, telling us to make sure we are in single procedure view, and asking if we want to see the message again. Selecting **Cancel** quits the function, and **Yes** or **No** means the user's choice is written to the Registry, for future reference. The procedure **ShowOptionsForm** simple shows this form.

Now have a look at **ReadFirstLine**. This reads the first line of procedure, to determine its type and name. We use **SendKeys** in here, which sends keystrokes to Access as though they had been typed on the keyboard. You might like to try these out to see them working. So the first one is *Ctrl-Home*—this sends the cursor to the top of the current screen, and this is why you need to be in single procedure view. If you were in normal view, you would always be sent to the top of the module declarations, and would always pick up **Option Compare Database**. This does also mean, however, that the procedure declaration must be on the first line, and there must be no comments before it. Next we do *Ctrl-Shift-→* to select the first word, and then *Ctrl-C* to copy the selected text to the clipboard. Once on the clipboard we can use **GetClipboardText** (as described earlier) to put this text into a string. Now we use a combination of **SendKeys** to select the actual procedure name, and this depends upon what type of procedure we are dealing with, as property procedures have a different layout to normal ones. At the end of the function, the actual procedure name is in a global string.

Let's look at **InsertHeader** now, the function that actually inserts the header. The first thing it does is to read the first line, thus getting the procedure name. Then we check each option from the options form (these are now stored in the registry) and, if selected, use **SendKeys** to send the text to the module. The last procedure is **InsertErrorTrap**, which inserts the error trapping code at the end of the new procedure, using the same method.

So you can see that although this looks quite complicated, with lots of API calls, it's actually fairly simple once you follow it through. Some of the coding has been necessary because the functionality just doesn't exist in Access. For example, the **Module** object has a method **InsertLines**, which seems an ideal replacement for **SendKeys**, but you can only insert lines at a specific line number. You cannot find the current line number or even insert at the current line. So near, yet so far.

One thing to watch for is changing add-ins when other databases that reference them are loaded. Before changing an add-in you should really un-load it from the database beforehand.

Let's now look at the other two add-ins supplied with the CD. These are completely different from the one described above, and we are only going to look at them working. Both of them work on forms and actually change the contents of the form. Back in Chapter 5 we looked at using the **Forms** collection to change the text to Italic, and if you remember, the **Forms** collection contains open forms. These two add-ins change the forms by opening them hidden in design view, looping through the **Controls** collection, and then closing them. Let's see what they do!

Try It Out—The Language Converter Add-In

Suppose you have just finished your all-singing, all-dancing new company application and the management are so impressed (it does happen occasionally!) that they have decided to use it in every other office world-wide. "Great, no problem " you say. "In the office's native language", they add. Great. Now you have to edit each form and keep a copy for each language. Not a pleasant task at all. But don't panic, there is a much simpler solution—you can use the Language Converter add-in.

1 Open **Whisky14.mdb** and use the Add-In manager to add the **Language.mda** to your add-ins. You can use the same procedure as you used for the Procedure Wrapper.

2 Select the Language Converter from the Add-Ins menu to see the Language Convert main form.

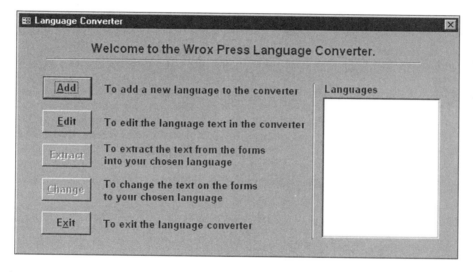

The buttons along the left side show the options, whilst the list on the right shows the languages available.

3 Press the Add button to view the Add Languages forms, and add a couple of languages.

If your language ability is better than mine you might wish to replace Gibberish with your favorite language. Once entered, close this form.

4 Select English from the list and press the Extract button. This will loop through all of the forms and extract the text from the controls. Nothing will change yet.

5 Press the Edit button to show the Edit Languages form.

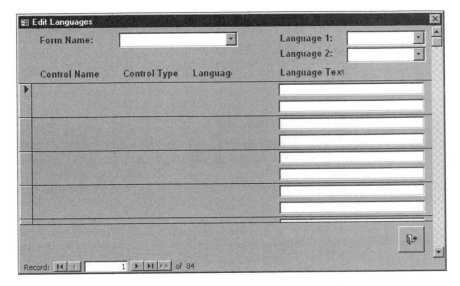

This has two main sections. The top allows the selection of a form, and the two languages you wish to edit text for. The bottom shows the controls and the text for each control. Select a form and languages at the top.

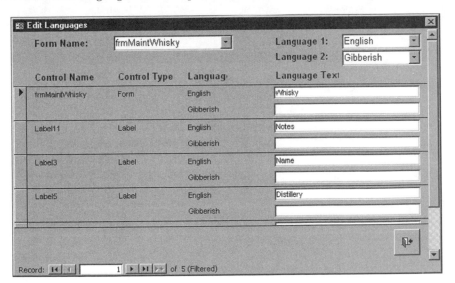

Notice how the details are filled in. The Text for English is the text that currently exists on your form, and Gibberish is empty. Type some text into the empty fields. You might like to do some more forms later, but for now close the form.

6 Back on the main form, select Gibberish (or your language) and press the Change button. This will change all of the text on the forms to that of the Gibberish language.

7 Exit the converter, and open the form you changed.

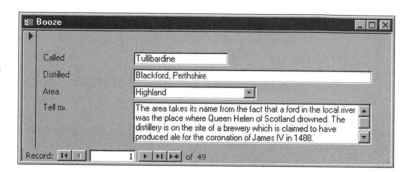

See how the text has changed to what you typed in. Notice that the text I typed in for the label for the Notes is too long for the field—this is something you will have to watch for when using this add-in, as many languages have longer words than English.

How It Works—The Language Converter

On your database, switch to the Tables tab and notice that there is a new table, Language. Open this to have a look at it.

FormName	ControlName	ControlType	DateUpdated	English	Gibberish
frmMaintWhisk	frmMaintWhisk	Form	/07/97 10:38:50	Whisky	Booze
frmMaintWhisk	Label11	Label	/07/97 10:38:50	Notes	Tell me about it
frmMaintWhisk	Label3	Label	/07/97 10:38:50	Name	Called
frmMaintWhisk	Label5	Label	/07/97 10:38:50	Distillery	Distilled in
frmMaintWhisk	Label7	Label	/07/97 10:38:50	Region	Area
frmOutsideWorl	cmdClose	Command butt	/07/97 10:38:50	&Close	
frmOutsideWorl	cmdExport	Command butt	/07/97 10:38:50	&Export	

The add-in has created a new table for you. The first column identifies the form, the second the control on the form, and the third the control type. The fourth column is the date the text was updated—it is not used in the current version of the converter, but could be used for enhancements. The last two columns are the languages you created, and the text for each control. If you run the converter again and add another language it would appear as another column.

So how does it work? Well, when you open the converter it checks for a table called Language, and if it exists it extracts the columns into the Languages list box, ignoring the first four columns. Adding a new language just adds another column, and editing languages just edits the entries. You could edit the entries in datasheet view as above, but the form gives a nicer interface.

When you press the Extract button, each form is opened hidden, in design view. We loop through the **Controls** collection and add a record for each one. When you press the Change button, the reverse is done. The form is opened in the same way, and the **Controls** collection used again, but this time the text for the control is taken from the Language table. It's quite simple really, and does not cover anything that you have not already learnt.

Try It Out—The Color Schemes Add-In

Do you like the way Windows 95 and NT 4 have color schemes for the display? Well I decided that it would be good to have a similar feature in Access for forms, so step forward the Color Schemes Add-In. The first thing we'll need to do is to register some ActiveX Controls.

 FYI

If you have trouble registering the controls, you may need to install the library msvbvm50.dll, which is on the CD accompanying this book. First, you should double click on the file COMMenu.reg, also supplied with the CD. Click OK on the dialog box. Then, move the file msvbvm50.dll to C:\Windows\System, and right click. Select Self Register from the context menu, and click OK—that's all there is to it.

1 From the Tools menu select ActiveX Controls.

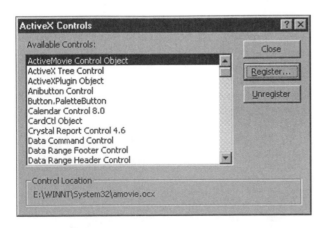

2 From the following dialog click the Register button

3 From the open dialog, move to the Color Schemes directory and select, one after the other, the following three OCX files.

FontControl.ocx

PaletteButton.ocx

PaletteWell.ocx

You will have to register each one individually. Once you've done this, these will appear as FontControl.ctlFonts, Button.PaletteButton, and PaletteWellControl.PaletteWell. You can now close the ActiveX Controls dialog.

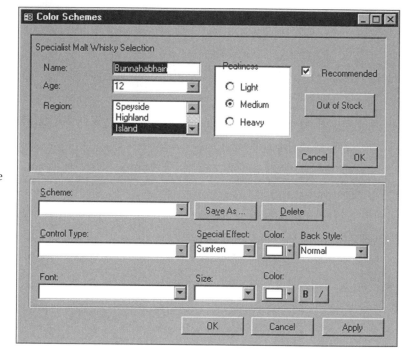

4 Now add the Color Schemes add in, and then select it from the Add-Ins menu.

There are two sections to this form. The top section is how the scheme will look, and the bottom section allows you to customize the controls. Notice that the label on the frame looks odd. This is because the default Back Style for the label is transparent—you may want to watch out for this if you wish to change this option for all of your forms. All of this should be very familiar, and will not need much explanation. The Scheme box allows you to select from a list of schemes, and you save the details to a new name or delete existing schemes. The Control Type allows you to select the type of control for which you wish to set the properties; form, text boxes, labels, etc., and you can change the style, font and color. Pressing OK will save the scheme, apply it to the forms and close the add-in, whereas pressing Apply will do the same but will leave the add-in open. Pressing Cancel closes the add-in without changing anything.

5 Try out some of the schemes provided, and try your own changes. Have a look at your forms afterwards to see how it has changed them.

How It Works

This works in a similar way to the Language Converter add-in, by looping through the **Controls** collection on each form. Instead of changing the **Caption** and **Text** properties it changes **BackColor**, **ForColor**, **Font**, etc.. It has been deliberately limited to selected controls, as these are the most commonly used, but more could be added. The scheme details are saved within the add-in itself so it does not add anything to the existing database.

You can see that a single idea—looping through controls—has produced two very different ideas, and can have a great effect on the usability of your application. Not only can your users have an application in their own language, but they can have their own preferred color scheme as well.

Creating Your Own Add-In

Creating your own add-in is just like creating a normal database, but with one exception. You need to create a new table—uSysRegInfo. This contains details that tell Access where your add-in should be stored, and what the entry function is.

Try It Out—Looking at System Tables

1 First close any open databases and open the Colour Schemes add-in (remember to change the type to add-ins on the Open dialog).

2 Select the Tables tab. Notice that the table uSysRegInfo isn't shown. It does exist, but it's a system table, so isn't shown by default. Select Options from the Tools menu, and pick the View tab. This gives you the option to see system tables.

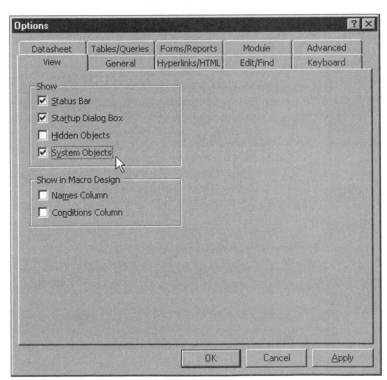

3 Make sure this option is checked and then press OK. Now you can see the table.

4 Open it up and have a look at what it contains.

How It Works

The first column, **SubKey**, is the place in the registry where these entries are stored. Every time you add an add-in, Access puts a new entry into the Registry so the details are available next time you start Access. This key is where those details are stored. HKEY_CURRENT_ACCESS_PROFILE is the position in the registry, which points to the current profile of Access—that is your settings for Access. Menu Add-Ins points at the Add-Ins section, and &Color Schemes is the name of the add-in. This is what appears on the menu.

The second column, **Type**, can be ignored for simple add-ins, but should contain the same values as shown above.

The last two columns point to the add-in itself. **ValName** is the name of the entry, and **Value** is the value of the entry. A **ValName** of **expression** means the expression called to run the add-in; in this case this is **wrox_ColorSchemes()**, which is a normal function in **Schemes.mda**. A **ValName** of **library** points to the **mda** file for the add-in. The |ACCDIR is replaced by the Access installation directory.

This may look rather complicated, but the easy way to do this when creating your own add-ins is to import the table from an existing add-in and just change what you need. All you will need to modify are the add-in description, the name of the **mda** file, and the function called.

General Issues

Listed below are some of the issues you need to consider when creating add-ins.

▶ Display all your Access forms as dialog boxes (set the Windowmode argument to `acDialog`) to prevent the user from continuing until all relevant information has been filled in.

▶ Remember that bound objects are bound to the data sources in the add-in. Use the `CurrentDb` and `CodeDb` functions to differentiate between the user database and the code database.

▶ Think about multi-user issues. Your add-in will generally be used by more than one person and must be able to cope with this.

▶ Don't let your add-in leave Access 97 in a different state to the one it was in when the add-in started. If you change any options, make sure you change them back again.

▶ Create error-handling code. Don't get into a situation where an error occurs but the user can't view details because they don't have permission on the add-in database.

Summary

You can see that through the use of libraries and add-ins you can increase the functionality of, not only your own applications, but of others as well. The ability to create self-contained routines promotes re-use, which in turn increases productivity.

This is one of the ways in which you can produce better applications. The use of library functions allows you to include many of the facilities available in Windows 95, but which Access 97 doesn't support directly. You can use the power of these low-level functions with just a few simple Visual Basic commands.

The use of add-ins is a great way to add functionality, not only to your applications but to Access 97 itself. The examples shown above are like this. The Procedure Wrapper extends the functionality of Access 97 for the developer, whereas the Language Converter and Color Schemes extend the functionality of the application for the user.

Exercises

1 For the language converter, check for the existence of the Language table in the user database, and make sure it is the correct one. After all, the user might have a table of the same name.

2 Add the ability for the language converter to modify reports as well as forms. This is often more important, as printed documentation very often has to be in the native language.

3 Make the language converter check for open forms. Any open forms should be switched into design view, the language details processed, and then saved and switched back. Would it be better to only run this add-in when there are no open forms?

4 Add the ability to change the **Status Bar Text** and **Control Tip Text** properties. This would need two extra columns in the Language table for each language.

5 Make the language converter truly multi-lingual by allowing it to work with the **InputBox** and **MsgBox** statements. This isn't as bad as it sounds, because you can just add the text to the language table as though it was another control, and create a new function to read it. So instead of:

```
MsgBox "Bzzt - wrong.  Don't press that button again."
```

You could have:

```
MsgBox LanguageText("FunctionName", "MsgBoxNumber1")
```

The overhead in reading the text is not noticeable at all.

6 Think about adding to the Language Converter and the Color Schemes run-time functions. This would allow the details to be changed on a more user-by-user basis. You could store the user preference and then apply that preference by calling a function from the Open event on each form

Multi-User Applications

So far we have looked at how VBA code enables us to do things that we would be unable to do with macros, queries, forms or reports. But we have really only concentrated on single-user applications. That is to say that the examples that we've looked at will work fine if you are the only person using the database, but what if someone else is using it at the same time? After all, the whole idea of an Access database is to provide a single repository of information that can be used by many people simultaneously.

In this chapter, we will be looking at some of the issues that can arise when you have several people using the same database at the same time. We shall then look at the issue of security within Access.

We will consider:

- What happens when two people want to view or change the same record
- How you can restrict which users can access the database that you have built
- How you can ensure that other people are able to use the objects that you have built, but not change them
- How to create new groups, users and passwords
- How to set different permissions for different users

Record Locking in Access 97

All too often, multi-user considerations are left until the end of a project. You build a database on your computer and it works fine when you test it on Friday night. You distribute it to half a dozen people on Monday morning, and when three of them try to use it at the same time, the whole thing grinds to a halt. That's the scenario we are trying to avoid in this section.

Record Locking Strategies

Access 97, like previous versions of Access, employs two methods of locking records—**optimistic** and **pessimistic** locking:

▶ With pessimistic locking, Access locks a record whenever someone starts to change the contents of that record

▶ With optimistic locking, Access only tries to lock a record when someone tries to save any changes that they have made

Let's look at an example to clarify the difference between the two. Suppose John and Mary are both using the same database and are editing records in the same table. If John decides to view record #30 then, irrespective of the type of locking strategy involved, Mary will still also be able to look at the contents of that record.

However, suppose John now decides to edit the contents of that record by typing a new value in one of the fields on his form. If **pessimistic** locking is being employed, Access will now lock that record so that only John can change it.

 FYI Pessimistic locking implies that when a user edits a record, Access pessimistically **assumes that someone else will also want to edit that same record and so it needs to lock it.**

Mary will now see the 'record locked' indicator on her form, which tells her that she can't edit the record. In fact, she will not be able to edit that record until John has finished with record #30 and has saved his changes.

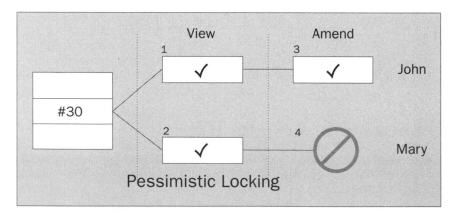

However, if an **optimistic** locking strategy were being used, Mary would have been able to make changes to record #30, even while John was editing it.

Optimistic locking implies that, when a user edits a record, Access optimistically assumes that no one else will want to edit the same record, and so it doesn't lock it.

This can be a very dangerous scenario. Assume that both John and Mary are now editing the same record—what happens when John tries to save the record? Nothing out of the ordinary... he is able to save the record as if nothing had happened. But what happens when Mary tries to save the record?

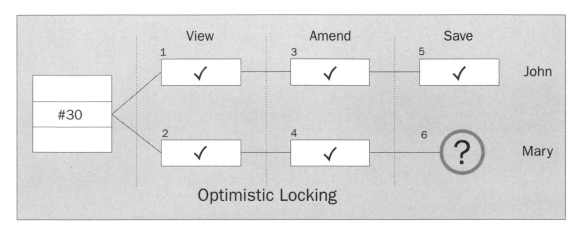

The answer is that when she tries to save a record that has changed since she opened it, she is presented with this dialog box:

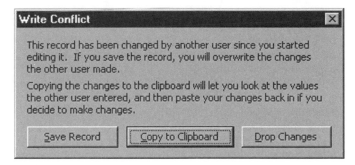

Sometimes, when a dialog box pops up you instantly know what is wrong and what you need to do. But this one carries a rather complicated message. You really need to think twice about how to respond to it and for those seeing it for the first time, it can be quite confusing. Essentially, the dialog box is telling Mary that she has three choices:

▶ She can save her record. This will overwrite John's changes without John being aware of the fact.

▶ She can copy her changes to the clipboard. She will then be able to see the changes that John has made and decide whether she still wants to make her changes.

▶ Or she can just call it a day and drop the changes she has just made. In this case, John's amended record will remain in the table but the changes that she has made will be lost.

Page Locks not Record Locks

In fact, there is a slight complication! Access 97 does not lock individual records. It locks data pages. A data page contains 2kb of data and may contain one or more records. The following diagram shows how data pages and records are related:

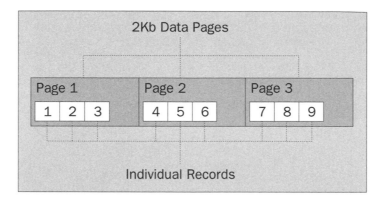

In the diagram above, records are roughly 600 bytes in length. Consequently, Access can fit 3 records on each data page. If a user locks record #3, the entire underlying data page is locked, so records #1, #2 and #3 will all be locked. Similarly, if a user locks record #5, then records #4, #5 and#6 will be locked.

In practice, records will vary in length depending on the data they contain. This in turn affects how many records will fit onto one page. The smaller the records are, the more records will fit on a page and, therefore, the more records that will be locked when a page is locked. The upside of having more rows to each page, however, is that it takes fewer page reads to access those records.

Note that records cannot span multiple pages. This means, in turn, that individual records cannot be more than 2kb in length and in practice, they are limited to a little less than this due to internal system overheads. Memo and OLE fields are stored on separate pages away from the rest of the data, and are limited to 1.2Gb in size.

Choosing a Locking Strategy

So which locking strategy should you choose? There is no simple answer, but in general:

▶ If it is unlikely that any two users will want to amend the same or adjacent records simultaneously, use optimistic locking.

▶ If it is likely that two or more users may want to amend the same or adjacent records simultaneously, choose pessimistic locking.

Setting the Default Record Locking Mechanism

To choose a particular locking strategy for your Access environment, you should select the appropriate option from the Advanced page of the Tools/Options... dialog box:

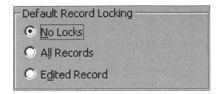

▶ No Locks invokes optimistic locking. A data page is locked only when a record on it is actually being saved.

▶ All Records (exclusive locking) causes the entire table or tables, which form the recordsource of the object, to be locked when any record is edited. This is fairly extreme and generally should only be used by the administrator, when performing maintenance.

▶ Edited Record invokes pessimistic locking. A data page will be locked as soon as someone starts to edit a record on it.

To set these options in code, you use the **SetOption** method of the **Application** object.

Try It Out—Changing the Default Locking Mechanism

1 Open up **Whisky15.mdb** and make sure the Default Record Locking option on the Advanced page of the Tools/Options... dialog box is set to No Locks. Click the OK button.

2 Type the following procedure into a new module:

```
Sub SetLocking ()

    Application.SetOption "Default Record Locking", 2

End Sub
```

3 Run this procedure by typing **SetLocking** in the Debug window.

4 Now open the Advanced page of the Tools/Options... dialog box again. The Default Record Locking option should now be Edited Record:

In previous versions of Access, the Default Record Locking information was saved in the Workgroup Information File—**System.mdw** in Access 95 and **System.mda** in earlier versions of Access. In Access 97, however, this information is stored in the Windows Registry. To find it, look at the following Registry key:

\HKEY_CURRENT_USER\Software\Microsoft\Office\8.0\Access\Settings

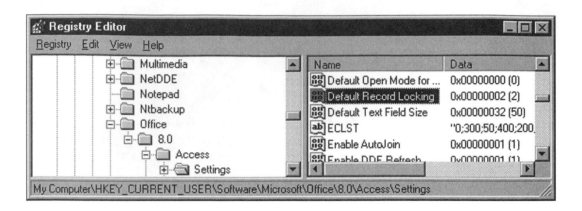

 You'll probably have heard this warning before, but I make no apology for re-iterating it: don't mess with Registry settings by editing them directly unless you are totally confident of what you are doing. Re-installing Windows is really very boring!

The table below shows the different options and the VBA statement that is used to set each of those options. As with all multi-select options, the value used in the **SetOption** method corresponds to the zero-based order in which the option appears on the dialog box.

This option...	...is also known as...	...and is set like this
No Locks	Optimistic Locking	`Application.SetOption "Default Record Locking", 0`
All Records	Exclusive Locking	`Application.SetOption "Default Record Locking", 1`
Edited Records	Pessimistic Locking	`Application.SetOption "Default Record Locking", 2`

In order to find what the current locking option is, you can use the **GetOption** method. Here's a procedure you can write to allow you to set and then read the Default Record Locking option:

```
Sub SetAndGetLocking(strLockType As String)

    Dim intLockIndex As Integer
    Dim strLockDesc As String

    'Convert the string argument into a option index
    Select Case strLockType
        Case "Optimistic"
            intLockIndex = 0
        Case "Exclusive"
            intLockIndex = 1
        Case "Pessimistic"
            intLockIndex = 2
```

```
        Case Else
            intLockIndex = -1
    End Select

    'Set default record locking option
    If intLockIndex <> -1 Then
        Application.SetOption "Default Record Locking", intLockIndex
    End If

    'Now determine and display default record locking option
    Select Case Application.GetOption("Default Record Locking")
        Case 0
            MsgBox "The default locking method is optimistic."
        Case 1
            MsgBox "The default locking method is exclusive."
        Case 2
            MsgBox "The default locking method is pessimistic."
    End Select

End Sub
```

If you run this procedure by typing the following in the Debug window,

```
SetAndGetLocking "Exclusive"
```

the default locking option will be set to Exclusive (All Records) and you will see this dialog box:

Implementing Record Locking on Forms

So far, we have only really considered the record-locking mechanism that applies to the tables in your database. But you can also specify the locking method used by individual forms, reports and queries. You do this by setting the **RecordLocks** property of the object concerned. For example, look at this code:

```
Dim frm As Form

DoCmd.OpenForm "frmMaintCountry"
Set frm = Forms!frmMaintCountry
frm.RecordLocks = 2
```

This will set pessimistic locking (Edited Records) for the **frmMaintCountry** form. In other words, as soon as someone edits a record using **frmMaintCountry**, Access will attempt to lock the data page that the record is on. This will prevent anyone else from editing that page, whether from **frmMaintCountry** or any other forms, or with a query or directly within the table where that record exists. This is the same as with record locking, as Access can't lock individual records—it can only lock data pages.

The **RecordLocks** property uses the same three arguments as the **Application.SetOption** method. They are described below:

This option...	...is set like this...	...and has this effect
No Locks	.RecordLocks = 0	Tries to lock a data page in the underlying table(s) when a user attempts to save an amended record on that page.
All Records	.RecordLocks = 1	Locks all records in the underlying table(s) whenever someone has the form open.
Edited Records	.RecordLocks = 2	Tries to lock a data page in the underlying table(s) whenever someone starts to amend a record on the form. The data page stays locked until the user finishes editing the record.

If you don't explicitly set the **RecordLocks** property for a form, report or query, the object inherits the default record locking option that was in place when the object was created.

Recordsets and Record Locking

Earlier in the book we looked at how we could create recordsets. The basic syntax for creating a **Recordset** object is as follows:

```
Set rs = db.OpenRecordset(source, type, option, lockedits)
```

The **source** argument simply defines where the records will come from that will populate the recordset. This can be the name of a table or query, or an SQL string. You should be familiar with this by now, but what of the other arguments? Well, let's take a more detailed look now at the other arguments that we can supply to the **OpenRecordset** method and, in particular, how these arguments affect the way that locking is handled.

The Type Argument

In Chapter 6 we said that there were five different types of recordset in Access 97. To specify the type of recordset we wish to open, we use the appropriate **type** argument with the **OpenRecordset** method. The following five intrinsic constants can be used for the type argument:

- **dbOpenTable**
- **dbOpenDynaset**
- **dbOpenSnapshot**
- **dbOpenDynamic**
- **dbOpenForwardOnly**

You should by now be familiar with the first of these three arguments. We looked at these in detail in Chapter 6. If you feel a little unsure of the differences between dynasets, snapshots and table-type **Recordset** objects, you should run through that chapter again. As far as we are concerned right now, however, the major difference is that you cannot edit the records in a snapshot.

We haven't yet said anything in this book about the last two types of recordsets, so we'll do that quickly now.

▶ A **forward-only** recordset is identical to a snapshot created with the **dbOpenSnapshot** argument except for one thing—you can only scroll through a forward-only recordset in a forward direction. In other words, once you have gone past a record, hard luck, you can't go back to it. This may sound restrictive but, if you think about it, quite often you start at the beginning of a recordset and only want to make one pass through it. And the advantage of forward-only recordsets is that, because they don't have the complex cursor functionality required for forward and backward scrolling, they are often quicker to open than normal snapshots.

▶ **Dynamic** recordsets are altogether different. Whereas snapshots, dynasets and table-type recordsets use the JET engine and Access tables, dynamic recordsets use a new technology called **ODBCDirect**, rather than the JET engine. This allows you to programmatically handle tables and queries that exist in non-Access databases as if they were in Access. This means that you can store your corporate data in a more robust and powerful database management system such as Microsoft SQL Server or Oracle, and yet still have the ease of programmatic access provided by the Data Access Object hierarchy.

To use a dynamic recordset, you must first make a connection to the non-Access database using the **OpenConnection** method of a **Workspace** object. This returns a **Connection** object. Then we use the **OpenRecordset** method against that **Connection** object. There is a whole load more that we could say about ODBCDirect in general and dynamic recordsets in particular, but it would be way beyond the scope of this book. If you want to know more about these topics, you should consult Access 97 Help under the keyword **ODBCDirect**.

The Option Argument

The second argument affects how updateable the recordset is, as a whole. Valid choices for this argument, together with their meanings, are shown below:

This option	...has this effect
dbDenyWrite	No one else can modify or add records while we have the recordset open.
dbDenyRead	No one else can read data in the table while we have the recordset open.
dbSeeChanges	If one person tries to save changes to a record that another user has modified since the first user started editing it, Access generates a run-time error.
dbAppendOnly	We can only add records to the recordset and cannot view or amend existing ones. We can only use this option with dynaset-type recordsets.
dbInconsistent	We can modify columns on both sides of the join in a dynaset built from multiple tables. This can leave the recordset in an inconsistent state.

Table Continued on Following Page

This option	...has this effect
`dbConsistent`	We can only modify columns that leave the dynaset consistent. So we can't alter the joined field on the 'many' side of a one-to-many join to a value that doesn't appear on the 'one' side.

There are a few other valid constants you can supply as the ***option*** argument, but they are either for use with non-Access databases or are present only for backwards compatibility.

The LockEdits Argument

The final argument is used to specify the type of record locking that will be used when we—or other users—try to edit records that appear in the recordset.

This argument	...has this effect
`dbReadOnly`	No one else can amend records that appear in our recordset so long as we have the recordset open.
`dbPessimistic`	A pessimistic locking strategy is applied (see earlier).
	No one else can amend records that appear in our recordset if we are in the process of editing them. Similarly, we can't edit a record in our recordset if someone else is already editing it.
`dbOptimistic`	An optimistic locking strategy is applied (see earlier).
	Two or more users can try concurrently to amend a record that appears in our recordset. However, only the first person to save his or her changes will be successful. When other users try to save a record that the first user has changed, Access generates a run-time error.

Again, there are another couple of arguments as well, but they are only for use with ODBCDirect, so we don't need to worry about them.

So, if we wanted to create a dynaset-type recordset based on the table `Country` that would allow us to add and edit records to the table, but didn't allow anyone else to view the records in `Country` while the recordset was open, we would use the following code:

```
Dim db As Database
Dim rec As Recordset

Set db = CurrentDB()

Set rec = db.OpenRecordset("Country", dbOpenDynaset, dbDenyRead)
.
.
.
rec.Close

db.Close
```

The LockEdits Property

Once a recordset is open, we can also change its locking behavior by setting its **LockEdits** property. To change the locking behavior for a recordset to optimistic locking, we set the **LockEdits** property of the recordset to **False**. To apply a pessimistic locking strategy, we set the **LockEdits** property of the recordset to **True**.

For example, the following piece of code opens a recordset and changes the locking behavior of the recordset to optimistic:

```
Sub ChangeLocks ()

    Dim db As Database
    Set db = CurrentDB ()

    Dim rec As Recordset

    'This opens a recordset with pessimistic locking (default)
    Set rec = db.OpenRecordset("Country", dbOpenDynaset)

    'This line sets the locking behavior to optimistic locking
    rec.LockEdits = False

    ...'Do something with the records

    rec.Close        'Close the recordset

    db.Close

End Sub
```

Although the **LockEdits** argument of the **OpenRecordset** method and the **LockEdits** property of a recordset do the same thing, the difference is when they are used. The **LockEdits** argument of the **OpenRecordset** method can only be used when you open a recordset, whereas you can set the **LockEdits** property of a recordset any time after the recordset has been opened, until the recordset is closed.

> *Some recordsets, such as those based on tables in ODBC data sources, do not support pessimistic locking. Attempting to set the LockEdits property of such a recordset to True will cause Access to generate a run-time error.*

Handling Record Locking Errors

It is all very well to say that, when a recordset is opened with the **dbDenyWrite** option, no one else can add or edit records in the underlying table(s), but what actually happens when a procedure attempts to open an exclusively locked table? The answer is that a run-time error occurs and, if we don't have any error handling, our application will stop. It is important, therefore, to know the types of record-locking errors that can occur at run-time, and how our error-handling code should deal with them.

Optimistic Locking Errors

With optimistic locking we should not encounter any errors when attempting to edit a record—only when we try to update or add one.

Likely Errors

If we are using optimistic locking, the three most common error codes we will experience are **3186**, **3197** and **3260**.

Error **3186** Couldn't save; currently locked by user <xxx> on machine <xxx>

This error only occurs when optimistic locking is being used. It indicates that we are trying to save a record on a page that is locked.

Error **3197** The database engine stopped the process because you and another user are attempting to change the same data at the same time.

This error occurs when we try to use the **Update** method but another user has changed the data that we are trying to update. The other user will have changed the data between the time we used the **Edit** method and the **Update** method. This is the same situation that led to the Write Conflict dialog box that we saw at the start of this chapter.

Error **3260** Couldn't update; currently locked by user <xxx> on machine <xxx>

This error will occur if we use the **Update** method to try to update a record we have added or changed, but where another user has since locked the page that the record is on.

It may also occur when we use the **AddNew** method to add a record to a recordset where the page on which the new record resides is locked.

You might have noticed that errors 3186 and 3260 have similar causes. In fact, although they can occur at subtly different times, as far as we are concerned we should handle them in exactly the same way.

How to Deal with Optimistic Locking Errors

For error codes **3186** and **3260**, we should wait a short period of time and then attempt to save the record again. If we still can't save the record after several attempts, we should cancel the operation, inform the user of what has happened and let him or her do something else.

For error code **3197**, we should requery the database to see what the new value of the record is, display it to the user and ask him or her if they want to overwrite the record with their own changes.

The following sample of code illustrates how we can gracefully handle the type of errors that occur when we are using optimistic locking:

```
    Function OptErrors() As Integer

        Dim db As Database
        Dim rec As Recordset
        Dim intLockRetry As Integer
        Dim i As Integer
        Dim intRetVal As Integer
        Dim recClone As Recordset

        Const LOCK_RETRY_MAX = 5
        Const LOCK_ERROR$ = "Could not save this record. " & _
                            "Do you want to try again?"
        Const SAVE_QUESTION$ = "Do you want to save YOUR changes?"

        On Error GoTo OptErrors_Err

        Set db = CurrentDb()
        Set rec = db.OpenRecordset("tblCountry", dbOpenDynaset)

        '
        ' This is the main body of your code
        '

OptErrors = True

OptErrors_Exit:
    Exit Function

OptErrors_Failed:
    OptErrors = False

        'This is where you put code to handle what
        'should happen if you cannot obtain a lock

        GoTo OptErrors_Exit

OptErrors_Err:
    Select Case Err
        Case 3197                           'Data has changed

            'Make a copy of the recordset
            Set recClone = rec.OpenRecordset()

            'Move to amended record
            '...

            'Display amended record
            '...

            'Ask user what to do
            intRetVal = MsgBox(SAVE_QUESTION$, vbExclamation + vbYesNo)
```

467

```
                            'If the user wants to save their changes
                  If intRetVal = vbYes Then
                      'Try to update again
                      Resume
                  Else
                      'Else just call it a day
                      Resume OptErrors_Failed
                  End If
            Case 3186, 3260

                  'Record is locked so add 1 to counter
                  'indicating how many times this happened
                  intLockRetry = intLockRetry + 1

                  'Have you already retried too many times?
                  If intLockRetry < LOCK_RETRY_MAX Then

                      'If you haven't, then wait for a short period
                      For i = 0 To intLockRetry * 1000
                      Next

                      'Now try again
                      Resume

                  Else

                      'But if you have already tried 5 times
                      'ask if user wants to retry.
                      'If they say yes then...
                      If MsgBox(LOCK_ERROR$, vbExclamation + vbYesNo) _
                                = vbYes Then

                          intLockRetry = 0  '...set counter to 0
                          Resume               'and do it over

                      Else        'But if they have had enough
                                  'just call it a day

                          Resume OptErrors_Failed

                      End If

                  End If
            Case Else            'Catch all other errors
                  MsgBox ("Error " & Err & ": " & Error)
                  Resume OptErrors_Failed
      End Select

End Function
```

Pessimistic Locking Errors

If we are using pessimistic locking, we can normally guarantee that we will be able to save any record that we have opened with the **Edit** method. For this reason, we shouldn't encounter error **3186**. However, we may come across the other two errors.

Likely Errors

Error **3197** Data has changed; operation stopped

When using pessimistic locking, this error occurs if we try to use the **Edit** method on a record but the data in the record has changed since it was last accessed. This may happen, for example, if someone has changed or deleted the record since we opened the recordset.

Error **3260** Couldn't update; currently locked by user <xxx> on machine <xxx>

Don't be misled by the word 'update' in the message. If we are using pessimistic locking, this error will occur if we try to use the **Edit** or **AddNew** methods on a record that is on a page locked by someone else.

How to Deal with Pessimistic Locking Errors

For error code **3260**, we should wait a short period of time and then attempt to edit the record again. If we still can't edit the record after several attempts, we should give the user the choice of continuing to attempt to edit the record or canceling the operation.

For error code **3197**, we should requery the database to see what the new value of the record is and try the **Edit** method again. If the record had only been changed, we should be able to edit it now. If it was deleted though, we will encounter error code **3167** (Record is deleted).

The function below contains an error handling routine that should take care of these errors:

```
Function PessErrors() As Integer

    Dim db As Database
    Dim rec As Recordset
    Dim intLockRetry As Integer
    Dim i As Integer

    Const LOCK_RETRY_MAX = 5
    Const LOCK_ERROR$ = "Could not save this record. " & _
                        "Do you want to try again?"


    On Error GoTo PessErrors_Err

    Set db = CurrentDb()
    Set rec = db.OpenRecordset("tblCountry", dbOpenDynaset)


    '
    ' This is the main body of your code
    '

PessErrors = True
```

```
PessErrors_Exit:
    Exit Function

PessErrors_Failed:
    PessErrors = False
    'This is where you put code to handle what should
    'happen if you cannot obtain a lock after many attempts

    GoTo PessErrors_Exit

PessErrors_Err:
    Select Case Err
        Case 3197              'If data has changed, then
            rec.Requery        'simply refresh the recordset
            Resume             'and try again.
        Case 3167
            'You have not got much choice
            'if someone else has deleted this record
            MsgBox "Someone else has deleted this record"
            Resume PessErrors_Failed
        Case 3260
            'But if the record is locked, add 1 to counter
            'indicating how many times you have retried
            intLockRetry = intLockRetry + 1

            'Have you already retried 5 times?
            If intLockRetry < LOCK_RETRY_MAX Then

                'If not then wait for a short period
                For i = 0 To intLockRetry * 1000
                Next

                'Now try again
                Resume

            Else
                'If you have already tried 5 times
                'ask the user if they want to retry
                'If they hit the yes button then...
                If MsgBox(LOCK_ERROR$, 'vbExclamation + vbYesNo) _
                          = vbYes Then

                    'Set counter to 0 and do it over again
                    intLockRetry = 0
                    Resume

                Else
                    'But if they have had enough
                    'just call it a day
                    Resume PessErrors_Failed

                End If
```

```
            End If
        Case Else
            MsgBox ("Error " & Err & ": " & Error)
            Resume PessErrors_Failed
    End Select

End Function
```

One of the errors that you encounter most frequently with both optimistic and pessimistic locking is error code **3260**. That is because Access always employs optimistic locking when you are adding a new record to a recordset. So even if the rest of your recordset is using pessimistic locking, you may find that users of your database will only discover that they cannot save their record after they have filled in every one of the fields on the form and hit the Save button.

Versions of Access which used version 2.x of the JET database engine (i.e. Access 2.x and earlier) were particularly prone to record-locking errors when you added new records because everybody who was trying to add new records was trying to lock the same page at the end of the recordset at the same time. However, the introduction of implicit transactions in Access 95, together with a different locking strategy for indexed pages, has resulted in significant improvements in this area.

Security

The first part of this chapter dealt with the way in which Access handles record locking, when multiple users are attempting to use the database at the same time. In the rest of this chapter, we will be looking at the other key issue that raises its head in a multi-user scenario—how Access enforces security.

Why Security?

The first question that needs to be answered is "Do I need to secure my database?" This is a question that you should ask when designing any database. Implementing a security mechanism adds a maintenance overhead—so does your application merit it? Quite often the answer will be that it doesn't. The ease with which database applications can be created with Access means that they are now frequently used for fairly trivial functions, which don't always require security. However, if you are concerned about any of the following issues, you should consider implementing some method of securing your application:

> **Your database contains confidential information which you don't want unauthorized personnel to view.**
>
> Frequently, databases are used to store confidential information about personal or financial details. Such data needs to be protected from accidental or deliberate access by people who aren't authorized to view it.

> **You want to protect your database objects from accidental change.**
>
> It may have taken you a lot of time to create your database application. The last thing you want is for one of the users of the application to modify the design of a form or query so that the application no longer works.

▶ **You want some of your users to be able to use certain functionality within your application but don't want this to be generally available.**

Often, your application will contain functionality which is only appropriate to a subset of users. For example, you may wish only Grade 3 managers to be able to use the application to approve expense checks.

▶ **You want to implement an audit trail to monitor who has been doing what in your application.**

As well as building an audit trail specifically for security purposes, you may find it useful to build one for use during the application's testing cycle or initial roll-out, so you can log how people have been using the application.

Security can be defined as a method of restricting the access that users have to a database and the objects within that database. You are probably already familiar with the methods of securing an Access database using the menu commands and standard Access dialogs. The main two ways of securing a database in this way involve:

▶ Creating a password for the database

▶ Establishing user-level security

Over 90% of the time you will perform these tasks through the user interface. These two options can be reached from the Security option on the Tools menu:

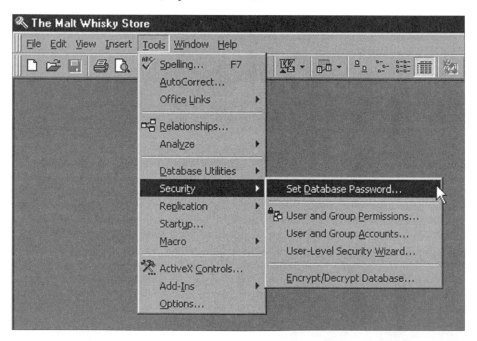

However, there may be rare occasions when it is preferable to administer these tasks from within VBA code. We will start by looking at how to set a database password from code, and then we'll examine the security model that Access employs and how it can be manipulated in VBA code.

Setting a Database Password from VBA

To set a database password from VBA, we simply apply the **NewPassword** method to a **Database** object representing the database. This method takes the existing password and the new password as its arguments.

```
Set db = CurrentDB()
db.NewPassword "", "Valerie"
```

The code above would add a password (**Valerie**) to a database which previously didn't have one. To change this password, we would use this syntax,

```
Set db = CurrentDB()
db.NewPassword "Valerie", "Smith"
```

and to clear the password, we would specify an empty string for the new password:

```
Set db = CurrentDB()
db.NewPassword "Smith", ""
```

 The **NewPassword** method can't be applied to non-Jet 3.0 databases. Attempting to do so will result in an error.

The Access 97 Security Model

The Access 97 security model consists of two elements:

- The workgroup information file
- User and group permissions

The workgroup information file contains:

- The names of all users in the workgroup
- The names of all groups in the workgroup
- Information about which users belong to which groups
- Each user's password (in encrypted form)
- A unique SID (Security ID) for each user and group (in a non-readable binary format)

In previous versions of Access, the workgroup information file also contained information about users' preferences as selected in the Tools/Options... dialog box. However, from Access 97 onwards, this information is now stored in the Windows Registry under the following key:

\HKEY_CURRENT_USER\Software\Microsoft\Office\8.0\Access\Settings

The location of the workgroup information file is specified in the registry under the following key, where it appears as **SystemDB**:

\HKEY_LOCAL_MACHINE\Software\Microsoft\Office\8.0\Access\Jet\3.5\Engines

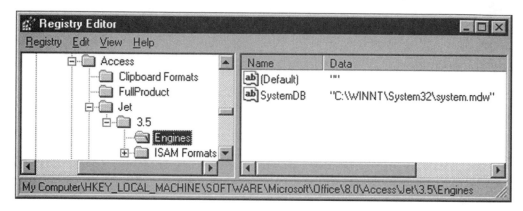

However, it is recommended that you don't change the location of the workgroup information file by editing the registry directly, but rather by using the workgroup administrator (**Wrkgadm.exe**) which is installed when you set up Access 97 on your computer.

Permissions for using individual data objects within a database are stored in the database which contains the objects. We'll look at how you modify these permissions a little later. First, we are going to look at how to modify the user and group information in the workgroup information file through VBA.

Manipulating Users and Groups

The Data Access Object hierarchy, which we have already noted to be central to VBA coding, contains the following security objects:

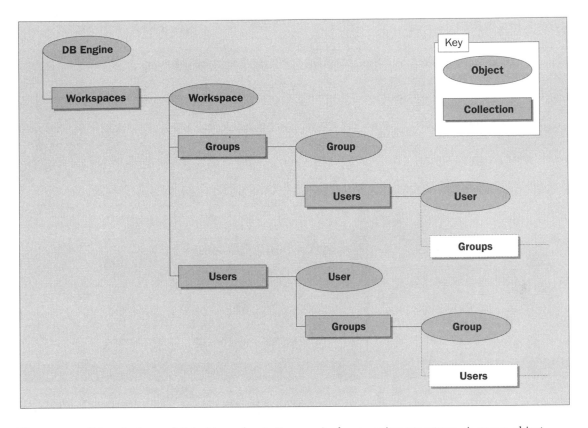

The most striking feature of this hierarchy is its seemingly recursive structure. A **User** object contains a **Groups** collection and a **Group** object contains a **Users** collection. The hierarchy is implemented in this way to cater for the many-to-many relationship between **Users** and **Groups**. A user can belong to one or more **Groups**, each of which can contain many users.

Let's have a look at how we can use these objects to perform the following tasks:

▶ Create new users and groups
▶ Add users to groups
▶ Change a user's password

Note that for the following examples to work, you must be logged in with the correct permissions for being able to create and modify users. The same rules apply for creating and modifying users and groups in VBA as they do when you use the **Security** menu options. Normally it is only members of the Admins group who should modify security options.

Creating a New User

Creating a new user is very straightforward—you simply use the **CreateUser** method against the **Workspace** object. For example, the following piece of code can be used to create a user called Mark Fenton:

```
Sub UserAdd()

    Dim wks As Workspace
    Dim usrMark As User
    Dim strUsersPID As String

    Set wks = DBEngine(0)
    strUsersPID = "1234abcd"

    'Start by creating a new User account
    Set usrMark = wks.CreateUser("Mark Fenton")

    'Now set the User's properties
    usrMark.Password = "Doctor"
    usrMark.PID = strUsersPID

    'Append User to the Users collection of this workspace
    wks.Users.Append usrMark

End Sub
```

As you can see, the first step is to create a new user object. You do this by applying the **CreateUser** method to the workspace object and supplying the name of the new user:

```
Set usrMark = wks.CreateUser("Mark Fenton")
```

The next step is to set the properties of the new user object. The properties you can set are the **Password** property, the **PID** property and the **Name** property. Note that we set the **Name** property of the user object when we created it with the **CreateUser** method.

The **PID** property is a string of between four and twenty characters which is used to uniquely identify a user:

```
usrMark.PID = strUsersPID
```

The **Password** property, a string of up to fourteen characters, corresponds to the password that the new user will need to enter. This is simply an additional way of verifying the user's identity and is *not* the same as the database password.

```
usrMark.Password = "Doctor"
```

After you have set these three properties, you are ready to append the user object to the collection of **Users** already defined in the current workspace. This will save the user, and its properties, in the workgroup information file.

```
wks.Users.Append usrMark
```

If you type the procedure into a new module and then run it, you can check the existence of the new user by going to the User and Group Accounts... section of the Security submenu on the Tools menu:

Creating a New Group

You can also create groups in VBA code. A group is used to collect together users to whom you wish to assign the same permissions. For example, you may have thirty different registrars who will use your database, each of whom you want to define as a user in an Access 97 workgroup. It would be very tiresome if you then had to assign permissions on every single database object to each of the thirty users. So, instead, you can create a group called **Registrars**, add the thirty users to it, and then assign database object permissions just to that group.

Wherever possible, you should assign permissions to groups rather than to individual users.

Creating a group is a very similar process to the one we employed above for creating new users:

```
Sub GroupAdd()

    Dim wks As Workspace
    Dim grpRegistrars As Group
    Dim strGroupPID As String

    Set wks = DBEngine(0)
    strGroupPID = "5678"

    'Start by creating a new Group account
    Set grpRegistrars = wks.CreateGroup("Registrars")
```

```
        'Now set the Group's properties
        grpRegistrars.PID = strGroupPID

        'Append Group to the Groups collection of this workspace
        wks.Groups.Append grpRegistrars

End Sub
```

First we create a group object within the current workspace:

```
Set grpRegistrars = wks.CreateGroup("Registrars")
```

Next we set the properties for the group. The only two properties of a group are the **Name** property and the **PID** property. We set the **Name** property when we create the group, just as we did when we created the new user.

```
grpRegistrars.PID = strGroupPID
```

And finally we save the group by appending it to the **Groups** collection in the current workspace:

```
wks.Groups.Append grpRegistrars
```

Adding a User to a Group

Once we have created the **Registrars** group, we want to add our new user to it. The following piece of code will achieve this:

```
Sub AddUserToGroup()

    Dim wks As WorkSpace
    Dim usrMark As User
    Dim grpRegistrars As Group

    Set wks = DBEngine(0)
    Set usrMark = wks.CreateUser("Mark Fenton")

    wks.Groups("Registrars").Users.Append usrMark

End Sub
```

First, we declare an object variable of type user and use it to reference the user object that we want to add to the **Registrars** group:

```
Set usrMark = wks.CreateUser("Mark Fenton")
```

All of the details concerning the user object Mark Fenton were set in the procedure **UserAdd**, so now it's just a case of appending the user object to the **Users** collection, which belongs to the **Registrars** group.

```
wks.Groups("Registrars").Users.Append usrMark
```

If you run the procedure and then look at the User and Group Accounts section again, you will see that Mark Fenton is now a member of the **Registrars** group.

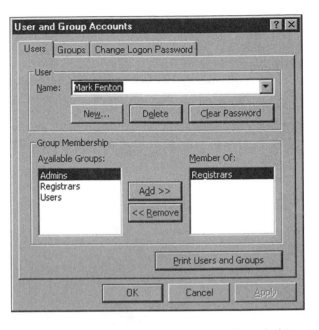

Also, if you refer back to the DAO hierarchy, you will realize that we could have achieved this the other way round:

```
Sub AddUserToGroup()

    Dim wks As WorkSpace
    Dim usrMark As User
    Dim grpRegistrars As Group

    Set wks = DBEngine(0)
    Set grpRegistrars = wks.CreateGroup("Registrars")

    wks.Users("Mark Fenton").Groups.Append grpRegistrars

End Sub
```

In this example, we append the **Registrars** group object to the **Groups** collection, which belongs to the user called Mark Fenton.

Changing a Password

To change our user's password we simply use the **NewPassword** method of the user object:

```
Dim wks As WorkSpace
Set wks = DBEngine(0)

wks.Users("Mark Fenton").NewPassword "Doctor", "Nurse"
```

And to clear Mark Fenton's password, we supply an empty string as the new password:

```
Dim wks As WorkSpace
Set wks = DBEngine(0)

wks.Users("Mark Fenton").NewPassword "Doctor", ""
```

FYI   To change a User's password you must be logged on to that database either as that User or as a member of the Admins Group.

Now that we have got this far, we should be able to create a form which allows the users of our database to change their password.

Try It Out—Creating a 'Change Password' Form

1 Open the **Whisky15.mdb** database and create a new blank form in Design view and set the following properties for it:

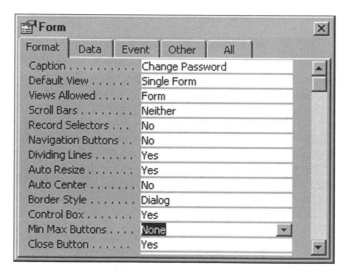

2 Add three text boxes. Call them **txtOldPwd**, **txtNewPwd** and **txtVerify** and change the text of their labels to read Old Password, New Password and Verify New Password.

3 Now select the three text boxes and change them to password input boxes by changing their Input Mask property to Password.

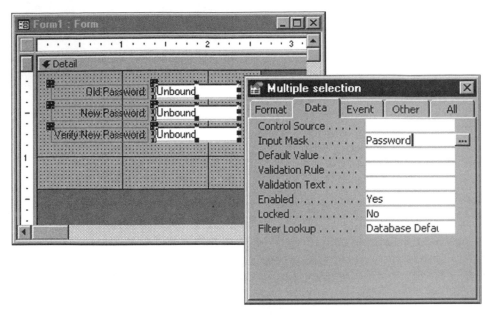

4 Add the following code to the form's **Load** event handler:

```
Private Sub Form_Load()

    Me.Caption = Me.Caption & " (" & CurrentUser & ")"

End Sub
```

5 Now add three command buttons. Call them **cmdCancel**, **cmdClear** and **cmdChange** and change their captions to Cancel, Clear and Change. Make sure that the Command Button Wizard isn't enabled when you create these buttons.

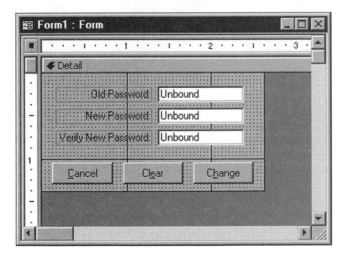

6 Next, add the following routines to the **Click** event handlers of the respective buttons. This code for the Cancel button:

```
Private Sub cmdCancel_Click()

    DoCmd.Close

End Sub
```

This code for the Clear button:

```
Private Sub cmdClear_Click()

    txtNewPwd = ""
    txtVerify = ""
    Call cmdChange_Click

End Sub
```

And finally this code for the Change button:

```
Private Sub cmdChange_Click()

    Dim sMsg As String
    Dim wks As Workspace
    Dim sErr As String

    On Error GoTo cmdChange_Click_Err

    Set wks = DBEngine(0)

    If IsNull(txtNewPwd) Or IsNull(txtVerify) Then Exit Sub

    If IsNull(txtOldPwd) Then txtOldPwd = ""

    sMsg = "Your new password and the verification of your "
    sMsg = sMsg & "new password do not match.  "
    sMsg = sMsg & "Please try again."

    If txtNewPwd <> txtVerify Then
        MsgBox sMsg, vbExclamation
    Else
        wks.Users(CurrentUser).NewPassword txtOldPwd, txtNewPwd
        If txtNewPwd = "" Then
            MsgBox "Password successfully cleared"
        Else
            MsgBox "Password successfully changed"
        End If
    End If
```

```
        txtOldPwd = Null
        txtNewPwd = Null
        txtVerify = Null

    cmdChange_Click_Exit:
        Exit Sub

    cmdChange_Click_Err:
        sErr = "Cannot change this password.  Please "
        sErr = sErr & "ensure that you have "
        sErr = sErr & "typed the old password correctly."

        MsgBox sErr, vbExclamation
        Resume cmdChange_Click_Exit

    End Sub
```

Beware! If Access does not ask you for a password when you start it up, then Access will log you on as **Admin** with an empty password. Once you change the **Admin** password to something other than an empty password, Access will always ask for a login and password when it starts. So when you use the password form, if you are changing the password for the **Admin** user, **make sure you write it down**, because if you forget it you won't be able to get back in.

> *To stop Access asking you for a login and password when it starts, set the password for* Admin *back to an empty string.*

7 Close the form and save it as **frmPassword**.

8 Finally, open the form and try it out!

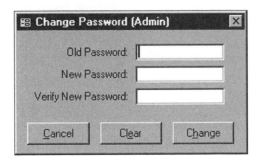

How It Works

If you followed the description of how to change passwords in the section above this example, you should have no problem understanding how the code works. The form simply allows a user to either enter a new password, change an existing one or clear the current password.

The code behind the **cmdCancel** button shouldn't need any explanation.

The **cmdChange** button is used to change the password of the user who is currently logged on. The user must enter their current password in **txtOldPwd** and new password in **txtNewPwd**. They then enter it again in the **txtVerify** box to ensure that no mistake has been made. When the **cmdChange** button is clicked, the procedure in the **Click** event of the button first checks that there is a value in both text boxes:

```
If IsNull(txtNewPwd) Or IsNull(txtVerify) Then Exit Sub
```

It then checks to see whether a value has been entered in the **cmdOldPwd** text box. If not, it converts the **Null** value of the text box to an empty string:

```
If IsNull(txtOldPwd) Then txtOldPwd = ""
```

Then it checks that both versions of the new password are identical:

```
If txtNewPwd <> txtVerify Then
    MsgBox sMsg, vbExclamation
```

If they are identical, it attempts to change the password:

```
wks.Users(CurrentUser).NewPassword txtOldPwd, txtNewPwd
```

If the attempt is successful, a message box informs the user of the fact:

```
If txtNewPwd = "" Then
    MsgBox "Password successfully cleared"
Else
    MsgBox "Password successfully changed"
End If
```

If all goes well, we exit the procedure after clearing all the text boxes:

```
txtOldPwd = Null
txtNewPwd = Null
txtVerify = Null

cmdChange_Click_Exit:
    Exit Sub
```

However, if an error occurs, it is trapped in the error handler. An error here will almost certainly be caused by the user supplying an incorrect current password, so we display a relevant message:

```
cmdChange_Click_Err:
    sErr = "Cannot change this password.  Please "
    sErr = sErr & "ensure that you have "
    sErr = sErr & "typed the old password correctly."

    MsgBox sErr, vbExclamation, "Cannot Change Password"

    Resume cmdChange_Click_Exit

End Sub
```

The code behind the **cmdClear** button is no more complicated. In fact, all we do is run the **cmdChange_Click** procedure after setting the New Password and Verify New Password boxes to an empty string. This removes the existing password from the database providing the correct current password has been entered:

```
txtNewPwd = ""
txtVerify = ""
Call cmdChange_Click
```

This form is still only very rudimentary in many ways, but it does illustrate how you can very quickly provide a simple interface to allow users to maintain their own passwords.

Setting Object Permissions with Visual Basic

The final aspect of security that we shall look at is the retrieval and setting of object permissions. We said earlier that permissions for using specific objects within a database are held within that database. But how do we find out what those permissions are and how do we set them?

The keys to retrieving and setting permissions are **Documents** and **Containers**. As you may know, a **Document** is an object which contains information about a specific object in the database. A **Container** is an object which contains information about a collection of objects in the database. You will not be surprised to know that some of the information held by **Document** objects and **Container** objects is information about permissions.

Try It Out—Retrieving Permissions

1 Create a new module or open an existing one and add the following procedure:

```
Sub ShowPerms()

    Dim objContainer As Container
    Dim objDoc As Document

    For Each objContainer In CurrentDb.Containers
        Debug.Print "--> Container: " & objContainer.Name
        For Each objDoc In objContainer.Documents
            Debug.Print "Document: " & objDoc.Name & "  ";
            objDoc.UserName = "Admin"
            Debug.Print "Perms: " & objDoc.AllPermissions
        Next
    Next

    Debug.Print "Done"

End Sub
```

2 Run the procedure from the debug window. You will get a large output similar to the following:

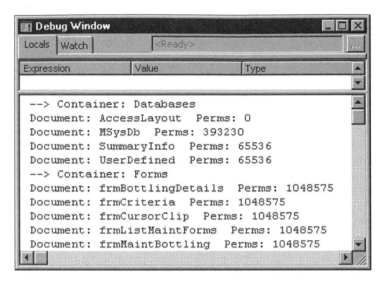

How It Works

The procedure loops through all the **Container** objects within the database and assigns a reference to each of them in turn to the variable **objContainer**. It then prints the **Name** of the **Container** object.

```
For Each objContainer In CurrentDb.Containers
    Debug.Print "--> Container: " & objContainer.Name
```

It then loops through all of the **Document** objects within the **Container** object referenced by **objContainer** and assigns them in turn to the variable **objDoc**.

```
For Each objDoc In objContainer.Documents
```

It then displays the name of the **Document** object and the permissions in that **Document** object for the **Admin** user:

```
Debug.Print "Document: " & objDoc.Name & "   ";
objDoc.UserName = "Admin"
Debug.Print "Perms: " & objDoc.AllPermissions
```

To display the permissions for a specific user you must first set the **UserName** property of the **Document** object you are inspecting to the user's name. The semicolon at the end of the first **Debug.Print** statement tells Access 97 not to move onto a new line for the next **Debug.Print** statement.

Note that we inspect the `AllPermissions` property of the document. The `Permissions` property only reflects the permissions that are explicitly and separately assigned to a user. The `AllPermissions` property reflects those permissions explicitly assigned to the user and those the user inherits from the group to which it belongs.

Analyzing the Output

Don't panic if you're a bit confused by the output you get in the Debug window. We'll go through this now.

Containers and Documents

Containers are not the same as collections. For example, the **Forms** collection contains references to those forms that are currently open and contains information about the design and properties of those forms. The **Forms** container, by contrast, has a document for every form in the database and this document contains information about the form's owner and permissions.

Each database will have within it the following eight containers: **Databases**, **Forms**, **Modules**, **Relationships**, **Reports**, **Scripts**, **SysRel**, **Tables**.

Now the contents of most of these containers are fairly obvious but you might be confused by the **Relationships** and **SysRel** containers. Well, the **Relationships** container holds information about all the relationships that have been defined between the tables in the current database, while the other container object, **SysRel**, is used internally by Access to store information about the layout of the System Relationships window. We need not concern ourselves with that here. You should also note that there is no separate container for queries. Instead, these appear within the **Tables** container.

So much for containers, but what about the documents? Again, looking at the names, you will recognize most of them as saved objects within the database. There are a few oddities, however, such as **AccessLayout**, **SummaryInfo** and **UserDefined**. These are all in the **Databases** container that refers to the current database.

The **SummaryInfo Document** has a **Properties** collection which contains the properties on the Summary page of the Database Properties... dialog box, found on the File menu. Similarly, the **UserDefined Document** has a **Properties** collection containing the user-defined properties, found on the Custom page of the same dialog box. Finally, the **AccessLayout Document** is a system document used internally by Access.

So that explains the unfamiliar documents and containers. The rest of them apply to familiar objects and collections within the database.

Permissions

The next thing we must explain is the permission values. What does a **Permissions** property of **1048575** for **frmCriteria** mean? To find out, we must use some intrinsic constants. Have a look at the following intrinsic constants which represent user permissions:

This constant	...equals	...and means that
dbSecNoAccess	0	The user can't access the object at all.
dbSecDelete	65536	The user is able to delete the object.
dbSecReadSec	131072	The user can read the security information about the object.
dbSecWriteSec	262144	The user is able to alter access permissions for the object.
dbSecWriteOwner	524288	The user can change the **Owner** property setting of the object.
dbSecFullAccess	1048575	The user has full access to the object.

You will no doubt have spotted that **1048575** is represented by the constant **dbSecFullAccess**, indicating that, in our previous example, **Admin** has full permissions for the form we created earlier, **frmCriteria**.

So, if we wanted, we could now alter our function so that it only shows whether or not a user has permission to, say, delete documents. In this case, it would read like this:

```
Sub ShowNoDelPerms()

    Dim objContainer As Container
    Dim objDoc As Document

    For Each objContainer In CurrentDb.Containers
        Debug.Print "--> Container: " & objContainer.Name
        For Each objDoc In objContainer.Documents
            If objDoc.AllPermissions And dbSecDelete Then
                Debug.Print "Can Delete Document: " & _
                            objDoc.Name & "  ";
                objDoc.UserName = "Admin"
                Debug.Print "Perms: " & objDoc.AllPermissions
            Else
                Debug.Print "Cannot Delete Document: " & _
                            objDoc.Name & "  ";
                objDoc.UserName = "Admin"
                Debug.Print "Perms: " & objDoc.AllPermissions
            End If
        Next
    Next

    Debug.Print "Done"

End Sub
```

To check whether the user has permission to delete a document, we compare the document's **AllPermissions** property with the constant **dbSecDelete** using the **And** operator:

```
If objDoc.AllPermissions And dbSecDelete Then
```

If the result of this expression is true (i.e. not **0**), the user has permission to delete the document. If you are a bit confused by that last statement, then we'll have another look at performing bitwise comparisons. We looked at this in Chapter 10 when dealing with the **VarType** property, but it can be a little confusing, and it will do no harm to run over the concept once more.

Bitwise Comparisons on Security Constants

Astute readers will have noticed that in the table of security constants above, many of the values of the constants are double that of the one above it. That is because the security constants represent bitmaps. A bitmap is simply a series of bit values in turn. Each bit can be either **1** (**True** or **On**) or **0** (**False** or **Off**). When we look at the binary representation of these numbers, things become a bit clearer (if you'll excuse the pun).

Constant	5	2	1	6	3	1	8	4	2	1	5	2	1	6	3	1	8	4	2	1	Value
	2	6	3	5	2	6	1	0	0	0	1	5	2	4	2	6					
	4	2	1	5	7	3	9	9	4	2	2	6	8								
	2	1	0	3	6	8	2	6	8	4											
	8	4	7	6	8	4															
	8	4	2																		
dbSecFullAccess	1	1	1	1	1	1	1	1	1	1	1	1	1	1	1	1	1	1	1	1	1048575
dbSecWriteOwner	1	0	0	0	0	0	0	0	0	0	0	0	0	0	0	0	0	0	0	0	524288
dbSecWriteSec	0	1	0	0	0	0	0	0	0	0	0	0	0	0	0	0	0	0	0	0	262144
dbSecReadSec	0	0	1	0	0	0	0	0	0	0	0	0	0	0	0	0	0	0	0	0	131072
dbSecDelete	0	0	0	1	0	0	0	0	0	0	0	0	0	0	0	0	0	0	0	0	65536
dbSecNoAccess	0	0	0	0	0	0	0	0	0	0	0	0	0	0	0	0	0	0	0	0	0

As you can see, each position in the bitmap represents a type of permission. If the permission is enabled, then the bit is set to **1**. If the permission is not enabled, the bit is set to **0**. So to determine what a permission value of 196608 represents, we need to split it into its binary format and see which bits are set.

5	2	1	6	3	1	8	4	2	1	5	2	1	6	3	1	8	4	2	1	Value
2	6	3	5	2	6	1	0	0	0	1	5	2	4	2	6					
4	2	1	5	7	3	9	9	4	2	2	6	8								
2	1	0	3	6	8	2	6	8	4											
8	4	7	6	8	4															
8	4	2																		
0	0	1	1	0	0	0	0	0	0	0	0	0	0	0	0	0	0	0	0	196608

By referring to the table showing the binary representations of the intrinsic security constants, we can see that the bits for **dbSecDelete** and **dbSecReadSec** are set. In other words, a permission value of **196608** means that the user can delete the object and can read the security information for it. However, the user cannot change security attributes or ownership of the object, since neither of these bits are set.

It's all very well converting these values into their binary equivalents on paper and determining which bits are set, but how do we do it in code? The answer is to use bitwise comparison operators. If you can remember back to Chapter 10, you'll remember that there are three main operators that we use.

This Operator	...has this effect
And	Combines two bitmaps into a new bitmap in which individual bits are set to **1** only if that bit is set to **1** in both the first **and** the second bitmap
Or	Combines two bitmaps into a new bitmap in which individual bits are set to **1** if that bit is set to **1** in either the first **or** the second bitmap
Not	Produces a new bitmap from an original bitmap in which the **1**s are changed to **0**s and the **0**s to **1**s.

So, let's look again at the statement in the **ShowNoDelPerms** procedure.

```
If objDoc.AllPermissions And dbSecDelete Then
```

This statement is logically equivalent to this:

```
If (objDoc.AllPermissions And dbSecDelete) <> 0 Then
```

Now, when we use **And** to compare a value with **dbSecDelete**, we end up with a bitmap which will have zeroes in every bit, except where that bit is **1** in both the values being compared. We know that **dbSecDelete** only has one bit set to **1**—the 17th bit from the right. It therefore follows that the only bit that could possibly be set to **1** in the resultant bitmap is the 17th bit. Furthermore, that bit will only be set to **1** if it is **1** in the value being compared with **dbSecDelete**.

In other words, **objDoc.AllPermissions And dbSecDelete** will only be non-zero if the 17th bit of **objDoc.AllPermissions** is set to 1. This is sometimes referred to as using bitmasks, because we are masking out all the bits that we are not interested in and exposing only the one we are interested in, namely the 17th bit.

Setting Permissions

We can also set permissions as well as retrieve them. Suppose we want to make sure that one of our users, Mark Fenton, doesn't accidentally delete **frmPassword** which we so carefully created earlier on. To do this, we can modify the **Permissions** property of the document for **frmPassword**. This is what the following procedure does:

```
Sub ProtectItFromMark()

    Dim db As Database
    Dim Doc As Document

    Set db = CurrentDb()
    Set Doc = db.Containers("Forms").Documents("frmPassword")

    Doc.UserName = "Mark Fenton"
    Doc.Permissions = dbSecFullAccess And Not dbSecDelete

End Sub
```

The first thing to notice about this piece of code is the way in which we select the document whose permissions we wish to alter. In the previous example, we simply looped through the container and document collections in turn. But if you want to, you can select a specific document or container by name. In this example, we are selecting the document for the object called **frmPassword**. Because this is a form, its document will be located in the container called **Forms**, hence the line:

```
Set Doc = db.Containers("Forms").Documents("frmPassword")
```

We then need to specify the user to whom these permissions should apply:

```
Doc.Username = "Mark Fenton"
```

Finally, we specify the permissions we want to give Mark. Here we are saying that we want Mark to be able to do everything but delete the form:

```
Doc.Permissions = dbSecFullAccess And Not dbSecDelete
```

To add one permission but revoke another you use the **And Not** operator with their constants. To see why this is, look at the tables below.

Constant	5	2	1	6	3	1	8	4	2	1	5	2	1	6	3	1	8	4	2	1	Value
	2	6	3	5	2	6	2	0	0	0	1	5	2	4	2	0					
	4	2	1	5	7	3	9	9	4	2	2	6	8								
	2	1	0	3	6	8	2	6	8	4											
	8	4	7	6	8	4															
	8	4	2																		
dbSecFullAccess	1	1	1	1	1	1	1	1	1	1	1	1	1	1	1	1	1	1	1	1	1048575
dbSecDelete	0	0	0	1	0	0	0	0	0	0	0	0	0	0	0	0	0	0	0	0	65536
Not dbSecDelete	1	1	1	0	1	1	1	1	1	1	1	1	1	1	1	1	1	1	1	1	983039
dbSecFullAccess And Not dbSecDelete	1	1	1	0	1	1	1	1	1	1	1	1	1	1	1	1	1	1	1	1	983039

To allow two permissions together you use the **Or** operator with their constants.

Constant	5	2	1	6	3	1	8	4	2	1	5	2	1	6	3	1	8	4	2	1	Value
	2	6	3	5	2	6	1	0	0	0	1	5	2	4	2	6					
	4	2	1	5	7	3	9	9	4	2	2	6	8								
	2	1	0	3	6	8	2	6	8	4											
	8	4	7	6	8	4															
	8	4	2																		
dbSecReadSec	0	0	1	0	0	0	0	0	0	0	0	0	0	0	0	0	0	0	0	0	131072
dbSecDelete	0	0	0	1	0	0	0	0	0	0	0	0	0	0	0	0	0	0	0	0	65536
dbSecReadSec Or dbSecDelete	0	0	1	1	0	0	0	0	0	0	0	0	0	0	0	0	0	0	0	0	196608

There are many other ways you can manipulate object permissions through VBA. After all, there are 25 security constants! But the principle is the same whichever you use. The full range of security constants is shown below:

acSecMacExecute	dbSecDBAdmin	dbSecReadSec
acSecMacReadDef	dbSecDBCreate	dbSecReadDef
acSecMacWriteDef	dbSecDBExclusive	dbSecReplaceData
acSecFrmRptExecute	dbSecDBOpen	dbSecRetrieveData
acSecFrmRptReadDef	dbSecDelete	dbSecWriteSec
acSecFrmRptWriteDef	dbSecDeleteData	dbSecWriteDef
acSecModReadDef	dbSecFullAccess	dbSecWriteOwner
acSecModWriteDef	dbSecInsertData	
dbSecCreate	dbSecNoAccess	

Workspaces

Finally, a quick note about workspaces. Many of the code snippets in this last section have started with the following line:

```
Set wks = DBEngine(0)
```

This means that any code that follows which uses the **wks** workspace object will execute in the current workspace. In other words, it will run in the security context of the currently logged on user. There are times, however, when we might want to run some code in the security context of a different user. For example, our database may contain a function which lists the groups to which the user belongs. The problem is that we need to be logged on with administrative privileges to do this.

The way to impersonate another user in code is to create a new workspace, which we do like this:

```
Set wks = DBEngine.CreateWorkspace("MyWorkspace", "Admin", "Glenfarclas")
```

This has the effect of programmatically logging us on as the user called **Admin** with a password of **Glenfarclas** and creates a workspace called **MyWorkspace**. Any operations performed on users or groups within that workspace will be executed as if they were being performed by the user called **Admin**, irrespective of how the current user is currently logged to Access.

In fact, if you want to try this out, you can have a go in one of the exercises at the end of this chapter!

Summary

In this chapter, we have looked at the many problems that can arise when more than one person wants to use a database at the same time. In fact they aren't so much problems, as issues. They only become problems when you ignore or forget about them.

The key to producing an Access database that will function as happily with ten people using it as with one, is to plan ahead. If you bear in mind the issues we have looked at in this chapter, and apply them to your databases from the moment you start building them, you should have very few problems. On the other hand, if you wait until the last moment to add a veneer of multi-usability on top of your database, you will spend some very long days and nights trying to iron out problems which wouldn't have arisen if you had been a little more far-sighted in the beginning!

This chapter has covered:

▶ The difference between optimistic and pessimistic locking

▶ How to apply locking

▶ The locking errors you are likely to encounter and how to deal with them

▶ How to use the user and group objects to secure a database

▶ How to set and change passwords

▶ Setting and retrieving permissions

Exercises

1 At the end of this chapter we looked at how it was possible to use the `CreateWorkspace` method to allow us to act in the security context of another user. One potential use of this is to allow us to create a procedure that lists all of the groups to which the current user belongs. The potential problem is that only members of the **Admins** group have permission to view this information. See if you can write a procedure that lists all of the groups to which the current user belongs even if the user is not a member of the **Admins** group.

2 The password form we created in this chapter is still fairly rudimentary. You can probably think of many ways to improve it. For example, some security systems force you to change your password at monthly intervals and will not allow you to reuse any of your, say, five previous passwords. See if you can modify the password form so that it enforces these two rules.

Hint: If you decide to store users' passwords in a table you need to make sure that you will be able to read the table from code, but that normal users won't be able to read the data in the table.

Communicating With
Other Applications

In Chapter 8, we looked at how you can get data into and out of Access and use that data in other applications, such as Microsoft Excel. The trouble with this method, however, was that it created a file, leaving you to import the data into Excel. This chapter is going to look at a better way of moving data between applications.

In particular, we will be looking at:

▶ Object linking and embedding
▶ Controlling other applications from Access
▶ Integrating with Microsoft Office

Object Linking and Embedding (OLE)

You have seen many examples of objects so far, such as recordsets, forms, etc., but what you may not realise is that other applications can act as objects too—OLE objects. An OLE object is simply a file or document created in another application, which retains a connection with its original application.

This feature allows you to link applications together so you can use bits of many different programs to create one larger program. For example, suppose you needed some spreadsheet capability in your database. Would you write lots of code to implement it? Of course not, when you can use OLE to link in Microsoft Excel—after all Microsoft has done a good job writing it, so why not use it?

In our hypothetical Excel-in-a-database example, when you double-click the spreadsheet, you'll see that Access *becomes* Microsoft Excel. That's right—becomes. What happens is that you **activate** the object and, because Excel is an **OLE server**, it takes control of the application, either by replacing some of the menus and toolbars or by starting a new instance of Excel. You don't have to do anything special because OLE handles the behind-the-scenes linking of the applications. One of the great things about OLE is that a whole host of applications support it. The Office 97 suite is especially good, so let's see how it can be used.

FYI Note that this behavior is only supported by OLE servers that use OLE2—some older applications may not open within the client application, but as a separate window instead.

Creating an OLE Object

There are two types of OLE object that can be used in Access 97: **bound** and **unbound** objects. The difference between the two is simple. A bound object resides in the database, i.e. there is a column in a table which has a data type of OLE object. Unbound objects, which can be used on forms and reports, are not stored in a database table, but are stored along with the form or report.

Try It Out—Creating an OLE Object

1 Create a new form, **frmExcel**, and select the Unbound Object Frame button on the toolbar.

2 Using the mouse, draw a square on the form to size the object, just as you would with any other control. This will open the Insert Object dialog.

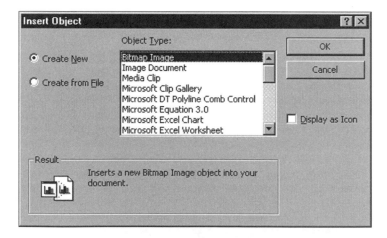

3 You can now select the type of object you require. You can select objects such as Word documents, Excel spreadsheets, charts or pictures. However, we want to insert the Monthly Sales spreadsheet that we created earlier, so select the Create from File option to use a file that already exists, rather than creating a new one. Type in the file name of the spreadsheet, or browse to find it, and make sure the Link box is checked. Then press the OK button.

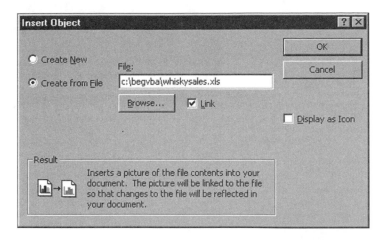

4 Change the Enabled and Locked properties to Yes and No respectively on the object's property sheet (on the Data or All tab), so that you can edit the object. By default, the new object is Locked and Disabled. Also change the Name property to **objExcel**, as we will use this to refer to the object later in the chapter.

5 Now switch to Form view and launch Excel. You can do this either by double-clicking on the object or by clicking the right mouse button when over the object to view the objects menu:

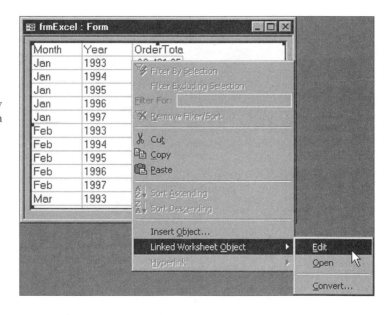

This will **activate** the object, here by launching Excel, the object's own application.

FYI Activation can either launch the object's application or change the Access menus (something we'll see in a moment). The former method is known as **external activation**, and the latter as **in-place activation**.

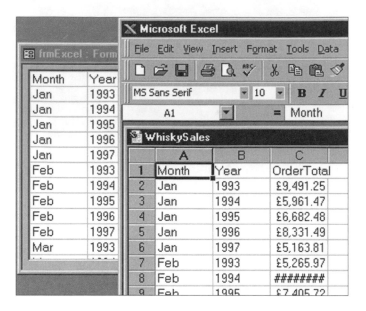

6 You should now see Excel launched:

Notice that if you type in the spreadsheet in Excel, the changes are automatically reflected on the form when you move off the cell. This is because the object is **linked** and it retains a connection with its source, that is the **WhiskySales.xls** file.

If you had not selected the Link option when inserting the object, it would have been **embedded**. An embedded object behaves in exactly the same way as a linked object, except that it does not retain a connection to its source file and, therefore, changes to the original object are not shown on the embedded object. Also, when you edit an embedded object, for example our spreadsheet, it is the embedded version of the spreadsheet to which you make changes, not the original spreadsheet. You should **embed** objects that won't change very often, such as pictures and **link** objects which may change regularly and whose changes you want to see. To see any changes in an embedded object you would have to re-embed it.

The OLE Object's Properties

OLE objects are just like other controls, in that they have properties which can either be set in the property sheet or from within code. The most important properties for OLE objects are listed below:

Property	Description
`Action`	This specifies what is to happen to the object, for example, whether it is to be linked, embedded or activated. This can only be set at run-time.
`Class`	This shows the application that the class belongs to. Our spreadsheet has a class of **Microsoft Excel 97**
`OLETypeAllowed`	This specifies whether the object can be embedded, linked, or both.
`SourceDoc`	The file to link when creating a linked object.
`SourceItem`	The data within the linked file, for example, a range of cells in a spreadsheet. The syntax for this is specific to the *server application*, so a range would appear exactly as it does in Excel.

The **Action** can be one of the following:

Action	Description
acOLECreateEmbed	Embed the object.
acOLECreateLink	Link the object.
acOLECopy	Copy the object to the clipboard.
acOLEPaste	Paste the object from the clipboard.
acOLEUpdate	Update the object with any changes from the source object.
acOLEActivate	Activate the object, that is, launch the object's application.
acOLEClose	Close the object.
acOLEDelete	Delete the object.
acOLEInsertObjDlg	Display the Insert Object dialog box. This allows the user to choose the object type to be inserted.
acOLEPasteSpecialDlg	Display the Paste Special dialog box.
acOLEFetchVerbs	Fetch a list of verbs that the object supports.

Activating the Object

To activate an object, you simply set the **Action** property to the action that you want to take place, such as **acOLECreateLink**, and then set it to **acOLEActivate**. This will first link the object to its source and then activate it.

Try It Out—Activating an Object

1 Add a frame/option group to the form with two option buttons to select between embedding and linking, and a command button to activate the object. Name the frame **fraAction**, and make sure the options have values of 1 for Embed and 2 for Link. Also, make sure you name the option buttons **optEmbed** and **optLink**. Name the command button **cmdActivate**.

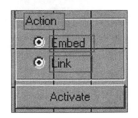

2 Create the code for the Activate button:

```
Private Sub cmdActivate_Click()

    Select Case fraAction
    Case 1
        objExcel.Action = acOLECreateEmbed
    Case 2
        objExcel.Action = acOLECreateLink
    End Select
```

```
        objExcel.Action = acOLEActivate

End Sub
```

This simply sets the action to either embed or link, depending on which option is selected, and then activates it—it really is that simple.

3 Switch into Form view and selected Link and press Activate. You should see the same as before.

4 Now select Embed and press Activate. Something different happens.

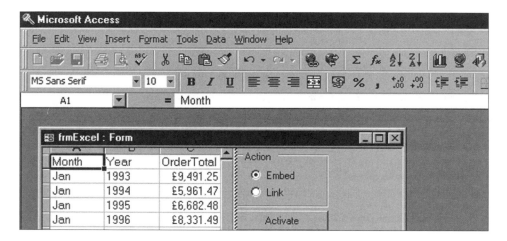

Notice how Excel is not launched as a separate application, but that it has been combined with Access. Look at the titlebar—it's still Access, but the Excel menus and toolbars have been combined with the Access ones. You are actually running Excel, but inside Access. When you click off the spreadsheet object onto any other control the Excel items disappear.

Updating the Object

By default, the object will automatically be updated whenever it changes, but there may be times when you wish to control this manually. This may be useful if you have an object that is changing often and the updating process is slowing your application down.

You can change how the updating works by changing the value of the **UpdateOptions** property for the object, setting it to one of two values:

Type	Value	Description
Automatic	**acOLEUpdateAutomatic**	Automatic updates occur, based on the number in the Refresh Interval field on the Advanced tab of the Options dialog.
Manual	**acOLEUpdateManual**	Updating takes place manually, by setting the **Action** property to **acOLEUpdate.**

You can also tell when an object is being updated, because the **Updated** event is triggered for the object.

Try It Out—Checking the Object for Changes

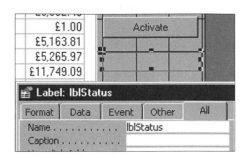

1 Add a label to the form to show the status of the object. Call it **lblStatus**.

2 Now add some code to the **Updated** event for the Excel object:

```
Private Sub objExcel_Updated(Code As Integer)

    Select Case Code
    Case acOLEChanged
        lblStatus.Caption = "Changed"
    Case acOLESaved
        lblStatus.Caption = "Saved"
    Case acOLEClosed
        lblStatus.Caption = "Closed"
    Case acOLERenamed
        lblStatus.Caption = "Renamed"
    End Select

End Sub
```

3 Open the object in linked mode. Make a change to one of the cells and notice how the label changes.

When an **Updated** event occurs, the value of the **Code** argument indicates what has happened:

Code	Description	Applies when...
acOLEChanged	The object has changed.	A linked object is modified in the server.
acOLESaved	The object has been saved.	The user chooses **Update** from the <u>F</u>ile menu in the server.
acOLEClosed	The object has been closed.	The server application closes the server document and updates changes to the client.
acOLERenamed	The object has been renamed	The user renames the document to which the client is linked.

Again, you can see how simple this is to use. People have been scared of OLE, but using OLE objects in your applications is very easy, and a great way to add functionality that you would otherwise have trouble providing.

Custom Controls

Access 2.0 was the first application to support custom controls (or OCX's), and although they have now been renamed ActiveX controls, they are, in fact, much the same. You know how much we like to extol the benefits of code re-use and encapsulation; well, custom controls are sections of self-contained code, encapsulating some functionality, that can be added to your application.

One of the first controls of this type was the calendar control, which shows a calendar, one month at a time, and has several useful events and properties. Let's have a look at how this can be used.

Try It Out—Custom Controls

In this exercise, you are going to create a generic calendar form using the Calendar ActiveX control.

1 Make sure you are in **Whisky16.mdb** and open the form **frmCompany**. This shows the company, location and contact details on one form, using the Tab control. Have a look at the Contacts page. It shows the date of birth for the person, and we want to add a calendar to allow selection of this date.

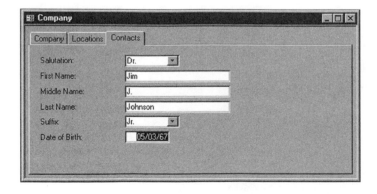

2 Create a new form and set the following properties so this will appear as a pop-up form. Call the form **frmCalendar**.

Property	Value
Caption	Date Selection
Scroll Bars	Neither
Record Selectors	No
Navigation Buttons	No
Auto Center	Yes
Modal	Yes
Control Box	No
Min Max Buttons	None
Close Button	No

3 Now you can add the control. The Calendar control is not on the ToolBox by default so you have to select the More Controls button:

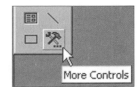

This shows you another window with a list of custom controls.

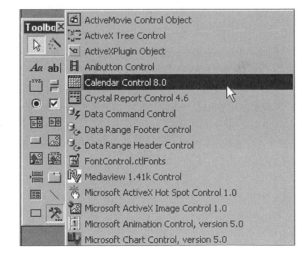

You might find yours differs slightly from this, depending upon which controls you have installed. The one you want is the Calendar control.

4 Add this to the form.

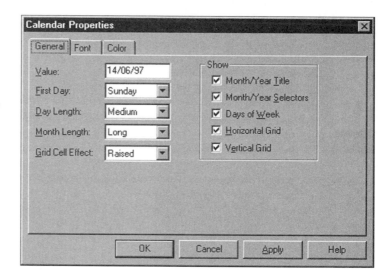

Change the controls name
to **ctlCalendar**. As this
is a custom control, it
has some of its own
special properties, and
you double-click on the
control to see these.

This allows you to change the properties for the calendar, such as how it looks. We are
going to leave it with the defaults, so Cancel this screen.

5 Now you are ready to add some code, so click on the Code button on the toolbar and
create a global variable. This needs to be placed in the **General (Declarations)** section.

```
Private mctlDate          As Control
```

This will be used to hold the control on the calling form (in this case the date of birth
field on the company form).

6 Now create a **Property Set** procedure for this control.

```
Public Property Set DateControl(ByVal ctlDate As Control)

    Set mctlDate = ctlDate

End Property
```

This will be called from the calling routine, just like any other form property. You will see
how this is done in a minute.

7 Now create another **Property Let** procedure, this time to set the initial date. This will be
the date we want the calendar to show when it first appears.

```
Public Property Let InitialDate(datD As Date)

    Me!ctlCalendar.Value = datD

End Property
```

This does not need to use a global variable, but sets the **Value** property of the calendar
control. This is the value that is highlighted when the control is visible.

8 We've got the properties now, but we need a way to get the selected value back to the
caller, so add a procedure for this.

```
Private Sub SetAndClose()

    If mctlDate Is Nothing Then
        MsgBox "The DateControl property has not been set", , _
                "Calendar Form Error"
    Else
        mctlDate = ctlCalendar.Value
    End If

    DoCmd.Close

End Sub
```

This first checks that the date field has been set, and if it hasn't, then an error message is
displayed. If it has been set then we simply store the date selected on the calendar control
into the date field.

9 Now that we can talk back to the calling form, we need a link between the date that has
been clicked and the **SetAndClose** function, so you need two more procedures. The first
is for the Click event of the Calendar control. Notice that the calendar control does not
have a Click event shown in the properties window (I suspect this is a bug), so you will
have to select this event from within the code window itself.

```
Private Sub ctlCalendar_Click()

    SetAndClose

End Sub
```

This simply calls the above routine. The date can also be selected with the keyboard so we need a routine for that too.

```
Private Sub ctlCalendar_KeyUp(KeyCode As Integer, ByVal Shift As Integer)

    Select Case KeyCode
    Case vbKeyReturn      ' carriage return
        SetAndClose
    Case vbKeyEscape      ' escape
        DoCmd.Close
    End Select

End Sub
```

In this case you only want to close if the return key is pressed, which has a value of 13, or if the escape key is pressed, which has a value of 27. In the case of the escape key though, we just close the form, and don't set the date.

That's it for this form. Close the form and save it. You now have a generic calendar form that can be called from anywhere. Now to the calling form.

10 Open the form **frmsubPerson** in Design view and add a new command button to the right of the date of birth field. Use a caption of ... (ellipsis), and call it **cmdCalendar**.

11 Add the following code to the **Click** event for this button.

```
Dim frmCal            As Form        ' calendar form
Dim ctlD              As Control     ' date control on this form

Set ctlD = Me!DoB
DoCmd.OpenForm "frmCalendar", , , , , acHidden
Set frmCal = Forms("frmCalendar")
With frmCal
    Set .DateControl = ctlD
    .InitialDate = ctlD.Value
    .Visible = True
End With
```

The first thing this routine does is to set a variable to point to the date of birth field. Then it opens the calendar form hidden. This is so it can set the properties before displaying it. We then set a variable to point to the form. This not only makes the code look better, but is faster too. Then we set the properties. The first is the **DateField** property, which stores the field that contains the date value. In this case we set it to the variable we set earlier, **ctlD**. Next we set the initial date, which ensures that when the calendar displays, it shows the initial date highlighted. Lastly, we then make the form visible. That's all there is to it in this form. Having set the properties for the calendar, it will fill in the appropriate field when it closes.

12 Save the form and close it (don't forget to compile the code first). Open the `frmCompany` form, switch to the Contacts tab and press your new button. You can select a date and it will appear in the Date of Birth field.

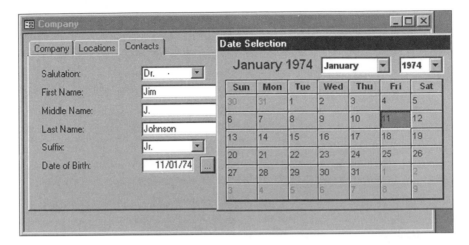

You could have implemented this by just putting the calendar control on the Contacts subform and you could then just set the **Value** property, which would have been simpler. However, you now have a generic form that can be used in any application.

Automation

So far, you have seen how to manipulate objects that are on a form but you can also create objects within code, and use their properties and methods to control them. This is called **Automation**.

An Automation object is created from a list of objects that the applications on your system expose, or make available, to the outside world. You have already seen some of these in action in a simple form. In the previous example the calendar form had four new properties, and you set those within another form. These properties are exposed to other forms because they are **Public**. The same principle applies to applications. The application that provides (exposes) the object is called the **object application** or **server application**, and the one in which you link or embed the object (i.e. the one contains the object) is called the **container application**. In the earlier examples of OLE objects, Excel is the object or server application and Access the container application.

The ability to use objects in VBA means that applications can be controlled by other applications. This gives even greater flexibility than embedded or linked objects because there you have limited control of the object application. With automation objects, you have complete control and can do anything that can be done in the object application's own macro or programming language.

Listed below are a couple of applications and a sample of the objects that they expose:

Application	Application Name	Objects Exposed
Microsoft Word	`Word`	`Application` `Document`

Microsoft Excel	`Excel`	`Application`
		`Chart`
		`Worksheet`
		`Range`

The application name and object are collectively known as the object's **class**, and are joined together when creating objects.

Creating Automation Objects

There are two methods for defining objects when using Automation, and, just like any other object within Access, they are declared with the **Dim** statement. The method you use depends upon how much you know about the object. For example, if you do not know what type of object is going to be stored (or perhaps you are going to use different objects at different times), then you can use the following:

```
Dim objObject    As Object
```

This defines a generic variable that can be used to store any object type, for example, when the user has the choice of selecting the object type. You can then use one of the following two methods to assign an object to this variable:

```
Set objObject = CreateObject ("Excel.Application")
```

Or:

```
Set objObject = GetObject ("C:\BegVBA\Sales.XLS")
```

The difference between these two is that **CreateObject** is used when you are creating a new copy of something, whereas, **GetObject** should be used when you need to start the application with an existing file. The example above will start Excel with the spreadsheet **C:\BegVBA\Sales.xls** already loaded. You can also use **GetObject** to return an existing instance of a class, for example, if Excel was already running. In this case you would use the following syntax:

```
Set objObject = Getobject(, "Excel.Application")
```

This skips the first argument, and uses the class of a running object to set the variable. In this case, this is the **Application** object of Excel. One thing to beware is that an error is generated if Excel is not already running. A good example of how to get around this is described in the On-Line help, under the **GetObject** topic.

As you can see, a variable is declared just like any normal variable, and **Set** just like other object variables. Think about the DAO objects; **Recordset**s, **Tabledefs**, etc. which are exactly the same. Using the `Object` variable—and `CreateObject` and `GetObject`—is known as **Late Binding**, as Access does not know what type of object it is to create until run-time.

A more preferable method is to use **Early Binding**, which is where you tell Access what type of object you are going to use as you declare it:

```
Dim objExcel    As Excel.Application
```

This declares the object as a specific type, after which you can assign the variable:

```
Set objExcel = Excel.Application
```

You can also insert the **New** keyword after the equals sign to instantiate a new copy of the object:

```
Set objExcel = New Excel.Application
```

This method has the flexibility to set a reference to a running copy from a link, or as shown above, create a new instance. If you know you are only ever going to use the one instance, you can use the **New** keyword to combine the declaration and assignment:

```
Dim objExcel As New Excel.Application
```

This declares a new copy of the object that is instantiated when you first refer to the object, so you don't need to use the **Set** statement. However, you may prefer to use the **Set** form, as this gives a clearer picture of where the object becomes instantiated. One thing to think about, though, is that processing takes place as the class is instantiated, and the method you use can have an impact on the apparent speed of your application. The slowdown appears when the object's application is loading, which is the moment the **New** keyword is used, so don't do this too often. For example, you may want to declare the object variable as a global, and only set it once. You could then use the object's application many times without the overhead of having to start it up.

The great benefit of early binding is that once you have the variable declared, Access knows everything about its class, and thus you can get help with the Quick Tips. However you need to set a **reference** to it first, so that Access knows what object you are talking about. You can achieve this by selecting References from the Tools menu.

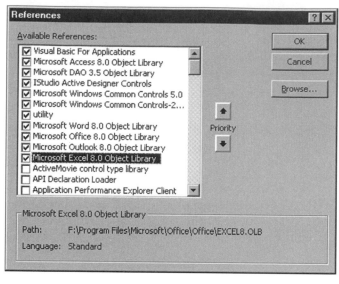

This gives you a selection of the applications that support Automation:

The list of references available may be different on your machines, as is depends upon what software has been loaded. All of the Office 97 applications are version 8.0. If you don't set a reference to the object, then you will get an error when you try to compile your module, as Access then thinks this is a user-defined type for which it has no definition.

Setting the Object's Properties

When it comes to properties, an object is just like the controls on a form with which you are already familiar. You can set the properties and use variables to hold their contents as normal. For example:

```
Debug.Print objExcel.Workbooks(1).Name
```

This would print the name of the first workbook open. The following lines set the value of a cell and format it to be bold:

```
objExcel.Cells(1, 1).Value = "10.75"
objExcel.Cells(1, 1).Font.Bold = True
```

Similarly, you can extract the information into a variable:

```
Dim strObjName As String
strObjName = objExcel.Name
```

Using the Object's Methods

Just as an object has properties, it also has methods. Remember that an Automation object is just a self-contained, hidden version of an application. You can, therefore, do most of the things that you would normally do in the application. For example, to save a worksheet in an Excel object you would use:

```
objExcel.ActiveWorkbook.SaveAs ("MonthlySales")
```

Or to create a new workbook:

```
objExcel.Workbooks.Add
```

Closing the Object

All Automation objects support a method that allows you to close the object and exit the application. This should always be done as soon as the object is no longer required since OLE objects can consume quite a lot of memory. This is especially true of out-of-process servers, such as Excel, but small in-process servers aren't always so big. If you are using an OLE Server that is designed to stay open all of the time, then you can leave it open—the Office Assistant is like this, as it sits around waiting to help.

Most likely, the method to close the object will be **Close** or **Quit**. For example, to close Microsoft Excel, you would use:

```
objExcel.[Quit]
```

Notice that the **Quit** has brackets around it. This ensures that the Excel, and not the Access 97, method is run.

If you are not sure what the method is called, set the object variable to **Nothing**. This is a special keyword that closes the application if no one else is using it and frees the associated memory:

```
Set objExcel = Nothing
```

Don't fear about closing the server prematurely, as the server will only close when the last person stops using it. This is handled automatically for you.

FYI The object and its application are not closed when an object variable loses scope. The **GetObject** function can be used to assign another object variable to the object if it is still active. If you do not intend to do this, always close the application and free up the memory that it is consuming.

So, to recap, one could create a new Excel spreadsheet, manipulate, save and close it with the following code:

```
Dim objExcel As Excel.Application

Set objExcel = Excel.Application
objExcel.Workbooks.Add

Debug.Print objExcel.Workbooks(1).Name

objExcel.Cells(1, 1).Value = "10.75"
objExcel.Cells.Font.Bold = True

Dim strObjName As String
strObjName = objExcel.Name
```

```
Debug.Print strObjName

objExcel.ActiveWorkbook.SaveAs ("MonthlySales")

objExcel.[Quit]

Set objExcel = Nothing
```

The Object Hierarchy

Before you can start to program using Automation, you really need to be familiar with the object model of the application. Remember how, when looking at Data Access Objects, we saw the hierarchy of objects? Well, Automation is no different from this. Every application in the Microsoft Office 97 suite, and many other programs, has a full model. In this section we are going to concentrate on Excel 97 and Word 97, as these will be the two most commonly used.

Much of the models have not been shown, because they are far too large to include here, but it is a good idea to get familiar with them if you are going to use Automation. The full diagrams, along with the other Microsoft Office Object Models are included on the CD, in the **Object Models** directory.

The Excel 97 Object Model

At a high level, the Excel object model looks like this:

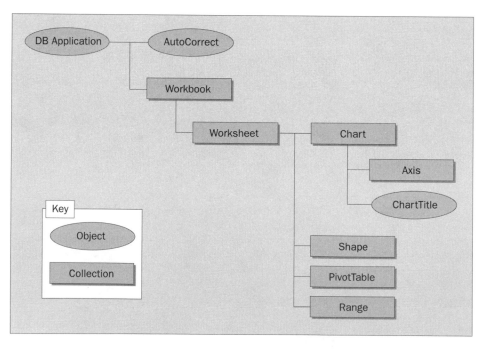

At the highest level is the **Application**, and under that a collection of **Workbooks**. Each **Workbook** has a collection of **Worksheets**:

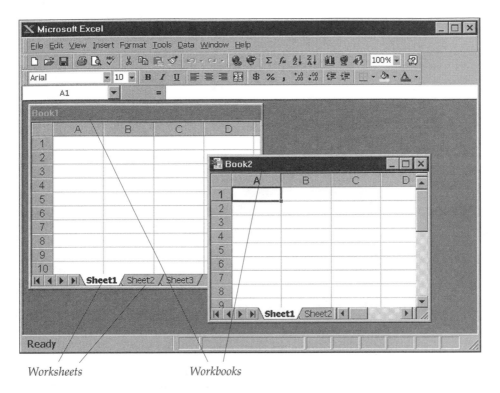

Worksheets   *Workbooks*

You can easily see how this hierarchy is arranged. A worksheet can contain charts, ranges of cells, etc..

The Word 97 Object Model

This is one of the fundamental differences with the 97 version of Office, as Word 97 is the first version of Word to support a full object model. Previous versions only supported the **Word.Basic** class, which meant that programming was done via Word macros. Although this method is still supported, and existing Automation programs will still work, the new object model provides a more structured approach. One difference is that using the new model starts Word invisibly, which is not how the **Word.Basic** method worked. There are also some small inconsistencies, so you should really convert any old code to the new method as soon as you can.

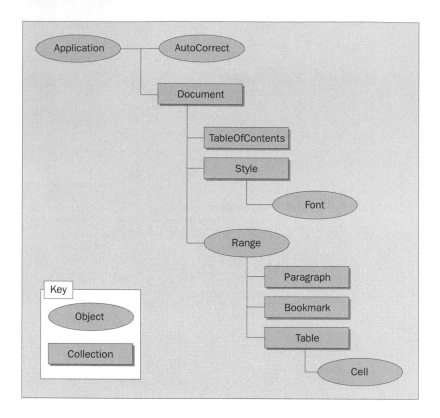

Try It Out—Creating a Chart in Excel

Hold on to your hats—this is where the programming gets exciting. The next example will use a crosstab query of all of the sales by month and year to generate some figures that will be inserted into Excel, and a chart based on these figures will then be saved. Sounds complicated, doesn't it? Follow the example carefully and you will see how easy it is. As the code needed for this is quite substantial, we'll assume that rather than typing it in, you will be using the version of the **CreateChart** procedure provided in Chapter 16 Code module.

1 Open up **Whisky16.mdb** and open the module Chapter 16 Code. The first thing to do is to ensure that you have set the references for Excel. Select the References... option from the Tools menu, and make sure you have the Microsoft Excel 8.0 Object Library ticked, as shown earlier.

2 Run the **CreateChart** procedure from the Debug window.

3 The procedure takes a couple of minutes to run but, once it's through, switch to Excel, and open the file **C:\BegVBA\MnthSale.XLS**.

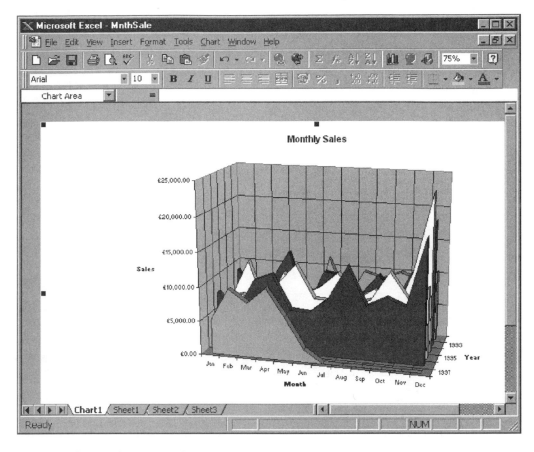

Impressive, eh? But how is it done?

How It Works—The Preparation

Let's examine the **CreateChart** procedure in detail.

```
Dim recSales      As Recordset          ' Recordset to create chart from
Dim varArray      As Variant            ' Array of entries from above
Dim objExcel      As New Excel.Application ' Excel object
Dim objChart      As Excel.Chart        ' Excel chart object
Dim intFields     As Integer            ' Number of fields in recordset
Dim intRows       As Integer            ' Number of rows in recordset
Dim intFld        As Integer            ' Loop index for fields
Dim intRow        As Integer            ' Loop index for rows
Dim strRange      As String             ' Range of Excel cells for data
```

The code starts, as always, with some variables. You can see that there are two object variables: one for Excel and one for the Chart. The use of the **New** keyword means that Excel will be started (hidden) as soon as the first property or method is referenced. This is not used for the

Chart object, as **New** creates a new instance of an object, and we won't want to do that for the chart, whereas Excel will create the chart for us, and we will reference it once it is created.

```
On Error GoTo CreateChart_Err

DoCmd.Hourglass True
Set recSales = CurrentDb().OpenRecordset("qryxMonthlySales")
```

The next thing we do is to set up the error handling and create the **Recordset** of the query. We turn on the hourglass to stop the user worrying that nothing is happening.

```
recSales.MoveLast
recSales.MoveFirst
varArray = recSales.GetRows(recSales.RecordCount)
```

Next, the **Recordset** is loaded into an array, using **GetRows**, which will allow faster access to the data later. There is a **MoveLast** at the beginning to ensure that the **RecordCount** is set correctly.

```
intFields = UBound(varArray, 1)
intRows = UBound(varArray, 2)
```

Now the number of fields and rows returned by the **Recordset** is calculated. The **UBound** function returns the number of elements in an array. We use **1** and **2** as the subscripts because this is a two-dimensional array—remember it came from a crosstab query.

```
objExcel.Workbooks.Add
```

Once the preparation is done, we can add a new workbook to Excel, as it starts without any workbooks.

How It Works—The Excel Object

```
recSales.MoveFirst
For intFld = 1 To intFields
    objExcel.Cells(intRow + 1, intFld + 1).Value = _
        recSales.Fields(intFld).Name
Next
recSales.Close
```

Now that a workbook is created we can add the titles for the year. As this is a crosstab query, these are the field names of the columns, so we use the **Fields** collection of the recordset to get the years, as shown below:

qryxMonthlySales : Crosstab Query

Month	1997	1996	1995	1994	1993	1992
Jan	£5,163.81	£8,331.49	£6,682.48	£5,961.47	£9,491.25	
Feb	£9,785.32	£5,593.75	£7,405.72	£11,749.09	£5,265.97	
Mar	£7,901.54	£10,460.53	£6,483.74	£4,397.43	£8,166.95	
Apr	£10,369.25	£11,643.21	£9,416.64	£10,379.37	£12,842.75	
May	£6,398.61	£6,589.93	£12,464.38	£7,205.00	£4,053.69	
Jun	£1,803.66	£6,451.01	£7,652.11	£8,469.26	£10,146.51	£11,543.34
Jul		£8,679.71	£7,504.25	£10,929.10	£9,625.96	£5,175.71
Aug		£13,583.52	£7,111.19	£7,122.88	£6,888.10	£9,781.16
Sep		£8,056.75	£8,039.74	£8,878.68	£10,215.98	£8,961.59
Oct		£9,422.17	£12,386.00	£5,050.51	£7,034.84	£10,062.03
Nov		£8,377.28	£8,454.27	£11,841.42	£11,988.53	£9,158.27
Dec		£18,227.38	£10,503.18	£23,399.46	£18,681.49	£10,512.95

Record: 12 of 12

We don't want to have the word Month is the spreadsheet, so we start at 1 for the **`Fields`** collection (it normally starts at 0). The Excel **`Cells`** collection is just like a two-dimensional array that starts at 1,1, so we just loop through the **`Fields`** adding the name of each to the first row in the spreadsheet, which now looks like this:

	A	B	C	D	E	F	G
1		1997	1996	1995	1994	1993	1992
2							

Now we can fill in the rest of the data.

```
For intFld = 0 To intFields
    For intRow = 0 To intRows
        objExcel.Cells(intRow + 2, intFld + 1).Value = varArray(intFld, _
             intRow)
    Next
Next
```

We place the data from the array into the active Excel object. These few lines cycle through the array and copy each element into an Excel cell. The first line is the loop that controls the fields, the second line is the loop that controls the rows. The third line uses the **`Cells`** collection of Excel, using the index numbers for the loop to identify the cell. One is added to the field (**`intFld`**) because the array index starts at 0, but the Excel cells start at 1, and an additional one is added to the row (**`intRow`**) as the first row contains the heading. The diagram below shows how this works:

var Array(1,0) var Array(1,1) var Array(2,0)

	A	B	C	D
1		1997	1996	1995
2	Jan	$5,163.81	$8,331.49	$6,682.48	$
3	Feb	$9,785.32	$5,593.75	$7,405.72	$1
4	Mar	$7,901.54	$10,460.53	$6,483.74	$
5	Apr	$10,369.25	$11,643.21	$9,416.64	$1
6	May	$6,398.61	$6,589.93	$12,464.38	$
7	Jun	$1,803.66	$6,451.01	$7,652.11	$
8	Jul		$8,679.71	$7,504.25	$1
9	Aug		$13,583.52	$7,111.19	$
10	Sep		$8,056.75	$8,039.74	$
11	Oct		$9,422.17	$12,386.00	$
12	Nov		$8,377.28	$8,454.27	$1
13	Dec		$18,227.38	$10,503.18	$2

var Array(0,0)

var Array(0,1)

var Array(0,2)

Note that the row and field indexes are reversed—this is because in the array, the numbers are stored in field/row order, whereas Excel uses row/field order.

```
strRange = "A1:" & Chr$(Asc("A") + intFields) & Format$(intRows + 2))
objExcel.Range(strRange).Select
objExcel.Range(Mid(strRange, 4)).Activate
```

Once the data is in Excel, a range is set up to cover the cells and is then activated.

Using **Chr$((Asc("A") + intFields)** is a standard trick to convert a number into a letter. The function Asc returns the ASCII number of **"A"** (which is 65). **Chr$** converts a number into a character.

We add **intFields** to the value of **"A"** (65). Remember that **intFields** is the upper bound of the array and an array starts at 0; therefore, **intFields** will be one less than the number of fields (in this case 6, as there are 7 fields). If we add 6 to 65 we get 71, which represents the letter G, so A-G is our field range. The number of rows is then added, giving A1:G13 for the range. This is then selected and a cell in the range activated.

```
objExcel.Application.Charts.Add
```

The next thing to do is to add a chart. **Charts** is a collection in Excel which specifies all of the charts in the workbook—there are none yet, so one is added which occupies a new worksheet, and makes it the active worksheet. It uses the selected cells in the original worksheet as its data, getting this from the currently active area selected earlier.

```
Set objChart = objExcel.ActiveChart
```

Next, the chart object is set to point to the currently active chart, so that some formatting can take place.

```
With objChart
    .ChartType = xl3Darea              'Line 1
    .HasTitle = True                   'Line 2
```

```
        .ChartTitle.Text = "Monthly Sales"       'Line 3
        .Axes(xlCategory).HasTitle = True                          'Line 4
        .Axes(xlCategory).AxisTitle.Caption = "Month"              'Line 5
        .Axes(xlValue).HasTitle = True                             'Line 6
        .Axes(xlValue).AxisTitle.Caption = "Sales"                 'Line 7
        .Axes(xlSeriesAxis).HasTitle = True                        'Line 8
        .Axes(xlSeriesAxis).AxisTitle.Caption = "Year"             'Line 9
        .HasLegend = False                                         'Line 10
    End With
```

So what do these lines do?

- Line 1 sets the type of the graph to a 3D area graph.

- Line 2 indicates that a title is to be used, and line 3 sets this title.

- The next two lines introduce the **Axes** object, which is a sub-object of the chart. Line 4 turns on the title for the category—this is the horizontal title nearest to you, running from left to right. Line 5 sets it.

- Line 6 turns on the vertical title, from bottom to top, and line 7 sets it.

- Line 8 turns on the titles for the depth axis, running away from you, and line 9 sets it.

- Finally, line 10 turns off the legend for the graph.

That's it for formatting. Although it consumes a fair few lines, you can see they are quite simple and extremely logical to follow.

```
    objExcel.ActiveWorkbook.Close True, "C:\BegVBA\MnthSale.XLS"
    Set objChart = Nothing
    Set objExcel = Nothing
    DoCmd.Hourglass False
```

All that is left to do is close the workbook and quit. The first argument to the **Close** method is whether the workbook is to be saved, and the second is the filename. Note that this does not automatically overwrite the file if it already exists—a dialog is displayed asking for confirmation.

That's all there is to it. You can see that using Automation is not that hard—you just need to get used to the object hierarchy and then practice a little.

Try It Out—Combined OLE

We've looked at embedded and linked OLE objects and Automation, but we haven't yet seen the two combined. This example demonstrates how to manipulate an OLE object on a form through Automation, and since we've used Excel thus far, let's continue with it for a while longer.

All of this code is contained within the form **frmExcelChart**. This contains Automation and has been implemented using the **Property Get** and **Property Let** procedures.

1 Open the form **frmExcelChart**. You will see that it contains an embedded Excel chart of the Monthly Sales figures:

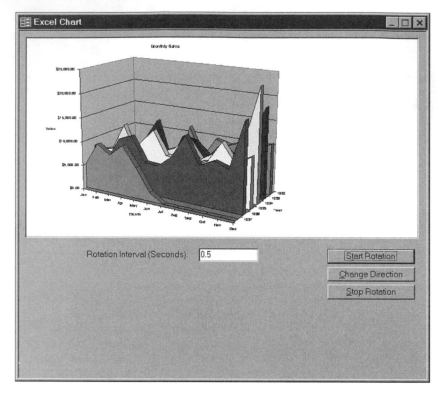

You can also see that there is a text box to specify the rotation time in seconds and three buttons—to start, stop and change the direction of rotation.

2 Try out the buttons to see what happens. Cool, huh! If this looks a bit flash, you will be surprised at how easy it is. Switch to Design view and have a look at the code.

How It Works

Start by having a look at the **General (Declarations)** section.

```
Private Const LEFT = 0
Private Const RIGHT = -1
Private Const DEFAULT_INTERVAL = 0.5

Private objChart        As Object
Private intDirection    As Integer
```

The code starts with a few module variables. The first three lines define some constants—two for the direction of rotation and one for the default rotation interval. The first variable defines an object variable to point to the chart object, and the second—an integer that will hold the current direction of rotation.

Now have a look at the new properties that have been added:

```
Public Property Let Direction(intDir As Integer)

    intDirection = intDir

End Property
```

This just sets the value of the variable to the required direction.

```
Public Property Let RotationInterval(dblInterval As Double)

    TimerInterval = dblInterval * 1000

End Property
```

This sets the value of the **TimerInterval**. It holds a figure in milliseconds and so has to be corrected for the figure of seconds that is being passed in. There are corresponding **Property Get** procedures for both of the above.

Now look at the new methods:

```
Public Sub RotationStart()

    RotationInterval = txtInterval

End Sub
```

The **RotationStart** procedure sets the value of the timer, by using the appropriate **Let** function. This in turn starts the rotation.

```
Public Sub RotationStop()

    RotationInterval = 0

End Sub
```

The **RotationStop** procedure sets the interval of the timer to 0, which stops any rotation.

```
Public Sub RotationDirectionChange()

    Direction = Not Direction

End Sub
```

RotationDirectionChange simply reverses the direction of rotation, by inverting the current direction. Since **0** and **-1** are used for the directions (hidden by the **LEFT** and **RIGHT** constants), the use of **Not** simply converts one to the other.

Now have a look at the code behind the command buttons:

```
Private Sub cmdStart_Click()

    Me.RotationStart

End Sub
```

To start the rotation, just call the start method. Similarly, to stop rotation, just call the stop method:

```
Private Sub cmdStop_Click()

    Me.RotationStop

End Sub
```

And to change direction—you guessed it—just call the **RotationDirectionChange** method:

```
Private Sub cmdChangeDirection_Click()

    Me.RotationDirectionChange

End Sub
```

Now to the meat of the code—the **Timer** event—which actually does the work of rotating the chart:

```
Private Sub Form_Timer()

    Dim intRot      As Integer
    Dim intAdd      As Integer
    Dim intLimit    As Integer

    intRot = objChart.Object.ActiveChart.Rotation

    If intDirection = LEFT Then
        intLimit = 0
        intAdd = -1
    Else
        intLimit = 44
        intAdd = 1
    End If

    If intRot = intLimit Then
        RotationDirectionChange
    Else
        objChart.Object.ActiveChart.Rotation = intRot + intAdd
    End If
    objChart.Action = acOLEUpdate

End Sub
```

The first thing to do is to get the current rotation value that is stored in the **Rotation** property of the chart. We use **objChart.Object** to point to the actual OLE object, rather than the control on the form. Since this could contain many other objects, we use **ActiveChart** to point to the currently active chart.

Next, decide upon the direction. If it is left, the value needs to be decreased by 1, and if it's right, the **Rotation** value needs increasing by 1.

Next, the current value is checked against the limit. The minimum value for **Rotation** is 0 and the maximum is 44. If the limit has been reached simply change direction. Otherwise, we increment or decrement the value (depending on the current direction) and update the object. The only thing left to do is to free the memory for the object variable when the form is closed:

```
Private Sub Form_Unload(Cancel As Integer)

    Set objChart = Nothing

End Sub
```

That's all there is to it—and you thought OLE was complicated. We've taken advantage of Excel's ability to display a chart at different rotations. All we have to do is update the argument that specifies the rotation angle we want each time the **Timer** event occurs.

Once again, this shows how powerful OLE can be with just a few simple commands. This could have been implemented with even less code but the property procedures make it more flexible.

The next few sections will show some of the other applications within Microsoft Office 97 that can be used as Automation servers, and the use to which they can be put. We are not going to examine the object models closely (remember, they are on the CD), but give you a taster of what's possible. An hors d'oeuvre, if you like, ready for you to cook the main course.

Try It Out—Creating a Letter in Word

The introduction of a full object model for Microsoft Word is a great leap forward for the programmer, and since this is new, we thought you might like to have an example. This example is going to create a letter in Word based upon a simple template. Create the code as detailed below, and then we'll have a look at how it works. If you're fed up with typing large amounts of code, you can find this code in the Word Functions module in **Whisky16.mdb**. Don't forget to add the reference to the Microsoft Word 8.0 Object Library, using the References option on the Tools menu.

1 Create a new module, and declare a constant in the declarations section

```
Private Const gconTemplate As String = "C:\BegVBA\Credit.DOT"
```

2 Create a new **Sub** called **CreditLetter**, and give it one argument:

```
Sub CreditLetter(lngPersonID As Long)
```

3 Now some variables:

```
Dim dbC         As Database             ' current database
Dim qryContact  As QueryDef             ' querydef of contact
Dim recContact  As Recordset            ' recordset of contact details
Dim objWord     As Word.Application     ' word object
Dim objDoc      As Object               ' document object
```

4 And now onto the code.

```
Set dbC = CurrentDb()
Set qryContact = dbC.QueryDefs("qryCompanyContacts")
qryContact.Parameters("PID") = lngPersonID
Set recContact = qryContact.OpenRecordset()
If recContact.EOF Then
    MsgBox "The person with an ID of " & lngPersonID & " could not be _
        found.", vbCritical, "Contact Not Found"
    Exit Sub
End If

' create word and a letter based on the template
Set objWord = New Word.Application
objWord.Visible = True
Set objDoc = objWord.Documents.Add(gconTemplate)

' fill in the details
InsertTextAtBookmark objWord, objDoc, "Contact", recContact("FullName")
InsertTextAtBookmark objWord, objDoc, "CompanyName", _
        recContact("CompanyName")
InsertTextAtBookmark objWord, objDoc, "Address", recContact("Address")
InsertTextAtBookmark objWord, objDoc, "Town", recContact("Town")
InsertTextAtBookmark objWord, objDoc, "PostCode", recContact("PostCode")
InsertTextAtBookmark objWord, objDoc, "Dear", recContact("FirstName")

' close up
objDoc.SaveAs "C:\BegVBA\CredLet"
objDoc.Close
objWord.Quit
recContact.Close
Set objDoc = Nothing
Set objWord = Nothing
```

5 That's it for this procedure, but next is another:

```
Sub InsertTextAtBookmark(objW As Object, objD As Object, strBkmk As _
        String, varText As Variant)

    ' select the required bookmark, and set the selection text
    objD.Bookmarks(strBkmk).Select
```

```
        objW.Selection.Text = varText

End Sub
```

6 Compile the module and save it as Word Functions. Open the Debug window and call the **CreditLetter** routine from the immediate pane:

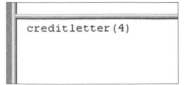

7 Now open Word and open the **CredLet** document that has just been created:

Pretty simple. Although this could have been accomplished by mail merge, this was created to give you an example of what can be done. Let's have a look at it in more detail.

How It Works

First, let's have a look at the Word template:

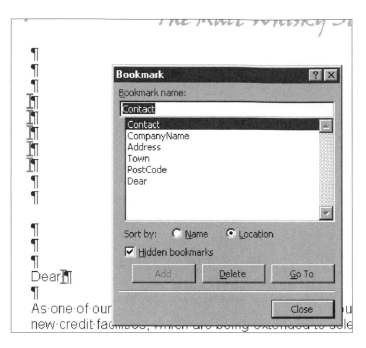

The icons that look like a large I are bookmarks, which act as placeholders (these bookmarks are only visible if the Bookmarks option has been selected under the View tab on the Options dialog, from the Tools menu in Word). There is one for the contact name, company name, address, town, zip code and first name of the contact. These will allow us to go to specific locations and insert text. Let's have a look at the code now.

We first create a constant for the credit letter template. This just makes it easy to change later.

```
Private Const gconTemplate As String = "C:\BegVBA\Credit.DOT"
```

Next we create a procedure and declare some variables:

```
Sub CreditLetter(lngPersonID As Long)

    Dim dbC          As Database           ' current database
    Dim qryContact   As QueryDef           ' querydef of contact
    Dim recContact   As Recordset          ' recordset of contact details
    Dim objWord      As Word.Application   ' word object
    Dim objDoc       As Object             ' document object
```

The first three variables should be familiar to you now; a database object, a querydef and a recordset, both for the contact details. The last two are the new ones. **objWord** is an object of type **Word.Application**—this will be the top level word object. **objDoc** will be used to store the Word document.

Now we can find the contact details:

```
Set dbC = CurrentDb()
Set qryContact = dbC.QueryDefs("qryCompanyContacts")
qryContact.Parameters("PID") = lngPersonID
Set recContact = qryContact.OpenRecordset()
If recContact.EOF Then
    MsgBox "The person with an ID of " & lngPersonID & _
      " could not be found.", _
      vbCritical, "Contact Not Found"
    Exit Sub
End If
```

You've seen this before. We open a connection to the database, and then open a query. This has a parameter so that we can select just one contact. The parameter name is **PID**. We then create a recordset based on this query, so we now have the contact details. Before continuing, we just check that a record exists in the recordset, and display a message if not.

Now comes the Word bits:

```
Set objWord = New Word.Application
objWord.Visible = True
Set objDoc = objWord.Documents.Add(gconTemplate)
```

First we create a new instance of Word, and set the **Visible** property to **True**. This allows us to see Word in action, as it normally starts hidden. Finally, we create a new **Document**. **Documents** is a collection of every document open in the instance of Word, and we have just added another to it. We pass in the template name, so that the new document is created based upon the template.

So now we have a document, we need to put some text into it.

```
InsertTextAtBookmark objWord, objDoc, "Contact", recContact("FullName")
InsertTextAtBookmark objWord, objDoc, "CompanyName", _
        recContact("CompanyName")
InsertTextAtBookmark objWord, objDoc, "Address", recContact("Address")
InsertTextAtBookmark objWord, objDoc, "Town", recContact("Town")
InsertTextAtBookmark objWord, objDoc, "PostCode", recContact("PostCode")
InsertTextAtBookmark objWord, objDoc, "Dear", recContact("FirstName")
```

This calls a new procedure to insert some text into a Word Bookmark. We pass into this procedure the **Word** object, the **Document** object, the Bookmark name and the text we want stored in the bookmark. We'll have a look at that procedure in a moment.

Now the data is in the document we can save and close it.

```
objDoc.SaveAs "C:\BegVBA\CredLet"
objDoc.Close
objWord.Quit
recContact.Close
Set objDoc = Nothing
Set objWord = Nothing
```

Firstly we save the document with the **SaveAs** method, using the name we wish to give the document. We then **Close** the **Document** object and **Quit** the **Word** object, close the recordset, and finally free up the memory use by the objects.

That's it for the main procedure, so let's look at **InsertTextAtBookmark**.

```
objD.Bookmarks(strBkmk).Select
objW.Selection.Text = varText
```

Bookmarks is a collection of the **Document** object (**objDoc** was passed into the procedure as the argument **objD**). This contains a list of all of the bookmarks in the document, as shown in the template earlier. Since we know the bookmark name, we can use this to index into the **Bookmarks** collection and use the **Select** method to select it. We then use the **Selection** object of Word and set the text to the required text. It's a simple as that.

Although a very simple example, you can see that you have a great deal of flexibility.

FYI If you look at the **Invoicing** module in the final Whisky database you will see how this can be harnessed. Although fairly complex, this module uses very similar techniques to read details from a recordset and insert the details into an invoice template. Where it differs is that instead of looking at specific bookmarks, it looks at every bookmark that exists in the document, and sees if there is a matching field in the recordset. If there is, the data from the recordset is inserted into the bookmark. This gives you a basic report writer, or a mail merge facility, allowing you to create recordsets full of data, and just select the bookmarks you require. If the code does not find a bookmark, then there is no error as the field is just ignored. Have a look at it, and use the techniques if you think they might work in an application you are writing.

Try It Out—Outlook

One of the great features of Office is Outlook—an integrated address book, diary, and mail application. Since it contains diary facilities, this could be used to add reminders, so that we can see when payment is due from orders. Once again we'll create it—and then have a look at how it works. Don't forget to add the reference for the Microsoft Outlook 8.0 Object Library.

1 Open the Outlook Functions module, and look at the procedure, **InvoiceReminder**; It has one argument:

```
Sub InvoiceReminder(strOrderNumber As String)
```

2 First, we declare some variables:

```
Dim objOutlook      As Outlook.Application      ' the outlook application
Dim objRem          As AppointmentItem          ' the new reminder
Dim qryI            As QueryDef                  ' the invoice query
Dim recI            As Recordset                 ' the invoice details
Dim datDue          As Date                      ' date payment due
```

3 And now the code:

```
Set dbC = CurrentDb()
Set qryI = dbC.QueryDefs("qryInvoiceDetails")
qryI.Parameters("OrderNum") = strOrderNumber
Set recI = qryI.OpenRecordset()
If recI.EOF Then
    MsgBox "This order was not found.  Please check the number and try _
            again", _
            0, "Order Not Found"
    Exit Sub
End If

Set objOutlook = New Outlook.Application
Set objRem = objOutlook.CreateItem(olAppointmentItem)

datDue = Format(recI("SentDate") + conMaxDelay - _
AveragePaymentDelay(recI("LocationID")), "dd-mmm-yyyy 10:00:00")
With objRem
    .Start = datDue
    .End = datDue
    .ReminderSet = True
    .ReminderOverrideDefault = True
    .Subject = "Payment Due: " & recI("CompanyName") _
                & vbCrLf & "Location: " & recI("LocationName") _
                & vbCrLf & "Order Number: " & recI("OrderNumber") _
                & vbCrLf & "Sent On: " & recI("SentDate")
    .Close(olSave)
End With

recI.Close
Set objRem = Nothing
Set objOutlook = Nothing
```

4 Run the procedure from the Debug window:

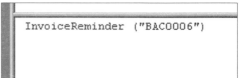

5 Now open Outlook and you should get an overdue reminder:

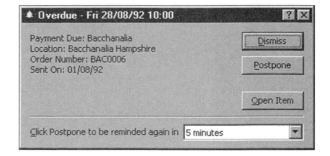

This pops up straight away because this is an old order and the appointment is in the past. However, with new orders it will only pop up when the date is reached.

> *Sometimes it may be necessary to have Outlook open before you run the code, in order that the Overdue notice be displayed. Otherwise, the notice is just displayed within the calendar somewhere in 1992!*

How It Works

This is very simple, but let's examine the code section by section. First, the procedure:

```
Sub InvoiceReminder(strOrderNumber As String)
```

This accepts an order number, which will be the order for which the reminder is to be created. Now the variables.

```
Dim objOutlook      As Outlook.Application      ' the outlook application
Dim objRem          As AppointmentItem          ' the new reminder
Dim qryI            As QueryDef                  ' the invoice query
Dim recI            As Recordset                 ' the invoice details
Dim datDue          As Date                      ' date payment due
```

The first is the Outlook Application object—you should be getting used to these now. The second is the **AppointmentItem** object, which will be used to create the reminder in Outlook. We then have **QueryDef** and **Recordset** objects for the invoice details, and lastly the due date. Now we have some variables we can get the invoice details:

```
Set dbC = CurrentDb()
Set qryI = dbC.QueryDefs("qryInvoiceDetails")
qryI.Parameters("OrderNum") = strOrderNumber
Set recI = qryI.OpenRecordset()
If recI.EOF Then
    MsgBox "This order was not found.  Please check the number and try _
           again", _
           0, "Order Not Found"
    Exit Sub
End If
```

This opens a recordset for the selected order number, displaying a message if the order is not found. OK, we now have the data, so let's create the reminder.

```
Set objOutlook = New Outlook.Application
Set objRem = objOutlook.CreateItem(olAppointmentItem)
```

Firstly we instantiate a new copy of Outlook, and use the **CreateItem** method to create a new item. The intrinsic constant **olAppintmentItem** tells **CreateItem** that we wish to create an appointment. Now that the appointment object is created, we can set some details for it.

```
datDue = Format(recI("SentDate") + conMaxDelay - _
AveragePaymentDelay(recI("LocationID")), "dd-mmm-yyyy 10:00:00")
```

The Whisky Shop has decided to use the average payment delay as part of its calculation for when payment is due. Thus the customers who pay quickly, actually get more time to pay next time. The function **AveragePaymentDelay** was already created for you and simply returns the average delay between the order being sent and the payment being received for that customer. This is then subtracted from a maximum value (45 in this case), giving a number of days, which is added to the sent date. It is on this new date that the payment is due. The date is formatted with a time of 10 o'clock in the morning, thus giving time for the post to arrive and be checked before the reminder pops up.

```
With objRem
    .Start = datDue
    .End = datDue
    .ReminderSet = True
    .ReminderOverrideDefault = True
```

Since this is only a reminder, the **Start** and **End** properties are set to the same date. These are the date and time that the appointment starts and ends. Then the **ReminderSet** property is set to **True** to force a reminder to pop up. We also set the **ReminderOverrideDefault** property to **True**, which forces the reminder on. This is necessary in this case as this is setting a reminder in the past, and Outlook disables reminders for these since the date has already gone.

```
    .Subject = "Payment Due: " & recI("CompanyName") _
             & vbCrLf & "Location: " & recI("LocationName") _
             & vbCrLf & "Order Number: " & recI("OrderNumber") _
             & vbCrLf & "Sent On: " & recI("SentDate")
    .Close(olSave)
End With
```

Lastly, for the reminder, we add some text. The **Subject** property is the Subject line in the reminder text, and we add a few of the order details to this before saving the reminder.

```
recI.Close
Set objRem = Nothing
Set objOutlook = Nothing
```

And finally the recordset is closed, and the object variables cleared.

As you can see this is extremely simple, and gives a great way of integrating diary functions into your Access applications. For another way of accomplishing this you might like to take a look at the Microsoft Exchange/Outlook Link Wizard, which we have provided on the CD. This is a standard Add-In supplied by Microsoft that enables you to link your Outlook items into Access, just like other linked items. You can have your diary, mail, contacts, etc., appearing as though they are normal Access tables, and you can then just use normal **Recordset**s to read and write data to and from them.

Try It Out—The Office Assistant

Finally, to end this section of examples into Automation, lets take a look at something really cool. You've probably used the Office Assistant by now, and whether you use it regularly or not, it is quite fun and useful for users. What you may not have realized is that this can be controlled using Automation too.

Try this little snippet of code, but make sure you add the Microsoft Office 8.0 Object Library to the references first.

```
Sub AnimateAssistant()

    With Access.Assistant
        .Visible = True
        .Animation = msoAnimationGoodbye
    End With

End Sub
```

Now call the procedure from the Debug window. Pretty cool, huh? I have to admit I laughed when I discovered this. It needs virtually no explanation. The **Assistant** is the object, **Visible** a property that just makes sure you can see your assistant, and **Animation** a method that you can set to one of several types. Have a go at some more—if you erase the equals sign and the type, a quick tip will appear showing you some more types. Try a few!

Although this is fun, it does have a serious function. It allows you to build on the standard functionality of Microsoft Office, and include it in your applications. Have a look at the Office Assistant module, and look at the **OfficeBox** function. One of the interesting features of the Assistant is that you can the Display Alerts option, which means that the Assistant takes over when message boxes appear. However, this only happens when the Assistant is active. The **OfficeBox** function works by checking for the Display Alerts property—if this is selected then the message is displayed in Assistant, and if not, then a standard message box is used. So, in your code, you could use **OfficeBox** everywhere you used to use **MsgBox**, and if the user has decided to use the Office Alerts, then the Assistant will pop up instead.

You can also create options from which the user can select—you can even replace some simple selection forms with the assistant. However, try not to go overboard. Remember that consistency is much better for the user than having one fancy module.

Access 97 as an OLE Server

Access 97 exposes its objects for use by other applications and these can be used from any language that can act as an Automation client, including Microsoft Excel, Microsoft Visual Basic, Microsoft Visual C++ and Microsoft Project.

We are not going to discuss Access as an OLE server in detail here. If you need to use Access in this way, you should use the same methods that have been used throughout this book. For example, in Microsoft Excel you could use:

```
Dim objAccess    As New Access.Application
```

Summary

This chapter has shown how you can use OLE to extend the power of your application. It has now become relatively simple to have automatically-updated graphs and spreadsheets on your forms, greatly increasing the potential of your application. The limits of OLE really lie with what you want it to do.

This chapter has covered how to:

▶ Embed and activate OLE objects within your Access databases

▶ Use ActiveX controls

▶ Use Automation objects that are hidden from the user and only exist in the code

▶ Use OLE objects (a.k.a. ActiveX controls) and Automation together to achieve impressive graphical results

▶ Integrate your application with the other programs in the Microsoft Office 97 suite

Hopefully, you've been convinced that all of these techniques are relatively simple and would easily benefit any applications you might create in the future.

Exercises

1 Create a procedure to output data to Microsoft Excel via Automation, and then create a Pivot Table from this data.

2 Use the Microsoft Exchange/Outlook Link Wizard to provide some diary facilities. Create a form based upon the Outlook Calendar to emulate a real calendar.

3 When adding a new contact, add an option that will include it in your Outlook Contacts at the same time.

The Internet

The Internet is probably the hottest, and most controversial, subject in the computer industry today. Many people see it as the savior of our society—the creation of a global community, with a wealth of information at our fingertips, 24 hours a day. Others see a Behemoth, waiting to swallow us whole once we've succumbed to its seductive wiles.

Whatever your view, the reality is that it's here, will be here for years to come, and, most importantly, can provide a useful business tool.

This chapter is going to look at how you can use the Internet features in Access 97. In particular we will be looking at:

- What the Internet is
- How to use Hyperlinks
- How to publish you data on the Internet
- Creating a Web Browser

What is the Internet?

The Internet is simply a collection of computers, all linked together—a very large collection, admittedly, but that's all. Before we look at how we can use the features of Access to connect to and from the Internet, let's look at a few definitions:

- HyperText Markup Language, **HTML**, is the format in which Internet documents are stored. It is a fairly simple language that was originally developed to layout text on the screen, providing formatting etc.. The hypertext feature allows different documents to be linked together, so that you can easily switch between documents, or follow links and references from one to another. HTML has evolved, and continues to do so, so that more and more features are built into it, but for the moment it's best just to think of it as the format for documents.

    For more information on how to write HTML documents, you may want to check out Instant HTML Programmer's Reference (ISBN 1-86100076-6), from Wrox Press.

> ▶ A **browser**, or web browser, is a program that displays HTML documents. The two most common are Microsoft Internet Explorer and Netscape Navigator.

> ▶ A **web site** is a computer (or computers) on the Internet that stores HTML documents. For example, the Wrox web site is `http://www.wrox.com`. The **www** stands for World Wide Web, which these days is just shortened to Web; **wrox** is the company name, and **com** stands for company or commercial. Other suffixes include **.edu** for educational establishments, such as universities and colleges, and **.gov** for government sites.

> ▶ A Uniform Resource Locator, or **URL**, is the name given to a particular web site, or to a document within it. The documents are stored in a fashion similar to your hard disk, with structured directories. So to have a look at the Access page at Microsoft, the URL would be: `http://www.microsoft.com/access`

A **web server** is the controlling machine at a web site. It accepts requests from web browsers and gives the browser the required document.

Protocols

To avoid confusion let's have a quick look at the main Internet protocols; what they are and how they work.

A protocol is just the name given by which computers can talk to each other. If you have a network, then the machines talk by way of a network protocol. When you talk to a machine on the Internet you are using a network protocol. Since the Internet can provide more than just HTML pages, there are also protocols that determine what you want to do. For example:

> ▶ When using a web browser to access HTML documents, you will be using the HyperText Transfer Protocol (**HTTP**). This is why URLs start with **http:**—this tells the web server you are talking to, what type of service you want.

> ▶ The other main protocol is the File Transfer Protocol (**FTP**). This allows you to download and upload programs and documents to a web server. In this case the URL would start with **ftp:**.

> ▶ The other protocol that you will probably use in Access is the **MailTo** protocol, which starts your email program to send mail messages. In this case a URL would start with **mailto:**.

There are many other protocols, but these are not as frequently used as the three we've listed.

The Hyperlink Data Type

Access 97 has a new data type to cope with the Internet facilities—the **Hyperlink**. This allows a URL to be entered as a field in a table, or a field on a form. This data type can take three pieces of information; some display text, an address and a sub address.

> ▶ The display text is the text you want to display. You have probably noticed when browsing the web that many links have some descriptive text rather than sharing the actual URL.

▶ The address is the actual URL of the item to be viewed.

▶ The sub-address is the section within the item.

The three parts are separated by the hash sign, so a **Hyperlink** looks like this:

> *Display Text#Address#Sub Address*

Let's look at some examples to see this more clearly.

URL	Displays	Action taken
`http://www.microsoft.com`	http://www.microsoft.com	Jumps to the Microsoft home page
`Microsoft on the Web #www.microsoft.com#`	Microsoft on the Web	Jumps to the Microsoft home page
`Hyperlinks#C:\Wrox\ BegVBA97\Internet.doc# Hyperlinks`	Hyperlinks	Open the document `C:\Wrox\BegVBA97\ Internet.doc` and jump to the bookmark `Hyperlinks`
`Whiskies#C:\Wrox\ BegVBA97\Whisky.mdb#Form frmMaintWhisky`	Whiskies	Open the form `frmMaintWhisky` in the database `C:\Wrox\ BegVBA97\Whisky.mdb`
`Whiskies## Form frmMaintWhisky`	Whiskies	Open the form `frmMaintWhisky` in the current database

Notice that the hyperlink data type does not restrict URLs to just HTML documents. You can also point to Word documents, Spreadsheets, Access forms, etc., giving you a great deal of flexibility. With the ability to open forms, you could even replace code behind buttons that open other forms with a hyperlink address. This would open a new form without the use of any code.

How to use Hyperlinks

Think how useful it could be if your application could contain hyperlinks, so users, with a click of the mouse, can be transported to a web site. Fortunately this is extremely simple, as Access provides a **Hyperlink** type, that can be included in tables and forms.

Try It Out—Adding a Hyperlink to a Table

1 Open the **Whisky17** database and open the **Whisky** table in Design view.

2 Add a new field of type **Hyperlink**, and call it **WebSite**.

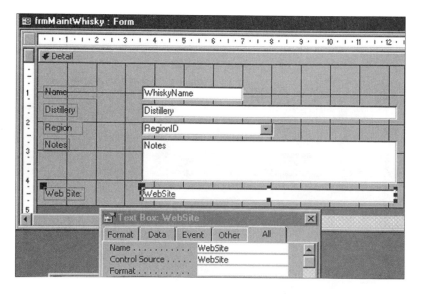

Whisky : Table

Field Name	Data Type
WhiskyID	AutoNumber
WhiskyName	Text
Distillery	Text
RegionID	Number
Label	OLE Object
Notes	Memo
WebSite	Hyperlink

3   Save the table and switch to table view. Find the Macallan whisky and add the following to the new WebSite field

http://www.regionlink.com/grampian/macallan/macallan.html/

This is the URL to the web site of the Macallan Malt Page.

4   Notice that once you've typed it in, when you place the cursor over this field it changes to a hand.

Whisky : Table

RegionID	Label	Notes	WebSite
Speyside		This is one of few distilleries to persist in the use of sherry casks for maturation of the whisky. It has long been one of the best-selling malts in England.	http://www.regionlink.com/grampian/macallan/macallan.html

5   If you have a connection to the Internet try clicking. Your web browser will be loaded and the appropriate site connected to. Notice that once a URL is entered you cannot click in the field to edit it. You will have to click into the previous field and press the *Tab* key to move into the WebSite field.

6   Close the table, open the form **frmMaintWhisky**, and add this new field to the form.

538

7 Now switch to Form view, and you can see you now have the **Hyperlink** as part of your form. Click this and your browser is launched as before.

Try It Out—Unbound Hyperlinks

As well as having hyperlinks stored in the table, they can be added on other controls to forms. The Command Button, Image and Label all support the new properties, so let's see these in action.

1 Open the form **frmSwitchboard** in Design view. This is the main menu form, to which we are going to add a web address.

2 Click on the image of Scotland, view the properties and add the following to the ControlTip Text property.

> **Click to jump to the Scottish Malt Whisky Society home page**

3 Now move to the top of the list and notice the two new properties:

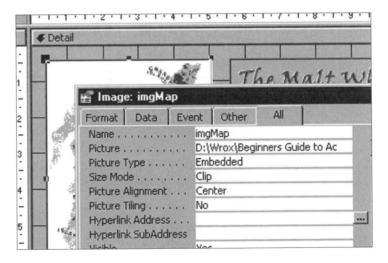

You can either type in a URL directly, or press the builder button to the right of the field to bring up the Insert Hyperlink window, where you can either enter the URL or browse for local HTML documents.

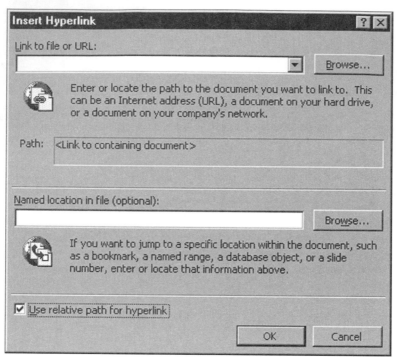

4 Enter the following into the Link to file or URL field.

www.smws.com

You can ignore the **http://** if you like, as this is added for you.

5 Press OK to close the dialog, save the form and switch to Form view. Notice how the cursor changes when you are over the image, and the status bar shows you the URL.

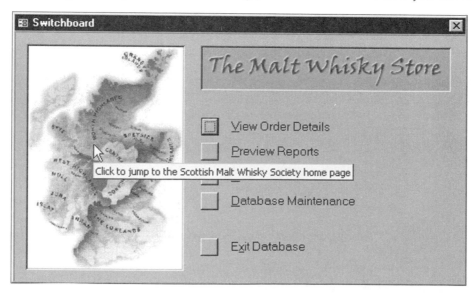

You can use the same technique for command buttons and labels.

That's all there is to adding hyperlinks to tables and forms in your application. You can see how this can be useful for providing links to related information, or even a list of web sites of your customers.

Hyperlinks from VBA

Now you have seen how easy it is to add hyperlinks to you tables and forms, you might be wondering how you can use these within your code. Well, the **Hyperlink** data type has several methods and properties, just like other objects.

Item	Type	Description
Hyperlink	Property	A property of the control bound to the hyperlink column that refers to the actual hyperlink object.
Address	Property	The main hyperlink address.
SubAddress	Property	The hyperlink sub-address.
Follow	Method	Follow the hyperlink to its destination. The same as clicking the control.
AddToFavorites	Method	Add the hyperlink to the Favorites folder.
FollowHyperLink	Method	Follow a hyperlink directly from the address. For use with controls that do not support the **HyperlinkAddress** property.
HyperlinkPart	Method	Parse the hyperlink into its constituent parts.

Because of the simplicity of using hyperlinks from tables and forms, you may not need to use the above functions from VBA code. As you have seen, clicking on a hyperlink in Access is the same as if you were viewing a web page with a hyperlink. However, there may be times when you want to manipulate hyperlink with code—and you can do this with the above methods, which are extremely simple to use.

The one that can make life a little simpler, though, is the **HyperlinkPart** function.

Try It Out—The HyperlinkPart Function

You have noticed that you cannot click into a hyperlink field without it following the link. But what happens when you need to edit a hyperlink? The only way is to tab into the field, which is a little cumbersome. Let's add a little builder form to help.

1 Open the form **frmMaintWhisky** in Design view and add a new button to the right of your **WebSite** field. Call it **cmdBuild**, and use a Caption of three dots, just like other builder buttons.

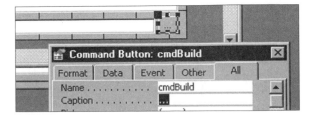

2 Since we are dealing with hyperlinks, let's use them instead of code to open a builder form. Add the following to the Hyperlink SubAddress property:

```
Form frmHyperlink
```

3 Save the form and close it. Create new blank form, and add three text boxes; **txtDisplayedValue**, **txtAddress**, **txtSubAddress** and a command button, **cmdClose**. Don't forget to give them captions.

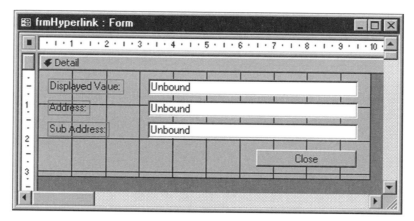

4 Now go to the **On Load** event for the form, and enter the following code:

```
Dim strHyperlink          As String

strHyperlink = Forms!frmMaintWhisky!WebSite

txtDisplayedValue = HyperlinkPart(strHyperlink, acDisplayedValue)
txtAddress = HyperlinkPart(strHyperlink, acAddress)
txtSubAddress = HyperlinkPart(strHyperlink, acSubAddress)
```

5 Now add the following code to the **Click** event for the Close button:

```
Dim strAddress          As String

strAddress = txtAddress
If LCase(Left$(strAddress, 7)) <> "http://" Then
    strAddress = "http://" & txtAddress
End If

Forms!frmMaintWhisky!WebSite = txtDisplayedValue & "#" & _
    strAddress & "#" & txtSubAddress
DoCmd.Close
```

6 Compile the code and save the form as frmHyperlink.

7 Open the form **frmMaintWhisky** in Form view and find The Macallan whisky again. This is the one that you typed the web address into earlier. Press the builder button to see the new form.

Notice that because there is no specific display value, the address is used.

8 Type over the displayed value with some nicer text, and press the Close button to return to the previous form.

Now you can see more meaningful text, but the hyperlink address stays the same. You can check this by placing the cursor over the Web Site field and looking at the status bar—it shows the web address.

How It Works—The HyperlinkPart function

Let's have a look at the code for when the form loads.

Firstly we declare a string and place the details from the **WebSite** field into it.

```
Dim strHyperlink         As String

strHyperlink = Forms!frmMaintWhisky!WebSite
```

Then we use the **HyperlinkPart** function to break down the hyperlink into its three constituent parts, and put these into the text boxes.

```
txtDisplayedValue = HyperlinkPart(strHyperlink, acDisplayedValue)
txtAddress = HyperlinkPart(strHyperlink, acAddress)
txtSubAddress = HyperlinkPart(strHyperlink, acSubAddress)
```

This function takes two arguments. The first is the hyperlink, and the second is the part of the hyperlink to return. The three values are intrinsic constants, and return the display text, the hyperlink address and the hyperlink sub-address.

Now we need the code to close the form. The first thing is to check that the beginning of the address is correct, so we declare a string and check it against **http://**. This should always be at the front of a valid hyperlink address, so if it's not there we add it.

543

```
Dim strAddress          As String

strAddress = txtAddress
If LCase(Left$(strAddress, 7)) <> "http://" Then
    strAddress = "http://" & txtAddress
End If
```

Once the address is checked, we can combine the three parts, using the # symbol to separate them, and place them back into the **WebSite** field.

```
Forms!frmMaintWhisky!WebSite = txtDisplayedValue & "#" & _
    strAddress & "#" & txtSubAddress
DoCmd.Close
```

That's it. Now you have an easy way to edit the hyperlink address.

Linking HTML Documents

You have previously seen how data from other applications can be linked into Access to provide you with another table, but you may not know that this can also be done with HTML documents. HTML can display tables, which are a bit like Word tables, and Access can link these in, just as it can with other types of data.

Try It Out—Linking an HTML Table

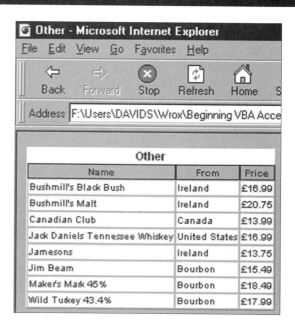

Although the Whisky Shop specializes in Malt Whiskies, they occasionally get requests to supply other whiskies. However, they do not keep these in stock, nor keep them amongst their price list. The Whisky Shop recently provided a list of these other whiskies on their web site, and decided that it would be useful to link these into their main application.

1 Close any forms you have open, and from the main database window select the File menu, then the Link Tables... option from the Get External Data option.

2 From the Open dialog, select HTML Documents from the Files of type field. Make sure you are pointing at the directory where you installed the sample files, and select the HTML document titled **Other**.

3 Now press the Link button to start the Link HTML Wizard.

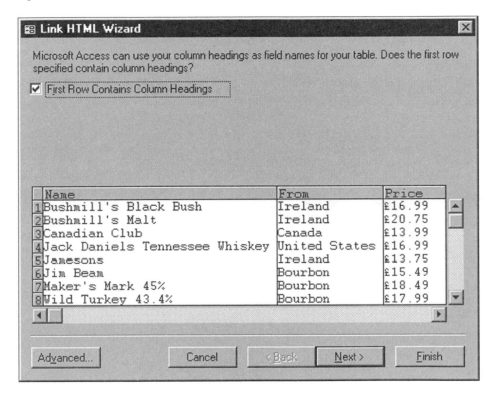

Make sure you have the First Row Contains Column Headings selected, so that the column headings are not included as part of the data. Notice that the HTML table is shown as a list of fields and rows.

4 Press the Next button.

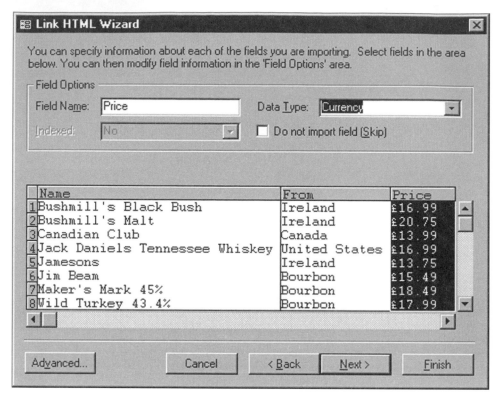

Select the Price column and set the Data Type to Currency.

5 Press Next again, and enter a table name. This will be the name that appears in Access. You can then press the Finish button, and press OK to close the notice dialog.

6 Open the table and you'll see it's just like any other table, except that it is not updatable.

Name	From	Price
Bushmill's Black Bush	Ireland	£16.99
Bushmill's Malt	Ireland	£20.75
Canadian Club	Canada	£13.99
Jack Daniels Tennessee Whiskey	United States	£16.99
Jamesons	Ireland	£13.75
Jim Beam	Bourbon	£15.49
Maker's Mark 45%	Bourbon	£18.49
Wild Turkey 43.4%	Bourbon	£17.99

Since the Internet is so popular, there is a great deal of information being published in HTML format. This method of linking allows you to quickly get access to some of that information without having to retype it.

Publishing on the Web

Now that you have seen that data can be linked from outside sources, you may be wondering how to get your data out to the waiting world. Access makes this very easy, but once again we need a few definitions before we start.

Static HTML Documents

A static HTML page is an HTML document that stands alone, showing data at the time the document was created. It is not linked to a database, and does not reflect any changes in the database. To update the data in a static HTML document, you have to recreate the document. Static HTML documents are fine for general text, but for database information they are a bit like snapshots, not showing the latest data. These have the **.html** suffix, and can be used on any web server.

You can save tables, queries, forms and reports to static HTML documents. For reports the formatting is kept, and the resulting document will look much like the report, but for the other object types, the document will look like a datasheet.

There are two ways to save data as an HTML document. The first is to select the item, and then select the Save As/Export... option from the File menu. Then pick To an External File or Database option from the following dialog.

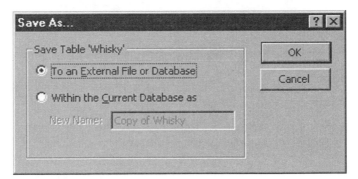

This shows the standard Save dialog. Change the Save as type option to HTML Documents.

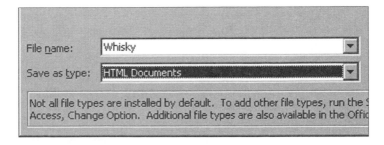

Enter a filename, and press Export button, and that's it. You can now open the file in a web browser. One thing to watch for is that any lookup fields only show their ID numbers, and not the lookup data. This is much the same as exporting the table to another database that was shown in chapter 8.

The HTML Export Wizard

The other way to export to HTML documents is to use the HTML Export Wizard. From the File menu, this time pick Save as HTML to launch the wizard. This guides you through the creation process, allowing you to pick the objects to save, and what type of export you require. There are various other options to allow you to pick templates, an ODBC data source or Access database, and where you want the document to be placed.

We are not going to delve into this, but the wizard brings together the three methods of saving to HTML documents into one central place.

Try It Out—Creating a Static HTML Document

1 Open the form **frmOutsideWorld** in Design view, and add another option button to the group. Checks its **Option Value** property is set to 7. Add the text to the label as shown.

2 For the **Click** event on the **Export** button add the following code to the bottom of the **Select Case** Statement.

```
DoCmd.OutputTo acOutputQuery, "qryWhiskyAndPrices", _
    acFormatHTML, "C:\BegVBA\Whisky.HTML"
```

3 Compile and save the form, then switch to Form view. Select the new option and press the Export button to create the document.

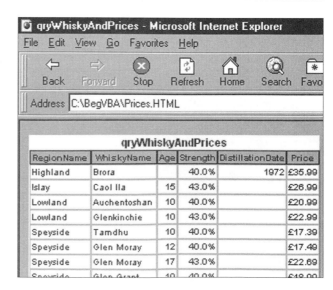

RegionName	WhiskyName	Age	Strength	DistillationDate	Price
Highland	Brora		40.0%	1972	£35.99
Islay	Caol Ila	15	43.0%		£26.99
Lowland	Auchentoshan	10	40.0%		£20.99
Lowland	Glenkinchie	10	43.0%		£22.99
Speyside	Tamdhu	10	40.0%		£17.39
Speyside	Glen Moray	12	40.0%		£17.49
Speyside	Glen Moray	17	43.0%		£22.69
Speyside	Glen Grant	10	40.0%		£18.00

It's as simple as that. If you have Microsoft Internet Information Server you might like to try the IDC and ASP options too, and these are described in more detail below.

Internet Data Connector

The Internet Database Connector (IDC) enables you to display a dynamic page, created from an HTML document that queries the database for the data, and therefore shows current data. Every time the page is opened, or refreshed, the database is requeried. The database can be any valid ODBC data source, but the web server must be Microsoft Internet Information Server (IIS). Two files are required for this, a **.idc** file and a **.htx** file.

For IDC files you can export tables, queries and forms, although they will all look like datasheets. You follow the same method as for static HTML documents, but this time select Microsoft IIS 1-2 in the Save as type field.

 Don't worry if you have IIS 3, as IDC files work with that and the latest version too.

File name:	Whisky
Save as type:	Microsoft IIS 1-2

Not all file types are installed by default. To add other file types, run the S
Access, Change Option. Additional file types are also available in the Offic

Press the Export button to see the following dialog.

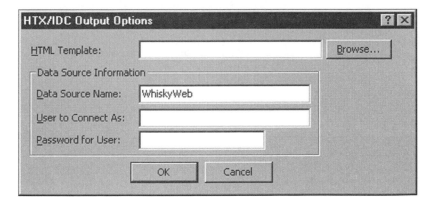

This allows you to select a template, but more importantly, the ODBC data source details. This is necessary so that when the document is opened, it has the correct details to connect to the database.

Active Server Pages

Active Server Pages, IDC's successor, is a technology for the creation of dynamic pages, as they show the database in its current state. But unlike the IDC they can emulate forms, allowing data to be entered, edited and deleted from a web page. The data can be from any ODBC data source, but, again, the web server must be Internet Information Server, this time at least Version 3.0, with Active Server Pages installed. Active Server Pages are stored with the **.asp** suffix, and, unlike the IDC method that creates two files, this only creates one per datasheet.

For ASP files you can export tables, queries and forms. Tables and queries are shown as datasheets, but forms are shown as HTML forms, that look very similar to your Access forms. Controls on the form are replaced with ActiveX controls, although the VBA code behind the form is not converted.

To position the controls on the HTML page, Access uses the Microsoft HTML Layout control. This is shipped with Internet Explorer 3.0 or later (and is available from the Microsoft web site), but does not run alone. This means that to create ASP pages you need IE 3.0, or later.

Listed below are the Access controls that are replaced by ActiveX controls, and how the replacement is handled.

Access Control	Corresponding ActiveX Control
Text box	Text box
Text box control bound to a Hyperlink field	Text box that displays the hyperlink text. However the hyperlink can't be followed.
List box	List box (single-column only)
Combo box	Combo box
Label	Label. If the label has **HyperlinkAddress** and/or **HyperlinkSubAddress** properties set, a hyperlink is created for the label.
Command button	Command button, but any code behind the button isn't saved. If the command button has **HyperlinkAddress** and/or **HyperlinkSubAddress** properties set, a hyperlink is created for the button.
Option group	Option group, but without a group frame
Option button	Option button
Check box	Check box
Toggle button	Toggle button
ActiveX control	ActiveX control, but any code behind the control isn't saved.

The following controls are not converted when saving a form as an ASP file and so are ignored:

- Tab controls
- Rectangles
- Lines

⬥ Page breaks

⬥ Unbound object frames

⬥ Bound object frames

⬥ Image controls

⬥ The background of a form set with the Picture property

Despite the fact there is some lack in functionality, you actually get a very serviceable form.

To save data as an ASP file you use the same method as before, but this time select Microsoft Active Server Pages in the Save as type field.

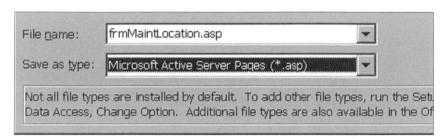

Press the Export button to see the following dialog.

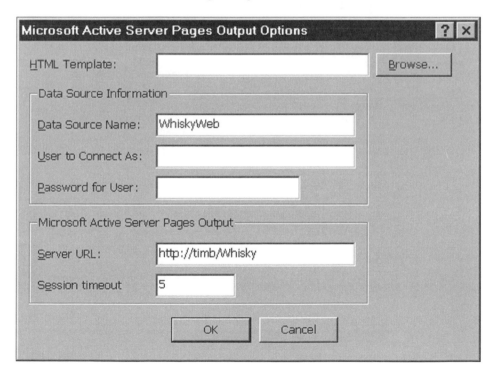

Once again there is space to enter the HTML template and ODBC data source details, but there is also a field for the address of the server. This should be the full address of where the document will be stored. Here, it's the address for an installation of Personal Web Server, which also supports the Active Server Pages.

If you have saved a form, you can open IE 3.0 to see it:

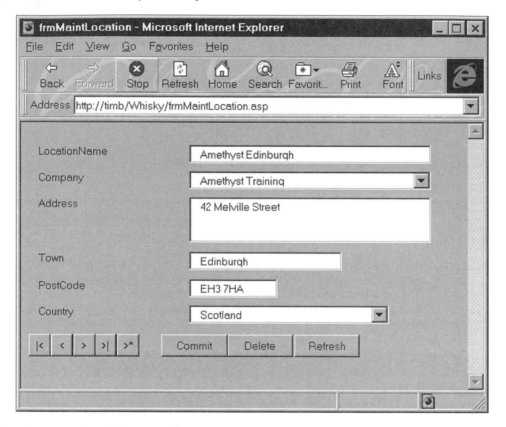

Although not perfect this goes a long way to providing web-based applications.

Creating a Browser

So far you have seen how easy it is to publish your Access data on the web, but what if you want to include web functionality in your applications. Well, that's very simple too, as Microsoft provides a Web Browser Control that can be added to your forms. This allows you to have a browser on your forms, instead of launching a separate one. One warning however—you must have Internet Explorer 3.0 or later installed to use this control.

Try It Out—A Web Browser

1 Open the table **Company** in Design view and add a new field call **WebSite**, of type **HyperLink**. Save and close the table.

2 Open the form **frmMaintCompany** in Design view. Resize the form so it's a little bigger.

3 Select the More Controls button from the Toolbox.

4 Now scroll down by placing the cursor over the arrow at the bottom of the form that pops up, and select the Microsoft Web Browser Control.

5 Add this to the form, just like any other control. You might need to resize the form to fit this in property. Name the control **ctlBrowser**.

6 Add a command button just above it, called **cmdWeb**, and give it a caption of **View Web Page**.

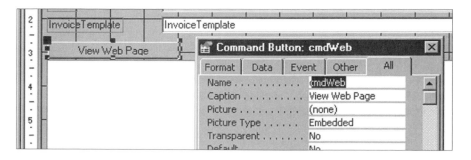

553

7 View the code for the **Click** event for the new button and add the following line of code.

```
ctlBrowser.Navigate HyperlinkPart(Me!WebSite, acAddress)
```

This uses the **Navigate** method of the browser control to navigate to the hyperlink. We use **HyperlinkPart** to extract the actual address from the **WebSite** field.

8 Close the form and save it.

9 Open the table Company, and add the following to the WebSite field for Bacchanalia:

```
file://C:\\BegVBA\\bacch.htm
```

This points to the Bacchanalia home page, stored locally on your disk.

10 Now open **frmMaintCompany** in Form view, and move to the record for Bacchanalia and press the View Web Page button. The browser will be filled with the web page.

Unfortunately there are some problems with the Browser control, and Internet Explorer 3.0. You might notice that it does not seem to size properly, so the web page does not look correct, and it does not refresh correctly. It will also look much better if you point it to a web site using **http** rather than **file**. These are known problems and will hopefully be sorted soon.

Despite the problems, the Web Browser control can view HTML documents that include any of the following:

- Standard HTML and HTML enhancements, such as floating frames and cascading style sheets
- Other ActiveX controls
- Most Netscape plug-ins
- Scripting, such as Microsoft Visual Basic Scripting Edition (VBScript) or JavaScript
- Java applets
- Multimedia content, such as video and audio playback
- Three-dimensional virtual worlds created with Virtual Reality Modeling Language (VRML)
- Microsoft Office Documents

I suspect this control would be more useful for intranet applications, where you have a chance to mix content. For those people with existing Access applications, but who are developing new Internet/intranet based applications, then this could pave the way for a mixed application during migration.

Summary

This chapter has shown some of the Internet facilities that are available in Access 97. The increased use of the Internet in everyday life and the general public awareness means that features like this will continue to be added and improved upon.

This chapter has covered:

▶ Hyperlinks and their use in Access

▶ How to import and export HTML documents

▶ How to create a Web Browser within Access

Exercises

1 Create a procedure that creates an HTML price list, once a week, for uploading to a web site.

2 If you have access to a web server running Microsoft Internet Information Server or Microsoft Peer Web Services, then create and IDC file so that the price list would always be correct.

Finishing Touches

In this final chapter, we take a quick look at a few of the things that we can do with our code to make sure that it is totally ready for release into a testing or production environment. They are things which are easily forgotten, but which can make a significant difference to the maintainability, performance and general 'polish' of your application.

We will start with a quick look at how we can tidy up our code through a final code review, to ensure that it is suitably commented, that all the error handling has been put in and all the dead code stripped out.

After that, we will look at the mechanics of code compilation and why it is so important both during the development process and once an application has been delivered into the production environment.

Finally, we will look briefly at the Windows Registry and how we can use it to store user preferences and gather usage statistics.

Tidying Up Code

It is always a good idea to review your application once you have finished the coding. This gives you a chance to tidy up the code and make sure that all the loose ends are tied up. During this final perusal, there are three main areas that you should be checking. You should make sure that:

- All the code is suitably commented
- Every procedure contains appropriate error handling
- All unused code has been deleted

Now no-one is saying that this is going to be great fun! If it were, you wouldn't need to check it in the final code review because you would have already done it! But even though it isn't the most exciting thing you will do, this final perusal is a very important process to undertake, if you want to deliver a polished application.

Check the Comments

It is very rare that the code behind an application, once written, will never be seen again. For a start, applications are seldom—if ever—perfect and most will need to be enhanced or re-written at some stage. Even if an application is perfectly suitable at the time it is delivered, business imperatives and the surrounding technology change. These are both powerful forces that contribute to the premature obsolescence of untended applications. Another reason for revisiting your code is that you may want to see how you did something last time so you can do it again in another database.

In both these situations you will be very grateful indeed if the code you are looking at is commented. It may seem like a chore to add comments at the time that you are writing the code but, believe me, it is a lot more boring putting them all in at the end! And it is even worse trying to wade through pages of uncommented code, trying to understand whether the reason that the code is so obscure is because the person who originally wrote it was exceptionally far-sighted and was avoiding problems which you can't see, or whether he just didn't know what he was doing. (And it's particularly annoying when you wrote the code yourself!)

But it is not enough simply to comment your code. There are, as with most things in life, two ways to comment a piece of code—a right way and a wrong way. There are four key dangers to watch out for when commenting code. We'll have a quick look at them now:

Too Few Comments

One of the problems we all come across when we add comments to our code is to know just how much detail to put into our comments. After all, it is to be hoped that **we** will know why we are doing what we are doing and in that situation it is sometimes hard to put yourself in the mind of someone who doesn't know. So be generous with your comments.

As a general guide, you should insert comments for four reasons:

> At the start of a procedure to identify who wrote the procedure, when it was written and what it does

> To identify a new logical step in the procedure

> To illuminate logic that operates in an unexpected manner

> To explain obscure or infrequently encountered procedures or syntax

The first two types of comment are useful for someone browsing through our code who wants to quickly get the gist of what our code is doing. The third type of code is useful for someone wanting to understand the intricacies of our program and to warn later revisers of our code that we did know what we were doing when we wrote it like this!

Too Many Comments

Of course, the other danger is to litter our code with too many comments. Don't comment the obvious. As a rule, you shouldn't need to comment variable declarations or simple variable assignations. (If you start commenting **Next** statements, something is going badly wrong!) Comments should always illuminate your code and having too many comments in a procedure can make the logic of code very difficult to follow.

Out of Date Comments

Another all too frequent tendency is to let our comments get out of date. When we modify code, we should also modify the comments to indicate what has changed. If the comments in a procedure are out of date, then they can be worse than useless.

Inconsistent Comments

Get into the habit of using a standard layout for the comments in your code. For example, you might place a header at the top of each procedure that looks like this:

```
'*****************************************************************************
'Purpose:       To determine the current screen resolution
'Parameters:    None
'Returns:       String variable indicating screen resolution (e.g. _
                640x480)
'Created By:    Robert Smith
'Created On:    01 Jul 97
'Comments:      This uses the APIs call GetDesktopWindow and _
                GetWindowRect
'               which need to be declared for this procedure to run
'*****************************************************************************
```

If your procedure headers all look the same it makes it much easier for those reading your code to **quickly** get to grips with what the procedures are meant to do.

Another area of consistency is in the use of block comments as opposed to inline comments.

```
'This is a block comment
Set rec = db.OpenRecordset(sSQL)
rec.MoveLast
lngCount = rec.RecordCount                  'This is an inline comment
rec.Close
```

I tend to prefer block comments on the grounds that they are neater and less liable to disappear off the right side of the page when printed or viewed on a screen with a low resolution. But whichever style you prefer, you should try to stick to it wherever possible. After all, it is a lot easier to read comments if you know where to look for them.

Check Error Handling

We looked in Chapter 11 at the need for error handling and how to best implement it. When you are reviewing your code at the end of the coding cycle, you should also make sure that all of your procedures contain appropriate error handlers. A typical error handler might look like this:

```
On Error GoTo MyFunc_Err

... main body of procedure
```

```
MyFunc_Exit:
    Exit Function

MyFunc_Err:
    Select Case Err.Number
        Case 3014
            MyFunc = False
        Case Else
            Call GlobalErr("MyFunc", Err.Number)
            Resume MyFunc_Exit
            Resume
    End Select
```

We need to review our code and ensure that all procedures have appropriate error handlers—but this does not mean that this is the best time to insert error handling. Always try to insert your error handlers when you first write the procedure. After all, the insertion of error handling can profoundly alter both the program flow within a procedure and the values that it might return. So, if you do add error handlers at this late stage of proceedings, you should test thoroughly the results that your code then produces.

> *The Procedure Wrapper add-in, which is on the disk accompanying this book, can be used to insert both error handlers and standard comment headers into new procedures and can be customized to suit your own preferences. For more information on using the Procedure Wrapper add-in, have a look at Chapter 14 where it is described in more detail.*

Delete Unused Code

A final task to undertake during your code review is the removal of unused procedures. If we are honest, most coding is a process of trial and error. It's just that the better you get, the fewer errors you make and the fewer trials you need. Even so, it is not unusual to find one's modules littered with the carcasses of defunct procedures that are either no longer used or never completed.

There is no place for these unused procedures in the production version of an application. Not only do they take up memory when the module they are in is loaded, but they can also be misleading for anyone browsing the code and trying to understand what the code does. So get rid of them.

> *One of the most frequent ways in which unused code is generated is when we delete a control that has an event handler but then do not delete the event handler code. This condemns the orphaned event-handler code to a purgatorial existence in the* **(General)** *section of the form's class module until either the code is deleted or it is associated with a new control of the same name. To avoid this situation, make sure that you delete event-handler code when you delete controls on forms or reports.*

If you want, you can move all of these unused procedures into a separate module and then save the module to a text file for future reference. But whatever happens, you should compile and then test the application after you have removed the unused procedures to check that they were really unused....

Compiling

We saw earlier in the book how compiling our code can alert us to any errors we may have made in our code. Some errors can be detected by Access as we are writing our code. For example, let's suppose we type the following line of code in a module:

```
docmd openform "frmSwitchboard"
```

As soon as we try to move off this line of code onto a new line, Access will alert us with a message box informing us that the line of code contains a syntax error.

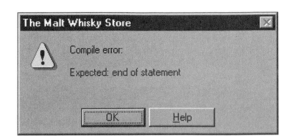

In this case, the error was generated because we missed out the period between the words **DoCmd** and **OpenForm**. Despite the misleading message box which Access displays, this isn't really a compile error; it is a **syntax** error. By default, Access will check the syntax of every line of code you enter and flag any errors it notices like the one above. If you want to, you can disable this automatic syntax checking by unchecking the Auto Syntax Check box on the Module tab of the Tools/Options... dialog.

Be wary of disabling automatic syntax checking. There are occasions when it can be useful to disable it. For example, you might be pasting a large chunk of code from, let's say, Visual Basic 3 into the module window and you know it will need a fair bit of rework before it will work in Access. In that case you won't want message boxes appearing every time you move from one line to another.

But in most other situations, you will want automatic syntax checking enabled. The majority of the errors it determines are genuine mistakes and are much more easily corrected on the spot.

Whereas syntax errors are easily recognizable as soon as they occur, there are other types of error that can creep into our code that cannot be detected until later on. For example, what if we create a **Do...Loop** structure and forget to put the **Loop** statement at the end? We certainly wouldn't want Access to flag the error when we move off the line containing the **Do** statement. So when should these errors be detected? The answer is that these are compile errors and are detected when all the code is fully compiled. We'll look now at what compilation actually involves and the implications of the different types of compilation afforded to us by Access. Then we'll look at ways of compiling our code programmatically.

What is Compilation?

So what happens when a code module in Access is compiled? Normally when programmers talk about compiling an application, they mean that the human-readable code is converted into native machine-readable code that can be executed directly. Access works slightly differently, in that the Visual Basic code that we write is not converted directly into machine-readable code but is instead converted into an intermediate format called p-code. When the application is run, the p-code is interpreted (i.e. translated into machine-readable code) line-by-line by a run-time DLL.

Many developers regard p-code as an unnecessary evil and bemoan the performance degradation that results from VBA not being compiled into native machine code. In point of fact, although native code can be substantially faster than interpreted p-code for computationally-intensive operations, which rearrange lots of bits and bytes all over the place, most of the VBA code we write is no slower in p-code than native code. After all, the VBA functions we use already reside in a run-time library which is highly optimized, so there won't be too much overhead there. And, in any case, once you start calling subprocedures, DLLs or other objects, the overhead of setting up things like stack frames makes the difference between p-code and native code performance negligible. Add to that the fact that the average application spends less than 5% of the time running code and you will see that the p-code versus natively compiled argument doesn't hold that much water when it comes to Access. (With Visual Basic it's a different argument as you are more likely to write apps in VB that are computationally-intensive and would therefore benefit from native machine code compilation—and that is why VB 5 Professional and Enterprise Editions now let you do just that.)

All the same, the process of compilation still causes the code we have written to be checked for syntax and integrity. And it's that stage of the process that is most noticeable to us. **If** structures without an **End If**, variables that haven't been declared, calls to procedures that don't exist—these are all the types of error that are detected and flagged to us when we compile our code. In fact, the whole process of checking the syntax and integrity of the code and then compiling it into p-code can be quite lengthy, especially where large amounts of code are involved.

> *If compiling code takes time and highlights errors in our code, the corollary is that uncompiled code will be slow to execute (all code must be compiled first before it is run) and may contain bugs. So, get into the habit of regularly compiling your code and **always** compile it before you distribute a finished application.*

How do we Compile Code?

If you open a code module and look at the Debug item on the menu bar, you will see that there are three commands available for compiling your code. Which of these should we use?

And then there is the Compile On Demand option on the Module tab of the Tools/Options... dialog. What exactly does that mean—and when should we use it?

Compile Loaded Modules

Well, to start with, the Compile Loaded Modules menu command does just what it says. It compiles the procedures in all the code modules that are currently loaded. In other words, it only compiles those standard code modules and form, report and standalone class modules that are currently open. It does this by checking every procedure in each loaded module and converting it into p-code. If any of the procedures in these modules call procedures in other modules, then the modules containing these procedures that are called are also loaded, checked and compiled.

The Compile Loaded Modules command is the one that you will use most often while you are developing—which is why it is the only compile command that also has a button on the default toolbar for the module window. When writing code, you should use the Compile Loaded Modules command as you go along to check that the procedures you have just written are free of errors.

Compile All Modules

The Compile All Modules command checks and compiles all modules in the database, whether or not they are loaded. This can take longer than the Compile Loaded Modules command if you have a lot of code or class modules, but it sometimes detects errors that the Compile Loaded Modules command doesn't. For example, if you delete a procedure in one module and then run the Compile Loaded Modules command, it won't pick up any procedures in other modules that call the deleted procedure, if those modules aren't loaded. Because the Compile All Modules command checks every module in the database it will detect this type of error.

Compile and Save All Modules

The Compile and Save All Modules command not only checks and compiles every module in the database—whether loaded or not—but it also saves the compiled version of the module. For this reason, this is the slowest of all the commands to complete. You should run this command when you have finished an application and are ready to distribute it. There is little point in using the Compile and Save All Modules command while you are still coding, because you will find that the next change you make to any of your code causes the module that the code is in to instantly decompile. We'll look in just a moment at what causes code to decompile.

Compile On Demand

Finally, we come to the Compile On Demand option on the Module tab of the Tools/Options… dialog. If Access needs to execute a procedure and the procedure is in a module that is not compiled, it will automatically compile the module before it runs the procedure. It has to because VBA code is not machine-readable, so the VBA has to be converted into p-code that can then be interpreted into a machine-readable format.

If the Compile On Demand option is checked, then Access will load and compile only those modules which contain procedures that are potentially called by the about-to-be-executed procedure.

However, if the Compile On Demand option is not checked, then Access will load and compile all modules which contain procedures that are potentially called by the any procedure in the module of the about-to-be-executed procedure. This can cause a notable performance hit, if your database contains a lot of uncompiled code, so you are advised to leave the Compile On Demand option checked at all times.

When does Code Decompile?

By this stage, you might be wondering whether the Compile On Demand option really makes much difference. Surely if you run the Compile and Save All Modules command before you ship your application you won't have any decompiled code, so you won't have to worry about how long it takes to compile. Most of the time that's fine. However, there are one or two things that your users can do that may cause code in your application to decompile.

- Adding a form, report, control or module
- Modifying the code in a form, report, control or module
- Deleting a form, report, control or module
- Renaming a form, report, control or module
- Adding or removing a reference to an object library or database

In Access 95, renaming a database, compacting a database into a target database with a new name or creating a copy of the database with a new name all caused the code in the database to decompile. Thankfully, this has been remedied in Access 97 and these actions do not now cause code in the database to decompile.

Programmatically Recompiling

If you are worried that code in your application might become decompiled, you could try to programmatically recompile your database. Have a look at the following portion of code. It is from the **AutoExec** function in the **Whisky18.mdb** database which is on the CD that accompanies this book. This procedure is called by the **AutoExec** macro and runs every time the database is opened.

```
Function Autoexec()

On Error GoTo Autoexec_Err

Dim strModule As String
Dim strProperty As String
Dim dtLastOpened As Date
Dim db As Database
Dim pty As Property
Dim lngDBTimesOpened As Long
Dim lngProfileTimesOpened As Long
Dim intRetVal As Integer

Set db = CurrentDb

'If the db is not compiled then open a module and
'force recompilation
If Not Application.IsCompiled Then
    'Display a message indicating we are compiling
    DoCmd.OpenForm "frmCompile", , , , acFormReadOnly
    'Turn off screen updating
    Application.Echo False
```

```
        'Get the name of any module
        strModule = db.Containers("Modules").Documents(0).Name
        'Open the module so we can use the Compile Modules menu command
        DoCmd.OpenModule strModule
        'Compile and save all modules
        Application.RunCommand acCmdCompileAndSaveAllModules
        'Set a database property to indicate last compile time
        MarkCompileTime
        'Give audible confirmation
        Beep
        'Close the module we opened
        DoCmd.Close acModule, strModule
        'Turn screen updating back on
        Application.Echo True
        'Remove the warning form
        DoCmd.Close acForm, "frmCompile"
    End If

    'Find out how many times this particular database has been opened
    IncrementTimesOpened
    lngDBTimesOpened = db.Properties("TimesOpened")
    'If this is the first time for this database, then show the greeting form
    If lngDBTimesOpened = 1 Then
        DoCmd.OpenForm "frmGreeting", , , , , acDialog
    Else
        'Else open the greeting form unless the user has deselected the _
                review check box
        If GetSetting("MWSDB", "Preferences", "StartUpDialog", True) Then
            DoCmd.OpenForm "frmGreeting", , , , , acDialog
        End If
    End If

    'Write information to the Registry to indicate usage for this user
    lngProfileTimesOpened = GetSetting("MWSDB", "Statistics", "UsageCount",
                                        1)
    SaveSetting "MWSDB", "Statistics", "UsageCount", lngProfileTimesOpened +
                                        1
    SaveSetting "MWSDB", "Statistics", "LastUsed", Format$(Now(), "yyyy.mm.dd
                                        hh:nn:ss")

    'And finally open the switchboard form
    DoCmd.OpenForm "frmSwitchboard"


Autoexec_Exit:
    Exit Function

Autoexec_Err:
    'Turn screen updating back on
    Application.Echo True
```

```
        'Now handle the error
    Select Case Err.Number
        Case Else
            Call GlobalErr("Autoexec", Err.Number)
            Resume Autoexec_Exit
            Resume
    End Select

End Function
```

The first thing that happens is that we check the **IsCompiled** property of the **Application** object.

```
If Not Application.IsCompiled Then
```

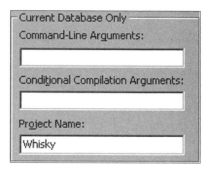

This returns **True** or **False** indicating whether all of the modules in the current project are compiled. The project contains all of the standard and class modules in the existing database. By default, the project has the same name as the database, but you can change the project name in the Advanced tab of the Tools/Options… dialog.

We noted above that renaming a database, compacting a database into a target database with a new name and creating a copy of the database with a new name no longer cause code in an Access 97 database to decompile. However, changing the name of the project does decompile all of the code in the modules that make up that project.

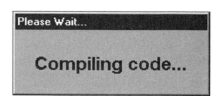

If the **IsCompiled** property returns **False**, the next step is to warn the user that we are going to recompile the code. We do this by displaying **frmCompile**, a simple popup form we have created.

We then turn off screen repainting, so the user does not see what we are up to.

```
Application.Echo False
```

Although useful, turning off screen repainting needs to be handled carefully. If our code breaks because of an error, screen repainting isn't automatically turned back on. This can lead to a hazardous situation, where we don't know where we are in our code and can't see where we are on screen. For this reason, we need to ensure that screen repainting is re-enabled when our code executes correctly and also when it breaks on an error. In other words, we need to make sure that we have got all the exit points from our procedure covered. So as well as turning on screen repainting if our code executes as it should, we also turn it back on as soon as an error occurs.

```
Autoexec_Err:
    'Turn screen updating back on
    Application.Echo True
```

Now that we have turned off screen repainting, we can get on with the actual compiling of the code. We do this with the **RunCommand** method of the **Application** object. This is the method we use when we want to execute a menu command and it replaces the **DoMenuItem** method of the **DoCmd** object that was in earlier versions of Access.

```
'Compile and save all modules
Application.RunCommand acCmdCompileAndSaveAllModules
```

The intrinsic constant **acCmdCompileAndSaveAllModules** tells Access that the command it is to run is the Compile and Save All Modules command. There is a slight complication, however. Access will only let us run this command if a module is currently open. So we need to open a module before we run the command. That's what these lines of code do.

```
'Get the name of any module
strModule = db.Containers("Modules").Documents(0).Name

'Open the module so we can use the Compile Modules menu command
    DoCmd.OpenModule strModule

'Compile and save all modules
Application.RunCommand acCmdCompileAndSaveAllModules
```

The **OpenModule** method of the **DoCmd** object opens, in Design view, a module whose name we pass to the method. If we wanted to, we could have passed the name of a specific module, such as the one which contained the **AutoExec** function. However, we might later change the name of that module and that would mean that we would need to change this code to reflect that change—which is something we might easily forget to do. So instead, we simply open the first module that appears in the Modules container for this database. It doesn't matter which module that is. We just need any module open to let us run the Compile and Save All Modules command.

Obviously, we don't want the user to see the module window flash open when the module is opened. So that's why we turned off screen repainting. It just makes it look a bit more professional. After all, most users naturally get a bit concerned when they see strange bits of code flashing onto their screen momentarily.

Once the code has compiled and been saved, all that is left is to close the module we opened, turn screen repainting back on, close our little alerter form and open the main database switchboard.

```
'Give audible confirmation
Beep

'Close the module we opened
DoCmd.Close acModule, strModule

'Turn screen updating back on
Application.Echo True
```

567

```
'Remove the warning form
DoCmd.Close acForm, "frmCompile"

End If
    .
    .
    .
'And finally open the switchboard form
DoCmd.OpenForm "frmSwitchboard"
```

> *Remember, the **AutoExec** macro—which runs the **AutoExec** function using the **RunCode** action—always executes after any startup options we might have specified in the Tools/Startup... dialog. So if we want our code to compile before the Switchboard form is displayed, we should open the form at the end of the **AutoExec** function, rather than from the Tools/Startup... dialog.*

Using MDE files

A new feature of Access 97 is the ability to save a database as an MDE file. When you save a database as an MDE file, Access creates a new database, into which it places a copy of all the database objects from the source database except for the modules. It then compiles all of the modules in the source database and saves them in their compiled form in the target database, which it then compacts. The target database does not contain a copy of the source VBA code, only compiled p-code.

There are three main benefits to be gained from creating an MDE file from a database:

▶ The p-code is smaller than the source VBA code, so the MDE file will take up less space and therefore have a smaller memory footprint

▶ The modules are already compiled, so performance of the database will be optimal

▶ Users are unable to perform certain modifications to MDE files (see Restrictions on MDE Files). This presents excellent opportunities for tightening the security of your application.

Saving a Database as an MDE file

Saving a database as an MDE file couldn't be easier. But you must meet certain prerequisites before Access will allow you to do so. The prerequisites are as follows:

▶ You must use a workgroup information file that contains users defined to access the database

▶ You must be logged on as a user with Open and Open Exclusive permissions for the database

▶ You must be logged on as a user with Modify Design or Administer privileges for tables in the database (or you must own the tables in the database)

▶ You must be logged on as a user with Read Design permissions for all objects in the database

In addition, you should note that you cannot convert a replicated database to an MDE file until you have removed all of the replication system tables.

If all these criteria are met, then you can save the database as an MDE file. The first step is to close the database. The process of creating an MDE file requires that Access should be able to exclusively lock the database, so you should make sure that no one else is using the database as well.

Then select the Make MDE File... option from the Database Utilities item on the Tools menu.

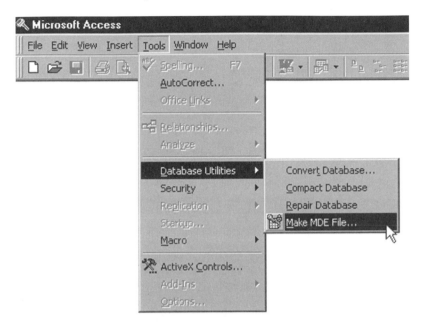

In the Database to Save as MDE dialog which then appears, you should type the name and location that you want for the new MDE file. And that's it!

Access 97 contains a bug which causes it to behave incorrectly if there is not enough disk space to create the MDE file. If, for example, you attempt to save the database as an MDE file on a floppy disk, and there is not enough room on the floppy disk, the attempt to save the MDE file fails silently without an error message informing you that it has failed. In addition, the status bar will still read "Make MDE" even after the failure. You need to close down Access and restart it to get rid of the message.

Restrictions on MDE Files

We noted earlier on that there are various actions that will cause code in a database to decompile. Because MDE files can only contain compiled code, those actions that cause code to decompile are not allowed in a database that has been saved as an MDE file. In other words, users cannot perform any of the following actions:

- Add a form, report, control or module
- Modify the code in a form, report, control or module
- Delete a form, report, control or module
- Rename a form, report, control or module
- Add or remove a reference to an object library or database
- Change the Project Name for the database in the <u>T</u>ools/<u>O</u>ptions... dialog

However, users are free to import or export tables, queries and macros to or from MDE or non-MDE databases.

Another caveat to heed, when using MDE files, is that Microsoft has stated that future versions of Access will not be backward compatible with Access 97 MDE files. In other words, if you create an MDE file with Access 97, you will not be able to open it or run it in future versions of Access, nor will there be a way to convert it to newer versions of Access.

> *These two limitations—the fact that you cannot modify forms, reports or modules, and that MDE files are not upgradable—should make you realize the importance of hanging onto your source code. When you save a database as an MDE file, you should **always** make sure that you keep a copy of the original source database, because you will need it if you want to make any changes to the design of forms, reports or modules or if you want to use the database with future versions of Access.*

Using MDEs with Add-Ins and Libraries

A final consideration applies if the database that you are saving as an MDE file contains references to other databases as either add-ins or libraries. In short, before you save a database as an MDE file, you should save as an MDE file any databases to which the source database contains references, and then redirect the references to the MDE files rather than to the original add-ins or libraries. Only then can you save the original database as an MDE file. The example below should clarify the situation.

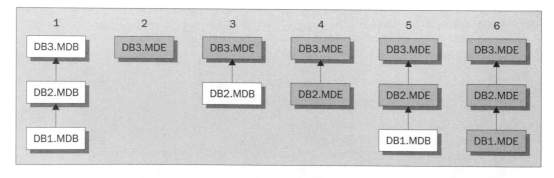

Let us suppose that we have a database **DB1.MDB**, which contains a reference to **DB2.MDB**, and that **DB2.MDB** in turn contains a reference to **DB3.MDB** (stage 1). The first step is to save **DB3.MDB** as an MDE file (stage 2) and then set a reference from **DB2.MDB** to the new compiled **DB3.MDE** (stage 3). Once you have set the reference, you can then save **DB2.MDB** as an MDE file (stage 4) and set a reference to it from **DB1.MDB** (stage 5). Only once you have done that, can you save **DB1.MDB** as an MDE file (stage 6).

Other Maintenance Tasks

Making sure that your code remains compiled is just one of the things that you can do to keep your database application running optimally, once it is in the hands of its users. There are, however, two other key tasks that need to be routinely performed if you want to get the best out of your application. These are compacting the database and repairing the database. Unlike compilation, however, although these tasks can be performed programmatically, they cannot be performed by a database on itself. All these require exclusive access to the database and so must be initiated from outside the current database.

Compacting the Database

Although your application may perform well when it is first delivered, over a period of time its performance may well degrade, especially if the tables within it frequently have records appended to and deleted from them. The reason for this is that Access does not recycle the space used by deleted records. In other words, when a record is deleted from an Access table, the disk space used by the record is not reused. So if records are frequently added to and deleted from an Access table, after a while the table will begin to resemble a Swiss cheese—full of holes. It is not damaged in any way, but because the data in the table will no longer be contiguous, scanning that data will take longer as more disk pages will need to be read in order to read the same number of records.

In order to reclaim the space taken up by these holes, we can compact the database. This effectively copies all of the objects in a database and writes them contiguously into a new database, so removing the holes. This, in turn, both reduces the size of the new database and makes access to the data in that database more efficient.

To compact a database from the menu bar, we select Compact Database from the Database Utilities item of the Tools menu. Another way we can compact a database is to use the **/compact** switch on the command line.

```
C:\WIN32APP\OFFICE\MSACCESS.EXE C:\WHISKY.MDB /compact
```

If we enter this line of code at the command prompt, Access will compact the database called **D:\Whisky.mdb** into itself. Alternatively, we can specify a target database.

```
C:\WIN32APP\OFFICE\MSACCESS.EXE C:\WHISKY.MDB /compact C:\WHISKY2.MDB
```

This line of code would create a new compacted database called **C:\Whisky2.mdb** from the source database **C:\Whisky.mdb**.

We can compact a database programmatically as well, by using the **CompactDatabase** method of the **DBEngine** object.

```
DBEngine.CompactDatabase "C:\Whisky.mdb", "C:\Whisky2.mdb"
```

You should note, however, that although you can compact a database into itself from the Compact Database item on the Database Utilities submenu of the Tools menu, you cannot compact the database you are in from VBA. In VBA, you can only compact another database. This can be frustrating. After all, it can be quite difficult to persuade users of the application, once it is delivered, that they need to close the database, compact it and open it again and do this at frequent intervals.

If you have partitioned your application, so that the tables are in a back-end database and each user has a copy of the queries, forms, reports and code in a front-end database, with the back-end tables linked into the front-end, then this is less of a problem. It will be the back-end that needs the more regular compacting and a database administrator can perform this task, or an overnight batch routine can be scheduled that runs while no-one is using the database. However, the Malt Whisky Shop application also contains a local table—**CriteriaHits**—which is emptied and repopulated whenever a user searches for an order. In this situation, the front-end database will also start suffering from 'database bloat' as the space taken up by the deleted records in the temporary table is not reclaimed.

So what can we do? Well, we could make sure that users of the Malt Whisky Shop database are regularly reminded of the need to compact the database.

The Malt Whisky Shop application reminds users to compact the application every five times that the database is opened. You can see this for yourself if you open and close the database a number of times. Every fifth time, a message appears as you close the database—when you close the Switchboard form, actually—reminding you to compact the database.

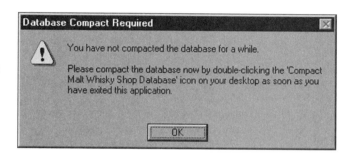

So how does it work? The answer is that it makes use of custom database properties. Have a look at the **IncrementTimesOpened** procedure that is called from within the **AutoExec** function whenever the database is opened.

```
Sub IncrementTimesOpened()

On Error GoTo IncrementTimesOpened_Err

Dim pty As Property
Dim lngDBTimesOpened As Long

lngDBTimesOpened = CurrentDb.Properties("TimesOpened")
CurrentDb.Properties("TimesOpened") = lngDBTimesOpened + 1

'Warn the user to re-compact every five opens
If lngDBTimesOpened Mod 5 = 0 Then
    booCompactTime = True
End If

IncrementTimesOpened_Exit:
    Exit Sub

IncrementTimesOpened_Err:
    Select Case Err.Number
        Case 3270                'Error code for "Property not found"
            Set pty = CurrentDb.CreateProperty("TimesOpened", dbDate, 0)
            CurrentDb.Properties.Append pty
```

```
            Resume
        Case Else
            Call GlobalErr("IncrementTimesOpened", Err.Number)
            Resume IncrementTimesOpened_Exit
            Resume
    End Select

End Sub
```

The purpose of this procedure is to increment a counter which indicates the number of times that the database has been opened. If the number of times it has been opened is a multiple of five, a flag (**booCompactTime**) is set to **True**. Then when the Switchboard form closes, the value of **booCompactTime** is inspected and, if it is set to **True**, the message is displayed warning the user to compact the database.

```
Private Sub Form_Unload(Cancel As Integer)

Dim sMsg As String
Dim CR As String

If booCompactTime Then
    sMsg = "You have not compacted the database for a while." & CR & CR
    sMsg = sMsg & "Please compact the database now by double-clicking"
            & " the "
    sMsg = sMsg & "'Compact Malt Whisky Shop Database' icon on your"
            & " desktop as "
    sMsg = sMsg & "soon as you have exited this application."
    MsgBox sMsg, vbExclamation, "Database Compact Required"
End If

End Sub
```

Let's look in a little more detail at the **IncrementTimesOpened** procedure. We looked at how to set custom database properties in Chapter 10. The first thing the procedure does is to retrieve the value of the **TimesOpened** property of the database and then increment it by one.

```
lngDBTimesOpened = CurrentDb.Properties("TimesOpened")
CurrentDb.Properties("TimesOpened") = lngDBTimesOpened + 1
```

Because this is a custom property, we cannot reference it using the normal syntax used for referencing properties:

```
CurrentDb.TimesOpened
```

Instead we have to retrieve it from the **Properties** collection of the database:

```
CurrentDb.Properties("TimesOpened")
```

If this is the first time that the database has been opened, the database will not have a custom property called **TimesOpened**. In that situation, Access would generate run time error **3270** when we try to inspect its value, so we have to handle the error to take care of that eventuality.

```
IncrementTimesOpened_Err:
    Select Case Err.Number
        Case 3270                'Error code for "Property not found"
            Set pty = CurrentDb.CreateProperty("TimesOpened", dbDate, 0)
            CurrentDb.Properties.Append pty
            Resume
        Case Else
```

The first line of the error handler determines what error has occurred.

```
Select Case Err.Number
```

If the error number is **3270**, it indicates that the custom database property does not exist, so we create the database property and assign it a value of **0** to indicate that the database has not been opened before.

```
Set pty = CurrentDb.CreateProperty("TimesOpened", dbDate, 0)
```

We then append the property to the database in order to save it.

```
CurrentDb.Properties.Append pty
```

Once the property has been saved, we can use the **Resume** statement to resume execution at the line which generated the error, as we know that this time round the property value can be inspected.

We then want to set the variable **booCompactTime** to **True** every five times that the database is opened. We do this by using the **Mod** operator, which returns the remainder when one number is divided by another.

```
If lngDBTimesOpened Mod 5 = 0 Then
    booCompactTime = True
End If
```

The variable **booCompactTime** was declared publicly, so it is visible throughout the database and still exists after the **IncrementTimesOpened** procedure exits. This means that it can be inspected in the **Unload** event handler for the Switchboard form.

Repairing the Database

Another maintenance task—as important as compacting—is repairing the database. Access databases can become corrupted from time to time. This can happen for a number of reasons, but most frequently it is because the database application was terminated ungracefully (i.e. crashed) in the middle of a write operation.

The first 2k page of data in every Access database is the header page and this contains something called commit bytes for each of the 255 potential users of the database. These are byte pairs which indicate the state of the database. Access checks these values whenever it opens a database and if it finds a non-zero value the database is regarded as suspect. For example, the commit bytes might indicate that one user was in the process of committing a transaction to disk when the database was last closed. If this is the case, Access displays a dialog warning the user that the database is in a suspect state and that it should be repaired.

However, sometimes the database might be in a corrupted state and Access doesn't realize it at the time. For this reason, it is a good idea to repair databases at frequent intervals, whether or not Access reports them as being damaged.

To repair an Access database, we select <u>R</u>epair Database from the <u>D</u>atabase Utilities item of the <u>T</u>ools menu. Alternatively, we can use a command-line switch when opening the database:

```
C:\WIN32APP\OFFICE\MSACCESS.EXE D:\WHISKY.MDB /repair
```

Like compacting, repairing a database is something that can be done programmatically, but not on the current database. The syntax for repairing another database from VBA code is quite simple, using the **RepairDatabase** method of the **DBEngine** object.

```
DBEngine.RepairDatabase "D:\Whisky.mdb"
```

Because we cannot programmatically repair the current database, the best way to ensure that users regularly repair a database is to suggest that they perform the repair whenever they compact the database. To make it easy for users to compact and repair databases, shortcuts can be provided on their desktops using the command-line switches stated above. If you do this, you might want to explain to users that although Access automatically exits when you compact a database this way, the user has to click an <u>O</u>K button to close Access when a repair is complete.

Using the Registry

In the example above, we used a custom database property to save a value which we wanted to preserve between sessions. Although this was appropriate in that situation, there is another better-known method to preserve values and that is the Windows Registry. The Windows Registry is a type of database used by Windows to store configuration parameters for users, machines and applications and it replaces **.INI** files which were so prevalent in earlier versions of Windows.

Registry vs. Ini files

In early versions of Windows, configuration information was stored in a single configuration file called **WIN.INI**. This was a simple ASCII file with the entries listed one after another, grouped by application name. Although this worked well early on, as more and more applications were installed on users' machines, and so more and more configuration information was required, the **WIN.INI** file became longer and longer. Apart from the fact that the **WIN.INI** file became slower and slower to read as it contained more and more information, there was also the problem of a fixed 64kb limit imposed on the file.

The next approach was to use a separate **.INI** file for each application. This provided some relief from the 64kb limit problem, but meant that users were left with a **Windows** directory full of numerous **.INI** files. Also, because applications each used different files, they were unable to share configuration information.

The next stab at the problem was the Registration database in Windows 3.1 and it is this that forms the basis of the Windows Registry in Windows 95 and Windows NT.

Structure of the Registry

Structurally, the Registry resembles a hierarchically organized tree. The tree contains nodes known as keys and each of these keys can contain either subkeys or data values. Each key has a name consisting of one or more printable ANSI characters and this cannot include a space, a backslash (****), or a wildcard character (***** or **?**). Key names beginning with a period (**.**) are reserved for use by Windows and subkey names must be unique with respect to the key that is immediately above it in the hierarchy.

You can see this for yourself if you run the Registry Editor (**regedit.exe**) which should be located in your computer's Windows directory. But be **extremely** careful when modifying values with the Registry Editor. If you modify a value incorrectly, Windows may not restart and you could be looking at one of those fun afternoons re-installing Windows… and your applications… and the data you lost… which you backed up, didn't you?

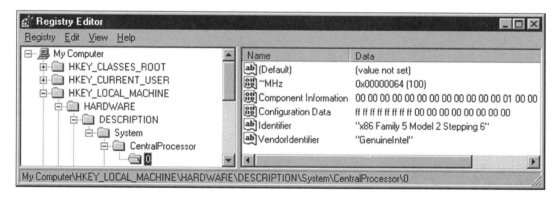

In the diagram above, the HKEY_LOCAL_MACHINE key has a HARDWARE subkey which includes a DESCRIPTION subkey. This has a System subkey which includes a CentralProcessor subkey with a subkey called 0. This has five unique values called ~MHz, Component Information, Configuration Data, Identifier and VendorIdentifier. You have probably guessed that this subkey provides information on the type of CPU that the computer contains—in this case a 100MHz Intel Pentium.

Saving and Retrieving Registry Values

We can use the Registry to save values that we want to preserve even when Access is not running. To do this, we use the **SaveSetting** and **GetSetting** functions. The **SaveSetting** function saves—or creates—a value under a given subkey and the **GetSetting** function retrieves a specified value. When we use these functions in VBA, the values we save are always placed beneath the following subkey:

HKEY_CURRENT_USER\SOFTWARE\VB and VBA Program Settings

To use the **SaveSetting** function, we need to specify in turn the application name, section name, value and data for that value. So, if we wanted to save a value in the Registry to indicate when the user last opened the Malt Whisky Shop database, we could use the following function in the **AutoExec** function we looked at earlier.

```
SaveSetting "MWSDB", "Statistics", "LastUsed", Format$(Now(), "yyyy.mm.dd
_ hh:nn:ss")
```

This would create a subkey called **MWSDB** for the Malt Whisky Shop Database, with a subkey called **Statistics**. In this subkey, it would place a value called **LastUsed** and data indicating when the database was last opened.

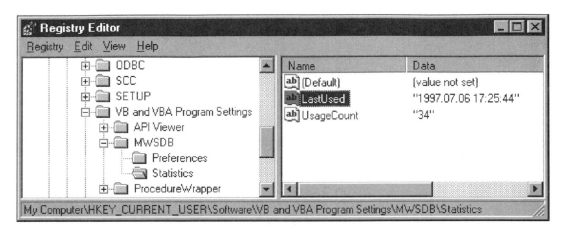

As a rule you should use the application name (MWSDB) to indicate the name of the application to which the values apply and use the section name to categorize the values for easy reference. You can see in the diagram above that the Malt Whisky Shop has a key called MWSDB that has two subkeys. One contains usage statistics—including when the database was last used—and the other subkey contains information about user preferences.

To keep an accurate note of how many times the current user has used the Malt Whisky Shop database, we could add the following code to the **AutoExec** function.

```
lngProfileTimesOpened = GetSetting("MWSDB", "Statistics", _
                                    "UsageCount", 1)
SaveSetting "MWSDB", "Statistics", "UsageCount", _
                                    lngProfileTimesOpened + 1
```

The first line retrieves the value of **UsageCount** under the **Statistics** subkey of **MWSDB**. The final argument indicates a default value that should be returned if the value or subkey cannot be located. The second line adds one to that value and saves it to the same place in the Registry.

Note that, because these values have been saved under the HKEY_CURRENT_USER key, they apply to the current user of the machine, rather than to the database or to the machine. This makes the Registry an excellent place to store user-related usage statistics or preferences. An example of a preference being stored is the StartUpDialog value.

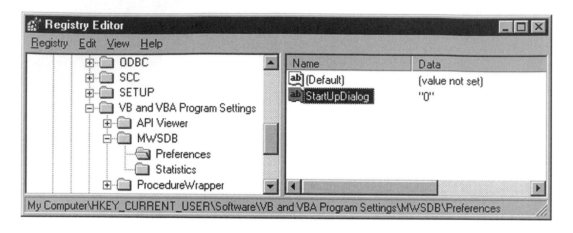

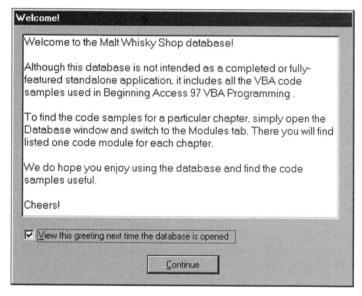

This value is used to determine whether or not the startup dialog should be displayed when the Malt Whisky Shop application is first opened.

The value of the StartUpDialog value is inspected in the **AutoExec** function, whenever the database opens.

```
If GetSetting("MWSDB", "Preferences", "StartUpDialog", True) Then
   DoCmd.OpenForm "frmGreeting", , , , , acDialog
End If
```

The final argument, **True**, indicates that if the value cannot be found—presumably because this is the first time that this particular user has opened the Malt Whisky Shop database—the value returned should be **True**. If **True** is returned, then the startup dialog is displayed.

Note that the startup dialog has a checkbox, which allows the user to indicate whether or not the form is to be displayed next time he or she opens the database. When the form is closed, we simply need to save the value of the checkbox to the StartupDialog value in the Registry. This is the code behind the Continue button on the startup dialog form.

```
SaveSetting "MWSDB", "Preferences", "StartUpDialog", (chkRepeat)
DoCmd.Close acForm, Me.Name
```

Now, the next time the database is opened and the **AutoExec** function runs, the startup dialog is only shown if the user wanted it to be and the value of HKEY_CURRENT_USER\SOFTWARE\VB and VBA ProgramSettings\ MWSDB\Preferences\StartUpDialog is **True**.

Conclusion

Wow! If you have made it this far, well done! (Unless you are one of those people who always flicks ahead to the last page of the book just to see if it really was the shifty-looking lift-attendant from Brazil who kidnapped the aging football star with the unconvincing limp.) We've reached the end of the book and if you have worked your way through from the beginning you'll realize that we have covered a heck of a lot of ground since we initially used VBA to create our 'intelligent' navigation button. And with a bit of luck, you'll have found it enjoyable as well as instructive. (If it hasn't and you have got this far, you deserve an award for perseverance!)

We started off with basic concepts and, in fact, the idea throughout the book has been to make sure that you gained a really solid understanding of the core ideas and techniques behind VBA in general and how VBA works with Access and DAO in particular. But as the book progressed we moved on to more advanced subjects, such as error handling and optimization and covered wider-ranging areas, such as OLE automation, class modules and working with the Internet.

We don't claim to have covered every topic in the utmost detail. There's a whole load more out there for you to learn! But what we hope we have done is to have given you a really solid platform from which to launch your foray into VBA programming.

So, well done for making it this far. Now it's up to you. Enjoy!

Events in Access 97

This section is a comprehensive list of all of the events that Access 97 can handle. It should give you an idea of just how much you can achieve in Access 97 through careful use of event handlers.

Events new to Access 97 are shown in **bold**.

Event Property	Belongs to...	Occurs...	Can be used for...
After Del Confirm	Forms	after the user has confirmed deletion of records or after the Before Del Confirm event is canceled.	determining how the user reacted to confirmation of the deletion of records.
After Insert	Forms	after the new record has been added.	requerying a form's recordset to show up-to-date data.
After Update	Forms; controls on a form	after the changed data in a control or record has been saved.	requerying a form's recordset to show up-to-date data.
Apply Filter	Forms	after the user has chosen to apply or remove a filter, but before the filter is applied.	changing the appearance of the form, depending on the filter criteria selected.
Before Del Confirm	Forms	after the user has deleted records, but before Access 95 has asked for confirmation.	creating your own messages asking the user for confirmation of records.
Before Insert	Forms	after the user types the first character in a record, but before the record is actually created.	allowing the developer to populate hidden ID fields in subforms.
Before Update	Forms; controls on a form	before the changed data in a control or record is saved.	validating data before it is saved.

Event Property	Belongs to...	Occurs...	Can be used for...
Initialize	Class	when a new instance of a class is created.	set default properties.
ItemAdded	Reference	when a reference is added to the project from Visual Basic.	to add extra references where dependencies occur.
ItemRemoved	Reference	when a reference is removed from the project with Visual Basic.	to clean up anything done when the reference was added.
On Activate	Forms; reports	when a form or report becomes the active window and gets focus.	triggering the display of custom toolbars.
On Change	Controls on a form	after the contents of a control change (e.g. by typing a character).	triggering the update of related controls on the form.
On Click	Forms; controls and sections on a form	when the user clicks the mouse button over a form or control; when the user takes some action which results in the same effect as clicking would (i.e. presses the spacebar to check a checkbox).	just about anything - this is one of the most used of all events and is about the only event used with command buttons.
On Close	Forms; reports	after a form or report has been closed and removed from the screen.	triggering the opening of the next form.
On Current	Forms	when the form is opened or requeried; after the focus moves to a different record, but before the new record is displayed.	implementing intelligent navigation buttons (see example in chapter 6).
On Dbl Click	Forms; controls and sections on a form	when the user depresses and releases the left mouse button twice over the same object.	implementing drill-down functionality in EIS applications.
On Deactivate	Forms; reports	when a form or report loses focus within Access 95.	triggering the concealment of custom toolbars.
On Delete	Forms	when the user attempts to delete a record.	preventing the user from deleting records.

Event Property	Belongs to...	Occurs...	Can be used for...
On Enter	Controls on a form	before the control receives focus from another control on the same form.	similar to On Got Focus.
On Error	Forms; reports	when a run-time database engine error occurs (but not a Visual Basic error).	intercepting errors and displaying your own custom error messages.
On Exit	Controls on a form	before the control loses focus to another control on the same form.	similar to On Lost Focus.
On Filter	Forms	after the user clicks the Advanced Filter/Sort or Filter By Form buttons.	entering default filter criteria for the user, or even displaying your own custom filter window.
On Format	Report sections	after Access 95 determines which data belongs in each section of a report, but before the section is formatted for printing.	displaying information on a report which is dependent on the value of other data on that report.
On Got Focus	Forms; controls on a form	after a form or control has received the focus.	highlighting areas of the form which you wish to draw to the attention of the user when editing that control.
On Key Down	Forms; controls on a form	when the user presses a key over a form or control which has the focus.	writing keyboard handlers for applications which need to respond to users pressing and releasing keys.
On Key Press	Forms; controls on a form	when the user presses and releases a key or key combination.	testing the validity of keystrokes as they are entered into a control.
On Key Up	Forms; controls on a form	when the user releases a key over a form or control which has the focus.	see On Key Down.
On Load	Forms	after a form has been opened and the records displayed.	specifying default values for controls on a form.
On Lost Focus	Forms; controls on a form	after a form or control has lost the focus.	validating data entered into a control.

Event Property	Belongs to...	Occurs...	Can be used for...
On Mouse Down	Forms; controls and sections on a form	when the user presses a mouse button.	triggering the display of custom pop-up shortcut menus.
On Mouse Move	Forms; controls and sections on a form	when the mouse pointer moves over objects.	displaying X and Y coordinates of the mouse pointer.
On Mouse Up	Forms; controls and sections on a form	when the user releases a mouse button.	triggering the concealment of custom pop-up shortcut menus.
On No Data	Forms; reports	after a report with no data has been formatted, but before it is printed.	suppressing the printing of reports which contain no data.
On Not In List	Controls on a form	when the user attempts to add a new item to a combo box.	creating a method for adding the item to the table which supplies values for the combo box.
On Open	Forms; reports	when a form or report is opened but before the first record is displayed.	setting focus on the form to a particular control.
On Page	Reports	after a page has been formatted for printing, but before it is printing.	drawing boxes, lines etc. on the page using various graphics methods.
On Print	Report sections	after a section has been formatted for printing, but before it is actually printed.	determining if a record is split across two pages.
On Resize	Forms	when a form is opened or resized.	preventing the user from reducing the size of a form beyond certain limits.
On Retreat	Report sections	during formatting when Access 95 retreats to a previous section of a report.	undoing actions you may have already instigated in the Format event handler.
On Timer	Forms	every time the period of time specified as the TimerInterval property has elapsed.	causing controls to 'flash'.
On Unload	Forms	after a form has been closed but before it is removed from the screen.	displaying a message box asking the user for confirmation that the form should be closed.

Event Property	Belongs to...	Occurs...	Can be used for...
On Updated	Controls on a form	after an OLE objects data has been modified.	determining if the data in a bound control needs to be saved.
Terminate	Module	when the instance of the class module is destroyed	to clean up any actions that occurred when the class was instantiated.

Functions

List of Functions by Name

Function Name	Function Group	What it does
Abs	Mathematical	Returns the absolute value of a number.
Array	Array Handling	Returns a variant containing an array.
Asc, AscB	Text Handling	Return the ASCII code of the first letter in a string.
Atn	Mathematical	Returns the arctangent of a number.
CBool	Conversion	Converts an expression to a boolean type.
CByte	Conversion	Converts an expression to a byte type.
CCur	Conversion	Converts an expression to a currency type.
CDate, CVDate	Conversion	Converts an expression to a date type.
CDbl	Conversion	Converts an expression to a double type.
Choose	Selection	Selects a value from a list of arguments.
Chr	Text Handling	Returns the character for a specified ASCII code.
CInt	Conversion	Converts an expression to an integer type.
CLng	Conversion	Converts an expression to a long type.
CodeDB	Miscellaneous	Returns the name of the current database.
Cos	Mathematical	Returns the cosine of an angle.
CreateControl	Object Handling	Creates a control on a form
CreateObject	Object Handling	Creates an OLE automation object.
CreateReport	Object Handling	Creates a report
CSng	Conversion	Converts an expression to a single type.
CStr	Conversion	Converts an expression to a string type.
CurDir	File & Disk	Returns the current drive path.
CurrentUser	Miscellaneous	Returns the name of the current user of the current database.

Function Name	Function Group	What it does
CVar	Conversion	Converts an expression to a variant type.
Date	Date & Time	Returns the current system date.
DateAdd	Date & Time	Adds a specified time interval to a date
DateDiff	Date & Time	Returns the number of time intervals between two dates.
DatePart	Date & Time	Returns a specified part of a given date.
DateSerial	Date & Time	Returns a date for a given year, month, and day.
DateValue	Date & Time	Returns a date type from a given string.
DAvg	Domain Aggregate	Calculates the average for a set of values.
Day	Date & Time	Returns the day of the month as a number.
DCount	Domain Aggregate	Counts the number of records in the domain.
DDB	Financial	Returns the depreciation of an asset.
DDE	DDE Commands	Define a DDE conversation.
DDEInitiate	DDE Commands	Initiate a DDE conversation.
DDERequest	DDE Commands	Request data in a DDE conversation.
DDESend	DDE Commands	Send data in a DDE conversation.
Dir	File & Disk	Find one or more a files or folders.
DLookup	Domain Aggregate	Return a value from a set of records.
DMax	Domain Aggregate	Calculates the maximum for a set of values.
DMin	Domain Aggregate	Calculates the minimum for a set of values.
DoEvents	Miscellaneous	Yield execution to the operating system.
DStDev	Domain Aggregate	Calculates the standard deviation for a set of values.
DStDevP	Domain Aggregate	Calculates the standard deviation population for a set of values.
DSum	Domain Aggregate	Calculates the total for a set of values.
DVar	Domain Aggregate	Calculates the variance for a set of values.
DVarP	Domain Aggregate	Calculates the variance population for a set of values.
Environ	Miscellaneous	Returns an environment variable setting.
EOF	File & Disk	Check for the end of a file.
Error	Miscellaneous	Returns the message for a given error number.
Eval	Mathematical	Evaluate an expression.
FileAttr	File & Disk	Returns information about the way a file was opened.
Fix, Int	Mathematical	Returns the integer portion of a number.
Format	Text Handling	Formats values according to instructions contained in the format expression.
FreeFile	File & Disk	Returns the next file number available.
FV	Financial	Returns the future value of an annuity.
GetObject	Object Handling	Retrieves an OLE object from a file

Function Name	Function Group	What it does
Hex	Conversion	Converts a hexadecimal number to a string.
Hour	Date & Time	Returns the hour of the day as a number.
HyperlinkPart	Object Handling	Returns the display name, address, or sub-address from a hyperlink
IIf	Selection	Returns one of two values, depending on the evaluation of an expression.
Input	File & Disk	Returns characters from an open disk file.
InputBox	Miscellaneous	Displays a dialog box and waits for the user to enter a value.
InStr	Text Handling	Searches for a string within another string.
IPmt	Financial	Returns the interest payment for a given period of an annuity.
IsDate	Examination	Tests whether an expression can be converted to a date.
IsEmpty	Examination	Tests whether a variable has been initialized.
IsMissing	Examination	Tests whether an optional argument has been passed to a procedure.
IsNumeric	Examination	Tests whether an expression can be evaluated as a number.
IsNull	Examination	Tests whether an expression contains valid data.
IsObject	Object Handling	Tests whether an expression references a valid OLE automation object.
IRR	Financial	Returns the internal rate of return for a series of cash flows.
LBound	Array Handling	Returns the lower bound (index) of an array.
LCase	Text Handling	Converts text to lower case.
Left	Text Handling	Returns the left part of a text string.
Loc	File & Disk	Returns the current position within a disk file.
LOF	File & Disk	Returns the size (length) in bytes of a file.
Log	Mathematical	Returns the natural logarithm of a number.
LTrim	Text Handling	Removes leading spaces from a string.
Max	SQL Aggregate	Returns the maximum of a set of values.
Mid	Text Handling	Returns the middle part of a text string.
Min	SQL Aggregate	Returns the minimum of a set of values.
Minute	Date & Time	Returns the minute of the hour as a number.
MIRR	Financial	Returns the modified internal rate of return for a series of cash flows
Month	Date & Time	Returns the month of the year as a number.
MsgBox	Miscellaneous	Displays a message dialog and waits for the user to press a button.
Now	Date & Time	Returns the current date and time.
NPer	Financial	Returns the number of periods for an annuity.

Function Name	Function Group	What it does
NPV	Financial	Returns the net present value of an investment.
Oct	Conversion	Converts an octal number to a string.
Partition	Selection	Returns a string indicating where a number occurs within a series of ranges.
Pmt	Financial	Returns the payment for an annuity.
PPmt	Financial	Returns the principal payment for an annuity.
PV	Financial	Returns the present value of an investment.
QBColor	Miscellaneous	Returns the RGB color code corresponding to a color number.
Rate	Financial	Returns the interest rate for an annuity.
RGB	Miscellaneous	Returns a whole number representing an RGB color value.
Right	Text Handling	Returns the right part of a text string.
Rnd	Miscellaneous	Returns a random number.
RTrim	Text Handling	Removes trailing spaces from a string.
Second	Date & Time	Returns the second of the minute as a number.
Seek	File & Disk	Sets the current position within a disk file.
Sgn	Mathematical	Tests the sign of a number.
Shell	Miscellaneous	Starts another application.
Sin	Mathematical	Returns the sine of an angle.
SLN	Financial	Returns the straight-line depreciation of an asset.
Space	Text Handling	Creates a string of a given number of spaces.
Spc, Tab	Text Handling	Used to position output when printing.
Sqr	Mathematical	Returns the square root of a number.
StDev	SQL Aggregate	Returns the standard deviation.
StDevP	SQL Aggregate	Returns the standard deviation population.
Str	Text Handling	Converts a number to its string representation.
StrComp	Text Handling	Compares two strings and returns a value.
String	Text Handling	Creates a string of a given repeating character.
Sum	SQL Aggregate	Calculates the total of a set of numbers.
Switch	Selection	Returns a value for the first expression in a list that is true.
SYD	Financial	Returns the sum-of-years' digits depreciation of an asset.
SysCmd	Miscellaneous	Carry out Access status actions.
Tan	Mathematical	Returns the tangent of an angle.
Time	Date & Time	Returns the current system time.
Timer	Miscellaneous	Returns the number of seconds since midnight.
TimeSerial	Date & Time	Returns the time for a given hour, minute, and second.
TimeValue	Date & Time	Returns a date type containing the time given in a string.

Function Name	Function Group	What it does
Trim	Text Handling	Removes leading and trailing spaces.
UBound	Array Handling	Returns the upper bound (index) of an array.
UCase	Text Handling	Converts text to upper case.
Val	Conversion	Returns a number contained in a string.
Var	SQL Aggregate	Calculate the variance.
VarP	SQL Aggregate	Calculate the variance population.
VarType	Examination	Returns a value indicating the type of data stored in a variable.
Weekday	Date & Time	Returns the day of the week as a number.
Year	Date & Time	Returns the year part of the current date.

List of Functions by Type

	Function Name	What it does
Array Handling	Array	Returns a variant containing an array.
	LBound	Returns the lower bound (index) of an array.
	UBound	Returns the upper bound (index) of an array.
Conversion	CBool	Converts an expression to a boolean type.
	CByte	Converts an expression to a byte type.
	CCur	Converts an expression to a currency type.
	Cdate, CVDate	Converts an expression to a date type.
	CDbl	Converts an expression to a double type.
	CInt	Converts an expression to an integer type.
	CLng	Converts an expression to a long type.
	CSng	Converts an expression to a single type.
	CStr	Converts an expression to a string type.
	CVar	Converts an expression to a variant type.
	Hex	Converts a hexadecimal number to a string.
	Oct	Converts an octal number to a string.
	Val	Returns a number contained in a string.
Date & Time	Date	Returns the current system date.
	DateAdd	Adds a specified time interval to a date.
	DateDiff	Returns the number of time intervals between two dates.
	DatePart	Returns a specified part of a given date.
	DateSerial	Returns a date for a given year, month, and day.

	Function Name	What it does
	DateValue	Returns a date type from a given string.
	Day	Returns the day of the month as a number.
	Hour	Returns the hour of the day as a number.
	Minute	Returns the minute of the hour as a number.
	Month	Returns the month of the year as a number.
	Now	Returns the current date and time.
	Second	Returns the second of the minute as a number.
	Time	Returns the current system time.
	TimeSerial	Returns the time for a given hour, minute, and second.
	TimeValue	Returns a date type containing the time given in a string.
	Weekday	Returns the day of the week as a number.
	Year	Returns the year part of the current date.
DDE Commands	DDE	Define a DDE conversation.
	DDEInitiate	Initiate a DDE conversation.
	DDERequest	Request data in a DDE conversation.
	DDESend	Send data in a DDE conversation.
Domain Aggregate	DAvg	Calculates the average for a set of values.
	DCount	Counts the number of records in the domain.
	DLookup	Return a value from a set of records.
	DMax	Calculates the maximum for a set of values.
	DMin	Calculates the minimum for a set of values.
	DStDev	Calculates the standard deviation for a set of values.
	DStDevP	Calculates the standard deviation population for a set of values.
	DSum	Calculates the total for a set of values.
	DVar	Calculates the variance for a set of values.
	DVarP	Calculates the variance population for a set of values.
Examination	IsDate	Tests whether an expression can be converted to a date.
	IsEmpty	Tests whether a variable has been initialized.
	IsMissing	Tests whether an optional argument has been passed to a procedure.
	IsNumeric	Tests whether an expression can be evaluated as a number.
	IsNull	Tests whether an expression contains valid data.
	VarType	Returns a value indicating the type of data stored in a variable.
File & Disk	CurDir	Returns the current drive path.
	Dir	Find one or more a files or folders.

	Function Name	What it does
	EOF	Check for the end of a file.
	FileAttr	Returns information about the way a file was opened.
	FreeFile	Returns the next file number available.
	Input	Returns characters from an open disk file.
	Loc	Returns the current position within a disk file.
	LOF	Returns the size (length) in bytes of a file.
	Seek	Sets the current position within a disk file.
Financial	DDB	Returns the depreciation of an asset.
	FV	Returns the future value of an annuity.
	IPmt	Returns the interest payment for a given period of an annuity.
	IRR	Returns the internal rate of return for a series of cash flows.
	MIRR	Returns the modified internal rate of return for a series of cash flows
	NPer	Returns the number of periods for an annuity.
	NPV	Returns the net present value of an investment.
	Pmt	Returns the payment for an annuity.
	PPmt	Returns the principal payment for an annuity.
	PV	Returns the present value of an investment.
	Rate	Returns the interest rate for an annuity.
	SLN	Returns the straight-line depreciation of an asset.
	SYD	Returns the sum-of-years' digits depreciation of an asset.
Mathematical	Abs	Returns the absolute value of a number.
	Atn	Returns the arctangent of a number.
	Cos	Returns the cosine of an angle.
	Eval	Evaluate an expression.
	Fix, Int	Returns the integer portion of a number.
	Log	Returns the natural logarithm of a number.
	Sgn	Tests the sign of a number.
	Sin	Returns the sine of an angle.
	Sqr	Returns the square root of a number.
	Tan	Returns the tangent of an angle.
Miscellaneous	CodeDB	Returns the name of the current database.
	CurrentUser	Returns the name of the current user of the current database.
	DoEvents	Yield execution to the operating system.
	Environ	Returns an environment variable setting.

	Function Name	What it does
	Error	Returns the message for a given error number.
	InputBox	Displays a dialog box and waits for the user to enter a value.
	MsgBox	Displays a message dialog and waits for the user to press a button.
	QBColor	Returns the RGB color code corresponding to a color number.
	RGB	Returns a whole number representing an RGB color value.
	Rnd	Returns a random number.
	Shell	Starts another application.
	SysCmd	Carry out Access status actions.
	Timer	Returns the number of seconds since midnight.
Object Handling	CreateControl	Creates a control on a form.
	CreateObject	Creates an OLE automation object.
	CreateReport	Creates a report.
	GetObject	Retrieves an OLE object from a file.
	IsObject	Tests whether an expression references a valid OLE automation object.
Selection	Choose	Selects a value from a list of arguments.
	IIf	Returns one of two values, depending on the evaluation of an expression.
	Partition	Returns a string indicating where a number occurs within a series of ranges.
	Switch	Returns a value for the first expression in a list that is True.
SQL Aggregate	Max	Returns the maximum of a set of values.
	Min	Returns the minimum of a set of values.
	StDev	Returns the standard deviation.
	StDevP	Returns the standard deviation population.
	Sum	Calculates the total of a set of numbers.
	Var	Calculate the variance.
	VarP	Calculate the variance population.
Text Handling	Spc, Tab	Used to position output when printing.
	Asc, AscB	Return the ASCII code of the first letter in a string.
	Chr	Returns the character for a specified ASCII code.
	Format	Formats values according to instructions contained in the format expression.
	InStr	Searches for a string within another string.
	LCase	Converts text to lower case.

Function Name	What it does
Left	Returns the left part of a text string.
LTrim	Removes leading spaces from a string.
Mid	Returns the middle part of a text string.
Right	Returns the right part of a text string.
RTrim	Removes trailing spaces from a string.
Space	Creates a string of a given number of spaces.
Str	Converts a number to its string representation.
StrComp	Compares two strings and returns a value.
String	Creates a string of a given repeating character.
Trim	Removes leading and trailing spaces.
UCase	Converts text to upper case.

Symbols

A

D

M

N

named arguments, creating code 64
:= 65

naming conventions, creating code 91
constants 94
controls 92
prefixes, listing 92
objects 93
prefixes, listing 93
variables 91
prefixes, listing 91

navigation buttons
application design 17
events 35
event properties 35
intelligence, adding to the buttons 55
recordsets 173

nesting, control structures 109
For...Next statement
If statement nested within 109

networks, optimization 423
attached tables, searching on indexed fields 423
AutoExpand, disabling 424
non-table objects, putting on local machine 424

New, multiple instances 391

NoData event, reports 275

Not, bitwise operator 490

NOT, If statements 101

Nothing, reclaiming memory 401

null pointers, functions in DLLs 303
ByVal 303

null value, variant variables 75

null-terminated strings, functions in DLLs 300
ByVal 300

O

object application, Automation 507

Object Browser 158

object linking and embedding (OLE) 495
Access 97, as OLE server 532
Automation 507
Automation objects, creating 508, 510 - 511
Automation/linking and embedding example 519
container application 507
creating a letter in Word, example 523
Excel chart example 514

object application 507
object hierarchy 512
Office assistant, example 531
Outlook, example 528
custom controls (ActiveX controls) 502
linking and embedding/Automation example 519
OLE objects
activating 499
bound 496
external activation 497
in-place activation 497
properties, listing 498
unbound 496
updating 500
OLE servers 495
Access 97 as OLE server 532

object variables, creating code 70

object-oriented programming (OOP) 133, 369
see also **classes** and **objects**
abstraction 371
Access 97 objects 135
data access objects (DAO) 135 - 136, 306
general objects, listing 135
advantages 134
encapsulation 134
reusability 134
classes 370
default instances 389
instances 370
multiple instances 389
custom methods, forms 389
custom objects
creating 374
designing 373, 374
writable properties 380
custom properties, forms 386
data hiding 379
encapsulation 319, 371
error minimization techniques 319
encapsulation 319
reusability 319
inheritance 372
objects
classes 134
collections 136
definition 370
methods 134
Object Browser 158
properties 134
referring to 154
special properties, representing objects 155
polymorphism 372

ObjectName, OutputTo 241

ObjectName, SendObject 243

objects
see also **classes**, **collections**, and **object-oriented programming**
(General) 40
declarations 41
Options 40
Base 40
Compare 40
Explicit 41
Private 41
Access 97 objects 135
data access objects (DAO) 135 -136
data, outputting from 241
OutputTo 241
general objects, listing 135
Automation
Automation objects, creating 508, 510 - 511
Excel chart example 514
letter in Word, example 523
object hierarchy 512
Office Assistant, example 531
Outlook, example 528
classes 134
definition 134
inheritance 134
instantiation 134 - 135, 371, 374, 378, 389
subclasses 134
code, creating
naming conventions 93
prefixes, listing 93
collections 136
custom objects 372, 373
creating 374
designing 374
interface 373
definition 134
encapsulation 134
manipulating. *see* **data access objects (DAO)**, manipulating
methods 134, 384
definition 134
Object Browser 158
object definition 370
object variables 385
object lifetimes 385
object-oriented programming (OOP) 133
abstraction 371
custom objects 372 - 374, 380
encapsulation 371
inheritance 372
object definition 370
object method 384
polymorphism 372
OLE
activating 499
bound objects 496
external activation 497
in-place activation 497
properties, listing 498

607

Beginning Java

Author: Ivor Horton
ISBN: 1861000278
Price: $36.00 C$50.40 £32.99
Available May 97

If you've enjoyed this book, you'll get a lot from Ivor's new book, Beginning Java.

Beginning Java teaches Java 1.1 from scratch, taking in all the fundamental features of the Java language, along with practical applications of Java's extensive class libraries. While it assumes some little familiarity with general programming concepts, Ivor takes time to cover the basics of the language in depth. He assumes no knowledge of object-oriented programming.

Ivor first introduces the essential bits of Java without which no program will run. Then he covers how Java handles data, and the syntax it uses to make decisions and control program flow. The essentials of object-oriented programming with Java are covered, and these concepts are reinforced throughout the book. Chapters on exceptions, threads and I/O follow, before Ivor turns to Java's graphics support and applet ability. Finally the book looks at JDBC and RMI, two additions to the Java 1.1 language which allow Java programs to communicate with databases and other Java programs.

Beginning Visual C++ 5

Author: Ivor Horton   ISBN: 1861000081
Price: $39.95 C$55.95 £36.99

Visual Basic is a great tool for generating applications quickly and easily, but if you really want to create fast, tight programs using the latest technologies, Visual C++ is the only way to go.

Ivor Horton's Beginning Visual C++ 5 is for anyone who wants to learn C++ and Windows programming with Visual C++ 5 and MFC, and the combination of the programming discipline you've learned from this book and Ivor's relaxed and informal teaching style will make it even easier for you to succeed in taming structured programming and writing real Windows applications.

The book begins with a fast-paced but comprehensive tutorial to the C++ language. You'll then go on to learn about object orientation with C++ and how this relates to Windows programming, culminating with the design and implementation of a sizable class-based C++ application. The next part of the book walks you through creating Windows applications using MFC, including sections on output to the screen and printer, how to program menus, toolbars and dialogs, and how to respond to a user's actions. The final few chapters comprise an introduction to COM and examples of how to create ActiveX controls using both MFC and the Active Template Library (ATL).

Beginning Linux Programming

Authors: Neil Matthew, Richard Stones
ISBN: 187441680
Price: $36.95 C$51.95 £33.99

The book is unique in that it teaches UNIX programming in a simple and structured way, using Linux and its associated and freely available development tools as the main platform. Assuming familiarity with the UNIX environment and a basic knowledge of C, the book teaches you how to put together UNIX applications that make the most of your time, your OS and your machine's capabilities.

Having introduced the programming environment and basic tools, the authors turn their attention initially on shell programming. The chapters then concentrate on programming UNIX with C, showing you how to work with files, access the UNIX environment, input and output data using terminals and curses, and manage data. After another round with development and debugging tools, the book discusses processes and signals, pipes and other IPC mechanisms, culminating with a chapter on sockets. Programming the X-Window system is introduced with Tcl/Tk and Java. Finally, the book covers programming for the Internet using HTML and CGI.

The book aims to discuss UNIX programming as described in the relevant POSIX and X/Open specifications, so the code is tested with that in mind. All the source code from the book is available under the terms of the Gnu Public License from the Wrox web site.

Beginning Visual Basic 5

Author: Peter Wright
ISBN: 1861000081
Price: $29.95 C$41.95 £27.49

The third edition of the best selling Beginner's Guide to Visual Basic is the most comprehensive guide for the complete beginner to Visual Basic 5. Peter Wright's unique style and humour have long been a favourite with beginners and, because the book has just the one author, you can be sure that the text has a consistent voice and flow.

As with all Wrox Beginning guides, every topic is illustrated with a Try It Out, where each new concept is accompanied by a focused example and explanatory text. This way, you get to create an example program that demonstrates some theory, and then you get to examine the code behind it in detail.

Peter starts with a lightning tour of the Visual Basic 5 environment, before moving on to the creation of a Visual Basic 5 program. Critical concepts such as events, properties and methods are given the attention they deserve. You'll find yourself starting with basics, such as "What is a control and how does VB5 use them?", but you'll quickly be able to move on to more complex topics such as graphics, object-oriented programming, control creation and creating databases. By the end of the book, you'll be able to build your own application from scratch, with very impressive results.

Supporting you on the web
http://www.wrox.com/

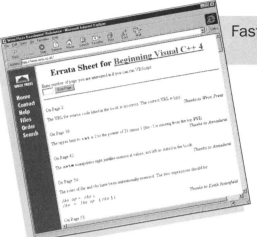

Fast download the source code to your book and collect updates on any errata

Preview forthcoming titles and test out some sample chapters

Get the full, detailed lowdown on any of our books - and read the reviews!

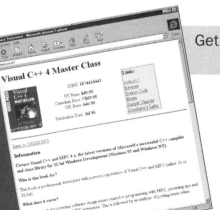

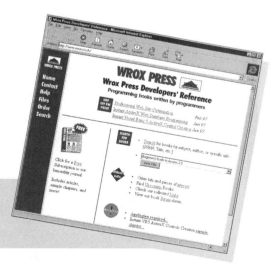

Sign-up for our free newspaper: "Developers' Journal" for Wrox activity, sample chapters and hot info on the industry

Drop into our mirror site at
http://www.wrox.co.uk

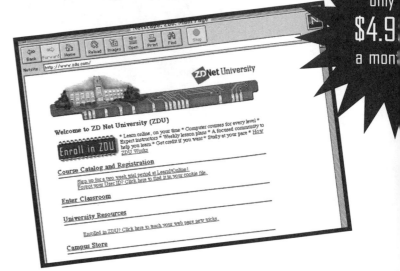

Register Beginning Access 97 VBA Programming and sign up for a free subscription to The Developer's Journal.

A bi-monthly magazine for software developers, The Wrox Press Developer's Journal features in-depth articles, news and help for everyone in the software development industry. Each issue includes extracts from our latest titles and is crammed full of practical insights into coding techniques, tricks, and research.

Fill in and return the card below to receive a free subscription to the Wrox Press Developer's Journal.

Beginning Access 97 VBA Programming Registration Card

Name _____

Address _____

_____

_____

_____

City _____ State/Region _____

Country _____ Postcode/Zip _____

E-mail _____

Occupation _____

How did you hear about this book? _____

☐ Book review (name) _____

☐ Advertisement (name) _____

☐ Recommendation _____

☐ Catalog _____

☐ Other _____

Where did you buy this book? _____

☐ Bookstore (name) _____ City _____

☐ Computer Store (name) _____

☐ Mail Order _____

☐ Other _____

What influenced you in the purchase of this book?

☐ Cover Design

☐ Contents

☐ Other (please specify) _____

How did you rate the overall contents of this book?

☐ Excellent   ☐ Good

☐ Average   ☐ Poor

What did you find most useful about this book? _____

What did you find least useful about this book? _____

Please add any additional comments. _____

What other subjects will you buy a computer book on soon? _____

What is the best computer book you have used this year? _____

Note: This information will only be used to keep you updated about new Wrox Press titles and will not be used for any other purpose or passed to any other third party.

Check here if you DO NOT want a subscription to The Developer's Journal or further support for this book ☐

WROX

WROX PRESS INC.

Wrox writes books for you. Any suggestions, or ideas about how you want information given in your ideal book will be studied by our team. Your comments are always valued at Wrox.

Free phone in USA 800-USE-WROX
Fax (312) 397 8990

UK Tel. (0121) 706 6826   Fax   (0121) 706 2967

—————— *Computer Book Publishers* ——————

NB. If you post the bounce back card below in the UK, please send it to:
Wrox Press Ltd. 30 Lincoln Road, Birmingham, B27 6PA

BUSINESS REPLY MAIL
FIRST CLASS MAIL   PERMIT#64   LA VERGNE, TN

POSTAGE WILL BE PAID BY ADDRESSEE

WROX PRESS
1512 NORTH FREMONT
SUITE 103
CHICAGO IL 60622-2567